# Communications in Computer and Information Science 1193

*Commenced Publication in 2007*
Founding and Former Series Editors:
Phoebe Chen, Alfredo Cuzzocrea, Xiaoyong Du, Orhun Kara, Ting Liu,
Krishna M. Sivalingam, Dominik Ślęzak, Takashi Washio, Xiaokang Yang,
and Junsong Yuan

## Editorial Board Members

More information about this series at http://www.springer.com/series/7899

Miguel Botto-Tobar · Marcelo Zambrano Vizuete ·
Pablo Torres-Carrión · Sergio Montes León ·
Guillermo Pizarro Vásquez ·
Benjamin Durakovic (Eds.)

# Applied Technologies

First International Conference, ICAT 2019
Quito, Ecuador, December 3–5, 2019
Proceedings, Part I

 Springer

*Editors*
Miguel Botto-Tobar ⓘ
Eindhoven University of Technology
Eindhoven, The Netherlands

Pablo Torres-Carrión ⓘ
Universidad Técnica Particular de Loja
Loja, Ecuador

Guillermo Pizarro Vásquez ⓘ
Universidad Politécnica Salesiana
Guayaquil, Ecuador

Marcelo Zambrano Vizuete ⓘ
Universidad Técnica del Norte
Ibarra, Ecuador

Sergio Montes León ⓘ
Universidad de las Fuerzas Armadas (ESPE)
Quito, Ecuador

Benjamin Durakovic ⓘ
International University of Sarajevo
Sarajevo, Bosnia and Herzegovina

ISSN 1865-0929        ISSN 1865-0937   (electronic)
Communications in Computer and Information Science
ISBN 978-3-030-42516-6        ISBN 978-3-030-42517-3   (eBook)
https://doi.org/10.1007/978-3-030-42517-3

This Springer imprint is published by the registered company Springer Nature Switzerland AG
The registered company address is: Gewerbestrasse 11, 6330 Cham, Switzerland

# Preface

The First International Conference on Applied Technologies (ICAT 2019) was held on the main campus of the Universidad de las Fuerzas Armadas (ESPE), in Quito, Ecuador, during December 3–5, 2019, and was jointly organized by the Universidad de las Fuerzas Armadas (ESPE), the Universidad Técnica Particular de Loja, and the Universidad Técnica del Norte, in collaboration with GDEON. The ICAT series aims to bring together top researchers and practitioners working in different domains in the field of computer science to exchange their expertise and discuss the perspectives of development and collaboration. The content of this three-volume set is related to the following subjects: technology trends, computing, intelligent systems, machine vision, security, communication, electronics, e-learning, e-government, and e-participation.

ICAT 2019 received 328 English submissions written by 586 authors from 23 different countries. All these papers were peer-reviewed by the ICAT 2019 Program Committee consisting of 191 high-quality researchers. To assure a high quality and thoughtful review process, we assigned each paper to at least three reviewers. Based on these reviews, 124 full papers were accepted, resulting in an acceptance rate of 38%, which was within our goal of less than 40%.

We would like to express our sincere gratitude to the invited speakers for their inspirational talks, to the authors for submitting their work to this conference, and the reviewers for sharing their experience during the selection process.

December 2019

Miguel Botto-Tobar
Marcelo Zambrano Vizuete
Pablo Torres-Carrión
Sergio Montes León
Guillermo Pizarro Vásquez
Benjamin Durakovic

# Organization

## General Chair

Miguel Botto-Tobar       Eindhoven University of Technology, The Netherlands

## Organizing Committee

Miguel Botto-Tobar       Eindhoven University of Technology, The Netherlands
Marcelo Zambrano Vizuete       Universidad Técnica del Norte, Ecuador
Pablo Torres-Carrión       Universidad Técnica Particular de Loja, Ecuador
Sergio Montes León       Universidad de las Fuerzas Armadas (ESPE), Ecuador, and Universidad Rey Juan Carlos, Spain
Guillermo Pizarro       Universidad Politécnica Salesiana, Ecuador
Benjamin Durakovic       International University of Sarajevo, Bosnia and Herzegovina
Jose Bucheli Andrade       Universidad de las Fuerzas Armadas (ESPE), Ecuador

## Steering Committee

Miguel Botto-Tobar       Eindhoven University of Technology, The Netherlands
Ángela Díaz Cadena       Universitat de Valencia, Spain

## Publication Chair

Miguel Botto-Tobar       Eindhoven University of Technology, The Netherlands

## Program Chairs

### Technology Trends

Jean Michel Clairand       Universidad de Las Américas, Ecuador
Miguel Botto-Tobar       Eindhoven University of Technology, The Netherlands
Hernán Montes León       Universidad Rey Juan Carlos, Spain

### Computing

Miguel Zúñiga Prieto       Universidad de Cuenca, Ecuador
Lohana Lema Moreira       Universidad de Especialidades Espíritu Santo (UEES), Ecuador

### Intelligent Systems

Janeth Chicaiza       Universidad Técnica Particular de Loja, Ecuador
Pablo Torres-Carrión       Universidad Técnica Particular de Loja, Ecuador
Guillermo Pizarro Vásquez       Universidad Politécnica Salesiana, Ecuador

## Machine Vision

| | |
|---|---|
| Julian Galindo | LIG-IIHM, France |
| Erick Cuenca | Université de Montpellier, France |
| Jorge Luis Pérez Medina | Universidad de Las Américas, Ecuador |

## Security

| | |
|---|---|
| Luis Urquiza-Aguiar | Escuela Politécnica Nacional, Ecuador |
| Joffre León-Acurio | Universidad Técnica de Babahoyo, Ecuador |

## Communication

| | |
|---|---|
| Nathaly Verónica Orozco Garzón | Universidad de Las Américas, Ecuador |
| Óscar Zambrano Vizuete | Universidad Técnica del Norte, Ecuador |
| Pablo Palacios Jativa | Universidad de Chile, Chile |
| Henry Ramiro Carvajal Mora | Universidad de Las Américas, Ecuador |

## Electronics

| | |
|---|---|
| Ana Zambrano Vizuete | Escuela Politécnica Nacional (EPN), Ecuador |
| David Rivas | Universidad de las Fuerzas Armadas (ESPE), Ecuador |

## e-Learning

| | |
|---|---|
| Verónica Falconí Ausay | Universidad de Las Américas, Ecuador |
| Doris Macías Mendoza | Universitat Politécnica de Valencia, Spain |

## e-Business

| | |
|---|---|
| Angela Díaz Cadena | Universitat de Valencia, Spain |
| Oscar León Granizo | Universidad de Guayaquil, Ecuador |
| Praxedes Montiel Díaz | CIDEPRO, Ecuador |

## e-Government and e-Participation

| | |
|---|---|
| Vicente Merchán Rodríguez | Universidad de las Fuerzas Armadas (ESPE), Ecuador |
| Alex Santamaría Philco | Universidad Laica Eloy Alfaro de Manabí, Ecuador |

# Program Committee

| | |
|---|---|
| A. Bonci | Marche Polytechnic University, Italy |
| Ahmed Lateef Khalaf | Al-Mamoun University College, Iraq |
| Aiko Yamashita | Oslo Metropolitan University, Norway |
| Alejandro Donaire | Queensland University of Technology, Australia |
| Alejandro Ramos Nolazco | Instituto Tecnólogico y de Estudios Superiores Monterrey, Mexico |
| Alex Cazañas | The University of Queensland, Australia |

| | |
|---|---|
| Alex Santamaria Philco | Universitat Politècnica de València, Spain |
| Alfonso Guijarro Rodriguez | University of Guayaquil, Ecuador |
| Allan Avendaño Sudario | Escuela Superior Politécnica del Litoral (ESPOL), Ecuador |
| Alexandra González Eras | Universidad Politécnica de Madrid, Spain |
| Ana Núñez Ávila | Universitat Politècnica de València, Spain |
| Ana Zambrano | Escuela Politécnica Nacional (EPN), Ecuador |
| Andres Carrera Rivera | The University of Melbourne, Australia |
| Andres Cueva Costales | The University of Melbourne, Australia |
| Andrés Robles Durazno | Edinburg Napier University, UK |
| Andrés Vargas Gonzalez | Syracuse University, USA |
| Angel Cuenca Ortega | Universitat Politècnica de València, Spain |
| Ángela Díaz Cadena | Universitat de València, Spain |
| Angelo Trotta | University of Bologna, Italy |
| Antonio Gómez Exposito | University of Sevilla, Spain |
| Aras Can Onal | Tobb University Economics and Technology, Turkey |
| Arian Bahrami | University of Tehran, Iran |
| Benoît Macq | Université Catholique de Louvain, Belgium |
| Bernhard Hitpass | Universidad Federico Santa María, Chile |
| Bin Lin | Università della Svizzera italiana (USI), Switzerland |
| Carlos Saavedra | Escuela Superior Politécnica del Litoral (ESPOL), Ecuador |
| Catriona Kennedy | The University of Manchester, UK |
| César Ayabaca Sarria | Escuela Politécnica Nacional (EPN), Ecuador |
| Cesar Azurdia Meza | University of Chile, Chile |
| Christian León Paliz | Université de Neuchâtel, Switzerland |
| Chrysovalantou Ziogou | Chemical Process and Energy Resources Institute, Greece |
| Cristian Zambrano Vega | Universidad de Málaga, Spain, and Universidad Técnica Estatal de Quevedo, Ecuador |
| Cristiano Premebida | Loughborough University, ISR-UC, UK |
| Daniel Magües Martinez | Universidad Autónoma de Madrid, Spain |
| Danilo Jaramillo Hurtado | Universidad Politécnica de Madrid, Spain |
| Darío Piccirilli | Universidad Nacional de La Plata, Argentina |
| Darsana Josyula | Bowie State University, USA |
| David Benavides Cuevas | Universidad de Sevilla, Spain |
| David Blanes | Universitat Politècnica de València, Spain |
| David Ojeda | Universidad Técnica del Norte, Ecuador |
| David Rivera Espín | The University of Melbourne, Australia |
| Denis Efimov | Inria, France |
| Diego Barragán Guerrero | Universidad Técnica Particular de Loja (UTPL), Ecuador |
| Diego Peluffo-Ordoñez | Yachay Tech, Ecuador |
| Dimitris Chrysostomou | Aalborg University, Denmark |
| Domingo Biel | Universitat Politècnica de Catalunya, Spain |
| Doris Macías Mendoza | Universitat Politècnica de València, Spain |

| | |
|---|---|
| Edison Espinoza | Universidad de las Fuerzas Armadas (ESPE), Ecuador |
| Edwin Quel | Universidad de las Américas, Ecuador |
| Edwin Rivas | Universidad Distrital de Colombia, Colombia |
| Ehsan Arabi | University of Michigan, USA |
| Emanuele Frontoni | Università Politecnica delle Marche, Italy |
| Emil Pricop | Petroleum-Gas University of Ploiesti, Romania |
| Erick Cuenca | Université Catholique de Louvain, Belgium |
| Fabian Calero | University of Waterloo, Canada |
| Fan Yang | Tsinghua University, China |
| Fariza Nasaruddin | University of Malaya, Malaysia |
| Felipe Ebert | Universidade Federal de Pernambuco (UFPE), Brazil |
| Felipe Grijalva | Escuela Politécnica Nacional (EPN), Ecuador |
| Fernanda Molina Miranda | Universidad Politécnica de Madrid, Spain |
| Fernando Almeida | University of Campinas, Brazil |
| Fernando Flores Pulgar | Université de Lyon, France |
| Firas Raheem | University of Technology, Iraq |
| Francisco Calvente | Universitat Rovira i Virgili, Spain |
| Francisco Obando | Universidad del Cauca, Colombia |
| Franklin Parrales | University of Guayaquil, Ecuador |
| Freddy Flores Bahamonde | Universidad Técnica Federico Santa María, Chile |
| Gabriel Barros Gavilanes | INP Toulouse, France |
| Gabriel López Fonseca | Sheffield Hallam University, UK |
| Gema Rodriguez-Perez | LibreSoft, Universidad Rey Juan Carlos, Spain |
| Ginger Saltos Bernal | Escuela Superior Politécnica del Litoral (ESPOL), Ecuador |
| Giovanni Pau | Kore University of Enna, Italy |
| Guilherme Avelino | Universidade Federal do Piauí (UFP), Brazil |
| Guilherme Pereira | Universidade Federal de Minas Gerais (UFMG), Brazil |
| Guillermo Pizarro Vásquez | Universidad Politécnica de Madrid, Spain |
| Gustavo Andrade Miranda | Universidad Politécnica de Madrid, Spain |
| Hernán Montes León | Universidad Rey Juan Carlos, Spain |
| Ibraheem Kasim | University of Baghdad, Iraq |
| Ilya Afanasyev | Innopolis University, Russia |
| Israel Pineda Arias | Chonbuk National University, South Korea |
| Jaime Meza | Universiteit van Fribourg, Switzerland |
| Janneth Chicaiza Espinosa | Universidad Técnica Particular de Loja (UTPL), Ecuador |
| Javier Gonzalez-Huerta | Blekinge Institute of Technology, Sweden |
| Javier Monroy | Universidad de Málaga, Spain |
| Javier Sebastian | University of Oviedo, Spain |
| Jawad K. Ali | University of Technology, Iraq |
| Jefferson Ribadeneira Ramírez | Escuela Superior Politécnica de Chimborazo, Ecuador |
| Jerwin Prabu | BRS, India |
| Jong Hyuk Park | Korea Institute of Science and Technology, South Korea |

| | |
|---|---|
| Jorge Charco Aguirre | Universitat Politècnica de València, Spain |
| Jorge Eterovic | Universidad Nacional de La Matanza, Argentina |
| Jorge Gómez Gómez | Universidad de Córdoba, Colombia |
| Juan Corrales | Institut Universitaire de France et SIGMA Clermont, France |
| Juan Romero Arguello | The University of Manchester, UK |
| Julián Andrés Galindo | Université Grenoble Alpes, France |
| Julian Galindo | Inria, France |
| Julio Albuja Sánchez | James Cook University, Australia |
| Kelly Garces | Universidad de Los Andes, Colombia |
| Kester Quist-Aphetsi | Center for Research, Information, Technology and Advanced Computing, Ghana |
| Korkut Bekiroglu | SUNY Polytechnic Institute, USA |
| Kunde Yang | Northwestern Polytechnic University, China |
| Lina Ochoa | CWI, The Netherlands |
| Lohana Lema Moreira | Universidad de Especialidades Espíritu Santo (UEES), Ecuador |
| Lorena Guachi Guachi | Yachay Tech, Ecuador |
| Lorena Montoya Freire | Aalto University, Finland |
| Lorenzo Cevallos Torres | Universidad de Guayaquil, Ecuador |
| Luis Galárraga | Inria, France |
| Luis Martinez | Universitat Rovira i Virgili, Spain |
| Luis Urquiza-Aguiar | Escuela Politécnica Nacional (EPN), Ecuador |
| Maikel Leyva Vazquez | Universidad de Guayaquil, Ecuador |
| Manuel Sucunuta | Universidad Técnica Particular de Loja (UTPL), Ecuador |
| Marcela Ruiz | Utrecht University, The Netherlands |
| Marcelo Zambrano Vizuete | Universidad Técnica del Norte, Ecuador |
| María José Escalante Guevara | University of Michigan, USA |
| María Reátegui Rojas | University of Quebec, Canada |
| Mariela Tapia-Leon | University of Guayaquil, Ecuador |
| Marija Seder | University of Zagreb, Croatia |
| Mario Gonzalez Rodríguez | Universidad de las Américas, Ecuador |
| Marisa Daniela Panizzi | Universidad Tecnológica Nacional Aire, Argentina |
| Marius Giergiel | KRiM AGH, Poland |
| Markus Schuckert | Hong Kong Polytechnic University, Hong Kong |
| Matus Pleva | Technical University of Kosice, Slovakia |
| Mauricio Verano Merino | Technische Universiteit Eindhoven, The Netherlands |
| Mayken Espinoza-Andaluz | Escuela Superior Politécnica del Litoral (ESPOL), Ecuador |
| Miguel Botto-Tobar | Eindhoven University of Technology, The Netherlands |
| Miguel Fornell | Escuela Superior Politécnica del Litoral (ESPOL), Ecuador |
| Miguel Gonzalez Cagigal | Universidad de Sevilla, Spain |
| Miguel Murillo | Universidad Autónoma de Baja California, Mexico |

| | |
|---|---|
| Miguel Zuñiga Prieto | Universidad de Cuenca, Ecuador |
| Milton Román-Cañizares | Universidad de las Américas, Ecuador |
| Mohamed Kamel | Military Technical College, Egypt |
| Mohammad Al-Mashhadani | Al-Maarif University College, Iraq |
| Mohammad Amin | Illinois Institute of Technology, USA |
| Monica Baquerizo Anastacio | Universidad de Guayaquil, Ecuador |
| Muneeb Ul Hassan | Swinburne University of Technology, Australia |
| Nam Yang | Eindhoven University of Technology, The Netherlands |
| Nathalie Mitton | Inria, France |
| Nathaly Orozco | Universidad de las Américas, Ecuador |
| Nayeth Solórzano Alcívar | Escuela Superior Politécnica del Litoral (ESPOL), Ecuador, and Griffith University, Australia |
| Noor Zaman | King Faisal University, Saudi Arabia |
| Omar S. Gómez | Escuela Superior Politécnica del Chimborazo (ESPOCH), Ecuador |
| Óscar León Granizo | Universidad de Guayaquil, Ecuador |
| Oswaldo Lopez Santos | Universidad de Ibagué, Colombia |
| Pablo Lupera | Escuela Politécnica Nacional, Ecuador |
| Pablo Ordoñez Ordoñez | Universidad Politécnica de Madrid, Spain |
| Pablo Palacios | Universidad de Chile, Chile |
| Pablo Torres-Carrión | Universidad Técnica Particular de Loja (UTPL), Ecuador |
| Patricia Ludeña González | Universidad Técnica Particular de Loja (UTPL), Ecuador |
| Paúl Mejía | Universidad de las Fuerzas Armadas (ESPE), Ecuador |
| Paulo Batista | CIDEHUS.UÉ, Portugal |
| Paulo Chiliguano | Queen Mary University of London, UK |
| Paulo Guerra Terán | Universidad de las Américas, Ecuador |
| Pedro Neto | University of Coimbra, Portugal |
| Praveen Damacharla | Purdue University Northwest, USA |
| Priscila Cedillo | Universidad de Cuenca, Ecuador |
| Radu-Emil Precup | Politehnica University of Timisoara, Romania |
| Ramin Yousefi | Islamic Azad University, Iran |
| René Guamán Quinche | Universidad de los Paises Vascos, Spain |
| Ricardo Martins | University of Coimbra, Portugal |
| Richard Ramirez Anormaliza | Universitat Politècnica de Catalunya, Spain |
| Richard Rivera | IMDEA Software Institute, Spain |
| Richard Stern | Carnegie Mellon University, USA |
| Rijo Jackson Tom | SRM University, India |
| Roberto Murphy | University of Colorado Denver, USA |
| Roberto Sabatini | RMIT University, Australia |
| Rodolfo Alfredo Bertone | Universidad Nacional de La Plata, Argentina |
| Rodrigo Barba | Universidad Técnica Particular de Loja (UTPL), Ecuador |

| | |
|---|---|
| Rodrigo Saraguro Bravo | Universitat Politècnica de València, Spain |
| Ronald Barriga Díaz | Universidad de Guayaquil, Ecuador |
| Ronnie Guerra | Pontificia Universidad Católica del Perú, Peru |
| Ruben Rumipamba-Zambrano | Universitat Politècnica de Catalanya, Spain |
| Saeed Rafee Nekoo | Universidad de Sevilla, Spain |
| Saleh Mobayen | University of Zanjan, Iran |
| Samiha Fadloun | Université de Montpellier, France |
| Sergio Montes León | Universidad de las Fuerzas Armadas (ESPE), Ecuador |
| Stefanos Gritzalis | University of the Aegean, Greece |
| Syed Manzoor Qasim | King Abdulaziz City for Science and Technology, Saudi Arabia |
| Tatiana Mayorga | Universidad de las Fuerzas Armadas (ESPE), Ecuador |
| Tenreiro Machado | Polytechnic of Porto, Portugal |
| Thomas Sjögren | Swedish Defence Research Agency (FOI), Sweden |
| Tiago Curi | Federal University of Santa Catarina, Brazil |
| Tony T. Luo | A*STAR, Singapore |
| Trung Duong | Queen's University Belfast, UK |
| Vanessa Jurado Vite | Universidad Politécnica Salesiana, Ecuador |
| Waldo Orellana | Universitat de València, Spain |
| Washington Velasquez Vargas | Universidad Politécnica de Madrid, Spain |
| Wayne Staats | Sandia National Labs, USA |
| Willian Zamora | Universidad Laíca Eloy Alfaro de Manabí, Ecuador |
| Yessenia Cabrera Maldonado | University of Cuenca, Ecuador |
| Yerferson Torres Berru | Universidad de Salamanca, Spain, and Instituto Tecnológico Loja, Ecuador |
| Zhanyu Ma | Beijing University of Posts and Telecommunications, China |

## Organizing Institutions

# Sponsoring Institutions

UNIVERSIDAD DE CUENCA
DEPARTAMENTO DE CIENCIAS
DE LA COMPUTACIÓN
FACULTAD DE INGENIERÍA

# Collaborators

# Contents – Part I

### Computing

# Contents – Part II

## Machine Vision

# Contents – Part III

## Electronics

## e-Learning

## e-Government and e-Participation

# Technology Trends

# Comparative Study of RDF and OWL Ontology Languages as Support for the Semantic Web

Marlon A. Altamirano Di Luca[1] (iD) and Neilys González Benítez[2](✉) (iD)

[1] Santa Elena Peninsula State University, Santa Elena 08544, Ecuador
[2] Pinar del Río Meteorological Center, 20100 Pinar del Río, Cuba
`neilys.gonzalez@pri.insmet.cu`

**Abstract.** Web services have been consolidated as technology for the use of the Internet, these services require integration mechanisms, to establish themselves as useful technological tools in the process of information and knowledge management and in dissimilar research activities, development of the organizations. In the process of modeling the Semantic Web, natural language processing algorithms are used, which improve the quality of the information stored in the digital repositories. The metrics of precision and completeness that contain the Weekly Web contribute to corroborate the quality, relevance and relevance of the information held on the internet. The objective of this paper is to compare the RDF and OWL ontology languages, in order to select the language that best fits the use of the Semantic Web, to carry out the process of managing the information, corresponding to the research activities with the greatest impact on the digital repositories of Ecuadorian universities.

**Keywords:** Algorithms of natural language processing · Information management · RDF and OWL languages · Ontology · Digital repositories · Semantic Web

## 1 Introduction

Information management was an almost exclusive domain of librarians, archivists and documentarists. The introduction of computers in the second half of the twentieth century, the continuous adaptation of work processes to new technologies and, mainly, the creation of the web in the nineties boasted the incorporation of new disciplines such as the theory of Information retrieval, to this environment.

The immediate consequence of such a situation caused the proliferation of multi-type research focused on the development of technologies and methods favorable to organizations and information management. However, in spite of the important advances made by the new technologies, the systems that allow processing and accessing the information contained in websites in a reliable manner are lacking in organizations.

In accordance with the above, the use of the Web is proposed as a well-defined model of information processing on the internet. The web has become a considerably practical tool for communication, commerce, entertainment, business, among others.

M. Botto-Tobar et al. (Eds.): ICAT 2019, CCIS 1193, pp. 3–12, 2020.
https://doi.org/10.1007/978-3-030-42517-3_1

Web design agencies have contributed to the opening of the Web field and in particular in the realization of pages and other functions.

Currently, the Web is a flexible medium, with a number of options that favor the development of New Information and Communication Technologies (ICT), existing in the market. These technologies constitute the instrument of everyday use, most used at all times.

The development of Information Technology and Communications has been continuous and there are more and more existing applications for use, example of this are the dynamic pages that are achieved through ICT, as well as the conception of these pages, which are cataloged as universal platforms for the evolution of applications, adaptation to user navigation forms and new trends in the digital world, to which web design agencies must adapt.

Web Services have been consolidated as an essential technology for Internet cooperation, but they require mechanisms for their integration, establishing themselves as a technological tool that contributes to the globalization and management of knowledge in organizational activities or in the field of research, with services that improve response times to users, in terms of efficient and fast searches.

According to the aforementioned, it is noteworthy that the web development is constant, which has led to the use of an extended and knowledgeable web called semantic Web. With the semantic web you can feel more and more technological innovations and the improvement of the traditional web itself.

The semantic Web is a paradigm that aims to overcome the current orientation of the Internet, where information is represented in a way that is understandable by people, towards a model where information is prepared for automated processing.

The model where the information is available and prepared for processing and use is called Ontology. Ontology, is the way to represent the knowledge of the Web in a way that is made readable and reusable by computers.

An Ontology is a hierarchy of concepts with attributes and relationships, which define a consensus terminology to detail semantic networks of interrelated information units. With Ontology, common vocabulary is defined to share information within a specific domain, said vocabulary being formed by classes or concepts, properties or attributes of classes and relationships between classes.

Ontologies provide the way to represent knowledge, it offers different advantages for modeling, generation, distribution and use of the knowledge produced and accumulated. Given these advantages for knowledge management, Ontologies are widely used to manage large volumes of information that come from different areas of knowledge.

The definitions of the basic concepts and relationships between the characteristics of the above-mentioned Ontologies, are made through the specific languages that support the ontologies in the semantic Web, which favor the interpretability between computers and information or knowledge. These languages are used to explicitly represent the meaning of the terms through vocabularies and the relationships between them.

Among the most used languages for the construction of ontology is OWL and RDF. The OWL language provides three sub-languages (OWL Lite, OWL DL and OWL Full), each with a higher level of expressivity than the previous one, designed to be used by specific communities of developers and users. The RDF language (SPARQL) is used to define the syntax and semantics necessary for a query expression on an RDF graph and the different forms of results obtained.

The work presented is related to the use of RDF and OWL ontology languages as a support for the Semantic Web, useful in the information management process of the digital repositories of Ecuadorian universities. For the development of the work, a study was carried out that showed that the languages commonly used for working with the Semantic Web, have variable characteristics and not all meet the required aspects to manage information quickly, organized and accurate in the repo - Digital sites.

For this reason, this paper proposes a comparative study of the languages that are frequently used in Ontology, RDF and OWL. These languages are the most used as a support for the Semantic Web for the processing and analysis of information, from the digital repositories, of Ecuadorian universities, making it possible to obtain better cataloged information to support decision-making, in the substantive processes universitarian.

The RDF and OWL ontology languages allow to specify concepts of different domains of knowledge through the use of languages based on symbolic and susceptible logic, if eventually interpreted by computers. These languages, being defined by various specifications, constitute the basis for work in W3C and are intended to build the semantic web [1].

The aforementioned author adds that, despite the important advances made by new technologies, the web user still lacks a system that allows to process and access the information contained in websites in a reliable way. Problem that is based on three aspects:

1. The web is a decentralized and heterogeneous system, completely different from the scenarios for which they were regularly prepared in accordance with the classic disciplines related to documentation and information retrieval.
2. What happens on the www is an information retrieval with adversario (adversarial information retrieval), another aspect never contemplated by the recovery of classical information.
3. The method of marking information, html, combines content elements with presentation elements.

On the other hand, the aforementioned authors refer that the web is a different scenario from those used by the classic disciplines linked to documentation. In order to facilitate the information management of new resources and control their heterogeneity, the use of Ontologies is proposed, useful for the design of tools that facilitate recognizing, comparing and combining web resources with different structures.

Ontologies have been traditionally used as a model of knowledge representation in Artificial Intelligence. According to the definition offered by [2] and subsequently extended by [3], an Ontology is an explicit and formal specification of a conceptualization.

They refer [2] and [3] that an Ontology is formed by a relational taxonomy of concepts and by a set of axioms or rules of inference by which new knowledge can be inferred. In this new context, one of the most cited definitions is that of [3] which completes the original of [2], for whom an Ontology is an explicit and formal specification of a shared conceptualization.

A complete conceptualization of Ontology, according to the aforementioned authors, is that Ontology is an abstract model of some phenomenon of the world constructed by identifying the concepts relevant to that phenomenon (usually a domain of knowledge). Explicit, which means that the concepts used in the ontology, and the restrictions for their use, are clearly defined.

Formal; It refers to the fact that it must be understandable for machines. Shared; it reflects the notion that it will contain knowledge agreed upon to some degree (in the case of a knowledge domain, it is assumed that it will be agreed by the experts in it) [4].

He refers [1] that for the specification of a domain to be considered an ontology, it must present at least two types of components: elements and relationships between them. The main components that define an Ontology according to [5] are:

- Classes: real world entities can be categorized into groups or sets of objects with similar characteristics, they form the ontology classes. Entities can be conceptual physical things. They constitute the core of an ontology and describe the concepts of a specific domain.
- Properties: entities that belong to a class have certain attributes. Therefore, the properties consist of attribute/value pairs and serve to conveniently describe the relevant characteristics of the entities that form the classes.
- Individuals, instances or copies: they consist of representations of objects or particular elements of a class. Individuals or instances of the class are called interchangeably.
- Class – Individual: associate individuals or instances with a class. They express themselves through relationships.
- Individual – Property: instances of a class have values associated with properties. These associations are expressed through relationships.
- Class – Property: the class as a set has properties. When applied to a class, these properties are called restrictions because they serve both to define it and to delimit the belonging of individuals to it.
- Class – Subclass: classes can have subclasses. This association is also expressed with relationships.

Other characteristics analyzed, as part of the study carried out in this research, to carry out the information management process, corresponding to the research activities, with the greatest impact on the digital repositories of Ecuadorian universities, through the Semantic Web, is that the Semantic Web is supported in the RDF and OWL ontology languages which are used to explicitly represent the meaning of the terms through vocabularies and relationships. The three sub languages (OWL Lite, OWL DL and OWL Full), provided by OWL, have a higher level of expression than the previous one, designed to be used by specific communities of developers and users [6].

OWL, is built on the basis of knowledge representation languages based on descriptive logic. This language is intended for those users who require maximum expressiveness, but guaranteeing computational completeness (possibility of reaching conclusions based on existing information) and inference in finite time [7].

The RDF language is a query language, it defines the syntax and semantics necessary for a query expression on an RDF graph and the different forms of results obtained. Its mission is to return all the triple-tas or components requested based on the comparison of a triplet passed as a parameter of the query (basic graph) with all the triplets that make up the RDF graph [8–10].

Based on the aforementioned, the RDF and OWL ontology languages are studied as support for the Semantic Web, to make use of this Web in Ecuadorian universities and manage information in digital repositories quickly and safely. Within the specific languages created for the definition of ontologies the most widespread is OWL [11]. The OWL language has been designed so that applications can automatically process and integrate information content on the Web. OWL is based on existing languages such as XML, XML Schema, RDF and RDF Schema, but includes new features to allow the creation of ontologies: vocabulary to describe classes and properties, relationships, constraints, cardinality, property characteristics, listed properties, and others.

In the RDF (Resource Description Framework) language, according to [11], XML serves as the basis for a knowledge representation language. Namespaces allow the possibility of shareable definitions, in this language a semantics associated with those definitions is required to separate the structure of the data from its meaning. RDF is a W3C standard defined on XML that allows to represent information about resources.

The main element of RDF is the statement, a define statement of what we know about a resource; relating it to another resource, declaring the values of the properties of a resource, making statements they receive, also the name of triplet. A triplet is made up of a subject, a resource identified by its URI, predicate, a property (also denoted by a URI) and object, a resource or literal with which the relationship is defined.

Other elements of RDF are resources, useful for referencing anything since it has a URI. The properties (properties), are characteristics, attributes or relationships that can be used to describe resources, are part of a vocabulary identified by a URI, the literal elements that are the values that belong to a primitive data type (usually one of the defined in xsd).

Containers/collections are RDF elements that allow you to reference resource groups, white nodes, another element that is recognized as a resource with no identifier used to group information or as variables in certain expressions.

On the other hand, in OWL the ontology becomes a first-order object) a resource, with this language the ontologies are important and extensible, they can annotate with meta-data, restrictions on classes and properties can be established, classes can be built from other classes and can be declared axioms of deduction on the ontology. The extension is defined in a new namespace; the ontologies are declared as objects of type ontology.

It is possible to import other ontologies, use type definitions in XML-Schema-Datatype (namespace xsd) and define properties to annotate ontologies. Instances are built from classes and properties.

Based on the characteristics described on the RDF and OWL ontology languages, as support for the Semantic Web, and the marked interest of its usefulness to carry out the information management process, corresponding to the activities of Research of greater impact in Ecuadorian universities, the comparative study for the selection of the ontology language that best fits to implement a Semantic Web on the digital repositories of Ecuadorian universities is carried out.

## 2  Materials and Methods

For the comparative study of the RDF and OWL ontology languages, which are frequently used to implement Semantic Web in the digital repositories of Ecuadorian universities, the Discrete Multi-Territory Decision Theory (DMD) was used, defined by [12] as a theory that contributes to select the language that best meets the criteria provided for carrying out the information management process, corresponding to the research activities with the greatest impact in Ecuadorian universities. The theory of DMD, is considered as a methodology for supporting decision-making, has been suitable in several fields of application, specifically where it is necessary to decide between several alternatives, taking into account various criteria or points of view [13].

Multicriteria evaluation and decision methods favor the process of finding possible, but not necessarily optimal, solutions, so the decision maker's preferences over predefined objectives play an important role in this process [13].

The aforementioned authors add that the following aspects must be taken into account for an adequate work with multicriteria methods:

1. Select the best alternative (s).
2. Accept good alternatives and reject bad ones.
3. Generate a ranking (ranking) of the alternatives considered (from "best to worst").

They emphasize that, to comply with the aforementioned aspects, there are different approaches, methods and solutions, to take into account, such as:

1. Linear Weighting (Scoring).
2. Multiatribute Utility (MUAT).
3. Relations of overcoming and processes of Hierarchical Analysis (AHP - The Analytic Process - Hierarchical Analytical Process).

For the comparative study of the RDF and OWL ontology languages that are frequently used to implement Semantic Web in the digital repositories, of the Ecuadorian universities that best fit to carry out the information management process, corresponding to the activities for research with the greatest impact, the linear weighting method (Scoring) is selected, where the decision maker plays an important role for each of the characteristics presented by the RDF and OWL ontology languages.

The method that was used in the investigation, has the purpose of defining a preference structure among the identified alternatives, as occurs in practice and in particular in the process of information management, corresponding to the major research activities impact. Linear weighting (Scoring), is a method with an orthodox and direct theoretical foundation, that is, according to utility theory and value theory, it contributes to the choice between a set of available alternatives so that satisfaction is maximized of what is desired.

Working with this method implies the knowledge of each of the alternatives and the evaluation capacity, which is achieved by defining a value (deterministic) function or a utility (probabilistic) function that represents preferences. In addition, it implies the transitivity of preferences or comparability. It is completely compensatory, and may be dependent on the allocation of weights to the factors or the scale of measurement of the evaluations [13].

The basic scheme that follows the linear weighting method consists in constructing a function of value $S_j$ for each alternative, according to as stated in Eq. 1. Results shown in Table 1.

**Table 1.** Results of the Linear Weighting of each selection criteria of the RDF and OWL ontology languages.

| Criteria | Weighing $w_i$ | RDF language $r_{i1}$ | OWL language $r_{i2}$ |
|---|---|---|---|
| Expressive power needed | 4 | 3 | 6 |
| Semantics for containers, collections | 5 | 2 | 6 |
| Possibility of checks for domain and range properties | 3 | 5 | 7 |
| Expression of all kinds of relationships | 5 | 4 | 7 |
| Obtaining results quickly and accurately | 5 | 7 | 8 |
| Degree of information organization | 4 | 7 | 8 |
| Characteristics of transitive and reflexive properties | 6 | 5 | 7 |
| Scoring $S_j$ | | 150 | 224 |

$$S_j = \sum_i W_i r_{ij} \qquad (1)$$

Where:

$w_i$; is the weight of the criterion $j$ y $r_{ij}$ the evaluation (rating) of the alternative $i$ regarding the criteria $j$.

The data used for the selection of RDF and OWL ontology languages for the information management process through the use of the Semantic Web, corresponding to the research activities of greater impact in Ecuadorian universities, correspond to the information extracted from the documentary analysis, which were quantified by assigning a weight (weighting) to make such a comparison. To establish the Satisfaction Rating for each alternative, a scale of 0–9 points is used, then the Scoring was calculated for each alternative, where the results obtained by applying the DMD theory are reflected in Table 1.

## 3 Results

Based on the analysis performed, the ontology language for the information management process through the use of the Semantic Web that reflected more appropriate results, for information management, corresponding to the research activities with the greatest impact in Ecuadorian universities, it corresponded with that of the OWL language. Result that corresponds to the state of the art related to the use of the Semantic Web for the management of information in digital repositories.

On the other hand, it should be noted that for the process of information management through the Semantic Web based on ontology it is important to use the OWL language, because with it the variants have a containing relationship, that is, all OWL Lite ontology is OWL DL, all OWL DL ontology is OWL Full.

The OWL language facilitates the creation and maintenance of metadata for learning objects, semantically relevant in the information management process, since this language is designed so that the applications that support the ontology-based Semantic Web, can Automatically process and integrate the information content on the Web, instead of simply presenting it for consumption.

OWL is based on existing languages such as XML, XML Schema, RDF and RDF Schema, but includes new features that allow to create onto-loggias: vocabulary to describe classes and properties, relationships, restrictions, cardinality, property features, properties listed, and others, that is why the use of this language is recommended for the use of the ontology-based semantic Web for the information management process corresponding to the research activities with the greatest impact on the digital repositories of the Ecuadorian universities.

## 4   Discussions

According to the results obtained through the comparative study, the functional requirements of the RDF and OWL ontology languages, required for the reuse of the Ontological Design Patterns, were addressed with the linear weighting methodology (ODPs, for its acronym in English), which are a way to help developers in the modeling of ontologies performed in OWL and are considered as a way to apply good practices.

It was obtained that the OWL ontology language, have advantages over the rest of the ontology languages for Semantic Web, and in particular for RDF, standing out:

- With OWL it is possible to represent and implement ontologies.
- It is a language of the evolution of two other languages OIL and DAML.
- OWL, is supported in the RDF vocabulary.
- The OWL language adds more vocabulary to describe properties and classes, including relationships between classes.
- The OWL language, supports using logical expressions.
- OWL, facilitates the definition of classes through conditions on its members.
- The OWL language, allows the Boolean combination of classes.
- OWL, provides the enumeration of the instances that belong to the class (by extension).
- OWL, grants the attribution of certain properties to relationships, such as cardinality, symmetry, transitivity, or inverse relationships.

On the other hand, OWL can be used to explicitly represent the meaning of terms in vocabularies and the (semantic) relationships between them. This language uses rdf to represent and encode ontologies, a recommendation that follows the characteristic tendency to proceed through "extensions". Therefore, OWL is an extension of rdf that adds elements such as those mentioned above to describe features and classes.

For this reason, the ontology-based semantic Web, for the information management process corresponding to the research activities with the greatest impact on the digital repositories of Ecuadorian universities, relies on universal mechanisms such as OWL, which provide infrastructure. global, and that contributes to solve the problems caused by a Web without semantics, in which the heterogeneity of information makes access to it can become a difficult task.

Also, the use of the OWL language, in the semantic Web based on ontology, has a disadvantage; the inability to define class conjunctions and the inability to define cardinality relationships. In order to address these problems, the W3C formed a working group that, based on an alternative language for the definition of knowledge called DAML + OIL, published OWL, a family of languages that extended the functionality present in the RDFS, which It was accepted as a W3C Recommendation on February 10, 2004 [14].

## 5  Conclusions

The RDF and OWL ontology languages are analyzed as support for the Semantic Web because of the importance it has in the information management process, corresponding to the research activities with the greatest impact in Ecuadorian universities.

To make the comparison between the ontology languages, the DMD theory was used, which is based on the results obtained on the characteristics that distinguish the compared languages OWL and RDF.

The result obtained with the DMD theory to determine the most appropriate ontology language to be used in the Semantic Web, to carry out the information management process, corresponding to the research activities with the greatest impact in the digital repositories of Ecuadorian universities, it is the OWL language.

The OWL language has the greatest advantages in the process of information management with the Semantic Web, because it is a language specially designed to structure knowledge about a reality issue, so that it can be easily shared in the net.

With OWL, it is possible to provide semantic content specification, which is important for the use of ontology in the information management process corresponding to the research activities with the greatest impact in Ecuadorian universities.

## References

1. Pedraza-Jiménez, R., Codina, L., Rovira, C.: Web semántica y ontologías en el procesamiento de la información documental. El profesional de la información **16**(6), 569–578 (2007). https://doi.org/10.3145/epi.2007.nov.04
2. Gruber, T.R.: A translation approach to portable ontologies. Knowl. Acquis. **5**(2), 199–220 (1993)
3. Studer, S., Benjamins, R., Fensel, D.: Knowledge engineering: principles and methods. Data Knowl. Eng. **25**, 161–197 (1998)
4. Gómez-Pérez, A., Manzano-Macho, D.: An overview of methods and tools for ontology learning from text. Knowl. Eng. Rev. **19**(3), 187–212 (2005)

5. Lacy, L.W.: OWL: Representing Information Using the Web Ontology Language. Trafford, Ann Arbor (2004)
6. Fernández, H.A.F.: Construcción de ontologías OWL'. Vínculos **4**(1), 19–34 (2013)
7. Matentzoglu, N., Bail, S., Parsia, B.: A corpus of OWL DL ontologies. In: Proceedings of the DL 2013, vol. 13, pp. 829–841 (2013)
8. Huang, J., Abadi, D.J., Ren, K.: Scalable SPARQL querying of large RDF graphs'. Proc. VLDB Endow. **4**(11), 1123–1134 (2011)
9. Horridge, M., Musen, M.: Snap-SPARQL: a Java framework for working with SPARQL and OWL. In: Tamma, V., Dragoni, M., Gonçalves, R., Ławrynowicz, A. (eds.) OWLED 2015. LNCS, vol. 9557, pp. 154–165. Springer, Cham (2016). https://doi.org/10.1007/978-3-319-33245-1_16
10. Du Charme, B.: Learning SPARQL. O'Reilly Media, Newton (2011)
11. Pollock, J.T.: Semantic Web for Dummies. Publishing and Editorial for Technology Dummies (2009)
12. Barba-Romero, S.: Evaluación multicriterio de proyectos. In: en Martínez, E. (ed.) Ciencia, Tecnología y Desarrollo: Interrelaciones Teóricas y Metodológicas, Ed. Nueva Sociedad, Caracas, pp. 455–507 (1994)
13. Martínez, E., Escudey, M.: Evaluación y Decisión Multiciterio. Reflexiones y Expe-riencias. Editorial Universidad de Santiago/UNESCO, Santiago de Chile (1998)
14. Schneider, P., et al.: OWL Web Ontology Language Semantics and Abstract Syntax (2004). http://www.w3.org/TR/2004/REC-owl-semantics-20040201/

# Model of Evaluating Smart City Projects by Groups of Investors Using a Multifactorial Approach

Lakhno Valeriy[1] ⓘ, Malyukov Volodymyr[2] ⓘ, Kryvoruchko Olena[3] ⓘ,
Tsiutsiura Mykola[4] ⓘ, Desyatko Alyona[3](✉) ⓘ, and Medynska Tetyana[3] ⓘ

[1] Faculty of Information Security, Computer Science and Communication, National University
of Life and Environmental Sciences of Ukraine, Kyiv, Ukraine
valss21@ukr.net

[2] Faculty of Computer Systems and Communications, National University
of Life and Environmental Sciences of Ukraine, Kyiv, Ukraine
volod.malyukov@gmail.com

[3] Faculty of Accounting, Audit and Information Technologies,
Kyiv National University of Trade and Economics, Kyiv, Ukraine
{kryvoruchko_ev,desyatko}@knute.edu.ua, medintan@ukr.net

[4] Department of Information Technology,
Kyiv National University of Construction and Architecture, Kyiv, Ukraine
teodenor@gmail.com

**Abstract.** In this paper the authors introduce a model for the mathematical support of the decision-making process during the evaluation of investment projects. As an example, the sphere of investing in Smart City development projects is considered. The emphasis in the model is placed on the multifactorial nature of the task in the search of rational financial strategies carried out by investor groups. The model particularly allows groups of investors (players) to evaluate the attractiveness and financial potential of the analyzed projects. At the same time, players can exercise control over a dynamic system in multidimensional project spaces. The model implies subsequent software implementation in a decision support system (DSS) or an expert system for cross-platform software products.

The results presented in the article have been obtained through computational experiments based on the solution of a bilinear multi-step quality game with several terminal surfaces. The scientific novelty of the research lies in the fact that, in contrast to existing solutions and related to conceptual direction of research, the article first considers a new class of multi-step bilinear games. The proposed solution provides an opportunity to correctly and adequately describe the investment processes, given the multifactorial nature of the problem statement. Computational experiments were performed in the MatLab system to search for sets of investors' preferences and their optimal financial strategies during the analysis of Smart City development projects. The results of computational experiments have proved and confirmed the correctness and adequacy of the model.

**Keywords:** Game theory · Investment strategies · Multidimensional case · Decision support · Multistep game · Bilinear equations

© Springer Nature Switzerland AG 2020
M. Botto-Tobar et al. (Eds.): ICAT 2019, CCIS 1193, pp. 13–26, 2020.
https://doi.org/10.1007/978-3-030-42517-3_2

# 1  Introduction

Conceptually, the idea of creating and developing smart cities (hereinafter referred to as Smart City) was declared in early 2000s. It should be noted that a lot of investors who are actively involved in the advanced digital technologies market have shown great interest in the development potential of Smart City. Since the beginning of the 21st century urban issues and the prospects for its development using new information technologies (IT) have been increasingly debated and have become issues of common concern at science forums devoted to advanced digital technologies of Smart City. A lot of players in the investment market, world-famous IT companies such as Google, IBM, Cisco Systems (USA), Siemens AG (Germany), Ericsson (Sweden), Schneider Electric (France) and many others, along with public institutions have begun to view Smart City from the perspective of investing in Smart technologies and creating new zones for mutually beneficial business cooperation among manufacturers of high-tech products through satisfying needs of the urban economy.

Thus, local authorities of large cities, primarily at the municipal level, announced strategies for investing in Smart City projects. The initiative mainly stems from the desire to improve the status of the city, as well as the ability to attract long-term investments. Consequently, the idea of localizing a high-tech business within the urban infrastructure has also become very promising and lucrative. At the same time, involved in this process companies have faced challenges aimed at solving local urban problems related to the use of new digital solutions. A vivid example can be illustrated by the company Google which has introduced a Flow system in order to monitor the local traffic in Columbus (Ohio). Basically, being based on the comprehensive analysis of various transport information this Smart system is designed to manage traffic as a whole. This accumulated information, for example, can be elicited from various sources such as smartphones, navigators, and other user devices. Analyzing this information, city authorities can easily forecast and successfully prevent traffic jams in a big city.

Undeniably, such investment projects are inherently risky and can be characterized by a high degree of uncertainty. The authors of the works [1, 2] state that, in order to increase the effectiveness and efficiency of evaluating such large projects, it is quite desirable to use the potential of various computerized decision support systems (DSS). This especially relates to situations when several groups of investors interact on the investment market pursuing, as a rule, quite diametrically opposed interests [3–5].

Rapid development of the Smart City technologies, actuality and relevance of our research was predetermined by the riskiness of new technologies development, particularly the need to develop new DSS models in purpose of investments in large innovative solutions. Such models, being implemented in the corresponding algorithmic and software development of DSS models, will definitely reduce the discrepancy between forecasting data and the actual return on investment in Smart City technologies.

# 2  Material and Method

Over the last 5–7 years, dozens of publications have been dedicated to financial, mathematical, algorithmic and other aspects of choosing well-grounded and prudent investor's strategies, in particular, for Smart City. A detailed analysis of these issues has been conveyed explicitly in [1–4]. In our research we have profoundly analyzed the publications that are significantly critical and conceptually relevant to the debate surrounding the issues. The scholars mainly review the related issues from the following aspects: mathematical and computer modeling, as well as selecting prudent investors' financial strategies [5–7]; in particular, exploiting modern DSS and expert systems. So as stated in [8–10], from the perspective of financial outcomes completely relying on traditional models and algorithms in calculating and optimizing options for investor actions in such inherently risky industries as investments in IT, cyber security, Smart City, enterprise digitalization, and the like, it is quite difficult for investors to achieve acceptable and expected outcomes.

At the same time, on the one hand the models introduced in the considered works enabled their users to obtain a certain forecast estimate for investors' actions, on the other one they still did not take into account the multifactorial nature of the investment process as a whole. Moreover, the obtained findings turned out to be frequently unworkable on the ground and did not result in program implementation; they mainly became a scope of academic interest rather than an appeal to real investors who require simple and effective tools for analyzing and choosing their financial strategies.

Some authors [10–12] claim that despite all its attractiveness, the hierarchy method (T. Saati method) [13] and expert methods [9, 10, 14] which are widely used in DSS, appear to be in most cases unsuitable for the synthesis of forecast estimates, issued by these software products to the investor. This factor becomes critical and especially noticeable for an investor or a group of investors when it comes to selecting rational and prudent strategies for channeling their financial resources in a particular project. It significantly relates to investing in large-scale and resource-intensive projects such as IT and Smart City.

Furthermore, after looking thoroughly into the issues discussed we can conclude that almost all the authors neglect or underestimate the impact of the multifactorial nature of the problem mentioned, as well as the fact that investors can equally act mutually on an agreed basis, being essentially allies, and being disagreed.

As pointed out in [7, 15, 16], there are models for DSS that notably relate to the analysis and evaluation of investor's strategies in the context of the actions of two parties (players). In accordance with [17, 18], the generally accepted approach to the model, which is namely based on the theory of games, implies that there exists the assumption that one of the parties involved in the investment process is viewed as a set of potential threats that may arise as a result of incompetent, uncoordinated actions of investors or groups of investors. But what is more critical is that such uncoordinated actions may result in a loss of capital. Consequently, the investor requires more accurate and adequate models that will prevent such a sad for him outcome.

Moreover, having analyzed the recent publications [1–3, 5, 12, 14, 16], we can state that investors in Smart City technologies can easily lobby for different areas of investment and, accordingly, defend their own vision of rational and prudent strategies for investing financial resources. Let us take a look at the following situations. One group of investors refers to the development of urban transport infrastructure on Smart City platforms and technologies as promising and quite lucrative. At the same time, another one longs for options for investing in energy-saving technologies that will reduce toxic emissions in Smart City, while the third group is increasingly interested in developing categories that characterize Smart City, such as healthcare or public safety. In fact, there can be various options creating different approaches to implementing well-known and successful Smart City investment projects exemplified by Melbourne, Tokyo, Seoul, San Francisco or Singapore.

There exists another suggestion that is introduced by the scholars in their works [16, 18] which holds that concerning the investigated issues surrounding this kind of problems, from the point of view of the logic the most suitable approach to describing the behavior of a complex system is to design models based on the game theory.

The thorough review of the related literature [1, 5, 9, 12, 15] has proved that most of the models and algorithms represented and examined in the works [13, 14, 17, 18] unfortunately do not contain valid and practical recommendations to investors in projects related to Smart City. This is especially true of aspects of the search of rational strategies for financial investment in such projects.

We can also encounter a separate trend in research concerning this particular area, it mainly relates to the works devoted to the use of various expert (ES) [19] and DSS [19, 20] for choosing rational investment strategies.

Thus, taking into account all the above mentioned factors determined our interest and the relevance of developing new models for DSS modules that will enable to support the decision-making process by a group or groups of investors in the search for rational investment strategies in the development of Smart City, considering the multi-factor nature of the task.

The suggested model is mainly based on the analysis of the financing procedure opportunities made by a group or groups of investors (hereinafter we use the terminology adopted in the theory of games - players) in the field of Smart City digital technologies development. The problem is solved by taking into account multifactorial nature, which is due to the multiplicity of possible strategies of the players and consequently the model logically continues our work [15, 16, 21]. In our research we put forward a designed approach which is based on solutions of bilinear multi-step quality games. Moreover, we would like to point out that a similar solution in the context of this article is considered for groups of players. Its core difference notably lies in the analysis of the outcomes obtained for several terminal surfaces.

## 3   Results

In our paper we set the following objectives, they are:

- developing models for intelligent support decision-making systems during the procedures for selecting rational strategies for investing by a group or groups of investors in projects related to the implementation of innovative Smart City technologies;
- carrying out a computational experiment within the environment of simulation modeling MatLab in order to verify the model's operability, as well as its adequacy, which will allow implementing the model programmatically in the form of a separate module for the support decision-making systems by a group or groups of investors in Smart City technologies.

Formulation of the problem. We believe that initially there is a situation when there are two groups of investors. These groups seek to invest in projects related to the development of Smart City. Each group of investors acts as a whole. However, we are confident that each investor in the group finances a certain digital technology as part of the development of Smart City, the suggested options for which have been analyzed above in the article. Let us look at these situations in more detail. The first player represents the first group and, accordingly, the second one is introduced by the second player. The suggested situation implies that players exercise control over a dynamic system in multidimensional spaces. This system will set changes in financial flows of players. Then, in accordance with the ideas noted in the works [15, 16, 21], the system can be described by bilinear multistep equations with dependent motions. It is necessary to find the sets of strategies $(U)$ and $(V)$, respectively, of the first and second player. We should remark that these strategies are defined by terminal surfaces $S_0$, $F_0$, respectively, for the first and second player. The goals of the players are defined as follows. The first player, using his management strategies (groups of players, hereinafter referred to as $Inv1$, for example, the Smart City investment object management of municipality or similar structure), tries to bring the dynamic system to the terminal surface $S_0$. The second player (groups of players), guided by his strategies, tries to bring the dynamic system to the terminal surface $F_0$. For players $Inv1$ and $Inv2$, it does not matter how the opposite side acts. The stated goals generate two tasks. They, respectively, are problems that must be solved from the point of view of the first ally player and from the point of view of the second ally player [15, 21].

In this paper, we consider only the solution to the problem from the point of view of the first ally player, since the solutions to the second problem are similar to [15, 16, 21]. At the same time, we should mention that the first player is introduced by a group of $M$ investors, while the second one is introduced by a group of $K$ investors.

At the moment of time $t = 0$ y $Inv1$ there is a set $h(0) = (h_1(0), \ldots, h_n(0))$, which consists of vectors $h_i(0)$. These vectors $h_i(0)$ are composed of $n$ components. The components characterize the amount of financial resources (hereinafter $FinR$), for the development $j$ of new technology for Smart City.

Similarly, we have the set $f(0) = (f_1(0), \ldots, f_n(0))$ ($f_i(0)$ for $Inv2$. This vector also consists of $n$ components. As in the first case, the components characterize the values $FinR$ aimed at $Inv2$ the development of $j$ Smart City technology.

The indicated sets will determine the predicted at the moment $t = 0$ values $FinR$ of the players (respectively $Inv1$ and $Inv2$). At the same time, the multifactor is taken into account in the sets $h(0)$ and $f(0)$.

## A. Numerical validation

Dynamics of changes $FinR$ for players can be described as follows:

$$h_1(t+1) = G_1^1 \cdot h_1(t) - U_1(t) \cdot G_1^1 \cdot h_1(t) - S_2^{11} \cdot V_1(t) \cdot G_2^1 \cdot f_1(t) - \ldots$$
$$-S_2^{1K} \cdot V_K \cdot G_2^K \cdot f_K(t);$$

$$\ldots\ldots\ldots\ldots\ldots\ldots\ldots\ldots\ldots\ldots\ldots\ldots\ldots\ldots\ldots\ldots\ldots\ldots$$

$$h_M(t+1) = G_1^M \cdot h_M(t) - U_M(t) \cdot G_1^M \cdot h_M(t) - S_2^{M1} \cdot V_1(t) \cdot G_2^1 \cdot f_1(t) - \ldots$$
$$-S_2^{MK} \cdot V_K \cdot f_K(t);$$
$$f_1(t+1) = G_2^1 \cdot f_1(t) - V_1(t) \cdot G_2^1 \cdot f_1(t) - S_1^{11} \cdot U_1(t) \cdot G_1^1 \cdot h_1(t) - \ldots$$
$$-S_1^{1M} \cdot U_M(t) \cdot G_1^M \cdot h_M(t);$$

$$\ldots\ldots\ldots\ldots\ldots\ldots\ldots\ldots\ldots\ldots\ldots\ldots\ldots\ldots\ldots\ldots\ldots\ldots$$

$$f_K(t+1) = G_2^K \cdot f_K(t) - V_K(t) \cdot G_2^K \cdot f_K(t) - S_1^{K1} \cdot U_1(t) \cdot h_1(t) - \ldots$$
$$-S_1^{KM} \cdot U_M(t) \cdot G_1^M \cdot h_M(t);$$

$$\tag{1}$$

where $h$ – financial resource value ($FinR$) for $Inv1$; $f$ – financial resource value ($FinR$) for $Inv2$;

$$h_1(t) \in R^n, \ldots, h_M(t) \in R^n, f_1(t) \in R^n, \ldots, f_K(t) \in R^n;$$

$U_1(t), \ldots, U_M(t), \quad V_1(t), \ldots, V_K(t)$ – square diagonal order matrices $n$ with positive elements
$\quad u_j^i(t) \in [0, 1], (i = 1, \ldots, n; j = 1, \ldots, M), \quad v_l^i(t) \in [0, 1], i = 1, \ldots, n; l = 1, \ldots, K$; on the main diagonals of matrices $U_j(t), V_l(t)$;
$\quad G_1$ – a matrix for transforming a financial resource $Inv1$ upon successful implementation in the field of digitalization of enterprises, taking into account multifactor nature; $G_2$ – resource conversion matrix $Inv2$; $S_1$ – a matrix characterizing the elasticity of the player's actions $Inv2$ in relation to player 1 ($Inv1$); $S_2$ – a matrix characterizing the elasticity of investments $Inv1$ in relation to $Inv2$; $G_1^j, G_2^l, S_1^{lj}, S_2^{jl}$ – square order matrices $n$ with positive elements $g_1^{km}, g_2^{km}, s_1^{km}, s_2^{km}, k = 1, \ldots, n; m = 1, \ldots, n$; respectively, $t = 0, 1, \ldots$
We assume that

$$S_0 = \bigcup_{i=1}^{K \cdot n} \{(h, f) : (h, f) \in R^{2 \cdot n}, h \geq 0, \quad f_i \prec 0\}, \tag{2}$$

$$F_0 = \bigcup_{i=1}^{M \cdot n} \{(h, f) : (h, f) \in R^{2 \cdot n}, \quad f \geq 0, h_i \prec 0\}. \tag{3}$$

where $S_0, F_0$ – terminal surfaces for $Inv1$ and $Inv2$, respectively;
$R^{2 \cdot n}$ – (2-n measured space).
The interaction $Inv1$ and $Inv2$ will end if the conditions are met:

$$(h(t), f(t)) \in S_0, \tag{4}$$

$$(h(t), f(t)) \in F_0. \tag{5}$$

If conditions (4) or (5) are fulfilled, then, accordingly, we believe that $Inv2$ and $Inv1$ did not have enough financial resources to continue financing procedures. If both conditions (4) and (5) are not fulfilled, we believe that the financing procedures will continue.

The process described by the system (1) is considered in the framework of the scheme of a multi-step positional game with full information [21].

The solution to problem 1 is to find the sets of "preference" $Inv1$, as well as its optimal strategies. It is similarly for $Inv2$. Here are the conditions under which the solution to the game is found. It means that we shall demonstrate how to find the sets of "preferences" and optimal strategies $u_*$ for $Inv1$.

We introduce the following notation.

$$G_1 = \begin{pmatrix} G_1^1 0 \ldots \ldots .0 \\ 0 G_1^2 \ldots \ldots 0 \\ \ldots \ldots \ldots \ldots \\ 0 \ldots \ldots \ldots G_1^M \end{pmatrix}; \; G_2 = \begin{pmatrix} G_2^1 0 \ldots \ldots .0 \\ 0 G_2^2 \ldots \ldots 0 \\ \ldots \ldots \ldots \ldots \\ 0 \ldots \ldots \ldots G_2^K \end{pmatrix}; \; U = \begin{pmatrix} U_1 0 \ldots \ldots .0 \\ 0 U_2 \ldots \ldots 0 \\ \ldots \ldots \ldots \ldots \\ 0 \ldots \ldots \ldots U_M \end{pmatrix};$$

$$V = \begin{pmatrix} V_1 0 \ldots \ldots .0 \\ 0 V_2 \ldots \ldots 0 \\ \ldots \ldots \ldots \ldots \\ 0 \ldots \ldots \ldots V_K \end{pmatrix}; \; S_1 = \begin{pmatrix} S_1^{11} \ldots \ldots \ldots S_1^{1M} \\ S_1^{21} \ldots \ldots \ldots S_1^{2M} \\ \ldots \ldots \ldots \ldots \\ S_1^{K1} \ldots \ldots \ldots S_1^{KM} \end{pmatrix}; \; S_2 = \begin{pmatrix} S_2^{11} \ldots \ldots \ldots S_2^{1K} \\ S_2^{21} \ldots \ldots \ldots S_2^{2K} \\ \ldots \ldots \ldots \ldots \\ S_2^{M1} \ldots \ldots \ldots S_2^{MK} \end{pmatrix}.$$

Define through $\hat{W}_1$ multitude: $\hat{W}_1 = W_* - \bigcup_{i=1}^{M \cdot n} W_i$,

$$W_* = \left\{ \begin{array}{l} (h(0), f(0)) : (h(0), f(0)) \in R_+^{(M+K) \cdot n}, \\ G_1 \cdot h(0) - S_2 \cdot G_2 \cdot f(0) \in R_+^{M \cdot n} \end{array} \right\}, \tag{6}$$

$$W_i = \left\{ \begin{array}{l} (h(0), f(0)) \in R_+^{(M+K) \cdot n}, \\ (G_1 \cdot h(0))_i = (S_2 \cdot G_2 \cdot f(0)))_i \end{array} \right\}. \tag{7}$$

Additional symbols:

$$R_1 = S_1, \; R_k = \{ (Q_{k-1} \cdot G_2 \cdot S_1 - R_{k-1} \cdot G_1)^+ + R_{k-1} \cdot G_1 \}; \tag{8}$$

$$Q_1 = E + S_1 \cdot S_2, \quad Q_k = (R_{k-1} \cdot G_1 \cdot S_2 - Q_{k-1} \cdot G_2)^+ \\ + Q_{k-1} \cdot G_2 + (Q_{k-1} \cdot G_2 \cdot S_1 - R_{k-1} \cdot G_1)^+ S_2. \tag{9}$$

We also assume that

$$1_j^{k,j} = \left\{ \begin{array}{l} 1, \; (Q_k \cdot G_2)_{ij} = 0, \\ \frac{(R_k \cdot G_1 \cdot S_2)}{(Q_k \cdot G_2)_{ij}}, \; (Q_k \cdot G_2)_{ij} \neq 0, \end{array} \right. \tag{10}$$

$$q_j^k = \left\{ \begin{array}{l} 1, \; (G_1 \cdot S_2)_{ik} = 0, \\ \frac{(S_2 \cdot G_2)_{ik}}{(S_2 \cdot G_1)_{ik}}, \; (S_2 \cdot G_1)_{ik} \neq 0, \end{array} \right. \tag{11}$$

$$m_k^i = \left\{ \begin{array}{l} \min_{1 \leq m \leq n, (Q_k \cdot B_2)_{im} \neq 0} \dfrac{\left\{ \sum_{j=1}^{n} \max((R_k \cdot G_1)_{ij}, (Q_k \cdot G_2 \cdot S_1)_{ij}) \times (S_2)_{jm} \right\}}{(\Psi)_{im}}, \tag{12} \\ or \; \exists \; m(i) : (\Psi)_{im(i)} \neq 0, +\infty, \forall m : 1 \leq m \leq n (\Psi)_{im} = 0; \end{array} \right.$$

$$q^*_{max} = \max_{1 \le k \le n, 1 \le i \le n} q^k_i, \quad m^*_i = \inf_k m^i_k, \quad (i = 1, \dots, n); \quad (Q_k \cdot G_2 = \Psi)$$

$$\bar{m}^i_k = \begin{cases} \min_{l \le m \le n, (Q_k \cdot B_2)_{im} \ne 0} ((Q_k \cdot G_2 \cdot S_1 \cdot S_2)_{im}/(\Psi)_{im}), \\ or \quad \exists \; m(i) : (\Psi)_{im(i)} \ne 0, +\infty, \forall m : 1 \le m \le n(\Psi)_{im} = 0; \end{cases} \tag{13}$$

$$\bar{m}^*_i = \inf_k \bar{m}^i_k, \quad (i = 1, \dots, n).$$

The lemma is valid. 1 [15, 16, 21].

**Lemma 1.** Within $\hat{W}_1$ 1-st player ($Inv1$) can achieve goals:

(a)  for the final quantity of steps $\hat{W}_1 \subseteq \bigcup_{m=1}^{N_*} W^n_1, \; 0 < N_* < +\infty,$

if $\lim_{\bar{T} \to \infty} \left( \min_{1 \le k \le n} (1^{T,i}_k) \right) > 1$, for $i : \quad 1 \le i \le n;$

(b)  at least in countable steps (or $\hat{W}_1 \subseteq \bigcup_{n=1}^{\infty} W^n_1$),

if $\lim_{\bar{T} \to \infty} \left( \min_{1 \le k \le n} (1^{T,i}_k) \right) = 1$, for $i : \quad 1 \le i \le n;$

The situation is quite possible if $\hat{W}_1$ $Inv1$ for a particular quantity of steps cannot achieve the goal:

(c)  for $\sup_T \left( \max_{1 \le i \le n} \left( \min_{1 \le k \le +n} (1^{T,j}) \right) \right) < 1.$

First of all, before formulating the theory of solving task 1 we shall illustrate one more lemma. To do this, consider a numerical sequence:

$$r_n = (1/q) \times m/\{m + (1 - r_{n-1})\}, \tag{14}$$

where $0 \le r_1 < 1, \quad 0 < q < 1, \quad 0 < m < +\infty.$

Values $r_1, q, m$ are related in accordance with the conditions (15)–(19):

$$\frac{2}{q} - 1 - \sqrt{\left(\frac{2}{q} - 1\right)^2 - 1} < m < \frac{2}{q} - 1 + \sqrt{\left(\frac{2}{q} - 1\right)^2 - 1}, \tag{15}$$

$$m \ge \frac{2}{q} - 1 + \sqrt{\left(\frac{2}{q} - 1\right)^2 - 1}, \tag{16}$$

$$m \le \frac{2}{q} - 1 + \sqrt{\left(\frac{2}{q} - 1\right)^2 - 1}, \quad r_1 \le \frac{(1+m)}{2} - \sqrt{\left[\frac{(1+m)}{2}\right]^2 - \frac{m}{q}}, \tag{17}$$

$$m \leq \frac{2}{q} - 1 + \sqrt{\left(\frac{2}{q} - 1\right)^2 - 1},$$

$$\frac{(1+m)}{2} - \sqrt{\left[\frac{(1+m)}{2}\right]^2 - \frac{m}{q}} < r_1 < \frac{(1+m)}{2} + \sqrt{\left[\frac{(1+m)}{2}\right]^2 - \frac{m}{q}}, \tag{18}$$

$$m \leq \frac{2}{q} - 1 + \sqrt{\left(\frac{2}{q} - 1\right)^2 - 1}, \quad r_1 \geq \frac{(1+m)}{2} + \sqrt{\left[\frac{(1+m)}{2}\right]^2 - \frac{m}{q}}. \tag{19}$$

**Lemma 2.** The sequence $r_n$ will be monotonically increasing, unbounded from above if condition (15) is satisfied. If conditions (16) or (17) are satisfied, the sequence will be monotonically increasing, having the limit $a$:

$$a = \frac{(1+m)}{2} + \sqrt{\left[\frac{(1+m)}{2}\right]^2 - \frac{m}{q}},$$

If condition (18) is satisfied – monotonically decreasing, having the limit $a$;
If condition (19) is satisfied – monotonically increasing, unbounded from above.
Notifying $r_1^i = \min_{1 \leq k \leq n} 1_k^{T,i}$. We assume that in (15)–(19) $q = q_{\max}^*$, $r_1 = r_1^i$, $m = r_*^i$ for some $i$, $1 \leq i \leq n$.

**Theorem 1.** The first player will achieve the goal (in the field $\hat{W}_1$):

(a) for a finite number of steps, for $i$ : $r_1^i > 0$, $0 < q_{\max}^* < 1$; for $i$ : $m_*^i > 0$, $0 < q_{\max}^* < 1$ and if one of the conditions (15), (16) or (19) is satisfied;
(b) at least in a countable number of steps for $q_{\max}^* = 1$ and the implementation of condition (16) or condition (17), in which $m_*^i = 1$ for some $i$ ;

The first player may fail to achieve his goal (in the field $\hat{W}_1$) in any number of steps $(\hat{W}_1 \not\subset \bigcup_{n=1}^{\infty} W_1^n)$:

(c) when $m_*^i = 0 \, \forall \, i = 1, \ldots, n$;
(d) for $m_*^i > 0$, for some $i$ and the implementation of condition (18) for the situation when $m_*^i \neq 1$.

**Remark 1.** The assertions of Theorem 1 will be fulfilled if, under its conditions, the quantity $m_*^i$ is replaced by $\bar{m}_*^i$. It is convenient for checking the conditions of Theorem 1 in specific problems. It should be noted that when considering investment procedures carried out by groups of investors, we have to bear in our mind that there might appear situations when in groups investors may act inconsistently. However, this inconsistency of actions in groups may lead to an option in which investors can fail to achieve their expected outcomes, which they could obtain if they acted consistently. Let us take a look at an example. We assume that the first group of investors consists of two investors, and the second one comprises only one investor. We shall record the dynamics of investor interaction:

$h_1(t+1) = (5/3) \cdot h_1(t) - u_1(t) \cdot (5/3) \cdot h_1(t) - 4 \cdot v(t) \cdot f(t),$
$h_2(t+1) = (5/3) \cdot h_2(t) - u_2(t) \cdot (5/3) \cdot h_2(t) - (1/3) \cdot v(t) \cdot f(t);$
$f(t+1) = f(t) - v(t) \cdot (1/4) \cdot f(t) - (1/4) \cdot u_1(t) \cdot (5/3) \cdot h_1(t) - 3 \cdot u_2(t) \cdot (5/3) \cdot h_2(t)$

where $u_1(t) \in [0, 1]$, $u_2(t) \in [0, 1]$, $v(t) \in [0, 1]$.

The initial position of the players of the first group are as follows: $h_1(0) = 2.7$; $h_2(0) = (7/19)$; the position of the player of the second group: $f(0) = 1$.

If you limit the time of the game to two steps, it is quite easy to conclude that the players of the first group must act consistently in order to achieve their goal in two steps, since with an uncoordinated method of action the first group can fail to achieve this goal. Indeed, the field $\hat{W}_1$ in our game is written like this:

$$\hat{W}_1 = \{(h_1(0), h_2(0), f(0)) : (h_1(0), h_2(0), f(0)) \in R_+^3, 5 \cdot h_1(0) \succ 12 \cdot f(0), 5 \cdot h_2(0) \succ$$

where $R_+^3$ – positive orthant in three-dimensional space;

A lot of preferences of the first group of investors in one step with an agreed method of action in the group:

$$W_{1,c}^1 = \{(h_1(0), h_2(0), f(0)) : (h_1(0), h_2(0), f(0)) \in R_+^3,$$
$$5 \cdot h_1(0) + 60 \cdot h_2(0) \succ 36 \cdot f(0)\}.$$

It should be notes that the ratio of the parameters is that the set of preference in two steps with the agreed method of action in the group coincides with $\hat{W}_1$, i.e. $W_{1,c}^2 = \hat{W}_1$.

The sets of preference with an uncoordinated way of players' actions in one and two steps are written as follows:

$$W_{1,H}^1 = \{(h_1(0), h_2(0), f(0)) : (h_1(0), h_2(0), f(0)) \in R_+^3,$$
$$5 \cdot h_1(0) \succ 24 \cdot f(0)\} \cup \{(h_1(0), h_2(0), f(0)) : (h_1(0), h_2(0), f(0)) \in R_+^3,$$
$$5 \cdot h_2(0) \succ 2 \cdot f(0)\},$$
$$W_{1,H}^2 = \{(h_1(0), h_2(0), f(0)) : (h_1(0), h_2(0), f(0)) \in R_+^3,$$
$$5 \cdot h_1(0) \succ 14 \cdot f(0)\} \cup \{(h_1(0), h_2(0), f(0)) :$$
$$(h_1(0), h_2(0), f(0)) \in R_+^3, 18 \cdot h_2(0) \succ 7 \cdot f(0)\}.$$

We can easily see that

$$h_1(0), h_2(0), h_3(0)) = (2.7, (7.19), 1) \notin W_{1,H}^1 \cup W_{1,H}^2 \cup W_{1,c}^1,$$

it relates to multitude $\hat{W}_1$. This situation shows that only with the coordination of their actions the investors of the first group will achieve their goal in two steps. It should be noted that if the actions of the players in the group are not coordinated, the first player (from the first group) with this initial state can achieve the goal in three steps.

**B. Computing experiment.** Computational experiments were performed by MatLab. Figures 1, 2 and 3 shows the results for test calculations during our computational experiments. The purpose of the experiment is to determine a lot of strategies of players and the multitude of preferences of investor groups.

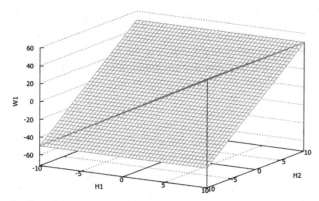

**Fig. 1.** The result of modeling the optimality set of the first group with the coordinated action of investors in the first group

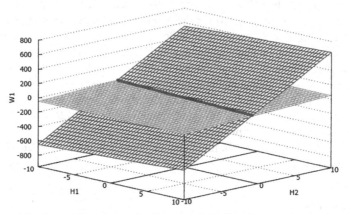

**Fig. 2.** The result of modeling the optimality set of the first investor in the first group with uncoordinated actions of investors in the first group

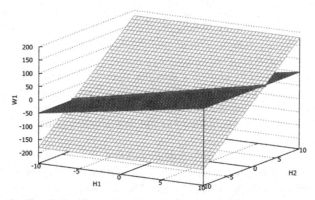

**Fig. 3.** The result of modeling the optimality set of the second investor in the first group in the first group with uncoordinated actions of investors in the first group

We should state that the results obtained during computational experiments demonstrate the correctness of the proposed model. However, slight differences of 5–8% can be explained by rounding of intermediate results in the MatLab program. This fact should be taken into account in the software implementation of the proposed model.

## 4   Discussions

Figure 1 shows the results of modeling the optimality set of the first group for the case of coordinated actions of investors in the first group. Figures 2 and 3 correspond to the optimality sets of the first investor in the first group and the second investor in the first group with their uncoordinated actions. Their union is "less" (by inclusion of sets) of the optimality set of the first group under the coordinated action of the players in the group. This is illustrated in Figs. 2 and 3. At the same time, we should point out that the disadvantage of the model lies in the fact that the data obtained using MatLab for predictive assessment when choosing a particular development strategy for investment projects in the development of Smart City will not always coincide with the actual data. However, at this stage of research, it is quite normal because so far only the model has been tested. With its successful testing and confirmation of correctness, several real projects will implement the corresponding software product in the form of DSS by groups of investors. After analyzing the results obtained using other models, for example, described in works [8, 12, 22, 23], we can state that the suggested solution improves the efficiency and predictability for the investor by an average of 7–12%.

We also assume that further prospects for the development of the study mainly relate to the implementation of models in the software product being developed - DSS when investing in Smart City.

## 5   Conclusions

The model is proposed for the mathematical support of decisions during the evaluation of projects for Smart City, taking into account the multifactorial nature of the task and potential financial strategies of investor groups. The model is aimed at subsequent software implementation in a decision support system (DSS) or an expert system for cross-platform software products. The model allows you to evaluate attractiveness for groups of investors (players) of the analyzed projects.

At the same time, players control a dynamic system in multidimensional project spaces. As an example of the applied scope of the model, investment projects for Smart City are considered. The results and the mathematical calculations presented in the article are obtained on the basis of the solution of a bilinear multistep quality game with several terminal surfaces.

The scientific novelty of the work lies in the fact that, in contrast to existing solutions and close in conceptual direction research, the article first considers a new class of multistep bilinear games. The proposed approach and the resulting solution for searching for a multitude of preferences of players allows us to correctly and adequately describe the investment processes, given the multifactorial nature of the problem statement. The designed software product in the form of a DSS module of investor groups provides the latest tools for finding optimal financial investment strategies.

Computing experiments were performed in the MatLab system to search for sets of investors' preferences and their optimal financial strategies during the analysis of Smart City development projects. The results of computational experiments confirmed the correctness and adequacy of the model for finding optimal strategies by a group of investors.

# References

1. Albino, V., Berardi, U., Dangelico, R.M.: Smart cities: definitions, dimensions, performance, and initiatives. J. Urban Technol. **22**(1), 3–21 (2015)
2. Angelidou, M.: Smart cities: a conjuncture of four forces. Cities **47**, 95–106 (2015)
3. Glasmeier, A., Christopherson, S.: Thinking about smart cities. Camb. J. Reg. Econ. Soc. **8**, 3–12 (2015)
4. Zanella, A., Bui, N., Castellani, A., Vangelista, L., Zorzi, M.: Internet of things for smart cities. IEEE Internet of Things J. **1**(1), 22–32 (2014)
5. Lakhno, V., Malyukov, V., Bochulia, T., Hipters, Z., Kwilinski, A., Tomashevska, O.: Model of managing of the procedure of mutual financial investing in information technologies and smart city systems. Int. J. Civil Eng. Technol. **9**(8), 1802–1812 (2018)
6. Paroutis, S., Bennett, M., Heracleous, L.: A strategic view on smart city technology: the case of IBM Smarter Cities during a recession. Technol. Forecast. Soc. Change **89**, 262–272 (2014)
7. Hollands, R.G.: Critical interventions into the corporate smart city. Camb. J. Reg. Econ. Soc. **8**(1), 61–77 (2015)
8. Mithas, S., Tafti, A., Mitchell, W.: How a firm's competitive environment and digital strategic posture influence digital business strategy. MIS Q. **37**(2), 511–536 (2013)
9. Tiwana, A., Ramesh, B.: E-services: problems, opportunities, and digital platforms. In: Proceedings of the 34th Annual Hawaii International Conference on System Sciences, pp. 8–pp. IEEE, January 2001
10. Mazzarol, T.: SMEs engagement with e-commerce, e-business and e-marketing. Small Enterp. Res. **22**(1), 79–90 (2015)
11. Solanas, A., et al.: Smart health: a context-aware health paradigm within smart cities. IEEE Commun. Mag. **52**(8), 74–81 (2014)
12. Mohammadzadeh, A.K., Ghafoori, S., Mohammadian, A., Mohammadkazemi, R., Mahbanooei, B., Ghasemi, R.: A Fuzzy Analytic Network Process (FANP) approach for prioritizing internet of things challenges in Iran. Technol. Soc. **53**, 124–134 (2018)
13. Selçuk, A.L.P., Özkan, T.K.: Job choice with multi-criteria decision making approach in a fuzzy environment. Int. Rev. Manag. Mark. **5**(3), 165–172 (2015)
14. Kache, F., Seuring, S.: Challenges and opportunities of digital information at the intersection of Big Data Analytics and supply chain management. Int. J. Oper. Prod. Manag. **37**(1), 10–36 (2017)
15. Akhmetov, B.B., Lakhno, V.A., Akhmetov, B.S., Malyukov, V.P.: The choice of protection strategies during the bilinear quality game on cyber security financing. Bull. Natl. Acad. Sci. Repub. Kazakhstan **3**, 6–14 (2018)
16. Lakhno, V., Malyukov, V., Gerasymchuk, N., et al.: Development of the decision making support system to control a procedure of financial investment. Eastern-Eur. J. Enterp. Technol. **6**(3), 24–41 (2017)
17. Smit, H.T., Trigeorgis, L.: Flexibility and games in strategic investment (2015)

18. Arasteh, A.: Considering the investment decisions with real options games approach. Renew. Sustain. Energy Rev. **72**, 1282–1294 (2017)
19. Gottschlich, J., Hinz, O.: A decision support system for stock investment recommendations using collective wisdom. Decis. Support Syst. **59**, 52–62 (2014)
20. Strantzali, E., Aravossis, K.: Decision making in renewable energy investments: a review. Renew. Sustain. Energy Rev. **55**, 885–898 (2016)
21. Lakhno, V., Malyukov, V., Parkhuts, L., Buriachok, V., Satzhanov, B., Tabylov, A.: Funding model for port information system cyber security facilities with incomplete hacker information available. J. Theor. Appl. Inf. Technol. **96**(13), 4215–4225 (2018)
22. Vilajosana, I., Llosa, J., Martinez, B., Domingo-Prieto, M., Angles, A., Vilajosana, X.: Bootstrapping smart cities through a self-sustainable model based on big data flows. IEEE Commun. Mag. **51**(6), 128–134 (2013)
23. Akhmetov, B., Balgabayeva, L., et al.: Mobile platform for decision support system during mutual continuous investment in technology for smart city. Stud. Syst. Decis. Control **199**, 731–742 (2019)

# Software Agents Meet Heterogeneous Ecosystems of Services and Resources for Controlling the Internet of Things

Pablo Pico-Valencia[1]([✉]), Juan A. Holgado-Terriza[2], and Evelin Flores-García[1]

[1] Pontifical Catholic University of Ecuador, Esmeraldas, Ecuador
{pablo.pico,evelin.flores}@pucese.edu.ec
[2] University of Granada, Granada, Spain
jholgado@ugr.es

**Abstract.** Service- and resource-oriented technologies have achieved a widely level of popularity and acceptance for the development of distributed systems. Most of the current processes executed on web, mobile and pervasive applications are generally developed by invoking heterogeneous services and resources through different models. This paper presents an analysis of the main approaches originated from the integration of Multiagent Systems (MASs) with service and resource architectures. The behavior of agents that explore and consume distributed services and resources on heterogeneous ecosystems was analyzed empirically in order to define a taxonomy of agents. Furthermore, a software tool for composing processes oriented to control IoT scenarios based on invoking services and resources is described. The experiments carried out show that the use of the artifice agent&services/resources is technically feasible and contributes significantly to the abstraction of the complexity of actions carried out in IoT environments.

**Keywords:** Multiagent System · Software agent · Internet of Things · Service · Resource

## 1 Introduction

In recent years, the integration of service- and resource-oriented technologies with software agents has been addressed by researchers to improve the level of interoperability and the distribution of intelligence in large multi-agent systems (MASs). New approaches such as MAS-Service Oriented Architecture (MAS-SOA) [20,27] and MAS-Resource Oriented Architecture (MAS-ROA) [7] have emerged in order to support the development of distributed systems (web, mobile and pervasive such as the Internet of Things, IoT [11,12]) that can model intelligent processes employing interoperable software components such as services and resources.

One of the limitations of services and resources is the lack of autonomy. This implies that services or resources cannot be executed on their own. Then, the

© Springer Nature Switzerland AG 2020
M. Botto-Tobar et al. (Eds.): ICAT 2019, CCIS 1193, pp. 27–40, 2020.
https://doi.org/10.1007/978-3-030-42517-3_3

execution of a service depends always on external entities such as applications, users or software agents that must be able to access and consume it. Software agents have associated intrinsic properties such as proactivity, autonomy, intelligence and collaboration that can be exploited if we can allow the access to the information sources provided by services and resources. Consequently, the execution of automation processes through software agents is feasible. In this sense, the integration of agents with ecosystems of services and resources becomes relevant in the domain of IoT because current objects, supported by an interface based on services and/or resources can be controlled in a proactive, intelligent and collaborative way. These aspects are being introduced into the field of IoT as detailed in [6,19]. These issues have motivated us to create a tool compatible with IoT middleware based on services and resources in order to facilitate the creation of complex agent behaviors that achieve automatic control tasks without embedding algorithms and intelligence within the structural components of the agents. For this reason, the aim of this paper is to demonstrate how beneficial it is to integrate agents with services and resources in the IoT domain.

The main objective of this study is to analyze, discuss and implement the main approaches arising from the integration of agents with services and resources in the IoT domain. We emphasize on the principal aspects associated with heterogeneity in ecosystems of Internet Services (IoS) and Internet of Resources (IoR) as well as the potential emerging entities that arise from the integration of these technologies to control IoT objects by setting a mechanism to distribute the algorithms and intelligence of the agents. Thus, the main contributions that this work makes to the literature are the following: (i) definition of new agent entities that can be modeled with services and resources, (ii) development of an application programming interface (API) oriented to simplify the invocation of heterogeneous services and resources uniformly and finally, (iii) presentation of the guidelines to build a MAS with the Java Agent DEvelopment Framework (JADE) [2] modeling agent behaviors employing distributed components such as services and resources.

This paper is organized in five sections. Section 2 describes the main entities involved in the process of integrating software agents with services and resources. Section 3 presents an API oriented to the modeling of blocks that define a sequence of invocations to heterogeneous services and resources. A case study in the area of Ambient Intelligence (AmI) implemented using IoT technologies based on DOHA (Dynamic Open Home-Automation [21]) services and RESTful resources has also been described in Sect. 4. Finally, in Sect. 6 main conclusions are outlined.

## 2   Background

Services and resources are aimed at supporting business processes and business automation based on Service Oriented Architecture (SOA) or Resource Oriented Architecture (ROA) using request-response or publish-subscribe schemes [Ref]. These components are distributed software pieces that have a standard and well-defined interface (API, Application Programming Interface), allowing them to interoperate between heterogeneous applications [8]. The execution or consumption of each component should be performed by another service/resource or user application. The use of a formal description of services and resources enables them to offer developers a high level of autonomy, interoperability, independence of development platform, encapsulation and availability [8,29]. Therefore, these features greatly favor the development of distributed systems.

On the other hand, software agents are potential entities especially designed for executing tasks with a certain degree of autonomy and intelligence just as a human being would. Its active nature helps the execution of coordination, collaboration and conflict resolution processes in distributed systems. This contributes significantly to develop systems with a high level of autonomy, sociability, rationality, reactivity, proactivity and adaptability [28]. These characteristics encourage the development of intelligent and collaborative systems. However, both aspects required in IoT ecosystems are not inherently supported by devices. In addition, software agents requires a common communication channel with data protocols known by all parties in order to share data to be processed.

Then, the integration of agent ecosystems with service/resource may benefit the development of distributed applications because agent technologies provide schemes to define agent behaviors in terms of processes or actions to be done while services/resources offer a common way to access data available in IoT devices. The natural coexistence between agent and service/resource is achieved when agent as active entity can invoke or consume one or more services or resources as passive entities.

## 2.1 Approaches

As Fig. 1 shows, benefits of both agents and services/resources can be exploited by modeling agent actions in two ways: including explicit services/resources or automatic discoverable services/resources. The first approach is focused on the design of agent actions based on blocks composed of orchestrated services and resources in order to achieve a specific goal [15]. In the second approach, the specific services/resources are discovered at runtime on catalogs, repositories, or directories which are generally distributed on the Internet [26]. This approach empowers agents to take advantage of services and resources with higher quality of service to enable self-adaptable systems. In both cases, the intelligence and algorithms associated with the agents can be distributed using cloud [3] or fog [13] computing technologies.

In order to materialize both approaches several specific software tools such as libraries, add-ons and APIs have been developed. Some of the most relevant add-ons are: JADE WSIG (*Java Agent Development Framework - Web Services Integration Gateway*) [1], WS2JADE (*Web Service in JADE*) [14] and JADE-WSDC (*JADE - Web Service Dynamic Client* [22]. However, these add-ons only support the consumption of a single service model (web services). This creates a limitation because in pervasive scenarios such as IoT, it requires not only the consumption of services but also resources, or both.

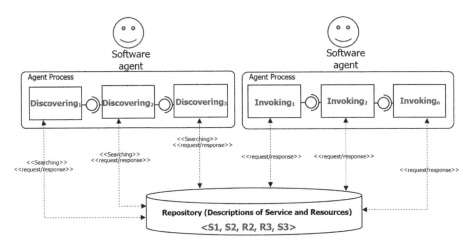

**Fig. 1.** Approaches originated from the integration of software agents with services and resources

With the purpose of providing an alternative solution to the limitation associated with the non-supporting of heterogeneity, Lee et al. [10] developed a framework oriented to enable mobile devices to perform invocations of SOAP (Simple Object Access Protocol) and OSGi (*Open Services Gateway initiative*) services, and resources using a REST interface. But this tool is not available on-line. That is why, an API is needed for providing programmers a uniform interface compatible with the consumption of heterogeneous services and resources linked to IoT.

### 2.2   Agents Meet Heterogeneous Ecosystems of Services and Resources

In general, heterogeneity of ecosystems of IoS and IoR is given by the inclusion of different computing technologies, vendors and models. In this sense, a heterogeneous ecosystem of services/resources ($E_i$) is defined as a collection of accessible services $S<S_1, S_2, S_3, ..., S_n>$ and resources $R<R_1, R_2, R_3, ..., R_n>$, where two or more of these components meet heterogeneity restrictions $<Rc_1, Rc_2, ..., Rc_6>$. These restrictions are described as follows:

- $Rc_1$: Being developed following the guidelines of different service/resource models (e.g., SOAP, RESTful, DPWS, DOHA).
- $Rc_2$: Being developed on different programming platforms or programming languages (i.e. Java, ASP .NET) or framework (e.g., Jersey, .NET Framework, Apache Axis2).
- $Rc_3$: Executing operations of a different nature or domain (e.g., scientific, management, general use).

- $Rc_4$: Running in different technological environments of execution or production (e.g., web servers, embedded systems, mobile devices, IoT objects, wearable devices).
- $Rc_5$: Using different levels of complexity to be modeled (e.g., microservices, composite services).
- $Rc_6$: Handling different extra components or aspects to the conventional ones (e.g., context sensitivity, semantic description, handling of temporal restrictions).

## 2.3 Towards Service- and Resource-Based Agents

By combining the benefits of agents (adaptability, proactivity, reactivity, rationality, sociability and autonomy), and services/resources (autonomy, interoperability, platform independence, encapsulation and availability/discovery) it is possible to model improved agents such as the T-matrix analysis of Table 1 shows.

**Table 1.** Emerging entities arising from the agent and services/resource approach.

| | | Self-adaptive | Intelligent-lightweight | Collaborative-flexible | Agile development | Standard-based | Fault-tolerant | Secure |
|---|---|---|---|---|---|---|---|---|
| **Agents** | Adaptability | * | | * | * | | | |
| | Proactivity | | * | | | | * | |
| | Reactivity | | | | | | * | |
| | Rationality | | * | | | | | |
| | Sociability | | | * | | | | |
| | Autonomy | * | | * | | | | |
| | Agents-services/resources | | | | | | | |
| **Services/Resources** | Autonomy | * | | * | | | | |
| | Interoperability | | * | | | | | |
| | Platform independence | | | | * | * | | |
| | Encapsulation | | * | | * | | | * |
| | Availability/Discovery | * | | * | | | * | |

Entities shown in Table 1 have new features and additional benefits compared with generic software agents. These entities can improve handling resources extending the capabilities of IoT devices. They are described as follows:

- **Self-adaptive agents.** Properties of the agents such as autonomy and adaptability together with properties of the services/resources such as discovery, enable the use of self-adaptive agents. Self-adaptation is achieved due to the fact that the building process of the agents is oriented to decouple the algorithms from their internal structure. Thus, the agents can modify their behavior according to the components discovered in ecosystems of services/resources.

- **Intelligent-lightweight agents.** Properties such as the reactivity and rationality of the agents, together with the interoperability and the capability of encapsulation associated with the services/resources, enable the use of lightweight intelligent agents. Lightweight intelligence enables agents can act coherently, executing complex logic processes based on rules or machine learning techniques without the need of encapsulating algorithms within the structure of the agent. This implies that the agent does not directly execute the processes associated with decision making. This capability empowers agents to become entities that optimize the use of computing and energy resources of the devices where they run.
- **Collaborative-flexible agents.** Collaborative-flexible entities arise from the combination of the social, adaptive and autonomic capacities of the agents, and properties such as autonomy and discovery associated with services and resources. These agents take advantage of the ability to communicate in order to establish relationships with a peer network for achieving their goals. These agents use service search mechanisms to support dynamic requests from their counterparts at runtime.
- **Agile development agents.** The agile development of agents is easily achieved thanks to properties such as platform independence and encapsulation associated with services/resources, and the adaptability of agents. Agents can be modeled as a set of behavioral artifacts [2] and deliberative elements [5] which can encapsulate services/resources already developed. These reused components used to build new agents save time and costs in terms of development.
- **Standard-based agents.** Services and resources have reached a high level of interoperability thanks to the standards used to describe these software components. However, the efforts made in the agent domain have not allowed achieving the interoperability levels as services and resources would. The platform independence of service/resource ecosystem enables the development of standard agents since their capabilities are described using similar standards used to describe services and resources.
- **Fault-tolerant agents.** The availability of the services and resources together with the reactive and proactive capability of the agents enable the use of fault tolerant agents. These agents analyze the changes occurred in their context in order to explore their ecosystem of services/resources and thus, recovering alternative components that satisfy the functionalities that have been affected. In this way, the system can continue to operate normally without requiring manual configuration.
- **Secure agents.** The security issue has caused much controversy in the field of agents. However, thanks to properties such as encapsulation associated with services, it is feasible to model secure agents because the algorithm is

not integrated into the structure of the agent itself. Security mechanisms of agents are inherited from security settings provided by the technologies of services and resources used to implement agents.

## 3   Modeling Agent Processes Using Services and Resources

We propose the definition of an API that allows the consumption of services and resources from web applications, mobile apps and IoT systems. For IoT systems, it is recommended that physical IoT devices have a communication interface based on services and/or resources. On the one hand, a specific case of devices compatible with a service-based interface are DPWS (Device Profile for Web Service [4]) devices. This interface is handled with DOHA services [21]. On the other hand, devices compatible with a resource-based interface are RESTful devices. OpenHAB (open Home Automation Bus [18]) is a tool compatible with this type of devices. This specific tool provides an interface based on uniform resource identifiers (URIs) for accessing heterogeneous devices of multiple brands (e.g., TV, temperature sensors, light-bulbs).

The invocations illustrated in (1) and (2) show how it is possible to use the developed interface to consume services and resources, respectively. In the case of the uniform service-oriented interface, it requires the specification of 4 arguments $<L, O, IA, DA>$, where $L$ is the server where the service runs, $O$ is the operation to be invoked, $IA$ is a list of input arguments and $DA$ is a list with the values of $IA$.

$$ansS = DOHA.InvokeServiceSTRING(L, O, IA, DA); \qquad (1)$$

Similarly, in the case of the resource-oriented interface, it requires 5 arguments $<L, R, M, IA, DA>$, where $L$ corresponds to the server where the resource is hosted, $R$ is the name of the resource, $M$ is the method (GET, POST, PUT, DELETE) to be invoked, and $IA$ and $DA$ are lists of arguments analogous to the lists used by services.

$$ansR = REST.InvokeResourceSTRING(L, R, M, IA, DA); \qquad (2)$$

Our API encapsulates the complexity inherent in the consumption of services and resources in IoT. Thus, for accessing the state of objects and capture data, programmers only need to define the parameters specified in the formalization previously described. The process to invoke a service or resource is independent of the model used for its implementation.

It is important to note that the proposed API returns data retrieved from services and resources in three different formats: plain text, XML (Extensible Markup Language) and JSON (JavaScript Object Notation) format. Programmers can use any of these formats according to their needs; that is, using a widespread format compatible with current systems such as XML, or using a more readable and optimized format such as JSON. Furthermore, we emphasize that our API is supported only for the development of Java applications.

# 4   Results

## 4.1   Scenario

We have defined a smart home as scenario for implementing our conceptual ideas. The goal of the application is to provide temperature comfort
in this scenario based on software agents supporting services and resources.
This application's general scheme, shown in Fig. 2, models the two possible
approaches originated from the integration of agents, services and resources;
that is, automation processes based on the composition of services and resources
(*temperature_comfort_agent*) or automatic discovery of services and resources
(*temperature_agent*). Both approaches were previously described in Sect. 2.1.

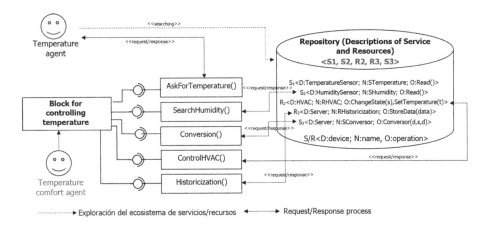

**Fig. 2.** General schema of the modeled scenario

## 4.2   Communication Model

How services and resources have been integrated with agents in the modeled
scenario shown in Fig. 2 is briefly described as follows:

- **Agents who discover services/resources**. The *temperature_agent* automatically discovers the service S1 (*STemperature*) on a distributed repository for accessing the temperature value of a physical IoT object installed
  inside the modeled scenario.
- **Agents who model their behaviors from a finite collection of ser-
  vices/resources**. The behavior of *temperature_comfort_agent* is driven by
  a process oriented to provide thermal comfort inside the room of the modeled
  scenario. This process invokes a set of 5 software components. The first one
  is a communication process with a counterpart agent (*temperature_agent*)
  oriented to get the temperature of the room of the scenario. The second
  one is an invocation to service S2 (*SHumidity*) in order to get the value of

humidity inside the room. The third one is a new invocation to the service *S*3 (*SConversor*) oriented to convert temperature value from Fahrenheit to Celcius. The fourth one is oriented to invoke a resource called *R*3 (*RHVAC*) oriented to apply a control mechanism to set the HVAC system based on the temperature and humidity inside the room. Finally, the fifth process invokes the resource *R*3 (*RHistoricization*) in order to save information regarding changes of the temperature of the scenario. This component creates a log from which audit processes can be addressed if necessary.

## 4.3   Implementation

The proposed MAS as well the ecosystem of services and resources were implemented on a Lenovo PC with a 2.50 GHz i7 processor and 16 GB of RAM. The computer had installed the 64-bit Linux Ubuntu 16.04 operating system and the Java 1.8 virtual machine.

On the other hand, in relation to the software tools used to implement the ecosystem of services and resources, the following frameworks were used: JAX-RS (Java API for RESTful Web Services) to create resources, JAX-WS (Java API for XML Web Services) to create web services, JMEDS (Java Multi Edition DPWS Stack) Framework to create services oriented to DPWS devices and DOHA to create specialized services for the automation-home. In addition, Glassfish Server 4.1 was used as the deployment server for the created ecosystem of services and resources. Also, the openHAB 2.0 tool was used to access the IoT devices based on resources.

**Temperature_agent.** The behavior of the *temperature_comfort_agent* was implemented directly. The block of actions of this agent consisted of a set of instructions oriented to make a search in the ecosystem of services and resources to discover a component that provided the temperature value. Once the ecosystem was explored, the agent recovered the *S*1 service and then proceeded to store it in order to avoid future searches. However, the agent performs again the process of exploring the ecosystem of services and resources when the current used component that provides temperature data stops working.

**Temperature_comfort_agent.** Implementing the process that drives the behavior of the *temperature_comfort_agent* is described in Listing 1.1. In short, this process is structured in 5 parts. In the first part (lines 5–6) the communication with the agent *temperature_agent* is made in order to request the value of the temperature of the room. This value is obtained by this agent using a service discovered by itself. The second part (lines 7–15) corresponds to the invocation of a service to obtain the humidity value of the room (line 15).

**Listing 1.1.** Snippet of the block for the tempeterature comfort agent

```
1.  import dynamicclients.DohaDC;
2.  import dynamicclients.RestDC;
3.  public class TemperatureComfortBehavior
4.  {
5.      /* AGENT COMMUNICATION - <<Ask for Temperature>> */
6.      String tempF = agentCommunication ("http://localhost:39982/
        IoARest/webresources/agent/communication?host=localhost&
        port=1099&sender=temperature_comfor&
        temperature_agent=Agent1&content=temperature");
7.      /* SERVICE INVOKING - <<Ask for Humidity>> */
8.      ArrayList p = new ArrayList ();
9.      p.add ("pINRED");
10.     ArrayList v = new ArrayList ();
11.     v.add (" QuitoMetropolitan ");
12.     DohaDC DOHA = new DohaDC ();
13.     DOHAservice.Initialize ();
14.     String loca="http://192.168.1.15:53859/SHummidity";
15.     String humi = DOHA.InvokeServiceSTRING(loca,"read",p,v);
16.     /* SERVICE INVOKING - Conversion */
17.     String locar = "http://192.168.1.15:53859/SConversor";
18.     ArrayList p1 = new ArrayList ();
19.     p1.add("pTEMP"); p1.add("pSOURCE"); p1.add("pCONVERSION");
20.     ArrayList v1 = new ArrayList ();
21.     v1.add(tempC); v1.add("F"); v1.add("C");
22.     tempC = DOHA.InvokeServiceSTRING(locar,"conversor",p1,v1);
23.     /* RESOURCE INVOKING - Control HVAC */
24.     ... control using tempC
25.     /* RESOURCE INVOKING <<Historicization>> */
26.     String locar="http://localhost:8080/RESTServices/";
26.     String resource ="webresources/resourcehisto/storedata";
27.     RestDC REST = new RestDC ();
28.     ArrayList p4 = new ArrayList ();
29.     p4.add("pINVALUE"); p4.add("pINPARAMETER");p4.add("pINRED");
30.     ArrayList v4 = new ArrayList ();
31.     v4.add(tempF); v4.add("H"); v4.add(" QuitoMetropolitan");
32.     REST.InvokeServiceSTRING(locar, resource, 1, p4,v4 );
33.     REST.Stop ();
34.  }
```

On the other hand, the third part (lines 16–22) corresponds to the invocation of a new service oriented to perform the conversion of the temperature value from Fahrenheit (F) to Celsius (C). This value is used by the next part of the block (lines 23–24) to establish an HVAC control measure, so that a comfortable temperature is maintained.

Finally, the last part of the process (lines 25–33) is the invocation to a resource oriented to historize the temperature value of the room. In this way, a log is kept of how the temperature has changed over time. It is important to point out that part 4 of the control block has not been detailed due to its similarity with the other blocks already described. This code illustrates the way that the proposed API performs the consumption of heterogeneous services in a uniform and easy way for programmers.

### 4.4    Evaluation

In order to empirically evaluate the functionality of the modeled system, Table 1 describes details of system behavior in terms of the integrity of communications between agents and the ecosystem of services and resources. In addition, a quantitative evaluation of the performance of the request/response processes applied to the services and resources that formed part of the ecosystem in the IoT domain was carried out. We use DOHA and RESTful models (Table 2).

**Table 2.** Evaluation of the process executed by the temperature_comfort_agent.

| # | Requester entity | Responser entity | Request/Response | Execution time (ms) | Losing data |
|---|---|---|---|---|---|
| 1 | Temperature comfort agent | Temperature agent | Successful | 7.97 ms (10 iterations) | No |
| 2 | Temperature comfort agent | S2 (SHumidity) | Successful | 639,58 ms (10 iterations) | No |
| 3 | Temperature comfort agent | S3 (SConversor) | Successful | 720,34 ms (10 iterations) | No |
| 4 | Temperature comfort agent | R2 (RHVAC-OpenHAB) | Successful | 24,19 ms (10 iterations) | No |
| 5 | Temperature comfort agent | R3 (RHistoricization) | Successful | 9,33 ms (10 iterations) | No |

First three columns of Table 1 show the two entities involved in the request/response processes performed in the modeled system: agent-gent, agent-service and agent-resource. In the case of item 1, the agent communication between $temperature\_comfort\_agent$ and $temperature\_agent$, was executed successfully and without reporting loss of data or messages. The following 4 communication processes, items 2–5, also correspond to request/response processes of type agent-service ($temperature\_comfort\_agent$ with $S_2$ and $S_3$) and agent-resource ($temperature\_comfort\_agent$ with $R_2$ and $R_3$). Similarly to the previous case, no message loss was reported in any of the communication processes.

Finally, the results obtained from the experimentation show the total time required for the execution of each of the request/response processes carried out to meet goals of the agent $temperature\_comfort\_agent$. Each experimentation was conduced during 10 iterations. Thus, the agent-agent communication required on average 7.97 ms. Also, in the case of agents who accessed IoT objects using DOHA services required on average 639.58 ms and 9.33 ms when the devices were accessed using a RESTful resource. The difference is considerable. However, given the heterogeneity handled in IoT it is important to give the opportunity to integrate IoT devices accessible through different interfaces.

## 5   Discussions

Modeling of agent actions based on services and/or resources is an useful method to distribute the intelligence of software agents [24,29]. This enables MAS to take advantage of Cloud Computing when distributing complex and specialized processes cannot carry out by agents themselves [9,23,25]. The consumption of services and resources has been technically feasible with the API proposed in this work. Processes such as monitoring (reading of sensors) and automatic control (updating of actuators) have been carried out successfully without reporting loss of data. The integrity of the reported data delivery in the system positions agents based on services and resources as useful entities in IoT scenarios. This aspect ensures in a certain way that control processes defined in agent behaviors can be applied in the IoT consistently.

Nowadays, the use of services and resources have been extended in the IoT domain thanks to the levels of interoperability provided in the development of distributed systems. The services and resources hide the complexity of accessing the physical devices of IoT. Add-ons such as: JADE WSIG [1], WS2JADE [14] and JADE-WSDC [22] could abstract this complexity by providing an easy-to-use interface for accessing and modifying the status of IoT devices as well as their resources. However, in general they do not consider the heterogeneity of services and resources as handled in IoT. This justifies the creation of an API like the one developed in this work. It is also expected that developers will be able to use this tool to develop intelligent agent-based IoT systems using services and resources as done in [17].

Additionally, novel agent models are including a component for ecosystem management of services and resources from which it distributes algorithms and intelligent automatic control processes. This is the particular case of the agent model Linked Open agent (LOA) [16] which describes 6 semantic components among which is the component *agent_service*. This component stores metadata of the services and resources it uses to achieve its goals. This stored metadata allows the LOA agent to complete its workflow to execute its actions invoking heterogeneous services and resources. The model contemplates the four models considered in this study, that is, SOAP, RESTful, DPWS and DOHA. The API proposed in this study is of importance to abstract the communications at the level of the interaction patterns agent-agent, agent-service and agent-resources.

## 6   Conclusions

Handling the heterogeneity of ecosystems of services and resources is an aspect that should be considered during the design of distributed systems such as IoT. Because IoT are ecosystems that consume public or private distributed software components, it is recommended to define for each functionality, what more convenient is to solve it, that is, a service or a resource. We recommend using DOHA and DPWS services, and RESTful resources because these components improve the performance of actions on IoT without losing data on message transmission. However, additional functionalities offered as web services can also be consumed with our API. This enables to cover more powerful and extended models of services and resources deployed on SOA and ROA.

As future work the creation of specialized repositories of services and resources in the area of IoT to facilitate the creation of agents and their behavior must be addressed. In addition, a GUI that allows the creation of agent behaviors through static (definition of services and specific resources of repositories) and dynamic (parameterization so that the agent searches in execution time for the most adequate services and resources) services- and resources-based processes must be built. This GUI should help developers to model agents that meet specific monitoring and automatic control goals on IoT ecosystems such as home automation systems.

# References

1. Bellifemine, F., Caire, G., Greenwood, D.: The Jade web services integration gateway. In: Developing Multi-Agent Systems with JADE, pp. 181–205 (2007)
2. Bellifemine, F., Caire, G., Poggi, A., Rimassa, G.: Jade: a software framework for developing multi-agent applications. Lessons learned. Inf. Softw. Technol. **50**(1), 10–21 (2008)
3. Bokhari, M.U., Makki, Q., Tamandani, Y.K.: A survey on cloud computing. In: Aggarwal, V.B., Bhatnagar, V., Mishra, D.K. (eds.) Big Data Analytics, vol. 654, pp. 149–164. Springer, Singapore (2018). https://doi.org/10.1007/978-981-10-6620-7_16
4. Cândido, G., Jammes, F., Barata, J., Colombo, A.W.: Generic management services for DPWS-enabled devices. In: 2009 35th Annual Conference of IEEE Industrial Electronics, pp. 3931–3936. IEEE (2009)
5. Chin, K.O., Gan, K.S., Alfred, R., Anthony, P., Lukose, D.: Agent architecture: an overview. Trans. Sci. Technol. **1**(1), 18–35 (2014)
6. Dar, K., Taherkordi, A., Baraki, H., Eliassen, F., Geihs, K.: A resource oriented integration architecture for the Internet of Things: a business process perspective. Pervasive Mob. Comput. **20**, 145–159 (2015)
7. Degroote, A., Lacroix, S.: Roar: resource oriented agent architecture for the autonomy of robots. In: 2011 IEEE International Conference on Robotics and Automation, pp. 6090–6095. IEEE (2011)
8. Erl, T.: SOA: Principles of Service Design. Prentice Hall Press, New York (2008). ISBN 0136042597
9. Gutierrez-Garcia, J.O., Sim, K.M.: Agent-based cloud service composition. Appl. Intell. **38**(3), 436–464 (2013)
10. Lee, J., Lee, S.J., Wang, P.F.: A framework for composing soap, non-soap and non-web services. IEEE Trans. Serv. Comput. **8**(2), 240–250 (2015)
11. Li, S., Da Xu, L., Zhao, S.: The Internet of Things: a survey. Inf. Syst. Front. **17**(2), 243–259 (2015)
12. Madakam, S., Ramaswamy, R., Tripathi, S.: Internet of Things (IoT): a literature review. J. Comput. Commun. **3**(05), 164 (2015)
13. Mahmud, R., Kotagiri, R., Buyya, R.: Fog computing: a taxonomy, survey and future directions. In: Di Martino, B., Li, K.-C., Yang, L.T., Esposito, A. (eds.) Internet of Everything. IT, pp. 103–130. Springer, Singapore (2018). https://doi.org/10.1007/978-981-10-5861-5_5
14. Nguyen, X., Kowalczyk, R., Chhetri, M., Grant, A.: WS2JADE: a tool for runtime deployment and control of web services as jade agent services. In: Unland, R., Calisti, M., Klusch, M. (eds.) Software Agent-Based Applications, Platforms and Development Kits, pp. 223–251. Birkhäuser, Basel (2005). https://doi.org/10.1007/3-7643-7348-2_10
15. Grau, J.P.P., Sanz, A.C., Crespo, R.G.: An evaluation of integration technologies to expose agent actions as web services. In: Wen, Z., Li, T. (eds.) Practical Applications of Intelligent Systems. AISC, vol. 279, pp. 259–270. Springer, Heidelberg (2014). https://doi.org/10.1007/978-3-642-54927-4_25

16. Pico-Valencia, P., Holgado-Terriza, J.A., Senso, J.A.: Towards an Internet of agents model based on linked open data approach. Auton. Agent. Multi-Agent Syst. **33**(1–2), 84–131 (2019)

17. Pico-Valencia, P.A., Holgado-Terriza, J.A.: An agent middleware for supporting ecosystems of heterogeneous web services. Procedia Comput. Sci. **94**, 121–128 (2016)

18. Portalés, C., Casas, S., Kreuzer, K.: Challenges and trends in home automation: addressing the interoperability problem with the open-source platform OpenHAB. In: Harnessing the Internet of Everything (IoE) for Accelerated Innovation Opportunities, pp. 148–174. IGI Global (2019)

19. Razzaque, M.A., Milojevic-Jevric, M., Palade, A., Clarke, S.: Middleware for Internet of Things: a survey. IEEE Internet Things J. **3**(1), 70–95 (2016)

20. Ribeiro, L., Barata, J., Mendes, P.: MAS and SOA: complementary automation paradigms. In: Azevedo, A. (ed.) BASYS 2008. ITIFIP, vol. 266, pp. 259–268. Springer, Boston, MA (2008). https://doi.org/10.1007/978-0-387-09492-2_28

21. Rodríguez-Valenzuela, S., Holgado-Terriza, J., Gutiérrez-Guerrero, J., Muros-Cobos, J.: Distributed service-based approach for sensor data fusion in IoT environments. Sensors **14**(10), 19200–19228 (2014)

22. Scagliotti, E., Caire, G.: Web service dynamic client add -on guide (2009). http://jade.tilab.com/doc/tutorials/DynamicClientGuide.pdf

23. Sim, K.M.: Agent-based cloud computing. IEEE Trans. Serv. Comput. **5**(4), 564–577 (2011)

24. Son, M., Shin, D., Shin, D.: Design and implementation of the intelligent multi-agent system based on web services. In: 2006 Seventh International Conference on Web-Age Information Management Workshops, pp. 20. IEEE (2006)

25. Talia, D.: Clouds meet agents: toward intelligent cloud services. IEEE Internet Comput. **16**(2), 78–81 (2012)

26. Tapia, D.I., Bajo, J., Corchado, J.M.: Distributing functionalities in a SOA-based multi-agent architecture. In: Demazeau, Y., Pavón, J., Corchado, J.M., Bajo, J. (eds.) PAAMS 2009. AINSC, vol. 55, pp. 20–29. Springer, Heidelberg (2009). https://doi.org/10.1007/978-3-642-00487-2_3

27. Vrba, P., et al.: A review of agent and service-oriented concepts applied to intelligent energy systems. IEEE Trans. Industr. Inf. **10**(3), 1890–1903 (2014)

28. Wooldridge, M.: An Introduction to Multiagent Systems. Wiley, Hoboken (2009)

29. Zhou, H., Cao, J., Guo, C., Qin, J.: The architecture of intelligent distribution network based on MAS-SOA. In: 2010 IEEE Power and Energy Society General Meeting, pp. 1–6. IEEE (2010)

# TDDM4IoTS: A Test-Driven Development Methodology for Internet of Things (IoT)-Based Systems

Gleiston Guerrero-Ulloa[1,2](✉) , Miguel J. Hornos[2] ,
and Carlos Rodríguez-Domínguez[2]

[1] Facultad de Ciencias de la Ingeniería, Universidad Técnica Estatal de Quevedo, Quevedo
120501, Ecuador
gguerrero@uteq.edu.ec
[2] Software Engineering Department, University of Granada, 18071 Granada, Spain
gleiston@correo.ugr.es, {mhornos,carlosrodriguez}@ugr.es

**Abstract.** This paper presents a development methodology for Internet of Things
(IoT)-based Systems (IoTS) that gathers ideas from several of the most outstanding
software development paradigms nowadays, such as Model-Driven Engineering
(MDE) and Test-Driven Development (TDD), in addition to incorporating the principles that govern agile software development methodologies, such as SCRUM and
XP. The methodology presented here, called Test-Driven Development Methodology for IoTS (TDDM4IoTS), has been proposed after an exhaustive review of
different software development methodologies, leading us to conclude that none
of them are specially oriented towards the development of IoTS. The methodology
mainly consists of eleven phases, whose order of application can be established
by the team that will develop the project in question. In this paper, we suggest an
order to follow, as well as existing software tools that could be used as support for
obtaining the corresponding deliverables at each phase.

**Keywords:** Software development methodology · Test-Driven Development ·
Model-Driven Engineering · Agile methodologies · Internet of Things (IoT) ·
IoT-based Systems

## 1 Introduction

In Software Engineering, proposals for new programming languages and paradigms
have always been the main issue, closely followed by methodologies. Thus, structured
programming emerged first, and then appropriate methodologies for Structured Analysis
and Design (SAD) were proposed. Likewise, object-oriented programming was firstly
proposed in 1972 [1], while proposals for Object-Oriented Analysis and Design (OOAD)
and a methodology for the development of Object-Oriented Software were published
in 1978 [2] and 1982 [3]. With the emergence of the Internet era and the World Wide
Web (WWW), developers were faced with the need to adapt existing methodologies
for the development of Web-based systems. The first documented Web development

M. Botto-Tobar et al. (Eds.): ICAT 2019, CCIS 1193, pp. 41–55, 2020.
https://doi.org/10.1007/978-3-030-42517-3_4

methodology was presented by Schwabe and Rossi in 2002 [4]. Thus, it has traditionally been considered necessary to review development methodologies after the emergence of new technological paradigms in Software Engineering.

Nowadays, IoT is one of the most prominent technological paradigms. This term, coined by Ashton [5], stems from the objective of "digitalizing physical objects" so that they can seamlessly interact with each other and with the people surrounding them to improve their lifestyles and productivity [6]. IoT is the result of the confluence/collaboration of several research areas, such as communication and cooperation, location and identification, sensor and actuator networks, integrated processing of distributed information, artificial intelligence and adaptive user interfaces, to name just a few of the most important converging fields.

The first IoTS were developed using ad-hoc methodologies specific to each development team, arising from the corresponding adaptation of methodologies employed in the development of more traditional information systems (IS).

However, the development of IoTS differs from the development of traditional computer systems in several key aspects. For instance, the development of IoTS necessarily involves deploying and setting up hardware components (sensors, actuators, controllers...) to interact with the physical and digital environment, which is not the usual case in traditional IS. Each of the hardware devices deployed in the environment (such as sensors, actuators and single board computers) requires a specific programming and configuration, as well as the implementation of information dissemination mechanisms (Publish/Subscribe or Request/Response are among the most common) to efficiently distribute data and create complex data flows between them.

On the other hand, in both traditional IS and IoTS, end-user client applications, mainly web-based [7] or mobile-based [8], must be implemented to interact with people, depending on the needs of the users themselves [9]. However, in the literature, the vast majority of IoTS development methodologies are focused exclusively on the implementation of either configuration software for IoT devices or a set of end-user applications, but they do not cover both aspects at the same time. In addition, none of the studied methodologies incorporate feasibility analysis or maintenance stages, instead they focus on software design and code generation. In this paper, we propose a methodology for the development of IoTS that covers all these aspects at the same time. Consequently, the main objectives of this paper are: (1) To present an exhaustive review of existing IoTS development methodologies, based on TDD, MDE and/or agile methodologies; (2) To check that there is no methodology specifically designed for the development of IoTS; and (3) To propose a new development methodology for IoTS that, in addition to the software in charge of business logic and user-system interaction, addresses the configuration and deployment of the hardware (sensors, actuators, processors,...) and the programming of single board computers (Arduino, Raspberry,...), so that they can perform an adequate pre-processing of the data captured by the sensors.

The remainder of this paper is structured as follows: Sect. 2 presents the state of the art on IoTS development methodologies based on TDD, MDE, and/or agile development methodologies. Section 3 proposes a new methodology for the development of IoTS that attempts to overcome the absence of a specific methodology for the development of IoTS. Finally, Sect. 4 outlines our conclusions and future work.

## 2 State of the Art

We searched for published papers on IoTS development methodologies at the Web of Science platform. Books, book chapters, and articles published in prestigious journals were selected, because they are considered more relevant, and in English, as this is the internationally adopted language for scientific publications. The search terms we used are shown in the central column of Table 1.

**Table 1.** Keywords and query strings used and number of search results obtained

| No. | Query structure | Results |
|-----|-----------------|---------|
| #1 | TS = (IoT OR "Internet of Things") | 15.597 |
| #2 | TS = (Framework OR Method*) | 8.957.432 |
| #3 | TS = (Development OR Deploy OR Implement* OR Design OR construct*) | 7.384.102 |
| #4 | TS = (Agile OR SCRUM OR XP OR "Extreme Programming" OR "Agile Inception" OR "Design Sprint" OR Kanban) | 14.452 |
| #5 | TS = (TDD OR "Test-Driven Development" OR MDE OR "Model-Driven Engineering" OR MDA OR "Model-Driven Architecture" OR MDD OR "Model-Driven Development" OR "Model-Driven Design") | 71.897 |
| #6 | #1 AND #2 AND #3 | 3.303 |
| #7 | #4 OR #5 | 86.224 |
| **#8** | **#6 AND #7** | **38** |

As a result, we obtained 38 documents (see last row of Table 1). After a thorough review of these documents, those that did not present a development methodology were discarded, and 12 papers (shown in Table 2) were finally selected for further analysis.

**Table 2.** Methodologies for the development of IoTS

| Ref. | Approaches | General IoTS | Domain |
|------|-----------|--------------|--------|
| [10] | MDE | ✓ | Intelligent street lights |
| [11] | MDD*, SOA♣ | ✗ | IIoT♠, Automobiles |
| [12] | MDD*, MDA♥ | ✗ | Mobile applications |
| [13] | Design based on components, BIP♦, Incremental design | ✗ | Wireless Personal Area Network Systems |
| [14] | MDD* | ✓ | Domotics, IIoT♠ |
| [15] | MDE | ✗ | Health monitoring |
| [16] | SOA♣, Principles of agile development | ✓ | Environmental and risk management systems for IIoT♠ |

*(continued)*

**Table 2.** (*continued*)

| Ref. | Approaches | General IoTS | Domain |
|------|-----------|:------------:|--------|
| [17] | SCRUM frame, Metamodels, SOA♣ | ✓ | Smart Homes |
| [18] | MDE, SOA♣ | ✓ | General |
| [19] | MDA♥ | ✓ | Wireless Sensor Network |
| [20] | Waterfall, Agile principles | ✓ | Not applied |
| [21] | Division by roles or responsibilities | ✓ | Intelligent Buildings |

*Model-Driven Development/Design; ♣Service-Oriented Architecture; ♥Model-Driven Architecture; ♠Industrial IoT; ♦Behavior Interaction Priority; ✓ Methodology for IoTS in general; ✗ Methodology for specific IoTS

## 2.1 Foundations of the Reviewed Methodologies

None of the analyzed TDD-related documents presented a development methodology for IoTS, unlike those related to MDE and agile development methodologies. Table 2 shows the references where the different methodologies were found, as well as the approaches they are based on, in addition to the type of IoTS and the domain for which they were developed or to which they were applied.

In TDD4IoTS, we have integrated some of the most common methodological stages that are proposed in the studied literature to solve the challenges of IoTS. In addition to them, we have incorporated the advantages of TDD to increase software quality (fulfillment of requirements, bug detection, improved software reliability, etc.).

## 2.2 Analysis of Existing Methodologies

The study of system requirements is the first step in the development of a system. Therefore, it should be the first phase in the methodology applied to its development. Table 3 shows a comparison of existing methodologies, focused on requirements analysis, detailing all the tools and models used for the development of IoTS.

Analyzing the state of the art on development methodologies for IoTS, we realized that some works [10, 11] do not mention the system requirements. Consequently, these methodologies do not consider the requirements analysis phase. The remaining of the reviewed methodologies agree on the importance of requirements analysis for the development of an IoTS. The methodology presented in [12] describes requirements analysis in greater depth, and presents some tools that developers can use to collect and analyze requirements. Whereas methodologies in [13–15] assume that the requirements are available before the development starts, conversely, those in [16, 17] consider that requirements are rarely available at the beginning of the development of an IoTS. In our contribution, we are more inclined towards the latter. Therefore, we propose TDD4IoTS as a methodology that sufficiently emphasizes the phase of obtaining and analyzing requirements.

The nature of IoTS makes it important to carefully consider all system states and transitions, since the system will have to react to events occurring in the environment

**Table 3.** Comparison of methodologies

| Reference | Requirement analysis | Use UML | UML diagrams | | | | | | Business Process Model and Notation (BPMN) |
|---|---|---|---|---|---|---|---|---|---|
| | | | Use cases | Activities | Classes | States | Sequences | Deployment | |
| [10] | ✗ | ✓ | ✗ | ✗ | ✗ | ✗ | ✗ | ✗ | ✗ |
| [11] | ✗ | ✓ | ✗ | ✗ | ✗ | ✗ | ✗ | ✗ | ✗ |
| [12] | ~ | ✓ | ✓ | ✓ | ✓ | ✗ | ✗ | ✗ | ✓ |
| [13] | ~ | ✗ | ✗ | ✗ | ✗ | ✗ | ✗ | ✗ | ✗ |
| [14] | ~ | ✓ | ✗ | ✗ | ✗ | ✗ | ✗ | ✗ | ✗ |
| [15] | ~ | ✓ | ✗ | ✓ | ✓ | ✓ | ✗ | ✗ | ✗ |
| [16] | ✓ | ✓ | ✓ | ✓ | ✗ | ✗ | ✗ | ✗ | ✗ |
| [17] | ~ | ✓ | ✗ | ✓ | ✓ | ✓ | ✓ | ✗ | ✗ |
| [18] | ✓ | ✓ | ✓ | ✓ | ✗ | ✗ | ✗ | ✗ | ✗ |
| [19] | ✓ | ✓ | ✗ | ✓ | ✓ | ✗ | ✗ | ✓ | ✗ |
| [20] | ~ | ✗ | ✗ | ✗ | ✗ | ✗ | ✗ | ✗ | ✗ |
| [21] | ~ | ✓ | ✗ | ✗ | ✗ | ✗ | ✗ | ✗ | ✗ |

✓ Used or considered; ~ Mentioned; ✗ Not specified

it controls. That aspect has only been taken into consideration by [15] and [17]. In addition, deployment diagrams, which can show interlinks between the (software- and hardware-based) system components, are only used in [19].

One approach that can reduce and alleviate the work of developers is specifying the context of the environment that IoTS must control: available networks, quality of service (QoS), privacy levels, the physical environment in which the system will be deployed, as well as the preferences that the user may have, such as aesthetic changes and accessibility parameters. This specification may also help in making decisions regarding the specific technologies and tools to use. These aspects are considered important in the present work, although they are not included in any of the reviewed methodologies.

Another widely forgotten aspect of the development of IoTS in the reviewed bibliography is information storage. Although most authors highlight the importance of information storage, they assume that it is ready to use at the beginning of the development, via existing software components that are not significant in the development process. However, we consider that the type of database (relational, NoSQL,...) that is used must be carefully chosen during the development process, in addition to adequately designing its structure and selecting the resources dedicated to its management (database engine, local server or in the cloud, etc.).

Consequently, we have reached the conclusion that existing methodologies have important shortcomings in terms of their applicability to IoTS. Therefore, we present a new methodological proposal to better tackle the specific requirements of IoTS in the next section.

## 3    An Overview of TDDM4IoTS

We present a new methodology specifically designed for the development of IoTS that integrates ideas from the most prominent software development methodologies and tries to mitigate the weaknesses found in the reviewed methodologies. In fact, it is based on the TDD methodology phases [22], while applying the fundamentals of MDE and the principles of agile methodologies. That is why we have named it Test-Driven Development Methodology for IoT-based Systems (TDDM4IoTS). Additionally, it emphasizes the use of tools that, according to experts, ensure that the software meets the requirements that the customer has provided.

We propose TDDM4IoTS as a methodology independent of specific automation tools or frameworks, so that developers are free to choose the appropriate tool(s) to be used, depending on their needs and preferences. Nonetheless, we are working on the development of an automated tool to support TDDM4IoTS in all its phases. For the requirements specification, we propose using use cases instead of describing the requirements in natural language, which is more usual and what makes them error-prone and full of ambiguities [16]. One of the goals of our automated tool will be to reduce ambiguities at this level. The use cases, together with the conceptual class model, will allow us to automatically generate both the tests and parts of the software that must pass those tests. The developers will focus on specifying and analyzing system requirements, as well as completing and adapting the automatically generated software.

The phases of the life cycle of TDDM4IoTS, shown in Fig. 1, take into account the development of all types of IoTS, which is why the order and frequency of application, as well as the allocation of resources for each phase will depend on both the nature of the project and the knowledge, skills, experience and number of project members. Nonetheless, the order of application suggested by the numbers shown in Fig. 1 would be valid for the development of a large number of IoTS.

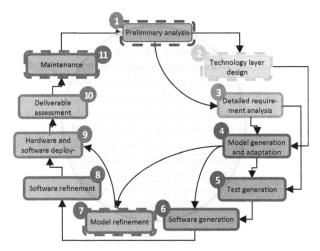

**Fig. 1.** Phases of the life cycle of TDDM4IoTS

These phases will be repeated iteratively for each deliverable. However, in the development of some deliverables, it may not be necessary to apply some of these phases (drawn with a dashed line in Fig. 1). For example, it may not be necessary to perform the preliminary analysis in a second iteration, or to carry out the refinement of the model in the development of a given deliverable. The development team must estimate the effort and duration of the process to obtain each deliverable or component into which any project is usually divided. Negotiation between the client and the development team on the priority (development order) of each deliverable will be of vital importance to the success of the project, unlike the SCRUM development framework, where the client (product owner) assigns development priorities to the deliverables (Sprints) [23–25].

TDDM4IoTS requires the *project facilitator*'s responsibility to be assigned to the member with the most experience in project management who possesses the characteristics of a leader. Developers who follow TDDM4IoTS are not subject to task impositions but to negotiations. The facilitator is not responsible for the whole project, s/he is just the manager of the negotiation between the development teams. The responsibility of the project rests with each of its members. Consequently, TDDM4IoTS adopts a horizontal management approach with shared responsibility, leaving the team members to self-organize. The number of developers will depend on the project size, and considering that we suggest "agile" teams, they should not exceed ten [23, 26]. The project members have different responsibilities, depending on their roles, shown in Table 4. Each development team is made up of a maximum of three developers, and should be balanced in terms of both knowledge and experience [26]. One of its members will be (informally) designated as a *counselor*, if necessary.

Consequently, while the participants can play three main roles in SCRUM, which are detailed in [29, 30], together with their responsibilities, we consider four roles in TDDM4IoTS, as shown in Table 4.

We can conclude that: (1) SCRUM is based on the principles for agile software development. (2) IoT encompasses different and varied aspects, such as the complexity of software development, hardware deployment, indispensable communications, cloud

**Table 4.** Roles and responsibilities in TDDM4IoTS

| Role[a] | Description | Responsibilities |
|---|---|---|
| Project facilitator | Expert with extensive experience in project management and in the agile development of IoTS. Conflict solver, trainer, facilitator and with the innate characteristics of a leader [27, 28] | (1) Support the development team in achieving its objectives. (2) Contribute with their experience to the development of deliverables. (3) Negotiate with the client aspects of the development (order of deliverables, time, resources,...)[b] |
| Counselor | Member of the development team that becomes a "leader" (without a formal designation) because of his performance | Instruct his/her teammates on the subjects of his/her domain |

(*continued*)

**Table 4.** (*continued*)

| Role[a] | Description | Responsibilities |
|---|---|---|
| Customer/End user | Person with good communication and knowledge of all the functionality of the IoTS who commissions the development team to develop it | (1) Contribute to the requirements of the IoTS. (2) Approve the functionality of the finished deliverables and the final IoTS |
| Development team | Multidisciplinary group of experts with knowledge of the different project domains, and which is responsible for the development of the IoTS. Facilitators of knowledge and experience | (1) Negotiate with the client on aspects of the IoTS development (order of deliverables, time, resources,...)[b]. (2) Create deliverables that fully meet customer requirements |

[a]Depending on the project, experts in other domains may be needed to provide their services for a specific time.
[b]This responsibility is shared by two roles.

storage and processing, and the intercommunication between these elements, among others. (3) SCRUM and XP ignore non-functional requirements, which are an important aspect in IoTS [31]. These three premises make it quite difficult to make a simple adaptation of SCRUM for the development of IoTS. This is why we intend to incorporate the best features of the manifesto for the agile development of software into TDDM4IoTS, adapting them to the particularities of IoTS.

The following subsections describe how to apply the foundations on which TDDM4IoTS is based and its phases, as well as the activities to be carried out and possible tools to be used in each of them.

### 3.1 Foundations of TDDM4IoTS

The main foundations on which TDDM4IoTS is based are described below.

**Values and Principles for Agile Software Development.** Agile software development is governed by four values, namely: (i) Individuals and interactions before processes and tools, (ii) Software working before extensive documentation, (iii) Collaboration with the customer before contractual negotiation, and (iv) Response to change before following a plan [29, 30]. Agile methodologies have revolutionized the software development process, demonstrating that development teams that have completed their projects successfully and on time did not respect rigid and heavy methodologies [30]. To comply with these values, twelve principles are detailed that a methodology must comply with to be qualified as an agile methodology [29, 30].

TDDM4IoTS complies with the twelve principles, bearing in mind that, as already said, IoTS comprise the deployment of a series of hardware devices in addition to the corresponding software. Therefore, a deliverable will be a finished element of the system, obtained as a result of an iteration, which is important for the customer.

**TDD as an Agile Methodology.** TDD [32–34] is one of the methodologies used for the development of traditional IS that has not been applied to the development of IoTS. As this type of methodology guarantees that the software of the developed system satisfies the requirements that the user has provided, we have incorporated it into our proposal. Nowadays, many integrated development environments (IDE) support TDD, such as IntelliJ IDEA, .Net, or Eclipse, to name just a few [35].

TDD, which is considered an agile methodology, is applied to ensure the quality of the deliverables. It has three phases in its development cycle [33]. By first writing the tests and then writing the code that has to pass the tests, it is ensured that the software does exactly what the customer wants (i.e., tests formally specify use cases) [22].

The agile software development methodologies that have been considered in this research are XP (eXtreme Programming) [36] and SCRUM [23]. We are interesting in how they approach software development projects, and especially in: delivery frequencies, acceptance of changes, giving greater importance to the deliverable than to an exhaustive documentation, and the quality of the software (tested and approved by the client) as one of the most important features, among other principles of agile methodologies that must be complied with. On the one hand, XP is one of the methodologies that has promoted TDD [35]. On the other hand, SCRUM delivers tested software, that is, software that has passed the tests, without specifying if the tests are written before or after the software code. However, it separates the tests from the development very well, as another (tester) team tests the software.

**MDE.** The heterogeneity of IoTS technologies and standards make MDE an important foundation for TDDM4IoTS. One objective is to reuse these models (with or without adaptations) in the development of other systems, for which these models could be converted into executable code [37].

### 3.2  Phases of TDDM4IoTS

The phases of TDDM4IoTS are designed so that the tools used by the developers in each phase are of their own choice. The tools that developers can use to meet the objectives of each phase are recommended. The first challenge to overcome is the communication among the project members and among the members of each development team. The best way to achieve an effective communication is face-to-face, as indicated in the agile manifesto [29, 30], involving periodic meetings set by the teams either at the beginning of the project or at the beginning of the development of the corresponding deliverable. Establishing the frequency of such meetings is the responsibility of all the project members. However, three to five meetings per week are recommended. Mechanisms should be sought so that development teams feel motivated and are at ease with their work, with the organization, with the rest of the project members and with their own team, in order to achieve a better performance [38].

**(1) Preliminary Analysis.** The objective of this phase is to obtain a feasibility study of the (complete) system regarding its technological, economic and operational aspects, as well as an analysis of the context in which the system will be deployed and the interaction with the end user, based on the requirements and objectives expressed by the client. The activities to be carried out may include:

- *Requirements analysis.* This analysis determines two types of requirements: (i) functional, which are the customer's specifications (list of deliverables), determining its implementation priority, and (ii) non-functional, also called quality attributes, such as scalability, intrusiveness, environment aesthetics (deployment, appearance, etc.).
- *Technology analysis.* This determines the technology to be used that meets the system requirements: (i) Hardware resources already available; (ii) Existing hardware, taking into account its characteristics and costs; (iii) Tools (software) for hardware configuration; (iv) Tools for both software development and storage management; (v) Third-party hardware for specific tasks, and (vi) First-party hardware development, if necessary and feasible.
- *Analysis of the environment.* The client can specify the characteristics of the environment in which the system will be deployed. For example, available and/or feasible power supply points, data communication networks – Internet access, customer's preferred methods of interaction, etc.
- *Feasibility analysis.* Among the types of feasibility to be analyzed are: (i) Technical feasibility, for which the questions to be answered would be: (a) Are there the technologies necessary to develop the project? (b) Are trained personnel available to develop the system? (c) Can the system be developed? (ii) Economic feasibility, where the question to be answered would be: Is there an adequate budget to develop the project? (iii) Operational feasibility, which is important for the system to remain in operation after it is implemented, so these questions must be answered: (a) Will it be possible to install the system once it is completed? (b) Will the system be able to operate with available resources? (c) Are there the necessary guarantees for the system to continue operating once installed? (d) Will the IoTS have a properly scheduled maintenance?

Since IoTS may involve the use of multiple technologies, the availability of each of them could alter the order or priorities of the deliverables. Therefore, it is necessary that this first phase is carried out globally at the beginning of the project, and reviewed at the beginning of the development of each deliverable, to consider the changes related to the technology (new devices, new tools, etc.) and requirements that might arise during the development of the project.

There are no specific tools to meet the objective of this particular phase. However, for the project planning, it is suggested to use a free software tool, such as OpenProj, GanttProject, dotProject, and for those who prefer proprietary software, MS-Project, among many others.

The result of this phase is fundamental for the first negotiations with the client, concerning deliveries, times, and budget. All this is preliminary and cannot be considered definitive, as it can be negotiated between both parties at the beginning of the development of each deliverable.

**(2) Technology Layer Design.** The objective of this phase is to obtain the first design of the global system that will serve as a guide for the development teams. This is very important, given that IoT involves emerging and heterogeneous technologies, and so far, it is difficult to find a professional who can master all the technologies involved in the development of IoTS [21].

For the system design, circuit design tools may be used that can represent as clearly as possible the elements that have been determined for the project. For example, if Arduino boards are used, online tools such as Circuito.io or Fritzing can be used. The development team may complement the designs that have been obtained. If necessary, the resulting design can be updated at the end of each deliverable. This will be one of the documents of greatest interest for all the development teams of the project. Therefore, it must always be accessible to all of them.

In this phase, the architecture with which the system will be implemented should be designed. Consequently, the outcome of this phase will serve as a guide for the entire development process.

**(3) Detailed Requirement Analysis.** The objective of this phase, which will be executed for each system deliverable, is to obtain the detailed requirements of the deliverable to be developed. In addition, the client will be asked to describe the tests together with the developers, to reduce ambiguities. For the requirements specification, it is recommended to use tools that are understandable for all the stakeholders, considering the customer as one of them. One of the notations to be used could be UML, with its different tools, such as use cases and semi-structured use cases, using pre-established templates, seeking to eliminate ambiguities, in addition to other tools, such as state and deployment diagrams, which help to understand the requirements provided by the client.

**(4) Model Generation and Adaptation.**
The purpose of applying MDE in TDDM4IoTS is to reuse models and thus improve the productivity of the development team. Therefore, in this phase, new models will be generated or existing models will be adapted. Using models abstracts out or at least minimizes the heterogeneity aspects of technologies, enabling a good communication between the development teams and the clients. Also, depending on the software tools used for modeling, the software can be automatically generated across models, from abstract models to specific models [10, 18]. One of the models is the class diagram, which is used to generate the database.

The suggested modeling languages are: UML, BPMN [12], the adaptation of one of them [14], their combination or the creation of a new one, always seeking to cover the particular characteristics of the IoTS to be developed and to be easily understood by those involved in the project. Among the automated tools for system modeling are StarUML, ArgoUML, MagicDraw and Visual Studio .Net, for example. For those who opt for BPMN, they can select tools such as Lucidchart or VisualParadigm, among many others.

**(5) Test Generation.** TDDM4IoTS follows the TDD paradigm, so it must generate the tests that the software must pass to ensure the quality of the system. The tests can be grouped into two groups: (1) The tests written by the developers, within which there are: (a) unit tests, which are the most exhaustive, to examine the complete functioning of a function, i.e., it is tested whether the function yields the results that it should yield and even whether it supports the exceptions that may arise; and (b) integration tests, which also involve system tests. And (2) tests documented by the client, which are basically acceptance tests, including functional tests [22].

The automated tools for this phase will depend on the IDE that has been selected for development, although so far no tool automatically generates tests based on requirements.

**(6) Software Generation.** This phase is based on models and tests. The developer must write/generate the code for the tests to be passed [33, 39]. The new models generated and/or the existing models adapted are part of the system documentation. Therefore, unlike SCRUM and XP methodologies, which suggest that the documentation related to the analysis and design of the solution should be written at the end of each deliverable development [30], TDDM4IoTS propose to do it before the code generation, as there are tools that, based on the models, help in this task. Also, when surveying software developers who work or have worked with SCRUM and/or XP methodology, most agree that the solution that will be implemented later should at least be sketched at the beginning of the life cycle of the methodology. This corroborates what is stated in TDDM4IoTS regarding the analysis and design of the solution, which should be carried out during the development of the deliverables.

Once the software has been generated, it is checked that it passes the corresponding tests, and then this phase finishes. The result of this phase is the software tested and working, though it will almost always have to be refined later.

To generate the code, some of the tools mentioned in the model generation and refinement phase can be used. In fact, there are several tools, both free software and proprietary software, which even allow simulation of the system behavior.

**(7) Model Refinement.** UML models facilitate model refinement. Note that the solution found is a functional solution, but not necessarily an optimal solution. Hence, it is important to make the necessary adjustments and refinements, such as improving the robustness, scalability or reusability of the deliverables that made up of the IoTS to be developed [40]. The result of this phase will be the definitive model, based on which the system code will be generated.

The tools recommended to perform the tasks of this phase are the same tools as in the model generation and adaptation phase.

**(8) Software Refinement.** The work of the developers in this phase will be to guarantee the software quality, eliminating redundancies and making the software easy to maintain. The tools that support this activity will be those provided by the chosen IDE. It must be ensured that the final software meets the specifications of a clean code [34].

**(9) Hardware and Software Deployment.** Once the software has been tested (simulated), it is implemented and deployed in the devices and resources to be used in the system, confirming compliance with the final requirements negotiated between the client and the development team. At this point, and for the first deliverable, both the information storage system and the applications that will serve for the user-system interaction will have already been configured [41, 42]. For subsequent deliverables, the necessary changes will be made to this assembled infrastructure to add the new deliverables. Since the subsequent deliverables depend on the technology already installed, the operation of the (new) integrated system must be guaranteed before continuing the development process.

The tools to be used in this phase will depend on the technology used (single board computers, embedded sensors...).

**(10) Deliverable Assessment.** Once the development of the deliverable is complete (it had to pass the necessary tests to guarantee its operation), the integration tests, the system tests and, of course, the functional tests must be performed once again at this stage [43, 44].

**(11) Maintenance.** IoTS combine the complexity of software maintenance with the minor complexity of hardware maintenance. If an IoTS physical component (e.g., sensor, actuator, board computer, among others) fails, it is replaced by some other similar device. However, if the software requirements change, the code has to be modified, given that it has no spare parts [45]. Additionally, IoTS need constant operational maintenance (batteries or power lines, and connectivity, among others).

## 4 Conclusions and Future Work

Based on a thorough review of the methodologies used for the development of IoTS, it has been found that there is no standard methodology for this application domain. This fact has led IoTS developers to use methodologies designed to develop other types of more traditional IS and to make ad-hoc adjustments to meet the particular needs of each project. Moreover, the use of these non-specific methodologies for the development of IoTS has overlooked the need to specifically consider important aspects of these systems, such as their special requirements and the particular characteristics of the hardware to be deployed in them.

Consequently, a new methodology called TDDM4IoTS has been proposed to specifically approach the development of IoTS, which includes the most important foundations of TDD, MDE, and agile development, and which tries to solve each of the aspects that have been detected as weaknesses in the reviewed methodologies that have been used for the same purpose.

One of our next projects will be to validate TDDM4IoTS, to determine its effectiveness and acceptance. In addition, a tool will be developed to support the automated generation of the deliverables corresponding to each phase of TDDM4IoTS. In particular, we will focus on test generation.

## References

1. Dahl, O.-J., Hoare, C.A.R.: Chapter III: Hierarchical program structures. In: Structured Programming, pp. 175–220. Academic Press Ltd. (1972)
2. Ingalls, D.H.H.: The Smalltalk-76 programming system design and implementation. In: Proceedings of the 5th ACM SIGACT-SIGPLAN Symposium on Principles of Programming Languages - POPL 1978, pp. 9–16. ACM (1978)
3. Pashtan, A.: Object oriented operating systems: an emerging design methodology. In: Proceedings of the ACM 1982 Conference on ACM 1982, pp. 126–131. ACM (1982)
4. Schwabe, D., Rossi, G.: The object-oriented hypermedia design model. Commun. ACM **38**(8), 45–46 (2002)
5. Ashton, K.: That 'Internet of Things' thing. RFID J. **22**(7), 97–114 (2009)
6. Ray, P.P.: A survey on Internet of Things architectures. J. King Saud Univ. – Comput. Inf. Sci. **30**(3), 291–319 (2018)
7. Leotta, M., et al.: An acceptance testing approach for Internet of Things systems. IET Softw. **12**(5), 430–436 (2018)

8. Benedetto, J.I., González, L.A., Sanabria, P., Neyem, A., Navón, J.: Towards a practical framework for code offloading in the Internet of Things. Future Gener. Comput. Syst. **92**(March), 424–437 (2019)
9. Cervantes-Solis, J.W., Baber, C., Khattab, A., Mitch, R.: Rule and theme discovery in human interactions with an Internet of Things. In: Proceedings of the 2015 British HCI Conference on - British HCI 2015, pp. 222–227. ACM, UK (2015)
10. Ciccozzi, F., Spalazzese, R.: MDE4IoT: supporting the Internet of Things with model-driven engineering. In: Badica, C., et al. (eds.) IDC 2016. SCI, vol. 678, pp. 67–76. Springer, Cham (2017). https://doi.org/10.1007/978-3-319-48829-5_7
11. Khaleel, H., et al.: Heterogeneous applications, tools, and methodologies in the car manufacturing industry through an IoT approach. IEEE Syst. J. **11**(3), 1412–1423 (2017)
12. Cai, H., Gu, Y., Vasilakos, A.V., Xu, B., Zhou, J.: Model-driven development patterns for mobile services in cloud of things. IEEE Trans. Cloud Comput. **6**(3), 771–784 (2018)
13. Lekidis, A., Stachtiari, E., Katsaros, P., Bozga, M., Georgiadis, C.K.: Model-based design of IoT systems with the BIP component framework. J. Softw.: Pract. Exp. **48**(6), 1167–1194 (2018)
14. Brambilla, M., Umuhoza, E., Acerbis, R.: Model-driven development of user interfaces for IoT systems via domain-specific components and patterns. J. Internet Serv. Appl. **8**(1), 1–21 (2017)
15. Harbouche, A., Djedi, N., Erradi, M., Ben-Othman, J., Kobbane, A.: Model driven flexible design of a wireless body sensor network for health monitoring. Comput. Netw. **129-2**, 548–571 (2017)
16. Usländer, T., Batz, T.: Agile service engineering in the industrial Internet of Things. Future Internet **10**(10), 100 (2018)
17. Pico-Valencia, P., Holgado-Terriza, J.A., Paderewski, P.: A systematic method for building internet of agents applications based on the linked open data approach. Future Gener. Comput. Syst. **94**, 250–271 (2019)
18. Sosa-Reyna, C.M., Tello-Leal, E., Lara-Alabazares, D.: Methodology for the model-driven development of service oriented IoT applications. J. Syst. Architect. **90**, 15–22 (2018)
19. de Farias, C.M., et al.: COMFIT: a development environment for the Internet of Things. Future Gener. Comput. Syst. **75**, 128–144 (2017)
20. Fortino, G., et al.: Towards multi-layer interoperability of heterogeneous IoT platforms: the INTER-IoT approach. In: Gravina, R., Palau, C.E., Manso, M., Liotta, A., Fortino, G. (eds.) Integration, Interconnection, and Interoperability of IoT Systems. IT, pp. 199–232. Springer, Cham (2018). https://doi.org/10.1007/978-3-319-61300-0_10
21. Patel, P., Cassou, D.: Enabling high-level application development for the Internet of Things. J. Syst. Softw. **103**, 62–84 (2015)
22. Martin, R.C.: Clean Coder Blog, TDD (2017). https://blog.cleancoder.com/. Accessed 11 Sept 2019
23. Rising, L., Janoff, N.S.: Scrum software development process for small teams. IEEE Softw. **17**(4), 26–32 (2000)
24. Heeager, L.T., Nielsen, P.A.: A conceptual model of agile software development in a safety-critical context: a systematic literature review. Inf. Softw. Technol. **103**, 22–39 (2018)
25. Abrahamsson, P., Salo, O., Ronkainen, J., Warsta, J.: Agile Software Development Methods: Review and Analysis. VTT Publications 478 (2002)
26. Holzinger, A., Errath, M., Searle, G., Thurnher, B., Slany, W.: From extreme programming and usability engineering to extreme usability in software engineering education (XP+UE→XU). In: 29th Annual International Computer Software and Applications Conference (COMPSAC 2005), vol. 2, pp. 169–172. IEEE, UK (2005)
27. Mowday, R.T.: Leader characteristics, self-confidence, and methods of upward influence in organizational decision situations. Acad. Manag. J. **22**(4), 709–725 (1979)

28. Koo, K., Park, C.: Foundation of leadership in Asia: leader characteristics and leadership styles review and research agenda. Asia Pac. J. Manag. **35**(3), 697–718 (2018)
29. Beck, K.: Manifesto for Agile Software Development (2001). http://agilemanifesto.org/. Accessed 11 May 2019
30. Hazzan, O., Dubinsky, Y.: The agile manifesto. In: Zdonik, S., et al. (eds.) Agile Anywhere. SCS, pp. 9–14. Springer, Cham (2014). https://doi.org/10.1007/978-3-319-10157-6_3
31. Sachdeva, V., Chung, L.: Handling non-functional requirements for big data and IoT Projects in Scrum. In: 2017 7th International Conference on Cloud Computing, Data Science & Engineering - Confluence, pp. 216–221. IEEE (2017)
32. Tort, A., Olivé, A., Sancho, M.R.: An approach to test-driven development of conceptual schemas. Data Knowl. Eng. **70**(12), 1088–1111 (2011)
33. Janzen, D., Saiedian, H.: Test-driven development: concepts, taxonomy, and future direction. Computer **38**(9), 43–50 (2005)
34. Martin, R.C.: Clean Code, A Handbook of Agile Software Craftsmanship, 1st edn. Pearson Education Inc., Boston (2011)
35. Madeyski, L., Kawalerowicz, M.: Continuous test-driven development: a preliminary empirical evaluation using agile experimentation in industrial settings. In: Kosiuczenko, P., Madeyski, L. (eds.) Towards a Synergistic Combination of Research and Practice in Software Engineering. SCI, vol. 733, pp. 105–118. Springer, Cham (2018). https://doi.org/10.1007/978-3-319-65208-5_8
36. Braithwaite, K., Joyce, T.: XP expanded: distributed extreme programming. In: Baumeister, H., Marchesi, M., Holcombe, M. (eds.) XP 2005. LNCS, vol. 3556, pp. 180–188. Springer, Heidelberg (2005). https://doi.org/10.1007/11499053_21
37. Sosa-Reyna, C.M., Tello-Leal, E., Lara-Alabazares, D.: An approach based on model-driven development for IoT applications. In: Proceedings of the 2018 IEEE International Congress on IoT, ICIOT, 2018 IEEE World Congress on Services, pp. 134–139. IEEE, San Francisco, EEUU (2018)
38. Rasch, R.H., Tosi, H.L.: Factors affecting software developers' performance: an integrated approach. MIS Q. **16**(3), 395–413 (1992)
39. Nyznar, M., Pałka, D.: Generating source code templates on the basis of unit tests. In: Grzech, A., Świątek, J., Wilimowska, Z., Borzemski, L. (eds.) Information Systems Architecture and Technology: Proceedings of 37th International Conference on Information Systems Architecture and Technology – ISAT 2016 – Part II. AISC, vol. 522, pp. 213–223. Springer, Cham (2017). https://doi.org/10.1007/978-3-319-46586-9_17
40. Chen, Z., Liu, Z., Ravn, A.P., Stolz, V., Zhan, N.: Refinement and verification in component-based model-driven design. Sci. Comput. Program. **74**(4), 168–196 (2009)
41. Monteiro, K., Rocha, E., Silva, E., Santos, G.L., Santos, W., Endo, P.T.: Developing an e-health system based on IoT, fog and cloud computing. In: 2018 IEEE/ACM International Conference on Utility and Cloud Computing Companion (UCC Companion), pp. 17–18. IEEE, Zurich (2018)
42. Guerrero-Ulloa, G., Rodríguez-Domínguez, C., Hornos, M.J.: IoT-based system to help care for dependent elderly. In: Botto-Tobar, M., Pizarro, G., Zúñiga-Prieto, M., D'Armas, M., Zúñiga Sánchez, M. (eds.) CITT 2018. CCIS, vol. 895, pp. 41–55. Springer, Cham (2019). https://doi.org/10.1007/978-3-030-05532-5_4
43. Latorre, R.: Effects of developer experience on learning and applying unit test-driven development. IEEE Trans. Softw. Eng. **40**(4), 381–395 (2014)
44. Shihab, E., Jiang, Z.M., Adams, B., Hassan, A.E., Bowerman, R.: Prioritizing the creation of unit tests in legacy software systems. Softw.: Pract. Exp. **41**(10), 1027–1048 (2011)
45. Pressman, R.S., Maxim, B.: Software Engineering: A Practitioner's Approach, 8th edn. McGraw-Hill Education, Boston (2015)

# Pseudoplastic Magnetorheological Fluid Flow on a Moving Horizontal Flat Plate

Roberto Silva-Zea[1]([✉]), Romel Erazo-Bone[2], Fidel Chuchuca-Aguilar[2], Ricardo Gallegos[2], Kenny Escobar-Segovia[3,4], and Ulises Gallegos Carrión[5]

[1] Universidad Industrial de Santander, Bucaramanga, Colombia
roberto.silva.zea2@gmail.com
[2] Universidad Estatal Península de Santa Elena, La Libertad, Ecuador
[3] Escuela Superior Politécnica del Litoral, Guayaquil, Ecuador
[4] Universidad Espíritu Santo, Guayaquil, Ecuador
[5] Halliburton Saudi Arabia, Al Khobar, Saudi Arabia

**Abstract.** In this article, the differential transform method has been used to solve the characteristic equation of the flow of a magnetorheological pseudoplastic fluid on a flat plate. Prior to this, other techniques were performed that allowed the transformation of the equation for the application of the method object of this investigation, considering a positive fluid deformation rate. The phenomenon of equal plate and fluid velocities with and without magnetic field was mainly taken into account. When the magnetic field is applied, the dimensionless velocity domain is drastically reduced, demonstrating that these types of special fluids are magnetorestrictive and their usefulness is under study for industrial and scientific applications.

**Keywords:** Differential transform · Pseudoplastic fluid · Magnetorheological fluid · Boundary layer · Nonlinear differential equations

## 1 Introduction

The boundary layer flow represents one of the problems of nonlinear differential equations that do not always have an exact analytical solution and require approximate solution methods. Among the approximation methods used to solve nonlinear differential equations are numerical and quasi-analytical methods. The most widely used numerical method to solve boundary layer problems is the shooting method. This method transforms the boundary value problem (BVP) into an initial value problem (IVP) with unknown initial values. From this, the problem is replaced with a system of first-order ordinary differential equations and is generally solved through the Runge-Kutta method. The shooting method in certain boundary value problems presents instability in the solution.

Quasi-analytical approximation techniques such as the homotopic analysis method (HAM), homotopic perturbation method (HPM) and the variational iteration method (VIM) represent valid alternatives to the numerical methods. In the present decade, the problems related to flows in the boundary layer have been solved using these approximation techniques, for example, HAM [1–6], HPM [7–12] and VIM [13–15]. In some

© Springer Nature Switzerland AG 2020
M. Botto-Tobar et al. (Eds.): ICAT 2019, CCIS 1193, pp. 56–69, 2020.
https://doi.org/10.1007/978-3-030-42517-3_5

of these articles, some modifications have been introduced to overcome non-linearity and the limit condition at infinity.

The differential transform method (DTM) is also one of the approximation methods used to solve differential equations. This method was originally introduced by Zhou [16] to solve initial value problems in the analysis of electrical circuits. The method consists of an iterative technique to find the solution to the problem based on the Taylor series. In this article, the DTM is used to solve the boundary layer flow equation of a magnetorheological pseudoplastic fluid.

To solve the problem and graphics, the symbolic language software MATHEMAT-ICA® has been used. The solution of the problem is presented here by the method proposed by Mosayebidorcheh [17] for the case of a boundary layer flow of a pseudoplastic fluid on a horizontal flat plate.

The objective of this investigation is to determine the behavior of the flow of non-Newtonian magnetic fluids in the presence of an external magnetic field in moving flat sheets using an appropriate mathematical approach method such as the differential transform where other approximation methods cannot be applied or that the results are not satisfactory. It is known that these types of fluids undergo a sudden change in their rheological behavior when they are in the presence of a magnetic field. The initiation of research on this subject is due to Rabinow [18], who investigated the application of this type of fluid in some types of instruments. The potential of magnetorheological fluid applications has been studied by Felt et al. [19], Mohebi et al. [20], Nakato and Yamamoto [21], Carlson et al. [22] and Weiss et al. [23] and covers such extensive fields as medicine, aeronautics, oil fields, oil refining, and others [24, 25, 26]. This is an original investigation, which represents the first of its kind, due to the degree of difficulty in solving the nonlinear flow equations for a non-Newtonian fluid.

## 2   The Differential Transform Method (DTM)

The differential transform is defined as:

$$F(k) = \frac{1}{k!}\left[\frac{d^k f(x)}{dx^k}\right]_{x=x_o} \tag{1}$$

Where f(x) is any function and F(k) is the transformed function. On the other hand, the inverse transform is defined as:

$$f(x) = \sum_{k=0}^{\infty} F(k)(x - x_o)^k \tag{2}$$

Substituting (1) in (2), we obtain:

$$f(x) = \sum_{k=0}^{\infty} \frac{(x - x_o)^k}{k!}\left[\frac{d^k f(x)}{dx^k}\right]_{x=x_o} \tag{3}$$

Which can be approximated to:

$$f(x) \approx \sum_{k=0}^{l} \frac{(x - x_o)^k}{k!}\left[\frac{d^k f(x)}{dx^k}\right]_{x=x_o} \tag{3a}$$

Where $l$ is the number of terms in the Taylor series that gives the solution of f(x) the most accuracy. Here are some properties of the differential transform and its inverse (Table 1).

**Table 1.** Properties of the differential transform

| Original function | Differential transformation |
|---|---|
| $f(x) = g(x) \pm h(x)$ | $F(k) = G(k) \pm H(k)$ |
| $f(x) = cg(x)$ | $F(k) = cG(k)$ |
| $f(x) = \frac{d^n g(x)}{dx^n}$ | $F(k) = \frac{(k+n)!}{k!} G(k+n)$ |
| $f(x) = g(x)h(x)$ | $F(k) = \sum_{r=0}^{k} G(r)H(k-r)$ |

## 3   Mathematical Formulation of the Problem

Consider the two-dimensional stationary flow of an incompressible pseudoplastic magnetorheological fluid flowing on a flat impermeable plate in motion with constant velocity $U_w$ in a concurrent direction or against current to the fluid direction. The two-dimensional equations that describe the boundary layer flow for the magnetoreological fluid are for this problem the following:

$$\frac{\partial U}{\partial X} + \frac{\partial V}{\partial Y} = 0 \tag{4}$$

$$U\frac{\partial U}{\partial X} + V\frac{\partial U}{\partial Y} = \frac{1}{\rho}\frac{\partial \tau_{XY}}{\partial Y} - \frac{\sigma B_o^2}{\rho}U \tag{5}$$

Where U and V are the components of the velocities on the X and Y axes respectively, $\tau_{XY}$ is the shear stress, $B_o$ is the magnitude of the vertically directed magnetic field, $\sigma$ and $\rho$ are the electrical conductivity and fluid density respectively. The boundary conditions are as follows:

$$\begin{aligned} U = U_w, \quad V = 0, \; at \; Y = 0 \\ U \rightarrow U_\infty \qquad as \; Y \rightarrow \infty \end{aligned} \tag{6}$$

$\tau_{XY}$ is defined as:

$$\tau_{XY} = m\left|\frac{\partial U}{\partial Y}\right|^{n-1}\frac{\partial U}{\partial Y} \tag{7}$$

The pseudoplastic Reynolds number is defined as:

$$Re = \frac{\rho U_\infty^{2-n} L^n}{m} \tag{8}$$

Where m is the fluid consistency coefficient, n is the power law index (for pseudo-plastic fluids $n \leq 1$), $U_\infty$ is the fluid stream velocity far field and L is the plate length. Then, the following dimensionless parameters are introduced:

$$x = \frac{X}{L}, y = \frac{Y}{L} Re^{\frac{1}{n+1}}, u = \frac{U}{U_\infty}, v = \frac{V}{U_\infty} Re^{\frac{1}{n+1}} \tag{9}$$

Combining Eqs. (7), (8), (9) into (5), we have:

$$u \frac{\partial u}{\partial x} + v \frac{\partial u}{\partial y} = \frac{\partial}{\partial y} \left( \left| \frac{\partial u}{\partial y} \right|^{n-1} \frac{\partial u}{\partial y} \right) - \frac{\sigma B_o^2 L}{\rho U_\infty} u \tag{10}$$

With the new dimensionless border conditions:

$$\begin{aligned} u &= \frac{U_w}{U_\infty}, v = 0, \, at \, y = 0 \\ u &\to 1 \qquad\qquad as \, y \to \infty \end{aligned} \tag{11}$$

## 4  Solution Method

The similarity variable $\eta$ and the current function $\Psi$ are introduced in order to transform (10) into an appropriately manageable equation:

$$\eta = \frac{y}{(nx(n+1))^{\frac{1}{n+1}}} \tag{12}$$

$$\Psi = (nx(n+1))^{\frac{1}{n+1}} f(\eta) \tag{13}$$

Where $f(\eta)$ is an arbitrary function to be found, which is related to the dimensionless velocity or as will be seen later. The velocities can be obtained from the current function $\Psi$, which are defined below:

$$u = \frac{\partial \Psi}{\partial y} = f'(\eta) \tag{14}$$

$$v = -\frac{\partial \Psi}{\partial x} = \frac{1}{(n+1)} \left( \frac{n(n+1)}{x^n} \right)^{\frac{1}{n+1}} [\eta f'(\eta) - f(\eta)] \tag{15}$$

Then applying the transformation by similarity in (10), we have:

$$\begin{aligned} [f''(\eta)]^{n-1} f'''(\eta) + f(\eta)f''(\eta) - M(n+1)f'(\eta) \\ = 0 \, para \, n \leq 1 \end{aligned} \tag{16}$$

In this case it has been taken that:

$$\frac{\partial u}{\partial y} > 0 \tag{17}$$

M is the local magnetic number defined as:

$$M = \frac{\sigma B_o^2 L}{\rho U_\infty} x \tag{18}$$

So the new boundary conditions transformed by similarity of (16) are:

$$f(0) = 0, \quad f'(0) = \frac{U_w}{U_\infty} = \epsilon, \quad f'(\infty) \to 1 \tag{19}$$

## 5  Problem Solution

The Differential Transform method is applied. First, in order to linearize (16) the method proposed by Mosayebidorcheh [17] is used, so:

$$s(\eta) = \left(f''(\eta)\right)^{n-1} \tag{20}$$

Which is equivalent to:

$$s(\eta)f''(\eta) = \left(f''(\eta)\right)^n \tag{21}$$

Deriving (21) we have:

$$s'(\eta)f''(\eta) + s(\eta)f'''(\eta) = n * f'''(\eta)\left(f''(\eta)\right)^{n-1} \tag{22}$$

Taking into consideration (20) and rearranging (22), it is corresponding that:

$$s'(\eta) * f''(\eta) = (n-1) * s(\eta) * f'''(\eta) \tag{23}$$

Applying the differential transform to (20) is therefore obtained:

$$\sum\nolimits_{r=0}^{k}(r+1)(r+2)(k-r+1)F(r+2)S(k-r+1)$$
$$= (n-1)\sum\nolimits_{r=0}^{k}(r+1)(r+2)(r+3)F(r+3)S(k-r) \tag{24}$$

Then the differential transform is taken to (16):

$$M(n+1)(k+1)F(k+1)$$
$$-\sum\nolimits_{r=0}^{k}(r+1)(r+2)F(r+2)F(k-r)$$
$$-\sum\nolimits_{r=0}^{k}(r+1)(r+2)(r+3)F(r+3)S(k-r) = 0 \tag{25}$$

The new transformed boundary conditions are therefore:

$$S(0) = (\lambda)^{n-1}, \quad F(0) = 0, \quad F(1) = \epsilon,$$
$$F(2) = \tfrac{\lambda}{2} \tag{26}$$

Where $\lambda$ is the value of $f''(0)$, which has been taken to change from initial value problem to a boundary value problem. The respective relationship is presented below to determine the value of $\lambda$ that allows to find the function $f(\eta)$ that fits the differentially transformed boundary conditions of the problem. The value of $\epsilon$ which is the ratio between the speeds of the plate and the free flow of the fluid will be taken in the range between 0 and 1 for convenience here in this investigation.

Solving the system of Eqs. (24) and (25), we obtain the $F$ values of the Taylor series for the function $f(\eta)$:

$$F(3) = \frac{\epsilon M(n+1)}{6\lambda^{n-1}}$$

$$F(4) = \frac{\lambda^{1-n}\left(M(1+n)\lambda - \epsilon\lambda - M^2(1+n)\left(-1+n^2\right)\epsilon^2\lambda^{-n}\right)}{24}$$

$$F(5) = -\frac{1}{120}\lambda^{1-3n}\left(-M^3\epsilon^3 + 4M^3n^2\epsilon^3 + 2M^3n^3\epsilon^3\right)$$
$$- 3M^3n^4\epsilon^3 - 2M^3n^5\epsilon^3 - 4M^2\epsilon\lambda^{1+n}$$
$$- 5M^2n\epsilon\lambda^{1+n} + 2M^2n^2\epsilon\lambda^{1+n}$$
$$+ 3M^2n^3\epsilon\lambda^{1+n} + 5M\epsilon^2\lambda^{1+n} + 2Mn\epsilon^2\lambda^{1+n}$$
$$- 3Mn^2\epsilon^2\lambda^{1+n} + \lambda^{2+2n}$$
$$\vdots$$

$$(27)$$

Now, considering similarly to (13) when $\lambda = 1$ a new function $g(\eta)$ is constructed such that:

$$\left[g''(\eta)\right]^{n-1}g'''(\eta) + g(\eta)g''(\eta) - M(n+1)g'(\eta)$$
$$= 0 \ for \ n \le 1 \qquad (28)$$
$$g(0) = 0, \quad g'(0) = \epsilon, \quad g''(0) = 1$$

Where the Taylor series coefficients for $g(\eta)$ are:

$$G(3) = \frac{\epsilon M(n+1)}{6},$$

$$G(4) = \frac{M(1+n) - \epsilon - M^2(1+n)\left(-1+n^2\right)\epsilon^2}{24}$$

$$G(5) = -\frac{1}{120}(-M^3\epsilon^3 + 4M^3n^2\epsilon^3 + 2M^3n^3\epsilon^3 - 3M^3n^4\epsilon^3$$
$$- 2M^3n^5\epsilon^3 - 4M^2\epsilon - 5M^2n\epsilon + 2M^2n^2\epsilon$$
$$+ 3M^2n^3\epsilon + 5M\epsilon^2 + 2Mn\epsilon^2 - 3Mn^2\epsilon^2$$
$$+ 1)$$

$$(29)$$

La relación entre $f(\eta)$ y $g(\eta)$ es la siguiente:

$$f(\eta) = \lambda^q g\left(\lambda^p\eta\right), \quad p = \frac{2-n}{3} \quad q = \frac{2n-1}{3} \qquad (30)$$

From the boundary conditions and with the aim of (30) it is then assumed that the value of $\lambda$ must be adjusted by the following expression:

$$\lambda = \left(\frac{1}{g'(\infty)}\right)^{\frac{3}{n+1}} \qquad (31)$$

## 6 Discussion of Results

For this problem, the Taylor series for both $f(\eta)$ and $g(\eta)$ developed to the order $O(\eta^{10})$ due to the large number of factors in each term to be handled in the series. On the other hand, we proceeded to use the 3D MATHEMATICA® graphing options to determine the value of $\lambda$ in the domain of the function $f'(\eta)$ corresponding to the dimensionless velocity $u$ in order to visualize the behavior of the $\lambda$ value obtained by the method proposed by Mosayebidorcheh [17] and adapted here for the solution of the problem. A value for $\eta$ of 30 has been considered for the calculation of $g'(\infty)$ to obtain greater representativeness of the trend in infinity. Emphasis was placed on equal velocities, for the plate and the fluid free current, especially with three indices of pseudoplastic behavior of the magnetorheological fluid before a local external magnetic field strength.

The comparison between Figs. 1, 4 and 6 allows us to observe the behavior of velocity versus the action of the local magnetic field. As can be seen, the speed domain is drastically restricted and falls below the value of $\eta$ considered here as infinite for the compliance of the boundary condition $f'(\infty) = 1$. This leads us to conclude that this type of fluids can be controlled under the action of an external magnetic field without the need for physical contact.

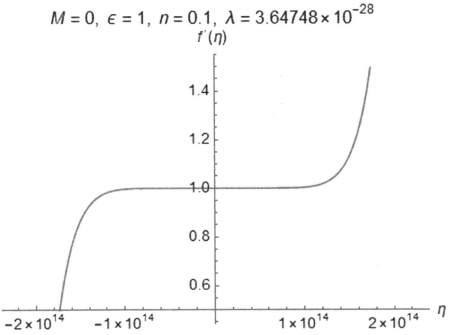

**Fig. 1.** Velocity profile of $f'(\eta)$ under the conditions shown. The value of $\eta$ is higher than assumed as infinite for calculations.

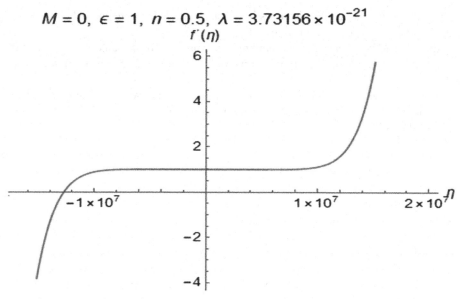

**Fig. 2.** Velocity profile of $f'(\eta)$. Notice the reduction in the value of $\lambda$ against an increment of n. $\eta$ it's practically infinite.

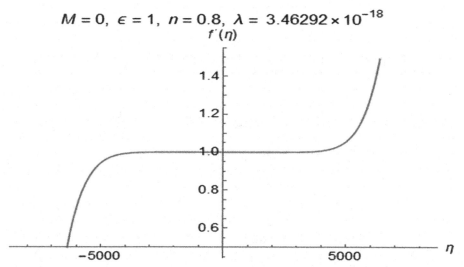

**Fig. 3.** Velocity profile of $f'(\eta)$. Notice the reduction of the domain against an increment of n compared to the Fig. 2.

On the other hand, in Figs. 1, 2 and 3 without the presence of a magnetic field, with a value of $\epsilon = 1$ for the three cases and gradually increasing the value of n, a gradual decrease in the domain of $\eta$ can be seen and also a del value growth. This means that when n grows, the value of λ also does it, as long as there is no magnetic field and the speeds of the plate and the fluid are equal.

Also when M is increased by maintaining constants $\epsilon$ and n, the value of λ is increased and the domain of $\eta$ is reduced to that considered as infinite, as can be seen in Figs. 4 and 6.

Figure 5 shows that when the velocity of the fluid is greater than that of the plate and in the presence of a local magnetic field the domain of $\eta$ practically disappears for a given value of n.

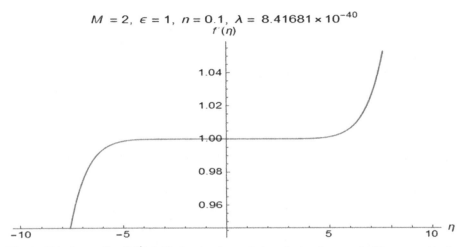

**Fig. 4.** Velocity profile of $f'(\eta)$. Notice the change in λ against an increase in M compared to the Fig. 1. The value of $\eta$ is less than assumed as infinity.

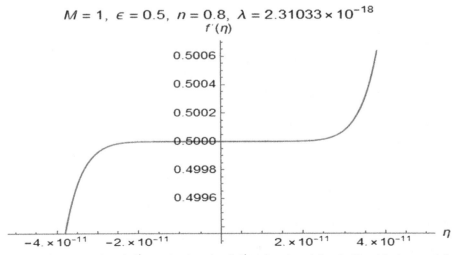

**Fig. 5.** Velocity profile of $f'(\eta)$. The domain of $f'(\eta)$ is reduced drastically with change of the rest of parameters of flow.

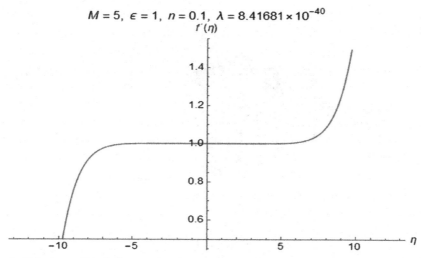

**Fig. 6.** Velocity profile of $f'(\eta)$. Notice the invariability in $\lambda$ against an increase in M with respect to Fig. 4. The value of $\eta$ is less than considered as infinity

A summary of the results obtained from $\lambda$ is found in Table 2.

**Table 2.** $\lambda$ values obtained

| M | $f'(0) = \epsilon$ | n | $f''(0) = \lambda$ |
|---|---|---|---|
| 0 | 1 | 0.1 | 3.64748E−28 |
| 0 | 1 | 0.5 | 3.731560E−21 |
| 0 | 1 | 0.8 | 3.462926E−18 |
| 2 | 1 | 0.1 | 8.41681E−40 |
| 1 | 0.5 | 0.8 | 2.31033E−18 |
| 5 | 1 | 0.1 | 3.73156E−21 |

Figures 7 and 8 show the behavior of $f'(\eta)$ against $\eta$ and $\lambda$ with respect to the conditions in Fig. 1. The 3D graph allows you to determine the range of values for $\lambda$, where the values are determined by the mathematical procedure described by Mosayebidorcheh [17], which serves to validate the results obtained.

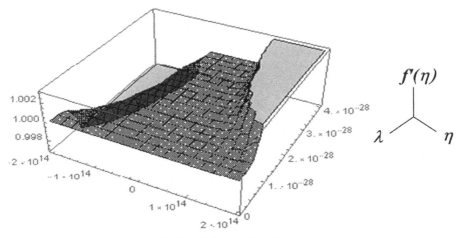

**Fig. 7.** 3D image 3D of Fig. 1.

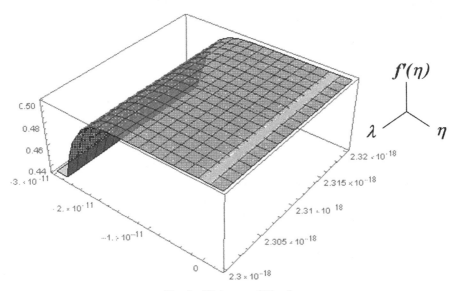

**Fig. 8.** 3D image of Fig. 5.

## 7  Conclusions

As has been observed, the DTM technique is a valuable tool for approximating non-linear differential equations, in this case with a greater degree of difficulty, due to the conditions of the problem. With this methodology implemented it was possible to find the solution of the differential equation representative of the boundary layer flow of a magnetorheological pseudoplastic fluid on a moving flat plate. Thanks to the help of a symbolic language software, it was feasible to perform the mathematical calculations and perform the traceability of the behavior of the approximate solutions to validate the results.

To make the decision to use the differential transform method, the use of numerical methods was first investigated, such as the trigger method, which yielded unsatisfactory results. Next, the combined MTD-Padé technique was used, with also not very encouraging results. Then, after an intensive literature review, he found the method proposed by Mosayebidorcheh [17], improving the results obtained under the conditions of the problem to be investigated.

The behavior of the fluid has been taken as the basis when the speeds of the plate and the free current are identical, the parameters such as the local magnetic field M and the index of pseudoplastic behavior n. A slight change was made in the ratio of plate speeds and fluid free current to observe its behavior.

It is concluded that when an external magnetic field is applied to the moving plate, the fluid velocity decreases. Likewise, when a local magnetic field is increased, the velocity of the fluid improves its distribution through the plate. It can also be concluded that before a unit value of $\epsilon$ without the presence of a magnetic field, with an increase in the rheological properties of the fluid represented in the value of n there is a gradual decrease in the domain of $\eta$ and also a growth in the value of $\lambda$. This could be significant, since by continuing to increase the value of n with these established conditions the speed domain can be limited until reaching the initially estimated. The special case is that presented in Fig. 5 where the domain is not initially estimated to determine the velocity, therefore it does not represent the fluid flow. This is important when designing a magnetorheological fluid and applying a magnetic field to control its flow on a moving plate.

## 8 Future Works

It is expected in a next phase of research the same phenomenon but against heat transfer through the plate, which would have a coupled system of partial differential equations, which must be solved simultaneously, so that the degree of difficulty in solving the problem is increased.

**Acknowledgement.** The authors are grateful for the financing of this research to the Sucker rod pump design project of the UPSE and especially to the evaluators of this article of the ICAT 2019 Congress.

## References

1. Motsa, S., Shateyi, S., Makukula, Z.: Homotopy analysis of free convection boundary layer flow with heat and mass transfer. Chem. Eng. Commun. **198**(6), 783–795 (2011). https://doi.org/10.1080/00986445.2011.534011
2. Rashidi, M.M., Momoniat, E., Rostami, B.: Analytic approximate solutions for MHD boundary-layer viscoelastic fluid flow over continuously moving stretching surface by homotopy analysis method with two auxiliary parameters. J. Appl. Math. (2012). https://doi.org/10.1155/2012/780415. (Mahomed, F.M. (ed.))

3.  Rashidi, M.M., Mohimanian Pour, S.A.: Analytic approximate solutions for unsteady boundary-layer flow and heat transfer due to a stretching sheet by homotopy analysis method. Nonlinear Anal.: Model. Control **15**(1), 83–95 (2010). https://www.mii.lt/na/issues/NA_1501/NA15107.pdf
4.  Nadeem, S., Hussain, A., Khan, M.: HAM solutions for boundary layer flow in the region of the stagnation point towards a stretching sheet. Commun. Nonlinear Sci. Numer. Simul. **16**(3), 475–481 (2010). https://doi.org/10.1016/j.cnsns.2009.04.037. (Chandre, C. (ed.))
5.  Nadeem, S., Lee, C.: Boundary layer flow of nanofluid over an exponentially stretching surface. Nanoscale Res. Lett. **7**(94), 1–6 (2012). https://doi.org/10.1186/1556-276x-7-94
6.  Rehman, A., Sheikh, N.: Boundary layer stagnation-point flow of micropolar fluid over an exponentially stretching sheet. Int. J. Fluid Mech. Thermal Sci. **3**(3), 25–31 (2017). https://doi.org/10.11648/j.ijfmts.20170303.11
7.  Dalir, N., Nourazar, S.: Solution of the boundary layer flow of various nanofluids over a moving semi-infinite plate using HPM. Mechanika **20**(1), 57–63 (2014). https://doi.org/10.5755/j01.mech.20.1.3406
8.  Esmaeilpour, M., Ganji, D.: Application of He's homotopy perturbation method to boundary layer flow and convection heat transfer over a flat plate. Phys. Lett. A **372**, 33–38 (2007). https://doi.org/10.1016/j.physleta.2007.07.002
9.  Nourazar, S.S., Habibi Matin, M., Simiari, M.: The HPM applied to MHD nanofluid flow over a horizontal stretching plate. J. Appl. Math. **2011**, 17 (2011). https://doi.org/10.1155/2011/876437. (Liu, Y. (ed.))
10. Jhankal, A.K.: Homotopy perturbation method for MHD boundary layer flow with low pressure gradient over a flat plate. J. Appl. Fluid Mech. **7**(1), 177–185 (2014). http://jafmonline.net/JournalArchive/download?file_ID=32462&issue_ID=216
11. Jhankal, A.K.: Application of homotopy perturbation method for MHD boundary layer flow of an upper-convected Maxwell fluid in a porous medium. Chem. Eng. Res. Bull. (18), 12–17 (2015). https://pdfs.semanticscholar.org/7d4b/8b13a969b95ba1458fee220e6bd1fadb7ffb.pdf
12. Jhankal, A.K.: MHD boundary layer flow near stagnation point of linear stretching sheet with variable thermal conductivity via He's homotopy perturbation method. J. Appl. Fluid Mech. **8**(3), 571–578 (2015). https://doi.org/10.18869/acadpub.jafm.67.222.20356
13. Aiyesimi, Y., Niyi, O.O.: Computational analysis of the non-linear boundary layer flow over a flat plate using Variational Iterative Method (VIM). Am. J. Comput. Appl. Math. **1**(2), 94–97 (2011). https://doi.org/10.5923/j.ajcam.20110102.18
14. Rabe Santatra, F.R., Solofoniaina, J.: Solutions of the boundary layer of a viscous fluid in forced convection on a flate plate by the variational iteration method. In: HAL, pp. 1–8 (2018). https://hal.archives-ouvertes.fr/hal-01693110/document
15. Xu, L., Lee, E.: Variational iteration method for the magnetohydrodynamic flow over a nonlinear stretching sheet. Abstract Appl. Anal. **2013**(4), 5 (2013). https://doi.org/10.1155/2013/573782
16. Zhou, J.K.: Differential Transformation and Its Applications for Electrical Circuits. Huazhong University Press (1986)
17. Mosayebidorcheh, S.: Solution of the boundary layer equation of the power-law pseudoplastic fluid using differential transform method. Math. Probl. Eng. **2013**, 8 (2013). https://doi.org/10.1155/2013/685454
18. Rabinow, J.: The magnetic fluid clutch. AIEE Trans. **67**, 1308–1315 (1948)
19. Felt, D.W., Hagenbüchle, M., Liu, J.: Rheology of a magnetorheological fluid. J. Intell. Mater. Syst. Struct. **7**, 589–593 (1996)
20. Mohebi, M., Jamashi, N., Flores, G.A., Liu, J.: Numerical study of the role of magnetic field ramping rate on the structure formation in magnetorheological fluids. Int. J. Mod. Phys. **13**, 2060–2067 (1999)

21. Nakato, M., Yamamoto, H.: Dynamic viscoelasticity of a magnetorheological fluid in oscillatory slit flow. Int. J. Mod. Phys. **13**, 2068–2076 (1999)
22. Carlson, J.D., Catanzarite, D.M., St. Clair, K.A.: Commercial magnetorheological fluid devices. Int. J. Mod. Phys. B **10**, 2857–2865 (1996)
23. Weiss, K.D., Carlson, J.D., Nixon, D.A.: Viscoelastic properties of magneto- and electrorheological fluids. J. Intell. Mater. Syst. Struct. **5**, 772–775 (1994)
24. Wahid, S.A., Ismail, I., Aid, S., Rahim, M.S.A.: Magneto-rheological defects and failures: a review. In: IOP Conference Series: Materials Science and Engineering, vol. 114, p. 012101 (2016). https://doi.org/10.1088/1757-899x/114/1/012101
25. Spaggiari, A.: Properties and applications of Magnetorheological fluids. Frattura ed Integrità Strutturale **23**, 57–61 (2013). https://doi.org/10.3221/igf-esis.23.06

# ICT as Part of the Training Process
# in Professional Practice

Camilo José Peña Lapeira[(⊠)] [iD] and Liliana Vargas Puentes[(⊠)] [iD]

Corporación Universitaria Minuto de Dios - UNIMINUTO, Cll 1 # 9-50, Bogotá, Colombia
{cjpena,liliana.vargas}@uniminuto.edu

**Abstract.** The present investigation makes an approach to the experiences of a group of students in the use, appropriation, and implementation of the TIC from the professional practice or internship carried out in the business sector and other entities and institutions constituted as a practice center located in the localities of Bosa and Kennedy of the city of Bogotá - Colombia, this with the objective of evaluating the degree of appropriation of these and their level of competence when it comes to solving problems that arise in the daily routine of professional practice. The type of research under which the project was worked was the case study, with a mixed approach through the use of qualitative and quantitative instruments such as the survey, the interview, the field diary, and the documentary analysis; Results were obtained that point to the improvement in the processes of appropriation of ICTs within the different academic programs that are currently offered in order to improve the way in which these technological tools are implemented at the time of to solve business problems, especially those that arise in newly constituted companies or with technological and budgetary limitations, in such a way that it can give good business support.

**Keywords:** ICT · Professional practice · Communication skills · Digital era · Innovation

## 1   Introduction

### 1.1   Relationship of ICT with Professional Practice

Education is a determining factor for the development of a country, not only because it is a fundamental right of every human being; but because it becomes a tool that allows transforming lives in order to consolidate peace, eradicate poverty and promote sustainable development in nations [1]. Thus, education becomes a central axis that allows the progress and progress of societies; where educational institutions have a high degree of social responsibility with individuals, since the globalized world in which we live demands professionals capable of facing the challenges of contemporary societies such as: the domain of science and technology [2], in such a way that the professional becomes a transforming agent that links his knowledge to the solution of problems in his communities.

Professional practices or what is known in other environments such as internships, is a space provided by academic institutions in which it seeks to link the student with

M. Botto-Tobar et al. (Eds.): ICAT 2019, CCIS 1193, pp. 70–84, 2020.
https://doi.org/10.1007/978-3-030-42517-3_6

their professional work in a real context, putting into practice what was learned inside the classroom and developing new skills at a professional level; However, at the time of starting professional practices, students find several barriers of which three stand out:

1. The salary payments of the practice centers do not supplement the economic needs of the students, since they are more given to transportation financing.
2. The activities carried out in the internship centers require the student to be competent in different fields complementary to their professional training, such as ICT competence, which in their vast majority are skills that are acquired by the student but that are very Little are formed in the academy as part of a curriculum or do not have a total relationship with the disciplinary component.
3. The evaluation of their professional practice process will largely depend on not only their performance in the field of discipline, but also depend on how they performed with their communication skills that depend to a great extent on the use of ICT resources.

For [3] "the profound transformations that we experience today in highly changing social contexts, typical of globalization, test the prevailing paradigms of professional learning in universities" (P. 2), which indicates that in today's world it is questioned in one way or another if the professional learning received by the students in the universities is in accordance with the needs of the environment in which these will unfold in the future, where being competent in ICT is almost an obligation for the students. Future professionals and their preparation in this field is not only a personal commitment on the part of the student but the educational infrastructure should gradually promote their development.

The incursion with the implementation of ICTs from the classrooms so that students develop technical skills in the various fields of application according to the basic training, will not only allow a change in the teaching mentality and pedagogical practices of educational institutions, It will provide different tools in the students during the development of their professional practice, aligned with the globalization components they face during their first approach to the working world that will mark an important guideline for their professional development.

## 1.2   ICT Skills in Professional Practice

The training of professionals currently involves competence and commitment to social development [4]; this taking into account that, it is not about training specialists in a specific field only, it is an imperative to train them integrally, which motivates them to be able to have an ethical and responsible performance with society. Here, competency training is understood as the permanent characteristics of people that are directly related to the successful execution of an activity, combining the cognitive, affective and behavioral [5]. This is because it is necessary to prepare them for the competitiveness of the changing world in which we find ourselves, where, in addition to the acquisition of knowledge, the professional motivation that invites them to have efficient, ethical and responsible actions is vital.

In this sense, higher education institutions are responsible for designing learning situations complementary to the training of the disciplinary area of future professionals through professional practices; These are considered as putting into practice the knowledge and skills acquired in the academic life of the professionals since they consist of a first approach to the working world on their part and are covered by educational regulations. For example, in Colombia, the Political Constitution establishes that "education will train Colombians in the practice of work", that is, it will facilitate their connection to an organization in such a way that they can carry out specific tasks in their disciplinary area. In this way, the objective is to contribute to the solution to the needs of the country.

Currently, Information and Communication Technologies (ICT) have revolutionized the business world and have taken us to the global world, because they allow us to be in contact and communicate with a number of people locally, nationally and internationally instantly. Therefore, ICTs have been consolidated as fundamental support tools for business management, thus strengthening the construction of strategies for competitiveness and innovation, generating sustainability for the organization and society [6]; for this reason, at a global level they are considered as a great generator of jobs; in fact they facilitate the growth of organizations because they constitute a strategic resource that helps companies find new opportunities in the market, with low costs and high probability of success [7], It is necessary to emphasize that their application needs partnerships strategies for obtaining expected results, for example, it is important to link ICT projects to generate synergies in the achievement of organizational goals and objectives; Likewise, a baseline should be established to compare the contribution of ICT to the performance of the organization [8] and thus establish the mechanisms that determine its functionality.

So then, ICTs integrate computing, telecommunications, and network media; therefore, they enable communication and interpersonal collaboration (person to person) and multidirectional collaboration (one to many or many to many) [9]; this allows a better and faster exchange of information between the parties involved in the process, while it is pertinent to have enough machinery and support to facilitate their appropriation in the organization and achieve maximum efficiency; that is, better results using fewer resources.

Because of this, ICTs have become a revolutionary instrument that has been accepted by different types of organizations, where governments of developed and developing countries have joined forces to consolidate and support sources of employment such as what are the companies of the different sectors; since these become an important support for the development and advancement of a country. In this sense, the linking of ICT in the training of future professionals must become an imperative for all institutions in the education sector, as it is clear that their domain, although it does not guarantee success for the insertion in the world of work, if it determines possibilities of linkage to it, because it is an added value that allows the professional to consolidate his specific and transversal competences.

## 2  Related Work

According to what has been described by [10], professional practices are generally part of the academic, curricular or training activities carried out during the university, these being the majority of the time required to obtain the academic degree (page 113).

Likewise, it emphasizes that professional practice and internships are mechanisms that serve as a "bridge" to bring young people to the labor market that allow young people to put into practice the theoretical knowledge acquired during their professional training in a "real" world, that is, in concrete and existing situations (page 114).

The aforementioned implies that students in the practice process develop competencies that, as he maintains [11]: "the development of a competence is a complex cognitive activity that requires the person to establish relationships between practice and theory"; transfer learning to different situations, learn to learn, pose and solve problems and act intelligently and critically in a situation. This interpretation, as mentioned by the author, is seen more clearly in the acquisition of experience and thus becomes a mechanism facilitating labor insertion and as an effective professional orientation device.

That is why throughout internships or internships, trainees go through a process of training and adaptation to new organizational forms of work [12], so these professional practices require constant support from tutors or teachers to follow up on the activities developed by the practitioners, for which there are alternatives associated with the use of ICTs which generate benefits from virtuality and advantages in the blended learning modalities, maintaining contact with practitioners who are in the professional scenario, orienting, facilitating or supporting the practices, through the provision of new documentation or information that the students demand for the development of their practice [11].

Proof of this is reflected in the study carried out by [13], which through the implementation of ICT tools for the monitoring and supervision of national and international internships of students of Production Engineering of the Simón Bolívar University (Caracas, Venezuela), obtained favorable results for both teachers and interns, by improving communication mechanisms through the implementation of instruments that include meetings by videoconference, email, digital documents, electronic bibliographic and newspaper resources, satellite maps, tools for programming activities and time conversion.

On the other hand, from fields of action such as Journalism and Social Communication, more and more have been venturing into the creation of online newspapers, blogs, web pages, virtual classrooms that are some of the web 2.0 tools currently being developed. In the classroom and function as tools that bring students closer to the environments of their future profession. From the use of these resources from the classroom, it can be established that the knowledge acquired in the pre-professional practices will also be strengthened, since students can work comprehensively in the different areas of communication and prepare for internships and links to public and private institutions and non-governmental organizations [14].

However, from the perspective of the admission of interns in organizations it is necessary to strengthen university-company relations, which allow improving the possibilities for students to actually apply the knowledge acquired during their training process and not only remain in operative tasks that prevent the proper application of theories to real situations in which they can intervene and encourage positive changes in organizations.

In relation to this, it is to be considered as part of the elements that large companies look for in students that can develop their professional practice in their facilities, [15] they mention that among other aspects, they consider the capacity and quality as a professional, that is, the solid basic knowledge that sustains its permanent updating and reclassification; skills in handling basic technologies for their professional work (computing, telecommunications); skills to work under pressure and to develop multitasking and multilevel work; experience and maturity to make decisions, and capacity to respond to questioning (p. 28).

This allows us to intuit that the use of ICT by students of professional practice becomes relevant in the development of tasks in the practice center, so the skill developed in the proper use of them will be a favorable aspect, even with the possibility of continuing a future contract once the period ends as a practitioner.

As a complement to the mentioned technical aspects, [16] it refers to the deontological code whose function is to guide the excellence of the profession, that is, to create a certain moral culture to guarantee that the assigned social function is fulfilled, for which it declares the ideal in which professionals should be guided, and determines the rules of professional behavior. In relation to this, these codes determine the demands of professional practice, that is, they guide professionals on the most appropriate forms of behavior to protect users from abuse or lack of honesty in professions whose mechanisms of action can be very aggressive.

The sum of these two components, ethical and technical, in the development of professional practice, must generate a synergy that allows multiple benefits for both the student, the educational institution and the company, being a source of feedback for all actors in the process which leads to the improvement of academic actions and social impact in organizations that allow the development of professional practices.

## 3    Methodological Approach

The general objective of the research is the evaluation of ICT competencies of Corporación Universitaria Minuto de Dios (UNIMINUTO) Vicerrectoría Regional Bogotá Sur students who perform professional internships in the organizational, marketing, administrative, accounting, training, advisory and consulting services, belonging to the centers of practice located in the towns of Kennedy and Bosa in the south of the city of Bogotá - Colombia, which allows the future not only to improve the academic programs but to contribute to the community in the business support processes based on the evaluation of the implementation of said competencies in the practices.

Case study was is the type of research under which the project was worked, with a mixed approach through the use of qualitative and quantitative instruments such as the survey, the interview, the field diary, and the documentary analysis, in which it is intended to provide a space aimed at SMEs in Bosa and Kennedy where La Regional Vice-Rectory Bogotá Sur and to be able to express not only what their needs are, but also to be able to make an evaluation on the performance of the students that are linked to these practice centers. In that sense, for [17, 18] this kind of research allows exploring, describing and/or explaining a particular reality based on initial data and reaching the discovery of new meanings; It has particular characteristics such as a. the case itself is the object of study; b. the important thing is the unit of analysis and not the subject; c. its intrinsic delimitation and d. do not claim for a particular data analysis collection. All this in order to contribute to its development and the change of political and social structures.

In what corresponds to the subject of the methods, it can be foreseen by the formulation of the objectives that there is a combined use of quantitative and qualitative methods, which makes use of the strengths of both types of methods, so that it serves, in the best understanding of the phenomenon. In this regard [19] they point out that although most researchers accept the need to use qualitative and quantitative methods of complementary forms, here it is insisted that there is a true triangulation between both. The qualitative should guide the quantitative, and the quantitative feedback from the qualitative in a circular process, but at the same time it advances, with each method contributing in the way that only he can.

For the study it was proposed to conduct a survey in digital format as one of the instruments to carry out the collection of information, in which students, owners, administrators and people related to SMEs were consulted, where it was collected Survey information as part of the process of characterization of the population under study and 10 questions that seek to assess the levels of satisfaction, relevance, and appreciation of the performance and management of ICT resources in companies. It also highlights the use of field diary to record the opinions of businessmen and teachers in meetings and interviews within the focus groups convened for this study as well as the use of a matrix of documentary analysis for the theoretical construct. The validity of the instruments depended on the piloting done with 5 students, teachers and businessmen as well as the validation by experts in the subject.

The target population of the study: students of the Virtual and Distance UVD programs of the Corporación Universitaria Minuto de Dios Vicerrectoría Bogotá Sur who enrolled in the first semester of 2019 the subject of Professional Practice (1041 students, which corresponds to 100% of the potential students). 437 was the sample or number of students who answered the survey. In the case of teachers, the sample was 12 of the 35 qualified to interview. In the case of companies, taking into account that there are 500 companies linked to the practice centers in the aforementioned locations through the different practice agreements, the sample was 252.

To carry out this exercise, it was necessary to determine the sample on which the survey should be applied, which is set out below. It should be noted that in order to establish the sample size, basic characteristics of the population studied should be taken into account, as well as establishing an acceptable maximum error and an estimated confidence level. In the case of error, the most commonly used levels are between 1% and 5% [20]; However, to the extent that the error is smaller, the size of the sample increases considerably, therefore, and taking into account that obtaining data is not an easy task, we choose to estimate an error of 5%. On the other hand, the probability of occurrence of the phenomenon is estimated based on what several similar samples in social sciences have established: a total certainty of 100% in which p + q equals 1; being p, means the occurrence of the event and q the non-occurrence [20].

The development of the project was implemented in three phases:

Phase 1: Documentary analysis to establish a bibliographic analysis matrix for the theoretical framework and state of the art of research
Phase 2: Fieldwork to assess ICT competence in professional internship students
Phase 3: Management of organizational development, for business evaluation and formulation of a proposal for improvement and training in ICT.

## 4   Results

The professional practice records of students of the Vice-Rectorate Bogotá South of UNIMINUTO were analyzed; according to these, between 2015 and 2018 the professional practice process was carried out by a total of 9465 students, which were linked to a total of 4007 practice centers or companies, as shown in Table 1.

**Table 1.** Total students who took professional practice and practice centers to which they were linked between 2015 and 2018

| Year | Number of students who did professional practice | Number of practice centers |
|---|---|---|
| 2018 | 3516 | 1349 |
| 2017 | 2999 | 1215 |
| 2016 | 2440 | 1189 |
| 2015 | 510 | 254 |
| Total | 9465 | 4007 |

Source: Own elaboration from data collected from the research

When dividing these students by units or academic areas, we find that the modalities in which these students have been linked are learning contract, special agreement (consists of the process of business strengthening), entrepreneurship proposal (Business or social) through a business plan, remunerated agreement in a foundation of a social order or educational institution (Monitoring), research (being a member of a seedbed group, monitoring research or accompanying a research project of a teacher), employment linkage as part of the process of practice and finally those who do not attend because their experience or work allows them to prove to be competent or sufficient in the exercise of profession (Homologation). According to the data reported in Table 2, he observes a marked tendency of the students to study their professional practice through a special agreement of business strengthening and employment linkage; they are followed by the learning and research contract, which has been having a significant upturn in the programs.

**Table 2.** Discrimination of students who studied professional practice between 2015 and 2018 by modality

| Year | Learning agreement special | Agreement (business strengthening) | Remunerated agreement (monitoring) | Entrepreneurship (business or social) | Research (seedling) | Validation of experience (homologated) | Labor linkage |
|---|---|---|---|---|---|---|---|
| 2018 | 194 | 1171 | 620 | 238 | 293 | 120 | 831 |
| 2017 | 223 | 1485 | 54 | 179 | 148 | 200 | 669 |
| 2016 | 272 | 641 | 83 | 178 | 131 | 174 | 949 |
| 2015 | 219 | 65 | 26 | 58 | 58 | 19 | 57 |

Source: Own elaboration from data collected from the research

For the purposes of this investigation, only the companies where the students were linked in the modalities of Learning Contract, Special Agreement (Business Strengthening), Remunerated Agreement (Monitoring) and Labor Linking that make up a total population of 7559 students were taken into account, of which 42% of these carried out their practice in the localities under study, considering a total of 3176 students linked to 500 practice centers, where students normally rotate period by period.

When asking the entrepreneurs about the competence of the student in the management of ICT resources the great majority agrees that obviously this is competent in their management, agreeing that what is appreciated is that they demonstrate the skills, skills, knowledge and attitudes applied to the use of information and communication systems, including the equipment that implies, coinciding with what is expressed by [21], as shown in the results shown in Fig. 1; However, this knowledge is not always well used or put into practice when it is necessary for it to contribute to the achievement of goals within the organization or company, since for evaluators there are not in many of the cases clear indications or evidence that The student will help significantly achieve organizational goals as shown in Fig. 2.

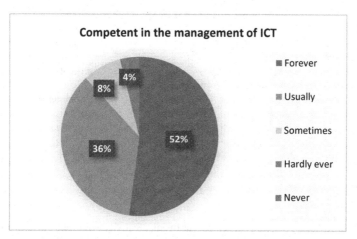

**Fig. 1.** The student demonstrates to be competent in the management of ICT courses such as email, social networks, computer resources and Blog?

The most relevant ICT skills for entrepreneurs are the management of specialized computer software such as simulators, modeling and diagramming software UML, ER and BPMN, management of financial and accounting software, social networks and business communication channels for merchandising.

In the same way, around the processes of innovation, as well as what happens around the contribution to institutional goals, from the formulation of innovative proposals through the use and application of creative processes, is evident in Fig. 3 that the majority of the student must act in a more participative way in the innovation processes applying knowledge in ICT; However, in large part this contribution will also depend on the fact that the practice centers are given an active role that enables confidence and the opportunity to contribute to it [22]. Learning in this environment, as evidenced in the

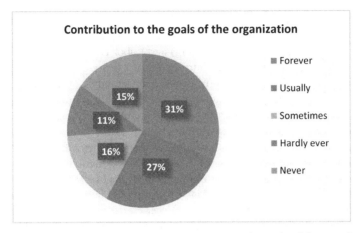

**Fig. 2.** With the help of the ICT resource contributes to the goals of the organization?

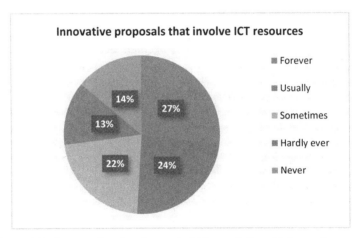

**Fig. 3.** The student shows a clear development of his creativity with innovative proposals that involve ICT resources

results presented in Fig. 4, however teachers and businessmen agree with stating that in many cases, students do not always know how to use them correctly when solving problems that demand their use or their response time to problems, they are not the ones desired to favor business performance, due in large part to the excessive use of simulators and practices in environments. And ideal conditions far from reality, but thanks to the self-learning supported by ICT, typical of this type d and students, also overcome their difficulties while sharing or contributing to their solution in learning communities such as social networks, forums, and student networks.

The perception of the entrepreneur is that even students need to be responsible for the management of ICTs, due in large part to the misuse of business environments and their high dependence on many mediation processes; however, it is recognized that students

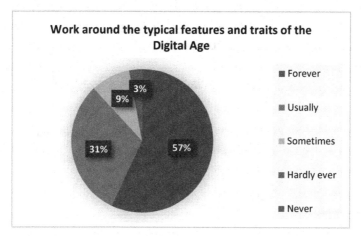

**Fig. 4.** Do you consider that students model their Work and learning around the typical features and traits of the Digital Age?

can improve in the processes of responsible promotion of technology use as digital citizens that are as shown in Fig. 5.

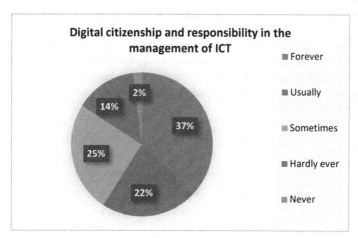

**Fig. 5.** Students in their own activities of the practice of professional practice promote and exemplify concepts of digital citizenship and responsibility in the management of ICT?

As a challenge for the students according to what is observed in Fig. 6, there is the commitment as future professionals to be leaders in the process of technological innovation mediated by ICT, in order to increase competitiveness and promote business growth [23]; however, as he states [24], since students of almost all educational levels use a part of this technology -especially social networks-, to encourage and increase their social life more than academic and professional life, they must also then overcome their own barriers that limit professional growth.

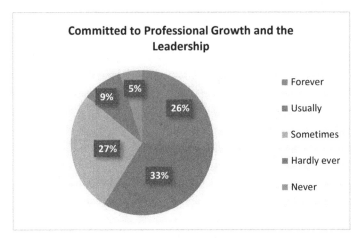

**Fig. 6.** The students are committed to Professional Growth and the Leadership of those who are immersed in ICT processes?

Regarding the assessment made by companies regarding the levels of satisfaction in relation to the participation of students in the development of ICT implementation within companies, professional competence, their level of receptivity to training in the process and their relationship of future potential to replicate what was learned based on business needs, the evaluation was quite positive, for this purpose a quantitative evaluation criterion was established between 1 and 5, 1 is the minimum value and 5 the maximum, the general average of the evaluation was 4.62 (Fig. 7), which indicates that although companies recognize the high potential that students have around the topic of ICT in their future growth, students must at the same time continue preparing in the same pace as these are growing.

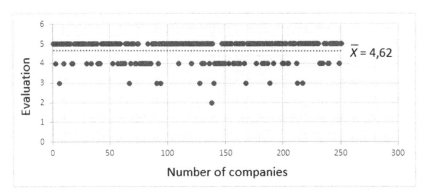

**Fig. 7.** Final evaluation of companies on the satisfaction of student participation in the ICT process

# 5  Discussion

Part of the debate is the responsibility of training in the proper management of ICT tools so that future professionals can exercise their profession, being competent in them and contributing significantly to business development, this because most university curricula do not it includes in-depth training in tools such as specific applications that students find in professional practice due to their commercial component, so they focus more on their general theoretical component of design or application.

The debate also focuses on establishing whether the practice centers help the student to become familiar with the future professional practice environment, helping him through his association with companies to manage resources in the hands of training environments for the application of knowledge that lead to solution of problems especially those related to the application of ICT or if on the other hand they only seek to solve the problem of having skilled labor in digital skills at a very low cost.

The question is raised as to why the contribution of students to the improvement of standards around ICT in professional practices is so low, since these are the first source of information about what can be improved in future processes students, people and organizations that wish to start improving advisory activities and provide information and guidance to entrepreneurs about new information technologies.

Starting from the premise that professional practices favor interaction between university, student, community, teaching, company, then spaces must be provided so that in consensus it contributes to the improvement of educational quality in the university, so that in the future the student may by developing their creativity and with innovative proposals that involve ICT resources can really contribute to business strengthening.

Every practice must be subject to an evaluation process as part of the continuous improvement processes, so it is necessary that both the student and the practice center carry out this process with the accompaniment of the institution, however, at the time to perform the evaluation of the competences of students in ICT, it is not yet known what is the best mechanism to do it nor have clear guidelines established by the Ministry of Information Technology and Colombian Communication regarding what are the main competences that must be evaluated, so that each institution is free to suggest the ones it considers most important to do so and are not necessarily the most consistent with the process.

# 6  Conclusions

The professional practice centers are a support strategy for the student. It consolidates the knowledge of the students in different fields such as companies, organizations or institutions. In the other hand, it allows a real contact with starting with real contact, exploring areas and processes and then raise and implement a process of continuous improvement of the work of the profession, however, is expected that the student with the help of the ICT resource contributes significantly to achieve the achievement of the goals of the organization.

Meanwhile, the scenario of professional practice must become the intersection curricular between the institution and the labor context, which allows the strengthening of skills and technological skills of future professionals, it is clear, the world is advancing by leaps and bounds and it is necessary that institutions, organizations, and companies are at the forefront of the technological challenges they face today and what better opportunity, the union between academia and the productive sector. The use of simulators, modeling software and participation in the design of applications contributes to achieving that goal. The aforementioned suggests that there are many opportunities to make research referred to the relation between ICT and professional practice because it involves two relevant aspect of the teaching: ICT and educational praxis.

Although professional practice is mandatory for any student pursuing a professional career in Colombia and in many countries, the mechanisms of choice of this and the options that students have for the development of these will depend exclusively on each of the institutions of higher education; in addition, each one is totally free to validate or evaluate the cases in which it is considered that this is homologated or not, just as the ICT competences of the students must be evaluated inside the practice centers.

The contribution made by students of professional practice in the fields of business consulting seeks to help companies with less income to improve the quality of their services or products, in order to increase their competitiveness in the market and be self-sustainable, it is clear that Students model their work and learning around processes and features characteristic of the Digital Age.

The ICT can be a great support in the professional practice; the ICTs provide different tools to develop the processes according to the world need.

The business practice centers seek the accompaniment and integral guidance through the provision of services that allow the continuous improvement of the companies and the living conditions of their owners and employees, taking into account the conditions and social environment in which they are located. The company, however, should also encourage spaces in which students can make significant contributions to the growth of these through the use of new technologies that place the Digital Age at the service, as members of the knowledge society that has grown Familiar with the subject.

## References

1. UNESCO: Education 2030: Incheon Declaration and Framework for Action: towards inclusive and equitable quality education and lifelong learning for all (2016)
2. Ventura, J.R.O., Amargó, V.E.S., Chinea, B.A.F., Obregón, J.M.R.: Las prácticas profesionales y la formación laboral en la carrera sistema de información en salud. Actualidades Investigativas en Educación **15**(3) (2015)
3. Díaz Barriga, F., Hernández, G., Rigo, M.A., Saad, E., Delgado, G.: Retos actuales en la formación y práctica profesional del psicólogo educativo. Revista de la educación superior **35**(137), 11–24 (2006). http://www.scielo.org.mx/scielo.php?pid=S0185-27602006000100011&script=sci_arttext
4. González Maura, V.: La formación de competencias profesionales en la universidad: reflexiones y experiencias desde una perspectiva educativa (2006). http://hdl.handle.net/10272/2010
5. Vargas, J.: Las reglas cambiantes de la competitividad global en el nuevo milenio. Las competencias en el nuevo paradigma de la globalización. Revista Iberoamericana de Educación. OEI (2001). https://www.riico.net/index.php/riico/article/view/1050

6. Albarracín, E.J.G., Erazo, S.C.R., Palacios, F.C.: Influencia de las tecnologías de la información y comunicación en el rendimiento de las micro, pequeñas y medianas empresas colombianas. Estudios Gerenciales **30**(133), 355–364 (2014). https://doi.org/10.1016/j.estger.2014.06.006
7. Shin, N.: Information technology and diversification: how their relationship affects firm performance. In: Strategic Information Systems: Concepts, Methodologies, Tools, and Applications, pp. 2460–2474. IGI Global (2010)
8. Plunkett, P.T.: Performance based management: eight steps to develop and use information technology performance measures effectively (2000). www.gsa.gov/gsa/cmattachments/GSADOCUMENT/eightstepsR2GX2-u0Z5RDZ-i34K-pR.doc
9. Ruiz, C.A.O.: Inclusión de las TIC en la empresa colombiana. Suma de negocios **5**(10), 29–33 (2014). https://doi.org/10.1016/S2215-910X(14)70006-0
10. Rueda, A.: Las prácticas profesionales y las pasantías desde la legislación comparada. Revista latinoamericana de derecho social (19), 111–132 (2014). http://www.scielo.org.mx/scielo.php?script=sci_arttext&pid=S1870-46702014000200111&lng=es&tlng
11. Tejada Fernández, J.: La alternancia de contextos para la adquisición de competencias profesionales en escenarios complementarios de educación superior: marco y estrategia. Educación XX1 **15**(2), 33–35 (2012). https://doi.org/10.5944/educxx1.15.2.125
12. Pacheco, A., Pupo, J.M.: Instructivo para la realización de prácticas pre-profesionales y pasantías en universidades del Ecuador. Revista Atlante: Cuadernos de Educación y Desarrollo (2016). http://www.eumed.net/rev/atlante/2016/07/pasantias.html
13. Torre Chalbaud, F.: Modelo de gestión para tutorías de pasantías industriales mediante tic. Revista de la Facultad de Ingeniería Universidad Central de Venezuela **27**(4), 25–32 (2012). http://ve.scielo.org/scielo.php?script=sci_arttext&pid=S0798-40652012000400004&lng=es&tlng=es
14. Estévez-Arias, T., Medina-Chicaiza, R., González-Hernández, W.: El desarrollo de la motivación profesional en la formación de los estudiantes de periodismo con el uso de las TIC. Revista iberoamericana de educación superior **7**(20), 191–201 (2016). http://www.scielo.org.mx/scielo.php?script=sci_arttext&pid=S2007-28722016000300191&lng=es&tlng=
15. Jaramillo Escobar, B.H.: Tesis: Evaluación del sistema de pasantías pre profesionales de los estudiantes de Cuarto Año de Economía para optimizar sus Competencias laborales y Propuesta de Reingeniería (2013). http://repositorio.ug.edu.ec/handle/redug/3113
16. Vilar, J.: Deontología y práctica profesional límites y posibilidades de los códigos deontológicos (2000). https://www.raco.cat/index.php/ArsBrevis/article/view/93659
17. Alzina, R.B.: Metodología de la investigación educativa, vol. 1. Editorial La Muralla (2004)
18. Jaramillo, I.D.T., Ramírez, R.D.P.: Fundamentos epistemológicos de la investigación y la metodología de la investigación: cualitativa. Fondo Editorial Universidad EAFIT (2010)
19. Briones, G.: Metodología de la investigación cuantitativa en las ciencias sociales. Bogotá: Instituto Colombiano para el Fomento de la Educación Superior – ICFES (2012)
20. Arras Vota, A.M.D.G., Torres Gastelú, C.A., García-Valcárcel Muñoz-Repiso, A.: Completencias en Tecnologías de Información y Comunicación (TIC) de los estudiantes universitarios. Revista latina de comunicación social (66) (2011). https://doi.org/10.4185/rlcs-66-2011-927-130-152. http://www.redalyc.org/articulo.oa?id=81921340018
21. Pedró, F.: The new millennium learners: Challenging our views on ICT and learning. Inter-American Development Bank (2006)
22. Peña Lapeira, C.J., Pereira Bolaños, C.A.: ICT and business inclusion in the Southern communities of the city of Bogotá – Colombia. In: Botto-Tobar, M., Barba-Maggi, L., González-Huerta, J., Villacrés-Cevallos, P., S. Gómez, O., Uvidia-Fassler, M.I. (eds.) TICEC 2018. AISC, vol. 884, pp. 253–265. Springer, Cham (2019). https://doi.org/10.1007/978-3-030-02828-2_19

23. Castro Tesén, R.: Manejo de tecnología e información científica en la formación universitaria. Inclusión & Desarrollo **5**(2), 63–82 (2018). https://doi.org/10.26620/uniminuto.inclusion.5. 2.2018.63-82
24. Araya, S.A.: Las redes sociales como instrumento de mediación pedagógica: alcances y limitaciones/Social networks as a tool for teaching mediation: scope and limitations. Actualidades investigativas en educación **13**(2) (2013). https://www.scielo.sa.cr/pdf/aie/v13n2/a13v13n2

# Q'inqu: Inclusive Board Game
# for the Integration of People with Disabilities

Janio Jadán-Guerrero[⊠], Hugo Arias-Flores[⊠], and Ileana Altamirano[⊠]

Centro de Investigación en Mecatrónica y Sistemas Interactivos, Universidad Tecnológica Indoamérica, Quito, Ecuador
{janiojadan,hugoarias}@uti.edu.ec, ile28.nov@gmail.com

**Abstract.** The educational inclusion of people with disabilities continues to be a great challenge for society. Due to the field's diversity and complexity, people with disabilities have few opportunities to be integrated into educational activities or even entertainment. This article describes a novel educational resource developed within the field of applied technologies. Q'inqu is an inclusive board game that encourages the family and educational inclusion of people with disabilities. Q'inqu is a Quechua word meaning "Labyrinth". This is a metaphor for the challenges faced by families living with a person with disabilities, and it also reflects its narrative structure based on the "Legend of the Incas' treasure". Q'inqu has the general theme of a traditional board game where turns are taken until the treasure is found. What makes it different is the integration of inclusive elements through the use of technology. There are cards with a braille code, a rectangular board with high relief, and a circular board with textures. An App reads QR codes and also patterns, which present additional information based on augmented reality. These features provide support to blind players and to those who are unable to read, making the game both entertaining and educational. Q'inqu was developed and tested by a multidisciplinary team of 80 people, which included students and professionals from design, education and pedagogy. The most relevant result was that out of 367 ideas that were presented, it was awarded first prize in the category Toys for children with disabilities in the CMA contest held in Ecuador.

**Keywords:** Q'inqu · Board game · Educational innovation · Disability · Family inclusion · Educational inclusion

## 1 Introduction

10% of the world's population, or about 700 million people, live with a disability. In Latin America and the Caribbean there are around 85 million people with these conditions, while in Ecuador about 1,800,000 people fall within this vulnerable group [1, 2].

The inclusion of people with disabilities in everyday activities requires practices and policies that are designed to identify and remove the barriers that hamper the individual's ability to participate fully in society. In Ecuador, the Organic Law on Disability [3] and the National Plan for Good Living 2013–2017 [4] cover issues of inclusion affecting several areas: education, health, housing, and decent work, among others [5]. In the educational

© Springer Nature Switzerland AG 2020
M. Botto-Tobar et al. (Eds.): ICAT 2019, CCIS 1193, pp. 85–94, 2020.
https://doi.org/10.1007/978-3-030-42517-3_7

area where our research is focused, Ecuador promotes inclusive education. The current Ecuador Constitution, Article 347, says that the State is responsible for "strengthening and [providing] the guarantee of the active participation of all the students, without any exclusion". However, although these laws exist to ensure the benefits of an inclusive education, this is yet to become the reality in education in Ecuador. The traditional educational model is still a "utopia" and is far behind in terms of diversity [6]. Against this, the Indoamérica University has made great efforts in the field of inclusive education, for example by developing learning and teaching technologies for people with disabilities [7] and a MOOC platform for disability awareness [8].

Building on work done in previous years, this article introduces a novel educational resource for the field of inclusive education: Q'inqu is an inclusive board game whose goal is to allow people with disabilities to play with other family members through its inclusive elements.

The rest of the paper is organized as follows. The second section describes the method applied in the study and the material used to build a prototype of Q'inqu. Section 3 explains and illustrates the proposed prototype, while Sect. 4 presents the results and impact. Section 5 discusses the evaluation of the prototype in a real situation, and finally, Sect. 6 presents the conclusions and makes suggestions for future work.

## 2   Materials and Method

The educational strategies were designed by 60 students doing their master's degrees in Education, Innovation and Leadership, divided into two groups of 30 students. The Design Thinking methodology was used, which is defined as an analytical and creative process that involves a person in opportunities to generate innovative ideas and that takes the perspective of the users as the center around which to experiment, model and create prototypes, to collect comments and to redesign [9].

The Design Thinking methodology has five phases: Empathize, Define, Ideate, Prototype, and Testing. To carry out each of these phases, a gamified virtual classroom was created on the Moodle platform using the metaphor of the legend of the hidden treasure in the Inca empire [10]. In the empathy phase, an activity called "The Camp" was created where participants were organized into groups of five. These groups were based on the tribes of the Inca Empire such as the Quitus, Paltas, Puruhaes, Panzaleos, Cañaris, and Shyris. The goal was to spend time getting to know the history of the Incas with a view to designing a relevant board game. Figure 1 shows the design of the metaphorical virtual classroom in Spanish.

In the Define phase, the activity "The Labyrinth" was created to raise the problem while bearing in mind the needs of the target population. In the Ideate phase, through the activity "The Compass", the explorers had to innovate concerning the strategies of the game. In the Prototyping phase, with the activity "The traveling cloud", the explorers put into practice the didactic strategies. Finally in the test phase, with the activity "The Inca Trail", all the groups evaluated the game, measured the time, and discussed the rules created by each group. These activities were carried out over five weeks, during which time, comments and collaborative work were recorded in forums. Once they had completed their five sessions, each group shared their findings and contributions. The general evaluation process ended with a survey of 20 closed and one open question.

## EL TESORO DEL ÚLTIMO EMPERADOR INCA

Cuenta la Leyenda que una cámara del tesoro repleta de oro y la momia del último emperador Inca esperan a quien sea capaz de localizar el lugar de descanso eterno de Atahualpa. Pero nadie hasta ahora ha sido capaz de descubrir la oculta ubicación del malhadado emperador y su inmenso rescate. Ahora ustedes van a formar varias expediciones para ir en busca del tesoro

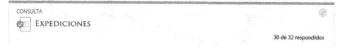

CONSULTA

EXPEDICIONES

30 de 32 respondidos

**Fig. 1.** Gamified metaphorical virtual classroom created on Moodle platform

## 3  Inclusive Q'inqu Board Game Description

Q'inqu is a Quechua word that means labyrinth and it is the name of a proposal that will integrate people with disabilities into home entertainment activities and into educational activities in educational institutions. The game is built around a traditional board game with a cultural theme from Ecuador, "The Legend of the Incas' Treasure", and it aims to generate interaction, entertainment, and learning.

The goal of the inclusive board game is to allow people with disabilities to play with other family members through technology-supported activities. The board game has traditional elements, but it is also integrated with a tablet or smartphone so that the audiovisual content of the game can be viewed through reading quick response (QR) codes. For example, when a card containing braille codes is viewed through a tablet, its meaning can be portrayed through both audio and video. Other cards have augmented reality patterns that provide additional information about the game's theme, and information that contributes to both entertainment and learning. Figures 2 and 3 show the inclusive board game, which has two boards: one of them is rectangular and is called "The Inca Trail" and the other is circular and is called "The Labyrinth". These two boards both have inclusive elements, such as high-relief routes and textured fields, that help people with visual disabilities to play and become integrated. The high relief board is oriented for players under 12 years old, while the round board is for players over 12 years old.

Like other board games, Q'inqu has challenges that are communicated by the color of the fields, each color meaning that you must take a card. The cards with a blue circle tell the legend in text format or through audio via QR codes. The green triangle cards

**Fig. 2.** Q'inqu inclusive board game, integrating braille code, QR codes and augmented reality (Color figure online)

**Fig. 3.** Q'inqu inclusive board game with the circular board (Color figure online)

introduce an amusing activity through augmented reality, for example, it may ask the player to imitate some animal shown in 3D. The cards with a red square transport you to a tunnel, and this is what makes the game entertaining. The yellow rhombus cards have history questions, which introduce a learning component.

### 3.1 Educational Metaphor

The educational element of the game involves the "Legend of the Incas' Treasure", which aims to present ancestral knowledge of Ecuador's history in a fun and inclusive way. The main goal of the game is to reach the treasure, which is in the center of the board. Each player starts with 10 corn kernels, which they can lose or win with their cards. An example of the content of the cards is shown in Fig. 4. A feature of these cards is that each has a braille code with a letter for the color.

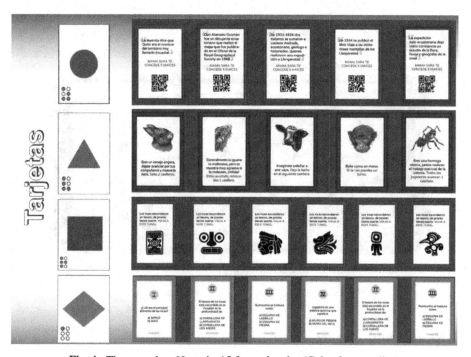

**Fig. 4.** The game has 60 cards, 15 for each color (Color figure online)

There are 4 gold coins, which are wildcards and can be used if a player lands on a black field. The black field means that the Inca is imprisoned, and in order to get his freedom back he can pay with one of these coins. These coins can be won if the player lands on a special field or they may be placed in the treasure field to make the game longer, as the game will not be finished until the first player reaches the goal. An interesting feature of the game is that different rules can be used, for example, the first one to reach the goal may win the game, or it may be the one with the most corn kernels who wins.

### 3.2  Innovative Nature of the Implemented Technology Solution

Several aspects of disabilities need to be considered when discussing accessibility and inclusion. This study presents an experience of educational innovation supported by augmented reality. Through the use of QR codes and braille writing on the cards, it allows people with visual, intellectual and language disabilities to be integrated into family recreational activities. Figure 5 presents an example of augmented reality as presented by the game. This is an innovative feature used in the design of hybrid interfaces.

**Fig. 5.** Green cards contain patterns that activate augmented reality elements (Color figure online)

## 4  Results and Impact

Through this project, the students from the Education, Innovation and Leadership master's degree course experienced the process involved in a research project. The topic was developed from a real problem and an empirical process was developed in an accessible and playful way. The students designed and built a state-of-the-art board game, having discovered that nothing similar existed in Ecuador and seeing this as an opportunity to contribute to a latent need.

By utilizing the Design Thinking and Game Thinking methodologies [9], the students were able to have an experience of educational innovation in the classroom. The objective was to introduce the use of disruptive technologies into the classroom through playful strategies and to design didactic applications for them. These methodologies allow innovative results to be generated, not only through their application but also through data generation that can be analyzed and processed. A user experience survey was completed by 60 students and the most relevant results are shown in Fig. 6. These results differentiate between the qualitative and the quantitative content, and show how the latter ratifies and complements the subjectivity that the former may display.

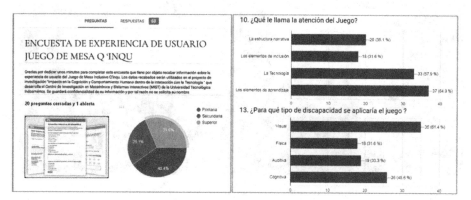

**Fig. 6.** User experience survey results

In order to evaluate this technological proposal more widely, in January 2019, the idea was registered with the Citi Microentrepreneurs of the Year (CMA) Toys' Contest, which is sponsored by several institutions in Ecuador, including the Citi Foundation, Conquito, Junior Achievement, Corporacion Favorita, Jugueton, Fybeca, TVentas, UDLA, Uniplex, and Sheraton [11]. Three hundred and eighty-seven proposals were received from all over the country and divided into three categories: Educational toys, Technological toys, Toys for the elderly or for people with disabilities. The contest was held in five stages over five months. The first was the selection of the idea, the second the generation of a proof of concept, the third the presentation of a prototype, the fourth was an evaluation, or "Testing Lab", and the fifth was called the "Shark Tank".

After a complex and competitive process, the final round was reached. Of 40 proposals selected for the evaluation stage, the best 13 were selected, and from these the three finalists were chosen. The inclusive board game Q'inqu was the finalist for the category Toys for older adults or people with disability. In the course of this process, several positive factors were highlighted regarding the creation of this technological solution. Figure 7 shows the Testing Lab and the grand final in the Shark Tank.

The Q'inqu board game achieved a remarkable position in the Ecuadorian contest, and the designers have been invited to participate in radio interviews due to the interest the project has raised. The public is expressing significant interest in acquiring the game, and this has prompted the creation of a spin-off from the University called Kiteracy Labs, which aims to commercialize the various technologies.

According to the marketing plan developed with the Canvas technique, a retail price of 45 USD should be obtainable. In order to recover the initial investment, 232 games will need to be sold.

**Fig. 7.** Evaluation round, Shark Tank and awards

## 5   Discussion

Accessibility and inclusion in board gaming is a topic little explored by academics or in the professional literature. It is also a very complex issue that is hard to discuss adequately because it covers game design, individual and group behavior under many different circumstances, and testing [12, 13]. Thinking of accessibility parameters for the players, such as a board that highlights the way forward, the use of textures to differentiate the fields, augmented reality technology, and cards with either a QR code or a braille code are all relevant contributions in this area.

Establishing differences in the board's level of complexity allowed us to consider the players' potential skills. For example, extra time is allowed for the accessibility media throughout the game.

A particular characteristic of the game is that it is pleasant and cooperative rather than competitive. The rules are not complex, which helps the less able participants. The use of technology to enable family and social inclusion in the recreational space was a success. This was evidenced in the survey carried out with the 60 master's students. These user tests would have provided better results if the game had been performed with disabled players, however, it was necessary to gather the players at a specific time and place, and including disabled players would have required a greater investment of time [12]. Figure 8 shows some fun scenes with the game.

Accessibility was not based on memory, although the participants had to answer questions posed by the game. The required cognitive input could be supplemented by support from the other participants.

There was no focus on a winner or loser. Games can trigger emotional discomfort in the participants. It was not even considered a priority for each player to move their own game piece; on the contrary, it was possible for any other player to help move it. It was

**Fig. 8.** Evaluation phase with master's students

designed as a game that integrates the players, that focuses on cooperation, and benefits from difference. Since the genre of the game is developed in a story, it allows groups of players to follow the same plot in the game [13].

## 6    Conclusion and Future Work

Board games are an easy way for family and groups of friends to enjoy a shared fun experience, providing a significant opportunity for creating social capital among friends and family. The board game offers opportunities for friends and family to enjoy each other's company, while the game offers a way to express emotions and awaken interaction.

The design of this game was considered pleasant and easy to play [13] for players both with and without disabilities, although the evaluation of accessibility in a board game is more complicated [12]. Tests were conducted in a real scenario with children to analyze their behavior and their acceptance of a girl with a disability. These results were encouraging, as the environment was one of entertainment.

Future work will involve the evaluation of the game in educational institutions through projects related to the wider society. For this, at least 30 games will be donated, and the educational intervention will be carried out with the participation of Psychology and Initial Education students. Through this rewarding experience, we want to reach as many homes as possible, we don't only want to sell the game, but we want to sell educational and family inclusion. In the future, we plan to propose a linkage project that will facilitate Q'inqu access for educational institutions in rural and vulnerable areas. All these initiatives leave us with gratifying experiences and an increased challenge to contribute to special education for children with disabilities.

**Thanks.** This work was financed by the research project "Impact on Cognition and Human Behavior within the Interaction with Technology (ICCHIT)". This is part of the "Interactive Multimodal Educational Technology (TIME)" program of the Center for Research in Mechatronics and Interactive Systems (MIST) of the Indoamérica University. The authors want to express their gratitude to the Graphic Design students and the students doing their master's degrees in Education, Innovation and Leadership for their participation in the project, as well as to Carolina and Hugo for always being a source of inspiration in generating new ideas to help people with disability.

# References

1. El Telégrafo. Personas con discapacidad cuentan con más derechos, Diario El Telégrafo (2017). https://www.eltelegrafo.com.ec/noticias/sociedad/6/plan-estatal-atiende-a-grupo-con-discapacidad. Accessed 12 Apr 2019
2. Conadis. Registro Nacional de Discapacidades. Registro Nacional de Discapacidades, recuperado de (2014). http://www.consejodiscapacidades.gob.ec/wp-content/uploads/downloads/2014/03/conadis_registro_nacional_discapacidades.pdf. Accessed 10 Apr 2019
3. Asamblea Constituyente de Ecuador: Constitución del Ecuador. Montecristi, Ecuador: Publicación Oficial de la Asamblea Constituyente (2008)
4. Senplades_Secretaría_Nacional_de_Planificación_y_Desarrollo_del_Ecuador:        Plan Nacional del Buen Vivir 2013–2017. Quito, Ecuador: Senplades (2014). http://www.buenvivir.gob.ec/
5. Romero, S., Bowen, K.K.: A challenge for teachers of inclusive higher education: faculty of humanistic and social sciences in UTM. Int. Res. J. Manag. IT Soc. Sci. 5(2), 129–135 (2018)
6. Bodero, L.: Carencia de metodología pedagógica en la educación inclusiva del ecuador. Espirales revista multidisciplinaria de investigación 2, 112–135 (2018)
7. Jadán-Guerrero, J., Altamirano, I., Arias, H., Jadán, J.: Designing assistive technologies for children with disabilities: a case study of a family living with a daughter with intellectual disability. In: Valencia-García, R., Lagos-Ortiz, K., Alcaraz-Mármol, G., del Cioppo, J., Vera-Lucio, N. (eds.) CITI 2016. CCIS, vol. 658, pp. 254–268. Springer, Cham (2016). https://doi.org/10.1007/978-3-319-48024-4_20
8. Lara-Alvarez, P., Jadán-Guerrero, J.J.: Plataforma virtual de sensibilización en discapacidades para instituciones públicas y privadas del Ecuador, Actas Encuentro Latinoamericano de e-Ciencia 2017, San José, Costa Rica (2017)
9. Arias-Flores, H., Jadán-Guerrero, J., Gómez-Luna, L.: Innovación Educativa en el aula mediante Design Thinking y Game Thinking. Hamut´ay 6(1), 82–95 (2019). http://dx.doi.org/10.21503/hamu.v6i1.1576
10. Jadán-Guerrero, J., Ramos-Galarza, C.: Metodología de Aprendizaje Basada en Metáforas Narrativas y Gamificación: Un caso de estudio en un Programa de Posgrado Semipresencial. Hamut´ay 5(1), 84–104 (2018). http://dx.doi.org/10.21503/hamu.v5i1.1560
11. CMA: Citi Microemprendedor del año (2019). https://www.concursocma.com
12. Heron, M.J., Belford, P.H., Reid, H., et al.: Meeple centred design: a heuristic toolkit for evaluating the accessibility of tabletop games. Comput. Games J. 7(2), 97–114 (2018). https://doi.org/10.1007/s40869-018-0057-8
13. Wilhelmsson, U., Engström, H., Brusk, J., et al.: Inclusive game design facilitating shared gaming experience. J. Comput. High. Educ. 29(3), 574–598 (2017). https://doi.org/10.1007/s12528-017-9146-0

# Integration of IoT Equipment as Transactional Endorsing Peers over a Hyperledger-Fabric Blockchain Network: Feasibility Study

Guillermo Andrade-Salinas[(✉)], Gustavo Salazar-Chacon[(✉)],
and Luz-Marina Vintimilla

Escuela Politécnica Nacional, Quito, Ecuador
{guillermo.andrade,gustavo.salazar,marina.vintimilla}@epn.edu.ec

**Abstract.** Internet of Things (IoT) experiences exponential growth in research and industry fields; the usefulness provided by IoT extends from critical applications such as intelligent transport systems and e-health to business-related applications such as banking and logistics. At the same time, faces privacy and security vulnerabilities becoming target of cyber-attacks, being necessary to mitigate them. Conventional security and privacy approaches tend not to be applicable for IoT, due to its decentralized topology and limited resources on its devices. Blockchain appears as a possible solution to the intrinsic security deficiency in IoT environments, since it has demonstrated its applicability in security and privacy fields over end-to-end networks with similar topologies as the ones used in IoT, thanks to its Defense-in-Depth approach is ideal for critical environments.

Blockchain is based on a ledger with capability to preserve an immutable record of all chronological ordered transactions processed in network, subsequently shared with members of the network. However, this technology requires high computational performance and high bandwidth, generating delays that are not found in most IoT applications.

This document examines the feasibility of implementing Blockchain considering IoT devices as endorsing peers and not only as users that invoke transactions. The results of proof of concept, bandwidth and performance measurements in several transactional tests are presented, applying the "Design Science Research" methodology. As a result, a high-level model for the implementation of IoT networks with Blockchain is proposed.

**Keywords:** Blockchain · Hyperledger Fabric · Internet of Things · IoT security · Raspberry Pi · Blockchain applications

## 1 Introduction

Internet of Things (IoT) implementations are growing rapidly due to large production of smart devices and high-speed networks. According to Juniper

© Springer Nature Switzerland AG 2020
M. Botto-Tobar et al. (Eds.): ICAT 2019, CCIS 1193, pp. 95–109, 2020.
https://doi.org/10.1007/978-3-030-42517-3_8

Research [9] and The Statistics Portal [18], around the world the are approximately 27 billion connected devices and more than 50 billion devices will be available by 2025.

Due to great acceptance of IoT, they have been the target of cyber-attacks. Due to limited computational performance, short storage capacity, and decentralized architecture, there are security issues difficult to resolve. Khan and Salah [12] list several security issues in OSI layers for IoT devices, but include Blockchain technology as a solution.

Blockchain is growing rapidly since its introduction in Bitcoin by Satoshi Nakamoto [15]. In IoT security researches conducted by Dorri [4,5], Minoli [13], Reyna [16] and Singh [17], several ways to improve security including Blockchain technology alongside communication protocols are introduced.

Although Blockchain's features are promising, some limitations on IoT devices don't allow full integration. Processor performance, ROM and RAM memory amount, and bandwidth are main limitations. Dorri [4], Minoli [13] and Reyna [16] have implemented Blockchain in IoT devices, coupling them as blockchain network users where IoT devices generate transactions that are sent to peer node to processes, approve and store in Ledger.

The actual research involves analyzing feasibility of integrate Blockchain in an IoT network communicating through MQTT protocol. Using a Raspberry Pi 2B+ as an endorsing peer node in blockchain network.

Article content is distributed as follows. Section 2 presents a review of the state of art, necessary to understand research carried out. Moreover, a description of used methodology. Section 3 describes the architecture and technical features of devices. Further, a mention of how blockchain was implemented. Section 4 presents results obtained in each test. Finally, conclusions and a model to implement Blockchain in Raspberry Pi devices are presented.

## 2 Context and Related Aspects

### 2.1 Internet of Things (IoT)

Fakhri and Mutijarsa [6] define IoT networks as a system of interrelated devices, i.e., the interconnection of several devices using embedded systems, sensors and artificial intelligence, providing environmental information and device status data through the Internet. IoT's main objective is to simplify daily life by providing a way of interaction between objects and objects with the human being. IoT devices are being used for implementations in smart homes, autonomous vehicles, remotely controlled equipment, among other applications that convert everyday objects into smart computers.

Singh [17] defines some security problems, one of them is cyber-attacks vulnerability. IoT devices must have affordable costs, that's why they violate several security policies that should be implemented to prevent invasive and non-invasive attacks such as Side-Channel Attack, Voltage Attacks, Temperature Attacks, being difficult having high security in IoT networks.

Chen [2] introduces three major problems into an IoT network:

- Central Server failures that can occur due to software defects or computer attacks.
- Single point of failure defining as a compromised device, which can cause system-wide failures.
- Lack of privacy of personal information stored on a central server that may be violated.

Some security in IoT networks is obtained by using several protocols in Application Layer on TCP/IP model (Layer 5, 6 and 7 on OSI model), including MQTT protocol [20]. MQTT is simple, fast and comes with a set of security features.

Security research on IoT networks conducted by Dorri [4,5], Minoli [13], and Reyna [16] presents several ways to improve security in similar networks using Blockchain with communication protocols.

## 2.2   Blockchain

Blockchain is a structured data replicated and distributed to all members of a network; it can be seen as a record where transactions (or information) are stored in blocks identified by their hash and bound to their predecessors by including its block hash in next block information. Singh [17] defines four basic pillars on which Blockchain is constituted. These ones represent great value in information security:

- **Consensus** verifies actions in networks,
- **Ledger** provides full details of transactions made on Blockchain networks,
- **Cryptography** ensures all data is encrypted, and only authorized users can decrypt it; finally,
- **Smart Contracts** use to verify and validate network members.

There are two basic types of Blockchain platforms [10]:

- **Private or Permissioned** platforms have control over network access. Only authorized applications or persons can participate in networks. Rules or agreements should be established between participants. Information is not public, is not accessible or consulted by anyone on networks. Some private platforms are Ripple Labs, Hyperledger, Tembusu, CryptoCorp or Tillit.
- **Public or Permissive** plataforms are those that anyone with a computer and network access can be joined. A configured computer based on blockchain criteria is necessary. Information is public in these platforms and can be consulted by external users. Anonymity is usually preserved. Some public platforms are Bitcoin, Ethereum, Augur, Tendermind or Litecoin.

Hyperledger Fabric project was implemented in this research, due to other platforms are cryptocurrency oriented and/or are not open source for implementation on external devices.

## 2.3  Hyperledger Fabric

Hyperledger Fabric [7] is an open-source Blockchain platform maintained by The Linux Foundation. Hyperledger was designed to support business transactions. A Blockchain network based on Hyperledger Fabric has a differentiation between nodes based on participation degree:

- **Client** is a node that submits a transaction-invocation. Represent the identity behind an end-user.
- **Peer** is a node that commits transactions and maintains the state and copy of Ledger. A peer node can have a special role, known as endorsing peer. An endorsing peer is responsible for approving transactions.
- **Orderer** is a node running communication service implementing a delivery guarantee. This node generates a communication channel between clients and peers, offering a message broadcast service that contains transactions.

Dorri [4], Minoli [13], Reyna [16] and Fakhri [6] have implemented Blockchain networks by coupling IoT devices as users of network, i.e. they only generated transactions and send them to a node to be endorsed.

## 2.4  Approach and Design Concept

Information systems research [1] (ISR) uses a variety of research methods to explore phenomena of interest; those methods have been developed by expert members in particular areas of Systems Information Community.

IS methodologies include Design Research or Design Science Research, which is suitable for the task of creating a new process model, known as an artifact. Vaishnavi [19] defines artifacts to algorithms, human/computer interfaces, and languages or system design methodologies.

This research aims to solve information security problems in IoT-MQTT environments using Blockchain. Further, propose a high-level model for the implementation of the Blockchain platform known as "Hyperledger Fabric" in IoT networks. "Design Science Research Methodology (DSRM)" [11] (see Fig. 1) was implemented in this research. Following DSRM, creation and subsequent evaluation of an IT artifact were carried out, maintaining its main objective, creation of an effective and useful artifact.

**Phase 1: "Problem Identification and Motivation".** This research focused on the following issue: "There is not a clear and simplified model for implementing information security with Blockchain in an IoT environment."

Based on Dorri's research [4,5], Blockchain was considered as a solution to information security problems in IoT networks, due to cryptography to secure information and Smart Contracts to identify network users, even with known limitations of IoT devices.

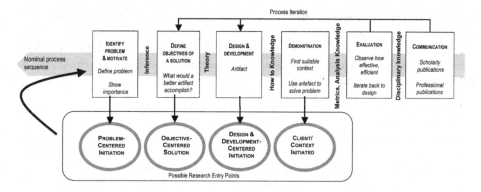

**Fig. 1.** Design Science Research Methodology (DSRM) [11].

**Phase 2: "Objectives of a Solution".** This research seeks to analyze the feasibility of implementing Blockchain as a method of information security and privacy in IoT-MQTT networks, which includes the following activities:

- Identify Blockchain's fundamental operation.
- Implement a basic IoT network prototype with Blockchain and MQTT.
- Test functionality of Blockchain in IoT-MQTT device by measuring and testing processor performance, traffic injectors and Blockchain performance.
- Propose a generic Blockchain implementation model for IoT networks.

**Phase 3: "Design and Development".** Researchers documentation from literary review and experts experience in related fields were a great helpful for designing of a generic Blockchain implementation model in IoT networks. Design and development stage was focused on the following substages:

- Identify Blockchain platforms applicable to IoT devices.
- Select and apply a Blockchain platform in an IoT network composed by a Raspberry Pi 2B+ and an Amazon Web Services (AWS) servers.

A shortlist of both private and public Blockchain platforms was detailed early. Hyperledger platform was selected to be used, due to two advantages related to objectives of this research:

- It is an open-source platform supported and developed by The Linux Foundation community.
- Multi-architecture, Hyperledger Fabric supports architectures such as amd64, s390x, ppc64le, and armv7.

Hyperledger aims to implement Blockchain on business operations, that's why its development is not geared towards cryptocurrencies, as many of Blockchain platforms.

**Phase 4: "Demonstration".** "Demonstration" phase will determine if Blockchain can be applied on an IoT device (Raspberry Pi 2B+) and an AWS server, both as complete nodes of a blockchain network. Transaction packets between network nodes were obtained. This phase includes basic operation of a prototype, contemplating Blockchain integration.

**Phase 5: "Evaluation".** Cleven [3] proposes that obtaining a useful artifact from Design Science Research, it is necessary to have two fundamental requirements: relevance and rigor. Relevance of artifact meets real commercial needs. Rigor requires the proper application of existing knowledge.

The relevance of high-level model (artifact), results of this research, care the need to implement Blockchain to protect information and decentralize IoT networks. In order to protect services offered by IoT from attacks on a single point of failure, moreover, distributing the computational load across thousands of devices in network. Rigor of artifact is met by implementing knowledge obtained from Blockchain (Hyperledger), IoT and MQTT for artifact creation.

Evaluating artifact by analyzing data collected to verify that implementation complies with the research requirements.

Data collected on the IoT device was:

- Logs demonstrating the correct functionality of MQTT protocol.
- Logs demonstrating communication and operation of the Blockchain network.
- Captured packets exchanged between network members for MQTT protocol and Blockchain, using a network sniffer, TShark software (Wireshark console version).
- Bandwidth measurement tests, using iPerf software.
- Performance measuring of Raspberry Pi processor and AWS server, using Htop software.

Stress tests were performed on the Blockchain network by increasing the number of transactions per second that nodes received until finding maximum of transactions were service encounters problems or stops.

**Phase 6: "Communication".** This document is set out research results.

## 3   Implemented System

Figure 2 presents the implemented system. A connection between t2.medium AWS-EC2 server and Raspberry Pi 2B+ through the Internet.

Node-Red software, which allows block programming, was installed on both devices. REST server, Blockchain network and MQTT broker interaction were programmed using Node-Red.

Raspberry and AWS server fulfilled a specific role in IoT-MQTT-Blockchain network. Raspberry Pi 2B+ works as an endorser peer and have a copy of Ledger

**Fig. 2.** Implemented system.

in Blockchain network. Besides working as an IoT device turning on/off a lamp through General Purpose Input/Output (GPIO) ports.

AWS server works as an endorsing peer, an orderer, and a Certification Authority Server (CA server) in the Blockchain network. Also, an MQTT broker is implemented.

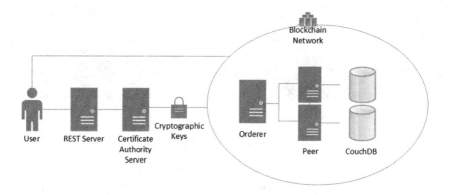

**Fig. 3.** Blockchain network using Hyperledger Fabric.

Figure 3 shows Blockchain architecture implementing Hyperledger Fabric platform. Hyperledger uses Docker images for deploying nodes (peer, orderer, among others). Hyperledger has a Software Development Kit (SDK) [8] used for the creation and configuration of REST service.

REST service communicates with Blockchain nodes in order to submit transactions and wait for an affirmative/negative response. Two transactions were programmed in REST service. The first one was getting the current value of Blockchain. The second one was making changes in the Blockchain state.

An MQTT broker is configured on AWS server to handles communication between Raspberry PI and AWS server. Comparative protection was applied to protect undesirable changes in MQTT. Comparative between MQTT and Blockchain states to prevent unauthorized changes in lamp state.

## 4    Results

Implementation and test results are detailed in this section.

### 4.1    Implementation

Building and deploying the newest versions of Hyperledger Fabric (>v1.2) on Raspberry Pi 2B+ has difficulties. Due to newer versions are developed for 64-bit architecture systems, so armv7 devices with 32-bit architecture present problems on implementation. Joe Motacek [14], on his website, propose a method to deploy Hyperledger Fabric on Raspberry Pi devices based on Fabric v1.0. His solution was deployed and adapted to research needs.

IoT prototype defined as a Raspberry connection to a lamp through GPIO ports (see Fig. 4) using a relay module to control lamp state (on/off).

(a) Off State.                                    (b) On State.

**Fig. 4.** IoT prototype.

Node-Red programming for AWS server is shown in Fig. 5. Generated transactions are based on information obtained from a graphical interface. The HTTP request is sent to REST server and its response is processed. If the answer is affirmative, a change is made in MQTT broker state.

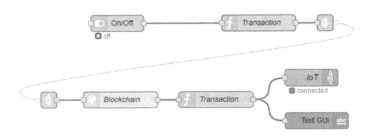

**Fig. 5.** Node-Red blocks in AWS server.

Raspberry block programming in Node-Red (see Fig. 6) receives change in the MQTT broker state and makes an HTTP request to REST server to get the current status of Blockchain. Both MQTT and Blockchain states are compared to finally performs change on GPIO port. The comparison is made in order to prevent unauthorized changes in the current state of GPIO ports.

**Fig. 6.** Node-Red blocks in Raspberry Pi.

## 4.2 Basic Operation

Basic operation of Blockchain and IoT-MQTT networks was demonstrated by network packets captured with TShark tool, where communication packet between nodes is shown (see Fig. 7).

| No. | Time | Source | Destination | Protocol | Port | Info |
|---|---|---|---|---|---|---|
| 131 | 9.220806735 | 3.17.180.159 | 10.10.0.212 | TCP | 7051 | 7051 → 42444 [PSH, ACK] Seq=5750 Ac... |
| 132 | 9.221175849 | 10.10.0.212 | 3.17.180.159 | TCP | 42444 | 42444 → 7051 [ACK] Seq=5758 Ack=614... |
| 133 | 9.308426901 | 3.17.180.159 | 10.10.0.212 | TCP | 7051 | 7051 → 42444 [ACK] Seq=6148 Ack=569... |
| 134 | 9.383814810 | 3.17.180.159 | 10.10.0.212 | TCP | 7051 | 7051 → 42444 [ACK] Seq=6148 Ack=575... |
| 135 | 9.406026101 | 3.17.180.159 | 10.10.0.212 | MQTT | 1883 | Publish Message (id=51571) [tesis/1... |
| 136 | 9.407163702 | 10.10.0.212 | 3.17.180.159 | MQTT | 37674 | Publish Received (id=51571) |
| 137 | 9.531000900 | 3.17.180.159 | 10.10.0.212 | TCP | 1883 | 1883 → 37674 [ACK] Seq=24 Ack=5 Win... |
| 138 | 9.531019441 | 3.17.180.159 | 10.10.0.212 | MQTT | 1883 | Publish Release (id=51571) |
| 139 | 9.533489486 | 10.10.0.212 | 3.17.180.159 | MQTT | 37674 | Publish Complete (id=51571) |
| 140 | 9.576925508 | 10.10.0.212 | 3.17.180.159 | TCP | 42444 | 42444 → 7051 [PSH, ACK] Seq=5758 Ac... |
| 141 | 9.692590593 | 3.17.180.159 | 10.10.0.212 | TCP | 1883 | 1883 → 37674 [ACK] Seq=28 Ack=9 Win... |
| 142 | 9.696898081 | 3.17.180.159 | 10.10.0.212 | TCP | 7051 | 7051 → 42444 [ACK] Seq=6148 Ack=580... |
| 143 | 9.696914852 | 3.17.180.159 | 10.10.0.212 | TCP | 7051 | 7051 → 42444 [PSH, ACK] Seq=6148 Ac... |
| 144 | 9.697319017 | 10.10.0.212 | 3.17.180.159 | TCP | 42444 | 42444 → 7051 [ACK] Seq=5802 Ack=621... |
| 145 | 9.776120927 | 3.17.180.159 | 10.10.0.212 | TCP | 7051 | 7051 → 42444 [PSH, ACK] Seq=6213 Ac... |

| No. | Time | Source | Destination | Protocol | Port | Info |
|---|---|---|---|---|---|---|
| 3552882 | 311295.81457... | 10.10.0.212 | 3.17.180.159 | TCP | 40584 | 40584 → 7051 [PSH, ACK] Seq=9492815... |
| 3552883 | 311295.93369... | 3.17.180.159 | 10.10.0.212 | TCP | 7051 | 7051 → 40584 [ACK] Seq=94266971 Ack... |
| 3552884 | 311295.94995... | 10.10.0.212 | 3.17.180.159 | TCP | 40584 | 40584 → 7051 [PSH, ACK] Seq=9492825... |
| 3552885 | 311296.06893... | 3.17.180.159 | 10.10.0.212 | TCP | 7051 | 7051 → 40584 [ACK] Seq=94266971 Ack... |
| 3552886 | 311296.14224... | 3.17.180.159 | 10.10.0.212 | MQTT | 1883 | Publish Message (id=3875) [tesis/la... |
| 3552887 | 311296.14341... | 10.10.0.212 | 3.17.180.159 | MQTT | 54084 | Publish Received (id=3875) |
| 3552888 | 311296.25920... | 3.17.180.159 | 10.10.0.212 | TCP | 1883 | 1883 → 54084 [ACK] Seq=107110 Ack=3... |
| 3552889 | 311296.25922... | 3.17.180.159 | 10.10.0.212 | MQTT | 1883 | Publish Release (id=3875) |
| 3552890 | 311296.26140... | 10.10.0.212 | 3.17.180.159 | MQTT | 54084 | Publish Complete (id=3875) |
| 3552891 | 311296.32077... | 3.17.180.159 | 10.10.0.212 | TCP | 7051 | 7051 → 40584 [ACK] Seq=9426697... |
| 3552892 | 311296.32119... | 10.10.0.212 | 3.17.180.159 | TCP | 40584 | 40584 → 7051 [ACK] Seq=94928531 Ack... |
| 3552893 | 311296.34274... | 10.10.0.212 | 3.17.180.159 | TCP | 40584 | 40584 → 7051 [PSH, ACK] Seq=9492853... |
| 3552894 | 311296.39472... | 10.10.0.212 | 3.17.180.159 | TCP | 40584 | 40584 → 7051 [ACK] Seq=9492857... |
| 3552895 | 311296.41869... | 3.17.180.159 | 10.10.0.212 | TCP | 1883 | 1883 → 54084 [ACK] Seq=107114 Ack=3... |
| 3552896 | 311296.45843... | 3.17.180.159 | 10.10.0.212 | TCP | 7051 | 7051 → 40584 [ACK] Seq=94267262 Ack... |

**Fig. 7.** Blockchain and MQTT network packages.

## 4.3 Performance

Different amounts of received transactions per second (Tx/s) were carried out in performance tests. Stress tests were performed in order to determine when the system presents processing problems or stops.

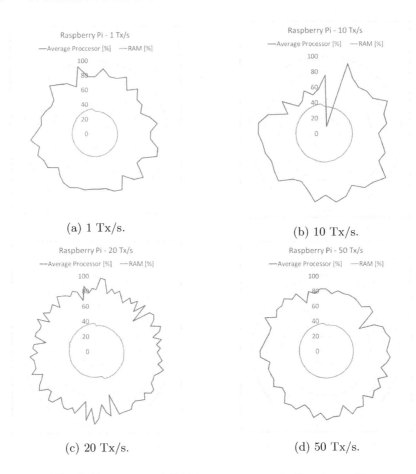

(a) 1 Tx/s.

(b) 10 Tx/s.

(c) 20 Tx/s.

(d) 50 Tx/s.

**Fig. 8.** Processor and RAM measurements in Raspberry Pi.

Figure 8 shows processor and RAM consumption in Raspberry. Processor resources consumption was high in each test but keeping an average of 80%.

Figure 9 presents processor and RAM consumption in AWS server. An increase in resource consumption is shown in each test. Figure 9d shows processor consumption fall, due to blockchain services stopped working. Orderer service caused a restart of blockchain services due to the consumption of available AWS server resources.

### 4.4 Bandwidth

Bandwidth (BW) was measured at the same time as performance tests. Additionally, a BW measurement was taken with occasional transactions condition, in order to have a reference of an almost inactive system.

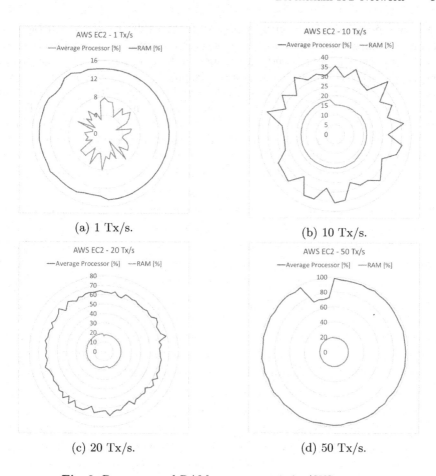

(a) 1 Tx/s.

(b) 10 Tx/s.

(c) 20 Tx/s.

(d) 50 Tx/s.

**Fig. 9.** Processor and RAM measurements in AWS server.

**Table 1.** Bandwidth resume.

|         | Occasional | 1 Tx/s | 10 Tx/s | 20 Tx/s | 50 Tx/s |
|---------|-----------|--------|---------|---------|---------|
| Max     | 282       | 282    | 256     | 282     | 256     |
| Average | 230.17    | 221.34 | 196.63  | 183.06  | 158.13  |
| Min     | 205       | 114    | 76.8    | 42.7    | 37.2    |

Table 1 shows the average, maximum and minimum values of BW obtained in each transactional stress test. Blockchain transactions did not overload bandwidth in-network, despite having a high number of transactions.

Occasional transactions test (see Fig. 10a) present average value of 230 Kbps, due to BW was only consumed when Blockchain nodes approve, save or query Blockchain information.

Measurements obtained with 1 Tx/s (see Fig. 10b) presents a little BW consumed, compared to measurements obtained in an almost inactive system. Increase transaction per second into values of 10 and 20 (see Fig. 10c and d respectively), BW consumption increases; despite it does not represent a large consumption of resources, increasing by 15% and 20% respectively compared to initial measurement. Figure 10e presents large BW consumption at the beginning of the test, after a while, there is an increase in available BW. Blockchain services stopped working due to the consumption of all processor resources.

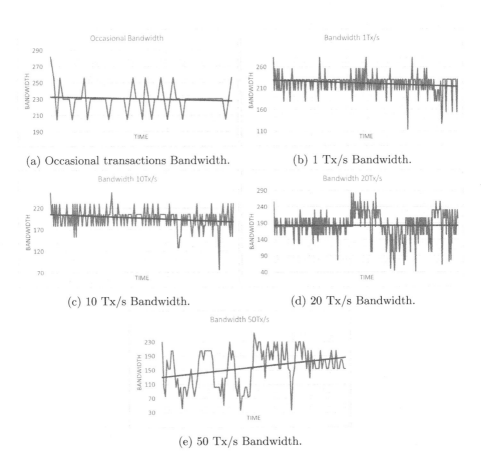

(a) Occasional transactions Bandwidth.        (b) 1 Tx/s Bandwidth.

(c) 10 Tx/s Bandwidth.        (d) 20 Tx/s Bandwidth.

(e) 50 Tx/s Bandwidth.

**Fig. 10.** Bandwidth measurements.

# 5   Conclusion

It is concluded that a Hyperledger Fabric platform implementation on a Raspberry Pi 2B+ as an IoT device can be developed with total success. This conclusion is based on the results presented in the previous chapter.

Hyperledger Fabric services integration in a Raspberry Pi 2B+ is possible if some considerations are taken. Fans or cooling systems are necessary to prevent overheating of processors in order to avoid restart or damage of devices. If it is planned to perform a large number of transactions over a Blockchain network, order service must be implemented on a dedicated server or as a distributed service on all network devices.

All Hyperledger services run on virtual machines based on Docker services, which represents additional security, thanks to a large number of advantages it has.

In this research, IoT device was not responsible for building data blocks to grant information security, in fact, IoT device worked as an endorsing peer. Raspberry Pi 2B+ has a large consumption of processor resources in testbeds presented, even in most basic proofs. RAM consumption in Raspberry Pi 2B+ device is very low; therefore, it does not suffer major inconveniences. In fact, RAM memory is not consumed at all. Therefore, SWAP memory would still available to improve RAM performance.

AWS server processor and RAM resources, in low transaction scenarios, does not represent a major impact. However, orderer service is running in AWS server, which is responsible for block creation. Due to its cryptographic algorithms, it generates a large computational load.

Bandwidth consumption is defined with an average speed between 180 Kbps for 50 transactions per second to 220 Kbps for one transaction per second. Therefore, it is considered an acceptable BW. Despite the amount of transactions produced a small amount of BW is consumed.

A high-level scheme is proposed for future implementations of Hyperledger Fabric platform in IoT devices implementing similar or superior technology of a Raspberry Pi 2 B+ (see Fig. 11).

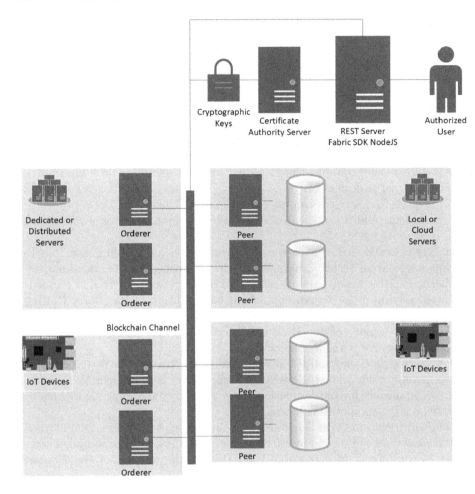

**Fig. 11.** High-level model implementing Hyperledger on a Raspberry Pi device.

# References

1. Association for Information Systems (AIS): IS Research, Methods, and Theories. https://aisnet.org/page/ISResearch
2. Chen, S., Wang, H., Zhang, L.-J. (eds.): ICBC 2018. LNCS, vol. 10974. Springer, Cham (2018). https://doi.org/10.1007/978-3-319-94478-4
3. Cleven, A., Gubler, P., Hüner, K.M.: Design alternatives for the evaluation of design science research artifacts, p. 1 (2009)
4. Dorri, A., Kanhere, S.S., Jurdak, R.: Blockchain in internet of things: Challenges and Solutions, August 2016. http://arxiv.org/abs/1608.05187
5. Dorri, A., Kanhere, S.S., Jurdak, R., Gauravaram, P.: Blockchain for IoT security and privacy: the case study of a smart home. In: 2017 IEEE International Conference on Pervasive Computing and Communications Workshops (PerCom Workshops), pp. 618–623. IEEE, March 2017

6. Fakhri, D., Mutijarsa, K.: Secure IoT communication using blockchain technology. In: 2018 International Symposium on Electronics and Smart Devices (ISESD), pp. 1–6. IEEE, October 2018

7. Hyperledger: A Blockchain Platform for the Enterprise. https://hyperledger-fabric. readthedocs.io/en/release-1.4/

8. Hyperledger Fabric: Hyperledger Fabric SDK for node.js. https://fabric-sdk-node. github.io/release-1.4/index.html#toc2_anchor

9. Juniper Research: IoT Connections to Grow 140% to Hit 50 Billion By 2022 (2018). https://www.juniperresearch.com/press/press-releases/iot-connections-to-grow-140-to-hit-50-billion

10. Kalinov, V., Voshmgir, S.: Blockchain A Beginners guide. BlockchainHub (2017). https://blockchainhub.net/blockchain-technology/

11. Peffers, K., Tuunanen, T., Rothenberger, M.A., Chatterjee, S.: A design science research methodology for information systems research. J. Manag. Inf. Syst. **24**(3), 45–78 (2007)

12. Khan, M.A., Salah, K.: IoT security: review, blockchain solutions, and open challenges. Future Gen. Comput. Syst. **82**, 395–411 (2018). https://linkinghub.elsevier. com/retrieve/pii/S0167739X17315765

13. Minoli, D., Occhiogrosso, B.: Blockchain mechanisms for IoT security. Internet Things **1–2**, 1–13 (2018)

14. Motacek, J.: Hyperledger Fabric v1.0 on a Raspberry Pi Docker Swarm. https:// www.joemotacek.com/hyperledger-fabric-v1-0-on-a-raspberry-pi-docker-swarm-part-1/

15. Nakamoto, S.: Bitcoin: A Peer-to-Peer Electronic Cash System (2008)

16. Reyna, A., Martín, C., Chen, J., Soler, E., Díaz, M.: On blockchain and its integration with IoT. Challenges and opportunities. Future Gen. Comput. Syst. **88**(2018), 173–190 (2018)

17. Singh, M., Singh, A., Kim, S.: Blockchain: a game changer for securing IoT data. In: 2018 IEEE 4th World Forum on Internet of Things (WF-IoT), vol. 2018-Janua, pp. 51–55. IEEE, February 2018

18. The Statistics Portal: IoT: number of connected devices worldwide 2012–2025. https://www.statista.com/statistics/471264/iot-number-of-connected-devices-worldwide/

19. Peffers, K., Rothenberger, M., Kuechler, B. (eds.): DESRIST 2012. LNCS, vol. 7286. Springer, Heidelberg (2012). https://doi.org/10.1007/978-3-642-29863-9

20. Zamfir, S., Balan, T., Iliescu, I., Sandu, F.: A security analysis on standard IoT protocols. In: 2016 International Conference on Applied and Theoretical Electricity (ICATE), pp. 1–6, October 2016

# Eliminating Gas Interference and Blockage in Sucker Rod Pumping Systems to Improve Oil Production

Romel Erazo-Bone[1,2]([✉]) [ID], Richard Gacía Vera[1], Fidel Chuchuca-Aguilar[1,2] [ID],
Juan Pablo Ramírez Yagual[1], Carlos Alberto Portilla Lazo[1],
and Kenny Escobar-Segovia[1,2] [ID]

[1] Universidad Estatal Península de Santa Elena, La Libertad, Ecuador
raerazo@upse.edu.ec
[2] Escuela Superior Politécnica del Litoral, Guayaquil, Ecuador

**Abstract.** Oil production in mature oilfields is affected by the decrease of reservoir energy; it generates free gas presence in reservoir and well. The free gas presence during the process of lifting fluid by sucker rod pumping systems can generates blockage or interference in the bottom pump, therefore, lowers the efficiency and the capacity to lift fluid in each oil wells production.

In this project it seeks to optimize the bottom hole equipment of the sucker rod pumping lifting system in the Petropolis oilfield.

The methodological process applied in this study was theoretical-experimental; the characteristics of the fluid and the pressure drop between the reservoir and the well were used to determine the optimal lifting flow in the system. Finally, was sized the bottom tool, it is consisting of a gas separator located in the bottom pump, in order to reduce gas interference and blockage.

Considering the implementation of the gas separator in each well analyzed, it was possible to increase oil production in all wells from 12% to 21% approximately.

Due to the maturity of the oilfield and the present conditions of each wells, the use of gas separation system in bottom well was implemented to optimize the pump's performance, managing to increase oil production and therefore increase economic income.

**Keywords:** Wells · Mature oilfields · Pumping · Production · Gas

## 1 Introduction

The following research project aims to optimize the underground equipment of the sucker rod pumping system in the wells of the Petropolis section through an analysis of fluid inflow in low production wells, for the optimization of hydrocarbon exploitation efficiency.

The wells analyzed in this investigation produce through sucker rod pumping unit and belong to the Petropolis Section of the Gustavo Galindo Velasco Field.

M. Botto-Tobar et al. (Eds.): ICAT 2019, CCIS 1193, pp. 110–124, 2020.
https://doi.org/10.1007/978-3-030-42517-3_9

By implementing the study of the behavior of the dynagraph charts and the use of the TAM (Total Asset Monitor) Echometer software, the aim is to obtain a higher production rate, improve pump efficiency and reduce production cost costs in each one of the selected wells [1].

Following the methodology applied, we proceeded to analyze the current state of the wells and subsequently determine what the main problem is during the process of fluid extraction from the bottom well, seeking to obtain an alternative that allows us to meet the established objectives.

According to the results obtained from each of the simulations in the TAM software, it was determined that the main problem in each of the wells was the presence of gas interference in the pump, resulting in: low pump efficiency, longer use of the pumping equipment, the bottomhole gas separator equipment is not efficient. Therefore, we proceeded to look for an alternative that, depending on the characteristics of each of the wells, minimizes the problems.

The alternative proposed by this research is to improve the background equipment (gas separator), through calculations and simulations that allow determining the size of an optimal separator for each well. By analyzing the influx of each of the wells, the optimum production flow of a well with natural flow was determined and the sizing of the mechanical pumping system with bottom separator was determined.

## 2   Sucker Rod Lift Systems

Crude oil production by sucker rod pumping systems represents 85% of all production worldwide. The sucker rod pumping system is a relatively simple piston pump, attached to the lower end of the string of pump rods. The oil is extracted by means of the piston and a traveling valve that moves from top to bottom inside a polished cylinder (barrel) with a fixed valve at the bottom. The piston is connected to the string of pump rods that extends to the surface, the upper end of the rod string is attached to a polished rod, which performs an upward and downward movement generated by a pumping unit (see Fig. 1) [2].

### 2.1   Dynagraph Charts

The dynamometer is a precision instrument, used in mechanical pumping systems to observe the behavior of the well during its production. Its components are elaborated thoroughly, in order to reduce inertia to a viable minimum [3].

For the measurement of the chart it is necessary to let the well pump for about ten minutes, or at least the time in which, the well was closed during the equipment installation process. A graph is obtained before this period of time elapses, the graph must be labeled.

When making a recording, it is advisable to let the pencil draw at least three times the graph, in order to show the slight variations.

**Interpretation of Basic Dynamometric Charts.** The records obtained during the taking of surface dynamometric charts are interpreted by a software, in order to obtain or calculate a dynamometer chart of the pump; and thus diagnose its behavior during the production of the well (see Fig. 2).

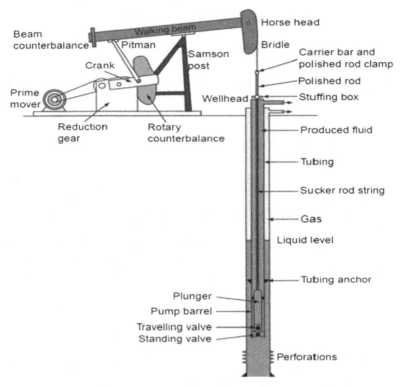

**Fig. 1.** Typical configuration of sucker rod pumping system.

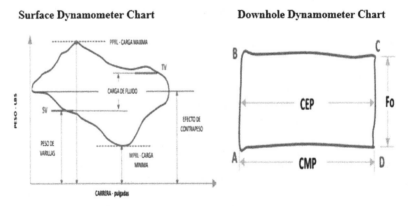

**Fig. 2.** Surface and downhole dynamometer charts.

Where:

TV: Traveling Valve.
SV: Standing Valve.

PPRL: Peak Polished Rod Load.

MPRL: Minimum Polished Rod Load.

A: Lower dead point of the plunger.

C: Upper dead point of the plunger.

CEP: Effective plunger travel (EPT).

Fo: Fluid load.

CMP: Maximum plunger travel (MPT).

CEP: Length of the piston stroke when the total fluid load is on the fixed valve.

Fo: Force acting on the piston due to the difference in pressure that exists on it.

CMP: Maximum length of piston movement relative to the barrel during a full stroke.

There are several problems present during the production process, whether due to equipment failures or formation characteristics, therefore, dynamometric charts will not always have the same behavior.

## 2.2 Well Inflow Behavior

To obtain the well flow behavior curve, it is necessary to know the Inflow Performance Relationship and Vertical Lift Performance curves, which can be determined by different methods and correlations [4].

**Inflow Performance Relationship (IPR).** The IPR curve is a mathematical tool used to evaluate the performance of the well using a graph that indicates the behavior of the flowing bottom pressure "Pwf" vs. the production rate of the "Q" well. The data is obtained by measuring different flows under different bottomhole pressures and the behavior of the curve will depend on the composition of the reservoir fluid. Mathematical equations to determine the behavior of the curve are based on productivity index models.

There are several methods for obtaining the IPR curve, established by several authors, including the method of Darcy, Vogel, Standing, among others.

To obtain the IPR curve of this work, the Standing method (Eq. 1) will be used for present and future IPR. The parameters for obtaining the IPR curve are presented below:

$$\frac{Q_o}{Q_{max}} = 1 - 0.2\left(\frac{P_{wf}}{P_r}\right) - 0.8\left(\frac{P_{wf}}{P_r}\right)^2 \tag{1}$$

Where:

Pr: Reservoir pressure.                    Qomax: Asolute open flow

Pwf: Bottomhole flow pressure.             Qo: Oil rate.

**Vertical Lift Performance (VLP).** As mentioned earlier, to determine the Inflow curve, it is generally based on productivity index models, while the outflow curve or also called VLP (Vertical Lift Performance) is obtained through correlations , the most common are: Hagedorn & Brown, Beggs & Brill, Duns & Ros. Once the outflow curve and the inflow curve are obtained, an intersection is generated, which indicates the optimal condition for the well under study. For the development of the outflow curve in this work, the Hagedorn & Brown correlation will be used. This requires knowing the following parameters [5]:

$$144\frac{\Delta p}{\Delta h} = \rho_m + \frac{f Q_L^2 M^2}{2.9652 X 10^{11} d^5 \rho_m} + \frac{\frac{\rho_m \Delta(v_m)}{2g_c}}{\Delta h} \tag{2}$$

$$\rho_m = H_L \rho_L + \rho_g (1 - H_L) \tag{3}$$

Where:

ΔP: Total pressure drop                    $\rho_m$: Mixture density

Ql: Liquid flow rate                        $\rho_g$: Density of gas

M: Total mass of oil                        f= Moody friction factor

Hl: Liquid holdup fraction                  Vm: average velocity of the mixture

Δh: Total depth drop                        $\rho_L$: Density of liquid

d: internal diameter of tubing              gc: gravitational constant

**The Correction of Gas Impact.** Accordingly, lifting costs get higher and production economy is considerably decreased. This is why gas interference is considered one of the biggest enemies facing the production engineer working in sucker-rod pumping.

Downhole gas separators used in sucker-rod pumping are often called gas anchors. All gas anchors operate on the principle of gravitational separation, because the pumping system does not allow the use of other separation methods. The force of gravity is utilized to separate the gas, usually present in the form of small gas bubbles, from the liquid phase. Liquids, being denser than gas, flow downwards, but gas, due to its lower gravity, tends to rise in the liquids. In order that this natural process can take place, the well stream has to be led into a space of sufficient capacity, from where the liquid is directed into the pump. The casing-tubing annulus offers an ideal way to lead the separated gas to the surface; this is why it is usually kept free in pumping wells [6].

When the pump inlet pressure is smaller than the bubble point pressure, gas will enter the pump and the pump can't be filled up. When the performance curve is applied in node analysis and optimization design, the effect of gas performance curve should be revised with the method of ESP. The correct method can be achieved by the calculation of filling level of pump [7].

### 2.3 Calculations of Gas Separators in Selected Wells

In gas separator designs, through tests, they indicate that the increase in pressure drop associated with increases in suction pipe length does not represent a problem during production. The focus on separator designs is to ensure that the suction pipe has sufficient volume for the separation process to take place within the separator [8].

In the GGV field, in wells that produce gas in the annular casing, the pump efficiency can often be significantly improved by using a better gas separator in the well. This, therefore, ensures that a minimum amount of gas enters the separator [9].

The gas separator inlet must be placed at least 10 ft below the inlet zone of the formation gas to allow the separation of free gas from the liquid between the outer diameter of the tube and the inner diameter of the casing. All these factors are considered for the design of the tool and preparation of this work [10].

The results of efficiency of the implementation of the tools indicate that they can separate between 90–100% of gas from the mixture, if the inlet of the pipe or the tool were completely submerged in the liquid phase of the mixture at all times [11].

The calculations for the gas separation system are based clearly on knowing the dimensions (length and diameter) of the suction pipes and mud pipes, and in turn the number of grooves that both pipes will have.

The following information is required to design the system:

- Production rate.
- Pump piston diameter.
- Stroke length.
- Fixed valve flow area.

It should be noted that not only the oil production of each well should be considered, but the amount of fluid entering the pump (Water and Petroleum) per day; In this case, the potential for each cycle is considered, because most wells in the GGV field produce that way.

## 3  Case Study

The Petropolis Section corresponds to the Northern Zone of the Field, has 28 wells, 5 of them are currently in a transitory inactive state, and 23 in a productive state, therefore, the production of the Petropolis Section comes from 82% of the wells.

The production of crude oil in the Petropolis section is carried out by means of two different types of artificial lifting, Sucker Rod Pumping and Local Tool, the sucker rod pumping being the most used in this section [12].

Figure 3 shows the percentage of the extraction system of the wells present in the Petropolis section, where it can be seen that the sucker rod pumping system is applied in 21 wells, while the local tool system is applied in 2 wells.

### 3.1  Methodology

The sizing of the proposed equipment was calculated theoretically and through the use of the TAM software in order to determine which of the two methods is more efficient and can be applied in each of the wells of the study following the methodology established in the Fig. 4. Once the sizing of the proposed equipment was obtained, a comparative analysis of production was carried out obtaining positive results that help to meet the proposed objectives.

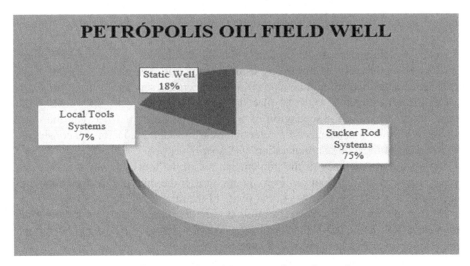

**Fig. 3.** Distribution of the petropolis section wells

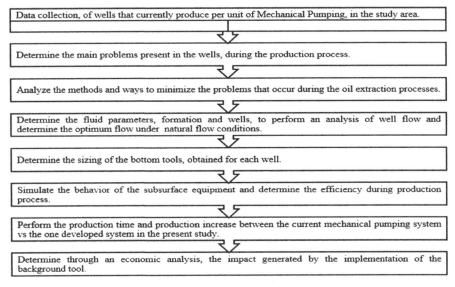

**Fig. 4.** Applied methodology

## 3.2 Results and Discussions

The results that will be presented in this study correspond to well PET0101. The selection of candidate wells to be intervened will be carried out by means of an analysis of dynograph charts, in order to determine the problems present during the production process and then optimize it.

The results of the simulation using the TAM echometer software are shown below:

**Well PET0101.** Figure 5 shows the surface (top figure) and bottom (bottom figure) Dynograph taken from the PET0101 well, which shows a maximum piston stroke of 31.36 inches, an effective piston stroke of 10.00 inches and a pump fill of 32%. It can be determined that during the downward stroke the traveling valve does not allow the entry of the fluid that is in the barrel until approximately the end of the stroke, the fluid entering the pump includes the presence of gas, therefore, it was determined that there is gas interference and fluid blow during oil extraction. The speed of the unit is 11.92 strokes per minute, it does not present data about the level of liquid in the well during the taking of the dynamometric chart.

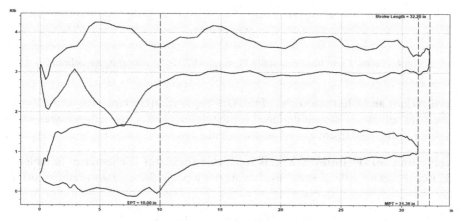

**Fig. 5.** Dynograph PET0101 Well

**Discussion.** The process of selecting wells for the present study was generally based on the following aspects:

– Wells must be in a productive state due to Mechanical Pumping.
– Wells must have current dynamometric chart information.
– Wells must present problems due to gas interference or gas blockage during the extraction process.

The last item is considered due to the inclusion of a tool in the bottom of the bottomhole pump, which allows to block the entry of gas into it, in order to optimize the performance of the pump and in turn the production.

**Obtaining the Inflow and Outflow Curves.** To obtain the inflow and outflow curves, the corresponding well test data was entered in an Excel data sheet (Fig. 6).

The optimum production for naturally flowing of the PET0101 well, according to the intersection of the IPR curves (red) and VLP (green), indicates that the appropriate production rate is approximately 7 bbl/d, at a pressure of 325 psig.

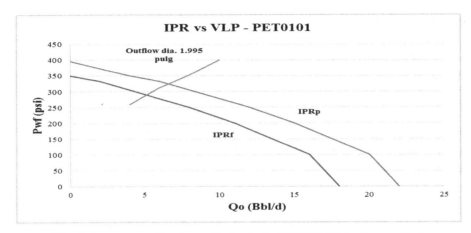

**Fig. 6.** Inflow vs. outflow (naturally flowing) – PET0101 (Color figure online)

**Specifications and Characteristics of the Gas Separation System.** The dimensions of each gas separation system designed for the different selected wells are presented in Table 1, using theoretical and simulated calculations.

**Specifications and Features of the Gas Separator Simulator - Echometer.** In Tables 1 and 2 it can be seen that the dimensions of the suction pipe and the separator are different for

**Table 1.** Dimensions and characteristics of the gas separation system, theoretical model

| | PET0101 | | PET0115 | | PET0120 | | PET0125 | | PET0129 | |
|---|---|---|---|---|---|---|---|---|---|---|
| Suction pipe | dia. ¾" | | dia. ¾" | | dia. ¾" | | dia. ¾" | | dia. ¾" | |
| | ID | 0.824 inch | ID | 0.824 inch | ID | 0.824 inch | ID | 0.824 inch | ID | 0.824 inch |
| | OD | 1.05 inch | OD | 1.05 inch | OD | 1.05 inch | OD | 1.05 inch | OD | 1.05 inch |
| | Long. | 13 ft | Long. | 8 ft | Long. | 12 ft | Long. | 13 ft | Long. | 8 ft |
| | #Ran. | 2 | #Ran. | 2 | #Ran. | 2 | #Ran. | 2 | #Ran. | 2 |
| Niple | $A_{Perf.}$ | 0.84 $inch^2$ | $A_{Perf.}$ | 0.97 $inch^2$ | $A_{Perf.}$ | 0.67 $inch^2$ | $A_{Perf.}$ | 0.67 $pulg^2$ | $A_{Perf.}$ | 1.12 $inch^2$ |
| | #Ran. | 3 | #Ran. | 3 | #Ran. | 3 | #Ran. | 3 | #Ran. | 3 |
| Separator | dia. 1¼" | | dia. 1¼" | | dia. 1¼" | | dia. 1¼" | | dia. 1¼" | |
| | ID | 1.38 inch | ID | 1.38 inch | ID | 1.38 inch | ID | 1.38 inch | ID | 1.38 inch |
| | OD | 1.66 inch | OD | 1.66 inch | OD | 1.66 inch | OD | 1.66 inch | OD | 1.66 inch |
| | $A_{flujo}$ | 0.63 $inch^2$ | $A_{flujo}$ | 0.63 $inch^2$ | $A_{flujo}$ | 0.63 $inch^2$ | $A_{flujo}$ | 0.63 $inch^2$ | $A_{flujo}$ | 0.63 $inch^2$ |

**Table 2.** Dimensions and characteristics of the gas separation system - software gas separator simulator

| Simulation data | | | | | | | | | | |
|---|---|---|---|---|---|---|---|---|---|---|
| | | PET0101 | | PET0115 | | PET0120 | | PET0125 | | PET0129 |
| Suction pipe | ID | 0.824 inch | ID | 0.824 inch | ID | 0.824 inch | ID | 0.824 inch | ID | 0.824 inch |
| | OD | 1.05 inch | OD | 1.05 inch | OD | 1.05 inch | OD | 1.05 inch | OD | 1.05 inch |
| Separator | ID | 1.38 inch | ID | 1.38 inch | ID | 1.38 inch | ID | 1.38 inch | ID | 1.38 inch |
| | OD | 1.66 inch | OD | 1.66 inch | OD | 1.66 inch | OD | 1.66 inch | OD | 1.66 inch |
| Casing | ID | 8.097 inch | ID | 4.560 inch | ID | 5.424 inch | ID | 4.560 inch | ID | 6.538 inch |
| | OD | $8^{5/8}$ inch | OD | 5 inch | OD | 6 inch | OD | 5 inch | OD | 7 inch |
| Gas velocity | 12 inch/seg | | 12 inch/seg | | 12 inch/seg | | 12 inch/seg | | 12 inch/seg | |
| SPM | 11.92 | | 11.46 | | 8.26 | | 9.89 | | 11.54 | |
| Pump displac. | 54.4 BPD | | 24 BPD | | 30.4 BPD | | 44 BPD | | 28.8 BPD | |
| Simulation results | | | | | | | | | | |
| Suction pipe length | 37.248 inch | | 38.743 inch | | 53.753 inch | | 44.894 inch | | 38.475 inch | |
| | 3.1 ft | | 3.2 ft | | 4.5 ft | | 3.74 ft | | 3.2 ft | |
| Separator capacity | 67 BPD | | 67 BPD | | 67 BPD | | 67 BPD | | 67 BPD | |

the same well, this is because through the equations it is considered that the separator must have twice the volume of flow that enters the pump, unlike the simulator, which calculates the volume of the separator according to the diameters of the suction pipe and the separator, for this reason, a different volume capacity is shown in the separator and length of the suction pipe for each calculation method.

For the present work, the measurements obtained by means of the design formulas of the separator will be considered, because when considering the length of the stroke, either bottom or surface for the calculation of the volume of the separator, a better appreciation of the volume of fluid is obtained that enters the pump for each stroke, therefore, the volume of the separator will be different for each well.

### 3.3 Pump Analysis Considering the Implementation of the Gas Separator

By using the separator a better filling of the pump is achieved, therefore, the desired production is obtained in a shorter time, which in turn results in a lower recovery time for each well (Table 3).

Considering aspects such as the production time and the time without producing (recovery time) of each well with and without a separator, it was possible to determine

**Table 3.** Analysis of well production efficiency - without gas separator vs implementation of gas separator.

| Well | Potential | MPT | Pump capacity | Production without separator | | | Production with separator | | |
|------|-----------|-----|---------------|------|-------------------|------------------|------|-------------------|------------------|
| | | | | EPT | Pump displacement | Production time | EPT | Pump displacement | Production time |
| PET0101 | 6 Bbls | 30.83 inch | 68 BPD | 8.87 inch | 22 BPD | 7–8 h | 25 inch | 54.4 BPD | 2–3 h |
| PET0115 | 8 Bbls | 14.58 inch | 30 BPD | 3.33 inch | 7 BPD | 27–28 h | 11.66 inch | 24 BPD | 7–8 h |
| PET0120 | 4 Bbls | 31.40 inch | 38 BPD | 15.23 inch | 6 BPD | 4 h | 25 inch | 30.4 BPD | 2–3 h |
| PET0125 | 3 Bbls | 30.57 inch | 55 BPD | 8.06 inch | 12 BPD | 6–7 h | 24.47 inch | 44 BPD | 2 h |
| PET0129 | 8 Bbls | 17.28 inch | 36 BPD | 4.31 inch | 10 BPD | 21 h | 13.82 inch | 28.8 BPD | 6–7 h |

how much oil production increases per day. Table 4 shows the percentage of production increase of each well, considering the production per day.

**Table 4.** Increase in daily production

| Well | Current production | Production with separator | Production increase | Production increase percentage |
|------|--------------------|---------------------------|---------------------|--------------------------------|
| PET0101 | 6 bbl/d | 7.25 bbl/d | 1.25 bbl/d | 20.83% |
| PET0115 | 1.6 bbl/d | 1.86 bbl/d | 0.26 bbl/d | 16.25% |
| PET0120 | 3 bbl/d | 3.13 bbl/d | 0.13 bbl/d | 4.33% |
| PET0125 | 3 bbl/d | 3.63 bbl/d | 0.63 bbl/d | 21% |
| PET0129 | 1.6 bbl/d | 1.8 bbl/d | 0.2 bbl/d | 12.5% |
| Total | **15.2 bbl/d** | **17.67 bbl/d** | **2.47 bbl/d** | **16.25** |

## 4   Economic Analysis

Through the implementation of the gas separator, an increase in production of each well analyzed according to time was obtained, obtaining an approximate increase of 74.5 barrels per month with respect to the production it normally presents. The objective of the economic analysis is to determine if the implementation of the bottom gas separator from the economic point of view is viable to be applied in each well, considering the average production obtained previously.

In order to conserve expenses, due to the low production of the section and the field, it will be considered that the equipment that is currently in each well does not present any change, unless it is necessary; that is, the tool proposed in the present investigation, will only be implemented to the bottomhole equipment.

The values of the indicators, in this work are presented below.

Considering an increase in production of 74.5 barrels per month in a period of 12 months plus the usual rate of each well, investment and maintenance expenses, and the value of the Internal Rate of Return (IRR) for this investigation is 43.56%. Additionally, it can be seen in Table 5, that in the second month the investment in each well is recovered.

**Table 5.** Cash flow forecast 1/2

| Months | Investment | Month 1 | Month 2 | Month 3 | Month 4 | Month 5 | Month 6 |
|---|---|---|---|---|---|---|---|
| Income | | | | | | | |
| Production (bbls) | | 530.5 | 530.5 | 530.5 | 530.5 | 530.5 | 530.5 |
| Price (USD) | | 58.00 | 58,00 | 58,00 | 58,00 | 58,00 | 58,00 |
| Total income (USD) | | 30,769.00 | 30,769.00 | 30,769.00 | 30,769.00 | 30,769.00 | 30,769.00 |
| Expenses | | | | | | | |
| Pulling unit (14 days) | −19,488.00 | | | | | | |
| Background separator (5 unit.) | −20,000.00 | | | | | | |
| Niple de Asentamiento (5 unit.) | −3,200.00 | | | | | | |
| Coupling (5 unit) | −2,400.00 | | | | | | |
| Corrective preventive maintenance | | | | | −2.000,00 | | |
| Total expenses (USD) | −45,088.00 | | | | −2.000,00 | | |
| Income (USD) | | 30,769.00 | 30,769.00 | 30,769.00 | 28,769.00 | 30,769.00 | 30,769.00 |
| Final Balance (USD) | −45,088.00 | −14,319.00 | 16.450,00 | 47.219,00 | 75.988,00 | 106.757,00 | 137.526,00 |

The Net Present Value (NPV) obtained in accordance with the cash flow calculated in Tables 5 and 6 of this project is 170,519.69 and the Profit - Cost ratio is 6.22, that is, for every dollar invested there will be a gain of $ 5.22.

The Cost-Benefit value in the present investigation is high because the current production plus the increase in production was considered for economic analysis, through the implementation of the gas separator.

**Table 6.** Cash flow forecast 2/2

| Months | Investment | Month 7 | Month 8 | Month 9 | Month 10 | Month 11 | Month 12 |
|---|---|---|---|---|---|---|---|
| Income | | | | | | | |
| Production (bbls) | | 530.5 | 530.5 | 530.5 | 530.5 | 530.5 | 530.5 |
| Price (USD) | | 58.00 | 58,00 | 58,00 | 58,00 | 58,00 | 58,00 |
| Total income (USD) | | 30,769.00 | 30,769.00 | 30,769.00 | 30,769.00 | 30,769.00 | 30,769.00 |
| Expenses | | | | | | | |
| Pulling unit (14 days) | −19,488.00 | | | | | | |
| Background separator (5 unit) | −20,000.00 | | | | | | |
| Niple de Asentamiento (5 unit.) | −3,200.00 | | | | | | |
| Coupling (5 unit) | −2,400.00 | | | | | | |
| Corrective preventive maintenance | | | −2.000,00 | | | | − 2.000,00 |
| Total expenses (USD) | −45,088.00 | | −2.000,00 | | | | −2.000,00 |
| Income (USD) | | 30,769.00 | 28,769.00 | 30,769.00 | 30,769.00 | 30,769.00 | 28,769.00 |
| Final balance (USD) | −45,088.00 | 168,295.00 | 197,064.00 | 227,883.00 | 258,602.00 | 289,371.00 | 318,140.00 |

## 4.1 Project Viability

The viability of a project is carried out considering three indicators, which are: Net Present Value (NPV), Internal Rate of Return (IRR) and the Benefit-Cost Ratio (B/C). The results are shown in Table 7 (Fig. 7).

**Table 7.** Project viability results

| Viability | Indicator | | |
|---|---|---|---|
| | VAN | TIR | B/C |
| Viable | VAN > 0 | TIR > i | B/C > 1 |
| Obtained values | 170,519.69 | 43.56% | 6.22 |

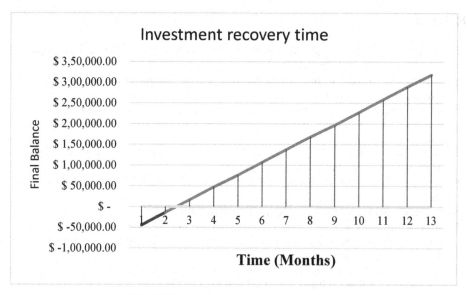

**Fig. 7.** Project investment recovery period

## 5 Conclusions

- Considering the implementation of the gas separator in each well analyzed, it was possible to increase oil production in all wells from 12% to 21% approximately.
- Due to the maturity of the oilfield and the present conditions of each wells, the use of gas separation system in bottom well was implemented to optimize the pump's performance, managing to increase oil production and therefore increase economic income.
- The main problems presented by the analyzed wells are due to the presence of gas interference and fluid shock; for this, the implementation of a gas separation system was determined, in order to optimize the efficiency of the pump during the extraction process. The presence of the fluid stroke is mainly due to the maturity of the field, which is reflected in its daily production; in this case, it is considerable to decrease the SPM.
- By simulating the implementation of the gas separation system in the selected wells of the Petropolis Section, it was possible to determine an increase in production in each of them compared to the design currently presented by each well. Considering the current production rate and maturity of the field, the increase in production is estimated as a favorable contribution.

# References

1. McCoy, J., Rowlan, L.: Gas Separator Simulation Program Information Condensed Version. Echometer Company, Wichita Falls (2014)
2. Camacho, W., Triana, J.: Impacto de la Producción de Gas Asociado a la Producción de Petróleo en los Campos Galán, Gala y Llanito en Pozos con Sistema de Levantamiento de Bombeo Mecánico. Universidad Industrial de Santander, Bucaramanga, Colombia (2011)
3. Slonneger, J.C.: Dynagraph Analysis of Sucker Rod Pumping. The Dynamometer Well Test. Gulf Publishing, Houston (1961)
4. Dale Beggs, H.: Reservoir Performance. Production Optimization Using Nodal Analysis. OGCI and Petroskills Publications, Tulsa (2003)
5. Brown, Kermit E., Dale Beggs, H.: Vertical Flow. The Technology of Artificial Lift Methods. PennWell Books, Tulsa (1977)
6. Takacs, G.: Sucker-Rod Pumping Manual. PennWell Books, Tulsa (2003)
7. Zhao, R., et al.: The new research of subsurface system performance curves of sucker-rod-pumping. In: International Petroleum Technology Conference (2013). https://doi.org/10.2523/iptc-17146-ms
8. Campbell, J.H., Brimhall, R.M.: An Engineering Approach to Gas Anchor Design. Society of Petroleum Engineers (1989). https://doi.org/10.2118/18826-ms
9. Podio, A.L., Mccoy, J.N., Drake, B., Woods, M.D.: Decentralized Continuous-flow Gas Anchor. J. Can. Petrol. Technol. (1996). https://doi.org/10.2118/96-07-03
10. Karmon, I., Panacharoensawad, E., Watson, M.: Quantifying a New Horizontal Well Gas Anchor Performance. Society of Petroleum Engineers (2019). https://doi.org/10.2118/195198-ms
11. Asociación Pacifpetrol S.A.: Master, Lista de Pozos Presentes en el Bloque "Gustavo Galindo Velasco". Sistema de Extracción de la Sección Petrópolis (2017)

# Quality Models: An Experience in the Software Industry

Sofía Gallardo-Cueva[✉], Gustavo Guaigua-Albarracín, and Rolando Reyes-Chicango

Department of Electrical and Electronics, University of the Armed Forces UFA-ESPE, "Quijano and Ordoñez" and Páez Sisters St., Latacunga, Ecuador
asofiagc@gmail.com, hgguaigua@espe.edu.ec,
rolandopreyesch@gmail.com

**Abstract.** At the moment in the software development companies, teams have been created to guarantee the quality of their products, applying methodologies that have resulted in successful companies, proposing to copy the model and replicate it in your organization strictly in some cases, or trying to adapt it to the reality of your company, into others.

In this article, the implementation is analyzed in a quality *"live model"*, a Quality Management System (QMS) comprehensive and based on the ISO 9001: 2015 "Quality Management Systems" Standard, with emphasis on "Projects Management" and "Service Management" processes of a medium-sized company dedicated to software development.

The application of this model called SPF (System Process Framework) implied, among other activities, the exact definition of the areas, procedures and tasks involved, determination of roles and functions of each member of the organization, implementation of technological tools, in general, activities that allowed evaluating indicators that are part of the methodology, tailored solution that is continually adapting and improving *"in hot"*.

By virtue of this, this article intends to present the results of the application of this *"live model"*, a concept based on the agile project management methodologies, this time applied to the quality assurance of the software product, with the objective that this experience, with its conclusions, be an input when choosing a quality model in the software development industry.

**Keywords:** Quality · ISO 9001:2015 · SGC · SPF · QMS

## 1 Introduction

Quality is undoubtedly one of the most important aspects that determine the commercial success of a product whatever its class.

Software as a result and as a process, of course doesn't escape from this reality, and it's like where each time companies allocate their effort more often to certificate their services and products that they offer to their customers, although this implies logically a greater investment, translated in costs, effort and time.

© Springer Nature Switzerland AG 2020
M. Botto-Tobar et al. (Eds.): ICAT 2019, CCIS 1193, pp. 125–138, 2020.
https://doi.org/10.1007/978-3-030-42517-3_10

One of the ISO standards most commonly used to manage and ensure the quality of software products has been the ISO 9001, since it's first release in 1987, to the last released in 2015, in his actual 10 fields of action, focused on achieving better results in profitability and productivity in the fields of human resources, infrastructure and work environment.

In this context that an experience lived in a medium-sized Ecuadorian company is analyzed, with a presence in 4 Latin American countries, dedicated to the development of customized IT solutions, where the implementation of a "live custom" model would be expected to obtain better results than the application of a "rigid model", in the quality of the software product.

This article aims to be a further contribution to the set of experiences lived by implementing Quality Management Systems (QMS) in software development companies, in order to have more elements of conviction when choosing and implementing a QMS.

For the purpose in a first chapter, the guidelines that constitute the ISO 9001: 2015 "Quality Management Systems" standard are reviewed in a general way, to then describe the SPF methodology proposed in this article, making an analysis of the results obtained and presenting finally a personal conclusion about the perceived impact.

## 2 Generalities

**General milestones of the ISO 9001:2015 Standard "Quality Management Systems" and its relationship in the quality of a software product.**

For this purpose, let's review in general terms the latest version of this standard, released in 2015, which proposes a new approach based on risks and oriented to meet the requirements not only of the client, but of the end user and in general to all the interested parts (stakeholders); This whole vision is based on its now 7 principles (see Fig. 1) of quality management [1]:

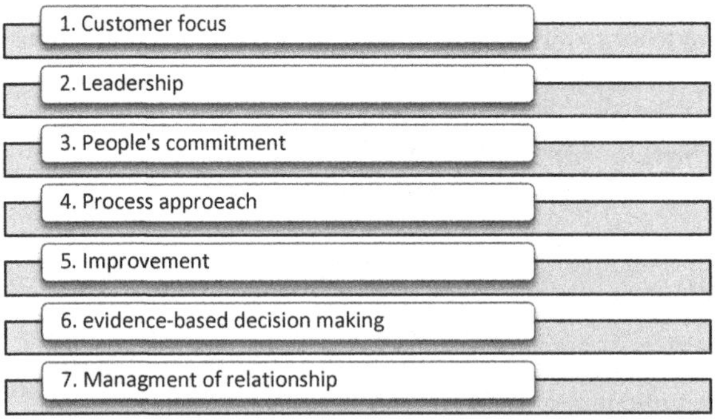

1. Customer focus

2. Leadership

3. People's commitment

4. Process approeach

5. Improvement

6. evidence-based decision making

7. Managment of relationship

**Fig. 1.** Seven principles of quality management of ISO 9001: 2015

It is necessary to consider that the ISO 9001:2015 standard is not exclusively for software products, this standard is responsible for verifying that all the wishes of a person are fulfilled in their client role and expressed in the form of requirements, in all the processes and in all the areas of management where a client intervenes, (Final concept of quality) is where it coincides with the purpose of a software product, satisfying the needs of a user.

## Continuous Improvement and SCRUM

This standard implements the methodology of the continuous improvement system of the PDCA Deming cycle (Plan - Do - Check - Act), which guarantees that the processes are reviewed again and again until a conformity is verified, this circumstance is aligned and perfectly matches with the agile project development methodology such as SCRUM that is used in the company under study for the development of its software applications, such a relationship perfectly overlaps the PDCA model with the Sprint SCRUM (see Fig. 2).

**Fig. 2.** Deming continuous improvement cycle in a sprint SCRUM

This standard indicates activities to manage the potential risks that arise and focuses them in such a way that these problems or obstacles can become opportunities, "Risk-based Thinking", that motivate the company to look for creative solutions.

## Object and Scope

Every company needs to demonstrate two things mainly: 1. Its ability to meet the needs and requirements of the customer and 2. Increase this satisfaction.

Although this IS (International Standard) is generic, in this case it fits perfectly for the software development area, since the satisfaction of customer requirements, is the unique objective to develop a computer application, no matter what technology is used, old or modern, what matters is that it meets the needs and strict order of the customer, determined in the form of Software Requirements Specification (SRS).

## Context of the Organization

The external and internal context of the organization must be clearly understood and specified, external factors such as legal, technological, competitive; and internal as values, culture and own performance; and above all have very clear organizational processes.

The scope of the QMS will be determined, considering the contexts referred to in the previous paragraph and the requirements of the stakeholders.

## Leadership

The QMS must necessarily be a "live" instrument, as proposed in the SPF, for this to happen it must necessarily have not only support but also supervision, control and commitment of senior management through a true organization policy based on effective leadership, in which everyone is involved, assigning them specific roles within the QMS.

## Planning

At this point, the standard requires us that both the requirements of the users and the audit findings, together with the risks and opportunities, are not only well defined, but that an action plan is planned, executed and controlled, and that its effectiveness is evaluated to ensure that the QMS achieves its objectives.

## Support for

Undoubtedly, the plans are strictly necessary, however, if there are no resources, infrastructure, people and results measurement instruments, a true QMS can hardly be organized and implemented.

The support of all organization is decisive, including a true knowledge of the organization itself and of the competition, organizational awareness, a noise-free communication between its staff, and of course having the respective and correct documentation.

## Operation

The organization must plan its changes, in addition it must review the consequences of the unforeseen changes that are found or requested in several ways, either at the request of the client, by audit findings or by change in the process or other causes.

In the software development, this whole process is carried out in an orderly and sequential way, one after the other, in the development of a product (see Fig. 3).

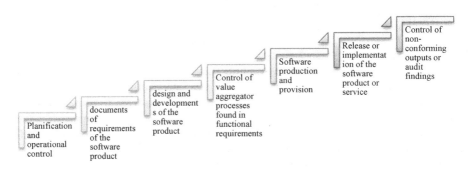

**Fig. 3.** Route of planning and operational control

## Performance Evaluation

The organization must comply with the roadmap of the activities that it will carry out with the audit findings or with the compliance or non-compliance reports.

In any case, the company must perform actions, answering these questions:

(a)  What do you need monitoring and measurement?
(b)  What is the monitoring, measurement, analysis and evaluation methods necessary to ensure valid results?
(c)  When should monitoring and measurement be carried out?
(d)  When should the results of monitoring and measurement be evaluated?

In response, activities should then be planned:

(e)  Monitoring, measurement, analysis and evaluation.
(f)  Internal audit.
(g)  Management review.

In a single sentence, which must always be present in a visible place of the company: *"The organization must always evaluate the performance and effectiveness of the QMS"*

In the case of the software industry, each development team integrates personnel responsible for quality assurance that will be present at all stages of the software life cycle.

**Improvement**
In order for this entire process of continuous improvement to fulfill its mission of achieving quality translated into customer satisfaction, the findings found in the audit cannot be left dead, it is imperative that the organization determines and implements actions necessary to achieve or increase satisfaction of the client, with actions such as: improvement of the product or service, prevention or correction of unwanted effects and, improves the performance of the QMS at all times.

# 3  Structure and Operation of the Quality Model "System Process Framework" SPF

## 3.1  SPF Quality Policy

It is very important for the organization to have established procedures and policies focused on delivering a quality service to its customers in the software product, for this reason the quality policy is a commitment acquired with the client, a commitment to continuous improvement, based on the abilities of the company smoking talent.

## 3.2  Quality Objectives

(a)  Comply with the levels of satisfaction and service agreed with customers.
(b)  Increase the adherence of the processes of the Quality Management System.
(c)  Continuously improve the Quality Management System.
(d)  Guarantee and maintain suitable personnel to support the strategy.

### 3.3 Context of the SPF Quality Model Processes

The SPF model is a comprehensive application framework, it means, it is used in all the processes of the company, for our efforts, we emphasize the processes of "Project Management" and "Service Management" that make up the area of "Software Engineering Practices" (see Fig. 4).

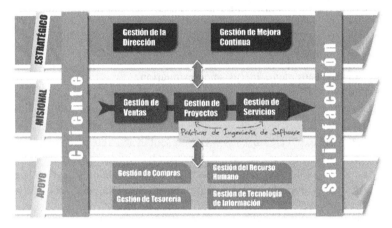

**Fig. 4.** Process map of the company under study

#### 3.3.1 Directorate Management

This process defines the main guidelines to ensure that Senior Management makes the strategic decisions of the Quality Management System based on its performance review.

#### 3.3.2 Continuous Improvement Management

This process defines the main guidelines to ensure the continuous improvement of the Quality Management System for all the processes that form it, that are responsible for designing and monitoring the implementation of the SPF quality model.

#### 3.3.3 Sales Management

This process defines the way in which the needs of both current and potential clients of the Andean Region are identified and addressed. Contact with a client can be established either by commercial campaigns, consultancies or visits, or if the same client seeks the company's services on its own initiative.

#### 3.3.4 Project Management

The objectives of this process are:

(a) Manage the life cycle of development and implementation projects.
(b) Finalize the projects within the agreed deadlines.
(c) Obtain the expected profitability and satisfaction of our customers.

### 3.3.5  Service Management

Manage the life cycle of the support line services in order to maintain the availability and stability of the systems developed for customers.

(a) Presale of Services: Design and estimate services based on the needs of the client and the catalog of services of the organization.
(b) Transition of Services: Start up the services taking into account the processes, people, tools, among others. It includes changes to the service that affect the main design established in the previous stage.
(c) Service Operation: Day-to-day processes established to meet the functional/technical requirements.
(d) Management and Control of Services: Ensure effective management of the service from the operational, financial, quality, human resources, customer satisfaction, among others.

### 3.3.6  Engineering Practices

The best practices of RUP and SCRUM are taken, the software engineering model is assembled according to the SPF quality model guidelines, for the customer improvement service, in a personalized life cycle (see Fig. 5).

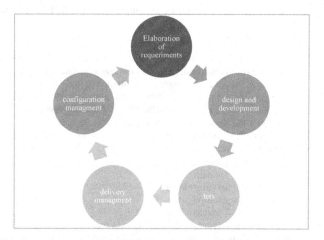

**Fig. 5.** Software engineering life cycle of a request for improvement.

### 3.3.7  Roles and Responsibilities of the Development Team

This is one of the most significant milestones of the SPF quality model, having well defined roles and responsibilities, in the case of the company under study, these are well defined (see Table 1), giving each role its specific responsibilities.

### 3.3.8   Customer Roles

In ensuring the quality of a software product, not only does the development team have to intervene, but the client plays an active and preponderant role in the proposed SPF model, providing constant feedback for continuous improvement (Table 2).

The flow of a requirement from its entry to the actual production pass can be defined in the following steps:

1. The requirement is created.
2. The Functional Analyst verifies that he has all the documents.
3. If everything is done, the quotation is given.
4. The quote is sent.
5. If the quotation is approved, the development and delivery to the client are planned.
6. Otherwise, the requirement is reclassified or closed.

### 3.4   Qualification of the Effort Invested in the Development of the Requirement

To keep track of the effort invested in development, it is a policy for developers to record their effort time from their activities in the JIRA tool. The time record is daily and for each requirement or activity developed.

**Table 1.**  Roles and responsibilities of the development team, RPF quality model.

| Role RUP [RUP role] | Responsibilities |
|---|---|
| **Architect** RUP [Architect] | • Ensure compliance with the guidelines and guidelines of the architecture<br>• Analyze the documentation received to identify the context and restrictions, detect risks and possible problems early, as well as optimizations to the software solution, and formally inform the Project/Account Leader<br>• Identify the constraints and the context of the problem<br>• Design the solution strategy: Decide on the technologies for the complete solution<br>• Develop the component model<br>• Develop the Domain Model<br>• Prepare the Services Model<br>• Develop the deployment model<br>• Prepare the Architecture document<br>• Collaborate on peer reviews for projects/accounts that request it<br>• It collaborates in reviews of the technical aspects of the requirements<br>• Review the Data Models<br>• Participate in the proposal to improve technical processes |

*(continued)*

**Table 1.** (*continued*)

| Role<br>RUP [RUP role] | Responsibilities |
|---|---|
| **Technical**<br>RUP [Designer] | • Ensure compliance with the guidelines and guidelines of the architecture<br>• Analyze the documentation received to detect risks and possible problems early, as well as optimizations to the solution; validates it with the Architect and, if necessary, formally informs the Project/Account Leader<br>• For cases of medium complexity, low for which the intervention of the Architect is not required, review and update the document the following topics of the Architecture document: restrictions and context of the problem, Component model, Service Model, Domain Model, and deployment model<br>• Details the analysis and design based on the requirements or use cases<br>• Prepare the detailed or technical Design document<br>• Analyze the technical feasibility of the requirements<br>• Perform code reviews<br>• Collaborate on peer reviews for projects/accounts that request it<br>• Manage your team's tasks in the available tool, generating periodic reports<br>• Ensure the correct application of the methodologies and the correct use of the selected tools<br>• Coordinates peer reviews, consolidates the results and ensures that corrections are made where appropriate<br>• Technically support the team of developers<br>• Ensure the correct versioning of the software and the correct deployment in the different environments<br>• Participate in customer interviews related to technical issues<br>• Analyze the documentation of the non-functional needs of the client<br>• Analyze non-functional requirements and propose alternatives and solutions<br>• Prepares the specification of non-functional requirements, designing/updating non-functional tests<br>• Review the results of the Smoke test<br>• Participate in customer interviews related to technical issues and answer questions to the customer about the specification of non-functional requirements<br>• Participate in the process improvement proposal |
| **Functional or Functional analyst**<br>RUP [Systems Analyst\|Requirements Specifier] | • Conduct customer interviews and presentations of current software (if any)<br>• Solve doubts about the requirements with the client<br>• Analyze the documentation of customer needs<br>• Analyze customer requirements and propose alternatives and solutions<br>• Make the specification document of the survey<br>• Perform the Functional Specifications, which may include realizing the use case model, identifying actors and detailing use cases<br>• Design or validate the Test Scenarios<br>• Verify Functional and Non-Functional Test Cases<br>• Participate in the process improvement proposal |
| **Project/Account Leader** | He is responsible for the project (Project Leader) or the service (Account Leader):<br>• Make assignments to your work team<br>• Plan the different activities<br>• It guarantees the effective development of activities<br>• Guarantees the capacity according to the planned demand<br>• Monitors performance and/or service level agreements |

(*continued*)

## Table 1. (*continued*)

| Role RUP [RUP role] | Responsibilities |
|---|---|
| **Business Specialist** RUP [Business Process Analyst] | • Identify objects and actors of the business<br>• Verify the Functional Specifications, in order to ensure their attributes<br>• Validate the proposed solution and non-functional requirements<br>• Validate the component diagram<br>• Participate in the process improvement proposal |
| **Test Leader** RUP [Test Leader] | • Design Test Plan<br>• Perform/Review estimates and schedule of test work<br>• Coordinate the operation of the test equipment<br>• Coordinate the installation in the test environment with the Integrator<br>• Determine the continuity of the tests based on the acceptance criteria<br>• Certify product quality as a result of the tests<br>• Consolidate periodic reports and closing report<br>• Analyze and evaluate the work done based on customer feedback<br>• Participate in the process improvement proposal |
| **Test Analyst** RUP [Test Analyst] | • Analyze the documentation received to detect risks and possible problems early, and validate them with the Test Leader<br>• Make estimates of the test work<br>• Design/update functional test cases for a set of Requirements or Use Cases<br>• Verify the execution of functional test cases<br>• Execute non-functional test cases<br>• Communicate results reports<br>• Participate in the process improvement proposal |
| **Tester** RUP [Tester] | • Execute Functional Test Cases<br>• Record defects and evidence of execution<br>• It supports the estimation of the test execution work<br>• Participate in the process improvement proposal |
| **Developer** RUP [Developer] | • Develop the solution code, coding a particular set of classes or class operations<br>• Perform unit or component tests<br>• Resolve software defects<br>• Participate in the process improvement proposal |
| **Deliverables Manager** | • Determine the scope of the Deliverable<br>• Define the strategy<br>• Plan tasks and resources<br>• Validate the Deliverable<br>• Participate in the process improvement proposal |
| **Responsible for Deliverables** | • Build the Deliverable<br>• Document the Installation Manual and the removal procedure<br>• Make the Delivery Note<br>• Execute the installation and removal steps<br>• Document the results and communicate to the Deliverables Manager Role<br>• Participate in the process improvement proposal |

In Table 3, we can appreciate and identify the number of requirements met by the area of operations of the organization, and the hours invested in the development of the requirements of the period.

**Table 2.** Roles and responsibilities of the client, RPF quality model.

| Role | Responsibilities |
|------|------------------|
| User | • Transmit and document business needs<br>• Clarifies and resolves l as doubts regarding the needs of the business<br>• Review and validate the documents of functional and non-functional requirements<br>• Formally validate the requirements |

**Table 3.** Requirements met in number of hours - JIRA tool.

| | | | |
|---|---|---|---|
| 200 | Periodo | 201908 | |
| 201 | Nombre de Cuenta | (Todas) | |
| 202 | Rol | (Varios elementos) | |
| 203 | | | |
| 204 | **Etiquetas de fila** | **Suma de Horas** | **Suma de Horas2** |
| 205 | ⊟ Manto Correctivo | 1.790,6 | 46,52% |
| 206 | Incidente | 364,6 | 20,36% |
| 207 | Problema | 17,0 | 0,95% |
| 208 | Petición de Servicio | 127,5 | 7,12% |
| 209 | Defecto | 948,7 | 52,98% |
| 210 | Soporte Emergente | 323,3 | 18,05% |
| 211 | Unificación | 1,0 | 0,06% |
| 212 | Unificación | 8,5 | 0,47% |
| 213 | ⊟ Manto Evolutivo | 411,4 | 10,69% |
| 214 | Devolución Cliente | 3,5 | 0,85% |
| 215 | Garantía | 7,3 | 1,76% |
| 216 | Mejoras OT | 400,7 | 97,39% |
| 217 | ⊟ Tareas Administrativas No Facturadas | 1.647,1 | 42,79% |
| 218 | Administrativa | 1.647,1 | 100,00% |
| 219 | **Total general** | **3.849,1** | **100,00%** |

## 3.5 Quality and Productivity Metrics

The organization to obtain the productivity and efficiency metrics are based on the following aspects:

(a) Developer cost
(b) Developer cost + fixed cost
(c) Amount of returns of the product delivered
(d) Number of Guarantees applied to the delivered product
(e) Planned hours
(f) Actual hours executed in the project
(g) Deviation from real hours

## 3.6 Incident Management

Two corresponding teams are assembled for the management of incidents, problems and improvements, in charge of the project leaders.

The data obtained and presented (see Table 3) with the JIRA tool, allows to identify the number of cases attended by module in the company.

# 4   Results

Taking the study time period from April to August of 2019 and based on the implementation of the SPF quality model, according to its indicators, in the 9 modules of an ERP software product developed for a customer whose Business line are insurance and reinsurance, the following results were obtained:

1. In the Accounting module, 12 findings were reported.
2. In the Collections module, 13 findings were reported.
3. In the Claims module, 10 findings were reported.
4. In the Reinsurance module, 6 findings were reported.
5. In the Commercial module, 2 findings were reported.
6. In the Billing - Income box module, 10 findings were reported.
7. In the Billing module - Cash outflow, 6 findings were reported.
8. In the SIE module, 6 findings were reported.
9. In the Reports module, 5 findings were reported.

The greatest number of findings were presented in the Collections module with 18.6%, Accounting with 17.1%, Claims with 14.36% and Billing - Cash Revenue with 14.3%. With this a priori data we can determine that the biggest problems arise in the processes and modules of the system that contain formulas, calculations and handle money, something to take into account in every information system.

The module where less problems were reported, is the Commercial, with only 2.9% of reports of findings, for the same reason stated in the previous paragraph, this module is dedicated to the management of contracts in the form of flow of the project, and has no complicated numerical calculations.

Something that attracts attention is the incidence of findings in the report module that despite being 5 cases and which constitutes 7.1% is relatively high. It's not programming defects; cases refer to changes in the structure of the reports.

There is a descending pattern in the cases reported per month (see Table 4).

**Table 4.**  Cases reported per month of study.

| Month/Year | Qty reports |
| --- | --- |
| April/2019 | 19 |
| May/2019 | 16 |
| June/2019 | 19 |
| July/2019 | 11 |
| August/2019 | 5 |

We can realize the pattern that has followed the number of cases in graphic form (See Fig. 6) where we appreciate that each month has been decreasing as the SPF quality model has been verified and modified "on the go".

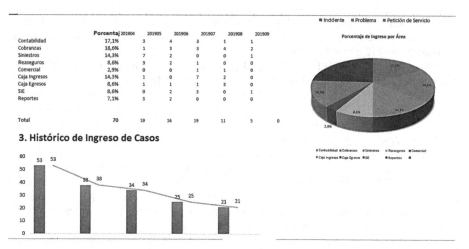

**Fig. 6.** General summary of the findings reported in the company's modules.

## 5 Conclusions

1. Since the SPF methodology was implemented in the company under study, there is a better control of incidents, based on indicators such as customer orders, inconsistency reports and audit findings, which, supported by the JIRA tool, allows to track these records, control that is made possible by taking corrective actions "on the go".

2. So far, with the implementation of the SPF, the amount of returns of software products by customers, maintains a downward trend every month, which would allow to infer that these are lower compared to previous years when this methodology was not used.

3. The largest number of reports and findings are related to the modules that handle mathematical calculations, this may suggest that greater control is needed in the development of the software product, in stages such as requirements and testing.

## 6 Future Works

To complement this work, it would be interesting to study the impact of this proposed model, in other companies or in a greater range of time, which would suggest changes to the current quality model.

## References

1. Michelena-Fernández, E., Cabrera-Monteagudo, N.: An experience in the implementation of the quality management system of a service company. Industrial Engineering 2011, XXXII January–April: consultation date: 30 January 2019. Michelena-Fernández (2011). ISSN 0258-5960

2. Manuel, G.P., Carlos, Q.A., Luis, R.G.: Continuous improvement of process quality. Industrial Data 6 August 2003: date of consultation: January 31 2019. http://www.redalyc.org/articulo. oa?id=81606112. ISSN 1560-9146
3. 90003-2018 - ISO/IEC/IEEE International Standard - software engineering - guidelines for the application of ISO 9001: 2015 to computer software (2018)
4. Velmakina, Y.V., Aleksandrova, S.V., Vasiliev, V.A.: Basics of forming an integrated management system. In: 2018 IEEE International Conference "Quality Management, Transport and Information Security, Information Technologies" (IT & QM & IS). IEEE Conferences (2018). https://ieeexplore.ieee.org/document/8524955
5. ISO, International Organization Standardization: ISO 9001: 2015 quality management systems – Requirements, Geneva, Switzerland. Online Browsing Platform (OBP) (2019). https://www.iso.org/obp/ui/#iso:std:iso:9001:ed-5:v1:es
6. Lizarzaburu Bolaños, E.R.: Quality management in Peru: a study of the ISO 9001 standard, its benefits and the main changes in the 2015 version. Universidad Empresa **18**(30), 33–54 (2016). https://doi.org/10.12804/rev.univ.empresa.30.2016.02
7. Callejas-Cuervo, M., Alarcón-Aldana, A.C., Álvarez-Carreño, A.M.: Software quality models, a state of the art. Lattice **13**(1), 236–250 (2017). https://doi.org/10.18041/entramado. 2017v13n1.25125
8. Aizprua, S., Ortega, K., Von Chong, L.: Software quality a continuous perspective. CENTROS Sci. Mag. **8**(2), 120–134 (2019). https://revistas.up.ac.pa/index.php/centros. ISSN: 2304-604X
9. Velez, A., Ormaza, M.: Quality management system for software production unit. Knowl. Pole **4**(3), 416–431 (2019). https://doi.org/10.23857/pc.v4i3.1091. https://polodelconocimiento. com/ojs/index.php/es. ISNN 2550-682X. Issue No. 31
10. Key, S.: Quality reference framework based on ISO 9001 and CMMI standards to optimize development time in software development SMEs. Technical University of Ambato. Ambato, Ecuador (2019)

# Biopotential Signals Acquisition from the Brain Through the MindWave Device: Preliminary Results

Iván Galíndez-Floréz, Andrés Coral-Flores, Edna Moncayo-Torres, Dagoberto Mayorca-Torres, and Herman Guerrero-Chapal[✉]

Facultad de Ingeniería, Universidad Mariana, Pasto-Nariño, Colombia
{igalindez,edmmoncayo,dmayorca,hhguerrero}@umariana.edu.co

**Abstract.** Brain Computer Interface (BCI) systems are the tools that allow the acquisition of biopotential signal spectra, with the most used attention, meditation and eye blinking signals. The main objective of BCI is to translate brain activity in digital form that can be used in different areas such as education, industrial, games, robotics, home automation and medical areas. In particular, this paper focuses on the acquisition and filtering of attention and meditation signals. For this, the variation and behavior of these signals are analyzed against external stimuli and in situations of stress and/or relaxation. EEG signals from the brain were captured by the MindWave Mobile device through the NeuroSky interface at a sampling rate of 1 Hz. The signals obtained are transmitted to two different devices, Arduino (At mega 328) and Raspberry Pi 3 through the Bluetooth module (HC-06) in order to compare the effectiveness of the sending and receiving times. The preliminary results in controlled scenarios allowed us identifying activities where complex mathematical calculations, meditation activities and listening to relaxing music are required. In this same sense, the comparison between the Arduino and Raspberry devices is shown.

**Keywords:** MindWave · Bluetooth · Biopotential signals · Acquisition · Attention · Meditation · Disability · Microprocessor

## 1 Introduction

The human brain is composed of a set of neural networks, which fulfill the function of transmitting information through electrochemical activity (differential electrical potential due to the change of existing ionic substances in the capture of an external stimulus in the neuron), generating the appearance of electric fields that can be called brain waves [1]. There are four main brain waves called Alpha, Beta, Theta and Delta. The brain wave or Beta rhythm can be captured in any area of the skull and is recorded in the parental and frontal areas, ". . . it has a low EEG amplitude pattern, but a high frequency" [2], it is present when a person is awake, excited or alert. The brain wave or Alpha rhythm, recorded

© Springer Nature Switzerland AG 2020
M. Botto-Tobar et al. (Eds.): ICAT 2019, CCIS 1193, pp. 139–152, 2020.
https://doi.org/10.1007/978-3-030-42517-3_11

in the region of the visual cortex (back of the head), is extremely rhythmic, but with an amplitude that increases and decreases constantly [3], it appears in people who are calm, resting in silence and especially with their eyes closed. The brain wave or Theta rhythm is identified as unconscious material, creative inspiration and deep meditation, and the brain wave or Delta rhythm, is related to deep sleep, childhood and serious illness.

BCI (Brain-Computer-Interface) systems have become a very useful tool for the development of several applications such as: trajectory and movement control, obstacle detection, lighting control, temperature, etc. We can highlight the use of BCI systems in home automation control, focused on the care of the human being through the use of biopotential signals of the brain. According to this, an EEG signal processing system is implemented in real time for the creation of home automation applications focused on people with motor disabilities. In this way, a better quality of life and lifestyle is achieved. Among the outstanding works we could mention "the implementation of biopotential signals in home automation rooms for quadriplegics" [4] and "Electronic lighting system (on-off) by controlling brai4 signals" [5] with the main objective in both works to generate a better quality of life for people with motor disabilities. One of the commercial devices that allow the collection of brain activity (using the Encephalographic recording technique) is the MindWave Mobile device which was developed by the NeuroSky company.

These measurements are carried out by placing the contact sensor on the forehead, or more specifically in the FP1 area of the brain, and the transfer node with the click on the ear, since as it works with a sensor there is only one channel to measure. The device fulfills the function of measuring the states of relaxation and attention through the use of the algorithm called eSsence that measures these levels on a scale of 0 to 100 through brain rhythms (alpha, beta, theta, etc.). The device can also capture blinking. For the acquisition and processing of EEG signals, UART communication (data transmission via Bluetooth) was performed between the MindWave Mobile device and a microprocessor, which was chosen by performing a measurement test between the Arduino and Raspberry pi, taking into account that it counts the parameters related to the collection time and data loss. In the second instance, the microprocessor defined (Raspberry pi), a study of attention and meditation was conducted with 11 people (3 men and 4 women, 50 to 60 years old), 3 older adults and a child to determine the possible differences, alterations and similar patterns that may exist in this type of measurement.

## 2    Materials and Methods

### 2.1    MindWave Mobile Interface

MindWave Mobile device acquires EEG signals; this is composed of a headband that collects brain activity and separates the signals according to the frequency. The device can be seen in Fig. 1.

**Fig. 1.** MindWave Mobile device [1].

It uses the ThinkGear AM module developed by NeuroSky, which serves as an interface between the brain and the computer. This module has a 98% reliability serving in the same way as a non-invasive medium and it is through this module that the filtration of brainwaves is done (alpha, beta, theta, etc.) obtaining the values of meditation and attention through the eSsence algorithm which works as the following: The data is sent by means of Network frame (successive series of bits, organized in cyclic form, that carry information and that allow the reception to extract this information) [6]. This data will be sent to the Serial COM port forming a package that the structure seen in Fig. 2.

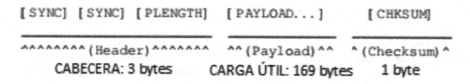

**Fig. 2.** Data package structure [7].

The Header section is composed of 3 bytes: two synchronizations [SYNC] bytes (0xAA 0xAA), followed by a [PLENGTH] (payload length) of bytes: "The two [SYNC] bytes are used to indicate the beginning of a new packet that arrives and are bytes with the value 0xAA (decimal 170). The synchronization consists of two bytes in length, instead of just one, to reduce the possibility that [SYNC] (0xAA) bytes that occur within the Package could be confused with the principle of a package" [4]. The [PAYLOAD] section has a range of up to 169 bytes in length, while each of [SYNC], [PLENGTH], and [CHECKSUM] is a single byte each, where the maximum bit value is 169 Bytes of length. It is in the [PAYLOAD] section where the meditation, attention and blinking data is sent.

## 2.2   Microcontroller-Based Data Acquisition Device

One of the microprocessors used for the acquisition and processing of the EEG signals is the Arduino which is a board based on the ATMEL microcontroller and is capable of recording programmed instructions, made by means of the arduino IDE programming language. Arduino is one of the most used microprocessors since it allows the construction of digital devices and their interaction with the real world [8], between the main features the following can be mentioned: Atmega328 microcontroller, 6 analog output pins, 14 digital pins, 32 KB flash memory, 5 v operating voltage, 7–12 v input voltage. Another of the microprocessors used for the acquisition and processing of EEG signals is the Raspberry pi which is a small board computer that is capable of supporting several necessary components in a common computer. It has an open source software where its operating system is Raspbian, but allows the use of other operating systems such as Linux or Windows 10 [9]. Among the main features can be mentioned: Broadcom processor, RAM, GPU, USB ports, HDMI, Ethernet, 40 GPIO pins, camera connector and SD card input.

### 2.3   Data Visualization

To determine and understand how the MindWave Mobile device works, NeuroSky offers a software package available for Windows, Mac and Android operating systems. As mentioned above, the device has a Bluetooth connection and it is necessary to pair the MindWave Mobile with the computer; sometimes the device requires a pairing code which is found in the instructions of the device. NeuroSky also provides a guide shown in Fig. 3 where it shows how the MindWave Mobile device should be connected, as well as the meaning of the device connection status symbols.

Through the interface shown in Fig. 4, you can see the variation of the signal that is being acquired by the MindWave Mobile device where you can observe parameters such as (Low Gamma, High Alpha, Delta, Theta, etc.) as well as the values of attention and meditation between ranges from 0 to 100.

Referring to meditation and attention, NeuroSky also provides a program called "MindWave Mobile Tutorial" whereby in addition to showing the level being measured, it also presents some tips or advice to obtain a better measurement of attention and/or meditation such as shown in Fig. 5.

Another parameter that can be meas-ured by MindWave Mobile is the blinking of the eyes by sending a value only when the subject blinks, it can be better observed in Fig. 6.

### 2.4   Data Acquisition and Processing with Arduino

For the data acquisition process of MindWave Mobile, it is necessary to decode the sent values since, as previously mentioned, these packages are sent through a net-work frame. In the case of Arduino, the NeuroSky company provides a reference code where the process of decoding and data acquisition is explained.

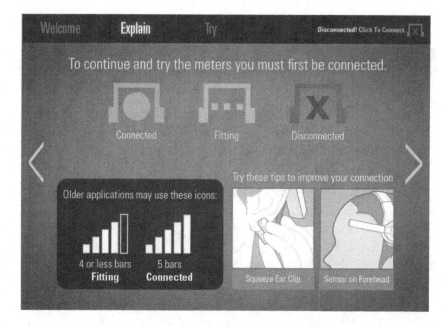

**Fig. 3.** MindWave Mobile connection guide.

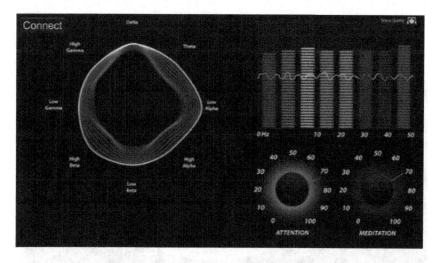

**Fig. 4.** MindWave Mobile interface.

First of all, it is necessary to perform the interface with the Arduino and since it does not have an internal Bluetooth device, it is necessary to connect an external Bluetooth device and configure it in "slave" mode so that in this way it receives the data sent from Mind-Wave Mobile. The interface is shown in Fig. 7.

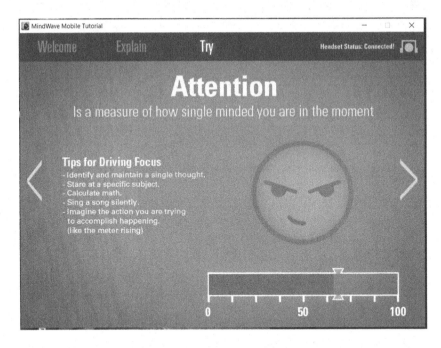

**Fig. 5.** MindWave Mobile attention tutorial.

**Fig. 6.** MindWave Mobile visualizer attention game.

**Fig. 7.** MindWave Mobile connection with Arduino and module HC-05.

The programming of the source code provided by NeuroSky begins by declaring the variables to be used and the speed at which the MindWave is already defined. It is worth mentioning the RadeOn Byte function that is used to read what the device sends and the payload length function used to determine the length of the useful data, since as the MindWave device uses the ThinkGear module for signal filtering and the sending of data, there needs to be a verification process of the data packet sent for the decoding process. This device sends the data encoded in 512 bits per second, when the Arduino detects the first bit input it has to start decoding the values and once it goes through the decoding process, it gives us the values of attention, meditation, blinking, the quality of the package (good or bad) and if there is loss of data packages.

### 2.5   Data Acquisition and Processing with Raspberry PI

For the process of acquiring data from MindWave Mobile through Raspberry pi, it is possible to use the NeuroPy library which is based on the mentality communication protocol published by NeuroSky. This library is written for Python 2.7, in which you get the values of attention, meditation, delta, theta, low Alpha, high Alpha, low Beta, high Beta, low Gamma, mid Gamma, lost signal and blinking. The programming of the source code begins by importing the NeuroPy library, then through the assignment of an object it is called the COM port where the MindWave Mobile was connected to the Raspberry pi and the speed defined by the device. Then, depending on the required value, the function is called (value required value) to then print the value obtained on the monitor. The interface is seen in Fig. 8.

**Fig. 8.** MindWave Mobile connection with Raspberry pi.

### 2.6    Experimental Setup for Attention and Meditation Signals

A study was conducted with the values of attention and meditation to determine the possible differences, alterations and similar patterns that may exist in this type of measurement. A sample of 7 people (4 Women and 3 men) with an age range of 40 to 50 years old was taken. To obtain more measurement parameters, a study was also carried out on 3 older adults (2 men and one woman) and one child. On the first instance, based on the code and ethical guidelines, an informed consent was made where the necessary and detailed information of the study is made known in an understandable way where it is specified that the use of the data obtained will be used only for educational purposes and cannot be used for commercial purposes, in the same way personal data will be handled anonymously.

**Test Attention.** The estimated time of this test was two minutes. First, the MindWave Mobile was placed on the subject's head and an initial test was performed to see if there was the sending of data, then he was asked to mentally perform a series of specific multiplication problems with a certain degree of complexity, initially with his eyes open and then with his eyes closed. After that, it was requested that with his eyes closed, he focuses on specific dates (birthdate or important moments) and finally, he was asked to try to describe a place with specific detail.

**Test Meditation.** The estimated time was two minutes. The subject was first asked to relax and start breathing slowly, then he was asked to breathe deeply and close his eyes. While in this state, he was asked to think about a nice time while listening to relaxing music and finally, the subject was asked to open his eyes slowly.

# 3  Results and Discussions

Around the decision that the microprocessor meets the needs required for the data acquisition and coding process of the MindWave Mobile, a sample of 71 data was taken from the attention variable in both the Raspberry pi and the Arduino. The resulting Arduino and Raspberry pi graphs are shown in Fig. 9.

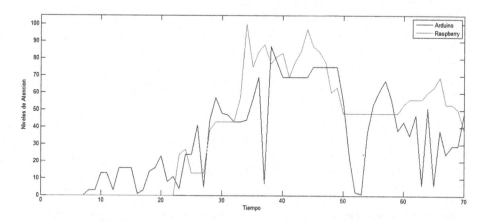

**Fig. 9.** Arduino vs Raspberry pi.

Figure 10 shows the resulting graph comparing the attention values obtained in the 3 men from 40 to 50 years old.

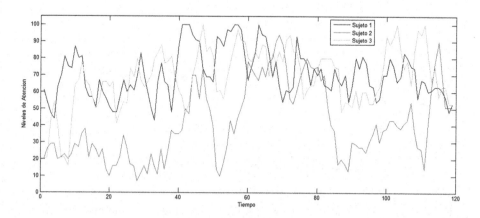

**Fig. 10.** Test men attention 40–50 years old.

Figure 11 shows the resulting graph comparing the meditation values obtained in the 3 men from 40 to 50 years old.

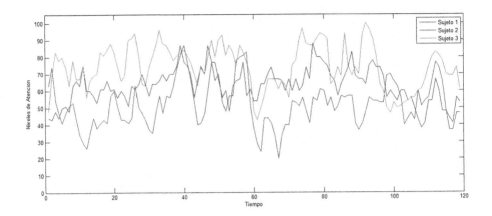

**Fig. 11.** Test men meditation 40–50 years old.

Figure 12 shows the resulting graph comparing the attention values obtained in the 4 women from 40 to 50 years old.

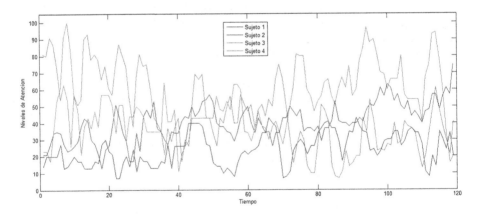

**Fig. 12.** Test women attention 40–50 years old.

Figure 13 shows the resulting graph comparing the meditation values obtained in the 4 women from 40 to 50 years old.

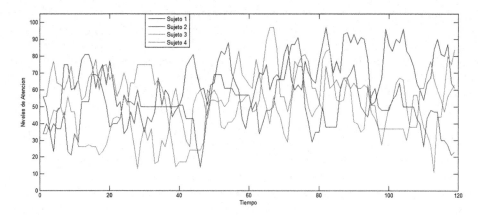

**Fig. 13.** Test women meditation 40–50 years old.

Figure 14 shows the resulting graph comparing the attention values obtained from older adults.

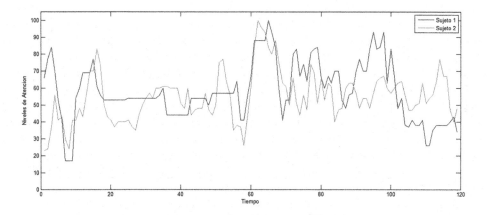

**Fig. 14.** Test older adults attention.

Figure 15 shows the resulting graph comparing the meditation values obtained from older adults.

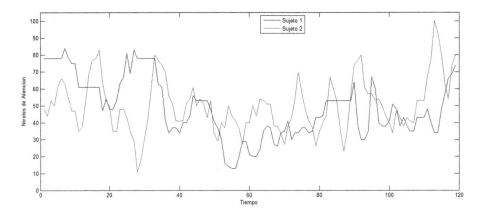

**Fig. 15.** Test older adults attention.

Figure 16 shows the resulting graph comparing the attention values obtained from the older adults and the child.

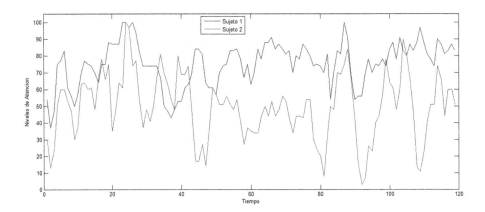

**Fig. 16.** Test older adults attention.

Figure 17 shows the resulting graph comparing the meditation values obtained from the older adults and the child.

As shown in Fig. 9, it can be seen that the Arduino obtains in a shorter time the data sent from the MindWave Mobile, unlike the Raspberry pi that needs a longer acquisition time. You can also see that with the Arduino, there is a greater loss of data and therefore there is a greater number of peaks and alterations, unlike the Raspberry pi that presents a greater stability in the data obtained. That is why the microprocessor Raspberry pi was used to study the values of attention and meditation. Another of the present advantages with the Raspberry pi is the making of the BCI system because this microprocessor presents the necessary capacities and characteristics for the creation of the domotic system.

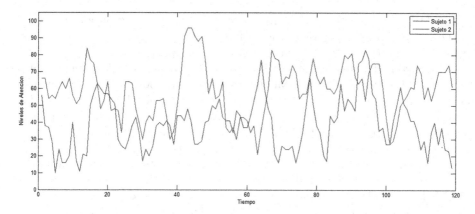

**Fig. 17.** Test older adults attention.

In Fig. 10, where the data for the men between ages 40–50 is expressed, it is observed that two of the three subjects have high values in comparison to subject 2; however, it is also observed that every time there is a peak, all the subjects are impacted, but in different amplitudes and therefore, at different times where you can see that there is a reason for the rise and fall, since the three subjects were subjected to the same procedure and under the same conditions. On the other hand, in Fig. 11, where the data for the meditation test of men between ages 40–50 is expressed, a reason for the rise and falls can also be observed, but this one instead has more alterations compared to Fig. 10. With the women between ages 40–50, the same comparison can be made with the men's graphs, although with the exception of subject 1 and subject 2 where a low amplitude and no reason for peaks can be seen (Fig. 12), where the values for the attention test are expressed, but it can be said that in comparison to this in Fig. 13, their meditation was higher. In the same way, Fig. 14 gives the reason to the previous figures of attention in which it has reason in the two subjects, but instead with this one, it's possible to note that there are slower and of lower amplitude and time. In Fig. 16, where the data for the two older adults' meditation test is expressed, a greater stability can be observed in both cases, few peaks in the data and finally, in comparison to Fig. 17, it has peaks of attention however it's not possible to differentiate very well since it is too close to the other signs.

The feasibility of the use of the MindWave Mobile device in the creation of BCI systems focused on domotic applications is validated in the study carried out and in the data collected on brain activity, since it presents the necessary requirements for a good acquisition and collection of EEG signals presented in attention and meditation values [5].

## 4   Conclusions

Analyzing the data obtained, it can be concluded that it is possible to use the Mind-Wave Mobile device for the acquisition and collection of brain activity.

It should be noted that it is possible to perform the acquisition and decoding of the signals through the use of the Arduino and Raspberry pi microprocessors (this being more suitable for the purposes of the project) and through these applications in the creation of a BCI system in home automation applications. In general, the use of biopotential signals for the creation of BCI systems can be determined, with the main objective of presenting an alternative to people suffering from motor disabilities, in order to provide them with an improved lifestyle and a better quality of life. Based on the study in particular, it was determined that the amplitude of the wave depends on the mood of the person and external factors (noise and ambient lighting). This is better reflected in the differences in age since a child can concentrate faster than an older adult, but unlike this he fails to maintain this concentration for a long time since he is more exposed to being altered by the above-mentioned factors. Unlike the case of meditation in which older adults can relax more easily than children but do not manage to maintain this state for a long time.

## References

1. Calderón, D.: Procesamiento de ondas cerebrales con microprocesador ARM para control de coche teledirigido (2016)
2. Vaca, E.: Prototipo de prótesis de un brazo con 12 DGL controlada mediante ondas cere-brales (2017)
3. Kolb, B., Whishaw, I.: Neuropsicología Humana, 5th edn. Panamericana (2017)
4. Ayala, J., Bautista, D., Espíndola A.: Implementación de señales electro encefálicas a un prototipo de habitación domótica para pacientes cuadripléjicos. Instituto Politécnico (2015)
5. Guevara, M.: Sistema electrónico de iluminación (on-off) mediante el control de señales cerebrales basado en tecnología eeg. Universidad técnica del Norte, Ibarra (2015)
6. Hernández, A.: Desarrollo e implementación de una interfaz de comunicación que permita la interacción entre un usuario y las señales emitidas por sus ondas cerebrales usando un dispositivo de eeg de NeuroSKy para controlar periféricos electrónicos (2014)
7. García, l.: Control del robot IRB120 mediante el casco de electroencefalografía Neurosky MindWave (2017)
8. Arduino. https://www.arduino.cc. Accessed 13 Oct 2019
9. Raspberrypi. https://www.raspberrypi.org. Accessed 13 Oct 2019

# Software Components of an IoT Monitoring Platform in Google Cloud Platform: A Descriptive Research and an Architectural Proposal

Billy Grados[(✉)] and Hector Bedon[(✉)]

Exponential Technology Group (GITX-ULIMA), Instituto de Investigación Científica (IDIC),
Universidad de Lima, Lima, Peru
{bgrados,hbedon}@ulima.edu.pe

**Abstract.** As software engineers, it is not an easy task to build a software solution that customers consider easy to use, cost-benefit balanced, secured, high available and prepared for high demand. There are many solutions for building a monitoring platform with these previous attributes and we need to consider all the technical factors to achieve this goal. We proposed an agile methodology for the project management approach, acquired the necessary equipment and services and hired the staff to design and develop a monitoring platform in Google Cloud Platform (GCP) with edge frameworks and technologies. We implemented a software working solution composed of five applications (app) or services and configured services in the GCP: IoT data web service, frontend web app, backend web app, IoT app, and mobile app. They were developed using Python, ReactJS, and Java and deployed in Google Cloud Platform for being used in personal computers, laptops, mobile devices, and IoT devices. We defined this architecture with its main basis in a cloud platform that used the publish/subscribe pattern for efficient data ingestion and reporting.

**Keywords:** IoT · MQTT · Monitoring system · Cloud computing · Software engineering

## 1 Introduction

As Drucker stated "What gets measured, gets managed" [1], the measurement of variables is important to improve the performance of our long-term goals. Internet of Things (IoT) is a technology trend that helps to measure domestic or industrial variables through Internet-connected devices like sensors, smartphones, computers, buildings, and home/work appliances [2]. For example, in smart buildings, if a temperature sensor is below an established limit, the air-conditioner increases its temperature to regulate it. This principle was the basis to achieve better performance rates in different industries: logistics [3], food [4], healthcare [5], sports [6], agriculture [7], fishing [8].

There are different ways to accomplish this process of measurement and it covers physical devices and software components from the connected things to the benefited

© Springer Nature Switzerland AG 2020
M. Botto-Tobar et al. (Eds.): ICAT 2019, CCIS 1193, pp. 153–167, 2020.
https://doi.org/10.1007/978-3-030-42517-3_12

end-users. One main component is where the data is stored, processed and computed. Edge computing [9] means that compute, storage and network are done locally (servers near the connected devices). Fog computing [10] is the computing done in large-scale connected devices to avoid high latency by sending to centralized servers. And Cloud computing is done in a centralized specialized data center like IBM Cloud [11], Amazon Web Services (AWS) [12], Microsoft Azure [13], and Google Cloud Platform (GCP) [14]. Every cloud service has its challenges and advantages. GCP was acquired as part of the project plan and it has more than thirty services, which were offered free in special usage rates. And, there are different frameworks for developing real backend, frontend and mobile software projects in the software industry [15]. However, what GCP services, what cutting-edge frameworks, what configuration, and how to use was not specified in any plan. We defined the backend software to help to manage the data by admin users, the frontend and mobile components to monitor the IoT data and all the necessary configurations for the cloud-computing platform in a detail proven manner. It is important to have the overall picture of the proposed architecture as explained in a study [16], but it is also relevant to have the specification. This research explains in Sect. 2 the elements that were considered for the development process, in Sect. 3 the overview of the architecture and a detail explanation of the software components (IoT app, IoT data web service, backend, frontend and mobile apps, and the datastore and SQL configuration), in Sects. 4 and 5, the conclusions and considerations.

## 2  Materials and Methods

We have proposed the design and development of an IoT platform for monitoring ecosystems for two projects: QSA "a real-time intelligent rural platform prototype to increase the productivity in the organic Quinoa value chain" (since January) and MPA "a real-time monitoring prototype to optimize artisanal fishing in order to improve the productivity of artisanal fishermen" (since November 2018).

In this research, we focused on the software development process, but this IoT platform had the administrative, hardware and software teams, and the end-users. For MPA, they were fishermen. For QSA, they were quinoa farmers.

As a software team, we used special equipment and materials to develop the IoT platform. Google Cloud Platform was acquired for developing and testing.

Nevertheless, these specifications were not limiting the use of other services. Therefore, we used other services as detailed in the Results section. We used the GCP console and gcloud command-line tool to configure the services.

We used SCRUM, an agile methodology for software development, as the framework for completing the goals in timeboxed iterations called sprints that last one week. During every sprint, we planned daily meetings from Monday to Friday and we used a whiteboard called Scrum board to centralize the status of the tasks. Each schedule was part-time and different from another team member. We communicate through WhatsApp in determined occasions. Every Friday, we showed the progress to all the team or to the administrative leader who was the coordinator of the projects.

The purpose of this IoT platform was the increment of productivity for farmers and artisanal fishermen. Both projects depended on a monitoring platform. In agriculture, for example, it helped to irrigate the soil if its humidity level is below a limit. In the fishing, it helped to gather data to elaborate a model for predicting the fish location in the sea. For that reason, the minimal requirements to accomplish were:

1. As an admin, I must manage users and IoT devices credentials in the system
2. As an IoT expert, I must configure the units of measurement, sensors, stations, and gateways in the backend app and the credentials in the IoT device app
3. As a researcher, I must visualize the monitoring data in the web and mobile apps
4. As a researcher, I must download the data in the web app.
   It is important for the projects that the platform must not lose the data.

# 3   Results

We build a monitoring platform to achieve the goals of the projects. We designed the components that Fig. 1 shows. All the main components were running or stored in the Google Cloud Platform (GCP). In the case of the Android mobile application (app), the users downloaded from the GCP and installed in their mobile devices with Android Operative System (OS). In consequence, the mobile app was the only one running on the user mobile device. In the case of the frontend web app or the backend web app, the users used their preferred web browser to interact with the system through their Personal Computers (PC) or laptops. For the frontend web app, the server sent the whole app to the browser and it stored the app in its cache (temporal storage in the web browser). These two apps depended on the IoT data web service and the API of the backend web app. For the backend web app, the server processed the Python code and sent a response in HTML5 (Hyper-Text Markup Language) along with other resources as images, CSS (Cascade Style Sheet), and JavaScript files to the web browser in every request of the users. Internally, the backend web app communicated to the IoT data web service to deliver IoT data through its API in a more convenient way to the frontend and mobile apps when it was necessary. In the case of the IoT app, we designed it to be a bridge between the software developed by the hardware team to gather the data from all the sensors and the GCP.

## 3.1   The Google Cloud Platform

We designed the components in the GCP as Fig. 2 depicts. The flow of the sensed data from the IoT device to the user web browser or mobile app was initiated from the software programmed by the hardware team to capture the data of the sensors and to send it to the GCP through the IoT app. The first component that received and processed that data was the IoT Core. We used its IoT Core registry to configure it with the authorized IoT devices. In the IoT device, e configured the IoT app with the GCP credentials and required parameters to send the data. The cloud Pub/Sub (Publish and Subscribe service) is a real-time messaging service that allows us to manage the data ingestion without bottlenecks and without dependencies. We subscribed a cloud function to a topic in the Pub/Sub service. Therefore, when a new message with the sensed data arrived at the IoT Core,

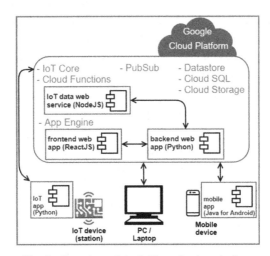

**Fig. 1.** Overview of the IoT monitoring platform

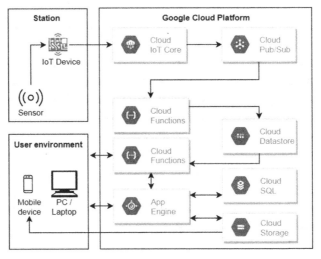

**Fig. 2.** Overview of the components in the Google Cloud Platform

it sent the data to our cloud function that executed the code and then stopped it without consuming resources as an entire application, container or virtual machine. The cloud function was programmed to store the data in the Cloud Datastore that is a NoSQL database. The other part of the flow that stored every new sensed data from the IoT device to the Datastore was initiated from the user that started the frontend or the mobile app in its user environment (PC/Laptop or mobile device respectively) to monitor the stations. These apps authenticated the user in the backend app and authorized the user to retrieve the sensed data from the Cloud Datastore through another Cloud function. The backend used the Cloud SQL to store the users' credentials and what stations they were authorized to monitor. The backend and frontend were running on an App Engine that permitted us to deploy them in Google servers. The mobile app was downloaded from the Cloud Storage. We stored the APK (Android application package file) in a specific folder that was linked from the backend app. Cloud Storage is a storage service in the GCP.

## 3.2   The IoT App

The purpose of the IoT app was to send the monitoring data to GCP. In spite of the details of the physical architecture are out of the scope of this research, we can include some general information about it. The flow of the data was in the following sequence. There were two ways of implementing a station. In the station way, the sensors were connected to the IoT Device in every station through a wire connection. In the station with a gateway, the sensors were connected to a station IoT device using wires. The IoT device was using Raspbian OS in a Raspberry Pi hardware. On the other hand, the communication between the station and the gateway was through XBee which is a radio module to communicate wireless between devices. The station was an Arduino based hardware and the gateway was a Raspberry based hardware.

The IoT app was developed in Python programming language. We used the MQTT protocol (Message Queue Telemetry Transport that is a machine-to-machine protocol or Internet of Things protocol). MQTT was designed as an extremely lightweight publish/subscribe messaging transport and IoT Core of the GCP supports it. We delivered it to the hardware team as a library. It has two main files: the config.py and the __init__.py. There are important lines that determined the endpoint where we sent the data.

- project_id and gcp_location are related to the GCP account and the GCP region
- registry_id is the name of the registry (we used quinoa for QSA project and monipez for MPA project)
- device_id is the device identifier.
- local_db_name is the name of the local SQLite database

We developed the library considering easy-to-use as its main advantage. They had to instantiate the library that we called IotSocket passing the mode parameter mode=Immediate to immediately send the data to GCP and has_log=True to show a log in the command line console. It had a station_data dictionary holding the following information: station_id, cruise (only for MPA), substation (only for MPA), timestamp, latitude, longitude, height, sensors. Every sensor data had the following information: id and its output. id was a unique identifier number that was generated in the backend system. The sensors attribute was a dictionary: one key per id and the sensor output as its value.

MQTT is well known to handle communication interruptions. Nevertheless, if the power supply powered off and MQTT had a queue with pending messages to send, this data was lost. For that reason, we implemented an algorithm to handle that scenario. We stored the data in a local SQLite database. We used the following statuses for every sent data: unsent, sent, and published. In this scenario, the data was in sent status. In the next restart of the IoT device, the program updated every sent data as unsent, and it retried to send them through MQTT until MQTT confirmed them as published.

We followed the façade pattern that is a software design pattern to encapsulate the interaction between the MQTTAdapter class responsible for the MQTT handling in the MQTTAdapter.py and the DBAdapter class in the DBAdapter.py responsible for storing the data in SQLite.

### 3.3  The IoT Data Web Service

IoT data web service had two cloud functions: one responsible for storing the sensed data in the Cloud Datastore and one responsible for retrieving the stored data and presenting to the requestor component.

**Storing Data Function.** It was a NodeJS function. The method sendPubSubToData-Store was defined in the main file index.js and was configured in the Cloud functions option in the GCP console where we defined: (1) Trigger: Pub/Sub. (2) Topic: monitoring. We had defined it in Pub/Sub option in the GCP console. We added the prefixes monipez or quinua for each project. (3) Function to execute: sendPubSubToDataStore.

The sendPubSubToDataStore method had the parameter with the sensed data from the IoT device sent through IoT Core and Pub/Sub. It had a data attribute with the Pub/Sub message encoded in base64. This message was decoded using the safe-buffer library and parsed to a JSON object. To store the data, we used one main entity called sensordata and three secondary stores to help the information retrieving. In order to create the entities, and to insert new data, we used the @google-cloud/datastore library. The method also processed the data and generated station entity, cruise, and cruise_substation. The last two were only generated for monipez project. Station had id, height, latitude, longitude, timestamp and sensor attributes. Sensor had the last values for that station. Cruise entity had station_id (the identifier for the station), cruise (a correlative number defined before every sea expedition), finish (timestamp) and start (timestamp). cruise_substation entity had the same attributes of the cruise except for substation that was a correlative number defined in every stop during the sea expedition.

**Retrieving Data Function.** It was a NodeJS application running on an express server. The main file was index.js that executed the werbserver.js file where we configured the express server with CORS (Cross-origin resource sharing) to avoid Chrome web browser blocks the frontend app to access an endpoint of different domain. webserver.js worked with the class Monitoring that worked with MonitoringDAO. It imported the underscore library to facilitate the data manipulation and @google-cloud/datastore library to retrieve the datastore data. It had the public methods: (1) getStations: it retrieved the information from station entity, (2) getSensorsByStation (id, since, until, cruise, substation, ids, config): it retrieved the information from sensordata entity and outputs array of JSON objects with id (identifier of the sensor), last_value, and values. Values was an array of JSON objects with timestamp and value (the sensor output). It accepted since and until parameter to filter the data in that timestamp range. It used the cruise and substation parameters to filter the data with these attributes. ids were used as separated comma values to filter what sensors were returned. Config helped to return the timestamps in seconds or milliseconds. (3) getCruises: it retrieved the cruise entity. It was an array of JSON objects with the start and finish timestamps of the sea expedition and an array of id of stations called station_id that were participating in the expedition. (4) getCruise (start, finish, station_id): it retrieve the cruise_substation entity. We used the parameters start, finish and station_id to filter the returned data.

The express server exposed the above methods through the following endpoints that were requested using HTTP GET method:

- getStations:/stations
- getSensorsByStation:
  /stations/{station_id}/sensors{?sensor_ids,since,until,cruise,substation}

  – station_id was a station identifier
  – sensor_ids, since, until, cruise, substation and millis were used concatenating with equals symbol (=) and its value. Every parameter was separated with ampersand symbol (&). millis=1 was used for expecting milliseconds in timestamp and millis=0 for seconds.

- getCruises:/cruises
- getCruise:/cruises/substations{?station_id, start, finish}

  – station_id was a station identifier
  – start and finish were used concatenating with equals symbol (=) and its value. Every parameter was separated with ampersand symbol (&)

As these requests used filters, the datastore queries had to use indexes that were defined in a file index.yml with the defined structure. kind_name refers to the datastore entity, property_one and property_two refer to properties that are indexed. We configured them using the command "gcloud datastore indexes create index.yml". The entities and its properties were: (1) monipez_cruise_substation: station_id, start. (2) monipez_sensordata: station_id, timestamp. (3) monipez_sensordata: cruise, substation, timestamp. (4) monipez_sensordata: cruise, timestamp. (5) quinua_sensordata: station_id, timestamp.

### 3.4  The Backend Web App

The admin users managed the access and the IoT experts managed the IoT data in this application written in Python programming language. The Fig. 3 explains that the Users entity has many Roles; an Association has many Users and many Zones. An Association is an organization where the user belongs to, and the Zone is the geographical location where the IoT monitoring hardware is deployed. There were two logical types of stations: gateways and stations (logical stations to avoid misunderstandings). Gateways were defined as a centralized station that had many logical Stations. However, we had two configurations for physical stations: (1) one gateway and one logical station corresponded to one physical station, and (2) one gateway corresponded to one physical station, and one logical station corresponded to one physical station.

Every Station had one or more Sensors. Every Sensor had one corresponding MeasurementMagnitudes. We managed the following data:

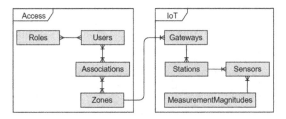

**Fig. 3.** The Entity-Relation diagram with Access and IoT modules

- Users: First name, Last name, Email, Password (an encrypted value handling by the app), Phone, Address, Active (True or False), Roles (one or more related to that entity), Associations (one or more related to that entity)
- Roles: Name, Description
- Associations: Name, Commercial name, Description, Email, Phone, Address
- Zones: Name, Description, Latitude, Longitude, Radius (around latitude and longitude), Association (one or more related to that entity). We related one Zone to one Association in practice.
- Gateways: Name, Description, Zone (one related to that entity)
- Stations: Name, Description, Gateway (one related to that entity)
- Sensors: Name, Description, Station (one related to that entity), Magnitude (one related to MeasurementMagnitudes)
- MeasurementMagnitudes: Name, Unit

This data was stored in a MySQL 2nd Gen 5.7 database that we configured its instance as "db-g1-small" machine type with one virtual CPU and 1.7 GB of RAM for development, testing, and production. "db-n1-standard-1" was the recommended configuration for the production environment. The storage configured was 10 GB. We disabled the backup and replicas for the development environment. Enabling backups was the recommended configuration for the production environment.

Backend application was deployed in the App Engine service of GCP using the command-line tool gcloud. The entry point was defined with "gunicorn-b:8081 main:app" in the app.yml file. Gunicorn is Web Server Gateway Interface (WSGI) HTTP Server that forwards requests to our Python application. GUnicorn called the main.py file that instance/__init__.py where was configured to use the following external libraries:

- Flask is a lightweight WSGI web application framework to build web services with very little overhead.
- Flask Admin is a micro-framework for Flask that builds a user-friendly admin interface on top of our existing data model. The framework was configured to let users to manage the explained data model for Access and IoT.
- Flask Security allows to quickly add common security mechanisms to a Flask application
- SQLAlchemy is the Python SQL toolkit and Object Relational Mapper used by Flask-Admin.

It had a login screen with email and password input boxes. The options showed in the admin interface were User, Role, Association, Zone for Access module, and Medition Magnitude, Gateway, Station, and Sensor for IOT module. Every option shows an admin interface for its corresponding Entity. A records list is the first shown screen with the options: "Create" (to insert a new record in the database), "Edit" (to update a record in the database. It is shown as a pencil icon) and "Delete" (shown as trashcan icon). It had a pagination button bar on the bottom of the screen. It was configured 20 rows per page; in consequence, button "2" retrieved the next 20 rows after the 20 rows of page "1". It also had a logout option in the top right part of the web page where the email of the logged user was.

The Create screen had the input fields for its respective Entity. For relationship fields, it had a select box with the related Entity id and name as an option. For example, "1-Test Station" was the first option for the station of id "1" and the name "Test Station" in Stations entity. It had "Save" option that returned to List screen after saving the data, "Save and Add Another" to save and execute the Create option again, "Save and Continue Editing" to save and stay in this same screen, and "Cancel" to return to the previous screen without saving. "Created" and "Updated" were automatic fields managed by the Flask-Admin framework.

"Edit" option in List screen showed a similar screen to "Create" but with the retrieved data. There was a new tab called Edit next to "List" and "Create" tabs. "Delete" option removed the record and displayed the message "Record was successfully deleted" inside a green box on the top of the list. In the case of many to many relationships, we configured an autocomplete input box to indicate the entities that the created or edited entity was related. The admin added or removed related entities in this box. For date-time fields that were not managed automatically by the framework, it had a date time picker that displayed a calendar and time select box.

In the file instance/__config.py used by instance/__init__.py, we had the main configuration for Flask, SQLAlchemy, and other values:

- Flask used SECRET_KEY to secure session
- SQLAlchemy used DATABASE_URI to define the connection string with the database engine, user, password, the database name, and the socket that had the project_id (GCP google account id), region and project name that was quinua or monipez. It also set up the engine options like the size of the open connections pool, and the seconds after the open connection were closed for recycling. All its values were prefixed by SQLALCHEMY_
- Flask Security extension needed the URL_PREFIX, password hash that was the algorithm used to encrypt and store the password using the salt value and other values. For example: if a user was able to register and receive a registration email; the routes or URL for security module. All its values were prefixed by SECURITY_

We had configured two environments: development and production. For that reason, the configuration file had a variable called app_config with the differentiated configurations: different database URI, if debug or test was activated.

### 3.5   The Frontend Web App

The frontend web app and the mobile app were more different between projects than the backend app. They have a different look and feel, and a different way to access the monitoring data. We had two types of physical stations: fixed and mobile. QSA only had fixed stations, on the other hand, MPA had fixed and mobile stations. The fish researcher used the mobile stations when they went to explore the sea to gather fish data. They called this exploration or sea expedition "cruise". Therefore, the users in MPA accessed the monitoring data through the expeditions for the mobile stations. The mobile stations had two types based on its monitoring duration: the whole cruise type and the type of the stop. This last type was also called "substations" in spite of the fish researchers were used to called "stations". We used the substations word to avoid a conflict with the stations definition already stated.

The frontend web app was accessed through the login form that had email and password fields. The monitoring option displayed a map with markers that were the fixed stations. For MPA, it displayed two options: "See cruises" and "See fixed stations". The last option was similar to QSA. The first one showed select boxes to choose the date and the cruise correlative number, and a map. After the user picked a date and cruise, it displayed a floating action button to show the whole cruise stations type and a polygon with markers in every stop of the cruise. After clicking the action button or the markers, it showed the sensors screen for the selected station, substation and cruise. A similar sensors screen was shown for QSA after clicking the markers. See Fig. 4 which is part of this screen. The users selected one or two sensors and optionally filtered the date range using a widget that had shortcuts for fast selecting date ranges: today, yesterday, this week, last week, this month, last month, this year. This widget allowed the user to pick a specific start date and finish date. After this step, the graph data appeared. The graph was a line chart with dots as the exact sensed values and the lines as the trend. The left Y-axis had the magnitude values of one selected sensor and the right Y-axis had values of the other one. X-axis had date-time values. In the case of MPA, the preferred selected sensor was depth for the left Y-axis and another sensor for the X-axis. Date time values were only used in fixed stations.

Frontend application was deployed in GCP App Engine service using the command "gcloud app deploy build/app.yaml". app.yml among the generated files by a tool called webpack were deployed. We used python 2.7 to handle static resource requests and sending the index.html as the main route which requested the *.js file and *.js.map files.

We used ReactJS as the main frontend framework with TypeScript programming language to build the web user interfaces and other libraries:

- ReactJS: the started file to inspect was src/index.tsx
- Bootstrap: an HTML, CSS, and JS toolkit to build the look and feel of the web. It was defined in the src/index.html file that imported bootstrap.min.css file.
- NPM (Node Package Manager): a tool for managing library dependencies. It also lets us create scripts in a package.json file. We executed webpack through npm.
- Webpack: a tool to bundle all our project assets like.tsx files. Its configuration was in webpack.config.js file. It bundled the entire ReactJS project into bundle.js, and

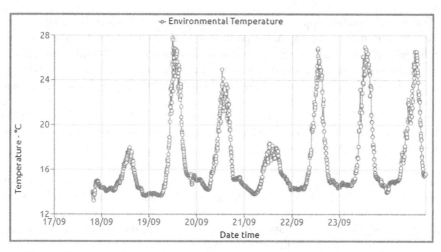

**Fig. 4.** Example of data graph for a selected sensor and range in the sensors screen

modifies the index.html file including the generated file. The bundle.js and the new index.html were generated in the build folder.

- JS: JavaScript programming language
- JSX: A JavaScript extension that lets the users write HTML code inside JS.
- TSX: similar to JSX but using TypeScript.
- TypeScript: ts or tsx were its file extension. It was configured with tsconfig.json that was used by the webpack loader "awesome-typescript-loader" to convert the.ts or.tsx files to.js files.
- Redux: a predictable state container for single-page applications. It was used with React and it stablished a scalable architecture. It defined one way to changes the application state with action objects and reducer functions. Reducers returned objects to control the way the state changed.
- Redux Thunk: it is a middleware for redux to let us use functions as actions in order to achieve things like executing asynchronous operations.
- UI components: react-date-range for choosing dates and date ranges with shortcut links, react-datepicker for picking a single date, recharts for graphs.

### 3.6 The Mobile App

The frontend web app and the mobile app were very similar in IoT monitoring terms. The mobile had the option to choose fixed or mobile stations, and to pick the cruise on a specific date for MPA. It had the same consideration for graphs: preferred depth in MPA, and date-time for fixed stations. The main difference was the dimensions of the screen. For that reason, we split the sensors screen: one for selecting, another to see overview data of that chosen sensor, and other to see the graph after clicking the see graph option in the overview screen. The overview screen showed the last, average, maximum and minimum value for the current day. For fixed stations, the graph screen showed two date pickers to filter the data by a date range.

The Android mobile app was developed with Android Studio in Java. There were two configuration files to compile the project in APK (Android Application Package) file: the build.gradle with two main dependencies (com.android.tools.build:gradle:3.4.1, and com.google.gms:google-services:4.2.0) and the app/build.gradle with minSdkVersion 23 (Marshmallow: Android 6.0–6.0.1), targetSdkVersion 28 (Pie: Android 9.0) and compileSdkVersion 28. The SDK was the Software Development Kit to compile the application. The minimum required version to run the app was 23 and the target was 28 that we used to compile the app. We used the Java 1.8 version to write the code. The dependencies to highlight were:

- AndroidX (androidx.appcompat:appcompat:1.1.0-beta01, androidx.constraintlayout: constraintlayout:2.0.0-beta1): It was recommended to add compatibility support to a new component for 23 version devices and above.
- Material Design (com.google.android.material:material:1.0.0-alpha1): library to give the material look and feel to the application.
- Google Maps (com.google.android.gms:play-services-maps:16.0.0): to show Google Maps in the monitoring screen
- MP Android Chart (com.github.PhilJay:MPAndroidChart:v3.1.0) for graphs.

We only requested INTERNET, ACCESS_FINE_LOCATION and ACCESS_COARSE_LOCATION in app/src/main/AndroidManifest.xml file to access the internet and GPS information of the mobile device. We configured two main activities: login and logged-in. Every screen detailed above were Fragment components.

Frontend and mobile apps were using the REST services of the backend to authenticate and authorize the users for stations and sensors. Then, these apps used the IoT data web service to retrieve the IoT data. The request and responses were in JSON format. Each client app parsed the data to present it to the users. In ReactJS, JSON objects were part of the code, in contrast, the org.json.JSONArray, and org.json.JSONObject was imported in the code to parse the data from JSON to Java objects.

After the APK file was generated, we used Google Storage to upload the file that was referenced by a single HTML page that was deployed with the backend application. We also used this Google Service to store additional files or assets that belong to other project modules.

### 3.7  The Cost

As we can see in Table 1, the more expensive is Cloud SQL. Stackdriver logging was part of the logging service for the deployed applications and Build was used in every deployment that the team made.

The Cloud SQL cost increased when we changed from micro to small machine type as shown in Fig. 5. The cost of a small instance is around three times of micro. For these projects, we determined a small instance as the instance to work. The Storage in Persistent Disk in Solid State Disk was $0.11 per day, the Micro was $0.25 per day, and the Small was $0.84 per day. This change occurred on August 27. Hence, the estimated average cost per month in the production environment was $53.7. Cloud Build, Cloud Functions, Cloud IoT Core, Cloud Pub/Sub, Stackdriver Logging were $0.00.

**Table 1.** Costs by products from July 2019 to September 25, 2019

| Google product | July | August | September | Total |
|---|---|---|---|---|
| Cloud SQL | $9.21 | $21.66 | $28.93 | $59.79 |
| Maps API | | $1.08 | $0.47 | $1.55 |
| App Engine | | $0.24 | $0.04 | $0.28 |
| Cloud Storage | | $0.01 | $0.01 | $0.02 |

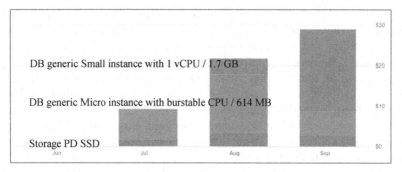

**Fig. 5.** Cloud SQL cost by SKU from June 2019 to September 25, 2019

## 4 Discussion

The main obstacle and the biggest expensive costs were trying to implement a pipeline of data ingestion through a more complex service called Dataflow. The costs were $20 per day only in this service. The project lost $600 in one month. We were notified when the estimated consumption of the credit was near 90%. We abandoned Dataflow approach. One way to reduce costs is to centralize all the backend information in one instance with one database per each project. GCP charges by the number of running instances, and not by the number of databases. IoT data storage cost was practically zero. We realized that using micro machine type in Cloud SQL was causing an out of memory error that generated unexpected database-closed connections provoking 500 error in the apps.

Two studies [2], and [17] considered cloud computing for IoT, but the later one implemented edge computing between IoT devices and cloud computing to improve the responses near the IoT devices. We didn't implement edge computing, but we are planning for further research. Both studies didn't have a detailed level as our study. We had explained in more detail how to implement our proposed architecture in a specific cloud like GCP.

GCP was easy to use (i.e. configure in admin panel) and deploy the solutions (through the command line tool) and it helped to control the authentication in the IoT devices through IoT Core.

TypeScript helped to identify bugs or logical problems, but it was difficult to set up libraries that did not have types. It added extra steps to configure them and more lines of code to implement features. ES6 as considered a better selection to start a ReactJS project. Redux is a simple library but the team did not understand clearly in the first weeks because it is a new paradigm for programing one single page applications.

## 5   Conclusions

This study shows the overview of the architecture and its detailed specification to accomplish the developing of an IoT Cloud monitoring platform by assembling different components: hardware, software, technologies, and cloud services. This approach is efficient in benefit-cost and is tested in two projects from the agriculture and fishing industries. We provide more detail than other studies for the benefit of researchers and developers that need an efficient solution for monitoring variables in its field of study or processes in companies, and the necessary information to accomplish it.

We explained all the elements that a software team should consider for running a monitoring platform with IoT devices and GCP: the overall architecture, the main frameworks and programming languages (Python, JavaScript, TypeScript and Java), the main cloud services from GCP (IoT Core, DataStore, Cloud SQL, Cloud Functions, App Engine) and the necessary configuration and implementation for the flow of the data from the devices to the end-user.

This proposed solution is not only useful for quinoa farmers and fishermen in Peru, but it is also useful for any farmer and for any industry and any country because a monitoring platform helps to optimize the processes in these industries through delivering the right information to make the best decisions. As researchers, we will apply this architecture to a third project for the aquaculture industry that will be executed in 2020.

**Acknowledgments.** This research was supported by the National Agricultural Innovation Program (PNIA) of Peru and the Institute of Scientific Research (IDIC) of the University of Lima.

## References

1. Drucker, P.F.: The Practice of Management, Reissue (2006)
2. Biswas, A.R., Giaffreda, R.: IoT and cloud convergence: opportunities and challenges. In: 2014 IEEE World Forum on Internet of Things (WF-IoT), pp. 375–376 (2014)
3. Lv, Y., Tu, L., Lee, C.K.M.: Tang, X.: IoT based omni-channel logistics service in industry 4.0. In: 2018 IEEE International Conference on Service Operations and Logistics, and Informatics, SOLI 2018, pp. 240–243 (2018)
4. Massaro, A., Manfredonia, I., Galiano, A., Pellicani, L., Birardi, V.: Sensing and quality monitoring facilities designed for pasta industry including traceability, image vision and predictive maintenance. In: 2019 II Workshop on Metrology for Industry 4.0 and IoT, pp. 68–72 (2019)
5. Chen, X., Rhee, W., Wang, Z.: Low power sensor design for IoT and mobile healthcare applications. China Commun. **12**(5), 42–54 (2015)

6. Kim, N.J., Park, J.K.: Sports analytics & risk monitoring based on Hana platform. In: 2015 International SoC Design Conference (ISOCC), pp. 221–222 (2015)
7. Dholu, M., Ghodinde, K.A.: Internet of Things (IoT) for precision agriculture application. In: 2018 2nd International Conference on Trends in Electronics and Informatics, ICOEI, pp. 339–342 (2018)
8. Dupont, C., et al.: Low-cost IoT solutions for fish farmers in Africa. In: 2018 IST-Africa Week Conference (IST-Africa), pp. 1–8 (2018)
9. Ngoko, Y., Cerin, C.: An edge computing platform for the detection of acoustic events. In: 2017 IEEE 1st International Conference on Edge Computing, pp. 240–243 (2017)
10. Hong, H.J.: From cloud computing to fog computing: unleash the power of edge and end devices. In: 2017 International Conference on Cloud Computing Technology and Science, CloudCom, December 2017, pp. 331–334 (2017)
11. IBM: IBM Cloud. https://www.ibm.com/cloud. Accessed 25 Sept 2019
12. Amazon: Amazon Web Services (AWS). https://aws.amazon.com. Accessed 25 Sept 2019
13. Microsoft: Microsoft Azure. https://azure.microsoft.com/. Accessed 25 Sept 2019
14. Google: Google Cloud Platform. https://cloud.google.com/. Accessed: 25 Sept 2019
15. RealWorld: RealWorld example apps. https://github.com/gothinkster/realworld. Accessed 25 Sept 2019
16. Pena, M.A.L., Fernandez, I.M.: SAT-IoT: an architectural model for a high-performance fog/edge/cloud IoT platform. In: 2019 IEEE 5th World Forum on Internet of Things (WF-IoT), pp. 633–638 (2019)
17. Pizzolli, D., et al.: Cloud4IoT: a heterogeneous, distributed and autonomic cloud platform for the IoT. In: Proceedings of the International Conference on Cloud Computing Technology and ScienceCloudCom, pp. 476–479 (2017)

# Mechanical Pain Assessment Through Parameters Derived from Photoplethysmographic (PPG) Signals: A Pilot Study

Andrés David Ramírez Mena[1] ⓘ, Leonardo Antonio Bermeo Varón[1] ⓘ,
Rodolfo Molano Valencia[2] ⓘ, and Erick Javier Argüello Prada[1(✉)] ⓘ

[1] Facultad de Ingeniería, Universidad Santiago de Cali (USC), Cali, Colombia
erick.arguello00@usc.edu.co
[2] Facultad de Salud, Universidad Santiago de Cali (USC), Cali, Colombia

**Abstract.** Based on the fact that pain modulates the contour of the photoplethysmographic (PPG) signal, several authors have used PPG-derived parameters, like the amplitude of the PPG signal (PPGA) and the variations of the inter-pulse intervals (i.e., the pulse rate variability – PRV), for pain measurement. However, all those studies were limited to use PPG-derived parameters to assess only thermally evoked pain and no recent studies seem to be available to examine whether it is possible to measure the intensity of the pain evoked by mechanical stimulation. The present study aims to analyze whether it is possible to assess the intensity of mechanically induced pain by using PPG-derived parameters. PPG signals were recorded from fifteen healthy subjects during 6 min, and three force stimuli (3, 6 and 9 N) were applied in ascendant order at 90 s intervals to induce three different levels of pain: low, medium and high. The PPGA, the heart rate (HR), and the high-frequency band (0.15 to 0.4 Hz) power of the pulse rate variability (PRV-HF) were computed before and after the initiation of mechanical stimulation and the percentage of change was calculated for each stimulus intensity. Results show that, even though all of the parameters varied considerably in response to painful stimuli, none of them were able to differentiate between three aforementioned levels of mechanical pain. Only HR was capable of differentiating between low and medium pain, as well as between low and high pain.

**Keywords:** Pain assessment · Photoplethysmography (PPG) ·
Mechanically-induced pain · Autonomic nervous system

## 1 Introduction

Pain is often considered as the most common reasons why individuals seek medical attention [1]. To provide effective pain treatment, an accurate assessment of the pain experienced by the patient is mandatory. However, reliable pain assessment can be especially difficult for patients who may not be able to communicate verbally or even express the sensation of pain.

© Springer Nature Switzerland AG 2020
M. Botto-Tobar et al. (Eds.): ICAT 2019, CCIS 1193, pp. 168–178, 2020.
https://doi.org/10.1007/978-3-030-42517-3_13

The autonomic nervous system (ANS) is severely influenced by the pain experience [2–4], so the signals derived from physiological processes modulated by autonomic activity can potentially be used in evaluating the perceived pain. Photoplethysmography (PPG) is an optical technique that can be used to measure changes in peripheral blood volume, which is also affected by pain experience. Based on that, several authors [5–7] have used PPG-derived parameters like the amplitude of the PPG signal (PPGA) to evaluate the balance between the depth of anesthesia and experimental pain stimulation. More recently, it has shown that variations of peak-to-peak intervals (PPI) extracted from PPG signals (i.e., the pulse rate variability – PRV) can be used to assess pain intensity in patients with chronic pain syndromes [8, 9]. On the other hand, all those studies were limited to use PPG-derived parameters to assess only thermally evoked pain and no recent studies seem to be available to examine whether is possible to measure the intensity of the pain evoked by mechanical stimulation.

Mechanical allodynia is an important feature of inflammatory, neuropathic and post-operative pain syndromes [10]. It may manifest whether by application of pres-sure on the skin (static allodynia) or after lightly stroking the skin surface (dynamic allodynia). Mechanisms underlying mechanical allodynia are still not fully under-stood, and methods for assessing pain in patients suffering that and similar conditions are based on subjective and even biased measurements [11]. In an attempt to provide physicians with a simple, objective and reliable method for measuring the intensity of pain evoked by mechanical stimuli, the present study aims to analyze whether it is possible to assess the intensity of mechanically induced pain by using PPG-derived parameters. A method like the one proposed in this work could be a good contribution to improve the efficacy of treatment options for patients suffering from mechanical allodynia or similar conditions, especially those who may not be able to report pain intensity.

## 2 Materials and Methods

### 2.1 Photoplethysmography-Derived Parameters for Pain Assessment

Photoplethysmography (PPG) is a simple, low-cost, non-invasive and reliable technique for measuring the changes in blood flow as changes in the intensity of the light reflected or transmitted through the tissues [12]. As illustrated in Fig. 1, the wave contour of the PPG signal is relatively simple (at least in comparison to the ECG). Nevertheless, it shows not only a high inter-subject variability but also a substantial body-site dependency. Likewise, several factors like changes in arterial blood pressure, body temperature and respiration can modulate PPG waveform.

Since PPG has been widely used to estimate HR and vasomotor tone, it is thought to be potentially useful for pain assessment. Based on that, the amplitude of the PPG signal (PPGA), the heart rate (HR), and the high frequency band (0.15–0.4 Hz) power of the pulse rate variability (PRV-HF) were used as pain indexes for this study.

**PPG Amplitude (PPGA).** Changes in PPGA have been found to occur either as part of the nociceptive response during general anesthesia [13], or as a result of experi-mentally induced pain [14]. Specifically, pain shifts the autonomic balance towards the sympathetic dominance, which in turn increases heart rate (HR) and causes peripheral vasoconstriction [15], which is reflected by the reduced amplitude of the PPGA [13, 16].

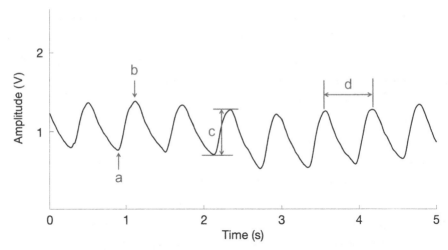

**Fig. 1.** An example of the PPG signal morphology. (a) Pulse onset. (b) Systolic peak. (c) Signal amplitude. (d) peak-to-peak interval.

**Heart Rate (HR).** An increase in HR as a response to pain has been previously reported [17, 18]. In addition, HR has been found to decrease after relieving pain in adult patients receiving assisted ventilation [19]. Although a possible influence of gender on the cardiovascular response to painful stimuli has also been observed [20], HR promises to be an important tool in revealing crucial information for pain assessment as long as it is used in combination with other physiological variables [7].

**Pulse Rate Variability-High Frequency (PRV-HF) Power.** The term heart rate variability (HRV) is used to describe fluctuations in the inter-beat intervals [21] also known as RR intervals. These oscillations reflect how the ANS modulates cardiac activity and it can provide relevant information about the patient's condition. It has been shown that the PRV can be used as a surrogate measurement of HRV, not only during stationary conditions [22, 23] but also under non-stationary conditions [24], although further research is needed to extend its use in clinical practice [25]. Regarding the effect of pain on the HRV, several authors [7, 26] have pointed out that experimentally induced pain in healthy adults produces an increase in the low frequency (LF: 0.04–0.15 Hz) spectral component of the HRV and a decrease in the HF component.

### 2.2  Data Acquisition and Processing

Figure 2 shows the electric diagram of the circuit used for this work. A NellcorTM adult finger clip (model DS-100A) was used to collect peripheral blood volume changes. The infra-red light-emitting diode (IR-LED) driving current is supplied by a 2N3904 NPN transistor and controlled by the potentiometer R2. A single pole, band-pass active filter with a lower cut-off frequency of 0.7 Hz, an upper cut-off frequency of 2.34 Hz, and a gain of 100 was used to filter and amplify the signal from the phototransistor. The output of the first stage is regulated by the potentiometer R7 and additionally amplified with a gain of 10. The whole circuit was powered with a rechargeable Ni-MH battery (3.6 V/1000 mAh, Huawei) and integrated into a single printed circuit board (PCB) using high-quality components, in order to reduce the signal contamination as much as possible. Second stage output was sampled at 100 Hz and digitalized by the 8-channel analogue-to-digital converter (10-bit resolution) of an Arduino Nano board. Once digitalized, the PPG signal is transmitted from the Arduino board to a portable PC (Acer TravelMate B113) via serial port. PPG recordings were processed off-line using Matlab R2013a (The Mathworks Inc., Natick, USA).

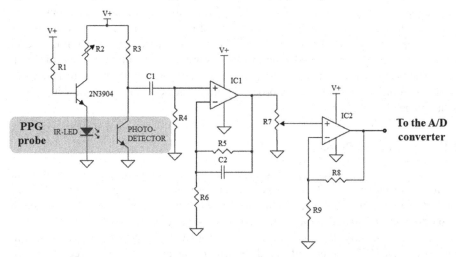

**Fig. 2.** Diagram of the circuit for acquisition and conditioning of PPG signals (Adapted from [28]).

Systolic peaks and pulse onsets (troughs) were detected by the peak detection method proposed in [27], which has also proved to be useful for HR estimation [28]. As done in [7], the PPGA signal was computed as the averaged difference between the peak and trough values in each beat over a 10-second window. The PPI signal was constructed from consecutive detected systolic peaks. HR was calculated by inverting the mean of the PPI in the previous 10-second window and multiplying by 60. Although at least 4 min are commonly required to compute HRV indexes, those metrics can be reliably and accurately estimated in 1–2 min windows when motion artifacts are not present, as demonstrated by [29]. The HRV-HF component was calculated from the previous 60-second window of PPI signals. Since interpolating and resampling unevenly spaced data can interfere in power spectral estimates [30], the Lomb-Scargle periodogram was used to estimate the Power Spectral Density (PSD) of the PPI series. For all parameters, the percentage of change was calculated as follows:

$$\%change = 100^{*}(average_{POST STIM} - average_{PRESTIM})/average_{PRESTIM}$$

$$(1)$$

where $average_{PRESTIM}$ and $average_{POSTSTIM}$ represent the average value of each parameter computed, respectively, before and after initiation of the mechanical stimulus. Prestimulus averages were calculated over a 30-seconds window.

## 2.3 Test Subjects

Fifteen healthy subjects (11 males and 4 females, with ages ranging from 18 to 45 years) were recruited for the study. After obtaining informed consent from the participants, they were all instructed to avoid smoking and consuming substances influencing cardiovascular system activity (e.g. alcohol) for 24 h before the experiment. Exclusion criteria were: (*i*) chronic or acute pain; (*ii*) neurological disease; (*iii*) serious cardiovascular disease (i.e., any type of disease involving the heart or blood vessels that might result in life-threatening medical emergencies, such as arrhythmias, infarct, and stroke); (*iv*) use of medications or recreational drugs; or (*v*) pregnancy. The study conformed to the Declaration of Helsinki and was approved by the Ethics Committee of the Universidad Santiago de Cali (registry code 009).

## 2.4 Experimental Protocol

At the day of the study, test subjects were asked to sit as comfortable as possible and not to talk or move, as well as to remain as still as possible during recording. Whereas the PPG finger clip was placed around the tip of left-hand index finger, the interdigital web (*Plica Interdigitalis*) between the index and middle fingers of the right hand were pinched with a locally-designed, mechanical stimulator. The device consists of a strain gauge with an HX711 breakout board, which acts as an interface between the strain gauge and an Arduino Nano board, as shown in Fig. 3a. Force stimuli were applied to the skin by a ~1.8 mm$^2$ flat-tip probe, which was attached at one end of the strain gauge whereas the other end was fixed to a customized plastic case (see Fig. 3b).

PPG signals were recorded during 6 min, and three force stimuli (3, 6 and 9 N) were applied in ascendant order at 90 s intervals to induce three different levels of pain: low, medium and high. Each stimulus lasted 2 s and all participants were informed that a stimulus would begin approximately 10 s before its initiation. The probe was placed on the skin 3 s before applying the stimulus. After stimulation, subjects were asked to numerically rate the perceived pain intensity by using a 1-10 numeric pain scale (1 = minimum; 10 = maximum). All experiments were performed at room temperature (20 °C) at the Robotics Laboratory of the Universidad Santiago de Cali.

## 2.5 Statistical Analysis

Analyses were performed using the Matlab scientific software. Given that all parameters were not normally distributed, the nonparametric Friedman test with post-hoc Wilcoxon signed ranks tests were conducted to assess the differences between the three pain levels. A $P$-value adjustment for Wilcoxon tests was applied, in order to avoid a type I statistical error due to multiple hypotheses testing.

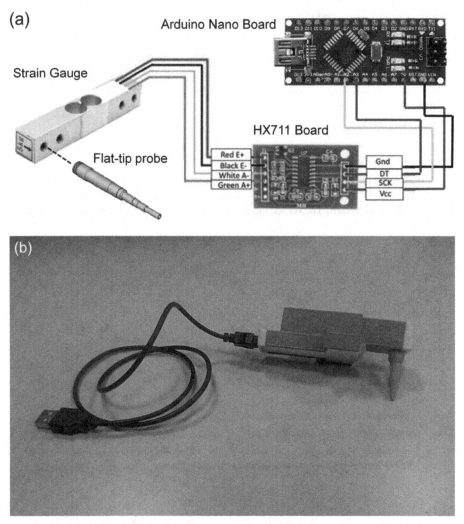

**Fig. 3.** The locally-designed, mechanical stimulator used in the present study. (a) Connection diagram. (b) The final appearance of the device.

## 3 Results

Figures 4 through 6 show the variations of normalized parameter values at low, medium and high pain (left panels). For the sake of clarity, error bars were omitted. As can be seen from Figs. 4 and 6, there was a pronounced decrease in PPGA and HRV-HF values when the stimulus was applied in comparison to the prestimulus average. For both parameters, negative peaks were followed by a gradual increase. On the other hand, there was a pronounced increase in the HR value when the stimulus was applied in comparison to the prestimulus average. The positive peak was followed by a gradual decrease (see Fig. 5).

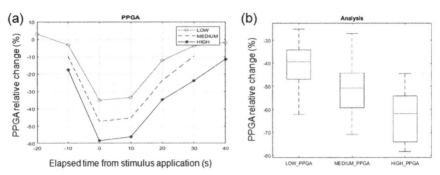

**Fig. 4.** The amplitude of the PPG signal (PPGA) as a function of three different intensities of mechanically induced pain. (a) The parameter variation before and after the application of force stimuli at each pain level. (b) The 60-second parameter values (median ± interquartile range) at each pain level.

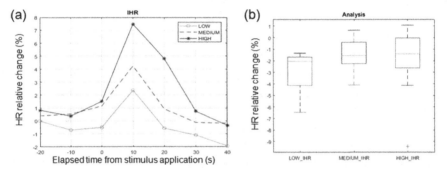

**Fig. 5.** The heart rate (HR) as a function of three different intensities of mechanically induced pain. (a) The parameter variation before and after the application of force stimuli at each pain level. (b) The 60-second parameter values (median ± interquartile range) at each pain level.

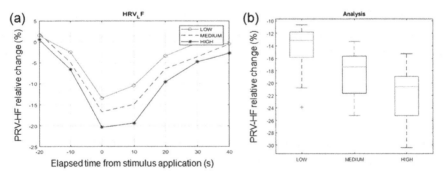

**Fig. 6.** The high frequency band power of the pulse rate variability (PRV-HF) as a function of three different intensities of mechanically induced pain. (a) The parameter variation before and after the application of force stimuli at each pain level. (b) The 60-second parameter values (median ± interquartile range) at each pain level.

Box-plots in Figs. 4 through 6 (right panels) show median values computed over the 60-second window after the stimulus onset (as done in [7]) at each pain level (median ± interquartile range). The difference between PPGA and PRV-HF values as a function of the stimulus intensity is more evident than that for HR values. However, no significant differences were found between parameter values at different pain levels. Table 1 summarizes the results of the Wilcoxon test. Significant results (P < .05) are emphasized with bold font.

**Table 1.** Degree of significance (P values) in differentiation between pain levels for each PPG-derived parameter.

| Parameter | Low vs medium | Low vs high | Medium vs high |
|-----------|---------------|-------------|----------------|
| PPGA | 0.1490 | 0.0734 | 0.4286 |
| HR | **0.0379** | **0.0175** | 0.5350 |
| PRV-HF | 0.3829 | 0.2593 | 0.5679 |

# 4 Discussion

Several authors [5–9] have reported that variations in parameters derived from PPG signals can be used to detect and even measure pain level. However, the majority of those studies were limited to assess only thermally induced pain. Decreases in PPGA have been found to occur as a result of mechanically induced pain [14], but whether it is possible to assess its intensity by using PPGA and other PPG-derived parameters, still remains unknown. The purpose of the present study is to shed some light on this issue and, ultimately, to provide an objective and reliable method for pain assessment by exploiting the easiness of use of PPG. Patients suffering from mechanical allodynia or similar conditions are capable of experiencing touch-evoked pain, and reliable pain assessment in such conditions is crucial for diagnosis and treatment.

The results of the present work show that none of the chosen PPG-derived parameters are able to differentiate between three levels (low, medium, and high) of mechanically induced pain. However, and according to the Wilcoxon test results, HR was able to differentiate between low and medium pain, as well as between low and high pain. Interestingly, the difference between HR values as a function of the stimulus intensity is less evident than that for PPGA and PRV-HF values (see Figs. 4 through 6, right panels). This is possibly due to the methodological differences between statistical analyses; i.e., whereas box-plots use the median values computed over the 60-second window after the stimulus onset (as done in [7]), the Wilcoxon test only took into consideration the peak values of each parameter at the different pain levels. For HR, peaks occur precisely during the 10-seconds after the application of the force stimulus. This is in good agreement with the results obtained in [7, 31], where it is pointed out that HR is able to differentiate pain levels, especially during the first 10 s after stimulus onset.

The inability of the chosen PPG-derived parameters for differentiating the intensity of mechanically induced pain could be attributable to several reasons. First, for all force stimuli, a fixed stimulus-free interval was used (90 s). Furthermore, test subjects were informed that a stimulus would begin approximately 10 s before its initiation. The utilization of fixed stimulus-free intervals is a common practice among experimental pain studies [6–8, 31, 32]. However, this might have caused predictability of stimuli and therefore anticipatory effects, which could modulate pain experience [33]. To avoid or minimize such effects, all stimulus intensities should be applied in a randomized order and participants should not be informed that a stimulus would be applied. Second, the neurophysiological mechanisms involved in the perception of mechanically induced pain are different from those underlying thermally induced pain [34]. When applying thermal stimuli, a select group of afferent fibers, also referred to as nociceptive (A$\delta$ and C), convey nerve impulses that might be decoded as pain. On the other hand, mechanical stimuli may activate not only nociceptive but also non-nociceptive afferent fibers (A$\beta$). As originally predicted by the Gate Control Theory (GCT), the activation of A$\beta$ fibers is able to suppress nociceptive transmission at the spinal level via a gating mechanism provided by lamina II inhibitory interneurons [35]. Therefore, the mechanical pain neural circuitry tends to be less sensitive than that involved in the perception of thermal pain. Third, the difference between stimulation intensities used in the present work (3, 6 and 9 N), as well as the stimulus duration (2 s), could be less than the required to provoke significant variations in PPG-derived parameters between different pain levels. And fourth, the emergence of adaptive mechanisms (e.g., habituation) supporting the balance between nociceptive and antinociceptive responses could cause pain attenuation over time [36], even in the short-term.

## 5   Conclusion

The purpose of the present study was to analyze whether it is possible to distinguish between three different levels of mechanically induced pain by using PPG-derived parameters. Even though all of the parameters varied considerably in response to painful stimuli, none of them were able to differentiate between three levels (low, medium, and high) of mechanical pain. Only HR was capable of differentiating between low and medium pain, as well as between low and high pain induced by mechanical stimulation. Further work should be extended to evaluate the effects of tonic (duration > 60 s) mechanical stimulation on a wider range of PPG-derived parameters and should be conducted such that all stimulus intensities are administered in a randomized order.

## References

1. Mobily, P.R., Herr, K.A., Kelley, L.S.: Cognitive-behavioral techniques to reduce pain: a validation study. Int. J. Nurs. Stud. **30**(6), 537–548 (1993)
2. Seifert, F., Schuberth, N., De Col, R., Peltz, E., Nickel, F.T., Maihöfner, C.: Brain activity during sympathetic response in anticipation and experience of pain. Hum. Brain Mapp. **34**(8), 1768–1782 (2013)
3. Schlereth, T., Birklein, F.: The sympathetic nervous system and pain. NeuroMol. Med. **10**(3), 141–147 (2008)

4. Benarroch, E.E.: Pain-autonomic interactions. Neurol. Sci. **27**(2), s130–s133 (2006)
5. Hamunen, K., Kontinen, V., Hakala, E., Talke, P., Paloheimo, M., Kalso, E.: Effect of pain on autonomic nervous system indices derived from photoplethysmography in healthy volunteers. Br. J. Anaesthesia **108**(5), 838–844 (2012)
6. Ye, J.J., Lee, K.T., Lin, J.S., Chuang, C.C.: Observing continuous change in heart rate variability and photoplethysmography-derived parameters during the process of pain production/relief with thermal stimuli. J. Pain Res. **10**, 527 (2017)
7. Treister, R., Kliger, M., Zuckerman, G., Aryeh, I.G., Eisenberg, E.: Differentiating between heat pain intensities: the combined effect of multiple autonomic parameters. Pain **153**(9), 1807–1814 (2012)
8. Ye, J.J., Lee, K.T., Chou, Y.Y., Sie, H.H., Huang, R.N., Chuang, C.C.: Assessing pain intensity using photoplethysmography signals in chronic myofascial pain syndrome. Pain Pract. **18**(3), 296–304 (2018)
9. Chuang, C.C., Ye, J.J., Lin, W.C., Lee, K.T., Tai, Y.T.: Photoplethysmography variability as an alternative approach to obtain heart rate variability information in chronic pain patient. J. Clin. Monit. Comput. **29**(6), 801–806 (2015)
10. Field, M.J., Bramwell, S., Hughes, J., Singh, L.: Detection of static and dynamic components of mechanical allodynia in rat models of neuropathic pain: are they signalled by distinct primary sensory neurones? Pain **83**(2), 303–311 (1999)
11. Barr, J., et al.: Clinical practice guidelines for the management of pain, agitation, and delirium in adult patients in the intensive care unit. Crit. Care Med. **41**(1), 263–306 (2013)
12. Allen, J.: Photoplethysmography and its application in clinical physiological measurement. Physiol. Measur. **28**(3), R1 (2007)
13. Korhonen, I., Yli-Hankala, A.: Photoplethysmography and nociception. Acta Anaesthesiol. Scand. **53**(8), 975–985 (2009)
14. Magerl, W., Geldner, G., Handwerker, H.O.: Pain and vascular reflexes in man elicited by prolonged noxious mechano-stimulation. Pain **43**(2), 219–225 (1990)
15. Awad, A.A., Ghobashy, M.A.M., Ouda, W., Stout, R.G., Silverman, D.G., Shelley, K.H.: Different responses of ear and finger pulse oximeter wave form to cold pressor test. Anesth. Analg. **92**(6), 1483–1486 (2001)
16. Shelley, K.H.: Photoplethysmography: beyond the calculation of arterial oxygen saturation and heart rate. Anesth. Analg. **105**(6), S31–S36 (2007)
17. Gélinas, C., Johnston, C.: Pain assessment in the critically ill ventilated adult: validation of the Critical-Care Pain Observation Tool and physiologic indicators. Clin. J. Pain **23**(6), 497–505 (2007)
18. Terkelsen, A.J., Mølgaard, H., Hansen, J., Andersen, O.K., Jensen, T.S.: Acute pain increases heart rate: differential mechanisms during rest and mental stress. Auton. Neurosci. **121**(1–2), 101–109 (2005)
19. Gélinas, C., Arbour, C.: Behavioral and physiologic indicators during a nociceptive procedure in conscious and unconscious mechanically ventilated adults: similar or different? J. Crit. Care **24**(4), 628-e7 (2009)
20. Tousignant-Laflamme, Y., Rainville, P., Marchand, S.: Establishing a link between heart rate and pain in healthy subjects: a gender effect. J. Pain **6**(6), 341–347 (2005)
21. Kleiger, R.E., Stein, P.K., Bigger Jr., J.T.: Heart rate variability: measurement and clinical utility. Ann. Noninvasive Electrocardiol. **10**(1), 88–101 (2005)
22. Lu, S., et al.: Can photoplethysmography variability serve as an alternative approach to obtain heart rate variability information? J. Clin. Monit. Comput. **22**(1), 23–29 (2008)
23. Lu, G., Yang, F., Taylor, J.A., Stein, J.F.: A comparison of photoplethysmography and ECG recording to analyse heart rate variability in healthy subjects. J. Med. Eng. Technol. **33**(8), 634–641 (2009)

24. Gil, E., Orini, M., Bailon, R., Vergara, J.M., Mainardi, L., Laguna, P.: Photoplethysmography pulse rate variability as a surrogate measurement of heart rate variability during non-stationary conditions. Physiol. Measur. **31**(9), 1271 (2010)
25. Georgiou, K., Larentzakis, A.V., Khamis, N.N., Alsuhaibani, G.I., Alaska, Y.A., Giallafos, E.J.: Can wearable devices accurately measure heart rate variability? A systematic review. Folia Med. **60**(1), 7–20 (2018)
26. Koenig, J., Jarczok, M.N., Ellis, R.J., Hillecke, T.K., Thayer, J.F.: Heart rate variability and experimentally induced pain in healthy adults: a systematic review. Eur. J. Pain **18**(3), 301–314 (2014)
27. Argüello-Prada, E.J.: The mountaineer's method for peak detection in photoplethysmographic signals. Revista Facultad de Ingeniería **90**, 9–17 (2019)
28. Argüello, E.J., Serna, R.D.: A novel and low-complexity peak detection algorithm for heart rate estimation from low-amplitude photoplethysmographic (PPG) signals. J. Med. Eng. Technol. **42**(8), 569–577 (2018)
29. McNames, J., Aboy, M.: Reliability and accuracy of heart rate variability metrics versus ECG segment duration. Med. Biol. Eng. Comput. **44**(9), 747–756 (2006)
30. Fonseca, D.S., Netto, A.A., Ferreira, R.B., de Sá, A.M.: Lomb-scargle periodogram applied to heart rate variability study. In: 2013 ISSNIP Biosignals and Biorobotics Conference: Biosignals and Robotics for Better and Safer Living (BRC), pp. 1–4. IEEE, Rio de Janeiro (2013)
31. Nickel, M.M., May, E.S., Tiemann, L., Postorino, M., Dinh, S.T., Ploner, M.: Autonomic responses to tonic pain are more closely related to stimulus intensity than to pain intensity. Pain **158**(11), 2129–2136 (2017)
32. Breimhorst, M., Sandrock, S., Fechir, M., Hausenblas, N., Geber, C., Birklein, F.: Do intensity ratings and skin conductance responses reliably discriminate between different stimulus intensities in experimentally induced pain? J. Pain **12**(1), 61–70 (2011)
33. Tursky, B.: Physical, physiological, and psychological factors that affect pain reaction to electric shock. Psychophysiology **11**, 95–112 (1973)
34. Koltzenburg, M.: Neural mechanisms of cutaneous nociceptive pain. Clin. J. Pain **16**(3 Suppl), S131–S138 (2000)
35. Melzack, R., Wall, P.D.: Pain mechanisms: a new theory. Science **150**(3699), 971–979 (1965)
36. Rennefeld, C., Wiech, K., Schoell, E.D., Lorenz, J., Bingel, U.: Habituation to pain: further support for a central component. Pain **148**(3), 503–508 (2010)

# Enterprise Digital Transformation in Ecuador: Strategic Options

Vicente Merchán[1,2](✉) and Víctor Paliz[1]

[1] Universidad de las Fuerzas Armadas ESPE, Sangolquí, Ecuador
{vrmerchan,vmpaliz}@espe.edu.ec
[2] Otavalo University, Otavalo, Ecuador
vmerchan@uotavalo.edu.ec

**Abstract.** Many companies in Ecuador are managing the opportunities and risks that digital transformation represents. To help them to better understand how to address this challenge, we describe the strategic options that 94 companies, which are among the 500 largest companies in Ecuador, have adopted to implement those independent aspects that digital transformation demands. With a quantitative-deductive approach of a descriptive type and based on a corporate digital transformation framework, we design a set of variables that senior management can use as guidelines when planning a digital transformation strategy. The results obtained yield important definitions and findings of the performance of senior management in relation to the challenges of business transformation. This work contributes to the knowledge of those who must make strategic decisions in particular business contexts to overcome the complexities of strategic business transformations.

**Keywords:** Digital transformation · Digital business · Digital innovation

## 1 Introduction

Digitalization is one of the most important and certainly most promising trends of the last decade. The organizations and mainly the companies of various profiles invest a lot of money and effort to digitally train their executives and employees, digitize business processes, implement sales infrastructure and digitize products and offers. Others, on the other hand, launch initiatives and projects with the uncertainty of how to proceed, what to do and how deeply and comprehensively the changes are implemented [16].

As defined by Berman [2], in the research carried out by IBM, companies that seek opportunities in an era of constant customer connectivity focus on two complementary activities: reshaping customer value propositions and transforming their operations using digital technologies to increase the interaction and collaboration with the client.

The Digital Transformation (DT) is the buzzword that emerges as the tendency to inject various forms of innovation into companies, institutions, governments or other public services [4], being a priority on the agendas of executive leadership in most business leaders in Ecuador where they seek that digital technologies make their strategic contribution in the coming years.

Integrating and exploiting new digital technologies is another of the biggest challenges that companies face today. No sector or organization is immune to the effects of

© Springer Nature Switzerland AG 2020
M. Botto-Tobar et al. (Eds.): ICAT 2019, CCIS 1193, pp. 179–190, 2020.
https://doi.org/10.1007/978-3-030-42517-3_14

DT. The market exchange potential of digital technologies is often broader than products, business processes, sales channels or supply chains; complete business models are being remodeled and frequently turned over [6].

The DT is a complex problem that affects all functional components within a company. Business leaders must simultaneously balance the exploration and exploitation of their companies' resources to achieve business agility [9], a necessary condition for the successful transformation of their businesses. This implies transformations of operations, as well as organizational structures, management concepts [11] (see Fig. 1), service management and customer service [8]. Companies need to establish management practices to govern these complex transformations. An approach to formulate a DT strategy that serves as a central concept to integrate all coordination, prioritization and implementation of digital transformations within a company.

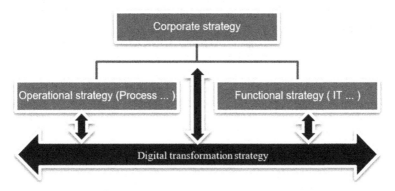

**Fig. 1.** Digital transformation strategy and company strategies [11].

The topic of the DT is important for Ecuador given the Digital Ecuador strategy for an innovative and competitive Ecuador [12]. However, the State policy for the DT in Ecuador faces a series of challenges that the Ecuadorian government must consider given the limited research evidence to successfully create the National Agenda of DT.

This study focuses on 94 effective companies that are among the 500 largest companies in Ecuador, because in 2017 they stood out for the level of income which was higher than the income of the previous year [3]. Therefore, the purpose of this research work is to know the strategic guidelines adopted by senior management of the companies investigated in the face of the DT challenge, in order to contribute to the knowledge in critical decision making and help senior management in the selection of the best options for the success of the digital company in Ecuador. With this objective, the following research question is posed:

*What are the strategic options that Ecuadorian companies have adopted to implement those independent aspects demanded by the DT?*

This document is structured. In Sect. 2 the literary review is presented. In Sect. 3, the research methodology is presented. In Sect. 4, the results are analyzed. In Sect. 5, the discussion is presented; and, in Sect. 5, the conclusions of the study are presented.

## 2 Literature Review

### 2.1 Digital Transformation: Introduction

Seen from its two conceptions: transformation and digital are described as a process that goes from an initial diagnosis to an improvement proposal driven by information technologies, with the characteristic that data is processed in real time and even used to derive information intelligently to provide their processes and products to those interested in a better knowledge [4].

As defined by [10], technological changes occur rapidly and the duration of many organizations is at stake due to the competition that exists. The main reason is that companies do not achieve technological growth. They need innovation models that guide the form of strategy, culture, processes and capabilities of an organization towards the design of an optimal digital strategy. In addition, digital transformation symbolizes talking about business transformation. It includes products and services within the business which will evolve having an added value: the use of new technologies to generate a direct impact on the income statement and the customer experience. What is more, it will find new optimal models that generate positive results based on customer demand and of course, the change in the company's internal culture. Most organizations resort to new skills and leadership to successfully promote this transition. The DT redirects the organization towards an effective digital relationship model in each of the contact points of the customer experience [15]. In other words, [1] it mentions that the DT is a set of facts aimed at improving and modernizing the processes, procedures, habits and behaviors of organizations and people who make use of digital technology. It improves the global competence of public administrations, companies and citizens, requiring organizations to review their business, operations and technology strategy models, implying a cultural change that must be led by the leadership. It also mentions that this transformation acts transversely in the society, the economy and in the day to day becoming the accelerator of change eliminating the boundaries between products and services. It shortens life cycles and increases customer expectations. Something to highlight is that the potential of digital technologies must be used to reinvent the organization itself in a way that adapts its products, processes and business models to the increasingly digital demand of users. For Hess et al. [6], a DT strategy affects a company in an integral way than an Information Technology (IT) strategy, and addresses the company's borders with potential customers, competitors and suppliers. Therefore, he argues that companies must have an independent digital transformation strategy.

The evidence of the digital transformation in other business and regional contexts is leading to an unprecedented economic scenario [17].

### 2.2 The Digital Business Transformation in Ecuador: Introduction

Jorge Cavagnaro in Vistazo magazine [3] confirms:

The commercial agreement with the European Union, the completion of the temporary 2% increase in VAT placed after the 2016 earthquake through the Organic Solidarity Law, the elimination of the tariff safeguard, and the brake on import quotas for vehicles, were some of the issues that marked the dynamics of the business sector in 2017. Additionally, the increase in GDP by 2.4%, the increase in non-oil exports, in the importation of consumer goods, raw materials and capital goods, and in the Final Household Expenditure, confirm the previous statement. On this occasion, the largest companies recorded 70 billion revenues, while in the ranking of 2016 they reached 65 billion. This highlights the positive performance of automotive companies: no one reduced their income and marked a 46% growth (p. 139).

Each of the companies chose the right perspective for digital transformation, depending on many circumstances such as the strategic vision of digital technologies that were available at the time.

## 2.3  Framework

Matt et al. [11] formulated the DT guidelines from a strategic perspective based on the knowledge and experience expressed by some German companies. The guidelines were grouped along four dimensions in the DTF Digital Transformation Framework: use of technologies, changes in value creation, structural changes and financial review (see Fig. 2).

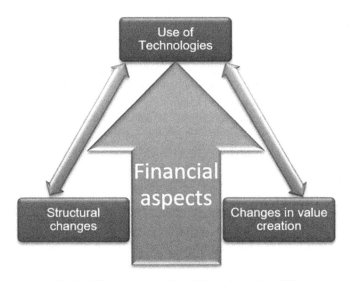

**Fig. 2.**  Dimensions for Digital Transformation [11].

In the previous figure, the DT framework represents the first step towards this vision. The framework focuses on the use of technologies which reflects the focus and ability of a company to explore and exploit new digital technologies. Then, the changes in value creation reflect the influence of digital transformation on the creation of value in a company. Next, the structural changes focus on the modifications of the organizational structure, processes, procedures and skill sets that are necessary to cope with and exploit the new technologies. Finally, the financial aspects are related to the need for the company to take strategic transformation actions in response to a central business that has financial difficulties due to the presence in the market of digital alternatives which erodes its margins.

The dimensions adhere to strategic guidelines that managers must observe to address a defined digital transformation program and to not lose it with critical decisions. These guidelines are considered according to the nature of the business, but in their context they provide a complete picture of the different options to opt for a DT strategy (see Table 1).

**Table 1.** Strategic options for digital transformation.

| Strategic options | Variables |
|---|---|
| Use of technologies | Importance of IT |
| | Focus towards new digital technologies |
| Changes in value creation | Digitization of the interface with customers |
| | Sources of commercial income |
| | Business scope |
| Structural changes | Responsible for DT |
| | Structure integration |
| | Types of operational changes |
| | New competencies |
| Financial aspects | Financial pressure |
| | Types of financing |

The set of strategic guidelines presented in the previous table emerges tied to a transformational model listed as one of the main strategic models for DT, which can be used by academics and experts.

## 3   Methodology

This research work had a quantitative-deductive approach of a descriptive type (non-experimental) [5] which basic research modality was the field; that is, the data were obtained from the same primary sources from where they were studied.

### 3.1   Survey

The survey was designed following the guidelines by [14] and the theoretical background of the work by [6]. The design includes 15 closed questions to obtain nominal and ordinal data (see Table 2).

Before the operation of the survey, an understanding analysis was carried out with researchers. As a result, the clarity and consistency of the terminology adopted in each question is confirmed.

**Table 2.** Survey

| Dimension | Question | Type |
|---|---|---|
| Demographic | Gender | Multiple – nominal |
| | Schooling | Multiple – nominal |
| | Job tittles | Multiple - nominal |
| | Activity sector | Multiple – nominal |
| Use of technologies | Importance of IT | Multiple – nominal |
| | Focus on new digital technologies | Multiple – nominal |
| Changes in value creation | Digitization of the interface with customers | Multiple – nominal |
| | Commercial revenue sources | Multiple – nominal |
| | Business scope | Multiple – nominal |
| Structural changes | Responsible for DT | Multiple – nominal |
| | Structure integration | Multiple – nominal |
| | Types of operational changes | Multiple – nominal |
| | New competencies | Multiple – nominal |
| Financial aspects | Financial pressure | Multiple – ordinal |
| | Types of financing | Multiple – ordinal |

### 3.2 Sample

The non-probabilistic sample [5] took into account 214 companies that were among the 500 largest companies in Ecuador by 2017, characterized by the level of income which was higher than the income of the previous year [3]. The different roles of those who participated included: IT managers, general managers, digital managers, among others. Participation was restricted to strategic level roles or their delegates. From the 214 business visits, 94 were complete, 14 were incomplete and 103 were only shown; representing a 43.9% of overall efficiency.

### 3.3 Analysis of Data

Survio´s website[1] was used to operate the survey, through which, the opinion data of the selected actors was consolidated. Then, with IBM SPSS Statistics 22 [7], we proceeded with the analysis of the nominal and ordinal variables applying cross tables [13].

## 4 Results

### 4.1 Demography

Table 3 shows the demographics results. This demonstrates that the male gender predominates in the survey with 90.4%. The level of schooling with the highest frequency

---

[1] https://www.survio.com/survey/d/estrategiadetd.

is engineering with 63.8%, followed by a master's degree with 27.7% and a doctorate degree with 5.3%. The most frequent functional positions are IT Manager or Director and IT Expert or Specialist with 36.2% and 26.6%, respectively. Finally, the information and communication technology sector is the most participatory economic activity with 20.2%.

**Table 3.** Demography

| Variable | Characteristic | Percentage |
|---|---|---|
| Gender | Male | 90.4% |
| | Female | 9.6% |
| Schooling | Technology | 2.1% |
| | Engineering | 63.8% |
| | Master | 27.7% |
| | Doctorate | 5.3% |
| | Other | 1.1% |
| Job tittles | General Manager | 7.4% |
| | IT Manager or Director | 36.2% |
| | Functional Manager or Director | 7.4% |
| | IT Expert or Specialist | 26.6% |
| | Functional Expert or Specialist | 2.1% |
| | Other | 20.2% |
| Activity sector | Agriculture, livestock, fishing or forestry | 1.1% |
| | Manufacture | 13.8% |
| | Financial and Insurance | 4.3% |
| | Administrative and services | 4.3% |
| | Education | 1.1% |
| | Petroleum | 5.3% |
| | Information and communication technology | 20.2% |
| | Foods | 14.9% |
| | Automotive | 6.4% |
| | Security | 2.1% |
| | Other | 26.5% |

## 4.2  Use of Technologies

Table 4 shows the use of technologies, which creates new opportunities for the company and generates competitive advantages. However, the importance and its strategic role varies substantially between them. The study reveals that 61.7% of the companies consider that IT is an enabler of strategic objectives (79% for IT companies). This means that it is an initial driver of change. They carefully monitor digital technologies and identify their potential to boost current operations or allow the creation of new business products and services; while 38.3% believe that the importance of IT lies in its function to support the change of process, supporting and meeting requirements, and defined commercial improvements. The approach to new digital technologies that the companies have adopted is different for the process of the new digital technologies diffusion. The research shows that 38.3% of companies act in an innovative way, creating and introducing new technologies in the market, other 33.0% believe that they implement new technological solutions in the early stages of their development. On the other hand, 28.7% of the companies which are more conservative believe that their policy is to adopt established and widely used technological solutions. The opinions expressed suggest that the ambition towards new business digital technologies is determined by the unique context; however, the ideal position in this regard should consider the existing technological competence, the extent of the IT spending and its size.

**Table 4.** Use of technologies

| Variable | Characteristic | Percentage |
|---|---|---|
| Importance of IT | Enabler | 61.7% |
| | Supporter | 38.3% |
| Focus on new digital technologies | Innovator | 38.3% |
| | Early adopter | 33.0% |
| | Follower | 28.7% |

### 4.3 Changes in Value Creation

Table 5 shows the opinions about the changes in the creation of value derived from digital technologies. This dimension is mainly related to the degree to which a company has already diversified its business in the digital world (levels 1 to 5), how it plans to generate revenue from digital technologies and its commercial or operational approach after the digital transformation. The companies think about their entry into new business areas which are conditioned on their financial statements and the size of their company. In all cases, 26.6% of respondents think they are in electronic sales channels (level 1), 10.6% in cross-media (level 2), 16.0% in rich media (level 3), 29.8% in platforms of content (level 4) and 17.0% in extended business (level 5). Therefore, it is inferred that the size of the companies can be an important determinant in the level of digital diversification that they have achieved so far. There are companies that think they are in full use of the possibilities offered by digital technologies in a customer-centric market, and others believe that they are making steady progress in their efforts to adopt the digital transformation. The focus on creating revenue from future business operations seeks to know how companies create value in an online world and, therefore, generate income. Consequently, 24.5% think that their source is paid content, 8.5% through "freemium" revenue models, 27.7% through advertising and 39.4% through the sale of complementary products or linked to their digital content. Finally, in the business field 10.6% focuses on content creation, 16.0% on content aggregation, 19.1% on content distribution, 27.7% on content platform management and 26.6% in other content management; therefore, most companies are managing content platforms in the way of creating important assets, as well as social media platforms do.

**Table 5.** Changes in value creation

| Variable | Characteristic | Percentage |
|---|---|---|
| Digitization of the interface with customers | Electronic sales channels | 26.6% |
| | Cross-Media | 10.6% |
| | Enriched-Media | 16.0% |
| | Content platforms | 29.8% |
| | Extended business | 17.0% |
| Commercial revenue sources | Paid content | 24.5% |
| | Freemium | 8.5% |
| | Advertising | 27.7% |
| | Selling complementary products | 39.4% |
| Business scope | Content creation | 10.6% |
| | Content aggregation | 16.0% |
| | Content distribution | 19.1% |
| | Content platforms | 27.7% |
| | Others | 26.6% |

## 4.4 Structural Changes

Table 6 shows opinions on the dimension of structural changes like who directs the DT effort, how they plan to create or maintain current structures, what type of operational changes are expected and how they plan to acquire new skills. Answering who is in charge of the DT effort, 52.1% think that the IT Manager of the business group has a total commitment to the strategy, 28.7% mention that it is in charge of the CEO of the business group, 10.6% indicates that it is the digital manager of the business group and, 8.5% think that it is the manager of a business unit. These data imply that, ideally, the CEO is fully responsible and adds authority to the DT strategy, the CIO can manage the transformation that is usually in cases where the focus is on business processes and IT infrastructure and the CDO addresses mainly digital technologies that involve services with customers. The focus on the integration of operations from the structural perspective presents a predominant opinion that represents 81.9%, this means that the companies face the effort of a less extensive and coordinated restructuring between the traditional and the new company. Regarding the expected types of operational changes, 41.5% supported the modified products and services, 37.2% operational business processes and 21.3% expressed skills changes based on digital technologies. In conclusion, operational changes depend on the scope of the business and future DT plans. Finally, 31.9% of the companies testify that the new competences will depend on the associations that are carried out in the majority of the companies, 28.7% mention the acquisitions, 23.4% think about the external supply and 16.0% mention internally. Senior management is evaluating the technological capabilities existing in companies and identifying the new skills that will be necessary.

**Table 6.** Structural changes

| Variable | Characteristic | Percentage |
|---|---|---|
| Responsible for DT | Group CEO | 28.7% |
| | CEO of business unit | 8.5% |
| | Group CDO | 10.6% |
| | Group CIO | 52.1% |
| Structure integration | Integrated | 81.9% |
| | Separated | 18.1% |
| Types of operational changes | Products and services | 41.5% |
| | Business processes | 37.2% |
| | Skills | 21.3% |
| New competencies | Internally | 16.0% |
| | Partnerships | 31.9% |
| | Takeovers | 28.7% |
| | External sourcing | 23.4% |

### 4.5  Financial

Table 7 shows the financial aspects, which is an important issue of DT's efforts. While the financial pressure on the company increases, this could be the trigger that motivates senior management towards a strategic transformation decision. The study reveals that 6.4% of companies consider the financial pressure in the business to be low, 74.5% think that the financial pressure is medium and 19.1% think it is high; in conclusion, there is a good predisposition of senior business management to undertake necessary efforts and accept the inherent risks of the DT that mostly depends on the competitiveness that businesses currently want to maintain in the presence of digital substitutes that erode their finances. The approach towards the type of financing, 76.6% believes that it will be with internal resources and 23.4% mentions that it will be with external resources; this implies that most companies will finance the DT effort according to their current well-being and future growth prospects. It is said that there is confidence in the DT and that this will bring benefits for the company and its investors, without ruling out the financial limitations of each company.

**Table 7.** Financial aspects

| Variable | Characteristic | Percentage |
| --- | --- | --- |
| Financial pressure | Low | 6.4% |
| | Medium | 74.5% |
| | High | 19.1% |
| Types of financing | Internal | 76.6% |
| | External | 23.4% |

## 5  Discussions and Conclusions

Structured research has been provided based on the digital transformation framework. Senior business management can observe the strategic guidelines identified above and understand how organizations are facing the DT effort in Ecuador; this will contribute to better actions and decisions that managers must make in their own business contexts. This research formulated a series of questions and strategic options that DT managers should take into account.

First, strategic options were investigated from the perspective of using technologies in which the majority of opinions points to IT empowerment and innovation. Then, in the changes of the creation of value, the content platform and the sale of complementary products are displayed. Next, in the change of structures, the figure of the IT manager, an integrated structure and an expectation for new products and services stand out. Finally, it highlights a medium financial pressure that must be addressed with internal financing, according to the majority. Previous studies highlight the particular use of big data, cloud computing, robotic customer service and blockchain [17].

We believe that a systematic approach would be the ideal way to propose a DT strategy. In addition, top management must be aware that a digital business demands a high level of uncertainty. There is no "recipe for cooking" on this topic, but rather a set of fully tested strategies.

Possibly, one of the limitations of this study is the low number of respondents and not that specific conversations with everyone were not held, but we believe that the work with companies from various sectors of activity gives the strength to understand how aspects of changes in the creation structural and financial values can be adopted without complications. However, getting a larger sample would help in more detailed studies, being able to create significant groups within the same sample size.

In the future, we will investigate how the profile of the person responsible for the digital transformation, level of use of technologies, changes in the creation of value, structures and financial decisions influence the performance of the digital company through modeling and, to what extent. Emphasis will be placed on technological solutions for digitalization.

## References

1. AMETIC: Transformación Digital: Visión y Propuesta de AMETIC|Ametic, 1 February 2017. Accessed 27 Aug 2019. http://ametic.es/es/publicaciones/transformaci%C3%B3n-digital-visi%C3%B3n-y-propuesta-de-ametic-0
2. Berman, S.J.: Digital transformation: opportunities to create new business models. Strategy Leadersh. **40**(2), 16–24 (2012)
3. Editores Nacionales S.A.: Vistazo No. 1226 (2018). https://www.vistazo.com/seccion/proyectos-especiales/500empresas
4. Gray, J., Rumpe, B.: Models for the digital transformation. Softw. Syst. Model. **16**(2), 307–308 (2017). https://doi.org/10.1007/s10270-017-0596-7
5. Hernández Sampieri, R., Fernández Collado, C., Baptista Lucio, P.: Metodología de la investigación, 6th edn. McGraw-Hill, México (2014)
6. Hess, T., Matt, C., Benlian, A., Wiesböck, F.: Options for formulating a digital transformation strategy. MIS Q. Executive **15**, 129–137 (2016)
7. IBM: Guía breve de IBM SPSS Statistics 22 (2011). ftp://public.dhe.ibm.com/software/analytics/spss/documentation/statistics/22.0/es/client/Manuals/IBM_SPSS_Statistics_Brief_Guide.pdf
8. Jäntti, M., Hyvarinen, S.: Exploring digital transformation and digital culture in service organizations. In: 2018 15th International Conference on Service Systems and Service Management (ICSSSM), pp. 1–6. IEEE (2018)
9. Lee, O.-K., Sambamurthy, V., Lim, K.H., Wei, K.K.: How does IT ambidexterity impact organizational agility? Inf. Syst. Res. **26**(2), 398–417 (2015)
10. Llorente, J.G.: Marketing Digital. Manual Teórico, Editorial Cep (2015)
11. Matt, C., Hess, T., Benlian, A.: Digital transformation strategies. Bus. Inf. Syst. Eng. **57**(5), 339–343 (2015). https://doi.org/10.1007/s12599-015-0401-5
12. Ministerio de Telecomunicaciones y de la Sociedad de la Información – Ecuador (2019). Accessed 18 Aug 2019. https://www.telecomunicaciones.gob.ec/
13. Newbold, P., Carlson, W.L., Thorne, B.: Estadística para administración y economía (2013). http://www.ingebook.com/ib/NPcd/IB_BooksVis?cod_primaria=1000187&codigo_libro=4485
14. Pfleeger, S.L., Kitchenham, B.A.: Principles of survey research: part 1: turning lemons into lemonade. ACM SIGSOFT Softw. Eng. Notes **26**(6), 16–18 (2001)
15. Sánchez, J.: Transformación e innovación digital. Recuperado de (2017). https://Incipy.Com/Ebooks/Transformacion-Digital.Pdf
16. Winkelhake, U.: Digital Transformation of the Automotive Industry. Springer, Cham (2018). https://doi.org/10.1007/978-3-319-71610-7
17. Zurdo, R.J.P., Torres, Y.F., Fernández, M.G.: Banca cooperativa y transformación digital: Hacia un nuevo modelo de relación con sus socios y clientes. REVESCO: Revista de Estudios Cooperativos, (129), 161–182 (2018)

# Twitter Opinion Analysis About Topic 5G Technology

Anibal A. Herrera-Contreras[1] , Eddy Sánchez-Delacruz[1(✉)] ,
and Ivan V. Meza-Ruiz[2]

[1] Instituto Tecnológico Superior de Misantla, Veracruz, Mexico
eddsacx@gmail.com
[2] Universidad Nacional Autónoma de México, Mexico City, Mexico

**Abstract.** Nowadays, Twitter has become a rich source for sentiment analysis and opinion mining data since every day thousand of users freely expresses their opinions in this social network. In this research, we analyze and classify the sentiment of shared publications that have the hashtag "#5G" as *positive, negative* or *neutral*. We use Google Cloud AutoML Natural Language Sentiment Analysis and we obtained a classification model with accuracy and recall of 80.89%, likewise applying Latent Dirichlet Allocation for the detection of topics. The result shows that is possible to identify main factors about public opinion in the acceptance or rejection of technology 5G, this information can be useful for technology companies.

**Keywords:** Twitter · Sentiment analysis · 5G technology

## 1 Introduction

5G is the new generation of mobile phone technologies, after of 4G technology. At the current state, it is not standardized and telecommunication companies are developing their prototypes. It is estimated that the first functional devices will be available in 2020, mainly in the cities that have 4G [20]. 5G network will allow for 400 megabits speeds at which you will be able to navigate through a mobile device. According to Agarwal et al., the advantages are: it possess high capacity and speed, global access and service portability, high resolution and bi-directional large bandwidth and 5G technology act as a backbone for multimedia, voice and internet. Disadvantages: in some parts of the world it is very difficult to get a high speed, privacy and security problems needed to be improved in 5G and old devices need to be renovated so they can support 5G technology [2]. In recent years a wide number of people use social networking like Twitter to express opinions about things, places or relevant topics. Recent studies have proven that with Twitter it is possible to get plausible information about opinions, in contrast to traditional ways [3,6].

This study has the goal of analyze the opinions of the Twitter users that used the #5G; this to identify the behavior of the people before the popularization

© Springer Nature Switzerland AG 2020
M. Botto-Tobar et al. (Eds.): ICAT 2019, CCIS 1193, pp. 191–203, 2020.
https://doi.org/10.1007/978-3-030-42517-3_15

of the technology. The data was obtained from the official API Twitter using the hashtags. After applying preprocessing the data, we perform an analysis of the sentiment using the Google Cloud Sentiment Analysis tool to perform the following tasks.

- Sentiment identification.
- Classification model.
- Model topic based classification.

Such model was used for the clustering of the words and to identify the main themes about the 5G network, this to be able to understand to your best the data.

The rest of the article is divided as follow: in Sect. 3 the materials and method implemented are described, the results are shown in Sect. 4 and, finally, the discussions and conclusions are presented in Sects. 5 and 6.

## 2 Related Work

In this section shows the related works to sentiment analysis on Twitter to analyze and determine the polarity of the tweets using machine learning techniques and text mining tools.

Loyola-Gonzalez *et al.* propose a classifier based on contrast patterns for the detection of Twitter bots. Their goal was to help the expert to take legal action against an account that has shown unusual behaviour. In the work they explore the use of Bayesian Network, k-Nearest Neighbor, C4.5, Naive Bayes (NBayes), Random Forest (RF), Support Vector Machine (SVM), Logistic Regression, Adaptive Boosting, Bagging, PBC4ci, Multilayer Perceptron. They were looking to identify the best classifier for bot detection. In their work they express that the best classifier was RF with an 99% Area Under the Curve (AUC) and a Matthews Correlation Coefficient (MCC). While the classifier based on patterns only achieved 90% AUC y 91% MCC [17].

Martin-Domingo *et al.* analyzed opinions on the Londres Heathrow in Twitter account from the point of view of sentiment analysis to identify new ideas that could improve the airport service quality (ASQ). They developed a system that could collect and analyze the data. Their design included a list of 108 key words for the identification of tweets that talk about the quality of tweets that task about the ASQ. Their sample consisted of 4,392 tweets. Their work concluded that there was 23 attributes about the ASQ. The sentiment analysis was performed using the tools *Theysay* and *Twinword*, they manually verified the results of both tools. They results showed that they could get a 78.7% and 69.6% Accuracy (ACC) respectively, having *Theysay* the best performance [19].

Saura *et al.* show a sentiment analysis based on the #BlackFriday Twitter hashtag using machine learning. This was the goal of identifying the identity the sentiment of the consumers in relation with the three classes: positive, negative and neutral. They were trying to link this sentiment to the offers published by different companies. They collected a total of 2,204 tweets using the Twitter API, the companies that were analyzed where selected because they belong the national rank of companies from "El Economista". They used the online tool

Monkeylearn, as a result the 32% of the tweets were identified as positive, 7.7% as negative and 60.2% as neutral. Their results aim to produce better marketing strategies [26].

Mane *et al.* propose a methodology to perform sentiment analysis using a Hadoop Cluster to analyze big amounts of not structure data. They used a distributed environment. Their main contribution is based in the speed, they also used the three classes for sentiment analysis: positive, negative and neutral. The collected data from the streaming API to collect tweets in real-time, they used SetiWordNet to create word dictionary; they used the information codified in WordNet to assign the sentiment analysis score. On the other hand, they used the OpenNLP tool to preprocess and label the data. They reported 72.27% ACC on the three sentiment classes [18].

He *et al.* analyze the opinion of three large Pizza chain: Pizza Hut, Domino's Pizza y Papa John's Pizza, this with the goal that the knowledge of the opinion could be useful to improve the products and service of the companies. For this the authors collected data from the social networks, and apply mining techniques to analyze the data. First, they preprocess the data to structure the information and to integrate the obtained data, transforming the obtained data in a usable format. They used the SPSS Clementine tool for the extraction, cluster and indexation of the data. They also used the Nvivo 9 to perform queries and to find pattern in the data. The result shoes that Domino's Pizza is more involve with their consumers this with the counts of post and answers. This showed that companies should keep an open dialogue with their clients, that they should monitor the conversation and answer the complaint and worries of their clients in a fast manner and prevent crisis related to increase of prices, changes on the recipes, etc. [13].

Chamlertwat *et al.* performed sentiment analysis of Twitter about some of the characteristics of smartphones using machine learning. This to discover the perception of the consuments and classify the comments in two classes: positive or negative. For this they developed a system divided in several stages. The first stage was in charge of collecting the data using the Twitter API. They proposed a list of keywords to collect tweets of the main products on the market. In the second stage, they filtering those tweets that were considered opinion, for that they perform a manual labelling and developed a SVM model to learn to differentiate between opinion and not. They use a selection of information gain evaluation, and they obtained a 84.5% ACC. In the stage three, they determined the polarity of the tweets using the SentiWordNet tool. Finally, in the fourth stage they classified characteristics of the product. In order to validate their methodology, they compare the identified characteristic by product with the ones obtained by experts, there was similarities among both analysis. Authors highlight that this type of studies provide information that helps industry in their decision taking strategies and to improve their products, they also mention that the more the data the best the results that can be reach [8].

Wang *et al.* studied a system for Twitter sentiment analysis in real-time for the presidential candidates in the 2012 USA elections, this to quantify the sentiment of the general public towards the candidates and the electoral events.

The implemented algorithm was a NBayes using unigrams. The results showed that it was possible to reach 59% of classification precision in for categories such as negative, positive, neutral and unknown [31].

Agarwal *et al.*, propose a mix of techniques and algorithms such as unigram, senti-features and tree kernels to base the sentiment analysis in Twitter. To validate the performance of each algorithm they implemented a SVM model in a cross validation setting. The results show that for a binary classification about the polarity, positive vs negative, the Three Kernel model present a better performance with an 73.93% ACC, on the other hand the mix of Unigram + Senti-features incrementally improves the performance up to 75.39% ACC [1].

Finally, Alec Go *et al.*, propose a machine learning technique to classify the tweets using distant supervising to create a binary class "positive and negative". They compare the NBayes, Maximum Entropy (MaxEnt) and SVM models with the Unigram, Bigram, Unigram + Bigram y Unigram + POS features. They found that suing Unigram was the best condition when an SVM model is using with a performance of 82.2% ACC, Bigram with NBayes reach 81.6% ACC. Additionally, the combination of Unigram + Bigram using MaxEnt has a performance of 83.0% ACC, finally Unigram + Tags POS got a performance of 81.9% ACC. They noted that the use of emojis was helpful to reach a score superior of 80% [11].

## 3    Material and Method

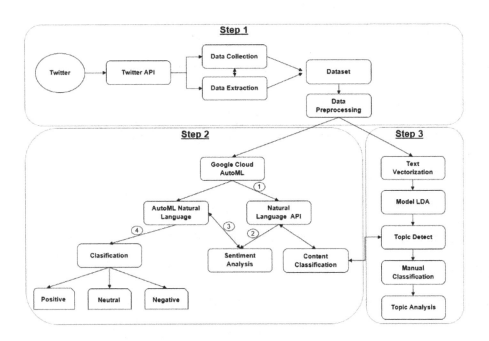

**Fig. 1.** Development of the methodological process.

Methodological process implemented in this research is described in Fig. 1. It is divided in three main steps; step one involves data collection from Twitter users by searching for the #5G hashtag using RStudio as programming language, connecting Twitter Search API. Step two draws upon in the classification of tweets into three categories, positive, negative and neutral, in addition, with the data gathered, a classification model was trained with machine learning using Google Cloud AutoML tool. Finally, in the step 3, we implemented Latent Dirichlet Allocation (LDA) Model in Python to detect various topics and develop their respective analysis.

### 3.1    Twitter

During the last years, social media has changed the way people interact [32], this because, it has become an ideal medium to share opinions, experiences, achievements, among many other things. Twitter is one of the social networks most popular in the world with 326 million active users [23]. This has resulted a strong interest on the part of researchers, companies and governments to analyze the opinions of the users on particular topics of their interests, trying to determine the contextual polarity, classifying the tweets into three categories, positive, negative and neutral. One of the great advantages of Twitter is that allow users create and share opinions instantly in one way publicly easy and accessible. It also allows the interaction among users sharing or interacting with the same hashtag about a particular topic. A hashtag is a label that is represented by the symbol "#". This label allows the users to participate in larger conversation about a particular theme [27]. The public openness of the platform makes Twitter ideal for the recollection of information contrary of other platforms [21].

### 3.2    Twitter API

For the collection of tweets we used the Rtweet library, this allows to connect to the Twitter API. A restriction is that the library only return the historic of the messages in the last 8 days, however another characteristic is that it allows to obtain the larger that 140 characters, up to 280 which is the new length allowed by the platform. We set up the parameter "retryonratelimit" to true, in this way consults continues trying after reaching the limits of the platform and we can collect data continuously. We also used the argument "max_id" to restart a collection from it stopped in the previous iteration. The nature of the obtained data is semi-structured, this allows for the realization of filter and queries on the data. For instance, to filter the data by date, geographic area, sort the users by number of post or followers among other characteristics.

### 3.3    Sample

In two previous studies, Cavazos-Rehg et al. [7] and Bermingham and Smeaton [4], the sentiment analysis was applied to two samples of tweets, one with 5,0000 tweets and another with 7,203 tweets. On the other hand, Reyes-Menendez *et al.* [24] collected 5,873 tweets related to the #WorldEnvironmentDay hashtag. Given these studies we decide to collect 8,102 tweets that used the #5G. At the beginning, the sample has composed by 46,559 tweets, but after removed duplicated tweets, mentions and retweets our collection is composed by 8,102 tweets. Following Saura et al. [25] and Reyes-Menendez et al. [24], the sample was validated using these factors:

- The user must have a profile picture and cover photo.
- Retweets are consider as duplicate information, so they were consider discarded.
- Tweets most have a localization name. Localization of names that where to precise were replaced by their country, for instance *california usa* was replace by *usa.*
- As a part of the cleaning preprocessing several aspects where cleaned, such as hashtags and links. Also the following characters: asterisks, parentheses, brackets, underscore, dash, tilde, apostrophe, single quotes and double quotes, greater than and less than symbols, numbers and whitespaces.
- Tweets should be at least 80 characters.
- Only tweets on English were considered.

It is important to notice that tweets come from different parts of the world. However, we only used those en English language since the processing tools only support this language.

**Table 1.** Publications of countries in percentage.

| Country | Percentage |
| --- | --- |
| United States | 22.94 |
| England | 10.82 |
| France | 3.93 |
| India | 3.92 |
| Finland | 1.48 |
| Sweden | 1.38 |
| Spain | 1.35 |
| China | 1.25 |
| Belgium | 1.07 |
| Canada | 1.03 |

The three more active counties were States, England y France. The three less active countries were China, Belgium y Canada. From China is understandable since the platform is not available.

### 3.4   Sentiment Analysis

The sentiment analysis allows to gain knowledge about the mental state of the user about a particular theme. This is a the that can be link with social networks for it is not exclusive to them. Liu [16] defines it a the field that analysis of opinions, sentiments, evaluations, attitudes and emotions of the people using the written text.

One the common ways to analyze the emotional behaviours contained in the text is using machine learning techniques; the machine learning is a subfield of the computer science and artificial intelligence. It inner working it is focus on patterns of data for the creation of intelligent algorithm that can learn without depend on the programming based on rules, but in the behavior codified in examples [22].

Additionally, the Google company has developed several application that have facilitated the work of several persons in different aspect of the digital life. Recently, the focus has been in the development of smart application using artificial intelligence, such is the case of the AutoML platform in the cloud. This tool can classify, extract and detect the sentiment using models of machine learning. It is focus on two [9]:

- Natural Language API: It has pre-trained models that allows the understand of the natural language, it includes sentiment analysis, name entity recognition, content classification and syntax analysis.
- AutoML Natural Language: It has a friendly interface for the user, so that she or he with the minimal effort and experience in the field can use it. The user can train their own personalized model, also they can load the data and test their model.

The sentiment analysis has been applied to several fields, such as the politics, technology, medicine, companies [10,13,15,30], to mention some. In this work, we analyze the tweets that contain the hashtag #5G, this to analyze the trends of the users toward this technology. We first use the Natural Language API from google to understand the language, the system classify the tweets into positive, negative or neutral. The API return the sentiment in two parameters, the score and the magnitude. The first one is number between $-1.0$ and $1.0$, where $-1.0$ is very negative, and $+1.0$ is very positive. The magnitude, shows the strength of the sentiment. We translate this score to three classes $-1$, $0$ and $1$.

With this classification, we train a new model using the AutoMl Natural Language with a split of 80% for training, 10% for validation and 10% for testing. We use the default setting.

### 3.5   Latent Dirichlet Allocation (LDA)

Natural Language Processing is a subfield of Artificial Intelligence that allows to deal process textual language [29]. On this field, the LDA technique is used to understand or identify the topics that a large collection of documents talk about.

This is done by identification a probability distribution over the vocabulary of the documents and the topics. This technique was proposed by Blei et al. [5].

In this study, we used LDA to identify the trends that are important to the users about the 5G. We did this with the 8,102 tweets sample that was described previously.

We create a list of all the tweets, we calculate the vocabulary and document representation using TF-IDF weighting. We only consider those words that appear more than 5 times, and we discard the 5% of the vocabulary more popular. We also discard common stopwords. These settings are common for NLP analysis [28].

We chose 30 topics for the collection, this because there has a better classification of the topics compared with other number of topics. We use that online version of LDA [14]. It is important to notice that LDA only identifies the vocabulary for topics, it can not tell us about the name of the topic. To deal with this situation we label the topics with two strategy one manual and one automatic using the Natural Language API from google using the classification of text that returns the name of a category with a score.

## 4   Results

This section presents the results that were obtained after implement the methodology described in the previous Sect. 3.

We also identify the hashtags that come together with the #5G hashtag. The most frequent are #iot, #technology and #huawei (see Table 2).

**Table 2.** Hashtags frequency

| Hashtags | Frequency |
| --- | --- |
| #iot | 1, 196 |
| #technology | 364 |
| #huawei | 339 |
| #digitaltransformation | 287 |
| #tech | 265 |
| #cybersecurity | 259 |
| #bigdata | 255 |
| #wireless | 232 |
| #mobile | 223 |
| #blockchain | 217 |
| #machinelearning | 197 |
| #innovation | 191 |
| #security | 189 |
| #smartcities | 174 |
| #telecom | 166 |
| #artificialintelligence | 163 |

Our classifier obtained a good score for the identification on positive tweets, while it was lower for neutral and acceptable for the negative class. In overall the performance was acceptable 80.89% (see Table 3).

**Table 3.** Sentiment analysis results.

| Sentiment | Tweets | Precision | Recall |
|-----------|--------|-----------|--------|
| Positive | 5,214 | 84.3% | 94.7% |
| Neutral | 905 | 54.5% | 20.2% |
| Negative | 1,983 | 73.6% | 69.0% |
| Total | 8,102 | 80.89% | 80.89% |

The result of automatically and manually label the tweets is presented in table (see Table 4). It can be notice that most of the topics focus on the innovation, finances, news. Surprising health is a concern of the public as well.

As an example of the obtained topics can be seen in Table 5 as can be seen they are consistent among themselves.

**Table 4.** Content classification: manual - natural Language API.

| | |
|---|---|
| Phone operators | Internet & Telecom/Mobile & Wireless |
| Health & Diseases | Health/Health Conditions/Cancer |
| Flights | Business & Industrial |
| Offers & Sales | No categories found |
| Technology Companies | No categories found |
| Electronic Devices | Internet & Telecom |
| Computer Hardware | Computers & Electronics |
| Journalism & News | News |
| Technological Innovation | Networking |
| Technological Publications | No categories found |
| Mobile Devices/Energy | Computers & Electronics |
| Entertainment/Fun | No categories found |
| Family & Hogar | No categories found |
| Confrontation | No categories found |
| Wireless/Antennas | No categories found |
| Shopping/Mall | Finance |
| Features Device | No categories found |

(*continued*)

**Table 4.** (*continued*)

| Phone operators | Internet & Telecom/Mobile & Wireless |
|---|---|
| Innovation & Countries | No categories found |
| Service Providers/Electronics | Mobile & Wireless |
| Health Conditions/Radiation | Computers & Electronics |
| Places/Locations | No categories found |
| Users Names | No categories found |
| Health/People | People & Society |
| Mobile Phones | Consumer Electronics |
| News/Business/Locations | Computers & Electronics |
| Health News | No categories found |
| Technology Business | No categories found |
| Discussion/Legislative Body | Law & Government |
| Finance | No categories found |
| Manufacture/Health | No categories found |

**Table 5.** Important topics.

| Health & Diseases |
|---|
| Radiation health effects cancer exposure risks microwave authorities skin harmful radiofrequency causing brain cause dangerous |
| Networking |
| 5 g new network technology future networks industry learn business mobile world great technologies data like |
| Technological Innovation |
| Huawei first new verizon technology phone us qualcomm network mobile wireless 2020 samsung market spectrum |

## 5   Discussions

Previous work have shown that the social network are a good option to analyze opinion of the users after the fact or in real time [12]. In particular, Twitter facilitates the interaction of comments by using hashtags, this has several advantages. One of them, is that a person could express their opinion using the same hashtag, this helps that we generate thousand of data cluster in a single label "#" [27]. Currently, there is one the largest platforms used for the extraction of date in different data, many of them to perform research.

The present study, focus in the sentiment analysis of tweets in which users expressed their opinion using the #5G in their publication in Twitter. We believe, that following this methodology (see Sect. 3) an analysis of sentiment analysis can be perform, in an adaptable fashion, identified the text in three categories: positive, negative and neutral. Also, we showed that a model LDA could be extracted to identify the themes on the conversation that can improve our understanding of the data. Our analysis shows that for a set of data composed of 8,102 tweets collected using the API of Twitter the tool AutoML Natural Language identify as positives the 64.35%, negatives 24.47% and neutral 11.17% (see Table 3). This shows that the classes are not balanced, since there is more tweets categorized as positives. This has a negative effect if a classifier would be train, since the performance for the classes is consistent among classes.

The results of this research show that the #5G technology is well positioned in with a 64.35% of positive tweets. However, the identified topics shade light in some concerns on the users such the effect of the radiation on the people, regarding a cancer an idea an rumor that it is part of the discussion.

Also, we could identify in the Table 2, that points to a perspective of impact once the 5G network is available for everyone. With faster networks there is the chance to use emergent technology such artificial intelligence, machine learning, internet of things, among others.

## 6   Conclusions

As has been mention through this work, Twitter has become an social network that can be exploited to extract the opinion and ideas of the user toward different topics. In this research, we use the social network twitter to analyze the publication about the 5G Network. This technology is the next generation of broadband for mobile communications; it promises a larger coverage, faster and better times when compared the 4G network. We obtained a sample of 8,102 tweets after cleaning the data. We perform an analysis using the Google Cloud AutoML Natural Language Sentiment Analysis tool for the classification of tweets in three categories: positives, negatives and neutral.

The analysis of sentiment and modeling of topics using LDA allow us to analysis the opinion of the users regarding their position of each person, we could see evidence about the advantage, disadvantages, promises, doubts and fears for the arriving of the 5G network.

The result of this research can be of utility for technology companies focus on the progress of technology, since with this companies could figure out future behaviours or stands regarding a topic. Based on this the companies could define strategies to deal with the sentiment of their users. The script and used data during this research is available in https://github.com/anibalhc/network5g.

## References

1. Agarwal, A., Xie, B., Vovsha, I., Rambow, O., Passonneau, R.: Sentiment analysis of Twitter data. In: Proceedings of the Workshop on Language in Social Media (LSM 2011), pp. 30–38 (2011)
2. Agarwal, A., Agarwal, K., Agarwal, S., Misra, G.: Evolution of mobile communication technology towards 5G networks and challenges. Am. J. Electr. Electronic Eng. **7**(2), 34–37 (2019)

3. Almeida, J.M., Pappa, G.L., et al.: Twitter population sample bias and its impact on predictive outcomes: a case study on elections. In: Proceedings of the 2015 IEEE/ACM International Conference on Advances in Social Networks Analysis and Mining 2015, pp. 1254–1261. ACM (2015)
4. Bermingham, A., Smeaton, A.: On using Twitter to monitor political sentiment and predict election results. In: Proceedings of the Workshop on Sentiment Analysis where AI meets Psychology (SAAIP 2011), pp. 2–10 (2011)
5. Blei, D.M., Ng, A.Y., Jordan, M.I.: Latent Dirichlet allocation. J. Mach. Learn. Res. **3**(Jan), 993–1022 (2003)
6. Castro, R., Kuffó, L., Vaca, C.: Back to# 6d: predicting Venezuelan states political election results through Twitter. In: 2017 Fourth International Conference on eDemocracy & eGovernment (ICEDEG), pp. 148–153. IEEE (2017)
7. Cavazos-Rehg, P.A., Zewdie, K., Krauss, M.J., Sowles, S.J.: No high like a brownie high: a content analysis of edible Marijuana Tweets. Am. J. Health Promot. **32**(4), 880–886 (2018)
8. Chamlertwat, W., Bhattarakosol, P., Rungkasiri, T., Haruechaiyasak, C.: Discovering consumer insight from Twitter via sentiment analysis. J. UCS **18**(8), 973–992 (2012)
9. Google Cloud: Google Cloud AutoML Natural Language Sentiment Analysis (2019). https://cloud.google.com/natural-language. Accessed 10 Sept 2019
10. Denecke, K., Deng, Y.: Sentiment analysis in medical settings: new opportunities and challenges. Artif. Intell. Med. **64**(1), 17–27 (2015)
11. Go, A., Bhayani, R., Huang, L.: Twitter sentiment classification using distant supervision. CS224N Proj. Rep. Stanford **1**(12), 2009 (2009)
12. Golder, S.A., Macy, M.W.: Diurnal and seasonal mood vary with work, sleep, and daylength across diverse cultures. Science **333**(6051), 1878–1881 (2011)
13. He, W., Zha, S., Li, L.: Social media competitive analysis and text mining: a case study in the pizza industry. Int. J. Inf. Manag. **33**(3), 464–472 (2013)
14. Hoffman, M., Bach, F.R., Blei, D.M.: Online learning for latent Dirichlet allocation. In: Advances in Neural Information Processing Systems, pp. 856–864 (2010)
15. Kanayama, H., Nasukawa, T., Watanabe, H.: Deeper sentiment analysis using machine translation technology. In: Proceedings of the 20th International Conference on Computational Linguistics, COLING 2004, pp. 494–500 (2004)
16. Liu, B.: Sentiment analysis and opinion mining. Synth. Lect. Hum. Lang. Technol. **5**(1), 1–167 (2012)
17. Loyola-González, O., Monroy, R., Rodríguez, J., López-Cuevas, A., Mata-Sánchez, J.I.: Contrast pattern-based classification for bot detection on Twitter. IEEE Access **7**, 45800–45817 (2019)
18. Mane, S.B., Sawant, Y., Kazi, S., Shinde, V.: Real time sentiment analysis of twitter data using Hadoop. (IJCSIT) Int. J. Comput. Sci. Inf. Technol. **5**(3), 3098–3100 (2014)
19. Martin-Domingo, L., Martín, J.C., Mandsberg, G.: Social media as a resource for sentiment analysis of airport service quality (ASQ). J. Air Transp. Manag. **78**, 106–115 (2019)
20. Mitra, R.N., Agrawal, D.P.: 5G mobile technology: a survey. ICT Exp. **1**(3), 132–137 (2015)
21. Neethu, M.S., Rajasree, R.: Sentiment analysis in Twitter using machine learning techniques. In: 2013 Fourth International Conference on Computing, Communications and Networking Technologies (ICCCNT), pp. 1–5. IEEE (2013)
22. Nilsson, N.J.: Introduction to Machine Learning: An Early Draft of a Proposed Textbook (1996)

23. Global Digital Report: Digital in 2019 (2019). https://wearesocial.com/global-digital-report-2019. Accessed 30 Aug 2019

24. Reyes-Menendez, A., Saura, J., Alvarez-Alonso, C.: Understanding# worldenvironmentday user opinions in Twitter: a topic-based sentiment analysis approach. Int. J. Environ. Res. Public Health **15**(11), 2537 (2018)

25. Saura, J., Palos-Sanchez, P., Martin, M.R.: Attitudes expressed in online comments about environmental factors in the tourism sector: an exploratory study. Int. J. Environ. Res. Public Health **15**(3), 553 (2018)

26. Saura, J.R., Reyes-Menendez, A., Palos-Sanchez, P.: Un análisis de sentimiento en Twitter con machine learning: identificando el sentimiento sobre las ofertas de #blackfriday. J. Espacios **39**, 16 (2018)

27. Small, T.A.: What the hashtag? A content analysis of Canadian politics on Twitter. Inf. Commun. Soc. **14**(6), 872–895 (2011)

28. Sunni, I., Widyantoro, D.H.: Analisis sentimen dan ekstraksi topik penentu sentimen pada opini terhadap tokoh publik. Jurnal Sarjana ITB bidang Teknik Elektro dan Informatika **1**(2) (2012)

29. Vásquez, A.C., Quispe, J.P., Huayna, A.M., et al.: Natural language processing. J. Comput. Syst. **6**(2), 45–54 (2009)

30. Vergeer, M.: Politics, elections and online campaigning: past, present... and a peek into the future. New Med. Soc. **15**(1), 9–17 (2013)

31. Wang, H., Can, D., Kazemzadeh, A., Bar, F., Narayanan, S.: A system for real-time Twitter sentiment analysis of 2012 US presidential election cycle. In: Proceedings of the ACL 2012 System Demonstrations, pp. 115–120. Association for Computational Linguistics (2012)

32. Yang, Y., Duan, W., Cao, Q.: The impact of social and conventional media on firm equity value: a sentiment analysis approach. Decis. Support Syst. **55**(4), 919–926 (2013)

# Design of an Autonomous Mobile Robot as a Base Platform for Research of Cyber Physical Systems

Andrés Toapanta, Fabricio Quinaluisa, Alexis Carrera, Henry Rivera, Luis Escobar$^{(\boxtimes)}$, and David Loza Matovelle

Universidad De Las Fuerzas Armadas-ESPE, Sangolquí, Ecuador
andres_toapanta@hotmail.com, edifabricio_quinaluisa@hotmail.com, ingalexiscarrera@hotmail.com, {herivera,lfescobar,dcloza}@espe.edu.ec

**Abstract.** The present article proposes the design and construction of a mobile robot for interiors with a Cyber Physical System (CPS) approach. It has the capacity to navigate in indoor environment and it also recognizes its surroundings by the Simultaneous Localization and Mapping (SLAM). In the generated map, the platform is able to navigate and to plan different trajectories towards the goal, recognizing obstacles, avoiding them and optimizing the routes. Besides, a docking station was built to charge and monitor the machine. It has a projection to work together with other robots and humans throughout IoT protocols.

**Keywords:** Unmanned ground vehicle · SLAM · Cyber Physical System

## 1 Introduction

Nowadays, there are commercial and research mobile robots that can navigate autonomous for purposes such as security and defense [1], services for the vulnerable people [2,3], or education and research [4]. Due to the high degree of autonomy of this kind of robots, it is difficult and expensive to obtain one in developing countries such as Ecuador, since they require a great variety of sensors and costly software platforms. This is the reason why there is an immediate need of low cost, scalable, easy to use and easy to build platforms.

A Cyber Physical Systems (CPS) approach ensures a low cost by increasing the capacity of sensors and actuators. Moreover, it also gives the opportunity to use wireless communication and increased bandwidth, a CPS complement a Mechatronic design due to its advantages such as: Scalability, Stability, Robustness among other [5].

A mobile machine has to accomplish tasks such as: navigate through an unknown place and avoid obstacles, calculate the best trajectory for each assignment, consider if it has to carry on a load, and how much energy has to spend in that kind of exercises. Furthermore, when a platform is autonomous, it also

© Springer Nature Switzerland AG 2020
M. Botto-Tobar et al. (Eds.): ICAT 2019, CCIS 1193, pp. 204–216, 2020.
https://doi.org/10.1007/978-3-030-42517-3_16

has to recognize all those tasks by itself and calculate every action needed to complete the current work without generating problems in its surrounding.

Indoor navigation requires, first, a recognizing function for the places where the platform needs to unwind through a strategy to solve the problem by simultaneous localization and mapping SLAM [6]. As part of the recognizing of any place: the position of walls, doors, hallways, and obstacles in the environment (tables, chairs, desks, etc.) are generated in the software. The map presents the information of places that the platform can reach and cannot. In order to navigate, the machine must establish a trajectory to the goal and refresh constantly to avoid any obstacle over its movement.

An autonomous mobile robot, as a complement, demands independence from human. For example, to charge batteries, the mobile robot must recognize the energy remaining in its cells and proceed to charge when needed.

This work shows the implementation of an autonomous mobile robot for interiors with the purpose of service using SLAM [1], Goal Navigation [7], and autonomous battery charging.

## 2    Cyber Physical System

This section shows a summary of Cyber Physical System (CPS) and how it is applied in the robot. CPS is defined as "physical and engineered systems whose operations are monitored, coordinated, controlled, and integrated by a computing and communication core" [5].

In [8], it is established some characteristics of the CPS in contrast to a Mechatronics System, which can be seen in the Table 1. The robot presents, in some degree, all of these characteristics. It is Autonomous because it recognizes all the surrounds whit SLAM in order to plan the trajectory and locate the docking station, being an example of energy efficiency. All the software was designed in ROS with the aim of scalability and stability. The mechanical design of the robot guarantees a Robustness desired.

As it is shown in [9], one of the main drivers for the development of a Cyber Physical System is the reduction of development costs. Some examples of commercial robots with their characteristics are shown in Table 2.

It can be seen that all of them have SLAM capabilities, goal navigation, and docking station [10]. Also, the price and payload is presented. In this way, the designed platform shows characteristics that challenge the first one named Kobuki whit better singularities like docking station and better price.

**Table 1.** Mechatronics and CPS parameters [5]

| Parameters | Type of products | |
|---|---|---|
| | Mechatronics | CPS |
| Maintainability/Availability | + | |
| Scalability | | ++ |
| Stability | | + |
| Robustness | | ++ |
| Efficiency | + | + |
| Autonomous | | ++ |
| Energy Efficiency | + | ++ |
| Safety | ++ | ++ |
| Compactness | + | |
| Reliability | ++ | + |
| Accuracy | ++ | + |
| Communication | ++ | ++ |

**Table 2.** Comparison of the simba robot proposal against other commercial robots with similar functions.

| Robot | Price | SLAM | Goal navigation | Docking station | Load capacity |
|---|---|---|---|---|---|
| Kobuki | $800, 00 | x | x | − | 4 Kg |
| RB1 | $2.500, 00 | x | x | x | 50 Kg |
| RB2 | $5.500, 00 | x | x | x | 200 Kg |
| Freight | $6.000, 00 | x | x | x | 100 Kg |
| Turtlebot3 | $1.400, 00 | x | x | x | 30 Kg |

# 3    Design and Constrution

## 3.1    Mechanical Construction

A configuration with the capacity to climb small slopes up to $10°$ and with the capability to navigate through different floors as carpet or ceramic was designed. Differential locomotion with a free wheel of 5 cm of diameter that allows the movement on irregular surfaces indoor environments were used. The structure of the mobile robot is circular in order to avoid closer obstacles, specially when turning over its own axis. Figure 1 shows the configuration of the robot SIMBA (Synergic Implementation of Mechatronics Base and Autonomy), (A) Driver TB6600, (B) Motors, (C) Batteries, (D) On board computer, (E) Wheels, (F) Bumpers, (G) Castor wheel.

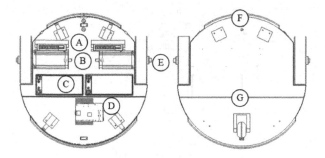

**Fig. 1.** Distribution of elements and differential drive configuration to the proposed robot.

**Fig. 2.** Mobile robot designed. (A) Lidar 360° (B) Sonar sensors and (C) Docking station.

The robot shown in Fig. 2 has a diameter of 40 cm, which gives the ability to go through doors and tight halls. The intern components are distributed in a way that turning center and gravity center are even. The mobile robot is equipped with front and rear bumpers to protect the integrity against shock and collect the information trough signals in the GPIO pins of a Raspberry PI2.

Steeper motors NEMA 23 were used with a direct coupling to rubber wheels of 14,5 cm diameter to mobilize the robot. The open loop control for the steeper motors was built by the implementation of the Accel Stepper [11] library in the Raspberry computer PI2, this is shown in Fig. 3. The control is established over the pulse frequency sent to drives TB6600, which enables the control for the angular velocity over each wheel and, moreover, the counting of steps for the required information for the odometry. These characteristics allow the SIMBA robot to undertake linear and angular trajectories with acceleration and deceleration.

On board, there are two batteries connected in series, each one with 7 AH capacity. The robot is energized with 24 V, which is necessary for the motors, and with a converter Buck LM2596, to reduce the voltage to 5 V when required for different elements of control and sensors.

A RPLIDAR 360 A1M8 sensor with a range of 12 m and resolution of 0,5 mm was acquired. The sensor RPLIDAR was installed in the upper area of the robot, resulting in a data measured 20 cm over the floor.

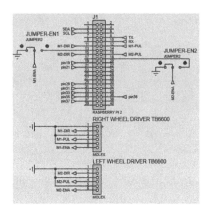

**Fig. 3.** Electric diagram for the connection of Driver TB6600 and the GPIO ports of the Raspberry PI2.

A ring of 12 ultrasonic sensors was implemented and connected to a microcontroller to obtain data of the distance where obstacles are presented. The microcontroller communicates with the on-board computer trough serial port at 115200baud. Figure 4 shows the robot that has been assembled.

**Fig. 4.** SIMBA - robot mobile SIMBA.

## 3.2 Simultaneous Localization and Mapping

The algorithm Fast SLAM 2.0 [12] present in the package Gmapping ROS [13] was implemented using the sensor RPLIDAR A1 in order to measure its environment. The algorithm requires the odometry data, which is calculated by the counting of steps over the motor and the Eqs. (1) and (2). With the pulses counting values for the lineal displacement $\Delta x$ is obtained by Eq. (3), $\Delta y$ by Eq. (4) and its angular displacement $\Delta\theta$ by Eq. (5).

$$\Delta S_r = \frac{\Delta steps_{right} \cdot 2\pi \cdot r_{wheel}}{400\dfrac{step}{rev}} \tag{1}$$

$$\Delta S_l = \frac{\Delta steps_{left} \cdot 2\pi \cdot r_{wheel}}{400 \frac{step}{rev}} \qquad (2)$$

$$\Delta x = \frac{\Delta S_r + \Delta S_l}{2} \left( cos \left( \theta + \left( \frac{\Delta S_r - \Delta S_l}{b} \right) \right) \right) \qquad (3)$$

$$\Delta y = \frac{\Delta S_r + \Delta S_l}{2} sin \left( \theta + \left( \frac{\Delta S_r - \Delta S_l}{b} \right) \right) \qquad (4)$$

$$\Delta \theta = \left( \frac{\Delta S_r - \Delta S_l}{b} \right) \qquad (5)$$

### 3.3 Navigation with Obstacle Avoidance

A navigation algorithm with obstacle avoidance and trajectory planner has been developed. The main goal of this algorithm is to navigate from an initial point to a goal, dodging obstacles and people present in the maps. The Dynamic Window Approach (DWA) [14] and the trajectory planner A* [15] makes it possible.

The Dynamic Window Approach algorithm (DWA) has a local planner that requires the robot to know the position all the time. This is the reason why an Adaptative MonteCarlo Localization particle filter [16] is used to adjust the robot position in real time- The AMCL position is assumed as real for the robot.

In Fig. 5 The action of the DWA algorithm and its simulated trajectories are shown in the map, the action of the RPLIDAR, with the information collected by the ultrasonic sensors the algorithm updates periodically. The sensors locate the position of the obstacles and the algorithm discards trajectories where a collision is detected. A search for the best command of velocity and acceleration with obstacle avoidance and minimum travel distance is done in real time.

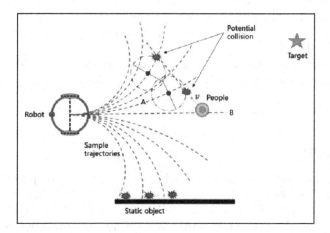

**Fig. 5.** The Dynamic Window Approach with simulated trajectories showed in broken line path. A Static object is shown like a wall or dynamic object like people [13].

## 3.4  Docking Station and Autonomous Charging

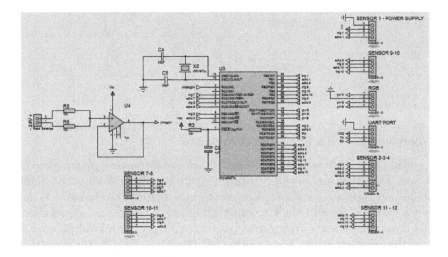

**Fig. 6.** Voltage reading with a divisor, the input mapped voltage is connected with the ADC converter. The ultrasonic sensors are connected to the digital ports in the microcontroller.

As part of the proposal a docking station was considered. SIMBA has the ability to recharge autonomously. The machine and the docking station have two contact points that allow the charging just by the correct placement of the robot. In order to achieve the correct position, a system with three infrared emitters was implemented in the docking station and four infrared receptors in the platform [16]. In this technique, synchronizing a signal of 38 KHz and the correct positioning of the anchorage are accomplished.

The robot requires the information about energy stored in order to start the automatic charging cycle. A circuit was used to measure the voltage in the batteries as shown in Fig. 6, by using a voltage divisor, an operational amplifier for impedance coupling and an analog-digital converter present in the PIC16F877A.

## 3.5  Controller

The mobile robot software was embedded into the on-board computer Raspberry PI2. It has 4 USB ports needed to connect the RPLIDAR A1M8 and it uses its GPIO ports to communicate with the PIC16F87A. The robot is connected to an Intel Core i5, 1,6 GHz with 8 GB RAM via Wi-Fi in a master-slave configuration based on the protocol XML – RPC for the communication between nodes and protocol TCP/IP to connect between computers. This architecture is exposed in Fig. 7.

The on-board computer executes all the functions of control over the motors and the sensor data. The master computer executes the SLAM, navigation, planning, trajectory, and auto positioning for the docking station algorithms. It also allows to monitor the position and sensors data in real time on RVIZ ROS. An architecture based on nodes was used in all the configuration for the controllers and algorithms.

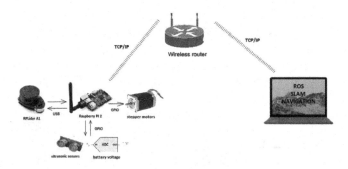

**Fig. 7.** Connection diagram between the Raspberry PI (on-board computer) and the master Computer over Wireless Network.

## 4    Experimentation

In order to evaluate the platform, three tests were performed to show its attributes. The first test was executed with the aim to determine an appropriate velocity for the robot navigation, and to also allow the machine to construct a map close to reality. The second test was to measure the navigation error, where a target is given. After the platform arrives to the objective, the robot position and the real position is taken and compared to get the trajectory accuracy. In the last test, the robot is placed 1 m away from its docking station, to exhibit the time that the platform requires to arrive at the station, and the charging status. In order to test its flexibility, the alignment of the docking station is modified.

### 4.1    SLAM Test

**Mapping Speed Test.** The SLAM test is done in a real ambient where different obstacles (tables, chairs, etc.) Fig. 8 exposed the results in an area of $90\,m^2$ at different velocities: (a) $0,5\frac{m}{s}$, (b) $0,35\frac{m}{s}$, (c) $0,2\frac{m}{s}$, (d) $0,17\frac{m}{s}$.

Figure 8c and d have similar quality, this relationship is given by the small difference on velocity between them.

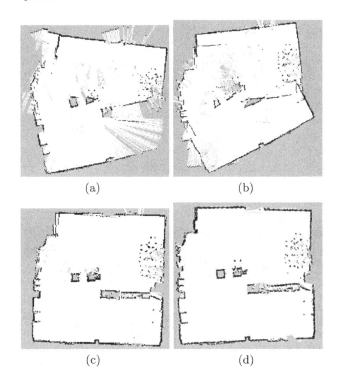

(a)                              (b)

(c)                              (d)

**Fig. 8.** Comparison of the map with SLAM over different robot velocities.

**Mapping Error Test.** The second test uses the SLAM. It shows errors obtained in an area of $53\,\mathrm{m}^2$, where four measurements were taken and compared against real measurements as shown in Fig. 9 and Table 2.

The maximum error shown in Table 3 is 3.56% and a minimum error of 0.54%.

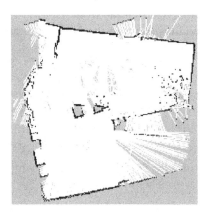

**Fig. 9.** Measurements L1, L2, L3, L4 in the map to compare the error that shows Table 3

**Table 3.** Error in the measurements for the map in the Fig. 8 against real measurements.

| | Distance | | Error % |
|---|---|---|---|
| | Real (m) | Measured (m) | |
| L1 | 11,74 | 11,5095 | 1,96% |
| L2 | 4,50 | 4,44547 | 1,21% |
| L3 | 4,77 | 4,6 | 3,56% |
| L4 | 1,88 | 1,86979 | 0,54% |

## 4.2  Path Planning and Navigation Test

Figure 10 is an example of an initial planned trajectory from point A to a goal, as the robot get closer to the goal the trajectory changes with a rate of 2 Hz.

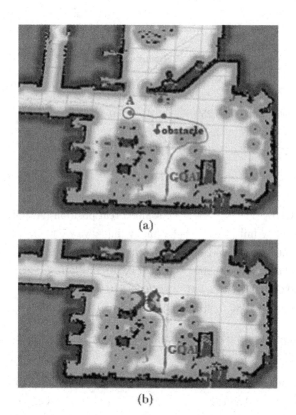

(a)

(b)

**Fig. 10.** Path planning from point A to a Goal. a. Initial planning, b. Adjusted trajectory and movement.

The sensors found a new obstacle in the proximity during the navigation planned in Fig. 10a the path change in real time and calculate the new path in Fig. 10b due because an obstacle is displaced and cleaned the path.

Tables 4 and 5 show the error in the goal given by the AMCL algorithm and the real one measured.

Position (x, y, yaw) is given in the plane respect to the docking station. Table 4 shows the comparison between the goal and the assumed real position; a $\pm 0{,}18$ m accuracy in position and $\pm 6°$ in yaw angle for orientation were obtained. Table 5 shows the comparison between real position and goal, a $\pm 0{,}13$ m accuracy in position and $\pm 4°$ in yaw angle for orientation were obtained.

### 4.3  Autonomous Battery Charging

The last test done is shown in Table 6, where the time to dock is taken from a distance of 1 m and a variable of its quality of alignment.

**Table 4.** Navigation goal error with respect to the Monte Carlo localization value.

| GOAL | | | Assumed real position (AMCL) | | |
|---|---|---|---|---|---|
| x [m] | y [m] | yaw [°] | x [m] | y [m] | yaw [°] |
| 3,000 | 0,004 | −2,000 | 2,860 | 0,003 | −2,180 |
| 0,990 | 0,000 | 0,250 | 0,970 | 0,001 | 0,200 |
| 3,027 | 0,997 | 32,340 | 2,943 | 0,981 | 33,440 |
| 4,024 | −0,986 | −49,000 | 4,022 | −0,865 | −55,000 |

**Table 5.** Navigation goal error with respect to the real goal achieved.

| GOAL | | | Assumed real position (AMCL) | | |
|---|---|---|---|---|---|
| x [m] | y [m] | yaw [°] | x [m] | y [m] | yaw [°] |
| 3,000 | 0,004 | −2,000 | 2,870 | 0,003 | −2,200 |
| 0,990 | 0,000 | 0,250 | 1,020 | 0,040 | 0,180 |
| 3,027 | 0,997 | 32,340 | 2,970 | 0,810 | 29,000 |
| 4,024 | −0,986 | −49,000 | 4,090 | −1,080 | −47,000 |

**Table 6.** Auto docking results with the initial pose achieved with the navigation and the final state over the docking station

| Test | Time [s] | Initial pose at 1 m | Docking position | Charging state |
|---|---|---|---|---|
| 1 | 40 | Aligned | Regular | Charging |
| 2 | 23 | Aligned | Bad | Charging |
| 3 | 24,7 | Aligned | Acceptable | Charging |
| 4 | 58 | Misaligned | Good | Charging |
| 5 | 67 | Misaligned | Good | Charging |

# 5 Conclusions and Future Work

A mobile robot was built with a cost of \$742,00 as a prototype, which represents an advantage over other commercial robots shown in Table 1, because Kobuki costs \$800 and it is a final product; moreover, it does not have a docking station as SIMBA do. The SIMBA robot is able to create maps with a maximum error of 3.56% with a velocity of 0,17 m/s, by the test realized in a 53 m². The robot has a navigation capacity to arrive to a goal from a starting point autonomously with obstacle avoidance in base of a trajectory planning using DWA and the capacity to dock to a station in a maximum time of 67 s. Furthermore, the objective to develop a base platform with standard parts and totally open source was accomplished. It is important to consider that the price of \$742,00 includes taxes and construction in Ecuador, being much more affordable for developing countries the construction of this kind of prototypes. Finally, as a CPS platform, it is shown that it has the capacity to connect throughout IoT protocols and be used as part of a more complex system in future work.

There are many areas of future work, the use of packages as Google Cartographer ROS, that allows the creation of 2D and 3D maps. In the same way, there is chance to recover the position of the robot to solve the Kidnapped Robot Problem. Some applications include office assistance, elderly care, building IoT platforms and the use as a platform to test algorithms and develop path plannings solutions.

**Acknowledgment.** This work is part of the Project "Autonomous robot mobile for indoors" from Research of the Mechatronic and Dynamic systems laboratory under the supervision of MSc. David Loza.

# References

1. Thing, V.L.L., Wu, J.: Autonomous vehicle security: a taxonomy of attacks and defences. In: 2016 IEEE International Conference on Internet of Things (iThings) and IEEE Green Computing and Communications (GreenCom) and IEEE Cyber, Physical and Social Computing (CPSCom) and IEEE Smart Data (SmartData), Chengdu, pp. 164–170 (2016)
2. Hengstler, M., Enkel, E., Duelli, S.: Applied artificial intelligence and trust-the case of autonomous vehicles and medical assistance devices. Technol. Forecast. Soc. Change **105**, 105–120 (2016). ISSN 0040–1625
3. Sikkenk, M., Terken, J.: Rules of conduct for autonomous vehicles. In: Proceedings of the 7th International Conference on Automotive User Interfaces and Interactive Vehicular Applications (AutomotiveUI 2015), pp. 19–22. ACM, New York (2015)
4. Merdan, M., Lepuschitz, W., Koppensteiner, G., Balogh, R., Obdržálek, D. (eds.): RiE 2019. AISC, vol. 1023, pp. 170–181. Springer, Cham (2020). https://doi.org/10.1007/978-3-030-26945-6
5. Escobar, L., et al.: Design and implementation of complex systems using mechatronics and cyber-physical systems approaches. In: 2017 IEEE International Conference on Mechatronics and Automation (ICMA), Takamatsu, pp. 147–154 (2017)

6. Gómez Gómez, D.H., de una técnica, D.: SLAM para ambientes dinámicos tridimensionales. Universidad Nacional de Colombia, Bogotá (2015)
7. Siegwart, R., Nourbakhsh, I.: Introduction to Autonomous Mobile Robots, Massachusetts Institute of Technology (2011)
8. Guerineau, B., Bricogne, M., Durupt, A., Rivest, L.: Mechatronics vs. cyber physical systems: towards a conceptual framework for a suitable design methodology. In: Mechatronics (MECATRONICS)/17th International Conference on Research and Education in Mechatronics (REM) (2016)
9. R. OSRF, Ros Components, [En línea]. https://www.roscomponents.com. Último acceso: 1 Junio 2018
10. DiCola, T.: GitHub, 27 Mayo 2016. [En línea]. Available: https://github.com/adafruit/AccelStepper. Último acceso: 15 Noviembre 2017
11. Gallardo López, D.: Aplicación del muestreo bayesiano en robots móviles: estrategias para localización y estimación de mapas del entorno, Alicante: Universidad de Alicante (1999)
12. Iralab, Iralab: [En línea]. http://irawiki.disco.unimib.it/irawiki/index.php/ROS_GMapping
13. Fox, D., Burgard, W., Thrun, S.: The Dynamic Window Approach to Collision Avoidance (1998)
14. Tian, L., Collins, C.: An effective robot trajectory planning method using a genetic algorithm (2003)
15. Vera Durán, J.: Sistema de recargar de energía de robots móviles con ROS, Málaga: Escuela Técnica Superior de Ingeniería Industrial - Universidad de Málaga (2016)
16. Pfaff, P., Burgard, W., Fox, D.: Robust Monte-Carlo Localization Using Adaptive Likelihood Models (2006)

# Development of a Mobile Application for the Integral Care and Attention of Elderly People

Paúl E. Vintimilla-Tapia[1]([envelope]), Jack F. Bravo-Torres[1],
Pablo E. Tamariz-Ordóñez[2], Yulissa R. Abad-Salinas[2],
Karina de L. Serrano-Paredes[3], Jenny A. Pacheco-Sarmiento[3],
and Sandra C. Salazar-Mostesdeoca[4]

[1] Grupo de Investigación GITEL,
Universidad Politécnica Salesiana, Cuenca, Ecuador
{pvintimilla,jbravo}@ups.edu.ec
[2] Grupo de Investigación GIRO,
Universidad de Cuenca, Cuenca, Ecuador
{pablo.tamariz,yulissa.abad}@ucuenca.edu.ec
[3] Grupo de Telemedicina, CEDIA, Unidad Académica de Salud y Bienestar,
Universidad Católica de Cuenca, Cuenca, Ecuador
{kserrano,jpachecos}@ucacue.edu.ec
[4] Instituto Superior Tecnológico "American College",
Cuenca, Ecuador
sandra.salazar@americancollege.edu.ec

**Abstract.** In recent years, the number of people reaching stages of ageing has increased considerably, reflecting a serious public problem. It is not enough to reach long ages, but to guarantee the integral care and attention of each individual. Thus, taking into consideration the difficulties faced by the elderly, States implement social security programs that seek to support their development. Ecuador follows this trend and presents proposals that address a number of fundamental rights, which are considered priority health care services. Although the measures implemented maintain the health, this reality changes when moving from an urban to a rural scenario. This is justified by the fact that in Ecuador, specialists who care for the elderly constantly change their location and, therefore, their patients, rather than maintaining a non-standardized data record on paper, causing inefficiency and waste of time. For these reasons, this article explains a proposal for a mobile application that seeks to standardize and digitalize the collection of medical data from the elderly in rural areas in order to increase the efficiency of current medical processes.

**Keywords:** Elderly care · Information and communication technologies (ICTs) · Multi-disciplinary work · Medicine · Nursing · Dentistry

M. Botto-Tobar et al. (Eds.): ICAT 2019, CCIS 1193, pp. 217–229, 2020.
https://doi.org/10.1007/978-3-030-42517-3_17

# 1   Introduction

The world's population is ageing rapidly. This demographic change presents both opportunities and challenges, as many people yearn for a long and healthy life. While ageing is likely to be associated with a declining workforce and a growing demand for health care, older adults can become valuable economic, social, cultural and family resources depending on their role in society [3]. This depends on their abilities and aspirations, since some want constant participation in social and occupational activities, while the unhealthy require medical assistance, which translates into a limitation in accepting commitments. On the other hand, despite the fact that life expectancy in old age is increasing in almost all countries, there is no assurance that the quality of these years will be adequate, making this stage the propitious context for long periods of morbidity [16].

Hence, while there are age-related difficulties such as walking or climbing stairs, the real deterioration begins with retirement, where the lack of work stands out [6]. The old man, in this life period, projects a negative self-concept of himself, and, having too much free time, experiences accelerated physical and psychological exhaustion, requiring activities that strengthen confidence. Therefore, it is essential to support the creation of continuous routines or work ventures that intervene in the exploitation of various skills and provide the right motivation to cope better every day. In summary, the role assumed with retirement could describe a scenario in which the holistic well-being of the elderly is undermined, generating feelings of worthlessness and little social recognition [2].

Consequently, based on Maslow theories [14], the needs of each elder can be grouped into 5 hierarchical levels [17]: (i) physiological, related to biological functions and attended by different areas of the Health Sciences (medicine, dentistry, nursing and gerontology); (ii) safety, which reflect a concern to maintain their own savings and have health insurance; (iii) love and relevance, aimed at stimulating social relationships with friends, family and partner; (iv) esteem, which focus on improving self-esteem and creating indifference to any negative opinion; and (v) self-realization, which lead physical experiences towards a spiritual dimension. When one level is satisfied, it is possible to move on to the next without forgetting that lower needs represent a physiological deficit (priority) and higher needs are related to requirements of rational development [4].

As can be seen, the needs of the elderly were described in a general way. However, transferring this situation to a rural environment gives rise to complications related to abandonment: a large part of the family, which has traditionally taken care of the elderly, does not live in the town as a result of emigration to the city; the remaining family still has other types of responsibilities; the neighbours, who were a source of care and support, change their residence in search of better opportunities; and the government's healthy services do not reach high levels of efficiency because of problems of access to remote areas. Then, as a derivative effect, it is observed that aging in a small town entails significant differences with respect to what happens in the urban environment, causing a marked perception of insecurity, loneliness and isolation [15].

In addition to the above, it is important to note that the main causes of death and disability in old age, for both urban and rural environments, are non-transmissible diseases [5]. Although many of them can be prevented or delayed thanks to strategies for the development of healthy behaviours, it is normal to find limitations when monitoring basic health habits in the elderly [3]. In that sense, an effective response to ageing must take into account the wide diversity in the health, social and economic circumstances of the population, relying on a multidisciplinary team that includes trained personnel [11,13]. However, within the country it is common for health professionals in rural areas to rotate or change patients after a certain period of time, causing difficulties in obtaining paper medical records, repeated measurements of vital signs and loss of time in any critical or care situation. In addition, adequate protocols and standards have not been established to correctly treat the data recorded in each visit, which leads to inadequate knowledge management on the part of health entities.

Based on this, a working group of four higher education institutions was formed in the city of Cuenca: Universidad Politécnica Salesiana with its research group GITEL, Universidad de Cuenca with its Dentistry career, Universidad Católica de Cuenca with its Nursing career, and Instituto Superior Tecnológico American College with its gerontology career, together with the support of Grupo de Telemedicina of the Corporación Ecuatoriana para el Desarrollo de la Investigación y la Academia (CEDIA), whose main objective is to design and implement technological solutions focused on improving the quality of life of the elderly. This article describes a proposal that seeks to solve many of the problems described through the development of a mobile application for digital data collection for the Integral Care and Attention of Elderly Person, known as ICAEP. Thus, its main contribution is based on providing a mobile tool that seeks to improve medical processes through timely management of clinical data of older adults living in rural areas, which are digitized to ensure integrity and easy access, to become a source of knowledge to predict risk scenarios and increase opportunities for efficient care and optimization of resources.

This article is organized as follows. Section 2 summarizes the policies that the government of Ecuador has implemented to ensure the well-being of older adults. Section 3 describes in detail the creation of the working group and the standardization of clinical data. In Sect. 4, the technical foundations of ICAEP and its expected functioning are presented. In Sect. 5, the main conclusions are presented.

## 2    Elderly Reality in Ecuador

The Consejo Nacional para la Igualdad Intergeneracional de la República del Ecuador defines older adults as those citizens who are 65 years of age or older, who represent 7% of the country's total population[1]. It also ensures that the aging process differs according to social, educational, cultural and economic conditions. Some elderly people enjoy a retirement and receive pensions that

---

[1]  https://www.igualdad.gob.ec/personas-adultas-mayores-situacion-y-derechos/.

allow them to live with dignity; others still work or have their own businesses, so they are economically independent; some collaborate with the care of their family, especially granddaughters and grandchildren; and, the most active, carry out sports, recreational or cultural activities, return to their studies to update their knowledge and even lend themselves to community work as volunteers. For its part, the Constitución del Ecuador considers older adults as a priority care group, which means that they must receive quality specialized care[2]. As a result, they are entitled to various benefits such as exemption or refund of tax payments, payment of reduced fares for public shows and transportation, and preferential access to various health services.

Although the above shows a generalized reality regarding ageing in the country, there are some cases, especially in rural areas, of elderly people who do not have a decent income and, as is characteristic of age, have diseases that threaten their health. Consequently, they suffer mistreatment and abandonment by their families, or they give up living accompanied because they do not feel useful, exposing themselves to scenarios of violence and begging. This stems from the fact that social security, whether public or private, is not a privilege enjoyed by the entire population. As a solution, the Government has defined the specific rights that guarantee the comprehensive well-being of the elderly, the following being particularly relevant:

- Free and specialized health care, as well as free access to medicines.
- Paid work, according to their abilities, for which limitations will be taken into account.
- Universal retirement.
- Discounts on public services and private transport and entertainment services.
- Exemptions in the tax system.
- Exemption from payment of notary and registration fees, in accordance with the law.
- Access to housing that ensures a dignified life, with respect for their opinion and consent.
- Right to receive food from relatives.

Currently, in order to comply with the aforementioned rights, the mission "Mis Mejores Años" and the integral care plan for the elderly person have been designed, which are briefly described in the following subsections.

### 2.1   Mission "Mis Mejores A nos"

In order to achieve active and healthy aging, the Ecuadorian state implemented the mission "Mis Mejores Años"[3]. Thus, it seeks to improve the quality of life of older adults, particularly those who are in conditions of vulnerability, extreme

---

[2] https://www.oas.org/juridico/mla/sp/ecu/sp_ecu-int-text-const.pdf.

[3] https://www.todaunavida.gob.ec/wp-content/uploads/downloads/2018/12/BrochureMisMejoresAn%CC%83os_L5.pdf.

poverty and who, if not for state action, would lack a minimum level of social security. Hence, the coverage of access to basic services is being expanded according to the chronological, physiological and cultural characteristics of the population. In fact, the aim is to increase the well-being of the elderly from a holistic perspective that recognizes their individual and social requirements.

In that sense, the pillars on which the mission is based are four:

1. Favourable environments and care services: shows that health, more than being understood as the absence of disease, refers to strengthening and preservation at the physical, mental and social level, satisfying vital needs such as autonomy, joy and solidarity. To this end, it is essential to implement policies and programs aimed at improving the interaction environments of older adults, contemplating systems of support and promotion of old age from a perspective of rights and active and healthy ageing that motivates participation in activities that dignify them.
2. Income security: the objective of the mission is to improve the quality of life of older people, especially those in conditions of extreme poverty and lack of social security. As a result, a cash transfer programme, known as "Bono Mis Mejores Años", is being implemented to help cover minimum requirements.
3. Skills and employability: education is one of people's fundamental rights. In addition, different approaches to ageing regard learning as a positive social determinant and require training. Therefore, Ecuador has policies to promote permanent education processes for older adults through the programs "Campaña Todos ABC" and "Alfabetización y Educación Básica Monseñor Leonidas Proaño", which seek to mobilize society to complete basic education and provide continuity to training throughout life. With respect to employment, activity rates remain high even after reaching retirement age, a reality specific to the peoples of Latin America and the Caribbean.
4. Health status: it is important to keep in mind that during old age there are variations in health conditions, so it is normal to find an increase in degrees of dependency and care. Added to this, dealing with the increased risk of having more than one chronic condition at the same time cannot consider the impact and treatment of each condition separately. Faced with this scenario, health systems must start from a health promotion and disease prevention approach, providing specialized care, long-term care and support mechanisms, with the objective of improving the quality of life. To this end, a package of services has been deployed for the care and follow-up of older adults, which considers two aspects: an initial assessment that identifies vulnerabilities and assigns a specialist physician according to the clinical picture; and an annual assessment by the geriatrician or the assigned physician.

## 2.2  Integral Care Plan for the Elderly Person

According to the technical norm for the implementation and provision of geronto-logical services in Ecuador[4], comprehensive care is an intervention aimed at older adults through promotion, prevention, recovery and rehabilitation activities at three levels: individual, family and community. Thus, based on the recommendations of the Pan American Health Organization (PAHO), three specific areas of action have been formulated for the creation of health programs and services:

1. Comprehensive community programs to provide a range of healthy ageing environments, supporting family care and dignity protection activities to avoid unnecessary institutionalization.
2. Programs designed to strengthen the technical capacity of social-sanitary services.
3. Programmes designed to provide incentives to encourage self-reliance, socially productive activities and the establishment of sources of income.

Punctually, in order to enjoy the service, a care unit must apply the card of acceptance and admission of each elderly person, verifying their identification data. In this way, it is possible to draw up an individual care plan that contains personal information, comprehensive assessment, intervention proposals, personalised support and recommendations for the elderly to acquire a greater degree of self-management over their lives. Based on the plan designed, the care unit organizes monthly activities that influence the achievement of established goals. Likewise, the family should be encouraged to start strengthening actions in the home, taking into account parameters such as health, care, rights, education and instrumental, cognitive and affective activities. Definitively, the integral evaluation is a systematic and dynamic process to stratify the users, taking into account multiple domains: health, functional state, mental, nutritional, social and economic, in addition to considering their resources and social-family environment. This assessment is carried out every six months, using the pillars that affect the life of the elderly: functional, cognitive-affective, social and physical.

From the proposals described, the country's intentions to meet the needs that arise during aging and ensure a proper development of life are evident. However, from a practical point of view, there are problems related to the management of information for older adults. Firstly, due to public processes, doctors, dentists and specialists visiting rural areas or GADs (from the Spanish "Gobiernos Autónomos Descentralizados") make notes on symptoms, diagnoses and treatments on paper, causing the data not to be immediately available. For example, a dentist may require certain studies that were previously performed by a general practitioner, but since there is no access, he repeats them wasting time and resources. Finally, a model for knowledge management has not been implemented, making it impossible for artificial intelligence algorithms to come into

---

[4] https://www.inclusion.gob.ec/wp-content/uploads/2018/12/Norma-T%C3%A9 cnica-para-Espacios-Activos.pdf.

play to optimize work and resource allocation. In order to face these inconveniences, the ICAEP application was designed, thanks to the joint work of several higher education institutions, which will be explained in the following section.

## 3   Working Group and Data Standardization

The Corporación Ecuatoriana para el Desarrollo de la Investigación y la Academia (CEDIA)[5], is an entity made up of universities, institutes, colleges and companies that seeks to foster, promote and coordinate the development of scientific research and academia, offering services related to information technologies focused on scientific, technological, innovative and educational progress in the country. Its members include the Universidad Politécnica Salesiana with its Grupo de Investigación en Telecomunicaciones y Telemática (GITEL), the Universidad de Cuenca with its Grupo de Investigación en Rehabilitación Oral (GIRO), the Universidad Católica de Cuenca with its Career in Nursing and the Instituto Superior Tecnológico American College with its Career in Gerontology, which noted the difficulties reflected in medical care protocols for older adults, especially in rural areas, which lead to inefficient data management. This gave rise to the idea of initiating a project to ensure the holistic well-being of the elderly.

After several meetings of the work teams of each institution, the specific objectives to be covered in a first phase of the project were established: (i) design and deploy a mobile application for the remote recording of medical data, known as ICAEP (Integral Care and Attention of the Elderly Person) and (ii) offer courses that cover topics related to living with the elderly. The first seeks to standardize the forms and protocols used by each area of Health Sciences (medicine, nursing, dentistry, psychology and gerontology) in order to digitize and optimize the management of each patient's information. Thus, any specialist can access examinations and diagnoses that their colleagues have made in past visits, in addition to implementing artificial intelligence algorithms that help predict risk scenarios. On the other hand, the second is based on the fact that families and some caregivers are unaware of the actions they should take in certain situations that an older adult may go through. Then, by taking the courses they will be able to train themselves on current issues of care and attention, improving their capacities and, therefore, the quality of life of themselves and of the people they care for. However, this article covers only the first objective, describing in the following subsections the standardization of data and the development of the mobile application.

### 3.1   Data Standardization

From a biological point of view, ageing occurs because of an accumulation of molecular damage influenced by genetic and environmental phenomena, a product of the passage of years [7]. This determines the appearance of multiple

---

[5] https://www.cedia.edu.ec.

alterations in health as progressive and non-lethal chronic-degenerative diseases, deteriorating the functionality of each individual and impacting their family environment and social participation [10]. For this reason, it is necessary that the assessment of the older adult be thorough, multidimensional and interdisciplinary to establish a follow-up and treatment plan. Thus, the measurable dimensions of geriatric assessment are grouped into four axes: physical health, functional state, psychological health and parameters, and can be measured with various instruments: social support networks, economic base and environmental safety [9].

First of all, it should be borne in mind that one of the key concepts for the assessment of older adults is their state of fragility, determined by a reduced functional reserve, increased risk of adverse events and mortality, as a consequence of the alteration that occurs at the cellular level and that affects the physiology of the systems, generating a lack of adaptation to internal and external stressors [1,8]. Another aspect to examine is functionality, which refers to a group of domains that interfere in the performance of daily activities to live independently and autonomously, the loss of normal functional skills affects social aspects. Finally, there are pluripathological patients with at least two chronic non curable diseases that generate progressive deterioration and gradual loss of functional autonomy with the risk of suffering new comorbidities and complications, causing important repercussions [12,18].

Taking into consideration the mentioned points, the variables to be determined include the following protocols:

1. Socio-demographic variables: age, gender, place of residence, employment situation and academic level.
2. Socio-family and/or caregiver-related variables: age, gender, and relationship to the primary caregiver.
3. Functional Dependency: Barthel Index, Pfeiffer, Lawton-Brody, Functional Gear Classification and Short Series of Physical Performance.
4. Socio-family risk measured by the Gijón scale, Yesavage index depression and family APGAR.
5. Clinical evaluation: general condition of the patient (anamnesis and physical examination), Charlson Index, Gohai Index, other comorbidities, falls in the last year and hospital admissions, risk of falls and mini nutritional.
6. Anthropometric variables: weight, height, body mass index, waist circumference, hip, waist hip index and blood pressure.
7. Complementary examinations.
8. Pharmacological variables: number and type of chronically prescribed drugs and new drugs after hospitalizations.
9. Fragility Variables: Frail screening tool y Gérontopôle Frailty screening tool.

Once the standardized parameters that will be registered in the visits to each elderly adult have been understood, the following section explains the architecture and operating mode of the ICAEP application.

## 4   ICAEP Application

The mobile application is focused on health professionals. Although its main objective is to intervene in the improvement of care processes for the elderly, only doctors, dentists, nurses, gerontologists and specialists in general will be able to access registers, medical records and other tools. For this first development, being the pilot of the research proposal, a modular architecture has been thought of that is hosted in a public cloud, in such a way that functionalities are added or eliminated without significantly modifying the structure of the application. Thus, initially there are 5 modules that are delivered under the Platform as a Service (PaaS) model. On the other hand, the core of the system complies with the characteristics of Infrastructure as a Service (IaaS), as an Ubuntu Server 16.04 will be deployed to host the HTML server, the database, the Web services and the VPN. The components and modules mentioned are specified in the following subsections and can be seen in Fig. 1.

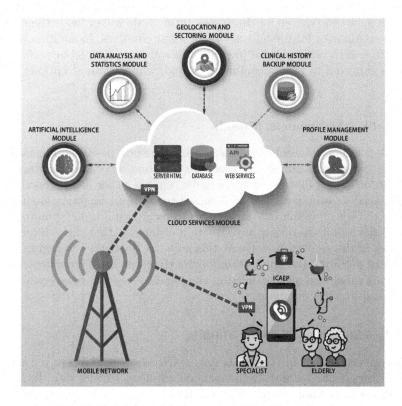

**Fig. 1.** Modular architecture of the ICAEP application.

### 4.1  Cloud Core

As it is a first implementation, it will work with a public cloud because of the facilities and flexibility it represents when installing servers and databases, in addition to the modular tools it offers. It should be noted that the core of the application is understood as IaaS and is conformed in a static way by 4 components: (i) an HTML server that keeps an informative Web page about the working group, mission, vision, projects, scientific articles and contact; (ii) Web services, known as REST API, that intervene in the handling of the data, both those sent from the application for storage and those that are requested to interact with the specialist; (iii) a database used to store information on the elderly, from the coordinates of their location to the medical histories of diagnosis and past treatments, following the defined standards; and (iv) a VPN to maintain privacy during the consumption of Web services, because it works with critical variables.

With respect to the initial modules, there will be PaaS tools to improve the efficiency of the health professionals in rural areas or municipal GADs. Although 5 modules have been chosen for this phase, future tests will evaluate their performance to continue or for use and rely on other alternatives. In addition, bearing in mind that each cloud service provider has countless options to perform any task, it is expected to form a community cloud, where the best options of each converge.

### 4.2  Profile Management Module

ICAEP is intended for health professionals. Therefore, it will be impossible to open it to the general public and therefore only one service administrator will be able to create profiles for each specialist. On the other hand, general users will have access to the patient data assigned to them, highlighting among their functions the consumption of Web services to record vital signs, symptoms and diagnoses, as well as to review any situation of interest that the elderly person could keep in the medical history. At this point, it is essential to highlight that the entry of data into the application follows the established standards, so that if the forms submitted are not filled in completely, they will be prevented from being loaded into the database.

### 4.3  Clinical History Backup Module

The information stored in the database is extremely important, as it forms the clinical history of older adults. In the event of any inconvenience with the nucleus, these records should not be compromised. Hence, to ensure high availability and persistence, a backup database will be established that can be deployed locally or through the services of another cloud provider. Users will then record the results of their visits in the kernel, which will automatically replicate them in the backup.

## 4.4    Geolocation and Sectoring Module

Considering that within the country rural areas cover large spaces, it is essential to optimize the specialists assigned to older adults. This module is responsible for analyzing the location of each patient and the distance it keeps from its peers to create a sector that helps better manage the time required to cover the planned visits and the number of staff who should do so. In this way, it is essential to consult the database before any assignment to check for changes in residences or transfers that reflect a new sectorization.

## 4.5    Data Analysis and Statistics Module

The intent of this tool is to predict any scenario that might arise based on the historical records of the elders. This is justified by the fact that, for example, during some months certain areas of the country experience low temperatures or the amount of rain increases, causing common symptoms. Then, knowing that there is a vulnerable group in a certain period of time, it is possible to reschedule the visits of specialists and allocate a greater amount of drugs. Likewise, communities could be found that due to their lifestyles develop special conditions that could be detected in time to prevent their propagation during the ageing of younger populations.

## 4.6    Artificial Intelligence Module

Finally, this module focuses on detecting specific problems in an older adult. Consequently, it is desired to group the historical symptomatology to find any pattern that could mean the development of a critical condition in time. To this end, based on the standardized variables, the entries that could produce a chronic disease will be defined so that a classification algorithm evaluates the possibility of complicating the state of health, threatening the patient's life.

## 5    Conclusions

Aging is a natural process that means a significant change in the lives of the people who go through it. In a physiological way, high probabilities of presenting a greater number of illnesses are reached, which reduces notably the quality of life. For this reason, States implement policies that try to address the problems that the elderly may face. Ecuador has implemented a series of proposals that include fundamental rights, including access to priority medical services. However, it does not take into account the difficulties of access that are found in rural settings, more than an inadequate handling of the information of each patient. As a solution, this article presented an application, known as ICAEP, which gives specialists the opportunity to standardize data collection, allowing continuous access to whoever requires it. In addition, by managing a modular design based on cloud computing technologies, functionalities can be added or removed without modifying their overall structure. Finally, for a first instance, 5 modules have been thought that intend to optimize the management of the profiles, support the clinical histories, group the elderly according to their location, predict temporary illnesses to provide resources and classify according to risk illnesses.

**Acknowledgment.** This project is supported by Universidad Politécnica Salesiana, Universidad de Cuenca, Universidad Católica de Cuenca, Instituto Superior Tecnológico American College and CEDIA. Special thanks to all members of the CEDIA foundation.

# References

1. Amblàs-Novellas, J., Martori, J.C., Brunet, N.M., Oller, R., Gómez-Batiste, X., Panicot, J.E.: Índice frágil-vig: diseño y evaluación de un índice de fragilidad basado en la valoración integral geriátrica. Revista Española de Geriatría y Gerontología **52**(3), 119–127 (2017)
2. Ayala Híjar, L.C.: Necesidades prioritarias de los adultos mayores según su percepción en un club del adulto mayor, Lima, Perú (2017)
3. Beard, H.P.J.R., Bloom, D.E.: Towards a comprehensive public health response to population ageing. Lancet (Lond., Engl.) **385**(9968), 658 (2015)
4. Bharti, R., Chandra, A., Tikku, A.P., Arya, D., Gupta, R.: Oral care needs, barriers and challenges among elderly in India. J. Indian Prosthodont. Soc. **15**(1), 17 (2015)
5. Bone, A.E., et al.: What is the impact of population ageing on the future provision of end-of-life care? Population-based projections of place of death. Palliat. Med. **32**(2), 329–336 (2018)
6. Chen, S., Cui, Y., Li, X., Ding, Y.: The unmet needs of activities of daily living and influencing factors among disabled older adults in Nanjing's elderly care agencies. J. Nurs. Sci. **32**(11), 70–73 (2017)
7. Cravens, D.: Comprehensive geriatric assessment for non-geriatricians. Mo. Med. **103**(2), 157–160 (2006)
8. García, C.E.: Evaluación y cuidado del adulto mayor frágil. Revista Médica Clínica Las Condes **23**(1), 36–41 (2012)
9. González-Domínguez, R., Castillo-Feliciano, L.M., Avilés, A.G.P.: Valoración gerontogeriátrica integral: comparación diagnóstica entre el módulo gerontológico y la consulta externa. Atención Familiar **21**(1), 2–6 (2014)
10. Jiménez-Aguilera, B., Baillet-Esquivel, L.E., Ávalos-Pérez, F., Campos-Aragón, L.: Dependencia funcional y percepción de apoyo familiar en el adulto mayor. Atención Familiar **23**(4), 129–133 (2016)
11. Lopreite, M., Mauro, M.: The effects of population ageing on health care expenditure: a Bayesian var analysis using data from Italy. Health Policy **121**(6), 663–674 (2017)
12. Loredo-Figueroa, M., Gallegos-Torres, R., Xeque-Morales, A., Palomé-Vega, G., Juárez-Lira, A.: Nivel de dependencia, autocuidado y calidad de vida del adulto mayor. Enfermería universitaria **13**(3), 159–165 (2016)
13. Majumder, S., et al.: Smart homes for elderly healthcare–recent advances and research challenges. Sensors **17**(11), 2496 (2017)
14. Maslow, A.H.: A theory of human motivation. Psychol. Rev. **50**(4), 370 (1943)

15. Pastor, M.Á.R., García, I.P., Serrano, V.O.: ICT solutions for elder people: manifested preferences in Spanish rural areas. Voters Change Profile Spain: Eur. Elect. 20D Gen. Elect. **6**(2), 137–177 (2017)
16. Ridgway, V.: Elderly persons health and wellbeing (2018)
17. Rowe, N., McMicken, D., Newth, T.: Dancing in the setting sun: performance, self-actualization and the elderly. In: Bond, K. (ed.) Dance and the Quality of Life. SIRS, vol. 73, pp. 527–544. Springer, Cham (2019). https://doi.org/10.1007/978-3-319-95699-2_30
18. Yépez-Ramírez, D., Jacinto-Becerra, B.F., Méndez-Bravo, E.G., Muñoz-López, D.E., Osornio-Mendoza, E.P., del Carmen Soria-Navarro, M.: Clinimetría geriátrica: propuesta de un instrumento integral en medicina familiar. Atención Familiar **20**(4), 106–110 (2013)

# SAFER-LIM: A Platform for Assistance, Care and Social Integration for the Elderly

Pablo A. Lema-Sarmiento[1]([⊠]), Paúl E. Calle-Romero[1],
Pablo L. Gallegos-Segovia[1], Paúl E. Vintimilla-Tapia[2], Jack F. Bravo-Torres[2],
and Esteban F. Ordóñez-Morales[2]

[1] Grupo de Investigación GIHP4C,
Universidad Politécnica Salesiana, Cuenca, Ecuador
{plema,pcalle,pgallegos}@ups.edu.ec
[2] Grupo de Investigación GITEL,
Universidad Politécnica Salesiana, Cuenca, Ecuador
{pvintimilla,jbravo,eordonez}@ups.edu.ec

**Abstract.** The steady increase in the world's older adult population is about to become one of the most critical social transformations of the 21st century, demanding significant adaptations of each nation's health and social systems. Consequently, from the various needs reflected by this demographic change, SAFER-LIM emerges, a Web platform based on three axes that guarantee the correct development of each individual during his/her aging: linkage with society, interaction with his/her peers and monitoring of the state of health. From there, a virtual space is created centralized in the elderly that is shared with doctors, caregivers and family members. On the one hand, the social requirements are satisfied thanks to the addition of friends, creation of events and recommendation of places, promoting the enhancement of spaces and places destined for the senescent. On the other hand, with respect to the state of health, has designed a network of e-Health sensors for doctors that process and record measurements on biological variables of each elderly, following a model based on user profiles. Finally, in general, caregivers or relatives can see in real time the geographic location of the older adult and receive alerts about the change of routes or the abandonment of safe areas (geofences). The results obtained on the deployment of SAFER-LIM in an elderly community show positive impressions about its use.

**Keywords:** Cloud computing · eHealth · Elderly care · Health monitoring · Social network

## 1 Introduction

Over the last few decades, the increase in individuals reaching stages of aging has become a demographic phenomenon of great interest to each nation. In that

M. Botto-Tobar et al. (Eds.): ICAT 2019, CCIS 1193, pp. 230–242, 2020.
https://doi.org/10.1007/978-3-030-42517-3_18

sense, the United Nations (UN) establishes as an older adult those persons whose age is from 60 years old [9]. Thus, today, this social group represents 13% of the world population and reflects an annual growth rate of 3%. Hence, according to data from the revision of the report entitled "World Population Prospects", the number of older people is expected to double by 2050 and triple by 2100, with a total of 3100 million [3].

At this point, it should be noted that senescence, inevitably, is about to become one of the greatest social transformations of the twenty-first century, with consequences for almost all sectors of society (for example, it took France almost 150 years to adapt to a 10% to 20% growth in the elderly population[1]). Therefore, taking into account that until 2050 the remaining time is decreasing, the main challenges to be faced are directly related to the holistic state of health of each elder. Thus, based on the constitution of the World Health Organization that seeks for each individual "a complete state of physical, mental and social well-being and not only the absence of disease and infirmity"[2], two key concepts can be contemplated for a correct development during old age: (i) the health of the elderly, which is seen as the functional capacity to take care of oneself and develop within the family and society, allowing, in a dynamic way, the performance of activities of daily living; and (ii) active aging, which is understood as the process of optimization of opportunities to fight for health, active participation in society and the security of reaching or maintaining an optimal quality of life in function of the years gained [10].

In addition to the above, it should be noted that large percentages of older adults suffer from isolation, depression, mistreatment, disconnection by their families and lack of socialization with their peers, reflecting factors unfavorable to healthy aging [11]. As a result, the elderly feel less useful and discouraged from carrying out daily activities, giving way to a social paradigm in which their main role is understood as a family burden that cannot contribute more to society. However, this idea is completely misleading, because the elderly can become an active pillar of society, contributing their wisdom and knowledge to future generations, so it is essential to ensure their welfare.

Based on the above, this work proposes the development of a Web platform, known as SAFER-LIM, whose main contribution focuses on ensuring the comprehensive development of the elderly. Thus, two fundamental axes are treated for the holistic well-being of any individual: socialization, to create personal ties with their peers to share and recommend places of interest, in addition to creating events; and the monitoring of the state of health, allowing doctors and caregivers to access a network of eHealth sensors, where biological variables of each elderly person are registered. Although the operation of this platform is centralized in the elderly, it indirectly creates a virtual space to also group doctors, caregivers and family members. Finally, it is important to point out that any indirect user (doctor, caregiver or family member) can know the location in real time of who is in their care and generate alarms in the event of

---

[1] https://www.who.int/news-room/fact-sheets/detail/ageing-and-health.

[2] https://www.who.int/about/who-we-are/constitution.

detect- ing abnormal movement patterns or the abandonment of a safe area known as geo-fence.

This article is organized as follows. In Sect. 2, related works are mentioned that reflect the proposals that have been developed based on the care of the elderly. Section 3 describes the proposal that contains the main ideas on which SAFER-LIM is based, giving way in Sect. 4 to the architecture that allows its deployment. In Sect. 5, there is an analysis of a first implementation, detailing the results achieved. The main conclusions are contemplated in Sect. 6.

## 2   Related Works

Currently, old age is becoming a social problem that threatens the well-being of each person, mostly due to the emergence of feelings of loneliness and abandonment. The first is closely linked to a personal dissatisfaction motivated by the total or partial lack of contact with other people; while isolation reflects objective characteristics of a situation marked by the scarcity of social relations. However, it is important to note that living alone does not lead to the triggering of these problems [4]. As a solution, there are countless studies in the literature that rely on technology as an ideal means to face the difficulties that arise hand in hand with aging [17].

Among the most relevant proposals are [6], which focuses on an IoT platform based on the Smart City concept for the care of the elderly and people with special abilities. One of its most notorious features is that it takes into consideration issues related to emotional or psychological health, although it does not specifically describe the tools they use. As part of its architecture, it indicates a dependence between the different sensors and a smart phone for sending data to services in the cloud, compromising its autonomy. Likewise, despite being conceived as an application open to the general public, access to stored data is only available to professionals and health institutions such as clinics, hospitals, doctors, insurers and caregivers.

Continuing with a similar thematic, the authors of [8] argue that the target audience for their research is older adults suffering from dementia. One of the main characteristics of individuals under this condition is the ease of getting lost, so it is essential to determine their geographical position in real time. Hence, the purpose of this work is to integrate radio frequency identification technologies with global positioning systems, mobile communications and geographic information systems (GIS) to build a preventive localization application that does not interfere with everyday activities. Thus, four monitoring schemes have been developed: residential, outdoor, rescue and emergency, and remote, which rely on mobile devices such as smart phones or laptops and communicate over the Internet with a database and web servers. As a result, family members or caregivers can identify the position of the elderly through a call center that will send relevant information through text messages.

For its part, in [13] describes the development and implementation of self-sustaining sensors that use wireless networks to recharge and send data. In general, its objective is focused on providing support to different applications related to the fields of medicine and elderly care. Although this article provides valuable information, since the main shortcoming of traditional sensors stems from the autonomy of their batteries, which at most support 24 hours without charge, no relevant information was found on the treatment and use of the recorded data. In addition, the number of available sensors is limited, so that only variables of temperature, acceleration and skin conductivity can be measured. Similarly, in [14] a device is implemented that includes a help button, light and humidity sensors that works specifically with older seniors. Hence, the aim is to automate the control over the lighting and the activation of the air conditioning of the elderly person's room, as well as to provide a panic button to intervene in the reduction of response times in the event of any eventuality. Likewise, any activity carried out by the device is notified through text messages. Although it is a useful project, it lacks user control, causing anyone who has access to the button to activate it and the caregiver or family member in charge to attend a false distress call.

Finally, the authors of [18] expose that poor medication management practices are a common problem leading to significant morbidity and mortality states in patients, especially in older adults. In consequence, they propose a socialized stimulus system that combines sensors in the home and social networks to improve adherence to medications. Sensors benefit the continuous monitoring of ingest behaviors; while social networks contribute to social incitement within a group with similar symptomatology, as reminders from people with the same interest are more effective than reminders from strangers. Therefore, there is competition among group members to improve social participation by reminding other members to take medications on time. Experimental results showed that adherence of test subjects to medication has improved markedly. The use of the application is intended only for the elderly, so there is no way for a third person such as a doctor, caregiver or family member to monitor or evaluate the health status of the elderly.

As can be noted, there are several alternatives that start from the difficulties presented by aging as research objectives. However, they cover specific points and do not treat the situation holistically. This is why SAFER-LIM is a platform that is born from the pillars of SAFER [2], and focuses on the integral care and health of the elderly, involving doctors, caregivers, family members and, of course, other older adults. On the one hand, from the point of view of physical care, SAFER-LIM equips each doctor with a network of 21 eHealth sensors, whose measurements are sent to a REST server via TCP protocol, where they are stored according to user profiles. With respect to psychological and social care, you can add friends, create events, add favorite places, promoting different types of interaction. In addition, by having recommendation functions to share favorite places, the existence of sites suitable for the elderly is disseminated, which can become meeting points or events. On the other hand, caregivers or family members have satellite tracking options that allow the creation of "geofences" thanks to a GPS device provided with a help button and GPRS connectivity. In this sense, it manages an alarm system that issues notifications to doctors, caregivers or family, and are grouped into 3 categories:

- Help: it is generated by the activation of the help button integrated in each GPS.
- Geofence Entry/Exit: Activated when the older adult enters or exits the geofence established by the caregiver or family member.
- GPS device status: indicates GPS status (online, unknown, moving, stopped).

The following section details in more depth the operation and the technological bases that allow the correct operation of SAFER-LIM.

## 3   SAFER-LIM: Description of the Proposal

SAFER-LIM is an upgrade of the SAFER platform, which provides tools to ensure the integral care of older adults. Its main difference from the original version is justified by the evolution of its features (see [1]), three key points are covered to avoid any type of alteration in the well-being of the elderly: linkage with society, interaction with people of the same age and monitoring of health status. As can be seen in Fig. 1, each point is part of a sequence that ensures a better quality of life, indirectly contributing to the process of adaptation to the aging of the world's population. For this reason, the following sections explain in a better way the mentioned aspects, as well the architecture that supports the deployment of the platform.

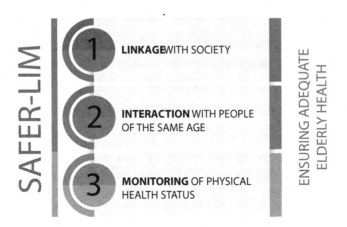

Fig. 1. Bases del desarrollo de SAFER-LIM

### 3.1   Linkage with Society

The time that users spend on social networks is increasing and growing exponentially. Nowadays, there are different alternatives that focus on every aspect of everyday life, passing from the more formal ones such as LinkedIn, Xing, About.me, where professional profiles are published to establish work relationships, to the more informal ones such as Facebook, Instagram, Snapchat, Zenly, which serve to share personal aspects. In essence, a social network is a virtual space that motivates to share information, photos, videos, links of interest, as well to intervene in aspects related to communication, exchanging ideas about their activities, tastes, affinities and even moods [12]. Another advantage is that connect people, establishing new relationships that reflect collaborative participation in events and activities.

SAFER-LIM offers its users a social health network where older adults, doctors, caregivers and family members can interact, each fulfilling a role and various functions to promote social participation, health care, leisure and culture.

### 3.2   Interaction with People of the Same Age

SAFER-LIM was designed so that the elderly have an accessible, intuitive and easy to manage space, known as "user friendly interface" [16], which facilitates the development of 3 tasks:

1. Create events: their purpose is to increase interaction between elders. For example, registering the event "Memory Workshop for Older Adults", each user establishes their interest in the event and, in the case of having previously attended, a rating can be assigned. This information is highly relevant, since through data analysis algorithms it is possible to establish specialized events to achieve specific objectives.
2. Add friends: fulfills the usual functions of add/delete friends like any social network. Thus, you can generate regular contacts to perform or attend joint activities.
3. Add places of interest: when a user finds a site that pleases or benefits him, he can save it in a list to recommend it to his contacts. This way, it is guaranteed that other users have knowledge of spaces in which they can feel comfortable.

### 3.3   Monitoring of Physical Health Status

The current advance and development of Information and Communication Technologies (ICTs) makes available to the population a number of tools, which are used in the implementation and development of SAFER-LIM. On the one hand, each adult is equipped with a GPS device that continuously sends positioning data to the REST server using the GPRS protocol. This information is monitored by caregivers or family members, as they are in charge of registering geofences[3]. Thus, when an elderly person enters or leaves a specific area, a notification is triggered, avoiding possible loss. In the Fig. 2, you can see an example of a geofence.

On the other hand, physical health monitoring is based on two technological currents: eHealth and mHealth. The first is defined by the World Health Organization as the cost-effective and safe use of TICs in support of health and

---

[3] Geofences define and assign geographic boundaries to points of interest on a graphical map [15].

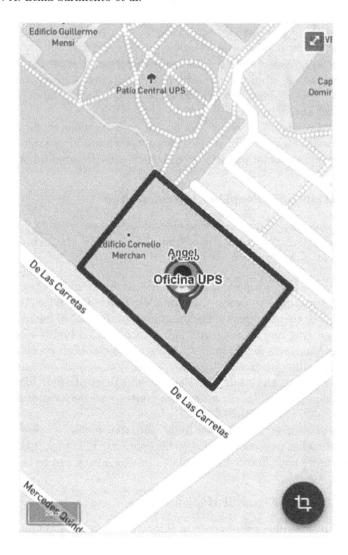

**Fig. 2.** Geofence created within SAFER-LIM

related fields [5]. While the second is conceptualized according to the Global Observatory of eHealth as medical and public health practice supported by mobile devices, such as telephones, patient monitoring devices, personal digital assistants and other wireless equipment [7]. Consequently, SAFER-LIM seeks to encourage doctors, caregivers and family members to become involved in the health of the elderly. For this purpose, it has two functionalities:

1. Add main doctor: A doctor can be registered to receive complete information on the health status of the elderly in real time. In this way, the aim is to prevent future illnesses or, if there is one, to make an optimal diagnosis in time.
2. Set caregiver/family member in charge: defines the users who will have access in real time to both the location of the older adult and notifications about their status.

Once the benefits of using SAFER-LIM have been described, the following section presents the architecture that supports its operation.

## 4    Proposed Architecture

SAFER-LIM is constituted by a series of components that allow to implement the described functions, which model the architecture client-server of four layers that is exposed in the Fig. 3, and is explained in the following subsections.

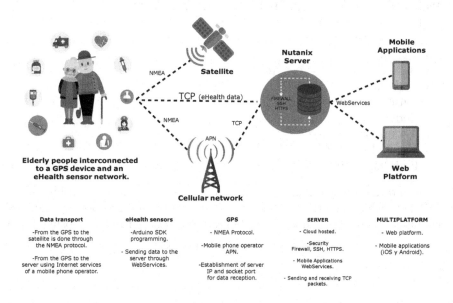

**Fig. 3.** SAFER-LIM architecture

### 4.1    Tracking Layer

Each older adult has a GPS device that registers positioning data and sends it to the REST server through GPRS. For this, the location data follows the NMEA (National Marine Electronics Association) standard because it handles a standard format of text strings, facilitating their interpretation. In addition, each device has a help button that, at the moment of being activated, emits an alert.

## 4.2 Sensors Layer

Elderly people who use SAFER-LIM have the facility to connect to a network of sensors that evaluate their health status. This was achieved thanks to the integration of Libelium's "MySignals HW BLE" solution[4], it has a wide range of tools at its disposal:

- Heart rate.
- Respiratory frequency.
- Oxygen in the blood.
- Electrocardiogram signals.
- Blood pressure.
- Signs of muscular myography.
- Glucose levels.
- Galvanic response of the skin.
- Lung capacity.
- Snore sensor.
- Patient Position (Sitting, Standing, Leaning, Left, Right).
- Airflow.
- Body Scale Parameters:
  - Weight
  - Bone mass.
  - Body fat.
  - Muscle mass.
  - Body Water.
  - Abdominal fat.
  - Metabolic index.
  - Body mass index (BMI).

The information obtained by each sensor is sent to the server through an API REST, which allows a direct interaction with the server for sending and receiving data. In addition, it is possible to use several formats, choosing JSON for this case.

## 4.3 Service Layer

The SAFER core is hosted on a NUTANIX server, where a UNIX server with a CentOS 7 distribution was virtualized. On the other hand, the application server is developed in NodeJS and is linked to the non-relational MongoDB database. Finally, a WebSocket is implemented for the continuous reception of positioning data, while a REST API is used to send, receive and process sensor information.

---

[4] https://www.cooking-hacks.com/mysignals-hw-ehealth-medical-biometric-arduino-complete-kit-ble.

### 4.4  Users Layer

SAFER is based on a hierarchical structure of users that enables certain functions according to the role that was assigned. Therefore, 3 types of user are handled:

- Doctor: in addition to accessing clinical history and consultations, visualizes reports on the data collected by the network of sensors, implementing a tele-consultation model. Likewise, family members and caregivers are contacted to disseminate results on consultations or medical indications.
- Family Member/Caregiver: observes in real time the geographic location, receives the state of the GOS and help alerts, also can create geofences. Like the doctor, it has access to reports of the data collected by the sensor network.
- Elderly: is the main user of SAFER-LIM and its role focuses specifically on improving social interaction with other elders. Therefore, the functionalities you access are related to keeping in touch with your friends, creating events or activities and generating recommendations on the sites of interest that have been visited.

## 5  Analysis of a First Implementation

To evaluate the performance of SAFER-LIM, a group of 10 older adults between the ages of 60 and 70, residents of the same neighborhood and with basic knowledge or willingness to operate a smartphone, were selected. After a brief talk, feelings of sadness, feelings of abandonment and low self-esteem became evident, since only 4 were maintained based on their retirement income and the rest depended on their families, losing self-sustainability. At the time of presenting the platform, they were asked to be accompanied by a relative or caregiver and 4 steps were followed:

1. Socialization and installation of SAFER-LIM with the work group and their family members/caregivers.
2. Demonstration and implementation of the main benefits of the application according to each role.
3. Delivery and training about GPS/GPRS device with help button, focusing on how to charge the device, send notifications and create geofences.
4. Training on the use of the eHealth sensor network.

After 15 days, an integral evaluation was carried out, in which the ease with which family members/caregivers used the eHealth sensor and GPS devices, was evident. On the other hand, older adults did not show any change. Although they were being monitored, they did not interact with their similars, giving way to the need to encourage the use of the mobile application. Thus, with the help of the neighborhood president, different activities were coordinated that were disseminated under the concept of events (therefore the importance of deploying the tests in users of the same neighborhood). After 30 days, they were interacting and creating their own events and meetings. Finally, the platform gained greater acceptance, demonstrating positive changes in the attitude of its users, as they began to socialize, organize events and know spaces of interest as recommended by their neighbors. In the Fig. 4 an example of event publishing within SAFER-LIM is presented.

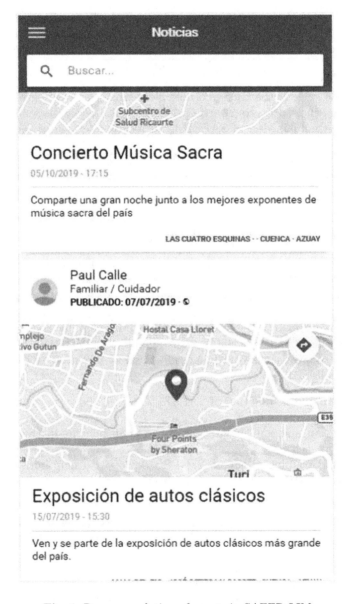

**Fig. 4.** Recommendation of events in SAFER-LIM

In a punctual way, a scenario was given in which a possible loss was avoided. An elder was to be realized medical examinations, so his son left him in a clinical laboratory and set up a geo-fence around the place. When the old man left, a notification was sent to his son, who observed that his father was taking an unknown route. He immediately called him and learned that he was not sure how to get home.

## 6  Conclusions

The strong integration of technologies to form a social network focused on the integral health of the elderly, such as SAFER-LIM, turned out to be a case of success. The evident improvement of the test group in the first implementation denotes the effectiveness of the application as a tool to progressively adapt to aging in society. For its part, the REST API on which this work is based provides the opportunity to obtain a large amount of information that can be analyzed with data mining tools, leaving the door open to future research based on trends, predictions and automatic recommendations.

**Acknowledgment.** To the *Universidad Politécnica Salesiana del Ecuador, Campus Cuenca*, especially to its Research Groups GIHP4C and GITEL for the support provided during this research.

## References

1. Bravo-Torres, J.F., Ordoñez-Ordoñez, J.O., Gallegos-Segovia, P.L., Vintimilla-Tapia, P.E., López-Nores, M., Blanco-Fernández, Y.: A context-aware platform for comprehensive care of elderly people: proposed architecture. In: 2017 CHILEAN Conference on Electrical, Electronics Engineering, Information and Communication Technologies (CHILECON), pp. 1–6. IEEE (2017)
2. Bravo-Torres, J.F., et al.: SAFER: a context-aware ubiquitous assistance platform for elderly care. CLAIB 2016. IP, vol. 60, pp. 349–352. Springer, Singapore (2017). https://doi.org/10.1007/978-981-10-4086-3_88
3. United Nations Department of Economic and Social Affairs: World population prospects: the 2017 revision, key findings and advance tables. Population Division working paper no. ESA/P/WP 241. United Nations Department of Economic and Social Affairs (2017)
4. Doblas, J.L., Conde, M.D.P.D.: El sentimiento de soledad en la vejez. Rev. Int. Sociol. **76**(1), 085 (2018)
5. Espinoza-Bautista, J., Álvarez-Ballesteros, S., Peón-Escalante, I.: Diseño idealizado para una salud sistémica a través de ehealth (2015)
6. Hussain, A., Wenbi, R., da Silva, A.L., Nadher, M., Mudhish, M.: Health and emergency-care platform for the elderly and disabled people in the smart city. J. Syst. Softw. **110**, 253–263 (2015)
7. Istepanian, R.S., Lacal, J.C.: Emerging mobile communication technologies for health: some imperative notes on m-health. In: Proceedings of the 25th Annual International Conference of the IEEE Engineering in Medicine and Biology Society (IEEE Cat. No. 03CH37439), vol. 2, pp. 1414–1416. IEEE (2015)
8. Lin, C.C., Chiu, M.J., Hsiao, C.C., Lee, R.G., Tsai, Y.S.: Wireless health care service system for elderly with dementia. IEEE Trans. Inf Technol. Biomed. **10**(4), 696–704 (2006)

9. María-Pozzi: Adulto mayor: un neologismo para disimular la ineludible vejez. Antenas Neológicas - Red de neología del español (2016)
10. Martínez Fuentes, A.J., Fernández Díaz, I.E.: Ancianos y salud. Revista Cubana de Medicina General Integral **24**(4) (2016)
11. Martínez-Mendoza, J.A., Martínez-Ordaz, V.A., Esquivel-Molina, C.G.,Velasco-Rodríguez, V.M.: Prevalencia de depresión y factores deriesgo en el adulto mayor hospitalizado. Rev. Méd. Inst. Mex. Seguro Soc. **45**(1) (2017)
12. Orihuela-Colliva, J.L.: Internet: la hora de las redes sociales (2008)
13. Paing, T., et al.: Wirelessly-powered wireless sensor platform. In: 2007 European Microwave Conference, pp. 999–1002. IEEE (2007)
14. Salgueiro, L.J.G., Gonzalez, A.A., Rodríguez, P.A.R.: Help button for elderly people on the Arduino platform (2018)
15. Sheha, M.A., Sheha, A.: Method and system for identifying and defining geofences, 13 September 2011. (uS Patent 8,019,532)
16. Tanghe, D., Hally, J.C.: Display screen with graphical user interface, 7 August 2012. (uS Patent App. 29/392,913)
17. Vines, J., Pritchard, G., Wright, P., Olivier, P., Brittain, K.: An age-old problem: examining the discourses of ageing in HCI and strategies for future research. ACM Trans. Comput.-Hum. Interact. (TOCHI) **22**(1), 2 (2015)
18. Yu, Z., Liang, Y., Guo, B., Zhou, X., Ni, H.: Facilitating medication adherence in elderly care using ubiquitous sensors and mobile social networks. Comput. Commun. **65**, 1–9 (2015)

# SCADA System Based on IoT for Intelligent Control of Banana Crop Irrigation

Jorge Berrú-Ayala[1], Dixys Hernandez-Rojas[1,2]($\boxtimes$) (iD), Patricia Morocho-Díaz[1],
Johnny Novillo-Vicuña[1,2] (iD), Bertha Mazon-Olivo[1,2] (iD), and Alberto Pan[2] (iD)

[1] Universidad Técnica de Machala, 5.5 km Pan-American Av., Machala, El Oro, Ecuador
{jberru_est,dhernandez,pemorochod_est,jnovillo,
bmazon}@utmachala.edu.ec
[2] Department of Computer Science, Universidade da Coruña, 15071 A Coruña (03082), Spain
apan@udc.es

**Abstract.** At present, precision agriculture involves a set of technologies for the optimal management of soil and crops to improve productivity. Banana cultivation is one of the leading export items in the province of El-Oro in Ecuador. However, most of the sprinkler and gravity irrigation systems used there are controlled by a manual operator. All of these raise the cost of operation and waste of resources, such as water and labor. Also, human errors and the inaccuracy of water control in irrigation generate stress on plants, and therefore, their growth and increase in humidity pests are affected. This work proposes a Smart Irrigation Control Panel (SICP), based on the Internet of things, as part of a SCADA system for automation of irrigation control of said crop, in the experimental farm "Santa Inés" of the Technique University of Machala. The SCADA proposed, has a dashboard, available in the IOTMACH cloud of the university, for real-time monitoring of the process variables and the remote control of the solenoid valves used for irrigation, an IoT gateway implemented in a Raspberry Pi 3 and a SICP installed in the field. The SICP is responsible for compiling the variables of temperature and humidity of the environment and the earth, water pressure, acquired through motes based on Arduino Mega. A radio link with Wimax technology was used to communicate the SICP with the cloud, to publish the variables mentioned. The tests of electrical continuity, insulation, and performance performed, allowed to verify the correct functioning of the entire system and the interaction time between the SICP, Gateway, and the IOTMACH Cloud.

**Keywords:** Smart Irrigation Control Panel · IoT · SCADA · Precision agriculture · Banana

## 1 Introduction

Internet of Things (IoT) is the assemblage of intelligent and self-identifiable objects, capable of interacting with each other and with the rest of the equipment through the internet, with or without human intervention. IoT consists of several domains or application fields such as smart cities, smart homes, smart health, Smart Agriculture, or also

© Springer Nature Switzerland AG 2020
M. Botto-Tobar et al. (Eds.): ICAT 2019, CCIS 1193, pp. 243–256, 2020.
https://doi.org/10.1007/978-3-030-42517-3_19

known as Precision Agriculture (PA), among others [1, 2]. The PA domain consists of a set of information and communication technology (ICT) and principles for efficient management of agricultural activities and resources, to guarantee the quality of production while maintaining the sustainability and environmental protection [3, 4].

The IoT and the PA ease the use of sensor networks to measure variables associated to weather, soil, water, crops, animals, etc; Sensor data is sent using networks and intermediate communication devices (Gateway) to a remote server (cloud computing) for monitoring and production control, from a terminal connected to the internet, such as a computer, tablet or smartphone [5, 6]. PA-IoT application data is also stored, processed, and enriched with other data to generate useful information that provides support to the decisions of agricultural entrepreneurs and end-users [7–10]. The areas or fields of application that PA assists are: agricultural crop management, soil management, irrigation control, fertilization, pest and disease control, planting and harvesting management, machinery control, cattle production management, etc. [11, 12]. The implementation of automated systems in agriculture requires the integration of technologies just as IoT, sensor networks, lightweight protocols for sensors [13], data networks, cloud computing or data center, plug-and-play mechanisms to auto detect sensors [14], big data analytics, data science, artificial intelligence, among others [7, 10, 15–18]. In PA, technologies like variable-rate management systems, agricultural drones, agrobots, geomapping, a global positioning system (GPS), and yield mapping are also integrated [19].

A Supervisory Control and Data Acquisition (SCADA) system integrated to IoT technologies facilitate efficient monitoring and control of physical components (machinery, hardware devices, sensors, and actuators). It is also a network of automatic data acquisition, processing, and administration of productive systems, highly efficient and profitable [1, 20]. The main applications of SCADA are in the industrial sector as factories. However, it can also be applied in the automation of agricultural sector processes, such as the case of crop irrigation control.

Ecuador is considered worldwide as a leading country in banana exports (*Musa spp.*) [21]. Banana is one of the most important tropical fruits for human consumption [22].

The types of irrigation that currently prevail in banana crops in Ecuador are by gravity (through the use of furrows or channels) and by sprinkling, controlled manually by an operator; In both cases, excessive resource consumption is evident. Manual irrigation control involves considerable problems. For example, if crops are located in remote locations and vast areas, costs and operating times are raised while resources such as water and labor are wasted. Besides, human errors like inaccuracy of water control during irrigation generates stress on plants. Therefore, their growth is affected, as well as the spread of pests and diseases in crops.

The purpose of this work is to develop and implement a SCADA system for the automation of banana crop irrigation based on the Internet of Things that optimizes resources. The research was carried out in an experimental banana farm of the Technical University of Machala (UTMACH) located in the province of El Oro-Ecuador. This document is organized in the following sections: Sect. 2 describes briefly the related work reviewed and which served as a starting point for our work. Section 3 explains the design and implementation of the proposed SCADA system; first, an architecture based on layers and components are presented, followed by the materials and tools used, then the design and implementation of the hardware and software components of the system. Section 4 shows the Experiments applied to test scenarios and evaluation metrics, and finally, Sect. 5 describes the conclusions of the work.

## 2 Related Work

SCADA systems are widely used in remote monitoring and control of industrial processes. The most prominent cases are public services such as distribution through water and gas pipes, power generation and distribution plants, environmental monitoring, telephone network monitoring, etc. [20, 23]. The benefits of SCADA lie in the control of different devices of the production system (or plant) such as opening or closing valves/switches, starting or stopping pumps, remote monitoring and control command stations, diagnosis and maintenance of machines, plant control and information resources integration, alarms activation and alert generation to the operator when significant changes have been detected, storage and display of continuous information on the states of devices and sensor measurements; historical system data generation, etc. [23].

PA, SCADA, and IoT technologies in the agricultural sector can be applied in the automation of processes such as crop irrigation control, fertilization, greenhouse control, fertilizer and compost production plants, storage warehouses of products, domestic animal production sheds, etc. [1, 3, 11, 24]. The automation of crop irrigation systems increases the yield of production, optimizes the use of resources, avoids irrigation inaccuracy due to human errors and, above all, avoids causing stress on the plants, a situation that can have significant effects on the yield of the production [25–27].

The most common types of crop irrigation are spray, gravity, drip, and micro-spray [28]. Sprinkler irrigation is characterized by carrying water through pipes and applying with pressure and in the form of rain on the crops [29]. In gravity irrigation, as water advances through furrows or channels, on the surface of the ground, infiltration in the soil profile co-occurs [30, 31]; it is frequently used in places with enough water and where little or no energy consumption is required. However, unnecessary infiltrations and loss of fluid occur [31]. Drip irrigation consists of the application of water under the surface of the soil using pressure pipes and various types of emitters, so that it only moistens the root zone of the plant in small quantities but more frequently. It is used for the irrigation of fruit trees, gardens, and trees. It is more efficient but implies more implementation costs [27].

In recent years it has been necessary to monitor variables that affect the crop such as temperature, humidity, and pH due to changes in environmental conditions, being essential for the implementation of a sensor network (SN) to collect environmental information and allow soil monitoring [32]. Several limitations can be found when implementing intelligent irrigation systems, for instance, high costs in electrical and electronic components, due to large areas of crops, additional protections in the installation of outdoor devices due to inclement weather (rain, sun, etc.), complex and expensive communication network infrastructures due to the vast distance in data transmission, security management due to theft of equipment, etc. Some works related to irrigation control are briefly described, which served to guide our research. The work [33] is a proposal of a prototype that reads soil moisture through a sensor connected to Arduino UNO [34] and sends the data to a Raspberry Pi device so that it can decide whether it activates or deactivates irrigation and finally sends an e-mail message to the administrator using GPRS/CDMA mobile technology.

In [35], they developed a Gateway prototype, through the use of IoT, for the simulation of packet routing at the RPL protocol level and to send sensor data located in the irrigation area to optimize the water consumption and the control and remote monitoring of the system. A WSN connects via Zigbee technology to the internet and sends messages to a mobile device, informing the state of the soil, so that the operator knows and makes the decision to irrigate the crop or not. In [36] they developed a system for monitoring the cultivation of a greenhouse using sensors for soil humidity, temperature-humidity of the environment and light, data that is sent to a web server through an NRF24LO1 and Ethernet transmitter; the data is stored in a MySQL database in JSON format; irrigation is automated using defined parameters of maximum and minimum values and the use of a data mining algorithm; Notifications are sent to a mobile phone where an operator can monitor field conditions.

In the work of [37], the authors carried out an experiment for the evaluation of different types of irrigation management in tomato plantations grown in greenhouses, using a sensor for ambient temperature and soil moisture; they collect data which is sent to a software developed for automatic irrigation management, by monitoring decision variables and the amount of water needed by the plant. In the system proposed by [38], for drip irrigation automation, they include humidity, temperature, rain level, and light intensity sensors, parameters that are sent via GSM to a microcontroller for irrigation management; in the same way, it sends land information via GSM to the farmer. Finally, in [39], they developed a low-cost intelligent system by using IoT so that the devices communicate with each other; for decision making, they used a neural network that processes soil data obtained through humidity and temperature sensors while for communication they used MQTT and HTTP to inform the user about the cultivation situation.

Our work contributes to the state of the art of banana irrigation, with an IoT based solution, which makes use of current communication technologies (Wimax), open hardware (Raspberry pi 3 and Arduino), data messaging with JSON and a cloud computing that provides us with a modern dashboard for monitoring and irrigation control of a plantation in real production of export bananas in the Santa Inés farm in Machala-Ecuador.

## 3 Design and Implementation of the SCADA System

### 3.1 SCADA System's Architecture

The proposed SCADA system is based on the Internet of Things architecture shown in Fig. 1, which consists of three layers: sensor network, communication network, and cloud computing. Consequently, each layer is explained:

1. **Sensor Network Layer (SNL).** It consists of motes, sensors, and actuators. Motes are devices with a minimal processing capacity that integrate sensors and actuators.

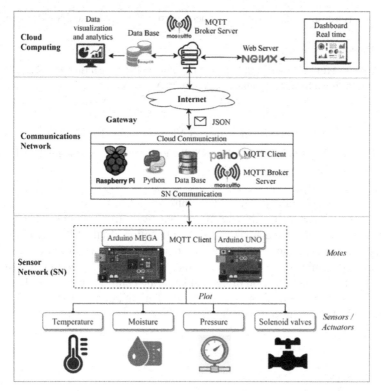

**Fig. 1.** SCADA system's architecture

2. **Network Communication Layer (NCL).** It covers the data communications network infrastructure, intermediary devices such as the Gateway and communication protocols.
3. **Cloud Computing Layer (CCL).** It consists of all servers, services, and applications necessary for the operation of the SCADA system, such as an MQTT Broker, database servers for data storage and processing.

### 3.2 Materials and Tools Used for the Design and Implementation of the SCADA System

Table 1 shows the hardware and software components that allowed the SCADA system implementation. They have been organized by the architecture layers proposed in Fig. 1.

### 3.3 Implementation of SCADA IoT Based System

Figure 2 shows the general diagram of the implementation of a SCADA system IoT-based for irrigation control of a banana plantation. An important element introduced in this implementation is the control panel, which constitutes the operator's natural

**Table 1.** Hardware and software components used in the SCADA and SICP systems.

| Layers | Components |
|--------|-----------|
| SNL | Arduino MEGA, Ethernet Shield board, Arduino UNO, Push Button ON and OFF, Sensor digital SHT, Pilot light, Breaker of 25 A, 110 V<br>Power supply, Relay module with 16 chanels, LCD display ($16 \times 2''$)<br>Pressure sensor, Solenoid valves, Arduino IDE, MQTT Client |
| NCL | Raspberry Pi 3, Nano Station, Python, SqLite, Mosquitto, Paho MQTT |
| CCL | IoTMach platform, Mosquitto, NGINX, Python and Node.JS, MongoDB, R language |

interface with the irrigation system. The control panel has a set of buttons, through which the operator can manually activate or deactivate the different solenoid valves installed to irrigate the desired areas within the plantation. As the SICP was installed in the plantation, operators can verify in situ the status and value of some variables such as temperature and humidity, water pump pressure, among others. Due to the ease of use and similarity to the manipulation of manual keys, the control panel is widely accepted by the operators and is the way for the acceptance of automation in productive processes, such as bananas for export in the Ecuador.

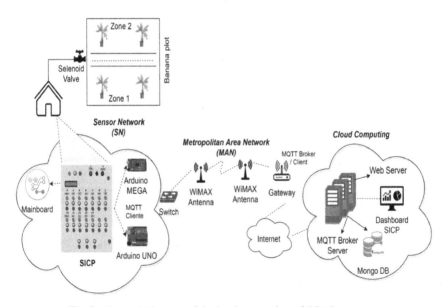

**Fig. 2.** General diagram of the implementation of SCADA system

The control panel's internal structure also has the motes used in the SN layer for the monitoring of the previously mentioned variables and others such as soil moisture and temperature and the control of actuators associated with the solenoid valves. All monitoring and control data is managed by the applications present in the cloud, such as the dashboard, web server, and MQTT broker. The distance between the SCIP and the cloud computing in our case was approximately 1 km, and we chose Wimax technology, widely used in signal repetition by local internet providers, to establish communication between them, which allows a generalization for similar solutions at a greater distance. The cloud receives the sensor data, validates it, stores it, processes and mediates a web dashboard, and displays it using representative graphs. The solenoid valves are also shown on the dashboard with icons (ON/OFF) according to their status. The user can control the actuators remotely by pressing the corresponding button.

### 3.3.1 SICP Hardware Design

The intelligent irrigation control panel (SICP) consists of a custom-designed mainboard for the connection of solenoid valves and in turn, serves as the basis for the Arduino Mega card that serves as the mote of actuators (solenoid valves). The mainboard has connector to each different zones like the solenoid valve inlet zone, zone to distribute energy to the peripheral components of the SICP, LCD screen and alarm zone. The SICP also integrates two more motes, implemented with Arduino UNO technology, were also implemented for the SHT sensors management that allows reading soil moisture and humidity located at two levels of depth, 25 and 80 cm, respectively, which were found in the banana field. All these components were located inside an electrical distribution board, as can be seen in Fig. 3. All the elements were adequately labeled for a secure location.

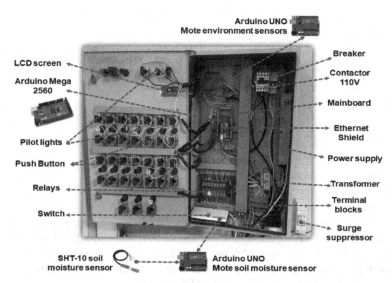

**Fig. 3.** Physical implementation of the Smart Irrigation Control Panel (SICP)

### 3.4  SICP Software Design

The software components of the implemented SCADA system are firmware for the Arduino MEGA mote and Arduino UNO engines, firmware for the Gateway, and Web application with dashboard-style located in the Cloud Computing. In Fig. 4, a diagram of activities is shown where the flows of actions are represented in Horizontal sections: Configuration, Sensing and Control, and interactions between the software components in Vertical Sections: Mote Firmware, Gateway, Cloud Computing, and Web user interface. Next, each horizontal section is explained:

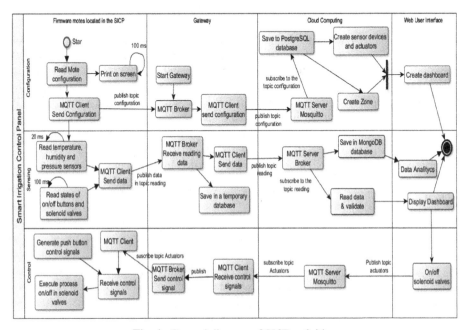

**Fig. 4.** General diagram of SICP activities.

1. "**Configuration**" section represents the actions performed when a mote is connected to the SCADA system for the first time, or its configuration has been modified. The configuration data such as all metadata were packaged in JSON format and sent to the cloud using the MQTT protocol so that they register in the PostgreSQL database.
2. "**Sensing**" section shows the data detection actions. The reading of sensor data and changes of the actuator status that are carried out from time to time are sent to the gateway through the MQTT protocol and then to the cloud. Once in the cloud, the data is published in the topics of the MQTT server.
3. "**Control**" section: Control signals designated to activate or deactivate actuators (solenoid valves) can be generated in two ways: (1) remotely through the SICP dashboard with a web interface, and (2) directly on the physical control board, pressing the pushbuttons as explained in the previous section.

## 4 Experiments

This section shows the operations carried out intending to assess the functionality and performance of the SCADA system IoT-based implemented in the banana farm "Santa Inés" in Machala-Ecuator. The first physical tests were electrical continuity and isolation, performed with the help of a digital multimeter. Then, the dashboard operation was checked in real-time. Finally, the efficiency tests were performed based on the latency metric of the control panel keypads and the installed pressure, temperature, and humidity sensors. The elements used in the described experiments were a Laptop (Lenovo 80E502A5SP G50-80), Arduino Mega 2560 (16 MHz), Ethernet Shield (W5500), Fluke-117, Arduino IDE (Version 1.8.10) and MQTTlens (Version 0.014). In the following section, the results and discussions of the defined experiments will be shown.

### 4.1 Continuity Tests and Electrical Insulation

The continuity tests carried out validated that all the internal connections of the SICP are operational, also guaranteeing all the input and output signals of the terminal block, which constitutes the physical connection interface with the rest of the SCADA elements proposed in Fig. 2, external to the SICP, such as the solenoid valves installed in the field and the temperature and humidity sensors. Although the SCIP was grounded with a copper rod, the electrical insulation between the components of the metal chassis was verified, where the lowest measured resistance was 74.9 k$\Omega$.

### 4.2 SICP IoT Dashboard Functionality

The SCADA monitoring and control functionality can be validated through the implemented dashboard, which constitutes the graphical interface of the system for monitoring and controlling irrigation in real-time remotely.

Figure 5(a) shows the dashboard widgets selected to monitor the analog variables in real-time and their historical variability over time. An example of these variables is soil moisture and temperature. Figure 5(b) shows the dashboard elements that allow us to know the current state of the digital input variables. For example, in the dashboard, we can see that the solenoid valves of zone 1: central, EV2 and EV4 are on, and the rest are in off. In the last block on the right, are the buttons that will activate the actuators associated with the solenoid valves of the irrigation system connected to the SICP. An essential element to highlight is the confirmation process implemented in our SCADA system, to validate that once the corresponding button was pressed, said actuator was physically activated. This validation is represented on the dashboard with the image of a green check.

### 4.3 Performance and Latency Tests

Performance and time delay tests were carried out to verify the interaction between the SICP, Arduino, Gateway, and the IOTMACH Cloud platform. In each of the experiments,

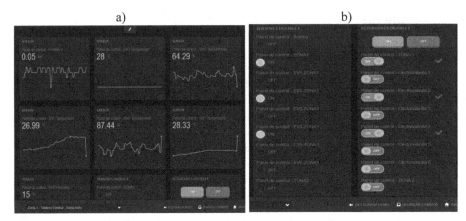

**Fig. 5.** Real-time dashboard (a) analog sensors monitoring, (b) sensors and digital actuators. (Color figure online)

four latencies were obtained. The first (T1) is associated with the time that the mote requires to read said input, either digital or analog. Then (T2) represents the latency between the mote and the gateway and (T3) the delay between the gateway and cloud computing. The last latency (TR), would be the sum of the previous ones represents the response time of the SCADA when a variation in its inputs is detected.

### 4.3.1 Digital Inputs Latencies

To obtain the digital inputs latencies, meaning the delay that a web user would experience when observing a change of status on/off on the dashboard, when an operator physically manipulates the corresponding button on the control panel to open or close a solenoid valve; 30 beats per minute were made, for a period of 5 days, obtaining a total of 4500 observations per day.

Figure 6 shows the minimum, maximum and average values of the four latencies for the keypads during the mentioned test period with an average of T1 of 2.5 ms, 53.9 ms for T2, 157.3 ms for T3, giving us an excellent response time, TR, of the buttons of just 213.7 ms.

### 4.3.2 Analog Inputs Latencies

To determine the SCADA's response time to the changes in the analog inputs, the pressure and temperature and humidity variables of two SHT type sensors were taken as samples. The pressure sensor delivers a 0–5 VDC voltage output, proportional to the pressure, and connected directly to the analog-to-digital converter of one of the SICP Arduino mote. Instead, SHT sensors deliver an I2C output. The results of this experiment are detailed in Table 2.

Comparatively, we can appreciate that the sensors' latencies with serial outputs are more significant than the real analog ones since they require greater processing to obtain the measured variable and also depend on the efficiency of the library used for I2C.

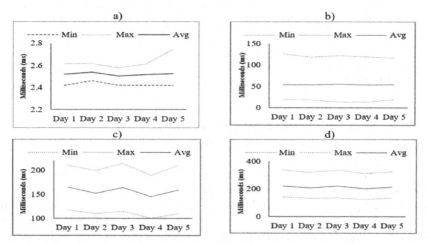

**Fig. 6.** Detection time of manual keypad states in Arduino and sent to the Cloud. (a) corresponds to the time of sending the message from the mote to the Gateway, (b) represents the time of sending the message from the Gateway to the MQTT server, (c) represents the time of sending the MQTT server to the Dashboard application, and (d) shows the response time.

**Table 2.** Analog inputs latencies.

| Variable (ms) | Time (ms) | Pressure | SHT-1 | SHT-2 |
|---|---|---|---|---|
| T1 | Min | 24,1 | 1507,9 | 1437,9 |
| | Max | 25,2 | 1508,2 | 1438,2 |
| | AVG | 24,3 | 1508,2 | 1438,2 |
| T2 | Min | 673.8 | 691.4 | 682.4 |
| | Max | 696.9 | 661.6 | 724.9 |
| | AVG | 703.4 | 721.4 | 687.4 |
| T3 | Min | 28,0 | 11,0 | 21,0 |
| | Max | 363,0 | 400,0 | 365,0 |
| | AVG | 163,5 | 160,4 | 191,3 |
| TR = T1 + T2 + T3 | Min | 725,9 | 2210,3 | 2141,3 |
| | Max | 1085,1 | 2569,8 | 2528,1 |
| | AVG | 891,2 | 2390,0 | 2316,9 |

On the other hand, we can see that the T2 latency is more prominent than those of T1 and T2, directly influenced by the means of communication used between SICP and the gateway. In our case, the latency of the communication channel of the radio link, based on Wimax technology, is reflected. However, we can indicate that a fast IoT-based SCADA was achieved with a latency seen by a web user from the cloud with less than

1 s for analog variables and less than 3 s for intelligent sensors with prior processing of the communication protocol used.

## 5 Conclusions

The article presented the design and implementation of an IoT-based SCADA system for irrigation control of a banana farm in Ecuador. However, the proposed solution can be replicated in any other agricultural production that requires irrigation control. The SICP developed as a part of SCADA's system, not only allowed the improvement of an irrigation control process based on the work of an operator who manipulates the keys within a plantation to section the irrigation. But also, with the acceptance of the agricultural staff of the control panel, allowed the possibility of using a dashboard for monitoring and opening or closing the solenoid valves remotely. Thus, achieving process automation. Leaving the doors open for future implementation of artificial intelligence techniques for an automatic irrigation decision, without the action of an operator. To determine the performance of the proposed SCADA, different experiments were carried out to obtain the response time of the system from a web user in the cloud, with an intuitive dashboard as an interface. The obtained results demonstrate a fast IoT-based SCADA with latencies lower than 1 s for pure digital and analog inputs, and less than 3 s for sensors with I2C serial outputs.

## References

1. Hernandez-Rojas, D., Mazón-Olivo, B., Escudero, C.J.: Internet de las cosas (IoT). In: Análisis de Datos Agropecuarios, Universidad Técnica de Machala, Machala, El Oro, Ecuador, vol. 1, pp. 71–100 (2018). ISBN 978-9942-24-120-7
2. Hernandez-Rojas, D., Mazon-Olivo, B., Novillo-Vicuña, J., Escudero-Cascon, C., Pan-Bermudez, A., Belduma-Vacacela, G.: IoT android gateway for monitoring and control a WSN. Technol. Trends **798**, 18–32 (2018)
3. Balafoutis, A.T., et al.: Smart farming technologies – description, taxonomy and economic impact. In: Pedersen, S.M., Lind, K.M. (eds.) Precision Agriculture: Technology and Economic Perspectives. PPA, pp. 21–77. Springer, Cham (2017). https://doi.org/10.1007/978-3-319-68715-5_2
4. Pedersen, S.M., Lind, K.M.: Precision agriculture – from mapping to site-specific application. In: Pedersen, S.M., Lind, K.M. (eds.) Precision Agriculture: Technology and Economic Perspectives. PPA, pp. 1–20. Springer, Cham (2017). https://doi.org/10.1007/978-3-319-68715-5_1
5. Hernandez-Rojas, D., Mazon-Olivo, B., Campoverde, A.: Cloud Computing para el Internet de las Cosas. Caso de estudio orientado a la agricultura de precisión. In: Proceedings of the Memorias Primer Congreso Internacional de Ciencia y Tecnología UTMACH 2015, pp. 47–53 (2015)
6. Campoverde, A., Hernandez-Rojas, D., Mazon-Olivo, B.: Cloud computing con herramientas open-source para Internet de las cosas. Maskana **6**, 173–182 (2015)
7. Ramírez-Morales, I., Mazon-Olivo, B., Pan, A.: Ciencia de datos en el sector agropecuario. In: Ramírez-Morales, I., Mazón-Olivo, B. (eds.) Análisis de Datos Agropecuarios, Universidad Técnica de Machala, Machala-Ecuador, pp. 12–44 (2018). ISBN 978-9942-24-120-7

8. Mazon-Olivo, B., Pan, A., Tinoco-Egas, R.: Inteligencia de negocios en el sector agropecuario. In: Ramírez-Morales, I., Mazón-Olivo, B. (eds.) Análisis de Datos Agropecuarios, Universidad Técnica de Machala, Machala-Ecuador, pp. 246–278 (2018). ISBN 978-9942-24-120-7
9. Mazon-Olivo, B., Rivas, W., Pinta, M., Mosquera, A., Astudillo, L., Gallegos, H.: Dashboard para el soporte de decisiones en una empresa del sector minero. In: Conference Proceedings - Universidad Técnica de Machala, vol. 1, pp. 1218–1229 (2017)
10. Ramirez-Morales, I., Ruilova Reyes, B., Garzón Montealegre, J.: Innovación tecnológica en el sector agropecuario, vol. 2, 1st edn. Universidad Técnica de Machala, Machala (2015). ISBN 0036-8075
11. Jones, J.W., et al.: Toward a new generation of agricultural system data, models, and knowledge products: state of agricultural systems science. Agric. Syst. **155**, 269–288 (2017)
12. Mazon-Olivo, B., Hernández-Rojas, D., Maza-Salinas, J., Pan, A.: Rules engine and complex event processor in the context of internet of things for precision agriculture. Comput. Electron. Agric. **154**, 347–360 (2018)
13. Hernandez-Rojas, D., Fernández-Caramés, T., Fraga-Lamas, P., Escudero, C.: Design and practical evaluation of a family of lightweight protocols for heterogeneous sensing through BLE beacons in IoT telemetry applications. Sensors **18**(1), 57 (2018). https://doi.org/10.3390/s18010057
14. Hernandez-Rojas, D., Fernández-Caramés, T., Fraga-Lamas, P., Escudero, C.: A plug-and-play human-centered virtual TEDS architecture for the Web of Things. Sensors **18**(7), 2052 (2018). https://doi.org/10.3390/s18072052
15. Muangprathub, J., Boonnam, N., Kajornkasirat, S., Lekbangpong, N., Wanichsombat, A., Nillaor, P.: IoT and agriculture data analysis for smart farm. Comput. Electron. Agric. **156**, 467–474 (2019)
16. Rivas-Asanza, W., Mazon-Olivo, B., Mejía-Peñafiel, E.: Generalidades de las redes neuronales artificiales. In: Rivas-Asanza, W., Mazon-Olivo, B. (eds.) Redes neuronales artificiales aplicadas al reconocimiento de patrones, Universidad Técnica de Machala, pp. 11–35 (2018). ISBN 978-9942-24-100
17. Rivas-Asanza, W., Mazon-Olivo, B., Tusa-Jumbo, E.: Reconocimiento de patrones en imágenes. In: Rivas-Asanza, W., Mazon-Olivo, B. (eds.) Redes neuronales artificiales aplicadas al reconocimiento de patrones, Universidad Técnica de Machala, Machala-Ecuador, pp. 61–126 (2018). ISBN 978-9942-24-100
18. Rivas-Asanza, W., Mazon-Olivo, B., Tusa-Jumbo, E.: Tecnologías utilizadas en el reconocimiento de patrones y clasificación de imágenes. In: Rivas-Asanza, W., Mazon-Olivo, B. (eds.) Redes neuronales artificiales aplicadas al reconocimiento de patrones, Universidad Técnica de Machala, pp. 36–60 (2018). ISBN 978-9942-24-100
19. Barnes, A.P., et al.: Exploring the adoption of precision agricultural technologies: a cross regional study of EU farmers. Land Use Policy **80**, 163–174 (2019)
20. Huda, S., Yearwood, J., Hassan, M.M., Almogren, A.: Securing the operations in SCADA-IoT platform based industrial control system using ensemble of deep belief networks. Appl. Soft Comput. **71**, 66–77 (2018)
21. FAO: Banana market review, preliminary results for 2017. http://www.fao.org/fileadmin/templates/est/COMM_MARKETS_MONITORING/Bananas/Documents/Banana_Market_Review_December_2017_update.pdf. Accessed 11 Oct 2019
22. FAO: Banana, land & water. http://www.fao.org/land-water/databases-and-software/crop-information/banana/en/. Accessed 11 Oct 2019
23. Mehta, B.R., Reddy, Y.J.: SCADA systems. In: Industrial Process Automation Systems, pp. 237–300. Elsevier (2015). ISBN 978-0-12-800939-0
24. Duran-Ros, M., Puig-Bargués, J., Arbat, G., Barragán, J., de Cartagena, F.R.: Definition of a SCADA system for a microirrigation network with effluents. Comput. Electron. Agric. **64**, 338–342 (2008)

25. Li, D., Hendricks Franssen, H.-J., Han, X., Jiménez-Bello, M.A., Martínez Alzamora, F., Vereecken, H.: Evaluation of an operational real-time irrigation scheduling scheme for drip irrigated citrus fields in Picassent, Spain. Agric. Water Manag. **208**, 465–477 (2018)

26. Jiménez-Buendía, M., Ruiz-Peñalver, L., Vera-Repullo, J.A., Intrigliolo-Molina, D.S., Molina-Martínez, J.M.: Development and assessment of a network of water meters and rain gauges for determining the water balance. New SCADA monitoring software. Agric. Water Manag. **151**, 93–102 (2015)

27. Katyara, S., Shah, M.A., Zardari, S., Chowdhry, B.S., Kumar, W.: WSN based smart control and remote field monitoring of Pakistan's irrigation system using SCADA applications. Wireless Pers. Commun. **95**, 491–504 (2017)

28. Goyal, M.R., Pandian, B.J. (eds.): Management Strategies for Water Use Efficiency and Micro Irrigated Crops: Principles, Practices, and Performance. Innovations and Challenges in Micro irrigation. Apple Academic Press, Oakville, Palm Bay (2019). ISBN 978-1-77188-791-5

29. Demin, P.: Aportes para el mejoramiento del manejo de los sistemas de riego. Instituto Nacional de Tecnología Agropecuaria, Catamarca - La Rioja, p. 24 (2014)

30. Frisvold, G., Sanchez, C., Gollehon, N., Megdal, S., Brown, P.: Evaluating gravity-flow irrigation with lessons from Yuma, Arizona, USA. Sustainability **10**, 1548 (2018)

31. Chavez, C., Fuentes, C.: Design and evaluation of surface irrigation systems applying an analytical formula in the irrigation district 085, La Begoña, Mexico. Agric. Water Manag. **221**, 279–285 (2019)

32. Bennis, I., Fouchal, H., Zytoune, O., Aboutajdine, D.: Drip irrigation system using wireless sensor networks, pp. 1297–1302 (2015)

33. Sahu, C.K., Behera, P.: A low cost smart irrigation control system. In: Proceedings of the 2015 2nd International Conference on Electronics and Communication Systems (ICECS), pp. 1146–1152. IEEE, Coimbatore (2015)

34. Novillo-Vicuña, J.P., Hernandez-Rojas, D.L., Mazon-Olivo, B., Correa-Elizaldes, K.D.: Monitoreo inalámbrico de señales eléctricas de voltaje 110/220 V a través de Arduino. Alternativas **19**(1) (2019). https://doi.org/10.23878/alternativas.v19i1.198

35. Khelifa, B., Amel, D., Amel, B., Mohamed, C., Tarek, B.: Smart irrigation using internet of things. In: Proceedings of the 2015 Fourth International Conference on Future Generation Communication Technology (FGCT), pp. 1–6. IEEE, Luton (2015)

36. Rajalakshmi, P., Devi Mahalakshmi, S.: IOT based crop-field monitoring and irrigation automation. In: Proceedings of the 2016 10th International Conference on Intelligent Systems and Control (ISCO), pp. 1–6. IEEE, Coimbatore (2016)

37. Rodriguez-Ortega, W.M., Martinez, V., Rivero, R.M., Camara-Zapata, J.M., Mestre, T., Garcia-Sanchez, F.: Use of a smart irrigation system to study the effects of irrigation management on the agronomic and physiological responses of tomato plants grown under different temperatures regimes. Agric. Water Manag. **183**, 158–168 (2016)

38. Barkunan, S.R., Bhanumathi, V., Sethuram, J.: Smart sensor for automatic drip irrigation system for paddy cultivation. Comput. Electr. Eng. **73**, 180–193 (2019)

39. Nawandar, N.K., Satpute, V.R.: IoT based low cost and intelligent module for smart irrigation system. Comput. Electron. Agric. **162**, 979–990 (2019)

# Resilience of Interconnected Infrastructures and Systems: The RESIIST Project

Daouda Kamissoko[1(✉)], Blazho Nastov[2], Vincent Chapurlat[3], Hélène Dolidon[4],
Aurelia Bony-Dandrieux[3], Bruno Barroca[5], Mickael Marechal[6], Jerome Tixier[3],
Matthieu Allon[2], Frederick Benaben[1], Nicolas Daclin[3], Alexis Muller[2],
Nicolas Salatge[1], and Valerie November[5]

[1] IMT Albi Mines, University of Toulouse, Toulouse, France
{douda.kamissoko,frederock.benabeb,
nicolas.salatge}@mines-albi.fr
[2] Axellience, Lille, France
{blazho.nastov,matthieu.allon,alexis.muller}@axellience.com
[3] IMT Mines Alès, Alès, France
{vincent.chapurlat,aurelia.bony-dandrieux,jerome.tixier,
nicolas.daclin}@mines-ales.fr
[4] CEREMA, Nantes, France
helene.dolidon@cerema.fr
[5] Université Paris-Est, Marne-la-Vallee, France
{bruno.barroca,valerie.november}@u-pem.fr
[6] SNCF, Toulouse, France
mickael.marechal@sncf.fr

**Abstract.** This paper introduces a methodology for resilience assessment of critical infrastructures based on massive data. The methodology is developed for the needs of the RESIIST research project. We start from the observation that the security of large cities has become a major issue. To ensure the proper functioning of critical infrastructures, it is essential to make the right decisions at the right time. To do this, managers are informed in their decision-making processes by several indicators such as resilience. As insecurity becomes more and more threatening with technological, natural and terrorist risks, it is essential to have an indicator of resilience of the infrastructures guaranteeing security. We therefore propose an innovative method of assessing resilience. It is innovative in that it combines both the genericity (it applies to all types of infrastructure), it takes into account several dimensions (economic, technical, social, human, regulatory etc.), it integrates massive data (from cameras, sensors, GIS, and social networks), it allows decision-making in an immersive environment in virtual reality.

**Keywords:** Resilience · Critical infrastructure · Decision making · Big data · Simulation · Virtual reality · Security · System

## 1 Introduction

This paper presents the proposal of the RESIIST project (https://research-gi.mines-albi.fr/display/resiist/RESIIST+Home). It addresses the issues of resilience assessment of

© Springer Nature Switzerland AG 2020
M. Botto-Tobar et al. (Eds.): ICAT 2019, CCIS 1193, pp. 257–270, 2020.
https://doi.org/10.1007/978-3-030-42517-3_20

critical infrastructures guaranteeing the security of territories. The term "critical infrastructure" is here-defines as "an infrastructure whose well-functioning is an issue for the stability and the functioning of a territory". Examples of critical infrastructure include power generation and distribution systems, water, gas, health services, banking, state (schools, laboratories, town halls, courts), or companies producing goods and services (industries, agribusiness, public services). The term "resilience" is here-defined as "the ability of an infrastructure to interact with other infrastructures and its environment in order to fulfill its missions and provide the expected services while facing different risks". Risk is used in the sense of a feared event (natural disaster, terrorist attack, internal dysfunction).

The idea of this paper is based on the fact that nowadays it is impossible to imagine a society without considering the preponderant role of critical infrastructures and systems that surround us. In an increasingly liberalized global economy, society needs are changing, but are still based on the assumption that critical infrastructures are functioning [1, 2]. Critical infrastructures show an increased vulnerability. From a resilience perspective, critical infrastructure observation makes the following finding. *The environment and needs are changing*: Critical infrastructures are evolving in environments where continuous delivery of goods and services is required. The demands that regulate their operations constantly evolve and affect the critical infrastructures in the execution of their societal missions. For example, in France, electricity consumption has increased by 350% in 40 years. *Everything is connected to everything*, and everything interacts with everything: Critical infrastructures, products and even entire cities become interconnected. They regularly provide some information on their statements and receive other information to fulfill their missions. Connectivity and interdependencies make infrastructures complex and lead to cascading failures and unpredictable behavior that can reduce the resilience [4]. *Risk situations are growing*: Whether in a critical infrastructure, a country, a city or a community, disruptive events occur daily. Instability has become the norm to integrate [1]. The assessment made by the company F-Secure in terms of computer security finally highlights 99 countries victims of computer attacks for the sole month of May 2017. In addition, the loss experience is diversified: The risks do not spare any structure. The specter of consequences is becoming wider: human lives, territory, economy, or branding are the targets with increasingly dramatic repercussions.

From this observation, several scientific and technological issues arise: The first is *"how to identify critical infrastructures and their limits?"*. Indeed, with connectivity and interdependencies, the boundaries of an infrastructure are not obvious to identify. There is a real need for all stakeholders to define the reasonable limits of their infrastructure. The second is *"how to understand the critical infrastructure at any time and in confidence, by crossing at best several data existing but not necessarily used?"*. This question considers the fact that infrastructures - interacting with each other, behaviors and properties that are difficult to deduce can emerge. There is therefore a need for data and models to improve the understanding of critical infrastructures. The third issue is *"how to decide and act effectively?"*. Cost has long been the key element in critical infrastructure decision-making. This reality is challenged by the need to consider other dimensions considered today as crucial for a better control of resilience (ecological, human, social, political). In addition, it is essential to consider several often-conflicting points of view (users, managers, communities, associations, lobbies). The fourth and last issue is *"how to justify decisions?"*. Since decision-making is not an end, to be accepted, every decision must be justified and rationalized. Rationalization gives a scientific argument to the decision and increases its acceptability.

Based on these observations and the resulting issues, our idea is to use big data to continuously evaluate the resilience of critical infrastructures. Data from various sources is interpreted to provide relevant indicators reflecting several dimensions. By using these indicators, models of infrastructure and resilience are developed. The intelligent visualization of these models makes it possible to take and justify decisions. Thus, the purpose of this paper is to propose a generic methodology for continuous resilience assessment that consider (i) model of a critical infrastructure (ii) continuous flows of big data (iii) the identification of decisions and their implementation (iv) the integration of several dimensions and several points of view. The big data sources used are from various natures (Cameras, Social Networks, Sensors, OpenData, GIS). From a societal point of view, with our proposal, it becomes possible to continuously monitor the critical infrastructures and territories on which they are called to function in any situation.

To fulfil this objective, several questions form the problematic of this paper: (1) Is it possible to continuously measure the resilience of an infrastructure, an organization, a territory with a generic approach? (2) How to prioritize infrastructures and determine the most critical one according to the context? (3) What differentiates one infrastructure from another for a given context and what is needed to put forward to characterize a critical infrastructure considering multiple points of view? (4) What are the risks likely to affect the proper functioning? (5) What are the actions to be defined preventively and correctively? (6) What could be the consequences of a decision and how can it be justified considering the analysis of the potential consequences?

To answer these questions, we propose a process that involves three steps: the interpretation of data into information, the exploitation of information into knowledge, the decision making for obtaining actions to do. The data streams are monitored continuously to obtain big data present in the data layer. The use of big data for the evaluation of resilience is the first originality of this approach. During the interpretation phase, the data provides indicators for infrastructure and risk. The indicators represent several dimensions including at least the technical, economic, environmental, regulatory, social and human dimensions. All these dimensions constitute the second originality. The context is enriched by a study of risks, impacts (resulting from the occurrence of the risk) and corrective and/or preventive treatment strategies. The implementation of these strategies has a systematic impact on the indicators and greatly reduces the consequences of the risk. This in-depth risk engineering is the third originality. The indicators are used in knowledge to obtain a model of resilience and a representation/simulation model of the infrastructure. The latter is represented by its digital twin and its resilience is evaluated considering the lack of knowledge, inaccuracies or uncertainties. It is thus possible to steer the infrastructure through its overall resilience. The use of the digital twin of the infrastructure is the fourth originality. Continuous evaluation of the infrastructure resilience in real time is the fifth originality. The decision-making process results in recommendations and a rational justification for them. Considering the points of view of all stakeholders is the sixth originality. Smart dashboards combined with virtual support the representation, steering and support for the implementation of the decision is the seventh and last originality of this paper.

For the relevancy of our proposal, we took care to make a state of the art on all issues related to the resilience of critical infrastructure. Then we built a case study to test the feasibility of our proposals. The next section describes the literature review.

## 2  Literature Review

This section presents the current state of the are concerning the needs mentioned above. We present three issues in the management of infrastructures in relation to the needs: the problematic of evaluation of the resilience, the problematic of modeling, and the problematic of decision.

### 2.1  Resilience Assessment

Resilience is a concept of growing interest to the scientific community. In Science Direct referencing of scientific articles, from 63 articles containing the word "resilience" in the title in 2007, we moved to 631 articles in 2017, an evolution of 1000% in just 10 years. The concept of resilience and the definitions that refer to it depend on the domain [2]. Whatever the field considered, the notion of resilience generally implies the presence of a risk and refers to the loss of a performance indicator. In the literature, there are different ways of dealing with infrastructure resilience issues: classical, qualitative, quantitative, data, expertise, and feedback. The traditional approach is to apply a traditional risk analysis approach to identify and address a risk for a specific infrastructure [3, 4]. Previous findings in terms of interdependence and connectivity make traditional approaches insufficient to adequately analyze the resilience of an infrastructure. The qualitative assessment family contains conceptual models and approaches based on the estimation of a semi-quantitative index. It is made particularly difficult by considering several dimensions or evaluation criteria and the possible inconsistency between these criteria. The family of quantitative methods can be decomposed into models of simulation, optimization, fuzzy logic, stochastic and deterministic. The reader is invited to see [5] for more information on this category. Evaluating resilience from data is done through data streams from various sources [6]. An evaluation by the transmitted data generates a complexity and issues related to the speed of emission, the quantity of the data emitted, and the diversity of their nature. In evaluation by expertise, the views of one or more experts are modeled and aggregated to obtain a global indicator [7]. In this evaluation category, the capture of antagonistic points of view and their conciliation constitute the main issue. Feedback assessment is mainly practiced in social resilience [8]. It consists of doing similarity analyzes in a situation from past cases. The identification of cases and similarities is the issue of this category.

### 2.2  Resilience Assessment

We mean by modeling the activity leading to the representation of the original infrastructure [9]. The problem of modeling is a crucial problem when it comes to critical infrastructure systems [10]. The systemic approach and several methods such as those proposed in [11, 12] or [13] are then recommended to be able to master, and to facilitate the understanding of the factors inducing this apparent or real complexity. In the field of engineering sciences, the System Engineering approach (ISO 15288) promotes standardized processes for the definition of specifications, design, analysis, verification and validation. and the use of models [14–17]. In this view, a system is usually modeled using a multi-view approach based at least on five points of view: (1) system, (2) need (3) functional and logical, (4) physical/organic and (5) behavioral. The system point of view represents the main features of the system as it currently exists (we are talking about AS-IS model) or as it should be (TO-BE model and sometimes TO-IMPLEMENT model) and its boundaries with the environment. The point of view needs defined the specifications and constraints of different stakeholders. The functional and logical point of view defines different functional architecture solutions of the system. The organic then physical point of view [18] allows the representation of the variants of the concrete architecture of the system. The definition or the choice of the DMSL (Design Specific Modelling Languages), favoring a systemic approach, and the construction of a numerical model is thus the first scientific issue of the modeling. The digital model must also be enriched with data, information and external knowledge, not necessarily easy to model. They must therefore be integrated and enrich the digital model to form what is then called the digital twin to meet the need for simulation and continuous evaluation of the resilience [19] of all or part of the critical infrastructure [20–22]. The mastery of data constraints used for the digital twin (temporalities, the risk of obsolescence) is the first issue of modeling. Transforming data models into indicators to build the infrastructure model is the second issue of the modeling.

### 2.3 Decision Support

Literature review in decision-making in the field of critical infrastructures reveals three types of problems: identification of criteria, procedure of aggregation of criteria, visualization of decisions and implementation of decisions. The identification of the decision criteria is a major stake in the management of the critical infrastructures [23, 24]. The criteria identification methodology proposed by [23] contains two essential steps: (1) determination of objectives and scope and (2) consultation, analysis of acceptability, reasonableness and realism. To our knowledge, there is no set of criteria or methodology applicable to each situation. This is explained by the principle of limited rationality in which (i) the decision-making environment is too complex to be comprehensively apprehended, (ii) the knowledge of the consequences of a decision is always partial, (iii) the rationality of an individual is limited due to lack of time and cognitive ability [25]. However, several authors agree that the criteria must consider several dimensions and check the axioms of completeness, cohesion and non-redundancy defined in [26]. The problem of aggregation lies in the search for a compromise between several criteria and/or the aggregation of the points of view of multiple decision-makers. There is a legion of aggregation procedures in the literature and so many ways of categorizing them. The most widely used methods are: Multi-Attribute Utility Theory, AHP (Analytic Hierarchy Process), Fuzzy Set

Theory, Case-based Reasoning, Data Envelopment Analysis, Goal Programming, ELEC-TRE, PROMETHEE, TOPSIS and the weighted sum [27]. (Triantaphyllou 2000) recommends a classification according to the type of data (Deterministic, Stochastic, Fuzzy) and the number of decision-makers (Mono decision-maker or group decision) [28]. Despite the availability of a certain amount of information, visualization for decision-making is a real scientific and technical problem [29]. The problematic of visualization has been described by [30] and summarized in these points: ergonomics, the comprehension of basic perceptual and cognitive tasks, prior knowledge for comprehension and interpretation, education and training, scalability, measurement of intrinsic quality, aesthetics, paradigm shift from structure to dynamics, causality, visual inference and prediction, visualization of a domain of knowledge. To these problems, [31] adds the human limit of the algorithms. Scientifically, various statistical and numerical methods are used to determine the fit of mathematical models with the data used in the exploratory data analysis. Data visualization provides graphical representations for manipulating and understanding data. Data mining mechanizes the process of identifying structures useful in the data. On a technical level, the visualization is done through the so-called classic dashboards and those called smart. Smart dashboards are means of representing and consolidating information in the form of a cumulative curve, semi-logarithmic graph, sawtooth, streamer, polar coordinates, Gantt, etc. They are used as a medium of decision and communication [32]. The boundaries of the dashboards were analyzed in [32]. They are related to the considering of the uncertainties in the interpretation of the visualization, to the quality of the data. Several technologies are used in the literature to help implement decisions: virtual reality, augmented reality, Cave Automatic Virtual Environment (CAVE), and smart dashboards. Virtual reality is a technology that makes it possible to immerse a person in a digitally created artificial world [33]. It has the advantage of being adapted to situations where information is heterogeneous, incomplete and imprecise. In addition, the input can be conventional data, but also logical relationships or any other knowledge structures [34]. The environment can be standardized, reproducible and controllable [35]. Latency, the distortion of certain input dimensions, constitute the main limits of virtual reality [35]. Augmented reality is an interface between data and the real world. It offers interaction possibilities by combining the real world and digital elements [36]. Current limitations are identification, tracking, provision of the right information in the user's environment, real-time visualization, preparation and implementation time. From a scientific point of view, decision-making issues are the number of criteria and decision-makers as well as uncertainties about data and potential decisions. Like modeling, the visualization of decisions is the technical issue to be lifted in decision-making.

The state-of-the-art elements related to the resilience assessment reported in this paper show that no detailed study or demonstrator considered all the ambitions set by this paper. The following section describes our proposal to remove all the issues identified above.

## 3 Proposal

In order to improve the current resilience of critical infrastructures, and especially to prepare the future in a context always uncertain, we propose in this paper to create and manipulate innovative representations to evaluate the resilience in continuous. The results of this paper are intended for companies operating critical infrastructures, communities and law enforcement, in the public and private sectors. Our proposal is a three-step process as shown in Fig. 1: Data Interpretation, Indicator Exploitation, and Decision making.

**Fig. 1.** Proposal.

### 3.1 Interpretation of Data

With the concepts of smart city, industry 4.0, big data everything becomes connected to everything and vice versa. The number of information exchanged and available continues to grow. For many authors, this high level of connectivity increases the instability of the system through interdependence [37], the emergence and non-linearity of new behaviors. The consequences of sources of instability are multiplied by the cascading failures where a small disturbance can lead to large consequences. Connectivity is also characterized by the availability of a large number of data in transmission as in reception. In this paper, we propose to use Big Data from various sources to evaluate the resilience in continuous. What is then considered as the source of the problem becomes the entry point of the solution. Our proposal to be generic, will consider rules and practices specific to each domain to instrument systems by sensors, collect and store data from various sources. These rules and practices are identified in this activity through data mining techniques. This activity helps identify the relevant data sources for each selected domain. On a technical level, the data will be centralized on a platform specially created to meet the scientific objectives. For the interpretation of data, there are two trends Machine Learning using neural networks to identify indicators (subset of data) and Event-driven architecture and complex event processing [38, 39]. This last approach is used in this paper through our software suite called R-IO (https://r-iosuite.com/). In this method family, the data is considered events.

### 3.2 Exploitation of Indicators

Many authors have proposed indicators for measuring resilience in the literature [6]. For the most part, the assessment of infrastructure resilience is based on a single parameter of the system [40]. Which is irrelevant from our point of view. In addition, because of the need for continuous measurement of resilience, integration of multiple dimensions, comparison to past situations, and aggregation of multiple viewpoints in evaluation, many models are unsuitable for operational use in real situations. In this activity, a resilience model is proposed and applied to the physical and behavioral model of the infrastructure. To do this, the family of simulation methods based on the resilience curve is recommended to represent the functional, behavioral and logical points of view. In this family we implement the proposition of [5]. The Multi Agent simulation implemented in the GAMA platform (http://gama-platform.org/) is used for this purpose. Several weaknesses identified in the literature are thus considered, notably: (a) the nonlinear behavior of the infrastructures, (b) the constraints and the objectives of operation, (c) the criteria (dimensions) of performance. The results of this evaluation will be an indicator of resilience for each criterion and an overall indicator of critical infrastructure. This indicator is normalized between zero (not resilient at all) and one (totally resilient).

### 3.3  Decision Making

In this activity, the objective is to follow the quantitative evolution of the resilience and the evaluation of the potential actions by simulation and projection on the resilience. However, the difficulty of making a decision based on resilience before, during, or after the disruption has been highlighted by many authors [41]. Thus, to choose an action, to visualize this choice and its consequences constitute real problems. To our knowledge, there is no operational tool dedicated to this theme except the [42] approach that uses the Personal Brain tool to visualize the hierarchy of concepts related to resilience. To meet this need, it is important to propose a methodology for decision support and to design appropriate interfaces to monitor and control resilience. The entry for this activity is a continuously updated multi-criteria table. For each pair of (Decision, Criterion) the model evaluates a resilience index. The decision to recommend is the one that will be the best on all the criteria. But the reality is that no action is better on all criteria at any given time. Thus, from this table, we identify the decisions that are not dominated by any other on all the criteria (Pareto Front). This reduces all decisions into a smaller subset. The recommendation of a decision from the multicriteria table requires the integration of additional information. This information can be found in the views of different stakeholders. We then use the multicriteria method of decision PROMETHEE. The PROMETHEE method has the advantage of being able to model several points of view through preference functions. Thus, the characterization and prioritization of infrastructures is a classification problem that can be solved by using the complete classification of PROMETHEE II.

## 4  Results and Discussions

In order to illustrate the feasibility of our proposal, we constructed a use case around a fictional city. The city contains all the infrastructures that a real city in 3D. Our job is to collect and assemble a variety of free templates to make them a coherent whole. The city is thus composed of building, road, airport, railway station, factory etc. Figure 2 (left) gives the overview of the city under unity. From a conceptual point of view, the structure of the city is modeled in the UML diagram below shown in Fig. 2 (right). As can be seen in Fig. 2 (right), the city is composed of networks (road, gas, electricity), Building (factory, home, public establishments, shopping center, town hall, public space) and People (Civilian, terrorist, police officer, security officer, doctors, gendarmes). Several scenarios can be simulated in this case study, but we only describe the scenario related to the risks of terrorist attack. It is possible to instantiate one or more terrorists in the city. The latter may possess three types of weapons: firearm, bomb and/or vehicle. The choice of weapons owned by a terrorist is done by the user. The damage caused will depend on the weapon used. All terrorists are represented by a class that has characteristics and behaviors that depend on the type of scenario. The behavior of the terrorist is translated into computer language in Unity. Thus, if it is equipped with a firearm, only the population category will be in danger (it is considered that bullets have no effect on other types of infrastructure). There is a delay between each shot at the population. When shooting at a target, there are two possibilities: either he misses his target, or he reaches it. The result of a shot will depend on the maximum range of the ball and its trajectory. Indeed, a target will be hit if (1) she is the first target on the trajectory of the ball; (2) the distance between it and the terrorist, at the moment of the shot, is less than or equal to the maximum range $P_{bal}$ of the ball. When a target is hit, either it dies, or it is injured. So, we define two areas on the trajectory of the ball. The first zone is defined by the distance $P_{1b} < P_{bal}$. If the distance between the target and the terrorist is less than or equal to P1b, the target dies. The second zone is that located between $P_{1b}$ and $P_{bal}$. If the distance between the target and the terrorist is within this range, the target will be injured. If the target is injured, it is possible to heal it and thus avoid death.

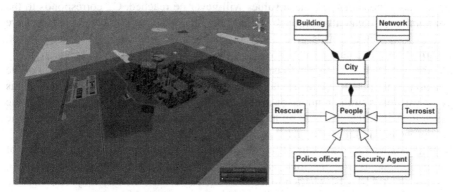

**Fig. 2.** Case study (left) and Concetual model (right).

## 4.1 Interpretation of Data

In the case study we simulated sensors in the city. The latter make it possible to determine: (1) the number of elements damaged by type; (2) the number of destroyed elements (among the elements belonging to the city). Each of these criteria may be interpreted differently for each critical infrastructure. For example, for the population, the number of items destroyed corresponds to the number of dead people; while for the factories, this criterion corresponds to the number of factories destroyed. For the population, the number of damaged elements will correspond to the number of wounded; while for buildings, this criterion corresponds to the number of buildings damaged. We define the values of each criterion over time, as well as the objectives and constraints.

## 4.2 Exploitation of Indicators

To exploit these indicators, we use the methodology proposed in [5]. The resilience is evaluated from several indicators called criteria. Each indicator induces a level of resilience. The value of each indicator comes from one or more sources (e.g., a sensor) and change between four parameters depending on the objectives. If the value of the indicator is between $f_{min}^m$ and $f_{max}^m$, the resilience induced by this indicator is 1. That is to say that it has no negative influence on overall resilience. If the value of the indicator is greater than $f_{max}$ or less than $f_{min}$, in this case, the resilience induced by this criterion is 0. This would mean that the negative impact of this indicator on overall resilience is maximal. If the value of the indicator is between $f_{min}^m$ and $f_{min}$ or between $f_{max}^m$ and $f_{max}$, in this case the value of the resilience induced by this criterion varies between 0 and 1. It is calculated according to the model proposed by [5]. In this case study, we have two criteria described below: the number of damaged elements (C1) and the number of destroyed elements (C2). C1 corresponds to the total number of elements damaged in the time interval [0, t]. For each infrastructure in the city, the goal is to have no damaged elements. This goal does not change over time and is the same for each infrastructure. The number of damaged elements cannot be negative; so theoretically and do not exist. But we rather consider that these values will never be reached. C2 corresponds to the total number of elements destroyed in the time interval [0, t]. The objective is to have no destroyed element. This goal does not change over time and is the same for all infrastructures. The number of destroyed elements cannot be negative; so theoretically and do not exist. But we rather consider that these values will never be reached. For the population it is considered that initially, the number of elements destroyed, which in this case corresponds to the number of deaths, must not exceed 25. It is assumed that due to certain events, the city may no longer be able to withstand as much casualties. The value of the maximum stress on the number of deaths, will therefore always be between 5 and 25 deaths. For other infrastructures, it is considered that initially, the number of destroyed elements, which in this case corresponds to the number of buildings destroyed, must not exceed 3. It is assumed that due to certain events, the city may no longer be able to authorize so much material loss.

## 4.3 Decision Support

In such a scenario, the role of the user will be to limit the number of deaths by implementing several decisions: (1) Send agents to the order to neutralize the terrorist: choose the number of agents, their means of transport (service vehicle or on foot), their weapons, their destinations and their positioning in relation to the terrorist; (2) Send rescue teams to treat the wounded: to choose the composition of the teams and to assign them wounded to take charge. To neutralize a terrorist, the user must place police officers, gendarmes and/or security agents in a strategic manner. The weapons used by officers (police, gendarmes, security guards) are considered to have the same characteristics as those used by terrorists. The user will have to choose several agents and manage their movements relative to the terrorist, while because a terrorist can move and that there can be several terrorists. But also considering the time before each shot. Regarding the care of the wounded. The user must deploy rescue teams so that the wounded are treated as quickly as possible. In fact, each inhabitant has a life gauge, which will be empty if the person dies. If a person is injured, his life gauge will gradually empty and depending on the level he will indicate, he will have some time left before he dies. The user must make his choice considering the state of the various wounded and the distance between a rescue team and the various wounded. A casualty taken in charge by a rescue team can be taken to the hospital; he will be considered out of danger if he arrives at the hospital before his life gauge is emptied. The rescue teams will be able to administer care that will delay the eventual death of the injured. At each moment the overall resilience indicator is displayed on a scale of 0 to 1. For example, Fig. 3 (left) show the evolution of the criterion continuously. As expected, as soon as the value of the criterion becomes greater than the maximum limit, the resilience becomes 0 (Fig. 3 – right).

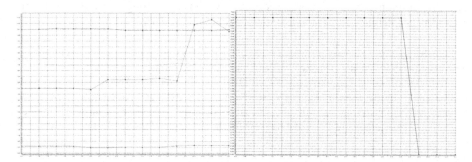

**Fig. 3.** Example of evolution of an indicator (left) and resilience (right).

This case study has been made for the purpose of developing a virtual reality application that is only a demonstrator. It illustrates the integration virtual reality technologies into resilience management. It does not consider the actual functioning of the various infrastructures mentioned there, the aim being first to show how the decisions taken can impact the level of resilience. Numerous simplifications have been made, particularly about the development of risks, the grouping of infrastructures by category, the calculation of resilience and the choice of resilience criteria.

## 5 Conclusions

The security and well-being of the territories depends heavily on the resilience of the hosted infrastructure. Given the growing needs of our societies, natural disasters, acts of terrorism, it is always essential to have a resilience assessment approach. The purpose of this paper was to present the approach proposed in the RESIIST project. The latter proposes a methodology and tools for (a) data collection, (b) modeling, (c) decision making (d) simulation and visualization (e) help with the implementation of decisions to evaluate in real time the resilience of critical infrastructures in order to define the possible strategies and to carry out analyzes on original criteria. Thus, with our proposal, the resilience of critical infrastructures is estimated more finely and continuously. Considering multiple dimensions, connectivity, interdependencies, integration of risk and uncertainties provides results that are very close to reality and based on a very complex reality. It greatly reduces the workload associated with low cognitive content activities in order to free up time for decision making and steering. It allows to study, evaluate and compare different technical solutions (alternatives) and to simulate different behaviors of the system. The proposal brings greater serenity to the person in charge of managing the infrastructure and reinforces the role of the human being at the center of this process. The following five contributions constitute the contributions of the methodology: (1) a generic approach, methods and tools; (2) a methodology for the identification, delimitation and prioritization of infrastructures; (3) on-going measurement indicators for resilience, based on big data; (4) a process and tool for multi-criteria decision support integrating several points of view; (5) an intelligent visualization of the system, its behavior, actions, risks in an immersive environment. Our proposal does not include some non-functional properties used in system engineering such as performance, reliability, availability etc. The integration of these properties is part of our perspective.

**Acknowledgments.** This paper shows a result of the RESIIST project (Résilience des infrastructures et systèmes interconnectés - Resilience of Interconnected Infrastructures and Systems https://research-gi.mines-albi.fr/display/resiist/RESIIST+Home [in French]). The RESIIST project is funded jointly by the French National Research Agency (ANR) and the General Secretary of Defense and National Security (SGDSN). The authors acknowledge these organizations for their support, and particularly, the industrial partners for the definition of the application cases.

# References

1. Ruault, J.-R.: Proposition d'architecture et de processus pour la résilience des systèmes: application aux systèmes critiques à longue durée de vie. Ph.D. thesis, Université de Valenciennes et du Hainaut-Cambresis (2015)
2. Hosseini, S., Barker, K., Ramirez-Marquez, J.E.: A review of definitions and measures of system resilience. Reliab. Eng. Syst. Saf. **145**, 47–61 (2016)
3. Johanson, J.: Risk and vulnérability analysis of interdependent technical infrastructures. Lund University, Department of Measurement Technology and Industrial Electrical Engineering (2010)
4. Giannopoulos, G., Filippini, R., Schimmer, M.: Risk assessment methodologies for critical infrastructure protection. Part I: a state of the art. JRC Technical Notes (2012)
5. Kamissoko, D., et al.: Continuous and multidimensional assessment of resilience based on functionality analysis for interconnected systems. Struct. Infrastruct. Eng. **15**, 427–442 (2018)
6. Barker, K., et al.: Defining resilience analytics for interdependent cyber-physical-social networks. Struct. Infrastruct. Eng. **2**(2), 59–67 (2017)
7. Taysom, E., Crilly, N.: Resilience in sociotechnical systems: the perspectives of multiple stakeholders. She Ji: J. Des. Econ. Innov. **3**(3), 165–182 (2017)

8. Winfield, L.F.: The knowledge base on resilience in African-American adolescents. In: Pathways Through Adolescence: Individual Development in Relation to Social Contexts, pp. 87–118 (1995)
9. Stachowiak, H.: Allgemeine modelltheorie (1973)
10. Jamshidi, M.: System of systems engineering - new challenges for the 21st century. IEEE Aerosp. Electron. Syst. Mag. **23**(5), 4–19 (2008)
11. Féliot, C.: Toward a formal theory of systems, Colloque d'Automne du LIX 2007 - CAL07 Complex Systems: Modelling, Verification and Optimization, Paris, Carré des Sciences, 3rd and 4th October 2007 (2007)
12. Penalva, J.M.: La modelisation par les systemes en situation complexes, Paris (1997)
13. Pederson, P., Dudenhoeffer, D., Hartley, S., Permann, M.: Critical infrastructure interdependency modeling: a survey of US and international research. Idaho National Laboratory, vol. 25, p. 27 (2006)
14. INCOSE: Survey of Model-Based Systems Engineering (MBSE) Methodologies, INCOSE TD-2007-003-01, Version/Revision: B, 10 June 2008
15. Lemazurier, L., Chapurlat, V., Grossetête, A.: An MBSE approach to pass from requirements to functional architecture. IFAC-PapersOnLine **50**(1), 7260–7265 (2017)
16. Micouin, P.: Model Based Systems Engineering: Fundamentals and Methods. Wiley, Hoboken (2014)
17. Nastov, B.: Contribution à une méthode outillée pour la conception de langages de modélisation métier interopérables, analysables et prouvables pour l'Ingénierie Système basée sur des Modèles (2016)
18. Crawley, E.: Introduction to System Architecture (2007)
19. Luglio, C.E.: Resilience of critical infrastructures: dynamic modeling of disruptive events in a European scenario (2017)
20. Ouyang, M.: Review on modeling and simulation of interdependent critical infrastructure systems. Reliab. Eng. Syst. Saf. **121**, 43–60 (2014)
21. FMI: Functional Mock-up Interface (2017). http://fmi-standard.org/. Accessed 26 Mar 2018
22. HLA: IEEE 1516-2010 – IEEE Standard for Modeling and Simulation (M&S) High Level Architecture (HLA) – Framework and Rules. IEEE Standard Association (2010)
23. Desmond, M.: Decision criteria for the identification of alternatives in strategic environmental assessment. Impact Assess. Proj. Apprais. **25**(4), 259–269 (2007)
24. Bacon, C.J.: The use of decision criteria in selecting information systems/technology investments. MIS Q. **16**(3), 335–353 (1992)
25. Simon, H.A.: Theories of decision-making in economics and behavioral science. Am. Econ. Rev. **49**, 253–283 (2000)
26. Roy, B.: Méthodologie multicritère d'aide à la décision. Economica (1985)
27. Velasquez, M., Hester, P.: An analysis of multi-criteria decision making methods. Int. J. Oper. Res. **10**, 56–66 (2013)
28. Triantaphyllou, E.: Multi-criteria decision making methods. In: Triantaphyllou, E. (ed.) Multi-criteria Decision Making Methods: A Comparative Study. APOP, vol. 44, pp. 5–21. Springer, Boston (2000). https://doi.org/10.1007/978-1-4757-3157-6_2
29. Zhu, B., Chen, H.: Information visualization for decision support. In: Zhu, B., Chen, H. (eds.) Handbook on Decision Support Systems. INFOSYS, pp. 699–722. Springer, Heidelberg (2008). https://doi.org/10.1007/978-3-540-48716-6_32
30. Chen, C.: Top 10 unsolved information visualization problems. IEEE Comput. Graphics Appl. **25**(4), 12–16 (2005)
31. 2016 at 9:35 pm Posted by Larry Alton on May 8 and V. Blog: 4 Potential Problems With Data Visualization (2016)

32. Matheus, R., Janssen, M., Maheshwari, D.: Data science empowering the public: data-driven dashboards for transparent and accountable decision-making in smart cities. Government Information Quarterly, February 2018

33. Steuer, J.: Defining virtual reality: dimensions determining telepresence. J. Commun. **42**(4), 73–93 (1992)

34. Valdés, J.J.: Virtual reality representation of information systems and decision rules: an exploratory technique for understanding data and knowledge structure. In: Rough Sets, Fuzzy Sets, Data Mining, and Granular Computing, pp. 615–618 (2003)

35. Morel, M., Bideau, B., Lardy, J., Kulpa, R.: Advantages and limitations of virtual reality for balance assessment and rehabilitation. Neurophysiol. Clin./Clin. Neurophysiol. **45**(4), 315–326 (2015)

36. Azuma, R.T.: A survey of augmented reality. Presence: Teleoperators Virtual Environ. **6**(4), 355–385 (1997)

37. Kamissoko, D.: Decision support for infrastructure network vulnerability assessment in natural disaster crisis situations. Doctorate, University of Toulouse, University of Toulouse 1 Capitole (2013)

38. Etzion, O., Niblett, P.: Event Processing in Action, 1st edn. Manning Publications Co., Greenwich (2010)

39. Luckham, D., Schulte, R.: Event Processing Glossary – Version 1.1, July 2008

40. Yodo, N., Wang, P.: Engineering resilience quantification and system design implications: a literature survey. J. Mech. Des. **138**(11), 111408–111408-13 (2016)

41. McDaniels, T., Chang, S., Cole, D., Mikawoz, J., Longstaff, H.: Fostering resilience to extreme events within infrastructure systems: characterizing decision contexts for mitigation and adaptation. Glob. Environ. Chang. **18**(2), 310–318 (2008)

42. Renschler, C., Fraizer, A.E., Arendt, L.A., Cimellaro, G.P., Reinhorn, A.M., Bruneau, M.: Framework for defining and measuring resilience at the community scale: the PEOPLES resilience framework, October 2010

# Simulation Tools for Solving Engineering Problems. Case Study

Fabián Cuzme-Rodríguez[✉], Ana Umaquinga-Criollo, Luis Suárez-Zambrano,
Henry Farinango-Endara, Hernán Domínguez-Limaico,
and Mario Mediavilla-Valverde

Carrera de Ingeniería en Telecomunicaciones, Universidad Técnica del Norte,
Av. 17 de Julio 5-21 y Gral. José María Córdova, 100105 Ibarra, Ecuador
fgcuzme@utn.edu.ec

**Abstract.** The areas of Engineering in Applied Sciences have contributed significantly to the social, economic and technological advances of the world, being of interest to the academy mainly in the university system and specialization in Ecuador and in several countries both in the teaching-learning process as well as in research, which makes it increasingly stronger and proposes better and new solutions to environmental problems. This article performs a quantitative, descriptive and systemic analysis, which combines with the analysis of the ISO/IEC 25010 standard considers criteria such as functionality, performance, compatibility, usability, reliability, maintainability, portability to evaluate the quality of the software; The analysis involves simulation tools immersed in the teaching-learning processes of the engineering area with the determination to identify the tools used to solve specific problems in this field, particularly in the Telecommunications Engineering Degree at the "Universidad Técnica del Norte" University. This study is based on the opinion of experts in the university and business field who validate the established criteria. The results of this article identify the use of the different simulation tools in the university education and research environment, in addition to promoting the inclusion of these tools in the process of training students so that they can propose solutions at a scientific level and/or technological.

**Keywords:** Simulators · ISO-25010 · NS2 · NS3 · MATLAB

## 1 Introduction

Simulation theory is one of the areas of study for the business sector, technology providers, research groups, among others, mainly due to the high cost of implementing an experimental network to study their behavior [1, 2]. For the most part, academic or corporate environments include limitations or restrictions on the quantity and variety of communication equipment and the possibility of modifying its design or implementation [3].

The study of the performance of communications networks through network simulators allows the technical user to "recreate systems and scenarios" in a software interface

M. Botto-Tobar et al. (Eds.): ICAT 2019, CCIS 1193, pp. 271–285, 2020.
https://doi.org/10.1007/978-3-030-42517-3_21

that allows him to study design and communication possibilities before they are put into production [4] which leads to the "complement to theoretical conceptualization" [1] considerable savings of type resources: time, cost [3], technological, human that benefits the quality of service of the institutions to their customers allowing them to maintain or improve their competitiveness.

Complex network simulation tools in the market are increasing, as well as the diversity of their services, usability of their interfaces, complexity, versatility; new topologies, type of license; advanced options such as: statistics, event viewer, among others [5], having to be necessary the study and diagnostic analysis of this type of software to know the opportunities and characteristics that these simulators require.

The use of telecommunication environment simulation tools allows users to create environments surrounded by reality and interpret them. Proposals as in [6, 7] that presents simulation environments with computational tools such as the NS2, which allows the use of mobile IPv6 protocols, applying quality of service (QoS) to evaluate data packets; It allows interpreting the capacity of simulation tools for research. In the same way, the simulation of environments for OSI model layers leads to the inquiry of finding the ideal tool to carry out research results and teaching purposes. In [8] it performs a simulation of a point-to-point link using MATLAB in which it performs an interface for the modification of different parameters concerning the transmission medium where it allows to analyze results using of graphs. It can be said that the simulation parameters of the tools can be in detail as for the analysis of a transmission medium that in this case implies the first layer of the OSI (Open Systems Interconnection) model.

This research presents the first phase of the study of the Research Project: Evaluation of communication protocols for Home Area Network (HAN) environments that are developed in the Telecommunications Engineering Degree at the Technical University of the North. This phase describes the quantitative, diagnostic and comparative analysis of the following Communication Network simulation software: *Ns2, Ns3, OPNET IT Guru, OMNET, GNS3, MATLAB,* the same ones that are studied in this institution in order to apply the synergy of evaluation methods in previous studies [4, 9] and to contribute with guidelines for an adequate selection of this type of software according to the needs of the users among them are: functionality, performance, compatibility, usability, reliability, maintainability and portability through a comparative analysis.

The rest of the document is organized as follows: In Sect. 2 the review and description of the Materials and Methods of the simulators previously selected are carried out, while in Sect. 3 the results obtained from the study are presented and finally in Sect. 4 the main conclusions.

## 2 Materials and Methods

The methodology applied is based on descriptive analysis and the opinion of experts who use the tools considered in this study. A guide is established to the analysis process that we wish to carry out in this article as shown in Fig. 1.

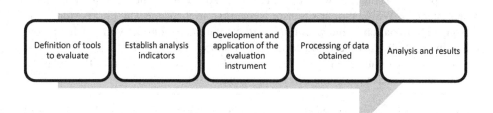

**Fig. 1.** The analysis process of simulation software tools

## 2.1  Software Tools Considered

The tools considered for evaluation are those used in the teaching-learning and research processes in the university environments of the Technical University of the North, considering the Telecommunications Engineering Career of the Engineering in Applied Sciences Faculty as a case study.

The considered tools are: NS2, NS3, OPNET, OMNET++, GNS3 and MATLAB, a brief detail of each of them is addressed.

**NS2 Simulator.** It is considered a discrete event simulator oriented to research in networks that provides substantial support in the simulation of TCP routing and multicast protocols over wired and wireless networks (local and satellite) [10], Fig. 2 shows a simulation of 4 nodes.

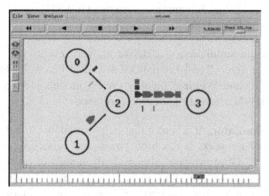

**Fig. 2.** Simulation screenshot in NS2

The simulations with which this tool works are related to the technologies handled at levels 2 and 3 of the OSI reference model. Studies such as [11] evaluate anti-collision protocols for Ultra High Frequency, RFID, on the other hand [12] simulate secure applications in vehicle area networks. While [13] simulate "different types of networks whether wired or wireless," the network model, "protocols and traffic sources". A specific practice is the simulation with wireless networks for protocol 802.11 [14], WLAN, Ah Hoc and Mobile-IP, the group of protocols: UDP, TCP, GPRS, MPLS, HTTP and FTP [9, 13, 15, 16] presents a complete work of the use of an extension for the simulation of a location systems in WSN (Wireless Sensor Networks), in the same way [17] performs the design and evaluation of the performance of a communications network for Intelligent Metering or AMI (Advanced Metering Infrastructure).

This tool facilitates the use of various modules and extensions for TCP simulation, routing and multicast protocols wired and wireless [18].

**NS3 Simulator.** NS3 and NS2 are two different simulators that are not compatible with each other; they are used to model how the Internet protocol and computer networks work. However, it is not limited to Internet computer network systems; it also allows to apply to non-Internet based systems. It can be read by the Wireshark software, to display the graphic mode requires the installation of Network Animator (NAM) [13]. Figure 3 shows a simulation of 4 nodes.

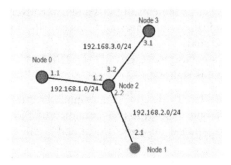

**Fig. 3.** Simulation screenshot in NS3

The tool allows the simulation of discrete network events with the objective of achieving emphasis on layers 2 and 4 of the OSI models [9], as well as the study of Long Term Evolution (LTE) and Wireless Fidelity (WiFi) models [18, 19], heterogeneous wireless networks (HWN) evaluating their performance.

**OPNET IT Guru Simulator.** It is a tool that helps simulate the behavior and performance of any type of network. It has high power and versatility compared to other simulators. OPNET IT Guru provides already built models of protocols and devices, allows to create and simulate different network topologies. Its set of protocols and devices is fixed, it does not allow to create new protocols nor to modify the behavior of the existing ones.

Allows scalability in hierarchical models for network structure and flexibility, supports layers 2 and 3 [9, 20], where there is a variety of implementations in this regard. It is the case of [21] that evaluates the performance of IEEE 802.11 in wireless networks with the variation of several parameters that the tool allows. Figure 4 shows a topology between routers and servers.

Supports LAN optimization designs that can be cableated and wireless with multi-scenario simulations [22] for persistence performance analysis. Significant advantages

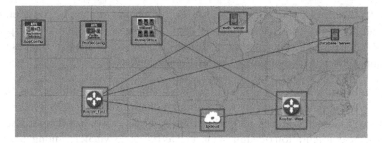

**Fig. 4.** Simulation screenshot in OPNET IT Guru

can be obtained in a WLAN in HTTP and FTP connections indicate the authors. To measure the performance of a network's services, traffic analysis for the subsequent implementation of QoS (Quality of Service) [23], which analyzes the queuing mechanisms, the behavior of the RSVP (Resource Reservation Protocol) and congestion avoidance algorithms [23].

**OMNET++ Simulator.** It allows to model the traffic on communication networks, network protocols, multiprocessors, distributed hardware systems, in the lower layers of the OSI model 2, 3 and 4, [24] analyzes the applicability of the software with respect to protocols with different routing schemes, [5] analyzes the data traffic flow of a sensor, file transfer, video and VoIP corresponding to the transport layer. Figure 5 shows a communication using the Zigbee protocol.

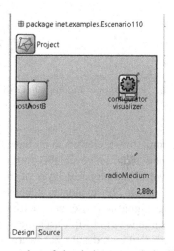

**Fig. 5.** Screenshot of simulation scenario in OMNET++

This tool carries out the simulation and creation of proposals for the different environments of communication networks, especially those that present problems in the influx of traffic such as wireless networks. In [25] a new framework called Cooperative Spectrum Resource Allocation (CSRA) is proposed for cognitive radio sensor networks

(CRSN) deployed for home energy control for a HAN environment. Consideration is given to an analysis of a CCC (Common control channel) concerning to a proposal with CSRA for a significant number of devices connected to achieve a fair spectrum distribution, sharing between sensors in intelligent homes.

**GNS3 Simulator.** GNS3 is a graphical network simulator that allows you to easily design network topologies and then run simulations. It supports IOS routers, ATM, Frame Relay, Ethernet Switches, and PIX firewalls, the latter work as decorative devices.

Allows the configuration of equipment such as routers, switches, among other active network devices through the IOS. Facilitates the design of network topologies and at the same time the execution of simulators. Supports ATM, Frame Relay, Switch Ethernet and PIX firewall, you can configure a network based on different protocols such as MPLS, VPN, RIP, BGP, OSPF, among others explain [9] and [26].

In addition, it performs traffic analysis of a network for layers 2, 3, and 4 with the ease of using different means of transmission intervening in layer 1 and the use of other linked simulators, where compatible services can be accessed on the network in the case of the different practices described in [26] and the simulation of [27]. Figure 6 shows a topology of an MPLS network.

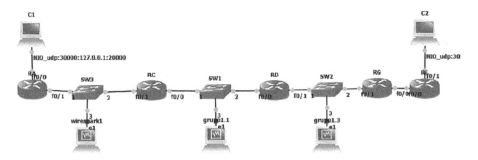

**Fig. 6.** Screenshot of topology in GNS3

**MATLAB Simulator.** The simulators reviewed so far have the uniqueness of allowing the user to model computer networks, however, this tool can be used to analyze the networks of sensors at the level of the physical layer of the OSI model is interpreted from [28] and [18]. For this reason [29] evaluates adaptive antennas simulating real conditions of a channel such as signal-to-noise, attenuation, and interference based on Bluetooth technology. In the same way in [30] it uses the Simulink tool for a complete simulation of a system for WSN that includes the hardware architecture of transmission nodes.

Figure 7 shows a simulation of the eye diagram together with a transmission constellation diagram.

Table 1 shows a summary of the main characteristics of each of the software tools considered:

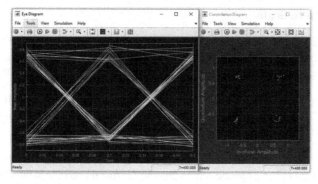

**Fig. 7.** Eye diagram simulation and transmission constellation diagram

**Table 1.** Main features

|  | NS2 | NS3 | OPNET | OMNET | GNS3 | MATLAB |
|---|---|---|---|---|---|---|
| License | Open-source | Open-source | Opensource | Open-source | GNU GPL v2 | Commercial |
| Language | English | English | English | English | 19 languages | English, Spanish, others |
| Integration with other types of software | OTCL, NAM | Linux Ubuntu Virtual machine | N/A | N/A | VMware (o VirtualBox), Dynamips, Qemu, putty y Wireshark. | N/A |
| Interface | Text (Graphical using NAM, OTCL) | Text | Graphical 32-bit and 64-bit and text | Graphical GUI: graphic (tkenv) y text (cmdenv) | GUI | |
| Programming language | C++, TCL | C++, Python | C++, C | C++ | N/A | IDE, text |
| Operative system | FreeBSD, Linux, SunOs, Solaris, Windows y Mac OS X | Windows, Linux, Mac OS, Free BSD | Windows, Linux, MacOS, Unix | Windows, Linux, MacOs, UNIX | Linux, Windows y Mac | M Language (own) |
| Version | 2.35 | NS-3.27 | 17.5 | 5.1 | 2.1.2 | Unix, Linux, Windows y Mac |

## 2.2 Evaluation Indicators

To evaluate the simulation tools, some indicators established in the ISO/IEC 25010 standard [31] that allow evaluating the software from some contexts were considered. Each of these criteria is described to understand what is sought in each of them:

**Functionality.** Represents the ability of the software product to provide functions that meet the stated and implied needs, when the product is used under the specified conditions. The items of functional completeness, correction, and functional relevance are considered.

**Performance.** This characteristic represents the performance relative to the number of resources used under certain conditions. The items of temporary behavior and use of resources are considered.

**Compatibility.** The capacity of two or more systems or components to exchange information and carry out their required functions when they share the same hardware or software environment. The items of coexistence and interoperability are considered.

**Usability.** The ability of the software product to be understood, learned, used and attractive to the user, when used under certain conditions. The following items are considered: the ability to recognize their adequacy, learning capacity, ability to be used, protection against user errors, aesthetics of the human interface and accessibility.

**Reliability.** The ability of a system or component to perform the specified functions, when used under certain conditions and periods. The items of maturity and availability are considered.

**Maintainability.** This feature represents the ability of the software product to be modified effectively and efficiently, due to evolutionary, corrective or perfective needs. The items of modularity and reusability are considered.

**Portability.** The ability of the product or component to be transferred effectively and efficiently from a hardware, software, operational or use the environment to another. The items of adaptability, capacity to be installed and capacity to be replaced are considered.

## 2.3 Measurement and Valuation Levels

The measurement levels allow comparison between some network simulators that are established by the previous analysis, which allows having a decision element when evaluating one or another tool:

- High. It has a high contribution to the indicator evaluated and the subsets fully comply.
- Half. It has a partial contribution with the indicator evaluated and the sub-assemblies partially comply.
- Low. It has a low contribution with the indicator evaluated and the subsets have lower compliance.

– Null. It does not contribute to the evaluated indicator and of the subsets, it has no compliance.

Each measurement level is assigned a numerical value in a range of 0 to 5; where zero (0) will be the lowest value and five (5) the highest value, Table 2 shows the allocation established in this study.

**Table 2.** Rating by level

| Level | Assessment |
|-------|------------|
| High  | 5          |
| Half  | 3          |
| Low   | 1          |
| Null  | 0          |

For calculating the value of each indicator described in Sect. 2.2 nomenclature is defined to identify follows Functionality ($V_{fun}$), Performance ($V_{des}$), Compatibility ($V_{com}$), Usability ($V_{us}$), Reliability ($V_{fi}$), Maintainability ($V_{man}$) and Portability ($V_{por}$). Equation 1 to calculate each indicator is described below:

$$V_{indicator} = \frac{\sum_{i=1}^{n} value_{indicator}}{nExpH} \quad (1)$$

Where, $n$ is the number of questions asked in each indicator, $i$ in the counter greater than zero (0), $value_{indicator}$ is the value (according to Table 2) assigned by the expert to each question and $nExpH$ is the number of experts They evaluated the same tool.

To obtain the total assessment of each tool that is most used according to the application of the survey, the following Eq. 2 is established:

$$Assessment_{total} = V_{fun} + V_{des} + V_{com} + V_{us} + V_{fi} + V_{man} + V_{por} \quad (2)$$

### 2.4 Development and Implementation of the Survey

The survey was defined in different sections that allow addressing the indicators to be evaluated and which were described in Sect. 2.2. the questions were grouped in the manner shown, in Table 3.

The survey was applied to experts who have used the tools described in Sect. 2.1, it was applied using the Forms tool of the Google Docs suite, which allowed to reach experts working in the academic and research field. See Fig. 8.

Table 4 shows the tools evaluated by 16 experts, which shows the scope in which it is used and the area of application in the field of engineering.

**Table 3.** Sections of the survey

| Section | Questions |
|---|---|
| General | – Mail<br>– Selection of the tool to evaluate<br>– Scope of use<br>– Application area in Engineering |
| Functionality | – Functionality level provided by the tool<br>– Functionality to work in several layers of the OSI model |
| Performance | – Level of efficiency provided by the tool |
| Compatibility | – Level of import or export of components to other tools, as well as reports and source files |
| Usability | – Ease of use of the tool<br>– Level of research/academic/business use provides the tool in your environment |
| Reliability | – Level of reliability provided by the tool<br>– Results attached to reality |
| Maintainability | – Level to make adaptations or modifications to develop improvements in simulation environments |
| Portability | – Portability level offered by the tool |

**Fig. 8.** Google Docs form

**Table 4.** Number of experts who evaluated the proposed tools

| Number of experts | Tool evaluated | Scope used | Application area |
| --- | --- | --- | --- |
| 1 | OMNET++ | Academic | Telecommunications |
| 2 | OMNET++ | Academic | Telecommunications |
| 3 | GNS3 | Academic | Telecommunications Communication Networks |
| 4 | OPNET | Academic | Communication Networks |
| 5 | MATLAB | Academic | Communication Networks |
| 6 | MATLAB | Research, Academic | Computer systems Mathematical modeling |
| 7 | MATLAB | Academic | Telecommunications Communication Networks |
| 8 | GNS3 | Academic | Telecommunications Communication Networks |
| 9 | GNS3 | Academic | Communication Networks |
| 10 | GNS3 | Academic Industrial-Business | Communication Networks |
| 11 | GNS3 | Industrial-Business | Communication Networks |
| 12 | GNS3 | Research Industrial-Business | Telecommunications Communication Networks |
| 13 | GNS3 | Academic | Communication Networks |
| 14 | MATLAB | Academic | Telecommunications |
| 15 | OMNET++ | Academic | Telecommunications Communication Networks |
| 16 | NS2 | Academic | Telecommunications Communication Networks |

## 3    Results and Discussion

The results obtained from surveys applied to experts provide a broad picture of the application of certain software tools described in Sect. 2.2 that many professionals in academia and research use. With the application of Eqs. 1 and 2 described in Sect. 2.3, the following results could be obtained as shown in Table 5.

**Table 5.**  Results obtained from the survey

| Tools | Functionality | Performance | Compatibility | Usability | Reliability | Maintainability | Portability | Assessment$_{total}$ |
|---|---|---|---|---|---|---|---|---|
| GNS3 | 4,1 | 3,6 | 3,9 | 4,1 | 3,4 | 4,4 | 3,0 | 26,6 |
| MATLAB | 2,8 | 4,0 | 3,5 | 4,0 | 3,8 | 3,3 | 2,3 | 23,5 |
| OMNET++ | 4,0 | 3,0 | 3,0 | 3,3 | 3,7 | 3,7 | 4,3 | 25,0 |
| NS2 | 3,0 | 3,0 | 1,0 | 3,0 | 3,0 | 5,0 | 1,0 | 19,0 |
| OPNET | 3,0 | 3,0 | 0,0 | 3,0 | 4,0 | 3,0 | 0,0 | 16,0 |

According to the results shown in Table 5, it is worth indicating some considerations, although GNS3 is the one that has the greatest value in most of its indicators and its total assessment, this is due to the fact that it is a software tool used to simulate many network and telecommunications scenarios without taking into account details of operation that communications perform at a low level, being a perfect tool for technical professionals who configure communication equipment for network and telecommunications inter-connectivity, and therefore its use in the academic and industrial/business environment. OMNET++ is another tool chosen by the experts to which they give a considerable value to each indicator, and which shows a structure to develop many more sophisticated solutions in terms of communication protocols, but that despite the fact that in our environment is being used within teaching-learning, is a good option to develop areas of research within telecommunications. MATLAB has already introduced its application in the part of mathematical modeling and is now the third referential option in the study. Being applied in the field of telecommunications as part of signal processing, introducing its use in academia and research. NS2, powerful tool but little considered by our experts, bearing in mind that new protocols can be developed and tested scenarios that cannot be developed in GNS3, this is because the diffusion of these tools is little and their use in the academy of the Faculty of Engineering of Applied Sciences. Finally, OPNET is considered, which despite being a commercial tool has a partial release for the academy and is not widely used for its use.

While another tool considered in this study was NS3 was not considered by any expert surveyed, this clearly shows the low diffusion of simulators that allow simulations in the telecommunications environment that go beyond just entering commands or assigning an IP address. NS3 is also a powerful tool whose strength can be exploited in LTE networks, although since it is not an update of NS2 and was a separate development it still has some instabilities in its versions.

There are many studies carried out with the software tools considered in this study such as GNS3 [27] which is used to create Virtual Private Networks, VPNs in Multiprotocol Label Switching environments, MPLS, but it should be noted that it is a powerful tool for testing certain configurations already defined on certain computers before applying it to a production environment, so to test new protocols or mechanisms for access to the medium is limited. In the case of OMNET it goes beyond just configuring equipment as it is applied in [20] where it is used to model and evaluate routing protocols in MANET networks with video applications, this allows being much more versatile when it comes to generating environments that improve existing protocols considering some variants. On the other hand, MATLAB, considering a referential study in the network environment is [32] where the performance of a wireless sensor network (WSN) is simulated and studied, another study such as [33] where a simulation framework including SIMULINK is analyzed; this also makes this tool strong in the field of networks and telecommunications although it has many other applications applicable to the field of artificial intelligence. NS2 as a referential study we cite [11], where an evaluation is made of the UHF RFID anti-collision protocols where different algorithms can be tested to compare their operating results. In the case of OPNET, the study cited is [34], which simulates and analyzes the performance of attacks on the MAC layer in underwater acoustic networks where some modules are tested in the MAC layer that indicate drops in performance. By NS3 that although it was not considered we present a study of [19], where it presents the design and implementation of a simulation system of a heterogeneous wireless network (HWN) where it tries to demonstrate a reliable and quantitative base of this environment.

## 4  Conclusions

This study clearly marks the commitment of the academy in promoting the use of simulation tools in the area of networks and telecommunications to develop capabilities that go beyond just configuring equipment at a technical level, this should be the guideline to develop solutions according to the needs of our environment, promoting autonomous learning, research and technological innovation, allowing the development of the academy at another level being competitive locally, nationally and internationally. On the other hand, the new requirements on the part of the control entities of higher education in terms of evaluation indicators that have to do not only with the understanding of the theoretical part, but that in practice allow students and researchers to propose solutions to the problems of the environment and that are attached to the real needs of institutions and companies at the local, regional and national level make this study applicable and valid.

## References

1. Hernández, W.E.C., Osario, M.E.C.: Utilización de herramientas software para el modelado y la simulación de redes de comunicaciones. Gerenc Tecnológica Informática **5**, 73–81 (2006)
2. Balasundram, A.: Poster: a comparison study of Wi-Fi direct and dedicated short range communication for intelligent transport services. In: MobiSys 2016 Companion - Companion Publication of the 14th Annual International Conference on Mobile Systems, Applications, and Services, p. 10 (2016)
3. Torres, J.A., Arias Figueroa, D., Díaz, J.: Herramientas de software de simulación para redes de comunicaciones (2016)

4. Dávalos, A., Paz, L., Cadavid, A., Mejía, A.: Método de evaluación y selección de herramientas de simulación de redes (2011)
5. Coello Ojeda, M.A., Sempere Paya, V.M., Rodríguez Hernandez, M.A.: Caracterización y Simulación de Fuentes de Tráfico en Smart Cities (2014)
6. Chileg, G., Vinicio, G.: Empleo de la herramienta computacional NS2 para simular el comportamiento de una red de telecomunicaciones móviles celulares cuando se utiliza el protocolo IP móvil v6 (MIPv6) en aplicaciones de voz (2009)
7. Gafur, A.M., Ben Saleh, A.: Capacity utilization based on contention window management in mobile ad hoc network. Int. J. Numer. Model Electron. Netw. Dev. Fields **32** (2019). https://doi.org/10.1002/jnm.2646
8. González, S., Javier, L.: Simulador de enlace de fibra optica punto a punto usando interfaz grafica de MATLAB, p. 122 (2012)
9. Calle, M.A., Tovar, J.D., Castaño-Pino, Y.J., Cuéllar, J.C.: Comparación de Parámetros para una Selección Apropiada de Herramientas de Simulación de Redes. Inf Tecnológica **29**, 253–266 (2018). https://doi.org/10.4067/s0718-07642018000600253
10. López Echeverry, A., García Quiroz, N.: Simulación de tráfico en redes inalambricasmediante NS2. Sci. Tech. **1**, 155–160 (2010). https://doi.org/10.22517/23447214.1805
11. Ben Fraj, R., Beroulle, V., Fourty, N., Meddeb, A.: An evaluation of UHF RFID anti-collision protocols with NS2. In: 2018 9th IFIP International Conference on New Technologies, Mobility and Security, NTMS 2018 – Proceedings, pp. 1–6 (2018)
12. Li, J., Zhang, Y., Zhao, J., et al.: NS-2 simulation of VANET for safety applications: issues and solutions. In: ACM International Conference Proceeding Series, pp. 67–72 (2017)
13. Carrión, B., Delgado, L.: Simulación y análisis de redes esporádicas móviles Ad-Hoc (2015)
14. Pan, J.: A survey of network simulation tools: current status and future development. CSE567M Comput. Syst. Anal. (2008)
15. Shin, J.Y., Jang, J.W., Kim, J.M.: Result based on NS2, simulation and emulation verification. In: Proceedings - 2009 International Conference on New Trends in Information and Service Science, NISS 2009, pp. 807–811 (2009)
16. Abu-Mahfouz, A.M., Hancke, G.P.: NS-2 extension to simulate localization system in wireless sensor networks. In: IEEE AFRICON Conference (2011)
17. Aranda, J.M.: Ingenieria. Universidad Distrital Francisco Jose de Caldas (2015)
18. Sharif, M., Sadeghi-Niaraki, A.: Ubiquitous sensor network simulation and emulation environments: a survey. J. Netw. Comput. Appl. **93**, 150–181 (2017). https://doi.org/10.1016/j.jnca.2017.05.009
19. Yu, H., Liang, G., Zhao, Y.: NS3-based simulation system in heterogeneous wireless network. In: 11th International Conference on Wireless Communications, Networking and Mobile Computing (WiCOM 2015), pp. 1–6. Institution of Engineering and Technology (2016)
20. Borja, N.: Simulación, modelamiento y evaluación de los protocolos de routing en redes MANET con aplicaciones de video mediante plataformas opensource de eventos discretos. Thesis (2017)
21. Kulgachev, V., Jasani, H.: 802.11 networks performance evaluation using OPNET. In: SIGITE 2010 - Proceedings of the 2010 ACM Conference on Information Technology Education, pp. 149–152 (2010)
22. Ayyoub, B.: Wired and WLAN Optimal Design Using OPNET$^{TM}$ IT GURU (2014)
23. del Rosario Cruz Felipe, M., Martínez Gómez, R., Hierrezuelo Pérez, C.: Análisis de tráfico en la red UCI mediante la simulación. Rev Telemática **12**, 76–89 (2013)
24. Morales Rodríguez, M., Calle Pérez, M.A., Tovar Vanegas, J.D., Cuéllar Quiñonez, J.C.: Simulando con OMNET, Selección de la herrameinta y utilización. Universidad ICESI (2013)
25. Aroua, S., El Korbi, I., Ghamri-Doudane, Y., Saidane, L.A.: A distributed cooperative spectrum resource allocation in smart home cognitive wireless sensor networks. In: 2017 IEEE Symposium on Computers and Communications (ISCC), pp. 754–759 (2017)

26. Carmona, J.G.: Propuesta de manual de prácticas de laboratorio de redes utilizando el emulador GNS3 (2017)
27. Djenane, N., Benaouda, A., Harous, S.: Simulation of a VPN implementation based on MPLS protocol, a case study: VPN-MPLS for MSN-AT. In: MoMM2009 - The 7th International Conference on Advances in Mobile Computing and Multimedia, pp. 589–593 (2009)
28. Rajaram, M.L., Kougianos, E., Mohanty, S.P., Choppali, U.: Wireless sensor network simulation frameworks: a tutorial review: MATLAB/Simulink bests the rest. IEEE Consum. Electron. Mag. **5**, 63–69 (2016). https://doi.org/10.1109/MCE.2016.2519051
29. Babich, F., Comisso, M., Dorni, A., et al.: The simulation of smart antennas in network simulator-2 using MATLAB. In: 2009 IEEE 14th International Workshop on Computer Aided Modeling and Design of Communication Links and Networks, CAMAD 2009 (2009)
30. Pau, G., Salerno, V.M.: Wireless sensor networks for smart homes: a fuzzy-based solution for an energy-effective duty cycle. Electronics (2019). https://doi.org/10.3390/electronics8020131
31. ISO: ISO 25010 (2011). iso25000.com
32. Ali, Q.I., Abdulmaowjod, A., Mohammed, H.M.: Simulation & performance study of wireless sensor network (WSN) using MATLAB. In: EPC-IQ01 2010 - 2010 1st International Conference on Energy, Power and Control, pp. 307–314 (2010)
33. Ali, Q.I.: Simulation framework of wireless sensor network (WSN) using MATLAB/SIMULINK software. In: MATLAB - A Fundamental Tool for Scientific Computing and Engineering Applications, vol. 2 (2012)
34. Zhang, J., Dong, Y.: Simulation and performance analysis of distributed attack against MAC layer of underwater acoustic network based on OPNET. In: 2017 IEEE International Conference on Information and Automation, ICIA 2017, pp. 1072–1076 (2017). https://doi.org/10.1109/ICInfA.2017.8079061

# Comparative Analysis Between Standards Oriented to Web Services: SOAP, REST and GRAPHQL

Jaime Sayago Heredia$^{(\boxtimes)}$, Evelin Flores-García, and Andres Recalde Solano

Pontificia Universidad Católica del Ecuador, Sede Esmeraldas, Ecuador
{jaime.sayago,evelin.flores}@pucese.edu.ec

**Abstract.** The use of web services has increased and has become the most widely used implementation today. The most crucial part of a web development project is the choice of the right tools for application development, this decision significantly influences the requirements to implement solutions for these services. The comparative analysis between SOAP, REST and GraphQL web services aims to assess the effectiveness of data transfer capabilities. The methods used were a systematic mapping to define the metrics to use for comparison such as response time and performance. A test environment was implemented, starting with the development of a web application using each of the technologies to be evaluated and in different programming languages. Then, the performance of web services was tested with the defined metrics and tools. We found, from experimental tests, that GraphQL has a faster response time and better performance than web services based on SOAP and REST. The result of the comparison can help developers choose the optimal and appropriate technology based on the performance of web services and other metrics that influence an essential aspect such as software quality.

**Keywords:** Web services · REST · SOAP · GraphQL · Java · C# · Php

## 1 Introduction

In today's society new technological tools have emerged, such as mobile devices and computers that have access to a diversity of programs and applications. However, the applications have had improvements in their storage and execution capacity, as well as in their architecture and development tools. These applications can currently be executed from a computer or smartphone, which in no case, these services would cease to be functional, fast, secure and dynamic. To allow access to an application you need a web service that acts as a network interface and uses protocols such as HTTP, XML, SMTP or Jabber [1]. A web service that could be defined as a software module offered by a service provider, available via the web and which is a key element in the integration of systems of different platforms, programming languages and technologies [2]. Web services provides flexibility to establish communication between our geographically separated devices [3]. Web services based on Simple Object Access Protocol (SOAP) include several standards such as WSDL, WSSecurity, WS-Transaction among others

© Springer Nature Switzerland AG 2020
M. Botto-Tobar et al. (Eds.): ICAT 2019, CCIS 1193, pp. 286–300, 2020.
https://doi.org/10.1007/978-3-030-42517-3_22

developed by W3C and enhanced by companies such as Microsoft and IBM that provide support tools to develop web services based on SOAP [4]. SOAP provides greater security and reliability, fewer errors, asynchronous requests, etc. so there are business, banking and payment information systems that use it today [2]. But Representational state transfer (REST) is not left behind because there is a strong number of advocates of this approach in which web services solutions can be developed simply representing and exposing the resources of the system, and transferring data over HTTP [3]. After developing and using it internally for three years, in 2016, Facebook released a specification and a reference implementation of its GraphQL framework [5]. This framework introduces a new type of Web-based data access interfaces that presents an alternative to the notion of REST-based interfaces [6]. Since its release GraphQL has gained significant momentum and has been adopted by an increasing number of users [5]. The comparative analysis between the SOAP, REST and GraphQL web services aims to evaluate the effectiveness of their data transfer capacities. Deciding on the style of service interaction is a very important choice for developers and designers as it significantly influences the underlying requirements for implementing web services solutions [7]. Comparing these standards is not a trivial task, although these paradigms are ways of creating web services, they differ in the way data is processed and in the services offered. SOAP is an XML-based message exchange protocol, while REST is a design principle that closely adheres to the client-server architecture and advocates the use of minimal HTTP methods, and GraphQL is a query language that is used to express the data retrieval requests issued to GraphQL-aware Web servers [5]. This document presents a comparison of GrahpQL technology with others, such as SOAP and REST, used for the development of web services. Comparison through metrics gives an important result. The result of the comparison can help the developers to choose which technology is the most optimal and adequate for the development of the web service, allowing them to comply with an essential aspect in the construction and execution of a web application such as the quality of the software.

## 1.1 Related Work

In this section we present several research works rigorously related to the topic of comparative analysis between the standards of web services SOAP, REST and GraphQL, which will give a significant contribution to the research. Bora and Bezboruah [3] mention that their main objective is to compare aspects and discover the factors that impact the performance of SOAP and REST web services, but not with GraphQL. For this they have developed, implemented and tested two prototypes of web services, one based on SOAP and another in REST focusing on the indicators: response time and performance. The authors conclude that the values of attributes such as performance and response time based on the REST architecture have better performance than the SOAP-based web service, the latter is stable up to 800 VU without errors, but when it reaches 1500 VU, the service shows poor performance with a 61% connection rejection and the experimental results above give researchers as well as software industrial practitioners an idea about the web services performance and the other metrics that influences the overall performance of the services. Pavan, Sanjay and Zomitza [4], describe that they created web services based on SOAP and REST that perform operations create, read, update and delete (CRUD) both services perform series of data exchange operations on a database server with wired and wireless clients. In this comparative analysis they used performance metrics to compare web services using throughput and time measurement indicators. They determined that the REST-based web service performed better than the service developed in SOAP with connected clients and the performance in KB per second with wireless clients. Where, on average, REST has better performance compared to SOAP, though not all results were statistically conclusive. As an ancillary outcome, they found that developing web services using SOAP was easier, due to considerable tool support. Helfer [8] categorizes to GraphQL as Web API technologies and brings them into a chronological sequence with REST and SOAP. In the study [9] they try to improve the interoperability of the Employment and Employability Observatory ecosystem (also known as OEEU), as they need to manage these data flows because the ecosystems need high levels of interoperability, and to allow collaboration and independence of internal and external components, for this they make implementations in API's REST and GraphQL, and thus analyze quantitatively the response time of each and determine the most optimal implementation. The research of Čechák [10] is a detailed study of GraphQL technology as a possible alternative to the Delivery API of Kentico Cloud. And for them the research is divided into four parts, in which the first part deals with an explanation of the current status and data structuring of the Kentico Cloud API, the second part compares the concepts REST and GraphQL for implementation, the third part describes the implementation of the proof-of-concept solution, and finally through the response time parameter a measurement of the two technologies (REST and GraphQL) is made and the results are presented. Vogel, Weber and Zirpins [11] have compared the performance of the web services development in REST and GraphQL in the context of an industrial case study and demonstrated the benefits of the data fetching approach with GraphQL. The evaluation was carried out through of performance tests. Resulting with a better GraphQL performance over REST. Observations have underpinned some of the conceptual benefits but also identified challenging aspects where further research is required. At the time of writing, no academic work exists on comparision entre SOAP and GraphQL. In our own work [12] we have studied how a web service depending on the technology chosen (in our case REST) can be decisive for the development of a web application. In which, we examined the performance implications in different types of requests applying different metrics such as performance and response time. In the following sections, we describe the result of testing between different technologies in a web application and provide a comparison of SOAP, REST and GraphQL.

## 1.2  Web Services

A web service consists of service and service description where service is a software module offered by a service provider, which is available through the Web. A service description contains the details of the service interface and implementations, including data types, metadata, categorisation information and the location where the service is exposed [2]. There are various Web service styles as SOAP (Simple Object Access Protocol) and REST (Representational State Transfer). These web services practice different interfaces and based on SOA (Service Oriented Architecture). In SOAP, the interface used to carrying the messages is SOAP, and to label services, it is WSDL (Web Service Description Language). In REST, interfaces are restricted to HTML (Hyper Text

Mark-up Language) by using well-known common methods of HTTP (PUT, DELETE, GET, and POST) to publish, consume and to describe resources [13]. The main goal of any platform of web service is to deliver the required interoperability level between various applications by using predefined web standards [14].

## 1.3  SOAP Web Services

SOAP is a lightweight XML-based protocol for exchanging information in a distributed decentralized environment [15]. It is used to transfer a message between web applications. It is built on xml format that access web services over HTTP. SOAP act as an envelope for sending the web services. The structure of SOAP envelope has two parts: header and body. Header is an optional part of SOAP. Header contains information related to applications data types that may be simple or complex. It contains user authentication for accessing the web services as well as the information about how sequencing of data elements is to be done. SOAP body is a mandatory part of SOAP envelope. It contains the data passed between calling and called services. When a client application calls a method from web service, the SOAP message is automatically generated by the web service and pass to the client [16]. SOAP implements technologies that are easy to adapt to a mobile device, since its limitation and consumption of resources is known, as well as the format in which messages are sent that generate a greater consumption of data and therefore demand a wider memory to have an optimal operation. The objectives that provide the fulfillment of SOAP services are based on a standard model that is to establish a protocol that is based on HTTP for transmission and XML for data encoding. Hardware platform independence, programming language and Web service implementation [15].

## 1.4  REST Web Services

These are considered as a style of architecture for distributed hypermedia systems generating in such a way an advance around the development of applications, considering that it is also taken as a model of Representational State Transfer or RESTful (implementation of REST), recognized by the optimization of resources and the improvement of the work around the applications and sites. Architectural style that consists of clients and servers and exposes functionalities through resources identified by URI, the clients interact with the resources through methods generating requests to the servers, these process it, generating a convenient response [1]. Around this, the construction of requests and responses are made around the transfer of resource representations, one of the most important being the representation of the captured resource in its current state. Unlike the SOAP Protocol, the data consumption is lower since it does not use the XML format, and it does not require headers. In this regard, it is established that the Restfull web service is a design that is based on the REST architecture, which is focused on building applications that explicitly use the protocol, and in relation to this optimize resources and improve the development of the work.

## 1.5  GraphQL

GraphQL is a query language for your API and a server-side runtime to execute queries by using a type system that you define for your data. GraphQL is not specified to any specific database or storage engine, but is backed by its specific code and data [17]. The query service is an instance that is executed separately from the client and can be considered as a web service. The GraphQL server allows the client to send more powerful queries than would be possible with another standard such as SOAP or RESTful. The GraphQL Query Language is a strongly typed query language developed by the social media company Facebook in 2012, provides a flexible syntax for describing data requirements and interactions for creating applications and from 2015 the service is publicly announced as a draft language specification [18]. The language was conceived for several general objectives such as reducing the overload of data transparency in relation to web service models similar to REST, in terms of both the amount of data unnecessarily transferred and the number of separate queries required to do so.

### 1.6  Performance Test, Benchmark Test and Load Testing

Software testing is defined as the ability to find errors, and a good test is one that has the highest probability to find a bug [19]. The software testing techniques can be broadly divided into various categories [20]. The performance test according to the Alonso [21] state that the purpose of the tests is to evaluate the response time of the system or memory it occupies. Tuya [22] determines, if the response times of the system, both under normal and special conditions, are within predefined limits. The purpose of the performance test is to verify the performance of the specified system (response time and service availability), where hundreds or more simultaneous user accesses are simulated during a defined time interval [23]. The benchmark test is a method for measuring the performance of a system, for which the system is tested with very demanding and varied tasks with the intention of measuring performance [24]. It is a program or set of programs that evaluates the performance of a computer system by reproducing a generic workload on that computer system [25]. For the construction of web application in order to improve the quality and performance is used load testing [26]. The load testing tests the response of the system under a normal load of work [27]. In the following sections, we carry out an analysis of the software tests to be considered for the comparison of SOAP, REST and GraphQL technologies.

## 2  Methods and Tools

The design of the research is comparative. Piovani [28] and Henao [29] mention that this type of research aims to identify differences and similarities around an event or in the same context. Because the tools will be contextualized to make comparisons, evaluate results obtained through the use of indicators and evaluation metrics, which will measure the performance of standards oriented to web services SOAP, REST and GraphQL. The research is quantitative as defined by Toro & Parra [30], considering that its purpose is to make exact and effective decisions that contribute to achieve the objective of the research and taking the idea of Hernandez, Fernandez & Baptista [31] where it uses structured procedures and formal tools for data collection and the study of generalization through statistical methods. The result of this research must be the comparative analysis of the impact of technologies oriented in the construction of web services such as SOAP,

REST and GraphQL. The inductive method is also used to establish the behavior of response time and load of architectures, as well as conceptualize that inductive logic starts mainly from the repeated observation of phenomena, and conclusions can be reached as a result of the inference of similarities observed in the cases studied. Moreover, two techniques have been applied, scientific observation [32] and the mapping study [33]. Scientific observation using has been applied together with computer tools to measure the behavior of the software in front of an overload of requests or data, and the performance based on the response time provided by consuming each web service built with each one of the SOAP, REST and GraphQL technologies. The result of analyzed data will provide truthful and concise information to determine the more optimal technology for the development of web applications. We used the mapping study technique, through the procedure of the three main stages as they are search, we obtained an initial selection of primary studies in which we assessed the quality in two stages. First the inclusion and exclusion criteria were taken into account, then information was extracted for a more precise and detailed review. Finally, the studies selected by the documentary analysis in which 232 investigations have been selected that are implicitly related to the topic and through the inclusion and exclusion method of the mapping study, 33 studies respond rigorously to the topic, from which 5 relevant studies were selected for this research in order to solve the question of this research. The analysis of these researches reflected in this first filter is limited primarily to identify the performance measurement metrics on websites and the form of analysis adopted by the authors. Based on the research it is worth mentioning that each author defined metrics to measure the performance of a web application, and in them we can highlight that they agreed on two of them, such as throughput and time to response [4, 9, 34].

### 2.1  Instruments

For the present research, an observation sheet and computer tools which allowed us to measure the behavior and performance of web applications based on SOAP, REST and GraphQL standards, these tools are: Apache JMeter which is an open source software to measure performance and behavior under load [35] and SoapUI which it is a tool for testing web service oriented applications such as SOAP and REST [36]. The define the metrics and parameters to analyze the web services, in the development of applications, is based on previous research [9, 34, 37]. Concluding that the parameter for the analysis of standards is performance because we can measure the response time provided by each service and the capacity that can support each standard. The test environment in order to apply the computer tools and test the performance of the SOAP, REST and GraphQL web service standards as shown in Fig. 1, an ideal test environment has been defined to avoid data and connection loss, in order not to alter the results.

The Java, C# and PHP languages the choice for developing of the web service. Its strong security mechanism, concurrency control and wide spread deployment in both client and servers makes it relatively easy to create web services [3]. The software and hardware specifications used in the comparative study are: Integrated Development Environment (IDE): Sublime 3.2.1, web browser: Google Chrome, web server: Apache, the database engine: Sql Server 2012. The client was hosted on a laptop with the following specifications Intel® Core™ i7-7500U CPU @ 2.70 GHz 2.90 GHz, RAM 12 GB,

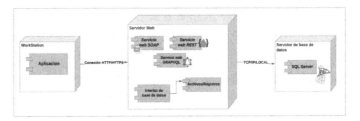

**Fig. 1.** Test environment deployment diagram

SO WIN Pro 64 Bits. The web services have been hosted on a 64-bit Windows Server 2016 R2 Standard operating system (OS). The hardware specifications are: Intel® i7-8565U® CPU at 6 GHz; 16 GB RAM and 512 GB SSD hard disk. The quality of the service is one of the most important factors, customer satisfaction causes the customer to remain in them creating a symptom of identity or decide to change to another that presumably offers better quality or comfort in the service [38]. In order to obtain information that helps improve performance, the benchmark is a continuous process that allows us to measure and compare systems or one of their components. Relating the methodologies of Patil [23] and Zhu [39], they perform procedures for the main activities of performance testing, and this is how the following benchmark activities are defined for the present research: Performance Testing. - It measures the response time of web services that have been developed in 3 programming languages (Java, C#, PHP), the test consists of simulating 50, 100, 500, 1000, 1500 virtual users. For the web services testing process, the SOAPUI tool was used to verify the proper functioning of the endpoints of each service and Apache JMeter to perform the stress and load tests for each application. For this purpose, the following metrics were defined by the mapping study: Response time: The average time is calculated in milliseconds for a set of results. And Throughput: performance measured in Kb/s of the server response. As an instrument it be used is Apache JMeter.

## 3 Analysis Results Comparison

### 3.1 Analysis of Experimental Data and Evaluation

To compare the performance of applications carried out under the standards of SOAP, REST and GraphQL web services, the tests designed in the previous chapter were executed; which consists of simulating 50, 100, 500, 1000, 1500 concurrent virtual users. In order to evaluate the results, 3 components provided by the tool were used. Summary Report, Aggregate Graph. The results were analyzed through a confidence interval with a 95% confidence level. For a first analysis, it is assumed that the population has a Normal distribution, for a second analysis, since the sample is large, it is not required to make the assumption that the sample has a Normal distribution since by the Central Limit Theorem (TCL), the averages of large and random samples are approximately normal.

### 3.2  Analysis of Experimental Data with CSharp

The first experimental analysis, the three web services are consumed under the programming language C Sharp, it has made an average of response times and performance offered under certain levels of concurrent users.

In the Table 1 it can be observed by means of the metric values analyzed by the tool, that the SOAP protocol with 1000 VU begins to generate a low performance with 6% of rejection of connection, when arriving at 1500 VU the protocol begins to increase the rejection of connection to 42%, in the case of the architecture REST and the language of schemes GraphQL, they are observed that the services are free of errors and stable up to 1500 VU. The first values show that the difference in response times with 50 and 100 concurrent users is a little convergent so the end user will not notice much difference.

**Table 1.** Comparison of experimental results with C Sharp.

| VUs | Parameter | SOAP | | REST | | GRAPHQL | |
|-----|-----------|------|--|------|--|---------|--|
| | | Average | Rejected % | Average | Rejected % | Average | Rejected % |
| 50 | Time response | 74000 | 0 | 56800 | 0 | 32200 | 0 |
| | Throughtput | 7144 | | 3603,1 | | 1420,8 | |
| 100 | Time response | 346800 | 0 | 269600 | 0 | 186400 | 0 |
| | Throughtput | 11580 | | 6981 | | 3520,4 | |
| 500 | Time response | 18850000 | 0 | 16742000 | 0 | 13140000 | 0 |
| | Throughtput | 25156,2 | | 15939,2 | | 10437,1 | |
| 1000 | Time response | 54604000 | 6,38 | 44516000 | 0 | 22524000 | 0 |
| | Throughtput | 229165,3 | | 177568 | | 122351,4 | |
| 5000 | Time response | 134550808 | 42,06 | 98164457 | 0 | 54057600 | 0 |
| | Throughtput | 197131,6 | | 225905,5 | | 162104,3 | |

In Fig. 2, it can be seen that from an amount greater than 500 VU concurrent can notice a big difference, this means that the more concurrent users there will be greater response times, so from 1000 users the SOAP protocol begins to generate a greater response time and guided by Table 1 where the web service begins to produce a rejection of 6% connection so it is difficult to meet several requests and generates a low performance, in the 1500 users happens something similar but in this amount the rejection of connection is much higher generating 42% so response times become very noticeable. Figure 3 evaluates the performance offered by each service, in it we can see that the three frameworks do not present a big difference from an amount less than 500 users,

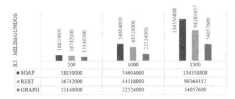
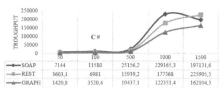

**Fig. 2.** Response time in the consumption of web services 500-1000-1500 VU's with C Sharp.

**Fig. 3.** Performance in the consumption of web services with C Sharp

reaching 1000 concurrent users where there is a rejection of 6% connection in SOAP, means that at this point the performance begins to decrease and in the 1500 VU's in SOAP already has a low performance so that the rejection of connection reaches 42% which means that you stop attending to several user requests to not get to complete the requests.

### 3.3 Analysis of Experimental Data with Java

The next analysis the web services are consumed under the Java programming language, just as the previous analysis has made the average response times and performance that this offers us of each web service. Observed by means of the values of the metrics

**Table 2.** Comparison of experimental results with Java

| VUs | Parameter | SOAP | | REST | | GRAPHQL | |
|---|---|---|---|---|---|---|---|
| | | Average | Rejected % | Average | Rejected % | Average | Rejected % |
| 50 | Time response | 127600 | 0 | 107400 | 0 | 54000 | 0 |
| | Throughtput | 18520,2 | | 12476,6 | | 3683,6 | |
| 100 | Time response | 483600 | 0 | 392000 | 0 | 206000 | 0 |
| | Throughtput | 22872,3 | | 15749,1 | | 8151,7 | |
| 500 | Time response | 21358000 | 0 | 16962000 | 0 | 11734000 | 0 |
| | Throughtput | 34385,9 | | 17659,9 | | 20587,8 | |
| 1000 | Time response | 46152000 | 4,16 | 41212000 | 0 | 24988000 | 0 |
| | Throughtput | 206897,3 | | 119968,7 | | 78462 | |
| 1500 | Time response | 97706000 | 43,34 | 64224000 | 0 | 44010000 | 0 |
| | Throughtput | 178950,1 | | 143948,1 | | 79553,1 | |

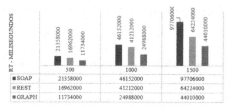

| ■SOAP | 500 | 1000 | 1500 |
|---|---|---|---|
| ■SOAP | 21358000 | 46152000 | 97706000 |
| ■REST | 16962000 | 41212000 | 64224000 |
| ■GRAPH | 11734000 | 24988000 | 44010000 |

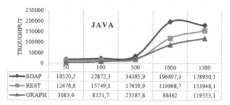

| | 50 | 100 | 500 | 1000 | 1500 |
|---|---|---|---|---|---|
| SOAP | 18520,2 | 22872,3 | 34385,9 | 196897,3 | 178950,1 |
| REST | 12476,6 | 15749,1 | 17659,9 | 119968,7 | 153948,1 |
| GRAPH | 3683,6 | 8151,7 | 23587,8 | 88462 | 119553,1 |

**Fig. 4.** Response time in the consumption of web services 500-1000-1500 VU's with Java.

**Fig. 5.** Performance in the consumption of web services with Java.

analyzed by the tool, that the protocol SOAP with 1000 VU begins to generate a low yield with 4.1% of rejection of connection, when arriving at the 1500 VU the protocol begins to increase to 43.3%, in the case of the architecture REST and the language of schemes GraphQL. Observed that the services are free of errors and stable up to 1500 VU. In the consumption of web services 50–100 VU's do not present a major and significant change and the end user will not notice great change or difference in response times. Figure 4 shows that response times become noticeable from a higher number of 500 concurrent users, from 1500 VU's begins to generate higher times and guided by table the SOAP protocol generates 43% connection rejection, while other services do not produce errors and remain stable. Figure 5 shows the performance produced by the three services with the Java language, therefore, it does not generate a major difference from an amount greater than 500 users, and is that from the 1000 users the SOAP protocol begins to generate errors and its performance begins to decline so it can't process 43% of assigned requests.

### 3.4 Analysis of Experimental Data with PHP

The third analysis of web services, it has come to consume under the programming language PHP, an average is made of response times and performance offered by such services. Can be observed by means of the values of the metrics analyzed by the tool, that the protocol SOAP with 1000 VU begins to generate a low yield with 6% of rejection of connection, when arriving at the 1500 VU the protocol begins to increase to 45%, in the case of the architecture REST and the language of schemes GraphQL, they are observed that the services are free of errors and stable up to 1500 VU. In the consumption of web services 50–100 VU's it can be defined that web services with a slight number of users does not generate a great notoriety in response times. Figure 6 shows us that from 1000 users it is reflected that the response times begin to look noticeable, guiding us by the data of Table 3 in which SOAP begins to generate a 45% connection rejection, even in PHP language, SOAP can't fully meet the requests given, while their counterparts do not show errors and generate shorter times. Figure 7 analyzes the performance of each service through the PHP language, it reflects that the SOAP protocol begins to decrease its performance when it reaches the number of 1500 concurrent users, this is because there is a connection rejection of 45%, while other services are stable without errors, noting that the schema language handles a better performance ahead of REST.

**Table 3.** Comparison of experimental results with PHP

| VUs | Parameter | SOAP | | REST | | GRAPHQL | |
|---|---|---|---|---|---|---|---|
| | | Average | Rejected % | Average | Rejected % | Average | Rejected % |
| 50 | Time response | 107800 | 0 | 102800 | 0 | 48800 | 0 |
| | Throughtput | 5938,1 | | 33339,7 | | 2680,9 | |
| 100 | Time response | 417600 | 0 | 284000 | 0 | 2228000 | 0 |
| | Throughtput | 15263,1 | | 6854,7 | | 5946,1 | |
| 500 | Time response | 30722000 | 0 | 25638000 | 0 | 19658000 | 0 |
| | Throughtput | 50205,7 | | 37743,5 | | 48727,5 | |
| 1000 | Time response | 62980000 | 6,04 | 48556000 | 0 | 31416000 | 0 |
| | Throughtput | 354937 | | 223645,7 | | 151329,2 | |
| 1500 | Time response | 173522000 | 45,38 | 109007422 | 0 | 72050000 | 0 |
| | Throughtput | 267412,2 | | 311580,6 | | 164182,8 | |

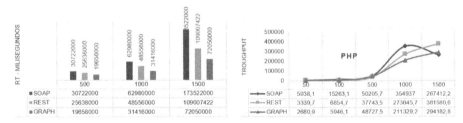

**Fig. 6.** Response time in the consumption of web services 500-1000-1500 VU's with PHP.

**Fig. 7.** Performance in the consumption of web services with PHP

## 4 Discussion

The results obtained in this research show that the response time of the GraphQL schema language is much better than the response time of REST and SOAP in the three languages in which they were examined. Web services based on REST show better times than SOAP. Bora & Bezboruah's [3] and Tihomirovs [2], performance tests on two web services in which the results coincide to a large extent with the present research, it can be seen that the response times and Throughput of the REST web service are lower than compared to the web service based on SOAP. In Vázquez's research [9] and Vogel, Weber & Zirpins [11], they perform an analysis study of the response times of the REST and GraphQL, show the performance results in which it reflects that GraphQL handles better response times than REST. In our study, the Tables 1, 2 and 3 show that the values of performance attributes such as throughput and response time in GraphQL are much lower than the performance attributes of REST and SOAP. It can be detailed that the SOAP based web service is stable between 850 VU and 930 VU and has no error, but offers low performance up to 1500 VU, with an average 43.59% connection rejection. In GraphQL and REST the services are error free and remain stable up to 1500 virtual users. Therefore, it is emphasized that GraphQL generates a lower overload making it efficient ahead of REST and SOAP. Statistical analysis of recorded performance metrics allows us to observe that response time suddenly increases or decreases for various levels of stress, this may be due to the partial release of data residues from the server side, which increases server stress. Web services based on SOAP consume the WSDL file of the provider that processes XML messages for their communications, and REST uses the HTTP URI of the resource available on the Internet that functions as the normal HTTP request and response methodology. GraphQL is much more flexible because it can describe exactly how the response should be, combining entities connected within a GraphQL data query. No additional server sends such as SOAP and REST are required.

## 5  Conclusions

This paper provides a comparison of SOAP, REST and GraphQL technologies based on performance tests and response time, allowing to analyze the impact of the technology used in the web service, has on the performance of applications. In the state of the art, a description of web technologies and services was made. An application was implemented with three programming languages; Java, C# and PHP, these languages consume the web services each one (SOAP, REST and GraphQL). A CRUD (Create, Read, Update, Delete) was built. In this analysis, metrics and tools such as Jmeter were selected for the test. It was confirmed that SI impacts the technology with which the web service was built on the performance of an application. As you can see, only when the amount oscillates between 800 and 900 VU the user will notice sharply the performance of the web application. The design of the test focuses on the metrics defined by the mapping study that are the performance and response time, with the help of benchmarking tools such as Apache JMeter and allows us to obtain the relevant values of each attribute. Figures 2, 4, 6 provide comparative results of the response time between SOAP, REST and GraphQL, in the figure it can be observed that the response time of GraphQL is lower in comparison with SOAP and REST. Figures 3, 5 and 7 show graphically the performance of each of the SOAP, REST and GraphQL standards in the test application. As a result, GraphQL has less response time and higher performance than SOAP and REST based web services. The experimental results allow researchers, as well as software professionals, an idea of the performance of web services and other metrics that influence the overall performance of web services. Situations where GraphQL should not be used should be mentioned, as more analysis criteria and measurement variables are required. An analysis of GraphQL's shortcomings would give us a better understanding and applicability. However, this document demonstrated that GraphQL has a better performance for the development of web services and allowing us to comply with an essential aspect such as the quality of the software.

## 6  Recommendations

The organization and selection of the different metrics to be evaluated, we recommend an extensive bibliographic review or the use of mapping study techniques that allow us to choose the most representative ones for research. In preparing a complete comparative analysis, it is advisable to establish common criteria by reviewing information from official sources. It is recommended that the benchmark methodology be carried out in similar scenarios in order to have a greater precision in the results of comparison of web services. It is recommended to minimize network traffic by grouping functionalities in the services in such a way that the number of necessary communications decreases. In order to do this, general services should be built that perform many tasks and return a lot of information, so that the network overload is reduced and there are better response times for the services. For the messages of SOAP services it is recommended to control the size as little as possible, since, when faced with complex messages, the processes of deserialization and the inverse consumes a lot of time and that is why the messages must be designed minimizing complexity.

Difficulties and limitations: When implementing the GraphQL service, several inconveniences arose due to the fact that it is a technology that has little time published on the web and does not have much documentation for development in several programming languages. There are limitations to our study. For example, our study does not show how GraphQL reacts with CPU and RAM intensive and high processing applications. Therefore, this document could benefit from the introduction of a case study dealing with the intensive and high processing use of CPU and RAM memory.

## References

1. Snell, J., Tidwell, D., Kulchenko, P.: Programming Web Service with SOAP. O'Reilly Media Inc., Sebastopol (2001)
2. Tihomirovs, J., Grabis, J.: Comparison of SOAP and REST based web services using software evaluation metrics. Inf. Technol. Manag. Sci. **19**, 92–97 (2016). https://doi.org/10.1515/itms-2016-0017
3. Bora, A., Bezboruah, T.: A comparative investigation on implementation of RESTful versus SOAP based web services. Int. J. Database Theory Appl. **8**, 297–312 (2015). https://doi.org/10.14257/ijdta.2015.8.3.26
4. Pavan, K.P., Sanjay, A., Zornitza, P.: Comparing performance of web service interaction styles: SOAP vs. REST. In: Proceedings of Conference on Information System Applied Research, pp. 1–24 (2012)
5. Hartig, O., Pérez, J.: An initial analysis of facebook's GraphQL language. In: CEUR Workshop Proceedings, vol. 1912 (2017)
6. Malik, S., Kim, D.H.: A comparison of RESTful vs. SOAP web services in actuator networks. In: International Conference on Ubiquitous Future Networks, ICUFN, pp. 753–755 (2017). https://doi.org/10.1109/ICUFN.2017.7993893
7. Pautasso, C., Zimmermann, O., Leymann, F.: RESTful web services vs. "Big" web services: making the right architectural decision. In: Proceeding 17th International Conference on World Wide Web 2008, WWW 2008, pp. 805–814 (2008). https://doi.org/10.1145/1367497.1367606

8. Helfer, J.: GraphQL - Evolution or Revolution ? (2017). https://speakerdeck.com/helfer/%0Agraphql-evolution-or-revolution. Accessed 27 June 2018
9. Vazquez-Ingelmo, A., Cruz-Benito, J., García-Penalvo, F.J.: Improving the OEEU's data-driven technological ecosystem's interoperability with GraphQL. In: ACM International Conference Proceeding Series Part F 1322, pp. 1–8 (2017). https://doi.org/10.1145/3144826.3145437
10. Čechák, D.: Using GraphQL for content delivery in Kentico Cloud. IsMuniCz (2017)
11. Vogel, M., Weber, S., Zirpins, C.: Experiences on migrating RESTful web services to GraphQL. In: Braubach, L., et al. (eds.) ICSOC 2017. LNCS, vol. 10797, pp. 283–295. Springer, Cham (2018). https://doi.org/10.1007/978-3-319-91764-1_23
12. Heredia, J.S., Sailema, G.C.: Comparative analysis for web applications based on REST services: MEAN stack and java EE stack. KnE Eng. 3, 82 (2018). https://doi.org/10.18502/keg.v3i9.3647
13. Jabbar, S., Naseer, K., Gohar, M., et al.: Trust model at service layer of cloud computing for educational institutes. J. Supercomput. 72, 58–83 (2016). https://doi.org/10.1007/s11227-015-1488-7
14. Rehman, B., Alam, K.A., Rehman, M., et al.: Combinatorial testing of web services: a systematic mapping. In: ACM International Conference Proceeding Series, pp. 1–6 (2019). https://doi.org/10.1145/3341325.3342009
15. IBM: SOAP 1.1 y 1.2. In: IBM Knowledge Center (2014)
16. Chawla, J., Ahlawat, A.K., Goswami, G.: A review on web services interoperability issues. In: 2018 5th IEEE Uttar Pradesh Section International Conference on Electrical, Electronics and Computer Engineering, UPCON, vol. 1, pp. 1–5 (2018). https://doi.org/10.1109/UPCON.2018.8596930
17. Facebook Inc.: Introduction to GraphQL. https://graphql.org/learn/. Accessed 9 Oct 2018
18. Facebook GraphQL: A data query language - Facebook Engineering. https://engineering.fb.com/core-data/graphql-a-data-query-language/. Accessed 9 Oct 2018
19. Dasoriya, R., Dashoriya, R.: Use of optimized genetic algorithm for software testing. In: 2018 International Students' Conference on Electrical, Electronics and Computer Sciences, SCEECS 2018, pp. 1–5 (2018). https://doi.org/10.1109/SCEECS.2018.8546957
20. Srinivasan, S.M., Sangwan, R.S.: Web app security: a comparison and categorization of testing frameworks. IEEE Softw. 34, 99–102 (2017). https://doi.org/10.1109/MS.2017.21
21. Amo, F.A., Normand Martinez, L.N., Segovia Pérez, F.J.: Introduccion a la Ingeneria del software. Delta (2005)
22. Tuya, J., Ramos Román, I., Dolado Cosín, J.: Técnicas cuantitativas para la gestión en la ingeniería del software. Netbiblo (2007)
23. Patil, S.S., Joshi, S.: Identification of performance improving factors for web application by performance testing. Int. J. Emerg. Technol. Adv. Eng. 2, 433–436 (2012)
24. Muñoz, A.: ¿Qué es un benchmark y para qué sirve? In: Tecnol. – Comput (2016)
25. Díaz Arberas, U.: Desarrollo y pruebas en entorno real de un smart reader Wi-Fi. Universidad del País Vasco (2016)
26. Liu, X., Hsieh, Y.J., Chen, R., Yuan, S.M.: Distributed testing system for web service based on crowdsourcing. Complexity (2018). https://doi.org/10.1155/2018/2170585
27. Khari, M., Kumar, P.: An extensive evaluation of search-based software testing: a review. Soft. Comput. 23, 1933–1946 (2019). https://doi.org/10.1007/s00500-017-2906-y
28. Piovani, J.I., Krawczyk II, N.: Los Estudios Comparativos: algunas notas históricas, epistemológicas y metodológicas, 821–840 (2017). https://doi.org/10.1590/2175-623667609
29. Arias Henao, D.P.: Investigación comparativa transcontextual en relaciones internacionales. Rev. Relac. Int. Estrateg. y Segur. 9, 77–99 (2006)
30. Toro Jaramillo, I.D., Parra Ramirez, R.D.: Fundamentos epistemológicos de la investigación y la metodología, 1st ed. Bogota (2011)

31. Hernández Sampieri, R., Fernández Collado, C., del Pilar Baptista Lucio, M.: Metodología de la investigación, 5ta Ed
32. Dieterich, H.: Nueva guía para la investigación científica. Mexico (2007)
33. De Souza Neto, J.B., Moreira, A.M., Musicante, M.A.: Semantic web services testing: a systematic mapping study. Comput. Sci. Rev. **28**, 140–156 (2018). https://doi.org/10.1016/j.cosrev.2018.03.002
34. Kumari, S., Rath, S.K.: Performance comparison of SOAP and REST based web services for enterprise application integration. In: 2015 International Conference on Advances in Computing, Communications and Informatics (ICACCI). IEEE, pp 1656–1660 (2015)
35. Apache JMeter - Apache JMeter$^{TM}$. https://jmeter.apache.org/. Accessed 13 May 2018
36. Beginner's Guide to SoapUI Projects—SoapUI. https://www.soapui.org/soapui-projects/soapui-projects.html. Accessed 15 Nov 2018
37. Burgos Suero, L.E.: Análisis y evaluación de las arquitecturas REST y SOAP para el desarrollo de servicios web aplicados al ERP AdrisERP y su versión móvil en Android. Universidad Señor de Sipán (2017)
38. Hernández Rodríguez, C., Flores, M.C.: La importancia del benchmarking como herramienta para incrementar la calidad en el servicio en las organizaciones (2017)
39. Zhu, K., Fu, J., Li, Y.: Research the performance testing and performance improvement strategy in web application. In: 2010 2nd International Conference on Education Technology and Computer, pp V2-328–V2-332. IEEE (2010)

# Portable Device and Mobile Application for the Detection of Ultraviolet Radiation in Real Time with a Low Cost Sensor in Arduino

Joe Llerena-Izquierdo(✉) ⓘD, Nebel Viera-Sanchez(✉) ⓘD,
and Bladimir Rodriguez-Moreira(✉) ⓘD

Universidad Politécnica Salesiana, Guayaquil, Ecuador
jllerena@ups.edu.ec, {nvieras,brodriguezm2}@est.ups.edu.ec

**Abstract.** This paper presents the design and implementation of a kit that involves a portable device and mobile application in order to detect and prevent ultraviolet radiation from any natural or artificial emission of UV rays, one of the invisible threats to human health. The prototype presents an adequate design in Arduino with low-cost components and portability for people, compared to other existing devices before the presentation of this article. The mobile application from the Android platform presents the data of the portable device during wireless connection with a friendly interface. Furthermore, the data from the prototype (UV index) are compared with the data of meteorological institute in the country http://186.42.174.236/IndiceUV2/. Such data, measurements in $mW/cm^2$, are taken from the north and south key points in Guayaquil, Ecuador, a distance of 10.7 km, in an understandable period on the 7th of April 2019 to this present date. The information is lodged on the site https://github.com/brodriguezm998/UV-Reader.

**Keywords:** UV radiation · UV index · Mobile device · Arduino

## 1 Introduction

Actually, the ultraviolet radiation (UV) is an ambience factor that affects the world population in a natural or artificial way [1, 16]. Multiple illnesses are diagnosed in high radiation levels, dangerous to health, especially to the skin because of the exposition to UV sources without protection. The human being is exposed daily to ultraviolet radiation (UV) in a natural and its factors that somehow provoke degenerative illnesses like skin, leissures, eye injuries, burns, photoaging [2] (freckles, solar lentigines, wrinkles, and aging) skin spots or alterations in the DNA. The excess of UV radiation and the effect of expositions the artificial or natural present new harmful factors for human beings [3]. The (ultraviolet) UV radiation is commonly identified in the means in an artificial form, with fluorescent lamps, in dermatology, disinfection and sterilization, UV in medicine, forensic analysis, chromatography, in dentistry, in museums, in the pharmaceutical industry, cosmetics, electrophoresis, semiconductors, technical equipment for potable water, imprint, window tint, germicide lighting in the food industry, artificial tanning and others [4]. The International Agency for Research on Cancer (IARC) considers

© Springer Nature Switzerland AG 2020
M. Botto-Tobar et al. (Eds.): ICAT 2019, CCIS 1193, pp. 301–312, 2020.
https://doi.org/10.1007/978-3-030-42517-3_23

that the factors which contribute to the increment of the cancer process keep adding up due to the high index of UV radiation [3].The mobile device have been introduced in health care and prevention themes considerably in technological conform that keep increasing; the portable and easiness of the combined usage with wireless technology allow to detect zones with a high index of UV radiation [5]. The design and implementation of a portable prototype for the detection and measurement of UV radiation levels in actual time that show about the population of Guayaquil in Ecuador are presented in this task. This device registers the longitude of short wave and allows the index display on a mobile application for Smartphones, the same that has been dominated as UVReader, providing data that come from a UV sensor which is referred to as "NeBla", the warning is created and presents the UV level. With this in mind, it is intended to deal with the prevention of illnesses that can be acquired once exposed to high levels of radiation.

## 2  Status of the Current Situation

### 2.1  Ultraviolet Radiation

The UV radiation (Ultraviolet) with its short wave longitudes is one of the natural factors that has a significant incidence in the world's health population. The (WHO) world health organization and its work "Ultraviolet radiation and health" [6], establishes the UV radiation levels in three types according to the interval of wave longitude in nanometers (nm), such intervals understand from the 100 nm to 400 nm [7]. The first band of wave longitudes ($\lambda$), Ultraviolet radiation type A (UVA), is established between 315 and 400 nm. The second band, Ultraviolet radiation type B (UVB), is established between 280 and 315 nm. The third band, Ultraviolet radiation type C (UVC), is established between 100 and 280 nm. From these, UVA (total) and a part of UVB (0.5%) [8, 16], affect the earth's surface with a direct impact, causing a biological, physiological and molecular incidence on living creatures [9], meanwhile the UVC radiation and a radiation percentage are caught by element of absorption capacities, oxygen, water vapor, ozone and carbon dioxide among these that are on the atmosphere [10] that affect gradually. The WHO, and its report of the year 2012, [11] determines that cancer represented 8.2 millions of death worldwide, which 55,000 reported cases were caused by skin cancer. (31000 men y 24000 women). The necessity and interest to develop automatic diagnostic tools based on prevention is urgent since no cure was found for such illnesses. It can help prevent among equipment that diagnosed such sources that generate the emanation of UV radiation and its excessive values.

### 2.2  Affect to the Human Being Because of the UV Radiation

One of the diseases that actually increases itself in the world population is Cancer and its many manifestations. [11] The excess to the UV (Ultraviolet) radiation exposure can generate Cancer in many different parts of the body and any of its external organs. There are different types of Cancer, especially skin cancer. Not that common but highly risked is melanoma [12]. Based on research done by the American Cancer Society, it is established that during a person's lifetime, the risk of suffering of melanoma (main risk) is the 2.6%. In other words 1 of every 38 people of fair skin, and one 0.58% for Latin Americans, which is approximately 1 in 172 people [13].

There are multiple risk factors for which a person can have melanoma for exposing himself to the ultraviolet light in an artificial form, whether these are fluorescent lamps, disinfecting or sterilization in medicine, like dentistry, germicide lightning in the food industry, artificial tanning among others, especially its maintenance and repair technicians for not having any type of industrial awareness. The birth marks on the skin represent a melanoma risk. With major frequency these are present in older people, but there are cases that have also detected such in younger people [14]; another disease is xeroderma pigment that has a high risk of melanoma, especially if the skin is exposed to the sun, specifically in parts of the body like the arms and legs [13].

**Table 1.** Devices for the detection of UV radiation.

| Digitals devices | | | |
|---|---|---|---|
| Device | Description | Distribution | Price |
| Solarmeter Model 6.5R Reptile UV | UV model 6.5 R ABS | In Amazon | $ 207.11 |
| Solarmeter Model 6.5 UV | Solar device for ranges of 280 to 400 nm with an index of UV 0–199.9 | In Amazon | $ 199.39 |
| Sper Scientific 850009 UV Light Meter | UVA/B light meter for forense analysis | In Amazon | $ 178.00 |
| Extech UV505 | Pocket light meter for UV-Ab ranges of 290 to 390 nm longitude tool | In Amazon | $ 161.31 |
| General Tools UV513AB | UV513AB, digital meter UVA/UVB, de 280 to 400 nm | In Amazon | $ 146.07 |
| AMTAST UV340B UV | Light meter UV: UVA and UVB, of 290 to 390 nm In Amazon | In Amazon | $ 139.99 |
| Sensitive UVB Meter for Reptile Lamps | Irradiance and aging testing Equipment to test irradiance and aging with UV and reptile lamps | In Amazon | $ 118.99 |
| SunFriend Personal UV Monitor | Activity UV personalize and waterproof meter | In Amazon | $ 45.00 |
| Nextav UV | Portable detector to measure the UV level of the Sunlight | In Amazon | $ 39.99 |
| Digital UV Index Sensor & Handheld UV Detector | Intensity meter of ultraviolet rays and sunlight detector | In Amazon | $ 38.99 |

The prices have been taken as references by the global distributor of Amazon without any delivery nor taxes to any country. In addition, the currency Exchange for each country has to be taken into account.

## 2.3   Devices and Applications to Detect UV Radiation

The high cost of technology and the interest for the prevention and risk theme that the emission sources of ultraviolet radiation, especially solar, render the amount of evidence that the existing devices present in the current means and worldwide (Fig. 1). On Table 1, it shows some of the actual devices, a brief description, the place of distribution and its cost.

The portable device NeBla has a cost of $31.10, arduino card UNO: $9.99, sensor ML8511: $7.99, module *Bluetooth HC-06*: $7.40, *Real-Time Clock* (RTC): $2.22, 9 volts battery: $2.00, o *Secure Digital module* (SD): $1.50, referential values in Amazon for components to wholesale Price (retail Price as well) The application of UV-Reader module and the source code for the device is free of charge. Available at: https://github. com/brodriguezm998/UV-Reader/tree/master/application.

**Fig. 1.** Mobiles applications of UV detection in Google Play

# 3   Materials and Methods

## 3.1   Methodology

For the development proposal for this applied investigation work, the authors chose the following methods: the empiric analytic method is utilized, for the elaboration of the portable design, the device, its function and connectivity. The radiation ranges criterion are established as world standards. Finally, the effectiveness testing of device data are tested. Sample of the north and south of the city from 10.7 km of distance between them in order to contrast the provided data of the National Meteor and Hydrology Institute (INAMHI) on the closest point of the province of Santa Elena in the Libertad County, $2°14'06.0''$S (South), $80°52'30.3''$W (West).

The theory method with a quantitative focus allows us to analyze related documentation with other previous Jobs and obtained data, do a comparison between devices and the implemented device just like functions between the mobile applications that are found in this field, so the best mobile applications are developed.

The satisfaction acceptance, by people in our means, is valid due to the elaboration of digital surveys through the Google forms, with a video introducing explanation where the usage of the device, its functions, data adapted by the portable device and the presentation in the mobile application. On the link: https://github.com/brodriguezm998/UV-Reader, the montage kit can be accessed, its design for its construction just like the emails of the authors to each collaboration or doubts of the data acquisition.

The objective population of the Project is addressed to the 100.000 people, inhabitants of the north and south of the city. The spots chosen are those where the two devices were placed for data receptionist, at a distance of 10, 7 km between them. In order to obtain level of reliability of 95% of the outcome, it is necessary to have samples of 375 people and with an error margin of 5.05%. The 375 are randomly selected and between the ages of 18 to 30 years (people that could go through the discharge, installation, usage and application process), for approximately 30 days.

A comparison between results is previously and post evidently about the use of the application. There is also the possibility to have a respective analysis in order to determine the acceptance level of the UV Reader kit and with the percentage given to reach and contribute to the prevention and protection of places where the ultraviolet radiation is exposed, especially specific locations.

### 3.2 Scope of the Study

This work is placed on the person-computer interaction, electronic device scope during the design of a kit that consists of a transportable device and a mobile application in order to detect and prevent ultraviolet radiation of any source whether natural or artificial emission of UV, one of the "invisible" threats to human health.

### 3.3 Structure and Architecture of the Portable Device

The UV-Reader kit consists of a portable device and mobile application. NeBla has an Arduino UNO card as its base badge which incorporates a microcontroller program with an architecture of pin connections that allow to establish communication with other cards of different technologies [15] such as: a Secure Digital (SD) card Reading module linked for saving light wave readings on a flat format, a Bluetooth module, a Real-Time Clock (RTC) module and the UV sensor model ML8511 which functions on a 5 V battery. This comes equipped with an amplifier that can make the conversation photoelectric dependable to a voltage of UV light that is caught. The NeBla portable equipment proportions an analogical amount of UV light which is detected and needs to be located in a place with a direct view line to an UV source (for this type of job, the UV emission sources are the sun or an UV lamp led). The experimental prototype is connected with Bluetooth wireless technology to a mobile UVReader application. The connections are visualized (see Fig. 2) to receive data during the UV (A) sensor and the transmission from a Bluetooth (B) to the mobile device. The portable device uses a feeding source of 9 V (E) and the RTC (C) to synchronize the system, SD (D) module is to load data received by the sensor and all the devices linked to the Arduino UNO card (F).

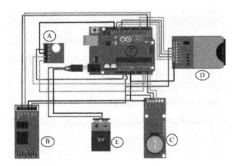

**Fig. 2.** NeBla connections prototype.

It is emphasized that the connection among components need a joint of program codes to allow effective communication between the hardware and the mobile application. The measurements according to the sensor are stored in the SD card and also uploaded in the inside storage of the mobile device. The dimensions of the portable NeBla kit are 2.95 in. wide, 2.76 in. long and 5.51 in. (see Fig. 3), the portable device NeBla uses the programming on the development interface (IDE) of Arduino version 1.8.21.0.

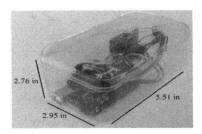

**Fig. 3.** NeBla portable device dimensions

### 3.4  Design and Development of Mobile Application

The mobile application nominated UV-Reader is developed by Android Studio and it is distributed in the three Java written languages. The first module is MainActivity, the main screed, where the UV meter is displayed and applied. The second module is ReportActivity, the screen of the visualization of the meter interactions in report form. The third module is AboutActivity, screen show the visualization of the information and recommendation on how to use it.

The following flow diagram, Fig. 4, specifies the logical function on the connection between NeBla and UV-Reader.

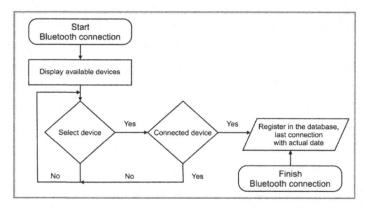

**Fig. 4.** NeBla and UV-Reader connection algorithm

The UV-Reader has on its main screen the state of the sensor if it is connected or not to the application. It shows the last registered connection and a needle as the indicator to the radiation index of UV on real present time (like the speedometer, design of the Javascript library named "Gauge.minjs") with a meter for each second and relapse of a second for every three hours. In the image (see Fig. 5), a value of the testing of 6.54 mW/cm$^2$ can be appreciated. This value was registered on September 18, 2019, 12:34 PM.

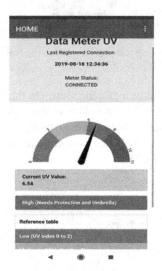

**Fig. 5.** Main screen of the UV-Reader application

The logical function on the writing and mapping of data can be visualized in Fig. 6.
Data is transmitted to a receptor in a Smart device where the application of the UV-Reader has been installed. The user can read the information and observe the ultraviolet UV radiation index in a determined location as it is shown in the image (see Fig. 7).

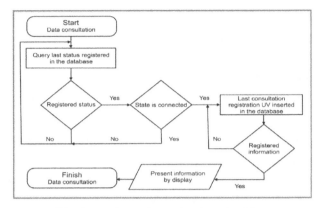

**Fig. 6.** Writing and mapping data algorithm.

**Fig. 7.** Transmission and reception from the NeBla UV-Reader

Data is processed to show it as a graphic view. On the right up hand corner named report, it shows the dimensions by date. The application shows the last 100 mobile registrations that have been entered in the database of the mobile device after the portable device transmission. The data is evaluated on a graphic chart averaging the last 30 min as it shows on the image (see Fig. 8).

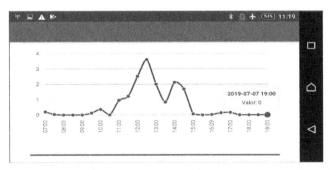

**Fig. 8.** Mobile application UV-Reader, radiation index expressed in mW/cm$^2$

The proposal of this paper is to obtain UV radiation measures of any means that produces it whether natural or artificial form in places where the user needs it or any other source that is in existence at home or industry alike, especially in those people that dedicate themselves to the maintenance of such equipment with UV technology and those that can be exposing themselves frequently so this risk could be reduced and prevent any type of cancer-related disease.

## 4    Data Acquisition

In order to have index values of UV radiation levels and confirmation of equipment functioning, we placed two NeBla prototypes, one in the north and the other one in the south of Guayaquil city at 2°09′25.8″S 79°56′01.8″W and 2°13′39.2″S 79°54′13.9″W respectively. Collecting sensor values every Sunday from the 7th to the 29 of September, 2019, from 07:00:00 to 19:00:00, such readouts are seen in the following image (see Fig. 9). The data is based in the digital Github repository: https://github.com/brodriguezm998/UV-Reader/tree/master/measurements.

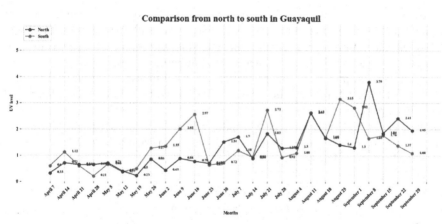

**Fig. 9.** Radiation index from the prototypes and their expressed values in mW/cm$^2$.

The solmaforo values are constracted (set equipment and the great structure) of the National Meteorology and hydrology institute (INAMHI) located in the Santa Elena province (closest measuring point) in the Libertad County at 127 km from the measuring point north and at 135 km from the measuring point south of Guayaquil. Currently, there are no equipment in Guayaquil in the INAMHI. The proportioned data is to show our comparative is at http://186.42.174.236/IndiceUV2/. It is known that our factors indicate how cloudiness can subdue the UV spectrum. In other words, the months of April and May when the weather changes and there is a cloudy sky, the values of the devices have an accentuated difference within the peninsula (see Fig. 10).

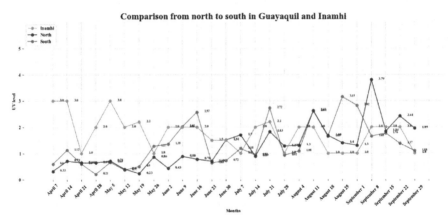

**Fig. 10.** Comparison of measurement in la Libertad (Inamhi) and Guayaquil (equipment NeBla).

## 5  Results and Discussion

The used technique in this paper determines the level of acceptance of the UV Reader equipment and its application, and it allows a reliability level of 95%, with a error margin of 5% of its value. A survey was given to three hundred and seventy-five people to see if the use of the application is of easy management. Furthermore, it was given to show if the kit contributes to the prevention and protection conscious to diseases of the skin because of the exposition to UV rays and the level of acceptance of the portable equipment and their mobile applications to be acquired.

In Fig. 11, 91.10% shows that NeBla and UV-Reader are an easy to use kit because of their size, structure for being transportable and simply applied, the 8.90% showed that its handling was a bit complexed.

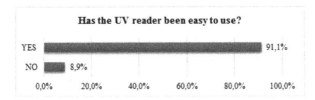

**Fig. 11.** Percentage of UV READER characteristics.

In Fig. 12, the 23.30% show that the UV-Reade kit furthers the prevention to the welfare of the skin to a 100%, the 46.50% shows that it furthers to a 75%, a 26.50% show that it furthers the welfare to a 50%. This shows that 96.3% of the population that has been surveyed has a high level of importance when it comes to the care and awareness to the exposure of UV rays.

Finally, in Fig. 13, 89.50% shows that it can be possible to acquire a NeBla kit and UV-Reader as a prevention device and health care to the exposure of ultraviolet rays.

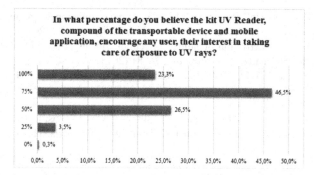

**Fig. 12.** Percentage of interest to the care of skin that has been exposed to UV rays.

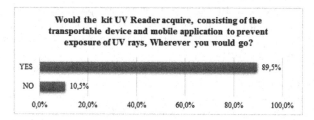

**Fig. 13.** Percentage to the acceptance of the equipment by the surveyed population.

## 6  Conclusions

Currently, the devices for the ultraviolet radiation detection are scarce and not easily found to the population Access. The mobile applications for UV radiation detection purposes that were used in this investigation require a type of device of high performance or that uses adaptable sensor to detect this type of radiation. In addition, the cost of the equipment (hardware) and application (software) are found with values above other devices that are for the prevention in health simulators. This paper presents an experimental prototype that has the ability to detect ultraviolet radiation in a kit and mobile application. The data that is received by the equipment and the application in the wireless form are presented in the mobile device in an adequate manner, using the index needle as a reference standard of WHO, helping the prevention of health risks due to the exposition of UV solar radiation The equipment acceptance by the population has reached high levels due to the creativity of the presented designer.

## References

1. Arnold, M., et al.: Global burden of cutaneous melanoma attributable to ultraviolet radiation in 2012. Int. J. Cancer **143**(6), 1305–1314 (2018)
2. Ventéjou, S., Bagny, K., Waldmeyer, J., Cartault, F., Machet, L., Osdoit, S.: Skin cancers in patients of skin phototype V or VI with xeroderma pigmentosum type C (XP-C): a retrospective study. Ann. Dermatol. Venereol. **146**(3), 192–203 (2019)

3.  Loomis, D., Guha, N., Hall, A.L., Straif, K.: Identifying occupational carcinogens: an update from the IARC monographs. Occup. Environ. Med. **75**(8), 593–603 (2018)

4.  Qiu, Y., et al.: UV inactivation of human infectious viruses at two full-scale wastewater treatment plants in Canada. Water Res. **147**, 73–81 (2018)

5.  Capela, N.A., Lemaire, E.D., Baddour, N., Rudolf, M., Goljar, N., Burger, H.: Evaluation of a smartphone human activity recognition application with able-bodied and stroke participants. J. Neuroeng. Rehabil. **13**(1), 1–10 (2016)

6.  Schwarz, M., Baumgartner, D.J., Pietsch, H., Blumthaler, M., Weihs, P., Rieder, H.E.: Influence of low ozone episodes on erythemal UV-B radiation in Austria. Theor. Appl. Climatol. **133**(1–2), 319–329 (2018)

7.  Riyanto, S.D.: Optimizing of electric power solar cell by various angle using the activator panel based on the timer and light sensor. In: 2018 International Conference of Applied Science and Technology, pp. 109–114 (2018)

8.  Park, D.H., Oh, S.T., Lim, J.H.: Development of a UV index sensor-based portable measurement device with the EUVB ratio of natural light, pp. 1–12 (2019)

9.  Oliveira, M.M., et al.: Dihydrocaffeic acid prevents UVB-induced oxidative stress leading to the inhibition of apoptosis and MMP-1 expression via p38 signaling pathway. Oxid. Med. Cell. Longev. **2019**, 1–14 (2019)

10. Hacker, E., et al.: UV detection stickers can assist people to reapply sunscreen. Prev. Med. (Baltim.) **124**, 67–74 (2019)

11. Ferlay, J., et al.: Cancer incidence and mortality worldwide: sources, methods and major patterns in GLOBOCAN 2012. Gynecol. Obstet. Fertil. **43**(1), 1–28 (2015)

12. Nicholson, A., Murphy, M., Walker, H., Tinker, R., Dobbinson, S.: Not part of my routine: a qualitative study of use and understanding of UV forecast information and the SunSmart app. BMC Public Health **19**(1), 1–9 (2019)

13. Whiteman, D.C., Green, A.C., Olsen, C.M.: The growing burden of invasive melanoma: projections of incidence rates and numbers of new cases in six susceptible populations through 2031. J. Invest. Dermatol. **136**(6), 1161–1171 (2016)

14. American Cancer Society: "¿Cuáles son los factores de riesgo del cáncer de piel tipo melanoma?" Facts & Figures (2017). https://www.cancer.org/es/cancer/cancer-de-piel-tipo-melanoma/causas-riesgos-prevencion/factores-de-riesgo.html

15. El Hammoumi, A., Motahhir, S., Chalh, A., El Ghzizal, A., Derouich, A.: Low-cost virtual instrumentation of PV panel characteristics using Excel and Arduino in comparison with traditional instrumentation. Renewables Wind Water Sol. **5**(1), 5 (2018)

16. Blumthaler, M.: UV monitoring for public health. Int. J. Environ. Res. Public Health **15**(8), 1723 (2018)

# Gamification as a Tool for Supporting Artificial Intelligence Development – State of Art

Zornitsa Yordanova(✉) 

University of National and World Economy, 8mi dekemvri, Sofia, Bulgaria
zornitsayordanova@unwe.bg

**Abstract.** Intelligence refers to the ability to learn and apply knowledge in new situations. Games have proven their capacity to support the process of learning as well as the ability of humans to apply knowledge in new and unknown situations. Artificial intelligence from the other hand definitely struggles to truly and fully emulate neurological functions and human intelligence. Following this logical equitation, gamification would probably may be in use for artificial intelligence development. This paper aims at examining if the concept of gamification would be a possible tool to support and boost artificial intelligence on its way of development. Reviewing the gamification literature, taking a deeper look at gamification in ICT, and examining contemporary artificial intelligence (AI) and gamification studies as concepts with some possible cross points, the paper exploits the idea of gamification as a pivotal tool to address some of the recent challenges of AI from a business perspective. The methodology in the research stepped on some already identified key challenges for AI development in the recent literature and results in a discussion of how gamification may support AI in its way to transform industries and humanity. The results of the discussion can be seen as starting points for future hypotheses and knowledge gaps for further study.

**Keywords:** Artificial intelligence · Gamification · Business to IT alignment

## 1 Introduction

Artificial intelligence (AI) has recently gained the interest of many sciences and research because of its wide application and promising results for achieving efficiency and transformation of economy and humanity as a whole. Many studies have already examined AI in multiple fields as games, robots, law, stock trading, remote sensing devices, education, management, information and communication technology, scientific inventions and even medicine and diagnostic procedures [1]. Surely, AI is and will be a transformation tool for industry and its future [2]. While many research explore how AI may impact all possible aspects of the existing life as we currently know it, pretty no one research focus on the supporters of this fast developing horizontally important science for the all other business sectors, governments, human aspects. As a result, many key challenges have recently arose as clear statements summarizing particular threats referring to the AI smooth development as a promising technology. This study is a conceptual one with

© Springer Nature Switzerland AG 2020
M. Botto-Tobar et al. (Eds.): ICAT 2019, CCIS 1193, pp. 313–324, 2020.
https://doi.org/10.1007/978-3-030-42517-3_24

the idea to arise some hypotheses for future proving on the possible impact and support of gamification as a tool for pillaring AI in its promising development road toward impacting almost all human-related areas of civilization.

Although several definitions of gamification can be found in the literature [3] they all have in common certain aspects and do certainly address similar aspects of the concept, i.e. the application of strategies, models, dynamics, mechanics, and elements of the games in other contexts than games, and the objective of producing a playful experience that fosters motivation, involvement, and fun [4]. In other words, gamification has been mostly explored only as an interaction instrument for achieving some particular goals [5]. In this paper, we examine the hypothesis that gamification may also be a tool in developing artificial intelligence and may serve as an instrument to solve some well-known issues for the faster development of this progressive area. The paper has a multidisciplinary approach since we explore gamification from management point of view and AI from technical perspective. The paper aims at analyzing and scoping the state of art of a possible use of gamification as a concept in the increasingly important topic of artificial intelligence. Gamification currently has been studied as a tool for engaging audience, students, employees, to activate passive listeners, to boost performance, to improve creative processes and to reveal some hidden strengths and weaknesses in business processes. Generally, gamification has been analyzed as a mediator between people and some of their natural functions as learning and working. Games, as a natural function of people have played the role of a bridge between their core interest and the work that should be done for achieving some results.

No one study has explored how gamification would impact as a tool the learning process in artificial intelligence or at least how gamification may be of use to solve potentially some of the key challenges which AI faces during its development. This paper aims at examining the state of art of this probability. For this purposes, both concepts are defined and some common points are discussed.

## 2 Material and Method

The use of gamification in ICT is not a new one area of research, on the contrary. Recent advances in serious games and computer game engines experimented with employing gamification mechanics and elements to impact in corporate management, administration, marketing, training, learning, education, beta testing, ecology incentives, programming development, etc. [6].

### 2.1 Gamification of the Learning Process

Play as a phenomenon is older than culture, economy, all socio-cultural and socio-economic system as we know them today prior to human society and human civilization [7]. Some authors have made an analogy with animal games that resemble and etymologically represent the same process, which suggests that games as a phenomenon may have existed even before the birth of mankind. Not a coincidence that we are discussing now games as a tool for artificial intelligence, which one itself is as far and in the same way close to humankind as animals are. Analyzing the game as a concept, Huizinga [7] concludes that it is more than just a physiological phenomenon or a psychological reflex. It goes beyond purely physical or purely biological activity. This is a significant feature – i.e. has some meaning and serves not only on its own, isolated from side factors and purposes, it is a function of human being. The importance of games as a phenomenon is also confirmed by pedagogical research, which determines games as an essential and critical element of the maturation process. After the brief preface, which puts the games at the center of human development since its inception, the concept of gamification is brand new, yet significant and promising for its development.

Among the first to define the concept of gamification as a modern concept is Nick Pelling [8, 9], who saw it back in 2002 as a process that makes the interface of different products, in his case, electronic transactions, more fun, faster and more playful. The gamification process defined by Deterding et al. [3] is the use of game elements in non-game contexts. In depth, this definition dealt with in another study of the same authors [10], where they explained that it is a matter of game elements, not a game in general. While games are usually played, play itself is a different and broader category than the game itself. Games, on the other hand, are characterized by rules and competition, or the struggle with concrete and persistent results or goals on the part of those involved. The authors make a distinction between the term "serious games" and "gaming". While serious games describe the use of incomplete games for non-entertainment purposes, the use of games and the use of gaming elements is a way of diversifying existing approaches for better performance. A link between the concept of gaming and serious games, however, is that both concepts use games for purposes other than their normal use for entertainment. In addition, gamification is also defined as a process of using gaming mechanisms and game thinking to solve problems from Deterding itself. The authors also claimed that gamification [10] as a term derives from the digital media industry. Lee and Hammer [11] believed that gamification is the use of gaming mechanisms, dynamics, and frameworks to promote desired behavior. Kapp [12] defined gamification as the use of game-based mechanics, aesthetics and playful thoughts to make people loyal, to motivate action, to encourage learning, and to solve problems. The key point of gamification is the inclusion of gaming tasks that players have to perform [13]. McGonigal [14] summarized in a study that, since the beginning of the 21st century, a lot of research interest has been on games as a phenomenon through which can be conveyed an element of joy and excitement in serious work situations and their solution. Shpakova et al. [15] defined gamification as "the process of doing activities in non-game contexts such as games." Another definition in the literature interprets gamification as an informal term for the use of video game elements in non-gaming systems to improve user experience and user engagement [16]. Huotari and Hamari [17] divided gamification into three parts: (1) implementing elements of the game in non-gaming activities, (2) making psychological changes, and (3) visible changes in user behavior.

As a summary of the analyzed definitions, it can be concluded that gamification is a concept for using game elements [3, 18, 19] in a different non-game context [15–17] for the purpose of increasing consumer engagement [3, 18, 19]. Again for the purpose of systemizing and summarizing, Jakubowski [20] concludes that he considers the following two definitions to be the most focused: (1) Gaming is the use of game elements in non-game contexts [3]; (2) Ignoring is the process of gaming and gaming mechanics

**Table 1.** Table captions should be placed above the tables.

| Authors | Definition |
|---|---|
| Pelling [8] | "A process that makes the interface of different products, more fun, faster and more playful" |
| Deterding et al. [3] | "Using game elements in non-game contexts" |
| Deterding et al. [3] | "The process of using gaming mechanisms and game thinking to solve problems by yourself" |
| Deterding et al. [10] | "Term for using video game elements in non-gaming systems to improve user experience and user engagement" |
| Lee and Hammer [11] | "Using gaming mechanisms, dynamics and frameworks to promote desired behavior" |
| Kapp [12] | "Use of game-based mechanics, aesthetics and playful thoughts to make people faithful, to motivate action, to promote learning and to solve problems" |
| Shpakova et al. [15] | "The inclusion of gaming tasks that players must perform" |
| Huotari and Hamari [17] | "Implementing elements of the game in non-games activities, making psychological changes and visible changes in user behavior" |
| Huotari and Hamari [17] | "A process of improving the service with the ability to play games to maintain the overall value creation of the user" |
| Zicherman and Cunningham [18] | "A process of using thinking and mechanics to engage users" |
| Burke [21] | "Using game mechanics and game design techniques in non-game contexts of design behavior, skills development, or engaging people in innovation" |
| Werbach and Hunter [19] | "Using gaming elements and game design techniques in non-gaming contexts" |
| Werbach [22] | "Process of turning activities into more playful situations" |
| Stieglitz et al. [23] | "Gamification for learning and game-based learning share common ground on the idea that game elements can make learning experiences more engaging" |
| Klabbers [24] | "Gamification is a business practice and a management method. It does not aim at making real-time business processes a playful game" |

for consumer engagement and problem solving [18]. The table below summarizes the definitions in the scientific literature since the slight difference between them explain the different aspects and characteristics of gamification and its application (Table 1).

Serious games on the other hand, no matter that some authors claim the concepts of gamification and serious games overlap sometime [25], are actually games that exclude fun, entertainment, and enjoyment from their important objectives [26].

## 2.2  Gamification in ICT

A lot of research on the topic of gamification in ICT actually explores again learning and education objectives by the prism of the possible use of ICT tools in combination with game elements and technics [27]. In academic context, especially in computing, the use of gamification is a mean for conditioning behaviors in the user [28]. Yordanova [29] summarized in a research the following possible applications of gamification in business software systems (Table 2).

**Table 2.**  Game elements, techniques and mechanism usage in business software systems

| Game elements, techniques and mechanism | Explanation for usage |
|---|---|
| Virtual goods | By promising virtual good for performing tasks accurately, the overall performance of business software system is better and users follow the right process more engagingly |
| Cooperation in the field of competition | Most of business software systems processes rely on good cooperation between users and different teams. That is why cooperation is stimulated by competition and thus brings better performance and minimizing mistakes |
| Achievements | Since users have usually been assigned to daily and routine duties and tasks in business software systems, different levels of achievements bring them more engagement and passion in work |
| Levels | Since users have usually been assigned to daily and routine duties and tasks, different levels of achievements bring them more engagement and passion in work in addition to the natural human desire for achievements |
| Opportunities for rewarding | Rewarding has been recognized in the literature and practice as one of the strongest motivators for achieving tasks and performance. The properly embedded opportunities for rewarding not directly related to payment gives other perspective of users and motivate their engagement better than extra payment on monthly basis. On the other hand, that approach stimulates each one of the performed tasks and the team work |
| Gifts | Gifts are almost as strong motivator for achieving performance and results as payment is. By providing gifts instead of extra payment, employers stimulate the inner employees' engagement |
| Challenges | The newly generations are more and more less susceptible to extra payment. The motivational factors for stimulating their work performance is a huge topic and challenges have been recognized as a tool for handling this problem |

## 2.3   Artificial Intelligence

Artificial Intelligence (AI) describes a set of advanced general purpose digital technologies that enable machines to do highly complex tasks effectively [30]. Artificial intelligence is seen from its perspective to be an important tool for industry in this research. In recent years, industry, the media, and political organizations have shown strong interest in AI, with AI-related research and applications rapidly increasing at home and abroad. Industry is interested in potential uses of AI [31]. The integration of AI with industrial demands has forced significant changes in services [32]. In the research of Hall and Pesenti [33] some common challenges have been summarized:

- Lack of access to data - sharing of data between organizations holding data and organizations looking to use data to develop AI
- Lack of appropriate skills for developing AI (in the sense of quality and quantity)
- Lack of student programs in AI (bachelor, master, PhD)
- Lack of support for AI research specifically
- Not clear and unified common policies and practices for licensing IP and forming spin-out companies in the area of AI
- a framework for explaining processes, services and decisions delivered by AI, to improve transparency and accountability

Garvey [34] summarized five strategies for a Framework for the Democratic Governance of Technology by Intelligent Trial and Error:

- Public deliberation about issues relevant to citizens' lives is central to all democracies
- Democratic Decision Making Process in business
- Common prudence rules
- Preparation for Learning from Experience
- Appropriate Expertise

Frank et al. [35] explored the impact of artificial intelligence on labor. They summarized these barriers:

- lack of high-quality data about the nature of work
- lack of empirically informed models of key microlevel processes
- insufficient understanding of how cognitive technologies interact with broader economic dynamics and institutional mechanisms

Smirnov and Lukyanov [36] stated that the development of the world market of artificial intelligence systems is at transitional stage, giving new opportunities for goods production improvement and economic growth all over the world.

## 3   Results - Artificial Intelligence and Gamification

All findings in previous research examined in the material and method section of the paper as AI challenges are discussed with AI experts. The study employed a focus group with subject matter experts in data science and AI. The reason for using this specific research technique is its usefulness in qualitative research [37] for depth understanding of the researched hidden possibilities for knowledge transfer between different fields. The choice of using subject matter experts is because of the required knowledge on data science and AI for the research purposes and also for extracting value with providing the understanding of different stakeholders, which permits the analysis to predict the reaction of potential groups on the field [38]. One focus group meeting was organized. It took place in September 2019 and it was formed by three specialists in data science and AI, each of them with 10 + years' experience. The literature analysis, performed above in the study, had been prior provided to the specialists for bringing more knowledge and understanding of gamification as a concept even though the three members of the focus group had declared their awareness of gamification. The awareness of gamification and its application were both criteria for selecting the subject matter experts as the main purpose was to discuss gamification for the purposes of AI development. The experts were also provided with the gamification tools described by Boer [39] since they are wide ranged enough for achieving diverse results. These are: limitations; emotional reinforcement; storytelling; progressive relationships; challenges; opportunities for rewarding; cooperation in the field of competition; cooperation; feedback, opportunity for a victory; achievements; leadership; avatars; levels; badges; points; fights; searches; collections; social graphics; combat the team; unlocking the content; virtual goods, gifts.

**Table 3.** AI challenges and gamification answer

| AI challenge in the literature | Gamification answer |
| --- | --- |
| Lack of access to data - sharing of data between organizations holding data and organizations looking to use data to develop AI | Win-win model of gamification would serve some stimulation initiatives for motivating organizations to share their data to AI developers and AI business product development |
| Lack of appropriate skills for developing AI (in the sense of quality and quantity) | Gamification technics, especially those applicable for learning purposes would definitely be useful for focusing learning of appropriate skills for developing AI (challenges, opportunities for rewarding, opportunity for a victory; achievements, collections, unlocking the content; virtual goods, gifts) |
| Lack of student programs in AI (bachelor, master, PhD) | Since AI is becoming so useful in industry, some gamification elements might be used so as more companies to give their data for research purposes and some scholarships to be provided |

(continued)

**Table 3.** (*continued*)

| AI challenge in the literature | Gamification answer |
| --- | --- |
| Lack of support for AI research specifically | This aspect has two perspectives: lack of support from governments and lack of private/business support. As for the second aspect, the usefulness of AI in industry presented by gamification for better understanding may be a tool for stimulating more companies to support AI research in diverse areas |
| Not clear and unified common policies and practices for licensing IP and forming spin-out companies in the area of AI | Governments must organize rankings and additional financial support to AI research (by the means of gamification) and to strengthen licensing and IP of AI methods and products based on AI |
| A framework for explaining processes, services and decisions delivered by AI, to improve transparency and accountability | Gamification is amongst the strongest tools for clarifying difficult information to stakeholders with no specific knowledge |
| Public deliberation about issues relevant to citizens' lives is central to all democracies | Citizen innovators with the support of gamification and AI incorporated within gamified tools may elicit first the main problems of citizens and then their best possible and optimal decision |
| Democratic Decision Making Process in business | Decision making in business is amongst the hardest business issue. Gamification has been researched as a possible tool not only to state a decision but also to use emotional and intuitive skills for it (cooperation in the field of competition; cooperation; feedback, opportunity for a victory; achievements; leadership) |
| Common prudence rules | Since the common prudence rules are difficult for analyses and systematization, gamification might be useful for elicit real values out of religion, personal perception, etc. |
| Preparation for Learning from Experience | Gamified platforms with incorporated AI features are possible tools for learning in close-to-real environment with almost real user experience |
| Appropriate Expertise | The increasing number of AI projects and research might be additional artificially boost by gamification by strengthen on specific skills and expertise as well as too direct education |

(*continued*)

**Table 3.** (*continued*)

| AI challenge in the literature | Gamification answer |
| --- | --- |
| Lack of high-quality data about the nature of work | Usually data about nature of work cannot be summarized by ordinary analytical tools and methods. Gamification would be useful for gathering data without respondent to be aware of the purpose of such experiments and thus to provide more high-quality data |
| Lack of empirically informed models of key micro level processes | Gamification would be of use in those cases where (1) Business cannot define the usefulness of AI at first glance and with no deep knowledge and (2) Gamification tools to be used so as to elicit details and specifics for key micro level processes with all dependencies, exceptions and curved processes |
| Insufficient understanding of how cognitive technologies interact with broader economic dynamics and institutional mechanisms | By stimulating (via gamification means) more individuals and companies to join AI platforms with their daily operations and cognitive perception, more economic dynamics and institutional mechanisms would be revealed |

The discussion had the purpose of answer how gamification would handle the selected challenges for the future development of AI (Table 3).

## 4   Discussion

In the discussion part of the research, the study goes through some common points between AI and gamification found in the literature since the discussion has already been started by other authors. Than a discussion over the results from the study examines the possible gamification instruments and methods.

Even though both Artificial intelligence and gamification are hot topics for academics and practitioners, very few are the science papers exploring the interaction and possible road map for developing their common way to new fields and possible collaboration. Arnold and Jantke [40] made an analysis of AI by the prism of how it may influence educational gamification. They assumed that Educational Gamification will succeed only if, Artificial Intelligence is incorporated within it. Their report intended to clarify how AI enables effective educational gamification. They concluded in their research about the current perspectives of Gamification & AI as a misunderstood area. Some other authors, exploring both concepts concluded that AI is increasingly important to gamification elements such as leader boards and points can be helpful to record students' progress and solving the problem of balancing pupils speed of understanding new academic material [41]. There are rare cases where authors dealing with gamification for e-learning who saw AI as an important or, at least, interesting approach, they excluded it explicitly from investigation and expected it to play a role only in the future [42]. For Chou [43] stated that through gamification, we can look through the lens of games to understand how to combine different game mechanics and techniques to form desired and joyful experiences for everyone. However, this study analyzes gamification as a tool in Artificial Intelligence and possible to solve the currently stated problems and issues which AI concept and knowledge area faces on the road of its development.

As a result, from the analysis, here is presented a diagram with describing the main gamification elements which might be of possible use in AI development. The main conclusions are presented in Fig. 1.

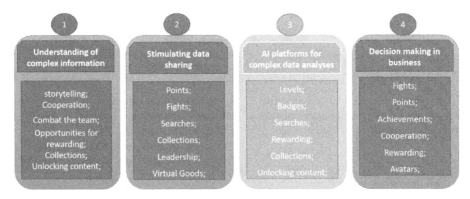

**Fig. 1.** Gamification elements for AI development and addressing AI challenges

## 5   Conclusion

Gamification has recently increased its popularity since there were only 8 articles in Scopus database mentioning gamification in 2011 (searched in titles, abstract and key words) and the accumulated number in 2019 is already 5517 [44]. The current paper contributes to the knowledge gap of how gamification might support the prominent role of AI development. Fourteen AI challenges were addressed and discussed from the perspective of their possible solving by gamification means and incorporating gamification elements and methods in AI solutions. As a result of the research findings and discussions conducted with the support of a focus group with subject-matter experts in the fields of data science and AI, a summary of gamification elements suitable for addressing the major points of intersection between AI and gamification is presented. The paper's results can be considered as a starting point for further research into their practical impact on the development of artificial intelligence.

**Acknowledgements.** The paper and the study is supported by NID NI 14/2018; BG NSF Grant No M 15/4 -2017 (DM 15/1), KP-06 OPR01/3-2018.

# References

1. Shukla, S., Jaiswal, V.: Applicability of artificial intelligence in different fields of life. Int. J. Sci. Eng. Res. (IJSER) **1**(1), 28–35 (2013)
2. Roblek, V., Meško, M., Krapež, A.: A complex view of industry 4.0. Sage Open **6**(2), 215844016653987 (2016). https://doi.org/10.1177/2158244016653987
3. Deterding, S., Dixon, D., Khaled, R., Nacke, L.: From game design elements to gameful-ness: defining gamification. In: Lugmayr, A., Franssila, H., Safran, C., Hammouda, I. (eds.) MindTrek 2011, pp. 9–15 (2011). https://doi.org/10.1145/2181037.2181040
4. Llorens-Largo, F., Gallego-Durán, F.J., Villagrá-Arnedo, C.J., Compañ-Rosique, P., Satorre-Cuerda, R., Molina-Carmona, R.: Gamification of the Learning Process: Lessons Learned. IEEE Revista Iberoamericana de Tecnologias del Aprendizaje **11**(4), 227–234 (2016). https://doi.org/10.1109/RITA.2016.2619138
5. Rice, J.: The gamification of learning and instruction: game-based methods and strategies for training and education. Int. J. Gaming Comput.-Mediated Simul. (IJGCMS) **4**(4), 302 (2012)
6. Tsihrintzis, G.A., Virvou, M., Watanabe, T.: Intelligent interactive multimedia systems and services. In: Proceedings of the 6th International Conference on Intelligent Interactive Multimedia Systems and Services (IIMSS2013), p. 41. IOS Press, Amsterdam (2003)
7. Huizinga, J.: Homo Ludens: A Study of the Play Element in Culture. Routledge & Kegan Paul, London, Boston and Henley, Second edition, (first edition published in German in Switzerland in 1944) (1949)
8. Pelling, N.: The (short) prehistory of gamification. Funding Startups (& other impossibilities). Haettu (2011)
9. Andrews, J.: Why Use Gamification: The Power of Games (2011). Article Source: https://www.zco.com/blog/why-use-gamification-the-power-of-games/. Accessed 20 Aug 2019
10. Deterding, S., et al.: Gamification: toward a definition. In: CHI 2011, Vancouver, BC, Canada, 7–12 May 2011. ACM (2011). 978-1-4503-0268-5/11/05
11. Lee, J., Hammer, J.: Gamification in education: what, how, why bother? Acad. Exch. Q. **122**, 1–5 (2011)
12. Kapp, K.M.: The gamification of learning and instruction: game-based methods and strategies for training and education. Pfeiffer, San Francisco (2012)
13. Kiryakova, G., et al.: Gamification in education. In: Conference: 9th International Balkan Education and Science Conference, Edirne, Turkey (2014)
14. McGonigal, J.: Reality is Broken: Why Games Make us Better and How They can Change the World. The Penguin Press, London (2011)
15. Shpakova, A., Dörfler, V., MacBryde, J.: Changing the game: a case for gamifying knowledge management. World J. Sci. Technol. Sustain. Dev. **14**, 143–154 (2017)
16. Deterding, S., et al.: Gamification: using game design elements in non-gaming contexts. In: CHI 2011, Vancouver, BC, Canada, 7–12 May 2011. ACM (2011). 978-1-4503-0268-5/11/05
17. Huotari, K., Hamari, J.: Defining gamification - a service marketing perspective. In: Proceedings of the 16th International Academic Mindtrek Conference, Tampere, Finland, 3–5 October 2012, pp. 17–22. ACM, New York (2012)
18. Zichermann, G., Cunningham, C.: Gamification by Design: Implementing Game Mechanics in Web and Mobile Apps. O'Reilly Media, Sebastopol (2011)
19. Werbach, K., Hunter, D.: For the Win: How game thinking can revolutionize your business. Wharton Digital Press, Philadelphia (2012)
20. Jakubowski, M.: Gamification in business and education - project of gamified course for university students. Dev. Bus. Simul. Exp. Learn. **41**, 339–341 (2014)
21. Burke, B.: Gamify: How Gamification Motivates People to Do Extraordinary Things. Routledge, London (2014)

22. Werbach, K.: (Re)Defining gamification: a process approach. In: Spagnolli, A., Chittaro, L., Gamberini, L. (eds.) PERSUASIVE 2014. LNCS, vol. 8462, pp. 266–272. Springer, Cham (2014). https://doi.org/10.1007/978-3-319-07127-5_23
23. Stieglitz, S., Lattemann, C., Robra-Bissantz, S., Zarnekow, R., Brockmann, T. (eds.): Gamification. PI. Springer, Cham (2017). https://doi.org/10.1007/978-3-319-45557-0
24. Klabbers, J.H.: The Magic Circle: Principles of Gaming & Simulation. Sense Publishers, Rotterdam (2009)
25. Susi, T., Johannesson, M., Backlund, P.: Serious games – an overview. Elearning **73**(10), 28 (2007)
26. Michael, D.R., Chen, S.L.: Serious games: games that educate, train, and inform. Education, vol. October 31, pp. 1–95 (2005)
27. Urh, M., et al.: The model for introduction of gamification into e-learning in higher education. Procedia Soc. Behav. Sci. **197**, 388–397 (2015)
28. Berengueres, J., Alsuwairi, F., Zaki, N., Ng, T.: Gamification of a recycle bin with emoticons. In: Proceedings of the 8th ACM/IEEE International Conference on Human-Robot Interaction, pp. 83–84. IEEE Press (2013)
29. Yordanova, Z.: Gamification application in different business software systems – state of art. In: Bhatia, S.K., Tiwari, S., Mishra, K.K., Trivedi, M.C. (eds.) Advances in Computer Communication and Computational Sciences - Proceedings of IC4S-2019. Springer, Cham (2020, in press)
30. Hall, D., Pesenti, J.: Growing the artificial intelligence industry in the UK (2017). https://apo.org.au/sites/default/files/resource-files/2017/10/apo-nid114781-1190661.pdf
31. Pan, Y.: Heading toward artificial intelligence 2.0. Engineering **2**(4), 409–413 (2016)
32. Zhou, J., et al.: Toward new-generation intelligent manufacturing. Engineering **4**(1), 11–20 (2018)
33. Hall, D., Pesenti, J.: Growing the artificial intelligence industry in the UK (2017)
34. Garvey, C.: A framework for evaluating barriers to the democratization of artificial intelligence. In: Thirty-Second AAAI Conference on Artificial Intelligence, pp. 8079–8080 (2018)
35. Frank, M.R., et al.: Toward understanding the impact of artificial intelligence on labor. PNAS **116**(14), 6531–6539 (2019)
36. Smirnov, E., Lukyanov, S.: Development of the global market of artificial intelligence systems. Economy of region **1**(1), 57–69 (2019). Centre for Economic Security, Institute of Economics of Ural Branch of Russian Academy of Sciences
37. Nyumba, W., Mukherjee, D.: The use of focus group discussion methodology: insights from two decades of application in conservation. Qual. Methods Eliciting Judgements Decis. Making **9**(1), 20–32 (2018). https://doi.org/10.1111/2041-210X.12860
38. Kahan, J.: Focus groups as a tool for policy analysis. Anal. Soc. Issues Public Policy **1**(1), 129–146 (2001)
39. Boer, P.: Introduction To Gamification, достъпна на (2013). https://cdu.edu.au/olt/ltresources/downloads/whitepaper-introductiontogamification-130726103056-phpapp02.pdf
40. Arnold, O., Jantke, K.P.: Technical Report: Educational Gamification & Artificial Intelligence, ADICOM Technical Report (2018). ISSN (Print) 2627–0749
41. Chassignol, M., Khoroshavin, A., Klimova, A., Bilyatdinova, A.: Artificial Intelligence trends in education: a narrative overview. Procedia Comput. Sci. **136**, 16–24 (2018)
42. Urh, M., Vukovic, G., Jereb, E., Pintar, R.: The model for introduction of gamification into e-learning in higher education. Procedia Soc. Behav. Sci. **197**, 388–397 (2018)
43. Chou, Y.-K.: Beyond Points, Badges, and Leaderboards. Octalysis Media, Fremont (2016)
44. Raitskaya, L., Tikhonova, E.: Gamification as a field landmark in educational research. J. Lang. Educ. **5**(2), 4–10 (2019)

# The Transformation of the Modelling & Simulation of Systems for the Training of the CAF: Design Requirements and New Functionalities

Manuel Antonio Fernández-Villacañas Marín[✉]

M&M Planning and Project Management & Technical University of Madrid, Madrid, Spain
`manuel.fernandez@mm-ppm.com`

**Abstract.** The rapid evolution of the technologies applied in modelling and simulation (M&S) of the operational activities of military systems has made simulation platforms fundamental. In the case of the combat air forces (CAF), the simulators mission so far has been the initial and advanced training of pilots in offensive and defensive air operations. A high operational hybridization between the real and the virtual has been achieved, incorporating the pilot's tactical-operational behaviour in air operations that reproduce circumstances of extreme hostility and lethality, adjusted to the effort that the aircraft would experience in a real flight, and applying the latest digital technologies. Yet the development effort has focused exclusively on comprehensive training solutions. However, the strategic development vector of M&S systems for CAF presents a much more ambitious spectrum, which transcends training and can become the core of the operational and logistic structures of the military forces in the future. This paper analyzes the main aspects that have conditioned the transition from the approach of the human-computer interaction (HCI) to the design of the user experience (UX), as well as the design requirements necessary for the development of the organizational architecture LVC-AI of M&S systems for CAF, and new functionalities beyond training systems. In this line, two examples of strategic development of these new functionalities in the field of logistics and in the operational field are developed. First, the case of obtaining, applying and managing logistic support intelligence related to the simulated effort of simulated hostile air operations and adverse weather conditions. Second, the case of the transformation of the LVC simulation platform into a real cabin on the ground, transforming the fighter aircraft into a remote pilot aircraft (RPA) capable of operating alternately in a conventional or remote way.

**Keywords:** Modelling and simulation · Digital transformation · LVC simulation · Intelligent system · Technology trends · Communications · Training

---

M. A. Fernández-Villacañas Marín — PhD Researcher and International Consultant in Logistics & Management, Associate Professor on the Technical University of Madrid, and Colonel of the Spanish Air Force (R).

© Springer Nature Switzerland AG 2020
M. Botto-Tobar et al. (Eds.): ICAT 2019, CCIS 1193, pp. 325–339, 2020.
https://doi.org/10.1007/978-3-030-42517-3_25

# 1  Introduction

The modelling and simulation (M&S) systems have become a fundamental tool for combat preparation in the armed forces, as well as for the planning and execution of their missions. The simulated platforms contribute decisively to improve and homogenize the degree of preparation of the combatants, reducing the cost and the environmental impact of their activities. Live, virtual and constructive simulation (LVC) is a taxonomy widely used to classify simulation platforms based on the degree of human participation and the degree of realism of the team. The systems simulate confrontations with enemy forces in adverse climatic environments and take into account allied and neutral forces, but in circumstances of hostile conflict that never or almost never occur in reality training.

In the case of the Combat Air Forces (CAF), the mission of the simulators developed so far has been mainly the initial and advanced training of pilots in offensive and defensive air operations. Fighter aircraft simulation systems have developed an operational hybridization of the real and the virtual, incorporating the pilot's tactical-operational behaviour in advanced air operations that reproduce circumstances of extreme hostility and lethality adjusted to the effort that the plane would supposedly experience on a real flight. There is a strategic development vector to promote an Integrated Training Solution (ITS) by applying the latest technologies and digital equipment, developing new training concepts for combat pilots and contributing to the improvement of offensive and defensive operational air capabilities.

LVC simulation platforms are socio-technical systems because of the permanent multidirectional interaction between people, not just users, and technologies. These people represent the stakeholders of all the communities involved in operations, training, testing, planning, analysis, experimentation, logistics, procurement and research and development. Therefore, the M&S must develop dynamically in relation to all the elements of the system of development and integration of the affected military capabilities and throughout their life cycle. The most appropriate integrated organizational architectures that allow the implementation of new hyper-connected and intelligent systems should be created.

During this decade, the objective in the development of M&S systems has been to create LVC and Artificial Intelligence systems capable of assembling models and simulations quickly, allowing the creation of operationally valid LVC environments for initial training and real missions, allowing a closest interaction between military operations and all the elements and structures of defence and security organizations. These M&S environments should be built with a scalable concept based on linkable components that interact in the integrated architecture to be developed.

The digital transformation of simulation platforms implies a complete organizational, cultural and strategic reinvention, which in the defence sector affects both military structures and companies that participate in it. The corresponding strategic development requires the M&S activities to evolve rapidly, thus creating an operationally valid LVC environment, which, beyond serving training processes, facilitate the development of doctrines and tactics, as well as the formulation of operational plans and the evaluation of situations of war. This promotes a closer interaction between operational commands, logistics and acquisition communities, and the industry responsible for the research and development processes of new aerospace weapons systems. These new M&S environments should be built from linkable components that interoperate in an integrated architecture, facilitating flexibility and rapid capacity to generate innovations. In this way, a strong M&S capability will allow the armed forces in general and the CAF in particular to meet operational and support objectives effectively in the various activities of military services, combat commands, and logistics organizations and of acquisitions.

## 2 Material and Method

### 2.1 Objectives, Methodology and Contents

This work aims to reflect the most significant conceptual elements of what the evolutionary transformation of the M&S training systems of the Combat Air Forces represents. It studies the requirements of the new hyper-connected and intelligent organizational architectures LVC-IA, as well as the new functionalities that, beyond the training activities, can be developed in the new systems within the foreseeable digital technological evolution.

In relation to the methodology, the research has been developed under a systemic conception through a systematized deductive process (Top-Down) guided by empirical evidence of the experience and operational research and logistics of the author, as well as in the evolution of his maturity professional in the air forces (Bottom-Up). The literature reviewed has been used to synthesize the essential concepts and approaches on the problem investigated, reviewing all this with a level of detail that is considered sufficient, seeking its original aspects to ensure objectivity and avoid interpretative biases.

To achieve the objectives, the work has been structured in two sections, after which the conclusions are presented. First, there is a conceptual reflection on the current situation of the simulation systems of the CAF, as well as the design requirements necessary to evolve the architecture of the M&S systems of the training systems. Second, the new potential functionalities that are generated are analysed through two examples within the strategic development of hyper-connected and intelligent CAF simulation platforms. The case of obtaining, applying and managing logistic support intelligence related to the simulated operations effort simulated hostile aerial and adverse weather conditions, as well as the case of the transformation of the LVC simulation platform into a real cabin on the ground, turning the fighter aircraft into an RPA capable of operating alternately in a conventional or remote way.

### 2.2 The Current Situation of the Simulation Systems for the Training of the CAF

*Meaningful Learning, Technologies and Simulation Systems*
Meaningful learning is the process according to which a new knowledge or new information is related to the cognitive structure of the person who learns, in a non-arbitrary and substantive or non-literal way. In this way, the student tends to compare and match the new knowledge acquired with the existing one, through a non-imposed process, where motivation or predisposition play a very important role. Thus, the cognitive phenomenon and the construction of meaning are carried out to achieve the above using virtual environments or simulators. It seeks to facilitate that connection of knowledge due to the

diversity of scenarios that can be managed, the application of unusual cases to solve, standardize and give uniformity to the training of experiences in defined groups, develop the problem-based learning and self-learning [1]. It is the type of learning in which the new information is related to what is already possessed, readjusting and reconstructing both information during this process, where technology plays an important role so that there is repetition or even practicing for several occasions if what is intended is to mechanize a procedure [2].

It is impossible to acquire large amounts of knowledge if there is no meaningful learning and for this to occur there must be two fundamental conditions. On the one hand, the main objective of all teachers is to have a predisposition to learn and on the other, obtain the motivation of the one who is learning and through the support of technology; it is considered possible to achieve this. The virtual reality is a simulation of a process, environment or situation and allows the interest of the students to be aroused by means of the handling of different scenarios with images, situations or sounds, making it possible to capture a better attention on what it tries to teach. On the other hand, the presentation of a relevant and significant material, that is to say with a logical meaning where there are adequate anchoring ideas in the subject that allow its relationship with the new material. This can be strengthened by using technology, such as augmented virtual reality and the support of simulators, which are tools that can make a student feel motivated to learn something due to its simple relevance and as a way to achieve autonomous learning [3].

In order to achieve the above, it is important that the right tools are learned, that is, that the student develops in increasingly complex real situations by doing and practicing and learning the necessary skills in safe and controlled environments, through the use of simulators or virtual environments to achieve more relevant or meaningful learning [4, 5]. This has strongly promoted cognitive psychology and meaningful learning, supported by educational technology, where the objective is for the instructor to know a goal that should be achieved by the students. Using the necessary tools such as e-learning and combined learning supported by simulators, the student discovers for himself what he would like to learn, practice and develop his skills, that is, the student himself involved in a technological user to develop the responsibility of his own learning, encouraging research habits [6]. This is precisely where technology emerges as an advanced organizer, to save the gap between what is already known and what is required to be known. Therefore, this offers the simulators the advantages derived from being able to represent the process of a phenomenon or a step-by-step explanation of a procedure, activity or task, through images that show in time the complex learning process [7, 8]. In this line of thinking, the development of Ramírez's research [9] on how these methodologies involve greater efficiency in the preparation of the armed forces is very enriching. His research is driven by the concern to improve and achieve meaningful learning particularly in its application in the performance and operations of flight crews, for its development with the highest level of effectiveness, efficiency and safety possible [10].

### The Simulation in the Pilot's Current Training in the CAF

The world of aviation is the frame of reference for the development of simulation media. The new disruptive technologies have allowed us to evolve into a completely new "virtual" world that not only complements the "real" world, but also becomes part of it in many professional activities and especially in everything related to aviation, applying the advancer mathematical Models [11]. Proof of this is the usual use of the expression "LVC training" (Live, Virtual and Constructive) [12].

Increasing the training of forces using simulators is a means to save budget [13]. Flight hours in a hunting simulator are not enough to train a pilot, but increasing those hours reduces overall costs, while allowing the pilot to gain in safety and skill, before training in a real fighter aircraft. It can be easy to quantify the fuel savings, maintenance of the weapon systems and personnel. This example not only provides us with an idea of the cost reduction, but also provides one more advantage, which is the greater flexibility-availability of the simulator in its use, compared to the restrictions on the number of flight hours on real aircraft. All of which is an increasingly limiting factor in the training capacity of all air forces, including for joint military space operations in which this limitation is very large [14].

As already mentioned, in the air forces a good part of the simulation efforts are focused on the CAF, trying to take advantage of the advantages offered by the simulators to the pilots for the acquisition of certain operational capabilities without the need to put the aircraft in the air. As we said, it is not only about saving costs, but also about improving the effectiveness of training by promoting the use of the simulator in certain practices focused on navigation and flight, and thus being able to spend more time on the real plane to exercise the operational aspects. Technology for training CAF teams has evolved through a convergence of advances in simulation technology for individual and collective training, methods for analyzing teamwork and designing training solutions, and intelligent tutoring technologies [15].

However, the fidelity of the simulator with respect to the aircraft it represents can be so high, that in the real flight it allows the learning of some of the capabilities offered by the weapons system to be ignored, especially in the field of navigation and flight. This even supports the firing of weapons, which allows the pilot to be trained in the launching of weapons without really firing them before being sent on a mission, After Action Review (AAR) [16].

Another characteristic of current flight simulators is the high degree of inhibition that the crewmember can achieve during simulated missions, that is, to get involved in them as if they were real. Two aspects, a physical one and a cognitive or psychological one mark this level of the pilot's immersion. The first refers to the exact replica of the cockpit instruments, the representation of the visual and sound environment and the movement or accelerations of the aircraft. The psychological one refers to the work in the cabin of the crew and the decision-making processes that would be adopted almost identically to that of a real mission [17].

The capabilities of M&S systems are used to support operational tests and systems analysis, taking into account the complexity of new air operations, multi-domain operations, and operations in highly controversial areas, where they cannot be done in live environments [18].

The Eurofighter simulator in the Spanish Air Force, called ASTA (Aircrew Synthetic Training Aids), is undoubtedly the most advanced in all of the air forces of the EU countries. This simulator is a key tool for training assigned fighter crews to the platform of the aforementioned air weapons system, both in its provision for instruction missions, preparation for the first flight, preparation of air and ground missions, release of weapons and fire, training for real missions, etc. In this regard, the dossier on simulation published in May 2015 by the Aeronautics and Astronautics Magazine of the Spanish Air Force [19] is of marked interest. Based on the experience gained during the first 10 years since the start-up of the ASTA, at the end of 2005 and with more than 10,000 h of training, the result of training in a synthetic environment of a combat pilot is analyzed through empirical research carried out in this simulator, and analyses the factors that integrate it. The final result that is obtained is as follows: types of training vs. mission flow, procedures, techniques, tactics, complete simulation of the "rehearsal mission", realism and stress in the mission flow, interactions with the rest of the elements, presence of human entities in the operating scenario, connection and interaction with other simulators, etc. [20–22].

## 3   Results: The Design Requirements in the Transformation of the Architecture of the M&S Systems of the CAF

### 3.1   From Human-Computer Interaction (HCI) to User Experience Design (UX)

Human-computer interaction (HCI) is a discipline related to the design, evaluation and implementation of interactive computer systems for human use and the study of the main phenomena that surround them. HCI surfaced in the 80s with the advent of personal computing. For the first time ever, sophisticated electronic systems were available to general consumers for uses such as word processors, games units and accounting aids. Consequently, as computers were no longer room-sized, expensive tools exclusively built for experts in specialized environments, the need to create human-computer interaction that was also easy and efficient for less experienced users became increasingly vital. Applied studies have been evolving for decades until today and have configured a multidisciplinary science that includes multiple fields that are encompassed in the following three disciplines: *Computer Science*, *Cognitive Science* and *Human Factors Engineering* [23]. The evolution of the systems has generated the multimodal human-computer interaction (MMHCI) concept, in which the fusion of MMHCI about related technologies has been progressively expanding [24].

Figure 1 presents in a generic way the interrelationships of the elements that are present in HCI [25]. Computer systems exist within a broader social, organizational and work environment (U1). Within this context, there are applications for which we wish to use computer systems (U2). However, the process of putting computers to work means that human, technical and labour aspects of the application situation have to adjust to each other through human learning, system adaptability or other strategies (U3). On the other hand, in addition to the use and the social context of computers, on the human side it is also necessary to take into account the processing of human information (H1), communication (H2) and the physical characteristics (H3) of users. On the computer side, a variety of technologies have been developed to support interaction with humans: the input and output devices connect the human and the machine (C1), which are used in a series of techniques to organize a dialogue (C2) and which are also used in turn to implement larger design elements, such as the interface metaphor (C3). By delving into the substrates of the machine that support the dialogue, the dialogue can make extensive use of computer graphics techniques (C4). Complex dialogues lead to considerations about the system architecture necessary to support features such as interconnectable computer application programs, windows, real-time response, network communications, corporate and multi-user interfaces, and multitasking of dialog objects (C5). Finally, there is the development process that incorporates the design (D1) of the dialogues, the techniques and the human-computer tools to implement them (D2), the techniques to evaluate them (D3), and a series of classic designs that are considered referents for the study (D4). Each of these components of the development process is linked with the others in a relationship of mutual and reciprocal influence through which the choices made in one area impact the choices and the options available in the others.

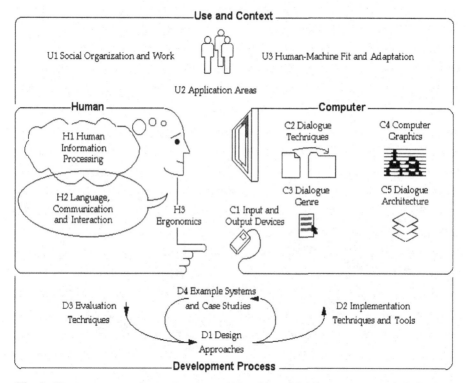

**Fig. 1.** Human-computer interaction: interrelationships of the elements present in HCI [25].

The evolution of these concepts gave rise to the user experience design (UX) methodology that is commonly used today [26]. The UX design is the design process used by the teams to create products that generate significant and relevant experiences for users, by involving them fully in the design of the entire product acquisition and integration process, including brand aspects, design, usability and function. User experience design is often used interchangeably with terms such as user interface design and usability. However, usability and user interface design are important aspects of the UX design, but they are subsets. A UX designer cares about the complete process of acquiring and integrating a product, including aspects of the brand, design, usability and function.

Products that provide an excellent user experience are designed by taking into account not only the consumption or use of the product, but also the entire process of acquisition, possession and even troubleshooting. Similarly, UX designers not only focus on creating products that are usable, but also towards other aspects such as user experience, efficiency and fun (Fig. 2).

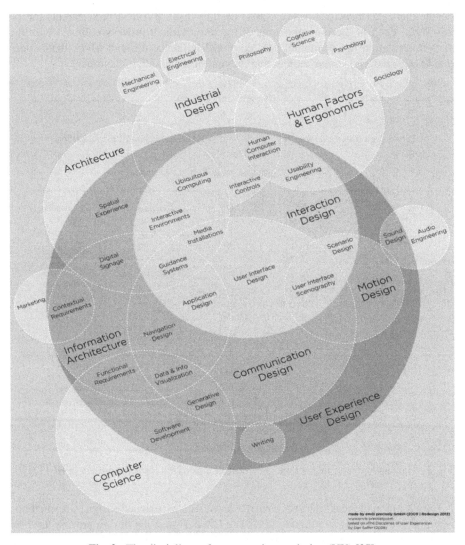

**Fig. 2.** The disciplines of user experiences design (UX) [27].

The UX designer considers the "why", "what" and "how" to use the product, "Why" involves the motivations of the users to adopt a product, whether they relate to a task they want to do with it or with values and points of view that users associate with the ownership and use of the product. "What" addresses the things that people can do with a product and its functionality. Finally, "how" relates to the design of functionality in an accessible and pleasant way. UX designers start with the "why" before determining "what" and then, finally, "how" to create products with which users can form meaningful experiences.

Using this new designs concept, one has to ensure that the "substance" of the product arrives through an existing device and offers a smooth experience. Since the UX design covers the entire user's journey, it is a multidisciplinary field: UX designers come from a variety of environments such as visual design, program programming, psychology, and interaction design. Designing for human users also means that one has to work with greater scope regarding accessibility and adapt to the physical limitations of many potential users. Typical tasks of a UX designer vary, but often include user research, profile creation, design of wired structures and interactive prototypes, as well as design proof. These tasks can vary greatly from one organization to another, but they always require designers to defend users and keep user needs at the centre of all design and development efforts. That is also the reason why most UX designers work in some form of user-cantered work process and continue to channel their best informed efforts until they address all relevant issues and user needs optimally [28].

### 3.2 The Design Requirements of the Architecture of the M&S Systems of the CAF

The aggregate representation of the fundamental elements of an LVC Organization includes hardware, software, networks, databases and user interfaces, policies, agreements, certifications, accreditations and commercial standards. The LVC integration architecture (LVC-IA) is intrinsically an organizational architecture given the "system of systems" environment it must support. LVC-IA links M&S technology to structures and people who need and use the information obtained through simulation. To achieve this, an LVC-IA training for CAF must meet three essential requirements: [29].

- **Integration** through simulation equipment, interoperability tools and support staff. The integration creates network-centric links to collect, retrieve and exchange data between live instrumentation, virtual simulators and constructive simulations, as well as between specific, joint and combined military command systems. Integration also unites data management, exercise management, exercise collaboration and the updating of training support systems.
- **Interoperability** through common protocols, specifications, standards and interfaces to standardize LVC components and tools for mission testing and training, testing, acquisition, analysis, experimentation and logistics planning.
- **Compostability** through common and reusable components and tools, such as post-action review, adapters, correlated terrain databases, multilevel security for multinational players and hardware and software requirements. Tolk [30] qualified its meaning by focusing on the need for conceptual alignment. The M&S community understands interoperability quite well as the ability to exchange information and use the data exchanged in the receiving system. Interoperability can be designed in a system or service after its definition and implementation.

The successful interoperation of the LVC component solutions requires the integrability of the infrastructures, the interoperability of the systems and the composability of the models [31]. LVC architectures must comprehensively address all three aspects in well-aligned systemic approaches. First of all, the most complex aspects related to Integration were technically solved with great solvency, and today they are not a problem in the development of M&S systems. Second, composability is different from interoperability. Composability is the consistent representation of truth in all participating systems. It extends the ideas of interoperability by adding the pragmatic level to cover what happens within the receiving system based on the received information. In contrast to interoperability, composability cannot be engineered into a system after the fact. Composability requires often significant changes to the simulation. Third, interoperability refers to methodologies to interoperate different systems distributed in a network system.

The development of the Levels of Conceptual Interoperability Model (LCIM) identified seven layers of interoperability among participating systems as a method to describe technical interoperability and the complexity of interoperations [32]. Zeigler's Modeling & Simulation theory extended it to the three basic levels of interoperability: pragmatic, semantic and syntactic [33]. The pragmatic level focuses on the receiver's interpretation of messages in the context of application relative to the sender's intent. The semantic level concerns definitions and attributes of terms and how they are combined to provide shared meaning to messages. The syntactic level focuses on a structure of messages and adherence to the rules governing that structure. The linguistic interoperability concept supports simultaneous testing environment at multiple levels (Fig. 3).

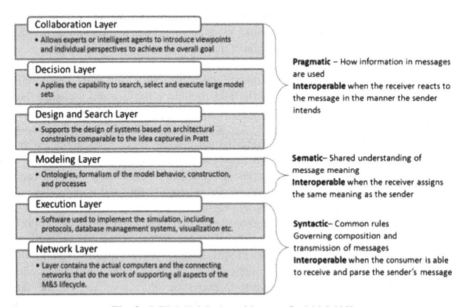

**Fig. 3.** LCIM: Zeigler's architecture for M&S [35].

The LCIM associates the lower layers with the problems of simulation interoperability, while the higher layers are related to the problems of reuse and composition of models. Simulation systems are based on models and their assumptions and restrictions. If two simulation systems are combined, these assumptions and restrictions have to be aligned accordingly to ensure significant results. Then, the interoperability levels that have been identified in the M&S area allow us to guide the way in which information is exchanged in general.

The Zeigler Architecture provides an architecture description language or conceptual model through which to analyze M&S systems. The LCIM provides a conceptual model as a means to discuss integration, interoperability and composability; the three linguistic elements relate the LCIM to the conceptual model of Zeigler. Architectural and structural complexity is an area of research in systems theory to measure cohesion and coupling and is based on the metrics commonly used in software development projects.

The M&S theory proposed by Zeigler, together with Kim and Praehofer, continues to provide a current conceptual framework and a valid computational approach associated with methodological problems in M&S [33] completely adequate for the development of simulation systems for the CAF.

## 4  Discussions: The New Functionalities to Be Generated Within the Strategic Development of the Intelligent and Hyper Connected CAF Simulation Platforms

Based on the extensive professional experience of the author of this work, as an Officer of the Spanish Air Force, and on the basis of the analysis of the EU Air Forces, it is possible to propose two new functionalities as an example that, among many others, could be developed within the LVC-IA of simulation systems for the CAF. (a) Obtaining, applying and managing logistics support intelligence related to simulated effort from simulated hostile air operations, and (b) Transformation the LVC simulation platform into a real cockpit on the ground, thus, turning the fighter jet into an RPA.

Both initiatives could be developed within the EU framework through R&D industrial projects proposed within the European Defence Industrial Development Programme (EDIDP).

Finally, the development of new functionalities and the expansion of simulation systems that integrate new distributive technologies, previously require cost-benefit analysis in detail, similar to any new technology integration, and before its large-scale implementation and use of limited resources susceptible to alternative uses [34].

### 4.1  Obtaining, Applying and Managing Logistics Support Intelligence Related to Simulated Effort from Simulated Hostile Air Operations

The mission that has been the focus on the development of state-of-the-art combat aircraft simulators at an international level is that of the initial and advanced training of combat pilots in both offensive and defensive military air operations under hostile environments and adverse weather conditions. However, these simulators are considered to be able to perform the logistical intelligence generation derived from simulated missions, but of high complexity and risk, as an added mission. Combat aircraft simulation systems have developed a real and virtual operational hybridization, incorporating the tactical-operational behaviour of the pilot in advanced air operations that reproduce circumstances of extreme hostility and lethality, through the effort that the aircraft would supposedly experience in real flight. The idea is to study and design other systems that are able to analyze the behaviour of the aircraft, in addition to the logistical and virtual support effort of all the elements of the airframe. These include, the engine, systems and armament, but based on simulated air operations of high hostility and lethality, which in the real world, would only occur in the event of serious conflicts.

The approach to obtaining logistical intelligence from combat pilot training simulators is completely new. With the exception of conclusions on logistical effort and costs that can be obtained in some very few real missions, combat aircraft flights are usually training flights in flight circumstances that are uncompromising in operational terms and with no adverse meteorology. It means having a system for generating alternative scenarios, in different air operations, both offensive and defensive, and according to the real behaviour of the pilots, and for estimating in each scenario the logistic effort of all the elements of the aircraft, systems and armament.

### 4.2 Transformation the LVC Simulation Platform into a Real Cockpit on the Ground, Turning the Fighter Jet into an RPA

The achievements obtained in the immersion of the pilots in their training on simulators, offers another interesting source of enrichment and profitability. That is to say, by transforming them into real cockpits on the ground, thus, converting the combat aircraft into a Remotely Piloted Aircraft (RPA), capable of operating alternatively in a conventional way or remotely in a cabin environment for the pilot, in exactly the same way. Operational empowerment is evident for high-risk attack missions in conflict situations, as it does not endanger the pilot's life, thus enhancing his operational aggressiveness. The aircraft significantly boosts its manoeuvrability, which is traditionally restricted by the physical resistance of the pilots on board. However, RPA also would carry out other important reconnaissance missions such as acting as intelligence platforms using radar, imaging systems, interception of communications, etc.

In this manner, with a transformation and empowerment investment that would have to be estimated, but which would probably be infinitely smaller than developing or acquiring new RPA, the aim would be to ensure that traditional combat aviation could also operate alternatively as RPA. Therefore, the strategy of transforming pilot training simulators into a real cockpit on the ground means the strengthening and greater profitability of traditional combat aircraft fleets. By giving them a new role to operate alternatively as RPA, they can also develop the missions that international military aerospace doctrine assigns to these latter aircraft, without the need to assume the large investments implied by their specific acquisition.

## 5   Conclusions

During the present decade, there has been a strong development of M&S systems in the field of training of the armed forces in general and of CAF in particular, which has been based on the application of the technological field of simulation to learning significant. Likewise, there has been a strong conceptual evolution from the human-computer inter-action (HCI) models, which integrated three essential disciplines (computer science, cognitive science and human factor engineering), to the user experience design (UX). This is the methodology that best responds to the current requirements of the M&S systems of the CAF training, which today incorporate, through a real and virtual operational hybridization, the pilot's tactical-operational behaviour in advanced air operations that reproduce circumstances of extreme hostility and lethality.

There is a strategic development vector to promote an integrated training solution by applying the latest digital technologies, with advanced equipment, developing new training concepts for combat pilots and contributing to the improvement of offensive and defensive operational air capabilities.

For this purpose, it is necessary to develop a LVC-IA integrated organizational archi-tecture, based in solid conceptual models that guarantee the levels of integration, inter-operability and composability, allowing a closer interaction between military operations and all the organisms present in the defence systems. These M&S environments should be built with a scalable concept based on linkable components that interoperate in that integrated architecture.

The continuous digital transformation of the simulation platforms implies a com-plete organizational, cultural and strategic reinvention, which in the defence sector affects both the military structures and the companies that participate in it. The corresponding strategic development requires the M&S activities to evolve rapidly, to create an opera-tionally valid LVC environment, which, beyond serving the training processes, facilitate the development of doctrines and tactics, the formulation of operational plans and the evaluation of war situations. Thus promoting an interaction approach between opera-tional commands, logistics and acquisition communities, and the industry responsible for the research and development processes of new aerospace weapons systems. These new M&S environments should be built from linkable components that interoperate in an integrated architecture, facilitating flexibility and the rapid capacity to generate innovations.

In this strategic development of M&S systems for CAF, it is necessary to propose new functionalities even beyond the training systems. Two of them have been proposed. The first one, in the case of obtaining, applying and managing logistic support intelligence related to the simulated effort of simulated hostile flight operations and adverse weather conditions. Secondly, in the case of the transformation of the LVC simulation platform into a real cockpit environment on the ground, turning the fighter plane into a remote pilot plane (RPA) capable of operating alternately in a conventional or remote way.

## References

1. Mayer, R.E.: Thirty years of research on online learning. Appl. Cognit. Psychol. **33**(2), 152–159 (2019)

2. Rodríguez, M.: La teoría del aprendizaje significativo: una revisión aplicable a la escuela actual. Revista Electrónica de Investigación e Innovación Educativa y Socioeducativa, Universitat de les Illes Balears, Spain, **3**(1) (2011)
3. González, C.S., Blanco, F.: Emociones con videojuegos: Incrementando la motivación para el aprendizaje. Videojuegos: una herramienta educativa del "homo digitalis". Revista Electrónica Teoría de la Educación: Educación y Cultura en la Sociedad de la Información, Universidad de Salamanca Spain, **9**(3) (2008)
4. Gómez, M.A., Gómez, P.P., González, P.A.: Aprendizaje Activo en Simulaciones Interactivas. Inteligencia Artificial. Revista Iberoamericana de Inteligencia Artificial, Asociación Española para la Inteligencia Artificial, Valencia, España (2007)
5. Contreras, G.A., García, R., Ramírez, M.S.: Uso de simuladores como recurso digital para la transferencia de conocimiento. Apertura, Revista innovación educativa, Universidad de Guadalajara, México, **2**(1), April 2010
6. Mason, G.S., Shuman, T.R., Cook, K.E.: Comparing the effectiveness of an inverted classroom to a traditional classroom in an upper-division engineering course. IEEE Trans. Educ. **56**(4), 430–435 (2013)
7. Ramírez, D., Macías, M.: Solving material balance problems at unsteady state using a remote laboratory in classroom. In: 120th ASEE Annual Conference & Education. American Society for Engineering Education, Atlanta (2013)
8. Santos, M.E., León, M.: El internet como herramienta de investigación en el Aprendizaje Significativo. Revista Internacional en Educación en Ingeniería **4**(1), 16–23 (2011)
9. Ramírez, R.: Capacitación con simuladores de vuelo para pilotos de la fuerza aérea en un ambiente de aprendizaje combinado. Tesis para obtener el grado de: Maestría en Tecnología Educativa, Tecnológico de Monterrey, México (2016)
10. Prats, M.: Prácticas docentes con simuladores de vuelo. A: II Jornadas de Innovación universitaria: el reto de la convergencia europea. Universidad Europea de Madrid, Madrid, Spain (2005)
11. Villacís, C., et al.: Mathematical models applied in the design of a flight simulator for military training. In: Rocha, Á., Guarda, T. (eds.) MICRADS 2018. SIST, vol. 94, pp. 43–57. Springer, Cham (2018). https://doi.org/10.1007/978-3-319-78605-6_4
12. Ejército del Aire de España: Combate aéreo simulado. Revista Española de Defensa N° 283, Ministerio de Defensa de España, Madrid, Spain, April 2012
13. Preámbulo de Editorial sobre Sistemas de Simulación: Simulación: la realidad más barata. Revista Española de Defensa N° 283, Ministerio de Defensa de España, Madrid, Spain, April 2012
14. Kasim, B., et al.: Modeling and simulation as a service for joint military space operations simulation. J. Def. Model. Simul. Appl. Methodol. Technol. (2019). https://doi.org/10.1177/1548512919882499. SAGE
15. Freeman, J., Zachary, W.: Intelligent tutoring for team training: lessons learned from US military research. In: Johnston, J. (ed.) Building Intelligent Tutoring Systems for Teams (Research on Managing Groups and Teams), vol. 19. Emerald Publishing Limited, Bingley (2018)
16. Aronsson, S., et al.: Supporting after action review in simulator mission training: co-creating visualization concepts for training of fast-jet fighter pilots. J. Def. Model. Simul. Appl. Methodol. Technol. **16**, 219–231 (2019)
17. Källström, J., Heintz, F.: Multi-agent multi-objective deep reinforcement learning for efficient and effective pilot training. In: Proceedings of the 10th Aerospace Technology Congress, Stockholm, Sweden, 8–9 October 2019
18. Hill, R.R., et al.: Open challenges in building combat simulation systems to support test, analysis and training. In: Proceedings of the 2018 Winter Simulation Conference, Gothenburg, Sweden, 09–12 December 2018

19. Martín, M.A.: Introducción del Dossier Simulación. Revista de Aeronáutica y Astronáutica, N° 843, Ejército del Aire de España, Madrid, Spain, May 2015
20. Saldaña, J.D.: La simulación de caza: El Eurofighter y el ASTA. Revista de Aeronáutica y Astronáutica N° 843, Ejército del Aire de España, Madrid, Spain, May 2015
21. Saldaña, J.D.: Reflexiones del entrenamiento en simulador. Revista de Aeronáutica y Astronáutica N° 843, Ejército del Aire de España, Madrid, Spain, May 2015
22. García-Mecerreyes, S.: Contribución de la psicología aeronáutica aplicada al ASTA. Revista de Aeronáutica y Astronáutica N° 843, Ejército del Aire de España, Madrid, Spain, May 2015
23. Human-Computer Interaction (HCI): Interaction Design Foundation. https://www.interaction-design.org/literature/topics/human-computer-interaction/. Accessed 06 Oct 2019
24. Liu, C., et al.: Considerations on multimodal human-computer interaction. In: Proceedings of the 5th IEEE International Conference on Cloud Computing and Intelligence Systems (CCIS), Nanjing, China (2018)
25. Chapter 2: Human-Computer Interaction. ACM SIGCHI - Resources HCI Bibliography. http://www.acm.org/sigchi/cdg/cdg2.html/. Accessed 06 Oct 2019
26. Benyon, D.: Designing User Experience: A Guide to HCI, UX and Interaction Design, 4th edn. Pearson, London (2019)
27. The Disciplines of User Experience Design. Made by envis precisely GmbH 2009, Redesign 2013. https://visual.ly/community/infographic/computers/disciplines-user-experience-design. Accessed 31 January 2020
28. User Experience (UX) Design. Interaction Design Foundation. https://wwwinteraction-design.org/literature/topics/topics/ux-design/. Accessed 06 Oct 2019
29. Miller, B.W., Lin, S.W.: Industrial internet: towards interoperability and composability. IIC J. Innov. Ind. Internet Consort. (2016). https://www.iiconsortium.org/news/joi-articles/2016-June-Industrial-Internet-Towards-Interoperability-and-Composability.pdf. 2nd Ed. June 2016
30. Taylor, S.J.E., et al.: Grand challenges for modeling and simulation: simulation everywhere - from cyberinfrastructure to clouds to citizens. Simulation **91**(7), 648–665 (2015)
31. Woong, T., Kim, K., Rabelo, L., Lee, G.: An agile roadmap for live, virtual and constructive-integrating training architecture (LVC-ITA): a case study using a component based integrated simulation engine (AddSIM). In: Proceedings of the MODSIM World Conference (2015)
32. Zeigler, B.P., Seo, C.H.: DEVS namespace for interoperable DEVS/SOA. In: Rossetti, M.D., Hill, R.R., Johansson, B., Dunkin, A., Ingalls, R.G. (eds.) Proceedings of the 2009 Winter Simulation Conference (2009)
33. Zeigler, B.P., Kim, T.G., Praehofer, H.: Theory of Modeling and Simulation: Integrating Discrete Event and Continuous Complex Dynamic Systems, 2nd edn. Academic Press, New York (2000)
34. Pope, T.M.: A cost-benefit analysis of pilot training next. Thesis for Degree of Master of Science in Logistics & Supply Chain Management, Air Force Institute of Technology USAF Air University, March 2019
35. Live, virtual, and constructive. In: Wikipedia, The Free Encyclopedia (n.d). https://en.wikipedia.org/wiki/Live,_virtual,_and_constructive. Accessed 31 Jan 2020

# Performance Evaluation of AMQP and CoAP for Low-Cost Automation

Gustavo Caiza[1], Carlos S. Leon[2], Luis A. Campana[2],
Carlos A. Garcia[2], and Marcelo V. Garcia[2,3(✉)]

[1] Universidad Politecnica Salesiana, UPS, 170146 Quito, Ecuador
gcaiza@ups.edu.ec
[2] Universidad Tecnica de Ambato, UTA, 180103 Ambato, Ecuador
{cleon9397,la.campana,ca.garcia,mv.garcia}@uta.edu.ec
[3] University of Basque Country, UPV/EHU, 48013 Bilbao, Spain
mgarcia294@ehu.eus

**Abstract.** A lot of communication protocols have been developed to support the efficient communication of the Industrial Internet of Things (IIoT) devices. These kinds of applications are intended to run with constrained resources. However, the selection of a standard and effective industrial messaging protocol is a challenging task for any shop floor integration because it depends on the nature of the IoT system and its messaging requirements. In this paper, two IoT protocols like Advanced Message Queuing Protocol (AMQP) and Constrained Application Protocol (CoAP) are compared using a low-cost hardware device for factory integration. The results show that the CoAP protocol is designed to be so small that it fits inside a microcontroller, but it can be fully applied in cyber-physical environments, in another aspect the AMQP protocol is more complex, there is no official support and you need bigger installation packages; but it provides a higher communication speed.

**Keywords:** AMQP · CoAP · Industrial Internet of Things (IIoT) · Low-cost automation

## 1 Introduction

The relationship between the IoT and computer technologies in the cloud allow effective decision making to improve the productive capacity of a factory. This improvement in the industry is called the fourth industrial revolution or Industry 4.0, which brings new capabilities in the environment [2, 4].

Industrial Internet of Things (IIoT) can be considered as the connection of industrial machine sensors and actuators to the Internet that can independently generate value [12]. IIoT protocols are used to develop Machine-to-Machine communication (M2M). One of the major factors that determine the performance of this M2M communication is the messaging protocol specially designed for M2M communications within the IoT applications. The selection of a communication standard and an optimized messaging protocol is a challenging task for

© Springer Nature Switzerland AG 2020
M. Botto-Tobar et al. (Eds.): ICAT 2019, CCIS 1193, pp. 340–353, 2020.
https://doi.org/10.1007/978-3-030-42517-3_26

any shop-floor integration. While selecting an appropriate messaging protocol for IoT systems, the pre-requisite is a better understanding of a target IoT system and its message/data sharing requirements [9].

Besides, IIoT applications that require a large network traffic, and consequently a greater bandwidth, would incur greater expenses to maintain the operation of the network infrastructure. Similarly, applications that generate a large amount of data require investments in computational resources (storage) proportional to the generated data [3]. Contrasted to the web systems, which use a single standard messaging protocol like HTTP. IIoT cannot rely on a single protocol for all its needs [5]. Consequently, hundreds of messaging protocols are available to choose for various types of requirements of the IoT system.

The aim of this research work is to evaluate and compared the use of two conventional communication protocols of IoT, AMQP, and CoAP, within an automated system. The main characteristics of this system are the requirement of real-time data transmission between the devices, as well as a diverse number of messages, due to the fact that the system consists of a sensor that partially sends the signal to activate the operation of the robotic manipulator arm (Scorbot). It should be noted that there is no intention of establishing which protocol is better than the other because the ideal protocol depends on the type of automation application being carried out. The aim is to capture the behavior of both protocols in the same automation environment [6, 7].

This document is organized as follows: In Sect. 2 is analyzed related works where the performance of the AMQP and CoAP protocols is evaluated and their contributions to research are highlighted. It describes the environment and the different work devices that are used in the implementation of both protocols. Section 3 shows the state of the art in the work, as well as the automation environment in which the protocols will be used. In Sect. 4, the case study and the automation environment in which the work is developed are presented. In Sect. 5 the results obtained from the research are discussed. Finally, in Sect. 6 conclusions of the project are established.

## 2  Related Work

In the following investigations and works carried out with the communication protocol CoAP and AMQP, the usefulness and versatility provided by these protocols are analyzed, as well as the applications and uses that have been developed by them.

The research developed by Alvear et al. [1] relates the IoT technology with artificial vision concepts in which it is intended to obtain data in real-time and at the same time remotely, which will be stored in databases. The authors denote that the collected data will be used to carry out statistical and probability studies in certain areas based on the activities or characteristics of people in environments or environments where the application of electronic systems is possible, either to improve processes or identify weak points them. This whole process started with the analysis of image processing and the capture of videos to be used in an algorithm focused on IOT, for this reason the authors address the application of the CoAP protocol, because it is a specialized protocol for data transfer. To be able to directly relate to HTTP and at the same time integrate into the Web.

In the study conducted by Naik [16] a comparison of IoT protocols is made, with communication standardization as a priority and, as an important factor, real-time transmission and transfer of data that are important aspects in IoT applications. The author mentions that the choice of a standard communication protocol that is also effective is a work that deserves considerable study because of the nature of the system to be implemented as well as the communication requirements that must be generated. The scientific article mentions an evaluation of communication protocols such as CoAP and AMQP used in IoT systems, to identify their strengths and limitations.

On the one hand, the author mentions that the communication systems that use the AMQP protocol are binary systems that generally use 8-byte headers with small or small messages, in addition that this protocol uses TCP as the default transport protocol and TLS/SSL and SASL for security. Similarly, the author mentions characteristics of the CoAP protocol that, unlike AMQP, uses fixed 4-byte headers with small messages and uses UDP as the transport protocol and DTLS for its security. An important point that the author considers is that these messaging protocols with the passage of time have been evolving according to the processes or needs that must cover, so it could be considered, devices, resources and the specific applications of IoT in which they will be employees [16].

On the other hand, a comparison made by the author refers to M2M/IoT compared to standardization, speaking of AMQP this study is successful worldwide and adopted the international standard ISO/IEC 19464: 2014 is currently used in projects of great importance as Nebula Cloud Computing from NASA and Indias Aadhar Project, however CoAP has not been left behind and in recent years has gained momentum and has been employed by large companies such as Cisco, Contiki, Erika and IoTivity in addition to having a specialized IETF standard to integrate IoT and the Web thanks to Eclipse Foundation. And when talking about security, AMQP presents a high level of security while CoAP uses DTLS and Ipsec useful tools for integrity, authentication and encryption [7].

Fernades [15] mentions that there are certain problems when talking about services or communications because a lot of data is commonly sent to databases and the agglomeration of data can affect the performance of the systems significantly; AMQP is a protocol that appears to address this problem and solve it. The study that the authors propose is the analysis of message exchange in a certain time, observing that when there is a high volume of message exchange the most favorable results are generated by AMQP because it can be connected with different applications and different platforms. In this analysis we use the AMQP protocol and the storage of data in a relational database created in MySQL, the exchange of data between clients and servers determined that when exchanging data in bulk the number of messages that can be sent per second it reduces with what causes a high consumption of resources and as a solution to this problem the AMQP is used.

As mentioned previously there are studies that to compared protocols IoT and certain characteristics presented by these protocols, varying according to the application or analysis that have been focused, is why the aim of this work is a comparison between CoAP and AMQP protocol as a way to help when making IoT systems and adopt the most appropriate protocol according to the requirements they must fulfill.

## 3   State of Art

### 3.1   Internet of Things

The IoT is based on three main foundations related to the capacity of objects that must have communication capabilities, computational capacity and may have interaction capacity [13]. It is called communication capacity because the IoT objects must have a minimum set of communication capacity. What we mean by this is not only a channel of communication, but also everything related to it, in order to make an efficient communication, such as an address, identifier and name. The objects can have all these characteristics or some of them [19]. The objects must have a basic or complex computational capacity to process data and network configurations. For example, receiving commands on the communications channel, administering network tasks, saving the status of a sensor, activating an effect, receiving signals and managing and controlling data.

### 3.2   CoAP (Restricted Application Protocol)

The CoAP communication protocol is used to communicate simple and inexpensive electronic devices such as PLC'S, RaspBerry and low power sensors. This protocol is a derivation of the HTTP protocol, but it is added several requirements such as multicast, overhead and simplicity, which are very important for the Internet of Things (IoT), reason why the protocol is applicable to develop the connectivity of intelligent objects using the Internet [6,12]. See Fig. 1.

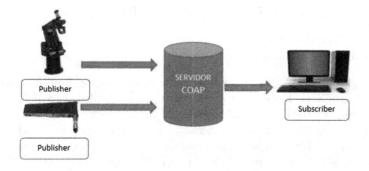

**Fig. 1.** CoAP architecture

It is a specialized protocol for the use of limited and limited low power wireless nodes that can communicate interactively through the internet, its client/server interaction model is similar to that of HTTP with the difference that CoAP performs these interactions (exchanges of messages) asynchronously by means of the UDP transport protocol [7].

### 3.3 AMQP (Advanced Message Queue Protocol)

The Advanced Message Queuing Protocol is also a publication/subscription protocol based on a reliable message queue. It has been commonly used in the financial sector. This community uses services such as commerce and banking systems that often require extremely high levels of performance, scalability, reliability and manageability [17]. AMQP uses TCP as its main transport protocol for the exchange of messages. Application level messages have a header to route them to the respective queue (see Fig. 2). The AMQP architecture is composed of two main components: Queues and Exchanges [17,18].

Queues represent the main concept of AMQP. All messages end in a queue that stores them before forwarding them to recipients. These queues can be organized by service levels with respect to implementation performance characteristics such as latency and availability [19].

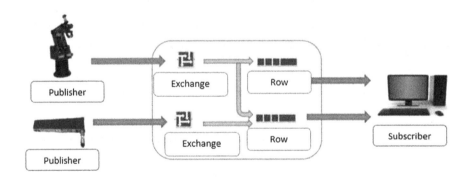

**Fig. 2.** Architecture AMQP

### 3.4 RabbitMQ Broker

Both AMQP and MQTT are communication protocols based on intermediaries. As discussed in Sect. 2, they contain a central entity, called an agent, in charge of managing peer-to-peer communication in the network. In this work, we use RabbitMQ, a popular open source message agent. RabbitMQ is an Erlang based technology that allows asynchronous communication between devices. Initially, it was developed to implement AMQP and then to support MQTT [12].

The exchanges distribute the messages to the respective queues according to the predefined rules. As a new message arrives at the intermediary, the exchange evaluates the message and stores it in a queue, ready to be forwarded. Figure 2 represents the main messaging process in an environment based on AMQP. First, editors who want to send messages to potential subscribers, send them to a broker. The intermediary has exchanges and queues. As mentioned above, the exchanges receive the messages and forward them to the respective queues. In turn, the queues send these messages to the clients that previously subscribed to the given queue [11].

## 3.5 Raspberry Pi 3

It is a low cost hardware platform that includes all the elements offered by a computer. Nowadays it has acquired great importance in the market due to its diversity of options for projects in computer networks, electronic circuits, robotics, domotics, security, programming, among other technological areas. Even some authors like Saari et al. [10] have used the Raspberry Pi as a solution for the Internet of Things (IoT).

The most current model of Raspberry Pi 3 is B, which has a storage unit with MicroSD Card Slot and is equipped with 35000 packages and pre-compiled programs in a format that facilitates installation. In addition, despite being adapted to the perfection of the board, it is not an operating system affiliated with the Raspberry Pi foundation [7, 14].

# 4 Case Study

The aim of this research work is to communicate a factory process made by a ScorBot ER-4U robot arm and a conveyor belt to control a palletizing process. In order to get the industrial information and compared IIoT protocols characteristics the control of industrial devices is made re-using a PLC industrial architecture. The PLC selected is an S7-1200. The ScorBot ER-4U robot arm is controlled by a PLC1 this PLC sends commands to the USB Controller that provides advanced control features for the ScorBot ER-4U robotic arm. The conveyor belt is controlled by a PLC2 that controls the electric motor to move pieces from a deposit to the robotic arm. The synchronization of the process is made by PLC1, this PLC sends commands to run or stop the conveyor. To read PLCs memories Raspberry Pi boards use the Snap7 library.

To implement the stack of AMQP and CoAP protocols the authors of this paper use low-cost boards like Raspberry Pi. The first Raspberry PI is used as a server (AMQP publisher or CoAP server) that sends information to all clients. The second one is used as the client (AMQP consumer or CoAP client) to integrate the information of the conveyor belt. Furthermore, a web client is developed to monitor the operation of the palletizing process.

The communication of all the components is given with a data transmission speed of 10 Mbps to have a minimum error rate in the communication, managing the processes in real-time and monitoring. Figure 3 presents the structure of the proposed communication architecture.

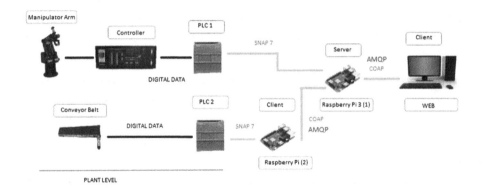

**Fig. 3.** Case study hardware architecture platform

### 4.1 SNAP 7 Implementation

Applying the Snap 7 (C++) library, it is intended to get data from the S7-1200 PLCs through the reading of the internal databases of the PLC using the Raspberry Pi 3. This library uses the Communication interface. S7 Siemens Ethernet for reading and writing PLC data (inputs, outputs, memories, timers, counters) and has three independent components: client, server and partner.

All Snap7 functions completely hide this concept, the data that a system can transfer in a single call depends only on the size of the available data. The Snap 7 stack library provides two main functions: Cli_FullUpload() to upload a full block from the PLC CPU and Cli_Upload() to upload only data from a data block, depending on the need of the software. These functions are asynchronous and executed in the same thread of the caller, i.e. it exists only when its job is complete. These functions consist of two parts, the first, executed in the same thread of the caller, which prepares the data (if any), triggers the second part and exits immediately. The second one is executed in a separate thread and performs the body of the job requested, simultaneously to the execution of the caller program. See Fig. 4.

The advantages of using the Snap7 library are many, because it is written in C++, reading data from Ethernet compatible PLCs, as long as the requests to Ethernet are not restricted. In the work done, the data is written and read through bytes, but you can use variables of type: Word, Double Word and Real used extensively in the programming of the Siemens language [8].

### 4.2 CoAP Protocol Implementation

The implementation of CoAP is based on libcoap library, an opensource C-library that is specifically targeted at low-cost embedded systems with constrained resources. This library provided support for the current working group drafts of CoAP as well as its optional extensions for block-wise transfer, resource observation.

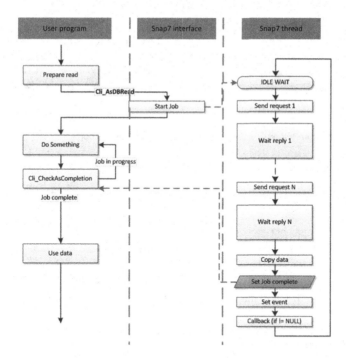

**Fig. 4.** Sanp7 communication function model

The library provides functions and data structures for parsing and in-place editing of CoAP protocol data units (PDUs) to minimize memory overhead in embedded systems. An additional application server and a multi-purpose command-line client built upon this library demonstrate the use of the API in stand-alone CoAP-enabled applications.

LibCoAP is compiled in Debian kernel into Raspberry Pi. The architecture of the software algorithm is described as follows: (i) When the client is initialized the CoAP-client class starts, this client has GET or PUT methods. The GET method is used to retrieve resources from PLCs. The resource is identified by the requested Uniform Resource Identifier (URI). The PUT method is used to modify an existing resource on PLC. CoAP uses the datagram-oriented UDP transport protocol to exchange messages.

(ii) When a request arrives at a resource from the client, the module of the server Server.on takes care of it according to what type of information requirement is, for example, the GET method receives information of the I0.5 input of the selected device, while the PUT method writes the value of each input and output of the PLC in which it is being executed. See Fig. 5.

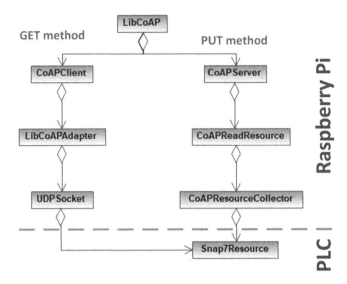

**Fig. 5.** Class diagram for CoAP PUT and GET methods

### 4.3 AMQP Implementation

The second protocol implemented in the low-cost hardware is AMQP. For this communication, rabbitMQ library was used. The RabbitMQ implementation of a sample dev/test event bus is boilerplate code. This library is a message-queueing software also known as a message broker or queue manager. The queue-manager software stores the messages until a receiving application connects and takes a message off the queue. The receiving application then processes the message.

The AMQP producer queueing up new messages of Snap7 library The consumer takes a message off the queue and starts processing the shop-floor information. Messages with shop-floor information are not published directly to a queue; instead, the producer sends messages to an exchange. An exchange is responsible for routing the messages to different queues.

The Message flow for AMQP protocol developed into low-cost hardware is as follows (see Fig. 6): (1) The producer publishes a message with ScorBot ER-4U robot arm to an exchange. (2) The exchange receives the message and is now responsible for routing the message. The exchange takes different message attributes into account, such as the routing key, depending on the exchange type. (3) Bindings must be created from the exchange to queues. In this case, there are two bindings to two different queues from the exchange. The exchange routes the message into the queues depending on message attributes. (4) The messages stay in the queue until they are handled by a consumer (conveyor device). The consumer handles the message.

The Listing 1.1 shows the function that sends the PLC states in AMQP, besides the String that stores the message, a simple message is created so that

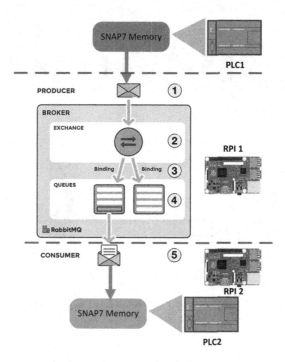

**Fig. 6.** Message flow for AMQP protocol

AMQP can send it. The created message is published to the corresponding device, which is PLC1 or PLC2.

```
void publishstatesPLC(string ipserver, string plc, string io,
    int number, bool data){
    message = "{\"protocol\": \"AMQP\", \"";
    AmqpClient::BasicMessage::ptr_t msg = AmqpClient::
    BasicMessage::Create(mensaje);
    connection->BasicPublish("", plc, msg);
}
```

**Listing 1.1.** Sending PLC states using AMQP protocol

# 5  Results Discussion

In the present study, different tests have been performed to compare both protocols and define in which situations they behave better. The first test is about the execution time introducing different bandwidths (5, 2.5, 1 Mbit), latencies (0, 5, 10 ms) and lost packet rates (0, 2.5 Y5)%, it should be noted that the tests were measured in seconds. Figure 7 shows a uniform behavior over time, with a variation between tests no greater than 7% the time. See Fig. 7(a).

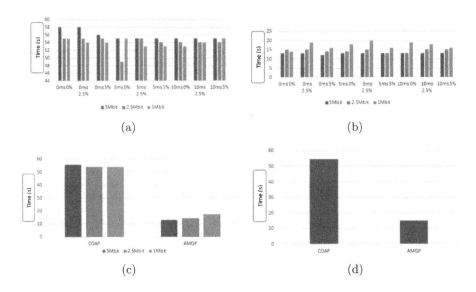

**Fig. 7.** Comparison of AMQ and CoAP protocols. (a) CoAP protocol execution time. (b) Execution time AMQP protocol. (c) Execution time per bandwidth. (d) Average execution times

As the main reason to be implemented the CoAP protocol is to run on hardware and minimal infrastructure, the execution time is clearly greater than AMQP due to the implementation problems required by this library. In the case of the AMQP protocol, the speed of execution is unparalleled, with an average of 0.09 s being much faster than CoAP, under normal conditions the protocol is optimal. The problem arises when the network conditions are less favorable, it shows a 17% variability with respect to the average. See Fig. 7(b).

Regarding the execution time, it can be noted that the AMQP protocol significantly exceeds the CoAP protocol with an average of 0.09 s under normal conditions, given the implementation problems required by the CoAP library. See Fig. 7(c). About the variability presented by the protocols, it can be noted that the CoAP protocol being restricted remains constant over time (variability of 1%), while AMQP suffers when the network conditions are not optimal (variability up to 30%). Figure 7(d) shows that AMQP is superior to CoAP.

In the 200 samples that were taken from the Scorbot Robot, it demonstrates a speed of 380% with respect to the process by CoAP. Throughput performance graphs, as they are done in a controlled and noise-free environment, have similar characteristics, so if you want to obtain a successful transfer of packets, both protocols fulfill their purpose. Due to the lack of compatibility, AMQP would not be compatible with small devices. In contrast, AMQP has reception feedback, so if it is implemented in the code, the rate of lost packets is zero in critical processes. See Fig. 8.

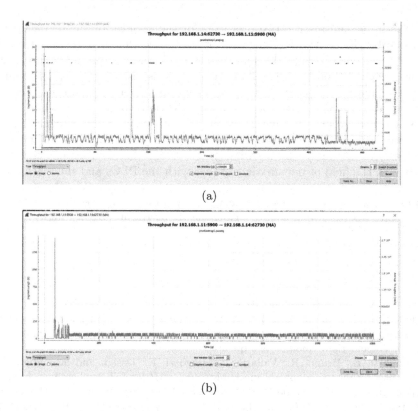

(a)

(b)

**Fig. 8.** AMQ and CoAP protocols performance. (a) CoAP protocol performance. (b) AMQP protocol performance.

## 6 Conclusion and Future Work

In the present work presents a study in order to make a comparison between two IoT communication protocols; AMQP and CoAP, due to the constant revolution in the industry and the implementation of Process Automation, where the Industrial Internet of Things (IoT) has been inserted as part of Industry 4.0, its development is on track.

In this way, the authors have developed research with the purpose of comparing both protocols and to give a verdict of which one is the most convenient in different types of scenarios, measuring the total time of the process (TPT) in the same conditions and for each protocol, for the analysis of AMQP the data is stored in MySQL, we have found that AMQP was faster than CoAP with an average of 0.09 s in normal conditions, however CoAP does not stay behind, since it does not require a broker and in the analysis of the variation in bandwidth, being a restricted protocol, it remains constant over time, for the case of AMQP, it presents variation is when the network conditions are not optimal.

When implementing the two protocols for the application of the palletizing of the Scorbot Er-4u Manipulator Arm, it was noted that AMQP is superior to the CoAP protocol in the 200 samples taken, showing a 380% higher benefit. However, each IoT protocol has its own characteristics, so each one of them in different scenarios can be of vital importance in terms of communication and in different cases, the CoAP protocol would be the best option.

As a future work, we have proposed to implement as an application the analysis of the FESTO parts sorting station with IoT protocols, since it makes use of sensors and actuators allowing us to change the environment and open ourselves to the field of pneumatic together with the PLCs and the mechanics.

**Acknowledgment.** This work was financed by Universidad Técnica de Ambato (UTA) and their Research and Development Department (DIDE) under project CONIN-P-256-2019.

# References

1. Alvear, V.: Internet de las cosas y visión artificial, funcionamiento y aplicaciones: revisión de literatura (Internet of Things and artificial vision, performance and applications: literature review). Enfoque UTE **8**(1), 244–256 (2017). http://ingenieria.ute.edu.ec/enfoqueute/
2. Ancillotti, E., Bruno, R., Vallati, C., Mingozzi, E.: Design and evaluation of a rate-based congestion control mechanism in CoAP for IoT applications. In: 19th IEEE International Symposium on a World of Wireless, Mobile and Multimedia Networks, WoWMoM 2018, pp. 14–15 (2018). https://doi.org/10.1109/WoWMoM. 2018.8449736
3. Andrade, L., Serrano, M., Prazeres, C.: The data interplay for the fog of things: a transition to edge computing with IoT. In: 2018 IEEE International Conference on Communications (ICC), pp. 1–7 (May 2018). https://doi.org/10.1109/ICC.2018. 8423006
4. Bahashwan, A.A.O., Manickam, S.: A brief review of messaging protocol standards for Internet of Things (IoT). J. Cyber Secur. Mobil. **8**(1), 1–14 (2018). https:// doi.org/10.13052/jcsm2245-1439.811
5. Batista, E., Andrade, L., Dias, R., Andrade, A., Figueiredo, G., Prazeres, C.: Characterization and modeling of IoT data traffic in the fog of things paradigm. In: 2018 IEEE 17th International Symposium on Network Computing and Applications (NCA), pp. 1–8 (November 2018). https://doi.org/10.1109/NCA.2018.8548340
6. Bhatia, R., et al.: Massive machine type communications over 5G using lean protocols and edge proxies. In: IEEE 5G World Forum, 5GWF 2018 - Conference Proceedings, pp. 462–467 (2018). https://doi.org/10.1109/5GWF.2018.8517086
7. Bolettieri, S., Tanganelli, G., Vallati, C., Mingozzi, E.: pCoCoA: a precise congestion control algorithm for CoAP. Ad Hoc Netw. **80**, 116–129 (2018). https://doi. org/10.1016/j.adhoc.2018.06.015
8. Din, S., Paul, A., Hong, W.H., Seo, H.: Constrained application for mobility management using embedded devices in the Internet of Things based urban planning in smart cities. Sustain. Cities Soc. **44**, 144–151 (2019). https://doi.org/10.1016/ j.scs.2018.07.017

9. Gohar, M., Choi, J.G., Koh, S.J.: CoAP-based group mobility management protocol for the Internet-of-Things in WBAN environment. Future Gener. Comput. Syst. **88**, 309–318 (2018). https://doi.org/10.1016/j.future.2018.06.003

10. Granjal, J., Silva, J.M., Lourenço, N.: Intrusion detection and prevention in CoAP wireless sensor networks using anomaly detection. Sensors **18**(8), 2445 (2018). https://doi.org/10.3390/s18082445. (Switzerland)

11. Halabi, D., Hamdan, S., Almajali, S.: Enhance the security in smart home applications based on IOT-CoAP protocol. In: 6th International Conference on Digital Information, Networking, and Wireless Communications, DINWC 2018, pp. 81–85 (2018). https://doi.org/10.1109/DINWC.2018.8357000

12. Kumar, A., Mozar, S. (eds.): ICCCE 2018. LNEE, vol. 500. Springer, Singapore (2019). https://doi.org/10.1007/978-981-13-0212-1

13. Herrero, R.: Dynamic CoAP mode control in real time wireless IoT networks. IEEE Internet Things J. **6**(1), 801–807 (2019). https://doi.org/10.1109/JIOT.2018.2857701

14. Iglesias-Urkia, M., Orive, A., Urbieta, A., Casado-Mansilla, D.: Analysis of CoAP implementations for industrial Internet of Things: a survey. J. Ambient Intell. Humaniz. Comput. **00**(2016), 1–14 (2018). https://doi.org/10.1007/s12652-018-0729-z

15. Fernandes, J.L., Lopes, I.C., Rodrigues, J.J.P.C., Ullah, S.: Performance evaluation of RESTful web services and AMQP protocol. In: 2013 Fifth International Conference on Ubiquitous and Future Networks (ICUFN), Da Nang, pp. 810–815 (2013). https://doi.org/10.1109/ICUFN.2013.6614932

16. Naik, N.: Choice of effective messaging protocols for IoT systems: MQTT, CoAP, AMQP and HTTP. In: 2017 IEEE International Symposium on Systems Engineering, ISSE 2017 - Proceedings (2017). https://doi.org/10.1109/SysEng.2017.8088251

17. Rathod, D., Patil, S.: Security analysis of constrained application protocol (CoAP): IoT protocol. Int. J. Adv. Stud. Comput. Sci. Eng. **6**(8), 37–41 (2017). https://search.proquest.com/docview/1947842952?accountid=17242

18. Talaminos-Barroso, A., Estudillo-Valderrama, M.A., Roa, L.M., Reina-Tosina, J., Ortega-Ruiz, F.: A Machine-to-Machine protocol benchmark for eHealth applications - use case: respiratory rehabilitation. Comput. Methods Programs Biomed. **129**, 1–11 (2016). https://doi.org/10.1016/j.cmpb.2016.03.004

19. Vallati, C., Righetti, F., Tanganelli, G., Mingozzi, E., Anastasi, G.: ECOAP: experimental assessment of congestion control strategies for CoAP using the wishful platform. In: Proceedings - 2018 IEEE International Conference on Smart Computing, SMARTCOMP 2018, pp. 423–428 (2018). https://doi.org/10.1109/SMARTCOMP.2018.00040

# Application of Reverse Engineering in the Manufacture of Prototypes of Mechanical Parts

Carlos A. Villarreal B.$^{(\boxtimes)}$, Fausto E. Tapia G.$^{(\boxtimes)}$, and Victor M. Cardenas$^{(\boxtimes)}$

Northern Technical University, 17 de Julio Avenue 5-21, Ibarra, Ecuador
{cavillarreal,fetapia,vmcardenas}@utn.edu.ec

**Abstract.** This paper presents the study of reverse engineering and three-dimensional printing as an alternative in the design of automotive parts, taking as a case study the distribution cover of the 2015 Chevrolet Spark car. For this, a 3D scanner "Scanner Handy" was used Scan" to capture the shape and characteristics of the distribution cover, and obtain a three-dimensional mesh (point cloud) for analysis, which is processed by using the "Geomagic Desing" software to obtain the three-dimensional CAD model; This model is imported into Siemens NX software to make dimensional adjustments through a comparative analysis between the constructed CAD model and the copied element, to perform prototyping by 3D printing. Finally, as a result, a prototype of the Spark 2015 distribution cover is obtained with the respective valuation of its mechanical properties, and an analysis of the degree of feasibility of this manufacturing process in the manufacture of automotive parts by means of 3D printing "FDM".

**Keywords:** Reverse engineering · 3D printing "FDM" · Three-dimensional digitization

## 1 Introduction

The conceptual design of a car has been changing based on technology, customer needs, safety, and resource optimization; which have allowed design engineering to start applying certain changes in their geometry according to their interior and exterior appearance. In past decades the doors of the cars were more robust, with upholstery and appearance that today have been modified through the use of new materials, manufacturing systems and design [1], which from the creation of modelling programs and Computer-aided design, they were revolutionizing, achieving models with more cosy and comfortable geometries according to user comfort.

Currently there are many drawing software that have engineering tools for design and simulation (CAE), which allow this type of analysis, such as: Inventor, Solid Works, NX, ANSYS, among others. The accuracy and veracity of their results depend on many factors, therefore, it is the responsibility of the engineer to properly use these design tools in solving problems and implementing applications in the field of engineering [2], which are very important in the technological development of the automotive company to meet customer demand.

© Springer Nature Switzerland AG 2020
M. Botto-Tobar et al. (Eds.): ICAT 2019, CCIS 1193, pp. 354–368, 2020.
https://doi.org/10.1007/978-3-030-42517-3_27

However, when you need to make designs from an existing product or system, direct engineering is not always the solution, since it is necessary to investigate its manufacturing and the engineering fundamentals applied in its creation, therefore, reverse engineering. It is a very important alternative that has allowed the reproduction of machine elements quickly and efficiently, allowing the acquisition of data in the reconstruction of models at the level of design and architecture, the quality control of the product while maintaining the traceability of its elements, code reuse and unauthorized cloning control [3]. Reverse engineering also allows you to investigate, create and innovate the manufacture of mechanical elements from elements previously designed and manufactured in the different fields of your application, becoming a very important design process in which you can use several methods to carry carried out an experimental procedure [4]. This methodology is applied in the industrial sector for the design and manufacture of new products, copies or replicas of models, dimensional inspection of mechanical elements subject to wear [5]; the measurement of displacements, deformations and stress analysis in the characterization of materials, vibration analysis, quality control, advanced engineering, art and restoration applications, etc. [6, 7].

At present, there are some optical metrology application techniques that offer a solution to these needs, since they allow a 3D digital survey of the topography and contour of the surface of the object by laser scanning [8]. Thus, Gopinath Chintala and Prasad Gudimetla investigate the application of 3D laser scanning, and their mesh processing using Ansys and Solid Works software in the design of a turbine blade in order to perform an analysis of efforts and displacements to optimize the material to be used in its manufacture [9], reverse engineering has also been applied in the modelling and redesign of cutting tools by using the 3D scanner "Structured Light Scanner" and different techniques of Additive Manufacturing, Fused Deposition Modelling (FDM), in order to optimize its geometry based on its manufacturing costs [4]. Another very important investigation is the application of reverse engineering in the study of geometries through the computational analysis of fluid dynamics (RE/CFD), in the modelling of a "scroll compressor", in order to study the adaptation of a Commercial spiral compressor as an expander in a micro ORC system [10]. Finally, Gameros et al. 2015, which presents a reverse engineering methodology for free-form surfaces can be cited by using an X-ray optical scanner to obtain the mesh using computed tomography (CT) to perform reconstruction of its geometry and the internal cooling system in a turbine blade [11].

Therefore, in the last decade, the application of reverse engineering in the manufacture and prototyping of parts in the automotive area, has new technologies that have important benefits, such as: ease of transport, the possibility of printing spare parts with customized technical specifications, and the reduction of material losses in their manufacturing [12]. These possibilities of reverse engineering increase together with the development of software and hardware, which are used in design and manufacturing [13]. Currently, there are different programs for reverse engineering, such as: Point Master v.5.3.3 to capture the point cloud, Gom Inspect v.7.5 to perform the alignment of the mesh, Geomagic Qualify v.12 for dimensional deviation analysis, 3D Remodeler v.7.1 for sizing, Rapidform XOV2 for a better fit and Polyworks inspector v.12 for documentation, etc. [6], which are very important tools in the field of reverse engineering in each of its stages.

An essential part in the modelling process is the 3D scanner [14, 15], for the time it takes to transfer the actual design to a 3D model and the training of the professionals who operate them in the verification of the dimensions and tolerances of the modelled part [16], that if necessary, this process can be carried out again, and executed under the same conditions, to verify by points the coincidences and possible defects, and take the necessary corrective actions [13]. However, another of the very important stages in the process of reverse engineering in the manufacturing industry of mechanical elements is the dimensional control and rapid prototyping through the generation and three-dimensional reconstruction (3D) of the objects under study [17]. The most interested sectors are the electronics, automotive, robotics, aerospace, oceanography, among others [15, 18]. The materials that are currently being used in Additive Manufacturing are: 51% Polymers, 19.8% Metals, and 29.2% composite materials (polymers plus metal) [18].

At present, the demand and use of custom components through the additive manufacturing of "PAM" polymers presents uncertainty about their mechanical properties [19, 20], therefore, many innovations are being made integrating new additive manufacturing technologies through implementation of fibbers to improve their properties and the quality of their products [21], thus, polymers reinforced with carbon fibbers improve their mechanical properties up to 435% [22]. However, thin-walled products are still a challenge in additive manufacturing [23], since there is a negative correlation between porosity, Young's modulus, and its slenderness [24]. Therefore, the control of printing variables for better efficiency in this 3D printing process is very important [20]. Currently, static tests have been carried out to characterize materials such as ABS, PLA, ABS plus P430, P400 ABS, ABS M-30, Polypropylene (PP), Polycarbonate (PC), among others [19], in order to improve its applicability in the manufacturing industry.

This paper presents a study of reverse engineering and three-dimensional printing in the design and manufacture of the distribution cover of the Spark 2015 car, with the aim of analysing its application in the manufacture of automotive parts that work under the influence of small efforts, and due to the demand for customized spare parts for their vehicles from users, environmental regulation standards, and the need to manufacture light cars is increasingly important. Currently, the global automotive industry needs greater competitiveness in the market and the incorporation of new systems in its mobility; considering this as an opportunity and necessity in the development of new technologies, and manufacturing processes of parts in the automotive sector.

## 2   Materials and Methods

The methodology followed in the modelling and prototyping of the distribution cover of the "Chevrolet Spark" car through the technique of reverse engineering and three-dimensional printing, was developed according to the following stages (Fig. 1):

(a)  Data processing and preparation.
(b)  Dimensional comparison.
(c)  Prototyping by 3D printing.
(d)  Evaluation of its mechanical properties.

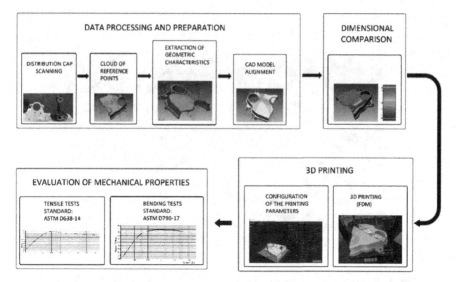

**Fig. 1.** Prototyping of the distribution cover by reverse engineering.

## 2.1 Data Processing and Preparation

Data preparation and processing is done by reverse engineering techniques with a "GO! SCAN 50 TM" 3D scanner, which is selected according to resolution (0.500 [mm]), scanning area (380 × 380 [mm]), portability, measurement speed (550000 [measurements/s]) and scanning and preparation time [25]. This scanner allows to copy the design geometry of the distribution cap and to store this information in a software ("VXelementsse") for the processing and reconstruction of this point cloud (Fig. 2), and to obtain a file in format stl, dae, fbx, ma, obj, ply, txt, wri, x3d, x3dz, and zpr.

This point cloud obtained as a digital file in stl format, is imported to the "Geomagic Design Direct" software, to continue with the processing and geometric reconstruction of the point clouds generated by this scanning system used, as shown in Fig. 2.

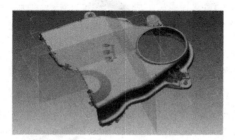

**Fig. 2.** Mesh obtained by Go Scan! SCAN 3D and imported into the software "Geomagic Design Direct".

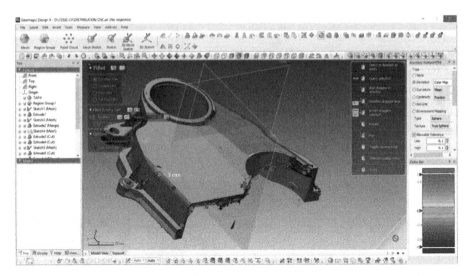

**Fig. 3.** Processing of the mesh using the "Geomagic Design Direct" software.

**Selection and Extraction of Geometric Characteristics.** At this stage, the mesh is processed through the "Geomagic Design Direct" software (Fig. 3), which through a set of CAD editing tools for modelling, allows applying treatment techniques and geometric reconstruction of the point cloud generated by the digitizing system (software VXelements) (Fig. 2). Once the 3D model has been obtained, a "stp" extension file is generated and imported into the design software, in which the last corrections are made until the required geometry is reached.

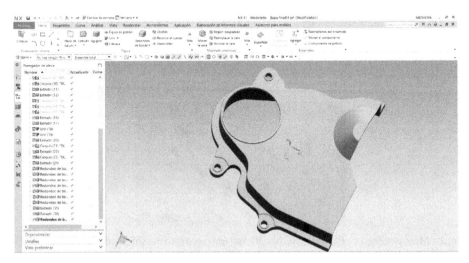

**Fig. 4.** CAD model of the distribution cover of the Chevrolet Spark 2015, imported into the "NX" software.

**Alignment of the CAD Model of the Distribution Cap by Means of Siemens NX Software.** In this stage the last corrections are made to the CAD model by means of NX software (Fig. 4), and a "stl" file is generated so that the additive manufacturing or 3D printing equipment by the FDM ("Fused Deposition Modelling") method can interpret the geometric information modelled in CAD.

**3D Printing by the "FDM" Method of the Distribution Cap, Spark 2015.** The prototype is made in the ANYCUBIC I3 MEGA printer (Fig. 5), for which it is necessary to know its technical characteristics (Table 1), its interface for the configuration of the printing parameters, as well as: the orientation of the printing filaments, the thickness of the printing layers, the filling percentage, the speeds and the auxiliary supports.

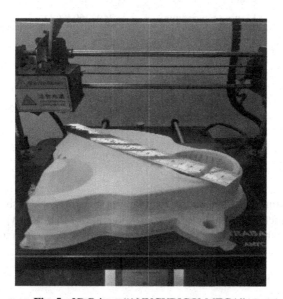

**Fig. 5.** 3D Printer "ANYCUBIC I3 MEGA".

**Table 1.** Technical characteristics of the anycubic i3 mega printer.

| Parameters | Value |
| --- | --- |
| Printer dimensions: | 405 mm × 410 mm × 453 mm |
| Technology: | FDM (Molten deposition modelling) |
| Size of construction: | $210 \times 210 \times 205$ (mm$^3$) |
| Layer resolution: | 0.05–0.3 mm |
| Positioning accuracy: | X/Y 0.0125 mm, Z 0.002 mm |
| Nozzle/Filament Diameter: | 0.4 mm/1.75 mm |
| Printing speed: | 20–100 mm/s (suggested 60 mm/s) |
| Supported materials: | PLA, ABS, HIPS, Wood |

**Mechanical Properties of the Filament Used.** In the Table 2 shows the mechanical properties of the filament used. The mass of the filament coils is 1 [kg], the diameter of the filament is 1.75 [mm], and its length is approximately 350 [m].

**Table 2.** Mechanical properties of the ABS filament used for the manufacture of the distribution cap.

| Parameters | Value |
|---|---|
| Printing temperature | 240 [°C] |
| Density | 1.5 [g/cm$^3$] |
| Diameter of filament | 1.75 [mm] |
| Melting temperature | 240–260 [°C] |
| Elongation at break | 45% |
| Dynamic friction coefficient | 0.5 |
| Traction module | 2.1–2.4 [GPa] |
| Tensile strength | 41–45 [MPa] |
| Izod impact resistance | 200–400 [J/m] |
| Water absorption | 0.3–0.7% at 24 h |
| UV resistance | Poor |

**3D Printing Parameters Used in the Prototyping.** In the Table 3 shows the different 3D printing parameters considered in the manufacture of the prototype, as well as the test specimens for their characterization of the mechanical properties in this case study.

**Table 3.** 3D printing parameters in the prototyping of the distribution cap

| Parameters | Value |
|---|---|
| Deposition pattern | |
| Deposition rate | 40 [mm/s] |
| Nozzle tip size | 0.4 [mm] |
| Diameter of filament | 1.75 [mm] |
| Orientation of the printing filaments | -45% +45% |
| Thickness of the printing layers | 0.2 [mm] |
| Deposition rate | 40 [mm/s] |
| Extrusion temperature | 240 [°C] |
| Deposition density | [100%] |
| Number of layers | Variable |

**Evaluation of the Mechanical Properties of the Prototype.** The evaluation of the mechanical properties of the prototype is carried out by means of mechanical tensile and bending tests according to ASTM D638-14 and D790-17, respectively, for which the universal testing machine "Tinius Olsen H25KS" with a maximum capacity of 25 [KN] and an accuracy of 0.01 [N] was used, as shown in Fig. 6.

**Fig. 6.** Universal machine (Tinius Olsen "H25KS) used in bending and tensile tests.

In the Fig. 7 shows the dimensions of the specimen for tensile tests and Fig. 8 shows the dimensions of the specimen for bending tests.

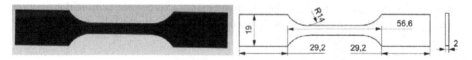

**Fig. 7.** Specimen dimensions for bending tests according to ASTM638.

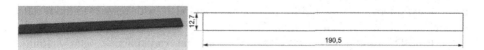

**Fig. 8.** Specimen dimensions for bending tests according to ASTM790.

**Conditions Under Which the Tensile Test was Performed.** The environmental conditions under which the tensile test was performed consisted of an initial temperature of 19.7 °C with an initial relative humidity of 52.9%, and a final temperature of 19.9 °C with a final relative humidity of 52.3%.

The procedure used is that described in ASTM D638-14, with a test speed of 2 [mm/min], a calibrated distance to measure deformation of 25 [mm] and a number of samples per test group of 5 samples.

**Conditions Under Which the Flexure Test was Performed.** The environmental conditions in which the flexure test was performed consisted of an initial Temperature of 19.7 °C with an initial Relative Humidity of 53.3%, and a final Temperature of 18.8 °C with a final Relative Humidity of 56.3%.

This bending test uses a group of 5 samples per test, and the method described by ASTM D790-17, Type of Procedure B, which specifies a relationship between the thickness and the distance between supports 1 to 16 respectively, and a test speed in accordance with Eq. 1 recommended by this standard (11 [mm/min]).

$$R = \frac{Z*L^2}{6D} \tag{1}$$

Where:

R,    is the moving head speed of the universal machine (mm/min).
Z,    is the deformation speed of the outer fibre (0.1 [mm/mm/min] for procedure B).
L,    is the distance between supports (mm).
D,    specimen thickness (mm)

## 3   Results and Discussion

This section presents the results obtained in each of the different stages of this research, and is detailed through images, diagrams, data tables, and information on the different processes in this stage of experimentation, in the manufacture of the bottom distribution cap of the Chevrolet Spark 2015, as well as a comparative analysis of the results obtained with respect to other researches.

**Manufacture of the Distribution Cap of Spark 2015.** In the Table 4 shows the results obtained in the manufacturing process of the distributor cap for the Chevrolet Spark 2015; obtaining a geometric variation of ±0.5 [mm] with respect to the original in the reverse engineering process, which is acceptable in comparison with the manufacturing dimensional tolerances required for this element and also, with respect to the results obtained in other investigations (Table 5).

In the 3D printing process "FDM", dimensional variations of 0.0034 [mm], 0.0104 [mm], 0.0080 [mm] and 0.0055 [mm] were obtained for nominal sizes of 12.6 [mm], 6 [mm], 2.6 [mm] and 2 [mm], respectively. These results are similar to the results achieved by other researchers (Table 6), therefore, it can be concluded that 3D printing by the "FDM" method is a very important technology in the rapid prototyping of mechanical parts.

**Evaluation of the Mechanical Properties of the Prototype.** In the Fig. 9 shows the ABS specimens printed in 3D after the tensile tests, and it can be observed that specimens 01 and 02 break outside the length calibrated for the use of the extensometer, therefore, the respective values of the deformations at the time of breakage are not recorded for specimens 01 and 05.

**Table 4.** Results obtained in prototyping.

| Results |
| --- |

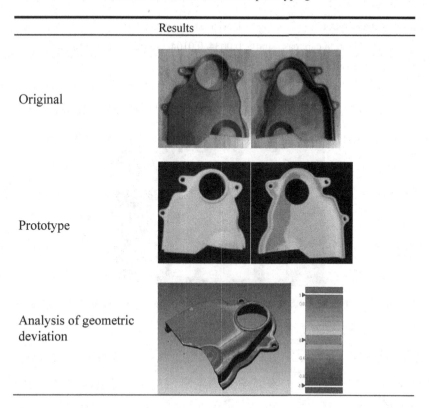

Original

Prototype

Analysis of geometric deviation

**Table 5.** Deviation achieved in the reverse engineering process with respect to other investigations.

| Investigation | Dimensional variation |
| --- | --- |
| Distribution cap; case study | ±0.5 [mm] |
| Turbinenschaufeln; Gameros [11] | ±0.85 [mm] |
| Propellerblätter in Bootsturbinen; Haimov [26] | ±0,05 [mm] |
| Verschlissene mechanische Teile; Li, Li, Tang and Du [5] | Worn parts; From 0.47 [mm] to 3.79 [mm]<br>Wear-free parts; From 0.04 [mm] to 0.09 [mm] |

According to the results obtained in the evaluation of the mechanical properties of the prototype distribution cap by means of 3D "FDM" printing with ABS filament (Fig. 10); the manufacture and replacement of mechanical parts by means of this technique is valid for those parts in which their functionality does not strictly depend on their mechanical properties, or in which the element can be reinforced to fulfil its function (Table 7).

**Table 6.** Deviation achieved in the 3D printing process with respect to other investigations.

| Investigation | Deviation achieved |
|---|---|
| Distribution cap; case study | 0.0034, 0.0104, 0.0080, y 0.0055 [mm] |
| Sokół and Cekus [27] | 0.05 [mm] |
| Nuñez et al. [28] | 0.000175 [mm] y 0.000262 [mm] |
| Ferro et al. [29] | 0.05 [mm] y 0.1 [mm] |

**Fig. 9.** ABS specimens printed in 3D after tensile tests.

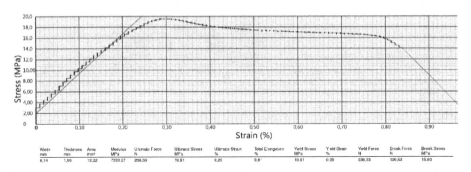

**Fig. 10.** Stress-strain diagram according to ASTM D638 - 14.

In the Fig. 11 shows the ABS specimens printed in 3D after the bending tests.

**Fig. 11.** ABS samples printed in 3D after bending tests.

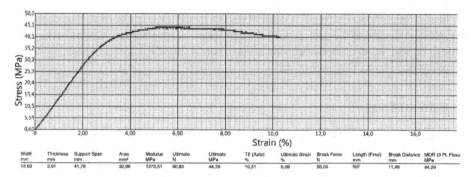

| Width mm | Thickness mm | Support Span mm | Area mm² | Modulus MPa | Ultimate N | Ultimate MPa | TE (Auto) % | Ultimate Strain % | Break Force N | Length (Final) mm | Break Distance mm | MOR (3 Pt. Flexu MPa |
|---|---|---|---|---|---|---|---|---|---|---|---|---|
| 12,63 | 2,61 | 41,76 | 32,96 | 1373,51 | 60,83 | 44,29 | 10,31 | 5,09 | 55,00 | N/F | 11,49 | 44,29 |

**Fig. 12.** Diagram flexural stress - % deformation according to ASTM D790 - 17.

**Table 7.** Results obtained in tensile tests with respect to other investigations.

| Investigation | Ultimate tensile strength (MPa) | Unitary deformation (%) | Elasticity modulus (MPa) |
|---|---|---|---|
| Distribution cap | 41–45 | | 2100–2400 |
| Distribution cap; case study (+45°/−45°), 100% | 19.51 | 0.29 | 7333.27 |
| Ziemian [30]; (+45°/−45°), 74.09% | 19.36 | | |
| Guamantario [31]; (+45°/−45°), 100% | 29.5 | 0.0233 | 1739 |
| Tymrak, Kreiger, y Pearce [32]; (+45°/−45°), 100% | 29.5 | 0.233 | 1739 |

**Table 8.** Results obtained in tensile tests with respect to other investigations.

| Investigation | Ultimate flexural strength (MPa) | Last bending force (N) | Ultimate flexural strength (MPa) | Resistance to 5% deformation (MPa) | Elastic modulus to flexion (MPa) |
|---|---|---|---|---|---|
| Distribution Cap; Case Study: (+45°/−45°), 100% | 44.29 | 60.83 | 44.29 | 43.68 | 1373.51 |
| Ziemian [30]; (+45°/−45°), 74.09% | 32.2 | | 32.2 | | 1438.6 |

In the Table 8 presents the results obtained in the evaluation of the mechanical properties to flexion of the prototype of the distribution cap; obtaining a ultimate flexion force of 60.83 [N], an ultimate flexion resistance of 44.29 [MPa], and an elastic modulus to flexion of 1373.51 [MPa] (Fig. 12).

# 4   Conclusions

Reverse engineering is a very important design methodology in the process of modelling, reproduction and geometric reconstruction of three-dimensional models of machine elements, which has been innovating in the last decade, which has allowed these systems to be increasingly easy to use and, in turn, to be able to copy increasingly complex shapes.

In the modelling process with the "Go! SCAN" 3D scanner and the "Geomagic Design Direct" software of the Spark 2015 distributor cap, a geometrical variation of ±0.5 [mm] with respect to the nominal dimensions of the part was obtained.

The 3D printing "FDM" of the distribution cap presents mechanical properties and dimensional variations that do not affect its functionality, however, on more complex surfaces such as ribs, perforations, furrows and hidden details where it was not easy to access in the digitization process, a greater deviation was obtained, however, these small details do not influence the total reproduction of its geometry with this process.

The mechanical properties of the prototype decreased approximately by half, and the dimensional variations were in the order of thousandths of a millimetre, therefore, it is considered that Reverse Engineering and 3D Printing is valid for the prototyping of automotive parts, however, is applicable in the manufacture of automotive parts subject to small efforts, or where it is possible to replace by another material that meets the design requirements.

**Acknowledgment.** We would like to thank the Technical University of the North for sponsoring the development of this research.

## Nomenclature

| | |
|---|---|
| CAD | Computer Aided Design |
| 3D | Three-dimensional |
| CAM | Computer-Aided Manufacturing |
| CAE | Computer-Aided Engineering |
| FDM | Manufacturing by molten deposition |
| ASTM D790-17 | American Society for Testing and Materials, standard 790, section 17 |
| ASTM D638-14 | American Society for Testing and Materials, standard 638, section 14 |
| PAM | Additive manufacture of polymers |
| CFD | Fluid Dynamics Computational |
| RE | Reverse Engineering |
| PE | Polyethylene |
| PLA | Acid polylactic |
| ABS | Acrylonitrile butadiene styrene |
| PP | Polypropylene |
| PC | Polycarbonate |

# References

1. Morales, J.A.H.: Revista iberoamericana de producción académica y gestión educativa, vol. 3, no. 6. Centro de Estudios e Investigaciones para el Desarrollo Docente, A.C (2014)
2. Pan, Z., Wang, X., Teng, R., Cao, X.: Computer-aided design-while-engineering technology in top-down modeling of mechanical product. Comput. Ind. **75**, 151–161 (2016)
3. Monroy, M.E., Arciniegas, J.L., Rodríguez, J.C.: Propuesta Metodológica para Caracterizar y Seleccionar Métodos de Ingeniería Inversa. Inf. Technol. **24**(5), 23–30 (2013)
4. Valerga, A.P., Batista, M., Bienvenido, R., Fernández-Vidal, S.R., Wendt, C., Marcos, M.: Reverse engineering based methodology for modelling cutting tools. Procedia Eng. **132**, 1144–1151 (2015)
5. Li, L., Li, C., Tang, Y., Du, Y.: An integrated approach of reverse engineering aided remanufacturing process for worn components. Robot. Comput. Integr. Manuf. **48**, 39–50 (2017)
6. Minetola, P., Iuliano, L., Calignano, F.: A customer oriented methodology for reverse engineering software selection in the computer aided inspection scenario. Comput. Ind. **67**, 54–71 (2015)
7. López-alba, E., Felipe Sesé, L.: Aplicaciones industriales de técnicas ópticas de campo completo para la medida de tensiones y deformaciones en elementos de máquinas industrial application of full field optical techniques to measure stress and strain in machine element, vol. 80, pp. 98–108 (2013)
8. Brown, G.M.: Overview of three-dimensional shape measurement using optical methods. Opt. Eng. **39**(1), 10 (2002)
9. Chintala, G., Gudimetla, P.: Optimum material evaluation for gas turbine blade using Reverse Engineering (RE) and FEA. Procedia Eng. **97**, 1332–1340 (2014)
10. Morini, M., Pavan, C., Pinelli, M., Romito, E., Suman, A.: Analysis of a scroll machine for micro ORC applications by means of a RE/CFD methodology. Appl. Therm. Eng. **80**, 132–140 (2015)
11. Gameros, A., De Chiffre, L., Siller, H.R., Hiller, J., Genta, G.: A reverse engineering methodology for nickel alloy turbine blades with internal features. CIRP J. Manuf. Sci. Technol. **9**, 116–124 (2015)
12. Böckin, D., Tillman, A.M.: Environmental assessment of additive manufacturing in the automotive industry. J. Clean. Prod. **226**, 977–987 (2019)
13. Dúbravčík, M., Kender, Š.: Application of reverse engineering techniques in mechanics system services. Procedia Eng. **48**, 96–104 (2012)
14. Tu, J., Wang, M., Zhang, L.: A shortcut to marking 3D target curves on curved surface via a galvanometric laser scanner. Chin. J. Aeronaut. **32**(6), 1555–1563 (2019)
15. Babu, M., Franciosa, P., Ceglarek, D.: Adaptive measurement and modelling methodology for In-line 3D surface metrology scanners. Procedia CIRP **60**, 26–31 (2017)
16. Chen, X., Possel, J.K., Wacongne, C., van Ham, A.F., Klink, P.C., Roelfsema, P.R.: 3D printing and modelling of customized implants and surgical guides for non-human primates. J. Neurosci. Methods **286**, 38–55 (2017)
17. Buonamici, F., Carfagni, M., Furferi, R., Governi, L., Lapini, A., Volpe, Y.: Reverse engineering of mechanical parts: a template-based approach. J. Comput. Des. Eng. **5**(2), 145–159 (2018)
18. Dizon, J.R.C., Espera, A.H., Chen, Q., Advincula, R.C.: Mechanical characterization of 3D-printed polymers. Addit. Manuf. **20**, 44–67 (2018)
19. Türk, D.A., Brenni, F., Zogg, M., Meboldt, M.: Mechanical characterization of 3D printed polymers for fiber reinforced polymers processing. Mater. Des. **118**, 256–265 (2017)

20. Ramezani Dana, H., Barbe, F., Delbreilh, L., Ben Azzouna, M., Guillet, A., Breteau, T.: Polymer additive manufacturing of ABS structure: influence of printing direction on mechanical properties. J. Manuf. Process. **44**, 288–298 (2019)

21. Heidari-Rarani, M., Rafiee-Afarani, M., Zahedi, A.M.: Mechanical characterization of FDM 3D printing of continuous carbon fiber reinforced PLA composites. Compos. Part B Eng. **175**, 107147 (2019)

22. Luan, C., Yao, X., Liu, C., Lan, L., Fu, J.: Self-monitoring continuous carbon fiber reinforced thermoplastic based on dual-material three-dimensional printing integration process. Carbon N. Y. **140**, 100–111 (2018)

23. Ahmed, N.: Direct metal fabrication in rapid prototyping: a review. J. Manuf. Processes **42**, 167–191 (2019)

24. De Ciurana, J., Serenó, L., Vallès, È.: Selecting process parameters in RepRap additive manufacturing system for PLA scaffolds manufacture. Procedia CIRP **5**, 152–157 (2013)

25. Rosicky, J., Grygar, A., Chapcak, P., Bouma, T., Rosicky, J.: Application of 3D scanning in prosthetic and orthotic clinical practice. In: Proceedings of the 7th International Conference on 3D Body Scanning Technologies, Lugano, Switzerland, 30 November–1 December 2016, pp. 88–97 (2016)

26. Haimov, E., Molinelli Fernández, E., Carrillo Hontoria, E.: Aplicación de láser escáner acoplado a brazos de medición para la inspección e ingeniería inversa. In: 52° Sesiones Técnicas de Ingeniería Naval, pp. 1–13 (2013)

27. Sokół, K., Cekus D.: Reverse engineering as a solution in parts restoration process. In: Procedia Engineering, vol. 177, pp. 210–217 (2017)

28. Nuñez, P.J., Rivas, A., García-Plaza, E., Beamud, E., Sanz-Lobera, A.: Dimensional and surface texture characterization in fused deposition modelling (FDM) with ABS plus. In: Procedia Engineering, vol. 132, pp. 856–863 (2015)

29. Ferro, C.G., Brischetto, S., Torre, R., Maggiore, P.: Characterization of ABS specimens produced via the 3D printing technology for drone structural. Curved Layer. Struct. **3**(1), 172–188 (2016)

30. Ziemian, C., Sharma, M., Ziemi, S.: Anisotropic Mechanical Properties of ABS Parts Fabricated by Fused Deposition Modelling. In: Mechanical Engineering, InTech (2012)

31. Calle Guamantario, W., Conejero, A., Ferrándiz, S.: Master universitario en diseño y fabricacion integrada asistida por computador influencia de los parametros de relleno en el comportamiento mecanico a la flexión de piezas fabricadas en impresoras 3-D de bajo coste (2014)

32. Tymrak, B.M., Kreiger, M., Pearce, J.M.: Mechanical properties of components fabricated with open-source 3-D printers under realistic environmental conditions. Mater. Des. **58**, 242–246 (2014)

# Computing

# Designing an Accessible Website for Palliative Care Services

Patricia Acosta-Vargas[1]([ᐅ]) [iD], Paula Hidalgo[1] [iD], Gloria Acosta-Vargas[2] [iD],
Belén Salvador-Acosta[1] [iD], Luis Salvador-Ullauri[3] [iD], and Mario Gonzalez[1] [iD]

[1] Intelligent & Interactive Systems Lab, Universidad de Las Américas, Quito, Ecuador
{patricia.acosta,paula.hidalgo,maria.salvador.acosta,
mario.gonzalez.rodriguez}@udla.edu.ec
[2] Pontificia Universidad Católica del Ecuador, Quito, Ecuador
gfacosta@puce.edu.ec
[3] Universidad de Alicante, Alicante, Spain
lasul@alu.ua.es

**Abstract.** There is no doubt that population growth and the increase in non-communicable diseases represent a challenge to society, especially for the health system, including palliative care. Maintaining accessible sites is essential for all kinds of people to interact on the web. Ecuador does not have websites on palliative care, and the existing ones in the area of health are not all accessible. To solve this need, we propose the design of a website in the area of palliative care, applying standards based on Web Content Accessibility Guidelines 2.1. By designing a website that applies the WCAG 2.1 standards, more people will be able to access healthcare, including people with disabilities. This research can contribute as a reference for the construction of more inclusive websites in the area of health.

**Keywords:** Accessibility · Palliative care · Design · Inclusive · Public health · Website · WCAG 2.1

## 1 Introduction

Accelerated global population growth and the increase in non-communicable diseases present significant challenges to society and health systems. It is estimated [1] that more than 40 million people worldwide require palliative care.

According to the Worldwide Palliative Care Alliance [2], in Ecuador, palliative care is not adequately developed or structured as part of the Public Health System. Currently, with the rapid development of technology, it is essential to better access information on palliative treatment and its benefits. Therefore, it is necessary to have timely information on the services and resources available to the country to achieve quality access to them.

At the beginning of 2019, the "We Are Social," reports on the Internet [3] claimed that Internet users increased by 8.6%, with approximately 350 million new users. On the other hand, [4] the World Health Organization (WHO) indicates that 15% of the people have some incapacity, and with the increase in age in the population, chronic diseases and thus disability rates have also increased.

© Springer Nature Switzerland AG 2020
M. Botto-Tobar et al. (Eds.): ICAT 2019, CCIS 1193, pp. 371–383, 2020.
https://doi.org/10.1007/978-3-030-42517-3_28

In this research, [5] we propose the creation of an accessible website for palliative care services in Ecuador, supported by the design of a website. However, having a website is not enough; to meet accessibility standards is also essential.

Consequently, a website to be successful must be visible in search engines, accessible, and inclusive, regardless of the technologies used. This research proposes a method for the design of an accessible website according to the Web Content Accessibility Guidelines 2.1.

The rest of the document contains: in Sect. 2, the review of the literature in which we narrate about accessibility and the tool applied in the evaluation of the websites. In Sect. 3, we propose the methodology and case study related to palliative care websites. In Sect. 4, we present the results and the discussion. Finally, in Sect. 5, we include the recommendations and future work suggested in this study.

## 2 Literature Review

Nowadays, the World Health Organization [6] argues that the global trend in life expectancy has increased, as has the population growth of the over-60 age group. Similarly, the prevalence of chronic diseases [2], such as cancer, dementia, and diabetes, has increased. Palliative care [7] refers to the increase of the condition of life on patients and families facing problems related to fatal diseases, through the avoidance and control of pain by early detection and appropriate therapy of distress, natural, psychosocial, or soul.

Candrian [8] argues that palliative care is a humanitarian necessity because of the support they propose for the relief of illness in patients and families. This care takes an interdisciplinary approach and is associated with less suffering, higher satisfaction, and lower hospital costs, along with better transitions between stages of progressive disease [9]. On the other hand, [10] it points out that the benefits are not only manifested in patients and family members but in health systems that regulate the use of services and reduce the unnecessary number of hospitalizations and costs.

In Spain, there are several palliative care websites including the site[1] of "Paliativos Sin Fronteras," which is a non-governmental organization, that offer documentation on the history of palliative care, clinical practice guide, and pain management. When analyzing with WAVE evidence, these sites are not accessible at a satisfactory level and have broken links and contrast errors. Another example is the website[2] of the "Escuela de Pacientes" of the Junta de Andalucía, it presents information on help in palliative care, but when analyzed with the automatic revision tool, the website presents accessibility errors related to empty and contrast links.

In Ecuador, despite trends in population growth, migration, and morbidity, the issue of palliative care is forgotten. Ecuador has national public health policies [11], but it does not officially report specialized palliative care services [2]. It does not include the operation of resources or multisector strategies, nor does it refer to the application of protocols to confront chronic diseases and their consequences.

---

[1] https://paliativossinfronteras.org/.

[2] https://escueladepacientes.es/mi-enfermedad/cancer/.

Concerning health websites, the authors share the following literature: Creixans-Tenas et al. [12] argue that the study was applied to assess the quality parameters of the websites of Catalan hospitals in the private area. The results indicate that studies related to accessibility, content, usability, and privacy policies are essential in the development of a website. Another study [13] indicates that factors influencing the visibility and quality of private services can be improved through adequate web accessibility with quality and accreditations.

Kaur [14] indicates that the most common problems of hospital websites in assessing safety, usability, and accessibility are the result of not correctly applying WCAG 2.0. Bouzas-Lorenzo et al. [15] analyzed some features of web browsing related to the ease of localization of websites, interaction, and accessibility to online services. The authors concluded that this research shows that the quality of e-health sites in Spain do not meet the minimum level of accessibility.

Acosta-Vargas et al. [16] argued that the trend of e-Health is to optimize to digital format the health care essential services that are increasing every day, in the same way, the consumers who access these essential services are people with incapacities and the senior. A scheme that can improve the quality of the community life cycle is health websites. In that study, the authors assessed 22 hospital health web pages according to the Webometrics position. The results indicated that health websites have many barriers for users; the study suggested that it is essential to consolidate valid code and execute quality practices with WCAG 2.0.

## 2.1 Web Accessibility

The World Health Organization [17] indicates that nearly 200 million people experience significant difficulties in its functioning. On the other hand, [17] the United Nations Convention, which deals with the rights of persons with disabilities, proposes to reinforce the conviction that disability is a priority in terms of human rights and development[3]. This vision drives us to design inclusive websites in which all human beings have the right [18] to live a life of health, comfort, and dignity.

To contribute to this altruistic goal, the WCAG 2.1 [5] established by World Wide Web Consortium in assistance with entities and corporations all over the world proposes guidelines where web accessibility is considered. These guidelines will happen the people's requirements, associations, and government policies at the international level.

As a result, web accessibility differs not only on accessible content subjects but also on web browsers, support tools, and customer interaction. It is, therefore, essential to contemplate[4] the User Agent Accessibility Guidelines 2.0. Another essential parameter are the authoring tools consisting of services and applications that "content creators" use to generate web content on stationary home pages, products, and the dynamic web. This includes[5] the Authoring Tool Accessibility Guidelines 2.0.

---

[3] https://www.un.org/spanish/disabilities/.

[4] https://www.w3.org/WAI/intro/uaag/.

[5] https://www.w3.org/WAI/standards-guidelines/atag/.

In June 2018, the W3C proposed WCAG 2.1 [5] consisting of four principles, 13 guidelines, and 78 compliance criteria. Each of these four principles is detailed below [5]:

*Principle 1: Perceptible*, refers to all users being able to perceive content in visual, sound, and perceptible behavior. It includes four guidelines and 29 compliance criteria. *Principle 2: Operable*, this principle refers to users being able to operate and navigate the interface elements. It comprises five guidelines and 29 compliance criteria. *Principle 3: Understandable*, this principle is related to the self-controls of the management interface; they must be comprehensible to all types of users. It comprises three guidelines and 17 compliance criteria. *Principle 4: Robust* means that the subject matter should be sturdy sufficient to be consistently understood by a wide-ranging multiplicity of users of applications that allow working with current and future technologies. Operators must be competent to access comfortable, as well as assistive machinery. It comprises one recommendation and three conformity criteria.

Besides, WCAG 2.1 proposes success criteria related to three levels [5] level "A" is a minimum; level "AA" is an intermediate, and level "AAA" is the maximum. An accessible website must comply with at least the "AA" level.

## 2.2  Web Accessibility Assessment Tools

The evaluation conducted out by Ismail et al. [19] on the homepages accessibility of Indian universities was evaluated with different assessment tools such as Web page Analyzer, AChecker, and WAVE.

Kimmons et al. [20] in assessing K-12 Websites in the United States applied WebAIM's WAVE because it supports a computerized accessibility metric for pages that contain many errors, as well as alerts to help website designers.

Acosta-Vargas et al. [21, 22], in their research on a combined web accessibility assessment method among the tools for assessing website accessibility, suggests WAVE because it helps in verifying the level agreement with WCAG 2.0.

Acosta-Vargas et al. [23], to assess accessibility on websites, suggest applying automatic tools and manual methods in the study to describe web accessibility problems identified on 348 university websites. In the research, the authors evaluated the most commonly used tools such as eXaminator, AccessMonitor, and TAW, Web Accessibility Checker, Tenon, AChecker, and WAVE[6]. In their study, they applied the WAVE. The results showed that the websites violate the WCAG 2.0 accessibility requirements. Nevertheless, WAVE is a tool that allows evaluating any website, even those that have authenticity problems.

Figure 1 shows a screenshot when evaluating the site https://www.hopkinsmedicine.org/ with WAVE in the left-hand panel showing the errors detected by the tool. Accessibility experts must review these errors manually. The main page is loaded to evaluate the website; once loaded, we run the WAVE plugin. The results obtained from the WAVE are essential to check manually and to correct any barriers detected.

---

[6] https://wave.webaim.org/.

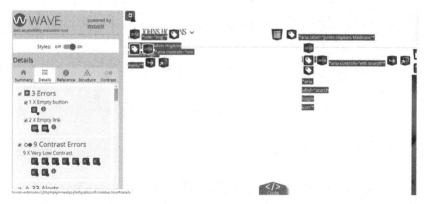

**Fig. 1.** Screenshot when evaluating https://www.hopkinsmedicine.org/ with WAVE.

## 3    Methodology and Case Study

This investigation utilizes WAVE, which consists of a plug-in component for the Google Chrome[7] browser, version 1.0.9, throughout the development process of the website. With this study, the authors identified the most frequent possible accessibility violations that apply to the palliative care directory. This research proposes to create an open and accessible website that specifies public and private resources for palliative care.

To evaluate the websites, the authors selected a sample with 16 health-related websites, of which 11 correspond to Ecuador and five to the health websites that occupy the first places in the world according to the ranking of Webometrics[8]. The authors compared the accessibility of the main pages of each site to take as reference and apply the WCAG 2.1 in the construction of an accessible website.

This research applies the stages of software development based on SCRUM [24] and User-Centered Design (UCD) [27], the development process is iterative in which website designers and programmers take control over the users and requirements of each phase during the creation process, from requirements planning to implementation and production of the application. Figure 2 contains the phases of developing software that includes four phases: (i) understanding the context of use, (ii) specifying consumer requirements, (iii) designing solutions, and (iv) evaluating based on requirements [25].

The method applied consists of 4 phases explained below:

**Phase 1: To understand the context of use.** We apply Scrum based on sprints, which includes intervals established to generate a deliverable product. This method involves the development of mini-projects to improve the effectiveness of the main project. Besides, in this first phase, we define the functionality, objectives, sprint risks, delivery times, among others. This phase is essential for changes, decision making, and improvements. We generate a structure of the services and resources of the palliative care website in Ecuador, as shown in Fig. 3.

---

[7] https://chrome.google.com/webstore/.

[8] https://hospitals.webometrics.info/en/Latin_America/Ecuador.

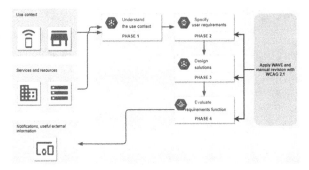

**Fig. 2.** Phases of development software

**Phase 2: Specify user requirements.** In this phase, we capture the information from phase 1 to adapt the website with the services for users of the palliative care website. Also, we apply an adaptive methodology to facilitate rapid prototyping, especially when there are changes requested by the site user [26]. At this phase, we involved development, where project managers ensure the inexistence of last-minute changes that affect the objectives of the project.

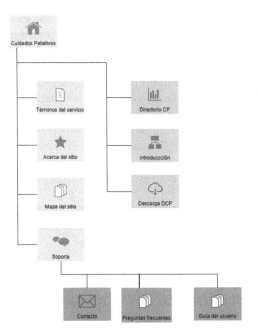

**Fig. 3.** Website structure for palliative care.

**Phase 3: Design the solutions.** At this phase, we apply the methodology with an agile process, as well as iterative and incremental. The architecture of the website allows understanding the elements and the interaction between them. Besides, at this stage, it is possible to analyze and evaluate the results by encouraging collaboration and feedback.

For example, the section of the "Palliative Care" website will include the "Palliative Care Directory," the authors suggest reviewing the design shown in Fig. 4.

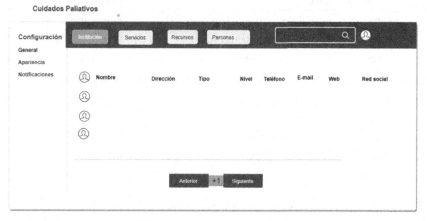

**Fig. 4.** Palliative care directory design.

**Phase 4: Evaluate according to the requirements.** In this phase, the end-user evaluates the model and application of each section of the website. During the website development cycle, we apply the WCAG 2.1, to verify the accessibility of the website up to the level "AA." During the evaluation of the website, web accessibility reports allow providing feedback. The lessons learned during each stage allows each sprint to be more productive and agile.

## 4 Results and Discussion

Table 1 registers the websites corresponding to the Webometrics classification; it contains the world classification, the URL, and the acronyms.

**Table 1.** Evaluated websites

| World rank | URL | Acronym |
| --- | --- | --- |
| 1 | http://my.clevelandclinic.org/ | my |
| 2 | http://www.stjude.org/ | stjude |
| 3 | http://www.hopkinsmedicine.org/ | hopkinsmedicine |
| 4 | https://www.mayoclinic.org/ | mayoclinic |
| 5 | http://umm.edu/ | umm |
| 3006 | http://www.hospitalalcivar.com/ | Alcivar |
| 5557 | http://www.hospitalmetropolitano.org/ | Metropolitano |
| 8364 | http://www.hospitalvernaza.med.ec/ | Vernaza |

(*continued*)

**Table 1.** (*continued*)

| World rank | URL | Acronym |
|---|---|---|
| 8863 | http://www.hospikennedy.med.ec/ | Kennedy |
| 9204 | http://www.hospitalrobertogilbert.med.ec/ | RobertoGilbert |
| 9400 | http://cort.as/ -KBc5 | EnriqueSotomar |
| 9483 | http://www.institutoneurociencias.med.ec/ | Neurociencias |
| 9909 | http://www.mediken.com.ec/ | Midiken |
| 11351 | http://www.hee.gob.ec/ | hee |
| 11730 | http://www.hospitalvozandes.org/ | Vozandes |
| 11959 | http://hvcm.gob.ec/ | hvcm |

The results of the websites evaluation were conducted on June 24, 2019, with the tool WAVE, Table 2 contains the acronym, the errors, the alerts, the features, the structural elements, HTML5 and ARIA, and the number of contrast errors.

**Table 2.** Assessment with WAVE

| Acronym | Errors | Alerts | Features | Structural | HTML5 and ARIA | Contrast errors |
|---|---|---|---|---|---|---|
| my | 0 | 33 | 6 | 24 | 23 | 17 |
| stjude | 0 | 70 | 37 | 65 | 185 | 16 |
| hopkinsmedicine | 3 | 32 | 51 | 41 | 56 | 15 |
| mayoclinic | 1 | 16 | 21 | 74 | 58 | 1 |
| umm | 23 | 32 | 16 | 39 | 37 | 19 |
| Alcivar | 42 | 23 | 110 | 67 | 15 | 64 |
| Metropolitano | 55 | 32 | 23 | 62 | 83 | 54 |
| Vernaza | 8 | 20 | 7 | 25 | 2 | 69 |
| Kennedy | 23 | 6 | 16 | 19 | 97 | 33 |
| RobertoGilbert | 8 | 20 | 9 | 25 | 2 | 65 |
| EnriqueSotomar | 30 | 9 | 21 | 15 | 26 | 2 |
| Neurociencias | 12 | 14 | 10 | 19 | 2 | 28 |
| Midiken | 14 | 31 | 0 | 29 | 48 | 13 |
| hee | 18 | 30 | 93 | 44 | 2 | 27 |
| Vozandes | 40 | 22 | 31 | 67 | 75 | 10 |
| hvcm | 13 | 62 | 47 | 33 | 0 | 22 |

Table 3 contains the acronym of the website with the type of success criterion, according to WCAG 2.1.

**Table 3.** Website and success criterion

| Acronym | 1.1.1 | 1.3.1 | 2.4.1 | 2.4.4 | 2.4.6 | 3.1.1 | 3.3.2 |
|---|---|---|---|---|---|---|---|
| my | 0 | 0 | 0 | 0 | 0 | 0 | 0 |
| stjude | 0 | 0 | 0 | 0 | 0 | 0 | 0 |
| hopkinsmedicine | 1 | 0 | 0 | 2 | 0 | 0 | 0 |
| mayoclinic | 0 | 1 | 0 | 0 | 0 | 0 | 0 |
| umm | 10 | 5 | 0 | 1 | 4 | 0 | 3 |
| Alcivar | 12 | 1 | 1 | 27 | 1 | 0 | 0 |
| Metropolitano | 30 | 6 | 0 | 18 | 0 | 0 | 1 |
| Vernaza | 7 | 1 | 0 | 0 | 0 | 0 | 0 |
| Kennedy | 11 | 1 | 0 | 11 | 0 | 0 | 0 |
| RobertoGilbert | 7 | 1 | 0 | 0 | 0 | 0 | 0 |
| EnriqueSotomar | 4 | 0 | 0 | 25 | 0 | 1 | 0 |
| Neurociencias | 8 | 1 | 0 | 3 | 0 | 0 | 0 |
| Midiken | 8 | 0 | 0 | 5 | 0 | 1 | 0 |
| hee | 1 | 1 | 0 | 15 | 1 | 0 | 0 |
| Vozandes | 25 | 1 | 0 | 0 | 1 | 0 | 1 |
| hvcm | 8 | 0 | 0 | 4 | 0 | 1 | 0 |
| **Total** | **132** | **19** | **1** | **111** | **7** | **3** | **5** |

The study dataset is available in Microsoft Excel format for review and replication in the Mendeley repository[9].

In Fig. 5 when comparing Ecuador's health websites with the first ones in the Webometric ranking, the Hospital Metropolitano has 55 errors, followed by the Hospital Alcívar with 42, in third place, is located the Hospital Vozandes with 40 errors, in fourth place, is located the Hospital Gineco-Obstétrico Enrique Sotomayor with 30 errors, in fifth place, is the site University of Maryland Medical Center with 23 errors. The websites with zero errors correspond to the Cleveland Clinic and St Jude Children's Research Hospital that is the range first in the webometrics ranking.

Table 4 contains the principle of WCAG 2.1, the guideline, the success criterion, the level, the total number of errors classified, and the percentage. Table 4 shows that the most frequently repeated error corresponds to the "Perceptible" principle with the "A" acceptance level of WCAG 2.1, with the criterion "1.1.1 Non-text Content" with a total of 132 errors corresponding to 47% within the evaluated sample. The second error is connected with the success criterion "2.4.4 Link Purpose," with a total of 111

---

[9] http://dx.doi.org/10.17632/8khd8g6789.1.

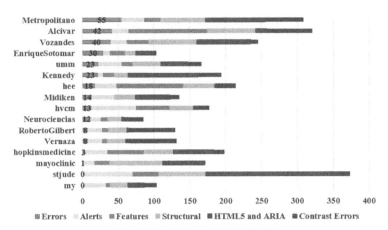

**Fig. 5.** Evaluation with the WAVE

**Table 4.** Principles revealed in the assessment of health websites

| Principle | Guideline | Criterion | Level | Total | % |
|---|---|---|---|---|---|
| 1. Perceivable [5] | 1.1 Text Alternatives [5] | 1.1.1 Non-text Content [5] | A [5] | 132 | 47 |
| 1. Perceivable [5] | 1.3 Adaptable [5] | 1.3.1 Info and Relationships [5] | A [5] | 19 | 7 |
| 2. Operable [5] | 2.4 Navigable [5] | 2.4.1 Bypass Blocks [5] | A [5] | 1 | 0 |
| 2. Operable [5] | 2.4 Navigable [5] | 2.4.4 Link Purpose (In Context) [5] | A [5] | 111 | 40 |
| 2. Operable [5] | 2.4 Navigable [5] | 2.4.6 Headings and Labels [5] | AA [5] | 7 | 3 |
| 3. Understandable [5] | 3.1 Readable [5] | 3.1.1 Language of Page [5] | A [5] | 3 | 1 |
| 3. Understandable [5] | 3.3 Input Assistance [5] | 3.3.2 Labels or Instructions [5] | A [5] | 5 | 2 |

errors that correspond to the 40%. The principles that are most violated are related to the principle of "Perceptible," "Operable," and "Understandable," there are no errors related to the principle of "Robust." The success criteria are mostly related to the "A" level of accessibility.

Figure 6 shows that all the errors of the evaluated health websites correspond to 3% of the "Understandable," 43% correspond to the "Operable," and 54% are related to the "Perceptible" principle.

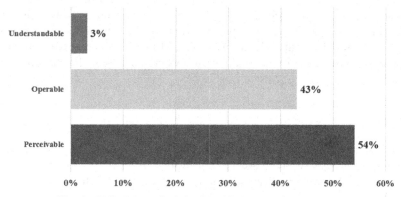

**Fig. 6.** WCAG 2.1 principles identified in the sites evaluated

From the analysis, we suggest improving (1) the design by inserting a text label for the form control. It is also essential (2) to use the element <label> to correlate it with the corresponding form control. (3) If there is no detectable tag, it is vital to support an associated tag. (4) Include a narrative title characteristic to the form control or refer to labels with "aria-labeled by." Besides, we suggest (5) removing empty links or providing script within the relationship that defines the functionality or purpose of that link. (6) It is essential to check that all headings include informative content. (7) It is essential to provide sufficient tags, clues, and guidelines for the needed interactive components. (8) The page language should be characterized by the HTML Lang attribute. (9) We suggest checking that the element referred to in the "aria-labeled by" attribute is present within the page and has an appropriate description. The results indicate that the websites did not accomplish an adequate accessibility level. Although we recognize that web accessibility assessment tools never replace review by a web accessibility expert, the use of automated tools should be used as a first step, throughout the website development cycle, but not as the only option.

## 5 Conclusions and Future Work

This study makes it possible to apply and conceive WCAG 2.1 from the beginning of the development of the website. Most health-related services could improve their websites and achieve greater visibility by improving the level of web accessibility. This research can, therefore, serve as a reference guide for the design of accessible and inclusive websites in such a way that the web contents published in public and private sector websites in Ecuador that provide services to the public are accessible and can fully satisfy the level of conformity "AA," according to the Ecuadorian Technical Standard NTE INEN-ISO/IEC 40500. This standard is an exact translation of WCAG 2.0.

In future work, we suggest the application of automatic evaluation tools with manual and heuristic methods to review possible violations that may occur on a website, and that represents accessibility barriers for people with disabilities or the elderly. We suggest applying automatic and manual evaluation throughout the web development cycle to ensure a satisfactory level of accessibility. Remember that the automatic tools to evaluate websites are not the perfect solution; it is always required having a review of experts in the field. Finally, we encourage website programmers to use the WCAG 2.1 standards as a reference in the design of future websites and to raise awareness about creating accessible sites with diversity in mind, because where there is no diversity, there is no innovation.

## References

1. World Health Organization: Cuidados paliativos. https://www.who.int/es/news-room/fact-sheets/detail/palliative-care. Accessed 23 Oct 2019
2. Worldwide Palliative Care Alliance: Global Atlas of Palliative Care at the End of Life, London (2014)
3. We Are Social and Hootsuite: Digital 2019: Global Internet Use accelerates - we are social. https://wearesocial.com/blog/2019/01/digital-2019-global-internet-use-accelerates. Accessed 18 Apr 2019
4. World Health Organization: Discapacidad y salud. https://www.who.int/es/news-room/fact-sheets/detail/disability-and-health. Accessed 28 June 2019
5. World Wide Web Consortium: Web Content Accessibility Guidelines (WCAG) 2.1. https://www.w3.org/TR/WCAG21/. Accessed 15 Sept 2019
6. World Health Organization: World Population Prospects: The 2017 Revision, New York (2017)
7. World Health Organization: National cancer control programmes: policies and managerial guidelines. (2002). https://doi.org/10.1016/S0885-3924(02)00463-3
8. Candrian, C.: Taming death and the consequences of discourse. Hum. Relat. (2014). https://doi.org/10.1177/0018726713485472
9. Morrison, S.: Health care system factors affecting end-of-life care. J. Palliat. Med. **8**, 79–87 (2005)
10. Saunders, C.: Hospice care. Am. J. Med. **65**, 726–728 (1978)
11. Ministerio de Salud Pública del Ecuador: Acuerdo Ministerial No. 00000101. Ecuador: Registro Oficial No. 415 (2011)
12. Creixans-Tenas, J., Arimany-Serrat, N.: Calidad de las web de los hospitales privados web quality of private hospitals. In: 2016 11th Iberian Conference on Information Systems and Technologies (CISTI), pp. 1–6 (2016). https://doi.org/10.1109/CISTI.2016.7521554
13. Creixans-Tenas, J., Arimany-Serrat, N.: Influential factors in the visibility and quality of the websites of private hospitals. In: Conference on Information Systems and Technologies, pp. 1–7 (2017). https://doi.org/10.23919/CISTI.2017.7975735
14. Kaur, A., Dani, D., Agrawal, G.: Evaluating the accessibility, usability and security of Hospitals websites: An exploratory study. In: 2017 7th International Conference on Cloud Computing, Data Science & Engineering – Confluence, pp. 674–680 (2017). https://doi.org/10.1109/CONFLUENCE.2017.7943237
15. Bouzas-Lorenzo, R., Mahou-Lago, X., Chao, L., Cernadas, A.: E-health and user experience in spanish public health portals. In: Proceedings of the 17th European Conference on Digital Government, pp. 47–57 (2017)
16. Acosta-Vargas, P., Acosta, T., Sergio-Luján, M.: Framework for accessibility evaluation of hospital websites. In: International Conference on eDemocracy & eGovernment, pp. 9–15. IEEE (2018). https://doi.org/10.1109/ICEDEG.2018.8372368
17. World Health Organization: Informe mundial sobre la discapacidad, https://www.who.int/disabilities/world_report/2011/es/. Accessed 11 Nov 2019

18. Naciones Unidas: El Programa de las Naciones Unidas sobre la Discapacidad, https://www.un.org/spanish/disabilities/default.asp?id=497#menu. Accessed 28 June 2019
19. Ismail, A., Kuppusamy, K.: Accessibility of Indian universities' homepages: an exploratory study. J. King Saud Univ. Inf. Sci. **30**, 268–278 (2018)
20. Kimmons, R., Smith, J.: Accessibility in mind? A nationwide study of K-12 Web sites in the United States. First Monday **24** (2019)
21. Acosta-Vargas, P., Luján-Mora, S., Acosta, T., Salvador-Ullauri, L.: Toward a combined method for evaluation of web accessibility. In: Rocha, Á., Guarda, T. (eds.) ICITS 2018. AISC, vol. 721, pp. 602–613. Springer, Cham (2018). https://doi.org/10.1007/978-3-319-73450-7_57
22. Acosta-Vargas, P., Salvador-Ullauri, L., Luján-Mora, S.: A heuristic method to evaluate web accessibility for users with low vision. IEEE Access **7**, 125634–125648 (2019). https://doi.org/10.1109/ACCESS.2019.2939068
23. Acosta-Vargas, P., Acosta, T., Lujan-Mora, S.: Challenges to assess accessibility in higher education websites: a comparative study of Latin America Universities. IEEE Access. **6**, 36500–36508 (2018). https://doi.org/10.1109/ACCESS.2018.2848978
24. López-Martínez, J., Juárez-Ramírez, R., Huertas, C., Jiménez, S., Guerra-García, C.: Problems in the adoption of agile-scrum methodologies: a systematic literature review. In: Software Engineering Research and Innovation, pp. 141–148. IEEE (2016)
25. Salvador-Ullauri, L., et al.: Development of an accessible video game to improve the understanding of the test of Honey-Alonso. In: Nunes, I.L. (ed.) AHFE 2019. AISC, vol. 959, pp. 289–298. Springer, Cham (2020). https://doi.org/10.1007/978-3-030-20040-4_26
26. Schwaber, K., Beedle, M.: Agile Software Development with Scrum. Prentice Hall, Upper Saddle River (2002)

# Web Application for the Management of Digital Diplomas in Training Centers Including Security QR Codes

Gustavo Eduardo Fernández Villacrés[1]([envelope]), Paola Cristina Pérez Fernández[2]([envelope]),
Víctor Manuel Pérez Rodríguez[2]([envelope]), and Leonidas Gustavo Salinas Espinosa[2]([envelope])

[1] Universidad Regional Autónoma de Los Andes, Ambato, Ecuador
ua.eduardofernandez@uniandes.edu.ec
[2] Universidad Técnica de Ambato, Ambato, Ecuador
paopf1005@gmail.com, {victormperez,leonidasgsalinas}@uta.edu.ec

**Abstract.** The processes have been diversifying over time, the virtual modality of training is the one that currently predominates, many public and private entities also hold events such as congresses of majority attendance, all these educational processes are guaranteed by certificates that normally must be printed as soon as these events culminate. The management of the certificates involves some difficulties such as high individual cost, errors in names are commented on several times and they must be redone. The project aimed to systematize this management to obtain digital certificates that can be easily downloaded from any part of the world at any time. The research was carried out in several entities that issue training processes and are committed to these difficulties. It was also possible to base the development tools and finally, a web application was obtained as a result that allows managing all the digital diplomas of one or several training processes. Also, it should be mentioned that the security in digital certificates is given by QR codes. The main conclusion is that web applications allow the improvement of the operational aspects of any training center.

**Keywords:** Web application · Training · Diplomas

## 1 Introduction

The training continues to be thought with the same guidelines and criteria as education in the University as if it were simply to insert it into the organizational field. The main difference between a process of training in the workplace and one of training at the University is that this form for a generically conceived environment, while on-the-job training needs to modify practices that are exercised in a particular organization. Any training action is a form of intervention in the organization. Install or change practices in the workplace, not only generate or build new skills. It also requires modifying the contexts that maintain and nurture existing practices, because everything that is done in an organization is subject to coordination between people and the follow-up of pre-established patterns and reciprocal expectations [1].

© Springer Nature Switzerland AG 2020
M. Botto-Tobar et al. (Eds.): ICAT 2019, CCIS 1193, pp. 384–394, 2020.
https://doi.org/10.1007/978-3-030-42517-3_29

Training and development are the main part of a continuous effort designed to improve employee competency and organizational performance. The training provides trainees with the knowledge and skills necessary to perform their current jobs. Teaching a worker how to operate a lathe or telling a supervisor how to schedule daily production are examples of training. On the other hand, development implies learning that goes beyond current work and has a long-term focus. Prepares employees to keep pace with the organization as it evolves and grows. The training generates employee satisfaction, improvement of morale, higher productivity and in general the criterion that satisfied employees produce satisfied customers [2].

In the simplest terms, services are actions processes and performances provided or co-produced by an entity or person for another entity or person. Customer service is the service provided in support of the products of a company. Many companies in the 21st century have taken service initiatives and promoted the quality of service as ways to differentiate and create competitive advantages. All this based on the managerial criterion that the quality service gave a good sense to the business [3].

The customer is the person to whom the company directs its actions using marketing to inform, guide and convince someone in the purchase of a product, service or brand. The company has to guarantee the quality of the product or service, it is the first of a series of steps aimed to achieve satisfaction and loyalty [4].

A center of continuing education is an entity usually assigned to a University, these centers have the purpose of issuing training processes at a private or business level, it must be taken into account that, given the technological advance and the modernization of business processes, the employees must be trained according to the demands of the companies. Among the main centers of continuing education, we have: la Politécnica Nacional, la ESPOL, la Universidad Técnica de Machala, la Universidad Católica de Cuenca, la Universidad Uniandes de Ambato (Ctt de Los Andes), it should also be mentioned that of the UTPL and so many others.

After several visits and observations made to the training centers of some educational institutions, it has been observed that the management of diplomas that certify this or that training process is handled manually, this generates some difficulties such as:

- Delays in the delivery of diplomas.
- High costs for printing expenses
- Cost increase due to corrections and reprinting
- The annoyance in the user for coming one or several times to take the respective diploma.
- Difficulties of sending when the student is from another region.

According to this symptomatology, the problem can be formulated, in the following sense: How to improve the management of Diplomas in a Continuing Education Center?

As a solution to this problem, it is thought about the automation of the management of diplomas to create a project to generate digital diplomas, the project had the following objectives:

General objective: develop a web application that allows the improvement of the management of diplomas in some centers of Continuing Education.

To achieve this general objective, the following specific objectives were considered:

- To research web applications bibliographically, their development tools and the management of diplomas.
- To diagnose the way to manage the diplomas in the different centers of continuous education.
- To prepare the web application with options to generate courses, teachers, students, and diplomas.

It can be assumed as a hypothesis that: With the automation of the management of diplomas at a Continuing Education center, customer service will be improved and operating costs will be reduced.

The justification for the development of the project essentially lies down in a solution that constitutes for the entity that provides educational services. An institution that issues academic events with massive assistance, it is logical to assume that it will have high costs and delays in the issuance of hundreds of certificates, with the technological solution certificates that can be issued in just one hour and with zero printing costs. If there are errors in names or dates in the certifications, they can easily be edited and corrected, while manually printing the corresponding delay. Occasionally, participants in a training event must return from distant cities to receive their certificate or often send it by mail generating additional expenses. All these difficulties are solved with the web application, also it generates an image of modernity to the entity since the user can download their digital diploma, from anywhere and at any time it is a great benefit for it. For everything described above, the realization of the project is justified.

The development of the project began with a theoretical foundation synthesized below.

Maximizing the profit for the investor is the main purpose of every company or company that generates profits, for two reasons, the first is that the owners provide a risk capital that allows the administrators to acquire the necessary resources to produce and sell goods or services [5].

The companies that provide services related to education are companies that compete with the service they provide, of course, they do not have a physical product but their competitive advantage will be related to the degree to which consumers value less tangible characteristics such as the speed of service, the image of modernity and more [6].

An information system is one that collects, processes, stores, analyzes and distributes information for a specific purpose or a general-purpose. In practice, the purpose of an information system is to obtain the correct information for the people who need it at the right time, and in the amount in addition to the appropriate format. It must be remembered that information systems must provide information for decision making, it is essential to remember the need to properly use the pyramid of knowledge (data, information, knowledge and decision making). The systems must facilitate the processing of the data, its conversion into information and through the appropriate context the conversion in turn into knowledge that will serve for decision making [7].

The analysis and design of systems is a systematic approach for the identification of problems, opportunities, and objectives analyzing information flows in organizations and designing computerized information systems to solve a problem [8].

A web application is a computer tool accessible from any browser, either through the Internet or through a local network. Through the browser, you can access all the functionality [9].

Among the advantages we have:

- It does not need any type of installation since it is accessed through a browser.
- It is a multiplatform and multi-device. This means that we can forget which software has each device that accesses, and that can also access a computer, a tablet, a smartphone [10].

The power is not in the accessing device, so even if we do not have a supercomputer, the application can be very powerful, since the weight is not supported by the computer from which it is accessed but by the server where it is hosted.

It can be in the cloud that would be accessible for any computer with internet access. It is very adaptable, visually intuitive and very easy to update if necessary [11].

PHP is a scripting language that runs on the server-side, whose code is included in a web page written in classic HTML. It can, therefore, be compared to other scripting languages that work according to the same principle: Asp (Active Server Pages) or JSP (Java Server Pages). This technology allows dynamic web pages whose content can be completely or partially generated at the time of the invocation of the page, thanks to the information obtained in a form or extracted from a database [10].

A web server is one that provides services to customers, one of its main functions is to store files belonging to a website and display them on the network and thus be able to be visited by users in the world [12].

The web server can also be defined in the following terms: it is a program that is permanently listening to the client connection requests through HTTP protocol. The server works in the following way: if it finds in its file system the HTML document requested by the client, it sends it and closes the connection; otherwise, it sends an error code and closes the connection. The web server also takes care of controlling the security aspects, checking if the user has access to the documents [13].

Apache is an application that allows us to implement a web server on our personal computer, assigning it a local server level, regardless of the operating system someone is in since it has open compatibility. Apache is considered an open-source web server with a free distribution that can be used in Windows, Linux, Macintosh, and other systems. Its closest competitor is the Internet Information Server, better known as IIS, which belongs to Microsoft and has the same Apache features, but is considered as a software owner too [14].

A database management system (DBMS) consists of a collection of interrelated data and a set of programs to access the data. The data collection, usually called the database, contains relevant information for a company. The main objective of a DBMS is to provide a way to store and retrieve information from a database in a way that is both practical and efficient. Database systems are designed to manage large amounts of information. Data management involves both the definition of structures to store information and the provision of mechanisms for the manipulation of information. Also, database systems must guarantee the reliability of stored information, despite system crashes or unauthorized access attempts. If the data are to be shared among different users, the system should avoid possible anomalous results [15].

Mysql is a relational database management system, which also offers compatibility with PHP, Perl, C, and Html, it has advanced functions for administration and optimization of databases to facilitate common tasks. To implement web functionalities, allowing safe and easy access to data through the Internet. It can be said that Mysql is a relational database administration client-server system designed for work in both Windows and Unix and Linux. In addition, certain statements can be fixed in PHP and Html code to design dynamic web applications [16].

The Internet has introduced important changes in the way in which companies operate their businesses. It has produced a dramatic drop in the cost of developing, sending and storing information while expanding the availability of information. Millions of people can exchange huge amounts of information directly, instantly and for free. In the past, information about products and services was closely linked to the physical value chain of such products and services [17].

## 2  Methods

A cross-sectional study of the problems related to the management of diplomas has been designed, it was proposed to carry out a qualitative-quantitative investigation, the same that was carried out in the place where the symptoms of the problem could be observed, in this case, the training entities of some places.

The methods used are:

Analytical-synthetic: To elaborate a theoretical framework based on the collection of information and the synthesis of it.
Inductive-Deductive: To induce a general solution from a particular.

The technique defined for the investigation is the survey of the respective Directors.
The population involved in the problem is composed of 15 entities that carry out training and issue certificates.
Since the population is very small, it is not necessary to define a sample.

## 3  Results

Next, the results of the research carried out (Table 1).
From the results obtained, the following analyzes can be made:

- 100% of those surveyed consider that the issuance of diplomas generates an expense.
- 80% of those consulted say that there are always delays in the printing of diplomas and that they are generally not ready when they are needed, especially when they are needed as urgent.
- 73% of respondents say that users are upset when they have to return to take a certificate since this implies expenses and time. Many entities assume the cost of home delivery but that increases the respective expense.

**Table 1.** Table captions should be placed above the tables. Results of the survey

| No. | Question | Yes | No |
|---|---|---|---|
| 1 | Does the generation of physical diplomas generate gas-coughs? | 15 | 0 |
| 2 | Sometimes there are delays in the printing of physical certificates? | 12 | 3 |
| 3 | Do users who must withdraw certificates sometimes get upset when they come and the certificate is not ready? | 11 | 4 |
| 4 | Do you sometimes have to repeat the certificates for mistakes in names or dates? | 14 | 1 |
| 5 | Would you consider a system that allows the rapid generation of digital type certificates to be useful? | 13 | 2 |
| 6 | Do you think it would be better for the user to be able to download a digital diploma from anywhere and at any time? | 10 | 5 |

Source: Researchers

- 86% say that a system that automatically manages diplomas will be very useful, especially when there are so many.
- 66% like the idea that users can download their diplomas from any-where and at any time.

Based on these results, it can be concluded that a computer system for the management of diplomas can be very useful in the centers of continuing education of several Universities of Ecuador. Based on this criterion, the web application began to be developed under the following criteria:

Software development methodology: The so-called cascade or linear methodology was applied, which has the four fundamental phases that are: analysis, design, development, and implementation.

In the previous analysis, essentially defined the processes that are part of the management of diplomas, then a scheme of the different processes (Fig. 1):

Once the processes are clearly defined, we proceed to define the modules that will contain the web application, these are:

- Teachers: here all the possible professors who can participate in the academic processes are registered.
- Courses: Defines the name and date of the course, as well as the assigned teacher.
- Students: Registers all enrollees who may participate in the academic course or event. An individual or massive registration can be made, the an-Excel format is used to mass register the enrollees.
- Enrollment: Individual or mass enrollment is here for students who have paid, this is only done with the ID numbers registered in the registration.
- Approvals. In this section the students who pass the course are registered, massive or individual approval can be made.
- Formats. You can upload the diploma format with the required measures, in addition, the format must have the necessary signatures

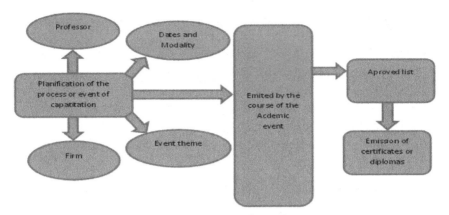

**Fig. 1.** Scheme of the different processes

- Reports: Reports are issued on the number of courses, participants and more.
- Users: registration of users who can access the system.

Once the modules were designed, we worked on the development of the web application, for which the following tools were defined: Mysql as a database, PHP as a programming language, Apache as a web server, and bootstrap as a working framework. After the respective black box and white box tests, the web application that has a free access module for downloading diplomas and the administrative compact with the previously defined modules was created (Fig. 2).

**Fig. 2.** Module for downloading diplomas

The certificate is generated and ready for downloading is displayed as follows (Fig. 3):

In the digital certificate, you can see a QR code that is generated automatically and that becomes an additional security element because it can be read by any mobile device

**Fig. 3.** Certificate generated

and be directed to the database of diplomas issued, this guarantees that, if the diploma is altered, its originality can easily be verified.

Next, the capture of the main menu of the system to the same that will have access to the administrator and from which it will be possible to manage the digital certificates (Fig. 4).

**Fig. 4.** The main menu of the system

Then a part of the coding of the web application is pasted, it is hosted on the servers of the company CYSSA and can be accessed easily for demonstration purposes.

```
<html lang="es" xmlns="http://www.w3.org/1999/html">
<head>
  <meta http-equiv="Content-Type" content="text/html; charset=UTF-8">
  <!-- Meta, title, CSS, favicons, etc. -->
  <meta charset="utf-8">
  <meta http-equiv="X-UA-Compatible" content="IE=edge">
  <meta name="viewport" content="width=device-width, initial-scale=1">
```

```
                <link        rel="shortcut        icon"        type="image/x-icon"
href="http://cyssaambato.com/cert/public/favicon.ico"/>
<! -- CSRF Token -->
                                <meta                    name="csrf-token"
content="LqpBlFrD5KwG2BK0Ej40BZEhDFTik5znPmcvrUv4">
<title>CYSSA - SISTEMA DE GESTIÓN DE CERTIFICADOS</title>
<link href="http://cyssaambato.com/cert/public/css/app.css" rel="stylesheet">
<! -- Bootstrap -->
<link href="http://cyssaambato.com/cert/public/css/bootstrap.min.css" rel="stylesheet">
<! -- Font Awesome --> <link href="http://cyssaambato.com/cert/public/css/font-
awesome.min.css"    rel="stylesheet">    <!    --    NProgress    -->    <link
href="http://cyssaambato.com/cert/public/css/nprogress.css" rel="stylesheet"> <! -- Datat-
ables --> <link href="http://cyssaambato.com/cert/public/css/dataTables.bootstrap.min.css"
rel="stylesheet">
        <link        href="http://cyssaambato.com/cert/public/css/buttons.bootstrap.min.css"
rel="stylesheet">
        <link        href="http://cyssaambato.com/cert/public/css/responsive.bootstrap.min.css"
rel="stylesheet">
        <link        href="http://cyssaambato.com/cert/public/css/scroller.bootstrap.min.css"
rel="stylesheet">
<! -- iCheck -->
<link    href="http://cyssaambato.com/cert/public/css/green.css"    rel="stylesheet">    <link
href="https://cdnjs.cloudflare.com/ajax/libs/animate.css/3.5.2/animate.min.css"
rel="stylesheet"> <! -- bootstrap-datetimepicker -->
```

## 4  Discussion

For Sutton [18] one of the parameters to define a quality service is the response capacity, this refers to the speed with which the company solves the customer's problems effectively. Based on this criterion, it is considered that the implementation of the web application will accelerate the delivery of diplomas and with this, the customer service is being improved. From the results of the research, it can be appreciated that the difficulties in the management of diplomas generate expenses and delays in the delivery, difficulties that are solved with the web application.

For the author Díaz [19] the customer service represents the constant effort that an organization must have to satisfy the needs that customers require, this is fully confirmed in the training centers where the web application for diploma management is installed. Due to the fact that some facilities are generated for the user, such as having his diploma at any time and at any time, this possibility generates customer satisfaction because it also prevents him from traveling to the place where the institution of training works and generates economic savings in the user.

It is also affirmed by Fernández [5] that competitiveness is established by the ability of companies to offer high-quality goods and services. These criteria are fully ratified in the investigation as it is affirmed by the majority of those investigated that with the automation of the processes the service is being accelerated, reducing the errors which imply raising the quality of the service to the client.

It is stated by Joyanes [20] that application software is used to solve specific actions or tasks, in this case, within the training entities, the issuance of a certificate is a frequent and very valuable process for the user, that is why it must be managed properly and quickly, all this is achieved with the web application since the possibility of issuing hundreds of digital diplomas quickly ensures a great service to the user. Also, the possibility of making quick corrections in the diploma allows the user not to have to return with the respective annoyances, it also prevents the company from returning to carry out the physical diploma, and it is even possible to avoid shipping costs if it is so the user has requested.

It can also be stated that according to Landou [17] the managers of the organizations have legal and ethical responsibilities in the security and confidentiality of the information that is why every web application must generate security in the storage of the data and the veracity of them. The backup of information before possible technological incidents or natural disasters must be conceived as an internal and automatic process, almost imperceptible for the user administrator of the system. The database must always be protected from improper access and inadequate handling. The backup of the information on different servers as well as in the cloud will be highly recommended.

## 5  Conclusions

The following conclusions can be drawn from the results obtained:

The management of diplomas implies expenses and time especially when they are in high number. This conclusion is generated from the manual management of diplomas, for example, there is a rapid training process that lasts just 3 days and is attended by 300 people, generally, in this type of event the inscriptions are made until the last moment, this implies that the data of the participants must be verified, the 300 physical diplomas must be printed and the deliveries made with respective agglomerations. The web application allows the rapid generation of diplomas, the correct correction in case of errors and the sending of the link to each user so that it can be downloaded. You can also save the sending of the link by putting a QR code in the event and having the participants access it to verify the veracity of the data of their diploma.

The automation of the management of diplomas produces an economic saving and a speed in the processes, which ends up in better attention to the client of the training entities. By improving the service, it is also improving by raising the image of the Institution and thereby adding value to the service received by the user.

The possibility of downloading a certificate from anywhere and at any time is attractive to users, it generates savings and the correction processes are very light.

The company can easily recover the investment made in the web application, this due to the savings that are had due to printing expenses, it is also saved in working time by corrections in the diploma data. To this must be added the flexibility of adapting the system to several types of mass training such as congresses and seminars. If the training processes are virtual and the students are in extremely distant regions of the company, the web application becomes an ideal resource to certify this training process.

The web application incorporates some security elements in its different modules, for example, it has a control related to the injection of malicious code, which ensures the permanence of the data in the database. It has also been considered important an automatic backup of the database every week and in the cloud, this process is internal and even goes unnoticed by the administrator of the web application.

# References

1. López, G.: Capacitación. Conciencia tecnológica **1**(2), 27–39 (2009)
2. Robbins, S., Judge, T.: Comportamiento oranizacional. Pearson, Prentice-Hall, México (2010)
3. Valero, A., Taracena, E.: La empresa de negocios y la alta dirección. Eunsa, Madrid (2000)
4. Paul, H., Kenneth, H. et al.: Adminsitración del comportamiento organizacional. Liderazgo situacional. Prentice Hall, México (2011)
5. Fernández, D., Fernández, E.: Comunicación empresarial y atención al cliente. Paraninfo, Madrid (2018)
6. María, S., Arrizabalaga, G.: Dimensiones de la responsabilidad social del Marketing. Revista venezolana de gerencia **18**, 434–456 (2013)
7. Diaz, L., Navarr, M.: Sistemas de información en la empresa. UAH, Alcalá (2013)
8. Littman, J.: API-based social media collecting as a form of web archiving. Int. J. Digit. Libr. **19**(1), 21–38 (2016)
9. Torres, M.: Desarrollo de aplicaciones web con PHP. Macro, Lima (2014)
10. Beati, H.: PHP, creación de páginas web dinámicas. ITMaster, México (2012)
11. Jimenez, J.: Fundamentos de programación. Alfaomega, Mexico (2014)
12. López, M., Sánchez, D., et al.: Programación web en el entorno cliente. Ediciones de la U, Bogotá (2016)
13. Van Lancker, L., Christophe, A.: HTML 5 y CSS3. Eni, Barcelona (2017)
14. Torres, M.: HTML 5 y CSS3. Macro, Lima (2014)
15. Reinosa, E.: Base de datos. Alfaomega, México (2012)
16. Heurtel, O.: PHP y MySql. ENI, Barcelona (2014)
17. Laudon, K., Guercio, K.: E-Commerce Negocios, tecnología y sociedad. Pearson, México (2014)
18. Thopson, A., Sutton, C., Janes, A., et al.: Administración estrategica, McGrawHill, México (2018)
19. Diaz, H.: Gestión de la cadena de suministro. Macro, Lima (2016)
20. Joyanes, L.: Sistemas de información en la empresa. Libro web, México (2015)

# Analysis of Essentially Non-oscillatory Numerical Techniques for the Computation of the Level Set Method

Israel Pineda$^{(\boxtimes)}$ (iD), Daniela Arellano$^{(\boxtimes)}$ (iD), and Roberth Chachalo$^{(\boxtimes)}$ (iD)

Yachay Tech University, Urcuquí, Ecuador
{ipineda,daniela.arellano,roberth.chachalo}@yachaytech.edu.ec
https://www.yachaytech.edu.ec

**Abstract.** In this paper, we analyze the Upwind Differencing and the Essentially Non-Oscillatory (ENO) schemes for the level set method during the evolution of interfaces. Our evolution experiments use different vector fields to test the behavior of the interface in different aspects. The experiments presented in this work are: evolution of a circle in a rotating field, shrinking and expanding of a square, Zalesak's disk revolution, and single-vortex evolution. Each one of them provides a different view of the strengths and weaknesses of the method. The experiments use the percentage of area loss, the $L_1$ error, and the order of convergence as accuracy metrics. We compare the different techniques, report our results, and provide conclusions.

**Keywords:** Essentially non-oscillatory · Level set method · Simulation

## 1 Introduction

Level Set Method (LSM) is a numerical technique that captures the evolution of an interface if this interface changes its topology, LSM easily can follow this variation (e.g., the interface splits in two or merges). The LSM has a variety of applications including, but not limited to, problems such as computer vision, fluid mechanics, combustion, image processing, simulation [8]. The key idea of the LSMs emerged from the Hamilton-Jacobi proposal to obtain numerical solutions of time-dependent equations to move implicit contours. Thus, we start by recalling the general Hamilton-Jacobi equation

$$\phi_t + H(x, t, \phi, D\phi) = 0, \quad \phi(x, 0) = \phi_0(x) \tag{1}$$

where $x \in R^d$ and $t > 0$. Crandall and Lions [1] introduced an relevant kind of monotone schemes for a simplified form of Eq. 1:

$$\phi_t + H(D\phi) = 0, \quad \phi(x, 0) = \phi_0(x) \tag{2}$$

© Springer Nature Switzerland AG 2020
M. Botto-Tobar et al. (Eds.): ICAT 2019, CCIS 1193, pp. 395–408, 2020.
https://doi.org/10.1007/978-3-030-42517-3_30

Unfortunately, monotone schemes can have at most first-order accuracy. Thus, Osher and Sethian [7] constructed a high-order upwinding scheme for Eq. 2 that mimics high order essentially non-oscillatory (ENO) schemes. Osher and Fedkiw [6] described a general numerical approach for each scheme: upwind differentiating, Hamilton-Jacobi ENO and weighted essentially non-oscillatory (WENO), which are used to get numerical solutions for Eq. 2.

In this paper, we implement and analyze the LSM to study a variety of surface motion problems, such as circle evolutions, expanding and shrinking squares, Zalesak's disks, and single vortices. These experiments allow us to evaluate the accuracy of the method in each scenario. To evaluate each experiment, we used the following metrics: the initial area, the loss of area after a revolution, error L1 and the order of convergence. The LSM is vulnerable to inaccuracies mainly due to numerically diffusion. For that reason, we can calculate the error in each experiment in such a way that the object to return to its initial state after some evolution time; in this way, the initial state can be used as the desired output in the error computation.

## 2    Methodology

### 2.1    Level Set Methods

The LSM is a technique which allows the evolution of an implicit function $\phi$ in time, this function represents a captured interface. This is a robust approach that supports topology changes of the surface. Figure 1(a) shows an example of the zero isocontour of a function $\phi$. The evolution of an implicit function $\phi$ is defined by the advection equation [6]:

$$\phi_t + \boldsymbol{V} \cdot \nabla\phi = 0 \tag{3}$$

where $\phi_t$ represents a temporal partial derivative in the time $t$, $\phi$ is a scalar field that contains a signed distance function, $\nabla$ represents the gradient of a function, and $\boldsymbol{V}$ is a vector field. This partial differential equation (PDE) is commonly known as the level set equation.

The second term of Eq. 3 is defined as

$$\boldsymbol{V} \cdot \nabla\phi = u\phi_x + v\phi_y + w\phi_z. \tag{4}$$

The discretization of Eqs. (3) and (4) is based on the construction of a grid that stores the information. Thus, the LSM represents an Eulerian approach to the interface evolution.

Figure 1 shows the state of a given interface $\phi$ at two different moments in time. The figure presents the intersection of the distance function with the two-dimensional domain plain, known as the isocontour. This isocontour is usually called the zero level set.

Figure 1(a) shows the initial state of a function while Fig. 1(b) shows the function after the evolution; there is an evident loss of area in this example. Additionally, Fig. 2 shows the surface defined by the function as well as the intersection with the domain.

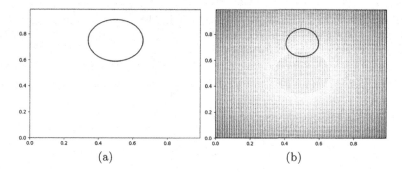

**Fig. 1.** (a) Isocontour of a distance function. (b) Isocontour after evolution together with the vector field that was used.

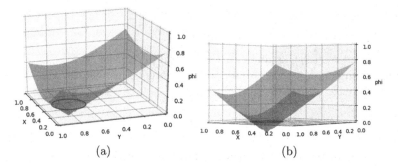

**Fig. 2.** Representation in three dimensions of the distance function (light blue) and its intersection with the domain (dark blue). (Color figure online)

**LSM Basic Upwind Differencing.** This numerical method is used to evolve an implicit function onward in time where the interface advances from one side to another on a grid. The grid needs to be preloaded with the distance function $\phi$ and the vector field $V$ at every grid point. Then, we can describe this method as follows.

We define the values of $\phi$ at a certain point in time $t^n$ as

$$\phi^n = \phi(t^n). \tag{5}$$

The value of $\phi$ in the next time step is

$$\phi^{n+1} = \phi(t^{n+1}), \tag{6}$$

after some time increment $\Delta t$, where $t^{n+1} = t^n + \Delta t$.

To discretize the time of Eq. 3, we employ the method of *forward Euler*, which is a first-order accurate scheme, denoted by

$$\frac{\phi^{n+1} - \phi^n}{\Delta t} + \overrightarrow{V}^n \cdot \nabla \phi^n = 0 \tag{7}$$

where, at time $t^n$, $\vec{V}^n$ stands for the external velocity field, and $\nabla \phi^n$ uses the values of $\phi$ at the same time to evaluate the gradient operator. Moreover, Eq. 7 can be seen in its expanded form:

$$\frac{\phi^{n+1} - \phi^n}{\Delta t} + u^n \phi_x^n + v^n \phi_y^n + w^n \phi_z^n = 0. \tag{8}$$

Considering the one-dimensional form of Eq. 8 for simplicity,

$$\frac{\phi^{n+1} - \phi^n}{\Delta t} + u^n \phi_x^n = 0. \tag{9}$$

In $R^1$, let $x_i$ be a discretization and distributed uniformly $\Delta x$; Eq. 9 can be defined at this specific grid point as

$$\frac{\phi_i^{n+1} - \phi_i^n}{\Delta t} + u_i^n (\phi_x)_i^n = 0 \tag{10}$$

where, at point $x_i$, $(\phi_x)_i$, stands for the spatial derivative of $\phi$.

To approximate $\phi_{x,i}$ at $x_i$, we use finite-difference techniques. Thus, a precise forward difference of first order is given by

$$\frac{\partial \phi}{\partial x} \approx \frac{\phi_{i+1} - \phi_i}{\Delta x}, \tag{11}$$

and a precise backward difference of first order is given by

$$\frac{\partial \phi}{\partial x} \approx \frac{\phi_i - \phi_{i-1}}{\Delta x}. \tag{12}$$

The differences of Eqs. 11 and 12 can also be written as $\phi_{x,i}^+$ and $\phi_{x,i}^-$, respectively. Osher and Fedkiw [6] described how to pick, based on the sign of $u$, the most suitable of these two options: if $u_i > 0$, $\phi_x$ is approximated with $\phi_x^-$, and similarly if $u_i < 0$, $\phi_x$ is approximated with $\phi_x^+$. When $u_i = 0$, $\phi_x$ does not need to be approximated because the $u_i(\phi_x)_i$ term vanishes.

**ENO Scheme.** In this section, the Hamilton-Jacobi essentially non-oscillatory (ENO) scheme is defined as a technique to approximate derivatives in space. This method enhances the numerical precision of the backward difference $\phi_x^+$ and forward difference $\phi_x^-$ approximations. Both are illustrated in Fig. 3. Also, a third-order accurate Runge Kutta approximation for time derivatives is presented to complement the numerical scheme.

We start by describing the Hamilton-Jacobi essentially non-oscillatory (ENO) scheme following the ideas described by Jiang [3]. In the one dimensional case, we work with a function $\phi$ which is continuous in $R^1$ and has piece-wise smooth derivatives.

The first step is to create a discretization of space $x_k$ with a uniform spacing $\Delta x$. Then, we have

$$\phi_k = \phi(x_k), \Delta^+\phi_k = \phi_{k+1} - \phi_k, \Delta^-\phi_k = \phi_k - \phi_{k-1}.$$

The $3^{rd}$ order accurate ENO scheme algorithm uses a left-biased stencil $\{x_k, k = i - 3, \ldots, i + 2\}$ to approximate $\phi_x(x_i)$. The algorithm selects one of the following:

$$\phi_{x,i}^{-,0} = \frac{1}{3}\frac{\Delta^+\phi_{i-3}}{\Delta x} - \frac{7}{6}\frac{\Delta^+\phi_{i-2}}{\Delta x} + \frac{11}{6}\frac{\Delta^+\phi_{i-1}}{\Delta x} \tag{13}$$

$$\phi_{x,i}^{-,1} = -\frac{1}{6}\frac{\Delta^+\phi_{i-2}}{\Delta x} + \frac{5}{6}\frac{\Delta^+\phi_{i-1}}{\Delta x} + \frac{1}{3}\frac{\Delta^+\phi_i}{\Delta x} \tag{14}$$

$$\phi_{x,i}^{-,2} = \frac{1}{3}\frac{\Delta^+\phi_{i-1}}{\Delta x} + \frac{5}{6}\frac{\Delta^+\phi_i}{\Delta x} - \frac{1}{6}\frac{\Delta^+\phi_{i+1}}{\Delta x} \tag{15}$$

In order to choose $\phi_{x,i}^{-,s}$ for $s = 0, 1, 2$ from Eqs. 13, 14, 15, the algorithm uses the relative smoothness of $\phi$ on the sub-stencils $\{x_k, k = i + s - 3, i + s - 2, \ldots, i + s\}$. The following equation provides the method to choose the appropriate approximation.

$$\phi_{x,i}^- = \begin{cases} \phi_{x,i}^{-,0} & if \; |\Delta^-\Delta^+\phi_{i-1}| < |\Delta^-\Delta^+\phi_i| \; and \; |\Delta^-\Delta^-\Delta^+\phi_{i-1}| < |\Delta^+\Delta^-\Delta^+\phi_{i-1}|; \\ \phi_{x,i}^{-,2} & if \; |\Delta^-\Delta^+\phi_{i-1}| > |\Delta^-\Delta^+\phi_i| \; and \; |\Delta^-\Delta^-\Delta^+\phi_i| > |\Delta^+\Delta^-\Delta^+\phi_i|; \\ \phi_{x,i}^{-,1} & otherwise. \end{cases}$$

Similarly, $\phi_{x,i}^+$ is approximated using the right-biased stencil $\{x_k, k = i - 2, \ldots, i + 3\}$ and sub-stencils $\{x_k, k = i - s + 3, i - s + 2, \ldots, i - s\}$ for $s = 0, 1, 2$.

To illustrate the ENO scheme, we show an example of the approximation of $\phi_x(x_i)$ by $\phi_{x,i}^-$, where $\phi$ is

$$\phi(x) = \begin{cases} \frac{1}{2}(1 - cos2\pi x) & if \; 0 \le x \le \frac{1}{2}, \\ \pi(\frac{1}{2} - x) + \frac{1}{2}(3 + cos2\pi) & if \; \frac{1}{2} < \pi x \le 1. \end{cases} \tag{16}$$

Figure 3 shows the results of this backward difference approximation as well as the forward difference approximation using the right-bias stencil.

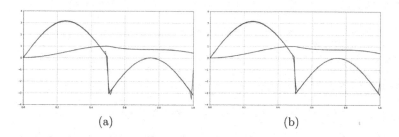

(a)                                                    (b)

**Fig. 3.** (a) Forward difference approximation. (b) Backward difference approximation.

The $3^{rd}$ order ENO approximation is a building block to construct higher-order schemes.

**Runge Kutta Scheme.** The next element of the scheme is time discretization. For time discretization, we apply the third-order Runge-Kutta scheme, which is described by Shu and Osher [9].

A high-order temporal discretization is essential for obtaining accurate numerical solutions. For that reason, Shu and Osher suggest total variation diminishing (TVD) Runge-Kutta (RK). TVD Runge-Kutta provides improved accuracy in the computation of time derivatives.

The TVD Runge-Kutta is an approach that performs several substeps before it reaches the following time step. First, an Euler step advances the solution to time $t^n + \Delta t$. Using the following expression

$$\frac{\phi^{n+1} - \phi^n}{\Delta t} + \boldsymbol{V}^n \cdot \nabla \phi^n = 0. \tag{17}$$

Next, a second Euler step advances the solution to time $t^n + 2\Delta t$,

$$\frac{\phi^{n+2} - \phi^{n+1}}{\Delta t} + \boldsymbol{V}^{n+1} \cdot \nabla \phi^{n+1} = 0. \tag{18}$$

Then, an averaging step takes the solution to time $\phi^{n+\frac{1}{2}}$,

$$\phi^{n+\frac{1}{2}} = \frac{3}{4}\phi^n + \frac{1}{4}\phi^{n+\frac{1}{2}}. \tag{19}$$

Later, another step advances the solution to time $t^n + \frac{3}{2}\Delta t$,

$$\frac{\phi^{n+2} - \phi^{n+2}}{\Delta t} + \boldsymbol{V}^{n+\frac{1}{2}} \cdot \nabla \phi^{n+\frac{1}{2}} = 0. \tag{20}$$

Lastly, a second averaging step advances the solution to time $t^n + \Delta t$,

$$\phi^{n+1} = \frac{1}{3}\phi^n + \frac{2}{3}\phi^{n+\frac{3}{2}}. \tag{21}$$

A comprehensive introduction of related topics is presented by Mazumder [5]. More up-to-date schemes are presented by Maciel and Andrade [4] and Sun and Shu [10].

## 2.2   Error Metrics

The error measure used to evaluate the accuracy is the $L_1$ norm, which is defined as

$$\|f - p\|_1 = \int_a^b |f(x) - p(x)| \, dx \tag{22}$$

where $f(x)$ is the desired function and $p(x)$ is the approximation, in our case the output of the numerical method.

Equation 22 is useful for working with analytic functions. However, we work with discrete functions in our experiments. Thus, the discrete version of Eq. 22 is

$$\sum_{i=0}^{n} |f(x_i) - p(x_i)| . \tag{23}$$

This equation shows the core idea of calculating the $L_1$ norm. However, to measure the accuracy of the level set method, a modified version that uses a multiplying normalizer is used. We first calculate a Heaviside function and then we calculate

$$\frac{1}{L} \int |H(\phi_{expected}) - H(\phi_{computed})| \, dxdy \tag{24}$$

as the error measurement, where $L$ stands for the perimeter of the interface.

Another important measurement is the order of convergence. The order of convergence is used to calculate how much the result of the simulation improves as the number of cells in the grid is increased. Thus, we calculate the order of convergence using

$$order = \frac{loge_2 - loge_1}{logr_2 - logr_1} \tag{25}$$

where $e_1$ and $e_2$ are the error of the two simulations, which, in our case, are computed using the $L_1$ norm, and $r_1$ and $r_2$ are the number of cells in each grid we are comparing.

## 3   Experiments

### 3.1   Circle Revolution

This experiment considers a rigid body rotation. The body is a circle within the unit square; it is centered at $(0.5, 0.75)$ and has a radius of 0.15. This function is given by

$$\phi = ((x - 0.5)^2 + (y - 0.75)^2)^{\frac{1}{2}} - 0.15.$$

The constant vorticity field is defined as by

$$u = \left(\frac{\pi}{314}\right)(0.5 - y),$$

$$v = \left(\frac{\pi}{314}\right)(x - 0.5).$$

This vector field has an interesting characteristic. Namely, it moves the body in a way that it comes back to the same position at unit time 628. More than one revolution is also possible.

Table 1 shows the time used to generate all images for one revolution. Depending on the number of disk operations, the time of the simulation changes considerably. The use of trial and error with this experiment and the analysis of the data in Table 1 helped us to save only every 10 time-steps.

Table 2 shows the results of using the upwind differencing scheme, mainly the area loss after one revolution for two different grids. The initial area and final area were calculated using the Heaviside function. Moreover, the $L_1$ norm was used to compute the accuracy of the interface. The error is computed following the method presented by Enright [2]:

1. Split the domain into many tiny pieces $1000 \times 1000$,
2. Interpolate the values of $\phi_{expect}$ and $\phi_{compute}$ onto the newly partitioned domain,
3. Numerically integrate Eq. 24 where $H(\phi) = 1$ if $\phi \leq 0$ and $H(\phi) = 0$ otherwise.

Details for the calculation of the error metrics are presented in Sect. 2.2.

**Table 1.** Circle experiment: execution time by disk writing operations.

|    | Time | Interval | Num. images |
|----|------|----------|-------------|
| v1 | 8 s | 0–5 | 51 |
| v2 | 19 min 9 s | 0–628 | 6280 |
| v3 | 10 min 36 s | 0–628 | 628 |
| v4 | 5 min 11 s | 0–628 | 0 |

**Table 2.** Result: circle revolution using upwind differencing

|  | Grid cells | Area | % Area loss | $L_1$ error | Order |
|--|-----------|------|-------------|-------------|-------|
| One revolution | Exact | 0.0696 | - | - | - |
|  | 50 | 0 | 100% | 0.0696 | N/A |
|  | 100 | 0.0283 | 59.34% | 0.0413 | 0.75 |

**Table 3.** Result: circle revolution using ENO-Runge Kutta

|  | Grid cells | Area | % Area loss | $L_1$ error | Order |
|--|-----------|------|-------------|-------------|-------|
| One revolution | Exact | 0.0706 | - | - | - |
|  | 50 | 0.0676 | 5.056% | 0.0036 | N/A |
|  | 100 | 0.0697 | 1.275% | 0.0009 | 2.0 |

By comparing the results between Tables 2 and 3 an abrupt change in the accuracy between both methods. So, we obtained the following differences: on the $50 \times 50$ grid, the interface disappeared before one revolution finalized, while for ENO with the identical grid, we got a considerable improvement of the solution, obtaining a 5.056 area loss. Furthermore, on the $100 \times 100$ grid, we observed that by using ENO-RK, 1.275 of the area was lost, as opposed to 59.34 of upwind differencing. Figure 4 shows the percentage of area that is preserved when using upwind differencing. Thus, these results show that upwind differencing fails on these grids, but if we increase the number of cells, it is possible that better results will be obtained. As we can see, the results of ENO are considerable on these grids; it means that for smooth interfaces, this method is a good solution.

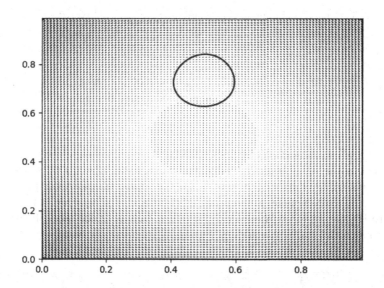

**Fig. 4.** Circle interface after one revolution (628 time units).

## 3.2    Expanding Square

A unit computational domain, consider the rigid body of square with edges of 0.60 centered at $(0.5, 0.5)$. In the case of a shrinking square, the velocity field is defined as

$$u = -N,$$

and as opposed to it, that is, in the case of an expanding square, the velocity field is given by

$$u = N,$$

Figure 5 illustrates the motion of the square through the velocity field using upwind differencing. Figure 5(b) shows rarefaction at the corners for both the expanding and shrinking square.

Comparing the results between Tables 4 and 5, we can observe important differences of the accuracy between both methods. So, we obtained the following differences: on the $50 \times 50$ grid, the interface in one revolution finalized with a $-25.49$ area loss, while for ENO with the identical grid, we got a considerable improvement of the solution, obtaining a 2.191 area loss. Furthermore, on the

**Table 4.** Result: shrinking and expanding square using Upwind Differencing

| Grid cells | Area | % Area loss | $L_1$ error | Order |
|---|---|---|---|---|
| Exact | 0.2601 | - | - | - |
| 50 | 0.3264 | −25.49% | 0.0663 | N/A |
| 100 | 0.2852 | −9.65% | 0.0251 | 1.40 |

**Table 5.** Result: shrinking and expanding square using ENO-Runge Kutta

| Grid cells | Area | % Area loss | $L_1$ error | Order |
|---|---|---|---|---|
| Exact | 0.2601 | - | - | - |
| 50 | 0.2544 | 2.191% | 0.0057 | N/A |
| 100 | 0.2622 | −0.807% | 0.0021 | 2.13 |

$100 \times 100$ grid, we observed that using ENO-RK resulted in a −0.807 area loss, as opposed to the −9.65 area loss observed when using upwind differencing. We consider this to be a small but significant reduction in area loss, thus we can observer which experiment give us better results. As we can see, the results of ENO are considerable on these grids, which means that for smooth interfaces, this method could provide a good solution for maintaining area.

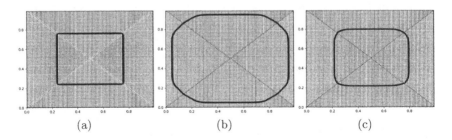

(a)                          (b)                          (c)

**Fig. 5.** The motion of the square through the velocity field. Both shrinking and expanding are shown.

### 3.3   Zalesak's Disk Revolution

The Zalesak's disk is a rigid body that is commonly used as an example to demonstrate the capabilities of the level set method. The interface is a slotted circle centered at $(0.5, 0.75)$. It has a radius of $0.15$. In this experiment, this body was moved through a constant vorticity velocity field.

The constant vorticity field used for this experiment is the same presented for the circle revolution experiment in Sect. 3.1.

**Table 6.** Result: Zalesak's disk revolution using Upwind Differencing

|  | Grid cells | Area | % Area loss | $L_1$ error | Order |
|---|---|---|---|---|---|
| One revolution | Exact | 0.0586 | - | - | - |
|  | 50 | 0 | 100% | 0.0586 | N/A |
|  | 100 | 0 | 100% | 0.0586 | 0 |

**Table 7.** Result: Zalesak's disk revolution using ENO-Runge Kutta

|  | Grid cells | Area | % Area loss | $L_1$ error | Order |
|---|---|---|---|---|---|
| One revolution | Exact | 0.0586 | - | - | - |
|  | 50 | 0.046 | 19.014% | 0.0148 | N/A |
|  | 100 | 0.0543 | 7.338% | 0.0065 | 1.2 |

By comparing the results between Tables 6 and 7, important differences in the accuracy between both methods can be observed. The following results were obtained: on the $50 \times 50$ grid, for the upwinding difference, the interface disappeared before one revolution finalize with a 100 area loss, while for ENO with an identical grid, we got a considerable improvement a 19.014 area loss. Furthermore, on the grid $100 \times 100$, we observed that using ENO-RK, 7.338 of the area loss, as opposed to 100 of upwind differencing. As we can see, the results of ENO are considerable on these grids, which means that for smooth interfaces, this method is an effective solution for reducing area loss (Fig. 6).

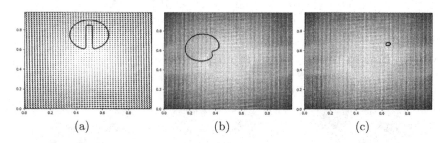

(a)                     (b)                     (c)

**Fig. 6.** Illustration of the loss of area by applying upwind differencing. Moreover, after one revolution of Zalesak's, the area is zero.

## 3.4   Single Vortex

Single vortex is a test case which entails resolving thin filaments on the mesh size that can happen in stretching and tearing flows to prove the ability of a Eulerian scheme. Then, the velocity field is defined by the stream function

$$\Psi = \frac{1}{\pi} sin^2(\pi x) sin^2(\pi y).$$

For implementation purposes, a unit computational domain is used with a circle with a radius of 0.15, set at $(0.5, 0.75)$. The expected result is to see the circle progressively stretched out toward the center of the computational domain. Figure 5a, b, and c illustrate the stretching using upwind differencing.

In order to analyze the error, the multiplication $\Psi \times cos(\pi t/T)$ is used to reverse the velocity field, where $T$ stands for the time at which the stream changes its direction [2]. To produce maximal stretching in the error analysis of the vortex test, we used the reversal period $T = 8$. Table 8 shows results about the poor performance of the tradition upwinding differencing scheme for this kind of extreme deformation. The experiments used $50 \times 50$ and $100 \times 100$ grids, and in both cases 100 area loss occurred (Fig. 7).

**Table 8.** Results with Single vortex using Upwind Differencing

| Grid cells | Area | % Area loss | $L_1$ error | Order |
|---|---|---|---|---|
| Exact | 0.0696 | - | - | - |
| 50 | 0 | 100% | 0.0696 | N/A |
| 100 | 0 | 100% | 0.0696 | 0 |

**Table 9.** Results with Single vortex using ENO-Runge Kutta

| Grid cells | Area | % Area loss | $L_1$ error | Order |
|---|---|---|---|---|
| Exact | 0.0706 | - | - | - |
| 50 | 0 | 100% | 0.0706 | N/A |
| 100 | 0.0301 | 57.36% | 0.0405 | 0.80 |

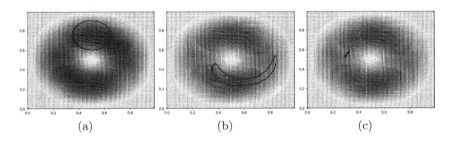

|     |     |     |
|:---:|:---:|:---:|
| (a) | (b) | (c) |

**Fig. 7.** Illustration of Single Vortex with $T = 8$ to return to its initial state.

By comparing the results between Tables 8 and 9, which are visible, we observed that the result for upwind differencing when the interface stretched was complete area loss. As we can see, even if we use a $100 \times 100$ grid, the result is the same. However, the results for ENO after the maximal stretching are minimum; we can see a 57.36 area loss using a $100 \times 100$ grid. Therefore, the results did not improve considerably as in the previous experiments; this means that for this type of test, using a different method or increasing the grid size for ENO is necessary to reduce area loss.

## 4   Conclusions

The level set method is used to smoothly capture moving interfaces. The method exhibits several strengths, but it also suffers from an excessive amount of area loss in under resolved regions of the interface. Experiments with upwind differencing yielded low accuracy results, while ENO-RK achieved improved accuracy for all our experiments. The grid size and the differentiation scheme directly affected the quality of the results. For example, with respect to the revolution of the circle, we lost all the area of the interface when testing with upwinding differencing on a $50 \times 50$ grid. However, the same experiment on a $100 \times 100$ grid was able to better preserve the area. Consequently, with a finer grid, the body does not disappear.

It is also possible to compare the results when using the same grid resolution but is not with a different method. In this case, the results using ENO-RK, with the same interface circle, had better conservation of area. This behavior was consistent for both grids. Thus, it is the low accuracy scheme that makes the interface vanish completely. Moreover, time affects the results; for that reason we used the Runge-Kutta scheme to increase the accuracy of the method.

We can summarize that all the interfaces that we considered in our experiments are better preserved when evolving with a high-order method such as ENO. High order time discretization schemes are also an important factor in the search for accuracy, as is the size of the grids.

In future experiments, we plan to use larger grids along with high performance computing (HPC) facilities as this approach requires more computational resources to execute. Another option to increase accuracy, that we will explore in future work, is to work with the WENO-RK scheme, which builds upon the $3^{rd}$ order ENO scheme described in this work. The WENO scheme is uniformly $5^{th}$ order accurate in smooth regions but will have the same stencil as the $3^{rd}$ order ENO scheme. It works nicely with the $3^{rd}$ order Runge-Kutta scheme for discretization time. Furthermore, we will use more interfaces, such as a deformation field, to test the best method for smooth regions. smooth regions. We also plan to use our results to create a hybrid method of the techniques described here and the particle level set method.

## References

1. Crandall, M.G., Lions, P.L.: Two approximations of solutions of Hamilton-Jacobi equations. Math. Comput. **43**(167), 1 (1984). https://doi.org/10.2307/2007396. http://www.ams.org/jourcgi/jour-getitem?pii=S0025-5718-1984-0744921-8

2. Enright, D., Fedkiw, R., Ferziger, J., Mitchell, I.: A hybrid particle level set method for improved interface capturing. J. Comput. Phys. **183**(1), 83–116 (2002). https://doi.org/10.1006/jcph.2002.7166. http://www.sciencedirect.com/science/article/pii/S0021999102971664

3. Jiang, G.S., Peng, D.: Weighted ENO schemes for Hamilton-Jacobi equations. SIAM J. Sci. Comput. **21**(6), 2126–2143 (2000). https://doi.org/10.1137/S106482759732455X. http://epubs.siam.org/doi/abs/10.1137/S106482759732455X

4. Góes Maciel, E.S., de Andrade, C.R.: Comparison among unstructured TVD, ENO and UNO schemes in two- and three-dimensions. Appl. Math. Comput. **321**, 130–175 (2018). https://doi.org/10.1016/j.amc.2017.10.026

5. Mazumder, S.: Numerical Methods for Partial Differential Equations: Finite Difference and Finite, vol. Methods. Elsevier, Amsterdam (2015)

6. Osher, S., Fedkiw, R., Piechor, K.: Level set methods and dynamic implicit surfaces **57** (2004). https://doi.org/10.1115/1.1760520

7. Osher, S., Sethian, J.: Fronts propagating with curvature-dependent speed: algorithms based on Hamilton-Jacobi formulations. J. Comput. Phys. **79**(1), 12–49 (1988). https://doi.org/10.1016/0021-9991(88)90002-2. http://www.sciencedirect.com/science/article/pii/0021999188900022

8. Pineda, I., Gwun, O.: Leaf modeling and growth process simulation using the level set method. IEEE Access **5**, 15948–15959 (2017). https://doi.org/10.1109/ACCESS.2017.2738032. http://ieeexplore.ieee.org/document/8007190/

9. Shu, C.W., Osher, S.: Efficient implementation of essentially non-oscillatory shock-capturing schemes. J. Comput. Phys. **77**(2), 439–471 (1988). https://doi.org/10.1016/0021-9991(88)90177-5. http://linkinghub.elsevier.com/retrieve/pii/0021999188901775

10. Sun, Z., Shu, C.: Strong stability of explicit Runge-Kutta time discretizations. Society **32**(5), 3020–3038 (2019)

# Software to Determine the Readability of Written Documents by Implementing a Variation of the Gunning Fog Index Using the Google Linguistic Corpus

Luis Carlos Rodríguez Timaná⬨, Diego Fernando Saavedra Lozano⬨,
and Javier Ferney Castillo García⁽⊠⁾⬨

Grupo de Investigación en Electrónica Industrial y Ambiental – GIEIAM,
Universidad Santiago de Cali, Cali, Colombia
javier.castillo00@usc.edu.co

**Abstract.** In English linguistics the Gunning Fog Index is used to determine the readability of texts. This methodology isn't as effective in the Spanish language because the complexity of words isn't determined by the number of syllables, unlike what happens in English. Therefore, a software was developed that allows us to estimate the readability of an academic text written in Spanish in a quantitative way. This software allows to compare the traditional methodology of the Gunning fog index and a modification to it, using the corpus linguistics for the Spanish language, based on thousands of texts digitized by Google, where the frequency of use of certain words is related. Texts produced by students from first to last semester were evaluated. Each text was subjected to the Gunning fog index assessment methodology and the corpus methodology, changing the percentage of complex words to the percentage of unknown words. In the evaluation of first semester texts it was found that the average fog index was 29.25, and an average of 37.9 complex words, for these same texts was found a modified fog index of 18.62 and 5.1 unknown words. On the other hand, for the evaluation of the texts produced in the last semester, the average fog index was 27.55 and an average of 51.4 complex words, with the modified fog index was an average of 15.08 and 7.1 unknown words. With this study, aspects related to the best use of punctuation marks and the increase of vocabulary related to the profession can be identified in a quantitative way.

**Keywords:** Corpus linguistics · Gunning · Fog Index

## 1 Introduction

Readability is the ease with which a reader can understand a piece of writing. In natural language, the readability of the text depends on its content (the complexity of its vocabulary and syntax) and its presentation (typographical aspects such as font size, line height and line length). The easier a text is to read, the more readable it will be. Readability depends on whether a text is composed of short sentences, if it uses structures that allow

© Springer Nature Switzerland AG 2020
M. Botto-Tobar et al. (Eds.): ICAT 2019, CCIS 1193, pp. 409–420, 2020.
https://doi.org/10.1007/978-3-030-42517-3_31

the reader to advance in the content of the text, to place the key words properly in the right place, to keep a logical order, among other characteristics [1].

The readability of texts is a matter of interest for educators, publishers, journalists and others who use written texts as a means of diffusion. On several occasions, all these people must make decisions about the material they are going to use or disseminate. Tasks that tend to be time-consuming for lack of judgment [2].

Currently there are different methodologies that allow quantifying the readability of a text, but these are oriented to the English language, so there is a need to implement a tool that allows a simple way to evaluate texts in Spanish. A software based on a variation of the Gunning fog index was developed for evaluate texts in Spanish, using Google Ngram by means of an API. The software was implemented in texts of 10 students of different semesters of the Faculty of Engineering of the Universidad Santiago de Cali. It was determined that first semester students had a lower readability in their texts than students in more advanced semesters.

**Theoretical Framework.** According to the dictionary of the "Real Academia Española", readability is the quality of being read. The easier a text is to read and understand, the more readable it will be, which is why it is a very important factor when creating content, especially when it is educational content [3]. There are different methodologies for quantitatively calculating the readability of texts. Some of them are mentioned below.

Flesch's readability test evaluates texts on a 100-point scale and considers the number of words per sentence and the average number of syllables per word. It does not consider any variable that may be affected by the language in which the text is written [3]. The formula for this test is mentioned in Eq. 1.

$$206.835 - 1.01 * \left( \frac{total\ words}{total\ sentences} \right) - 84.6 * \left( \frac{total\ syllables}{total\ words} \right) \qquad (1)$$

The Flesch-Kincaid School Placement Test evaluates textbooks based on U.S. school placement. Because we are looking for an index that fits the Spanish language, it is rejected [3]. The formula for this test is mentioned in Eq. 2.

$$0.39 * \left( \frac{total\ words}{total\ sentences} \right) - 11.8 * \left( \frac{total\ syllables}{total\ words} \right) - 15.59 \qquad (2)$$

The Flesch-Szigriszt readability index is an adaptation to the Spanish language of the Flesch index, mentioned above [3]. The formula for this test is mentioned in Eq. 3.

$$206.835 - 62.3 * \left( \frac{total\ words}{total\ sentences} \right) - \left( \frac{total\ syllables}{total\ words} \right) \qquad (3)$$

All the indexes mentioned above consider the total syllables per total words of the text, but it was considered more important to study readability in terms of word length, since its simplification considers that short words imply a minor difficulty of understanding. The Gunning fog index uses this methodology and it is possible to adjust the formula. It is an index that indicates the readability of a text using a series of characteristics of it. In order to determine readability, the subject matter of the text is not considered. Common parameters are used, such as the number of syllables of the words that make up the text. This index is established by an equation formulated by Robert Gunning in 1952 to identify the audience to which a given text can be directed. This method was created for the English language and is not as accurate for Spanish-language texts [4].

Although in Spanish the words are generally longer than in English, the frequency with which they appear in the texts in both languages is very similar, as seen in Fig. 1. This allows the Gunning Fog Index to be used to evaluate the readability of texts written in Spanish. However, since in Spanish longer words are used, a slight change was made in the Gunning formula. Through the Google Linguistic Corpus long words are chosen based on the frequency of occurrence in this and not based on its longitude. Obtaining as a result a more robust algorithm to measure readability in the Spanish language. The development of the methodology will be explained in later sections.

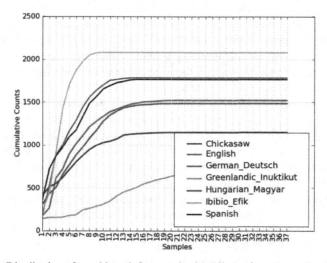

**Fig. 1.** Distribution of word length frequencies in different languages. Source: [4].

A distinction must be made between linguistic readability, which deals with verbal aspects, and typographical legibility, which refers to the visual perception of the text (layout of the text on the page, size of the letter, use of italics, bold, etc.). In this case, the linguistic readability will be evaluated, that is why some concepts must be known firsts.

The syllable is each of the phonological divisions into which a word is divided. It is the second smallest division of the spoken string. The phonological units into which a word is divided are called syllables, according to the minimum grouping of its articulated sounds, which means the union of a vowel and one or more consonants. In other words, these are the sound fragments into which a word can be divided, respecting the logic of its pronunciation [5].

The hiatus occurs when the accentuation of a word or its pronunciation forces to separate in different syllables a diphthong or a triphthong. This happens when there are two strong vowels, as well as when in a diphthong or in a triphthong the tonic vowel is a weak one [5].

A diphthong is a sound chain that is based on the articulation of two vowels, one followed by the other, without interruption and producing a smooth transition in the sound frequencies that characterize the timbres of each of the two vowels. Phonologically, two vowels articulated in this way are part of the same syllable. In a diphthong the acoustic formants have a smooth transition from one point of the vowel area to another, which gives them their diphthong nature. This is due to an articulation in which the tongue moves between different points during the emission of the diphthong. The two end points of the joint are perceived as the two vowels forming the diphthong. In the spectrogram of a hiatus the transition zone is not observed, that is why phonetically they are different [5].

The triphthong is the sequence of three vowels in the same syllable: closed vowel (u/i) + open vowel tonic (a/e/o) + closed vowel (u/i) [5].

Another fundamental concept is the Linguistic Corpus, because the implemented software makes use of it. A linguistic corpus is a broad and structured set of real examples of language use. These examples can be texts (the most common), or oral samples (generally transcribed) [6]. A linguistic corpus is a relatively large set of texts, created independently of their possible forms or uses. This means, in terms of its structure, variety and complexity, a corpus must reflect a language, or its mode, as accurately as possible; in terms of its use, concern that its representation is real. These corpora have similarities with the texts because they are composed of them, on the other hand, they are not texts in themselves, because unlike these, it does not make sense to analyze them in their entirety. A corpus lacks such characteristics because it does not have a structure, only a composition. For this reason, it is convenient to analyze a corpus using our own tools and methodology [6].

Each person writing a text forms his own style according to his knowledge and years of study. The selection of words and style will make a text clear, short and precise, or otherwise heavy or not very readable. On the other hand, a text must have unity, coherence and emphasis. Directly, the fog index does not measure the coherence of a text, because each person must evaluate if it is coherent under their own concept. The style is clear when it is readable. It is short when it does not contain useless words in the text. It is precise when a word cannot be removed without affecting the meaning of the sentence. Figure 2 shows how style relates to the quality of a text.

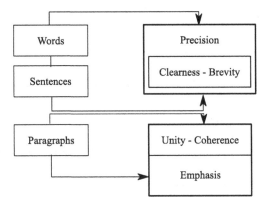

**Fig. 2.** Relation of writing style to words, sentences and paragraphs [7].

Readability tests were created to estimate the easy in which a text can be read, commonly expressed in years of study necessary to understand a text. Being able to measure the readability of a text allows educators to select texts that are relevant to their students by grade level, or their level of language proficiency for people who are learning a new language. In addition, readability tests help writers and publishers to verify that their texts meet the level of readability required for the target audience. Evaluating texts is increasingly important, due to the increasing variety, volume and complexity of written texts [8].

Since the popularization of personal computers, tools for writing analysis have been implemented. For example, the Word text editor performs document analysis if the user enables the option, in addition to correcting spelling, congruence and other errors. This tool uses the Flesch readability test and the Flesch-Kincaid grade level test. However, these are not enabled for the Spanish language [9].

Analysis of the readability of the texts has been used to verify that health-related materials have an appropriate level for most patients. For example, in [10] and [11] readability formulas are used to evaluate texts addressed to patients, so that thresholds can be established to guarantee the greatest readability for patients. Different hospitals, such as in [12] or in articles such as [13], have used readability tests to verify that documents of great importance, such as consent forms, have adequate readability for patients. Likewise, in web pages or health information documents, readability analyses have been carried out, finding that they are not optimal since they exceed the readability average [14]. Readability tests have also been applied in subjects related to: Parkinson's disease information [15], web-based cancer information [16], online educational materials for otolaryngology patients [17], orthopedic-related health topics [18], and others.

Readability tests have been used in conjunction with other tools to identify useful product reviews, due to the extensive proliferation of user-generated content, there has been a need to select useful information automatically. A wider range of classification characteristics is achieved through readability testing [19]. Because these same reviews are one of the main guides used by many users to decide which product to buy, they are often subject to manipulation, which is why in [20] used rating, readability and sentiment analysis to detect online review manipulation.

**Related Works.** The work of [22] describes a readability assessment approach to support the process of simplifying text for low-literate readers. Given an input text, the aim is to predict its level of readability, which corresponds to the level of literacy expected of the target reader, classified as rudimentary, basic or advanced. In this paper was explored the traditionally used characteristics plus the assessment of readability with several new characteristics and experimented with alternative ways of modeling the problem.

This article from [23] presents a different approach to the assessment of readability through classification. Through automatic learning a comparator is generated that judges the relative readability between two texts, and through this a set of given texts is ordered. The proposal solves the problem of the lack of training data, because the construction of the comparator only requires training data annotated with two levels of reading. The proposed method is compared with regression methods and a last generation classification method. An application called Terrace was developed, which retrieves texts with readability like that of a given input text.

In the work of [3], a tool was developed to analyze the readability of educational contents. The Gunning Fog Index was used to evaluate the texts. It was recommended to improve the formula that calculates the readability index in order to better adapt it to the Spanish language. On the other hand, in the work of [9], a Corpus in the Spanish language was used, constructed from Google Ngram and the Harvard university, the fog index was found by changing the long words for unknown words according to the frequency of appearance in the created corpus. So, the unknown words are calculated according to their frequency in the downloaded corpus.

## 2    Materials and Methods

### 2.1    Materials

In this research we used as materials a laptop with the following technical specifications: Intel core i5 processor, 8 Gb RAM and 1 Tb hard disk. The laptop must have internet access to be able to make requests to Google Ngram.

### 2.2    Methods

The fog index is an equation that measures the readability of an English text. It results in years of study necessary for a person to understand a text in a reading. Usually the fog index is used to adjust a text according to the level of the target audience. This idea was conceived by the American Robert Gunning, who considered that the use of long sentences and long words made it difficult to understand a text. Based on this, the fog index in paragraphs with a length of about one hundred words is calculated according to Eq. 4 [21]:

$$0.4\left[\left(\tfrac{N.\ words}{N.\ sentences}\right) + 100\left(\tfrac{N.\ long\ words}{N.\ word}\right)\right]\#  \tag{4}$$

Where the terms:

- N. words represents the number of words in the paragraph.
- N. sentences is the number of sentences in the paragraph.
- N. long words corresponds to the number of long words in the paragraph.

A word is considered long, according to the Gunning Fog Index, if it has a length of three or more syllables. Except for proper pronouns, compound words and words that turn from three syllables when conjugated with English suffixes such as -ed, -es, or -ing [22].

Using Gunning fog index, you get a scale of values for English text, which correspond to: 5 as easy to understand, 10 more complicated, 15 difficult to understand and 20 very difficult to read. For example, most of the Bible has a fog index between 6 and 7. Magazines for the general public have an index of about 10. It should be noted that although a person with several years of study may understand a text with a fog index of 17 does not mean that it is pleasant to read these types of text.

Although the Gunning Fog Index is a practical and brief way to assess the complexity of compressing a text. It relates important characteristics of readability, such as sentence length and the use of long words. It has limitations in considering all long words as difficult. Since not all long words are complicated to understand. For example, the following long words are common and easy to understand in English, elephant, population, billion, etc. From the above, it can be deduced that the more common a long word is, less trouble it causes to the average reader [21].

The Zipf-Mandelbrot law was formulated in 1940 by George Kingsley Zipf. Establishing an empirical relationship between the frequency of a word, being inversely proportional to the nth word elevated to a value slightly greater than one [23]. So, the frequency of the second most repeated word will be about half of the first, the third word a third of the first, and so on. It is convenient to evaluate the frequency of the words in a logarithmic scale due to the non-linear variability between the frequency of a set of words.

Google Ngram Viewer, is a web page that shows a graph of the frequency of words separated by commas, using the annual count of N-grams in the different printed resources between 1500 and 2018, the Corpora has the languages: English, Spanish, Chinese, French, German, Hebrew, Italian and Russian. The algorithm can search by word or phrase, even if they have spelling errors or are meaningless [24].

The corpus of Google Books has limitations due to cultural popularity. One of its main problems is that the corpus is a library. It contains one of each book. So, a recognized author can significantly insert new words or phrases into Google Books vocabulary. Another problem lies in the inclusion of scientific texts, which have become an increasingly significant part of the corpus throughout the twentieth century. This results in phrases typical of academic articles, but less common at the general level [25].

## 3  Results

Initially, a program was implemented in Java to calculate the fog index according to Eq. 4. The algorithm enters a text into it and separates it into an array of words. The number of words is obtained according to the number of spaces and the number of sentences according to the number of points. Then, going through the arrangement of words is the number of long words, depending on whether the number of syllables of the word is greater than or equal to three. Finally, it is applied from the Gunning fog index parameters obtaining the readability of the text.

To separate the syllables a part of the algorithm in JavaScript was translated from [26] to Java, this code separates a word in syllables. Identifying correctly the formation of hiatuses, diphthongs and triphthong.

This program was applied for different texts in Spanish, of representative authors at world and local level, obtaining values greater than 17 for all. This shows that the index is not scaled for the Spanish language. According to the direct calculation of the fog index, much academic experience would be required to read texts such as "*100 years de soledad*" and "*El ingenioso hidalgo don Quijote de la Mancha*", which are texts commonly read in the literature area of colleges and universities. The comparative texts and their results can be seen in Table 1.

**Table 1.** Gunning fog index for different texts in Spanish.

| Text | Author | paragraph | Fog index | Long words |
|------|--------|-----------|-----------|------------|
| *El ingenioso hidalgo don Quijote de la Mancha* | Miguel de Cervantes Saavedra | Cha 1/paragraph 1 | 22.35 | 54 |
| *100 años de soledad* | Gabriel García Márquez | Cha 2/paragraph | 24.75 | 67 |
| *El canto de las sirenas* | William Ospina Buitrago | paragraph 2 | 27.88 | 96 |
| *Hace tiempo. Un viaje paleontológico ilustrado por Colombia* | Carlos Jaramillo Muñoz y otros | Several | 22.22 | 40 |
| *La Biblia* | | psalm 30 | 17.08 | 50 |

A clear limitation is that the Gunning fog index is not directly applicable to all languages. In the case of Spanish, words tend to be longer, resulting in much higher values for the fog index equation compared to the general fog index indicators. The book *"100 años de soledad"* would require approximately 25 years of study to understand the text in a single reading, which is equivalent to approximately one person with a post-doctorate.

A change was made in the Gunning equation, varying the long words to complex words. Considering the complex words which have a lower percentage of frequency of appearance compared to a defined threshold. To determine this threshold, a list of 60 words was made, classifying the words according to whether they were easy or complex. With the list of complex words, it was determined that the frequency value corresponded to 0.00015%, establishing this value for the threshold. Figure 3 below shows the words classified on a logarithmic scale, based on the threshold.

In Java, an API was made to obtain data from the Google Ngram page. Through requests using the package "org.json", which allows light and language-independent data exchange, including the ability to convert between JSON and XML, HTTP headers, cookies and CDL. So, you can send data to a page and receive its response. To make requests to Google Ngram, it relied on the API developed by [14], in which an API was developed to make requests by making modifications to the URL of Google Ngram.

Through the API, a Software was implemented that processes the entered text. Obtaining the number of sentences, number of words, and the number of complex words. For this, a paragraph is divided into words and organized into an arrangement, filtering the language signs, such as punctuation marks, question marks, exclamation marks, quotation marks, etc. With this arrangement you get the number of words and by passing it through a filter, you remove the words that are in the word buffer, which is constantly updated with the words that have been searched before. This buffer was used because the maximum number of words that can be done per query is 12 and generating many

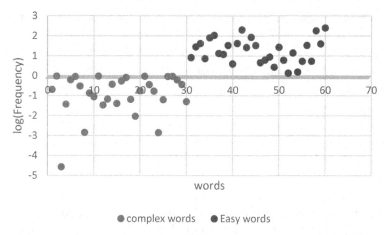

**Fig. 3.** Determination of the threshold for classifying words as complex or easy.

requests can make the page block the service momentarily. The algorithm scheme is shown in Fig. 4.

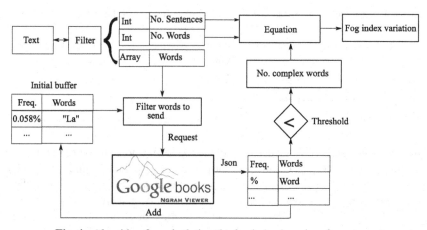

**Fig. 4.** Algorithm for calculating the fog index based on frequency.

The calculation of the fog index based on frequency was made for the same texts analyzed (with the Gunning fog index). Results were lower than the obtained using the Gunning fog index. On average the results differ by approximately 8 years, being a significant result, because they represent years of study equivalent to more than one university degree. Although the index decreases notably its value for the different texts, it is still a little high for the analyzed texts. The results can be seen in Table 2.

The slight increase in the fog index based on frequency is because Google Ngram tends towards academic literature. In order to verify the variation in the fog index, academic texts were collected from 10 university students over the course of their careers. They were asked to write at least two texts, the first in the first semesters of their careers,

**Table 2.** Comparison of the Gunning fog index and the variation performed.

| Literary work | Fog index | Fog index based on frequency |
|---|---|---|
| *El ingenioso hidalgo don Quijote de la Mancha* | 22.35 | 17.00 |
| *100 años de soledad* | 24.75 | 15.43 |
| *El canto de las sirenas* | 27.88 | 17.17 |
| *Hace tiempo. Un viaje paleontológico ilustrado por Colombia* | 22.22 | 11.76 |
| *La Biblia* | 17.08 | 12.44 |

and the second at the end of their careers. The criteria for the inclusion of the collected texts was that they had paragraphs of around 100 words. Texts of any academic subject, as exact sciences, humanities and thesis, were valid. In addition, the year or semester of completion of the text was requested. In total, all the students analyzed belonged to engineering careers. On average, the time difference in the elaboration of the evaluated texts was 6 semesters. The results obtained are shown in Table 3.

**Table 3.** Average score for the text at the beginning and end of the university course.

| Text | Fog index | Long words | Fog index based on frequency | Complex words |
|---|---|---|---|---|
| 1 | 29.25 | 37.90 | 18.62 | 5.10 |
| 2 | 27.55 | 51.40 | 15.08 | 7.10 |

Table 3 show that there was a decrease in the fog index and an increase in long words of text 1 to 2. However, it is confirmed that the directly applied Gunning fog index is not correct, because it does not have the appropriate scale. On the other hand, the fog index based on frequency showed an increase in readability in the students writing and an increase in the number of complex words used for writing, due to the process of university formation of each of these. This decrease can be explained due to the improvement of the style of each student, making more precise, coherent texts and making correct use of punctuation marks.

## 4   Discussions

Due to the boom in scientific literature on Google Ngram some words that are not considered difficult decrease in frequency. Some words in Spanish had a much lower frequency than the threshold, e.g.: "*escondiste*", "*clamé*", "*cantad*", etc. Although these words are not quotidian are easy to understand, but because Google Ngram has a more academic tendency they decrease in frequency. Academic texts often speak in the third person and use words that are more focused on scientific contexts. Therefore, the developed algorithm was only tested in academic contexts.

As a future work it is expected to make a comparison of all the existing readability tests adapted to the Spanish language. In addition, it is planned to develop a tool to evaluate the readability of a text for the writing of essays and scientific articles. As well as allowing to measure the level of writing of a student, to verify that he has the necessary tools to start his university education process, and then follow its evolution.

## 5 Conclusions

A software was implemented to determine the readability of academic documents written in Spanish. Through a variation of the Gunning fog index using the Google Ngram linguistic corpus. It was possible to measure the readability level of different literary texts in Spanish. The results were verified with literary texts and documents made by university students at the initiations and finals of their careers. An average improvement of 3.54 in textual readability and an average increase of 2 complex words was evidenced.

Having a tool that allows quantifying the readability of documents written in the Spanish language, allows to generate processes to improve the written production of academic texts, helping to improve the readability of documents and their reception, by verifying that they meet the required level according to the target audience. On the other hand, knowing the level of readability of a text allows teachers to select the most appropriate documents for their students, according to their years of study or level of language proficiency, in the case of foreign students who are learning Spanish.

It is important to offer tools to improve the writing conditions of students, also improve the readability of academic institutions such as universities and publishing houses. Institutions that have as their main measurement standards the publication of scientific articles and literary texts, and deal with different levels of education.

## References

1. Ferrando Belart, V.: La legibilidad: un factor fundamental para comprender un texto. Aten. Primaria **34**(3), 143–146 (2004)
2. Brucker, C.: Arkansas tech writing. English **2053**(June), 109 (2009)
3. Mata San Juan, H.: Herramienta de análisis de legibilidad de contenidos educativos. Graduate theses, Departamento de Informática, Universidad Carlos III de Madrid (2017)
4. Frías Delgado, A.: Distribución De Frecuencias De La Longitud De Las Palabras En Español. A Survey of corpus-based Research, pp. 756–770 (2009)
5. Coserio, E.: Introducción a la Lingüística (1983). https://www.csub.edu/~tfernandez_ulloa/spanishlinguistics/introduccion%20a%20la%20linguistica%20general.pdf
6. Pitkowski, E.F., Vásquez Gamarra, J.: Tinkuy Boletin de investigación y debate. El uso los corpus lingüísticos como Herram. pedagógica para la enseñanza y Aprendiz. ELE*, no. 11, pp. 31–51 (2005)
7. Mac Lean, A.: Comunicacion Escrita, pp. 5–17 (1975)
8. Zamanian, M., Heydari, P.: Readability of texts: state of the art. Theory Pract. Lang. Stud. **2**(1), 43–53 (2012)

9. Felipe Ovares, B., José Alberto, R.B.: Variación del Índice de Niebla Usando un Corpus Obtenido a Partir de los Libros Digitalizados por Google (2010)

10. Barrio-Cantalejo, I.M., Simón-Lorda, P., Melguizo, M., Escalona, I., Marijuán, M.I., Hernando, P.: Validación de la escala INFLESZ para evaluar la legibilidad de los textos dirigidos a pacientes. An. Sist. Sanit. Navar. **31**(2), 135–152 (2008)

11. Wang, L.W., Miller, M.J., Schmitt, M.R., Wen, F.K.: Assessing readability formula differences with written health information materials: application, results, and recommendations. Res. Soc. Adm. Pharm. **9**(5), 503–516 (2013)

12. Navarro-Royo, C., Monteagudo-Piqueras, O., Rodríquez-Suárez, L., Valentín-López, B., García-Caballero, J.: Legibilidad de los documentos de consentimiento informado del hospital La Paz. Rev. Calid. Asist. **17**(6), 331–336 (2002)

13. Simón Lorda, P., Barrio Cantalejo, I.M., Carro, L.C.: Legibilidad de los formularios escritos de consentimiento informado (1996)

14. Blanco Pérez, A., Gutiérrez Couto, U.: Legibilidad de las páginas web sobre salud dirigidas a pacientes y lectores de la población general. Rev. Esp. Salud Publica **76**(4), 321–331 (2002)

15. Fitzsimmons, P.R., Michael, B.D., Hulley, J.L., Scott, G.O.: A readability assessment of online Parkinson's disease information. J. R. Coll. Phys. Edinb. **40**(4), 292–296 (2010)

16. Friedman, D.B., Hoffman-Goetz, L.: A systematic review of readability and comprehension instruments used for print and web-based cancer information. Heal. Educ. Behav. **33**(3), 352–373 (2006)

17. Svider, P.F., et al.: Readability assessment of online patient education materials from academic otolaryngology-head and neck surgery departments. Am. J. Otolaryngol. - Head Neck Med. Surg. **34**(1), 31–35 (2013)

18. Badarudeen, S., Sabharwal, S.: Assessing readability of patient education materials: current role in orthopaedics. Clin. Orthop. Relat. Res. **468**(10), 2572–2580 (2010)

19. O'Mahony, M.P., Smyth, B.: Using readability tests to predict helpful product reviews (2010)

20. Hu, N., Bose, I., Koh, N.S., Liu, L.: Manipulation of online reviews: an analysis of ratings, readability, and sentiments. Decis. Support Syst. **52**(3), 674–684 (2012)

21. Seely, J.: Oxford Guide to Effective Writing and Speaking: How to Communicate Clearly (2013)

22. Aluisio, S., Specia, L., Gasperin, C., Scarton, C.: Readability Assessment for Text Simplification (2010)

23. Montemurro, M.A.: Beyond the Zipf-Mandelbrot law in quantitative linguistics. Phys. A **300**, 567–578 (2001)

24. Michel, J.-B., et al.: Quantitative analysis of culture using millions of digitized books. Science **331**(6014), 176–182 (2011)

25. Pechenick, E.A., Danforth, C.M., Dodds, P.S.: Characterizing the Google Books corpus: strong limits to inferences of socio-cultural and linguistic evolution. PLoS ONE **10**(10), e0137041 (2015)

26. Cofré, N., Arce, J.: Librería para obtener las silabas, posición de la silaba tónica, tipo acentuación, hiato, diptongo y triptongo de una palabra. https://github.com/ncofrem/silabajs. Accessed 14 Oct 2019

27. Fisher, J.: API for Google Ngram Viewer. https://jameshfisher.com/2018/11/25/google-ngram-api/. Accessed 14 Oct 2019

# Quality Assessment Approaches for Ambient Assisted Living Systems: A Systematic Review

Lenin Erazo-Garzon[1,2]([⊠]), Jean Erraez[1], Priscila Cedillo[1,2],
and Lourdes Illescas-Peña[2]

[1] Universidad del Azuay, Av. 24 de Mayo 7-77, Cuenca, Ecuador
lerazo@uazuay.edu.ec, jeanka181@es.uazuay.edu.ec
[2] Universidad de Cuenca, Av. 12 de Abril, Cuenca, Ecuador
{priscila.cedillo,lourdes.illescas}@ucuenca.edu.ec

**Abstract.** Ambient Assisted Living (AAL) aims to improve people's quality of life through the use of information technologies. Due to the critical nature of AAL systems, quality is a priority. However, as AAL is a relatively new domain, its main limitation is the lack of consensus and standardization in quality assessment. This work presents a systematic review to determine the state of the art on the quality assessment of AAL systems from a multidimensional vision (software product, in use, data and context). Initially, 1308 primary studies were extracted, from them 21 relevant studies related to models, frameworks, taxonomies and other approaches of quality assessment were selected after applying the corresponding inclusion and exclusion criteria. The selected studies were subject to a comparative analysis that determined the most recurrent and critical quality attributes for AAL systems, being an important contribution to generate consensus in the construction of more complete quality models. Furthermore, this work allowed to recognize the strengths and limitations of the quality proposals studied and to identify research gaps and challenges.

**Keywords:** AAL · Ambient Assisted Living · Assessment · Context quality · Data quality · Quality attribute · Quality in use · Software product quality

## 1 Introduction

Ambient Assisted Living (AAL) solutions' purpose is to improve the quality of life of people through the use of the information and communication technologies [1]. The AAL systems are mainly oriented to vulnerable groups, such as: elders, people with disabilities, children, chronic patients, among others; to increase their independence and to support them during daily activities (e.g., home activities). It is important to take into account that the families, informal caregivers, care organizations or healthcare providers, are also indirect beneficiaries of this technology; therefore, improving the quality of life from a holistic approach [2].

From a technological perspective, AAL systems are made up of sensors, actuators, computer hardware, software and databases, all of them interconnected through communication networks to exchange data and provide services. The sensors are interconnected

© Springer Nature Switzerland AG 2020
M. Botto-Tobar et al. (Eds.): ICAT 2019, CCIS 1193, pp. 421–439, 2020.
https://doi.org/10.1007/978-3-030-42517-3_32

with the AAL applications and routers in order to send data to locally located computers or to the cloud for their corresponding analysis and interpretation. This with the objective of generate responses adjusted to the environment and behavior of the user through the use of actuators [3]. Along this process, errors in the collection, transmission and processing of data can result in incorrect contextual knowledge and, therefore, infer false positive or false negative events. These could lead to AAL systems operational defects, even in the critical systems, which could compromise and endanger people's lives [4].

Thus, due to the critical nature of AAL systems and their highly distributed, heterogeneous and dynamic environment, quality assurance and in particular of non-functional requirements must be a priority aspect during the process of development of these systems. However, as AAL is a relatively new domain, its main limitation is the lack of consensus and standardization in the quality assessment of AAL systems.

With this background, this article presents a systematic review with the purpose of get to know the state of art on the quality assessment of software product, in use, data and context for AAL systems. To carry out this research, the methodological guide of Kitchenham [5] has been used. Initially, 1308 articles were obtained and through the application of several filters, based on inclusion and exclusion criteria, 21 primary studies related to the construction of models, frameworks, taxonomies and other approaches of quality assessment for AAL systems were selected. Then, methods of analysis and synthesis were applied to understand how those proposals address the evaluation of quality, identifying the measurable concepts, standards and attributes that most frequently appear in the studies, with the purpose of determining the degree of relevance for the quality assurance of AAL systems.

The structure of this article is as follows: Sect. 2 presents a review of the literature related to the subject. Section 3 describes the research method used in the systematic review. Section 4, includes the results obtained in the review, as well as presents a discussion on the main findings and challenges related to quality assessment in the AAL domain. Finally, Sect. 5 presents the conclusions and lines of future work.

## 2    Related Work

In the scientific literature there are several systematic reviews or mappings that aim to provide knowledge about the state of the art on the quality assessment of AAL systems. A brief description of these secondary studies is presented below.

Memon et al. [3] present a systematic review focused on frameworks, platforms, standards and quality attributes within the AAL domain. The results of the review show that standards are used in a limited and isolated manner, while quality attributes are often addressed insufficiently. The authors conclude that interoperability, usability, reliability, data accuracy and security are the main challenges for AAL systems; requiring more inter-organizational collaboration, user-centered validation studies and increased standardization efforts.

Then, Garcés et al. [6] present a systematic mapping identifying the main quality attributes used by the selected primary studies, the way in which the attributes were evaluated and the AAL subdomains where they were proposed. The authors conclude that a greater effort by the scientific community is required to establish a more complete quality model that includes the quality attributes relevant to AAL systems with their respective metrics.

Calvaresi et al. [1] provide an overview of the AAL domain, presenting a systematic analysis of more than 10 years of literature focused on the stakeholders' needs. The findings of this review show that researchers neglect the view of the entire AAL ecosystem, focusing only on the study of information technologies rather than supporting the various stakeholders' needs. Another important problem that this review points out is the lack of an adequate evaluation of the proposed solutions.

El Murabet et al. [7] present an overview of the current state of the art of AAL oriented layouts and identify the main requirements and challenges that reference models and architectures in AAL must meet, by the defining a set of quality attributes in several dimensions, in order to improve and consolidate future designs.

Although the non-functional requirements for AAL systems have been analyzed by the aforementioned secondary studies, it has been observed that several works on quality assessment for AAL systems have not been considered in these secondary studies. Further, there is no complete systematic review of the quality assessment for AAL systems from the perspectives of software product, use, data and context. For this reason, this work has performed a comprehensive, updated and multidimensional systematic review of the quality assessment for AAL systems that contributes to generate consensus in determining the quality attributes that should be considered relevant and critics in the construction of AAL systems.

## 3   Methods and Materials

The methodological approach applied in this paper is based on Kitchenham's guidelines [5], which guarantee a reliable, rigorous, replicable and auditable process. This procedure consists of three phases: (i) planning the review, (ii) conducting the review; and, (iii) reporting the review.

### 3.1   Planning the Review

**Research Question.** "How is the quality of AAL systems addressed from the perspectives of: software product, in use, data and context?".

**Data Sources and Search Strategy.** The digital libraries used to search the primary studies were: IEEE Xplore, ACM Digital Library, Springer Link and Science Direct. For the manual search, the most representative conferences, workshops, journals and books on the subject of AAL were selected. The search was conducted from 2007, because this is the date when the study of technologies to support the daily activities of people in their natural environment within the area called Ambient Assisted Living began. The preparation of the initiative-169 "Ambient Assisted Living" of the European Treaty was implemented on 2007 and provided the necessary instruments so the European Commission can contribute with funding and political support for the execution of research projects in this area [8]. For the search in the digital libraries the search string presented in Table 1 was used. This string was applied to the metadata of the paper: title, abstract and keywords.

**Table 1.** Search string.

| Concept | Sub-string | Connector |
|---|---|---|
| Quality | Quality | AND |
| Ambient Assisted Living | Ambient Assisted Living | OR |
| AAL | AAL | OR |
| e-Health | e-Health | |

**Search string:** *("Quality") AND ("Ambient Assisted Living" OR "AAL" OR "e-Health")*

**Selection of Primary Studies.** The primary studies obtained from the automatic and manual search were evaluated and selected by four researchers based on the title, abstract and keywords. Discrepancies in the selection of studies were resolved by consensus, after reviewing the full paper.

Primary studies that meet at least one of the following criteria were included:

IC1. Studies presenting models, frameworks, taxonomies and other approaches of quality assessment for AAL systems from the perspectives of software product, in use, data and/or context.

IC2. Studies presenting quality attributes or non-functional requirements to assess the quality of AAL systems from the perspectives of software product, in use, data and/or context.

IC3. Studies presenting quality metrics to assess AAL systems from the perspectives of software product, in use, data and/or context.

Primary studies that meet at least one of the following criteria were excluded:

EC1. Editorials, prologues, opinions, interviews, news or posters.
EC2. Duplicate reports of the same study in different sources.
EC3. Short papers with less than five pages.
EC4. Papers written in a language other than English.

**Quality Assessment of Primary Studies.** A questionnaire consisting of 10 questions was used to evaluate the primary studies according to methodological rigor and the credibility and relevance of the results for the scientific community and/or industry. The questionnaire is available in the following url: https://bit.ly/33tbQrH.

Each question was evaluated by the researchers using the following scoring scale: (i) the study complies with the research question (1 point); (ii) the study partially complies with the research question (0.5 points); and (iii) the study does not comply with the research question (0 points). The total score of each question was calculated based on the arithmetic mean of the scores assigned by each researcher. To calculate the total score of each study, the scores obtained by the 10 questions were added. The score served only to order the studies according to the scientific rigor and relevance, to correctly focus the analysis and presentation of the results of the systematic review.

**Data Extraction Strategy.** For the extraction of data, a form was designed (see Table 2), whose structure is intended to answer the research question posed in the review. This strategy guarantees the application of the same data extraction criteria to all selected studies and facilitates the analysis and synthesis of the results.

**Table 2.** Data extraction form.

| | | |
|---|---|---|
| EC1 | Measurable quality perspective or concept | ( ) Software product quality<br>( ) Quality in use<br>( ) Data quality<br>( ) Context quality |
| EC2 | Alignment with quality standards | ( ) Yes Name(s): _____<br>( ) No |
| EC3 | Software product quality attributes[a] | ( ) Functional Suitability<br>( ) Performance efficiency<br>( ) Compatibility<br>( ) Usability<br>( ) Reliability<br>( ) Security<br>( ) Maintainability<br>( ) Portability |
| EC4 | Quality attributes in use[b] | ( ) Effectiveness<br>( ) Efficiency<br>( ) Satisfaction<br>( ) Freedom from risk<br>( ) Context coverage |
| EC5 | Data quality attributes[c] | Inherent Data Quality<br>( ) Accuracy<br>( ) Completeness<br>( ) Consistency<br>( ) Credibility<br>( ) Currentness<br>Inherent and System-Dependent Data Quality<br>( ) Accessibility<br>( ) Compliance<br>( ) Confidentiality<br>( ) Efficiency<br>( ) Precision<br>( ) Traceability<br>( ) Understandability<br>System-Dependent Data Quality<br>( ) Availability<br>( ) Portability<br>( ) Recoverability |
| EC6 | Context quality attributes | Specify: _____ |

[a] ISO/IEC 25010: Software product quality.
[b] ISO/IEC 25010: Quality in use.
[c] ISO/IEC 25012: Data quality.

**Methods of Analysis and Synthesis.** The methods applied are: (i) *quantitative*, frequency calculation of the primary studies for each extraction criterion, with the corresponding construction of bar graphs; and, (ii) *qualitative*, descriptions that highlight the strengths and limitations of quality approaches, as well as research challenges.

## 3.2  Conducting the Review

During this phase, the primary studies were identified, selected and ordered using the inclusion, exclusion and quality criteria defined in the review protocol. The procedure performed is described below (see Fig. 1):

1. *Automatic search.* The search string was adapted according to the engine syntax of each of the digital libraries. Subsequently, the searches were executed, obtaining 1308 primary studies. Additionally, duplicate studies (111) were eliminated, finally leaving 1197 primary studies for further analysis.
2. *First selection.* The pertinence of the titles, abstracts and keywords of the studies with respect to the inclusion and exclusion criteria defined in the review protocol was verified. As a result, a repository with 69 studies was obtained.
3. *Second selection.* Discrepancies and doubts regarding the selection of certain studies were resolved by consensus among the researchers, after reviewing the full document. As a result, the repository was reduced to 19 studies. In turn, the manual search of papers was carried out; and, the snowballing technique was applied to the selected papers, being able to include 2 additional studies.
4. *Quality Assessment.* As a final activity, the selected primary studies were ordered according to their level of scientific rigor and relevance.

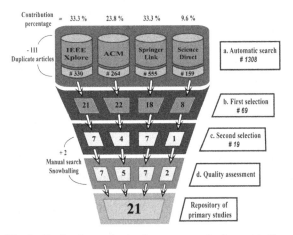

**Fig. 1.** Evaluation and selection process of primary studies.

## 4   Results and Discussion

The 21 selected primary studies can be synthesized in 17 proposals related to the construction of models, frameworks, taxonomies and other approaches of quality assessment for AAL systems. Table 3 shows the quality proposals (QP#), indicating the measurable quality concepts or perspectives that they address (software product quality, in use, data and/or context), as well as the quality standards on which is based the construction of each of the proposals. The following subsections present the results of the review based on the extraction criteria.

**Table 3.** Quality assessment proposals or approaches for AAL systems.

| ID | Quality proposal | Reference to primary study | EC1: Measurable quality perspective or concept | | | | EC2: Alignment with quality standards |
|---|---|---|---|---|---|---|---|
| | | | Software product | In use | Data | Context | |
| QP1 | Quality model for AAL software systems - QM4AAL | [9] | × | × | | | ISO/IEC 25010 |
| QP2 | Framework for evaluating AAL technologies | [10] | × | × | | | ISO/IEC 25010 |
| QP3 | Evaluation of AAL platforms according to architecture-based quality attributes | [11] | × | | | | ISO/IEC 9126, 25010 |
| QP4 | Evaluation framework for EU research and development e-health projects' systems | [12] | × | × | | | ISO/IEC 9126, 14598 |
| QP5 | Elicitation of quality characteristics for AAL systems and services | [13] | × | × | | | ISO/IEC 9126 |
| QP6 | OptimAAL quality model | [6] | × | | | | ISO/IEC 9126, 25010 |

*(continued)*

**Table 3.** (*continued*)

| ID | Quality proposal | Reference to primary study | EC1: Measurable quality perspective or concept | | | | EC2: Alignment with quality standards |
|---|---|---|---|---|---|---|---|
| | | | Software product | In use | Data | Context | |
| QP7 | Unified methodology for the evaluation of e-health applications | [14] | × | | | | |
| QP8 | Taxonomy of functional and non-functional requirements for remote healthcare | [15] | × | × | | | |
| QP9 | Quality requirements framework for the evaluation of middleware systems in the AAL domain | [16] | × | | | | |
| QP10 | Quality model for the evaluation AAL Systems | [17] | × | | × | | ISO/IEC 25010, 25012 |
| QP11 | Quality model for service delivery in AAL and AT (assistive technology) provision | [18] | | × | | | |
| QP12 | AAL system multilayer model to evaluate the quality of data, information and contextual knowledge | [4] | | | × | × | |
| QP13 | Data quality-oriented taxonomy of AAL systems | [19] | | | × | | |

(*continued*)

**Table 3.** (*continued*)

| ID | Quality proposal | Reference to primary study | EC1: Measurable quality perspective or concept | | | | EC2: Alignment with quality standards |
|----|------------------|----------------------------|------------------|------------|------|---------|---------|
| | | | Software product | In use | Data | Context | |
| QP14 | Data quality-oriented efficacy evaluation method for ambient assisted living technologies | [20] | | | × | | |
| QP15 | Data reliability and quality in body area networks for diabetes monitoring | [21] | | | × | | ISO/IEC 25012 |
| QP16 | Quality of context evaluating approach in AAL e-health systems | [22–26] | | | | × | |
| QP17 | Evaluation method for context-aware systems in u-health | [27] | | | | × | |

### EC1: Measurable Quality Perspective or Concept

Table 3 and Fig. 2 show that a large part of the research efforts have been directed towards software product quality, with 10 proposals. In this sense, it is not surprising that software product quality is a prevailing factor in AAL systems, since attributes such as: reliability, security and usability are non-functional requirements of vital importance to ensure the quality of AAL systems. In addition, it can be seen that the quality in use and data quality have been addressed at a medium level by the researchers, identifying 6 and 5 proposals, respectively. Finally, the measurable concept less studied by the scientific community is the context quality, with only 3 proposals. Therefore, it is suggested to deepen this line of research, since it is essential to know the environment or context in which they operate for the correct functioning of the AAL systems.

### EC2: Alignment with Quality Standards

In general, 10 of the 17 proposals studied, that is 58.82%, align with a quality standard, while 41.18% of the remaining proposals raise quality approaches based on knowledge and/or experience of the authors in projects, such as: UniversAAL or BRAID. In Table 3

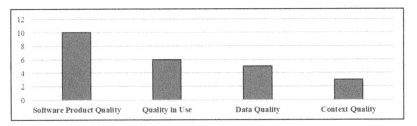

**Fig. 2.** Frequency of quality proposals by measurable concept.

and Fig. 3, it can be seen that in relation to the software product quality, of the 10 proposals analyzed, 2 are the product of the combination between the ISO/IEC 25010 and ISO/IEC 9126 standards, 3 are based solely on the ISO/IEC 25010 standard, 2 are based solely on the ISO/IEC 9126 standard; and, 3 do not align with a standard. Regarding the quality in use, of the 6 proposals studied, 2 are based on the ISO/IEC 25010 standard, 2 on the ISO/IEC 9126 standard; and, 2 do not align with a standard. About data quality, of the 5 proposals analyzed, 2 are based on the ISO/IEC 25012 standard and 3 do not align with a standard. Finally, with regard to the quality of the context, none of the proposals identified have been constructed based on an existing standard.

These data show the lack of consensus among quality proposals, beginning with the absence of a common nomenclature to name the characteristics, sub-characteristics and attributes of quality to the AAL domain. Also, the diversity of hierarchical relationships among these, influential aspect in the measurement and evaluation of the quality at global level (system) and partial (characteristics).

In order to have more homogeneous evaluation approaches, it is recommended that researchers build quality models with a hierarchical structure based on existing standards. First, the relevant characteristics and sub-characteristics for the AAL domain must be selected from the quality standards, complying with the nomenclature and relational structure proposed by the standard. Then, it is necessary to specialize the quality model, identifying the quality attributes and metrics specific to the AAL domain. The results of the extraction criteria: EC3, EC4, EC5 and EC6 are presented in the following subsections and will be very useful to guide this process.

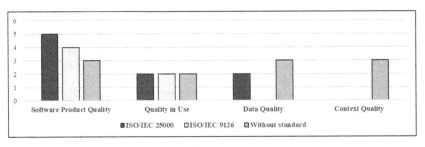

**Fig. 3.** Frequency of quality proposals by quality standard.

Additionally, there are quality proposals that are based on the ISO/IEC 9126 standard, although the ISO/IEC 25000 standard had already been published, hence an additional effort is required to update these proposals.

One of the challenges identified in this research is related to building a context quality standard or deepening the study of the characteristic *context coverage* of the ISO/IEC 25010 standard for quality in use, breaking it down into attributes more specific which could improve its measurement.

### EC3: Software Product Quality Attributes

The purpose of this extraction criterion is to know the most relevant characteristics or attributes for the evaluation of the quality of AAL systems from the software product perspective. In this sense, a comparative analysis was performed between the proposals of software product quality and the ISO/IEC 25010 standard, in order to determine the level of recurrence of the characteristics and sub-characteristics included in said standard (see Table 4). For the analysis it was necessary to map the characteristics and sub-characteristics of quality according to the similarity of their meaning and objective of evaluation, despite having different names in the proposals.

The characteristics *reliability, security* and *usability* are the most used by the approaches to evaluate the quality of AAL systems with 100%, 80% and 70%, respectively; followed by the characteristics *functional suitability, performance efficiency* and *portability* with 60%; as well as the characteristic *maintainability* with 50%; and finally, the characteristic *compatibility* is the least considered with 30%.

A result that attracts attention is that only 30% of the studies consider the *compatibility*, despite the fact that AAL systems have a highly distributed and heterogeneous ecosystem, based on internet platforms of things. Hence, related attributes, such as: *interoperability* and *co-existence* should be studied in future research.

Despite not being included in the ISO/IEC 25010 quality standard, the characteristic *scalability* has been considered relevant, due to its level of recurrence in several studies

**Table 4.** Comparative analysis of software product quality proposals.

| Characteristics and sub-characteristics ISO/IEC 25010* | Q P 1 | Q P 2 | Q P 3 | Q P 4 | Q P 5 | Q P 6 | Q P 7 | Q P 8 | Q P 9 | Q P 10 | Recurrence Percentage |
|---|---|---|---|---|---|---|---|---|---|---|---|
| **Functional suitability** | x | x | | x | x | | x | x | | | **60%** |
| Functional completeness | × | × | | | | | | | | | 20% |
| Functional correctness | × | × | | | | | | | | | 20% |
| Functional appropriateness | × | | | | | | | | | | 10% |
| **Performance efficiency** | x | x | x | x | x | x | | | | | **60%** |
| Time behavior | × | × | | | | | | | | | 20% |

*(continued)*

**Table 4.** (*continued*)

| Characteristics and sub-characteristics ISO/IEC 25010[*] | Q P 1 | Q P 2 | Q P 3 | Q P 4 | Q P 5 | Q P 6 | Q P 7 | Q P 8 | Q P 9 | Q P 10 | Recurrence Percentage |
|---|---|---|---|---|---|---|---|---|---|---|---|
| Resource utilization | × | × | × | | | | | | | | 30% |
| **Compatibility** | **×** | **×** | | | | | | **×** | | | **30%** |
| Co-existence | × | × | | | | | | | | | 20% |
| Interoperability | × | × | | | | | | × | | | 30% |
| **Usability** | **×** | **×** | | **×** | **×** | | **×** | **×** | **×** | | **70%** |
| Appropriateness recognizability | × | × | | | | | | | | | 20% |
| Learnability | × | × | | | | | | | | | 20% |
| Operability | × | × | | | | | | | | | 20% |
| User error protection | × | | | | | | | | | | 10% |
| User interface aesthetics | × | × | | | | | | | | | 20% |
| Accessibility | × | | | | | | | | | | 10% |
| **Reliability** | **×** | **×** | **×** | **×** | **×** | **×** | **×** | **×** | **×** | **×** | **100%** |
| Maturity | | × | | | | | | | | | 10% |
| Availability | × | | | | | | | | | × | 20% |
| Fault tolerance | × | × | × | | | | | | | | 30% |
| Recoverability | × | × | × | | | | | | | × | 40% |
| **Security** | **×** | **×** | **×** | | | **×** | **×** | **×** | **×** | **×** | **80%** |
| Confidentiality | × | | × | | | | | | | × | 30% |
| Integrity | × | | | | | | | | | × | 20% |
| Non-repudiation | × | | | | | | | | | | 10% |
| Authenticity | × | | | | | | | | | × | 20% |
| **Maintainability** | **×** | **×** | **×** | | **×** | **×** | | | | | **50%** |
| Reusability | × | | | | | | | | | | 10% |
| Analysability | × | × | | | | | | | | | 20% |
| Modifiability | × | × | × | | | | | | | | 30% |
| Testability | × | × | | | | | | | | | 20% |
| **Portability** | **×** | **×** | **×** | | **×** | | | **×** | **×** | | **60%** |
| Adaptability | × | × | | | | | | | | | 20% |
| Installability | × | × | × | | | | | | | | 30% |
| Replaceability | | × | | | | | | | | | 10% |

[*]  Only sub-characteristics of the ISO/IEC 25010 standard used by proposals are included.

(QP1, QP7), whose purpose is to assess the capacity of AAL systems to incorporate new functionalities with a high degree of abstraction.

In relation to the sub-characteristics included in the ISO/IEC 25010 standard, of the 10 quality proposals identified, only proposals QP1, QP2, QP3 and QP10 specify a tree of quality requirements at this level. In turn, none of the proposals raise a tree of quality requirements of more than two levels, decomposing the sub-characteristics in quality attributes specific to the AAL domain. In conclusion, the fundamental challenge is to build more complete quality models, which specify the particular non-functional requirements that AAL systems must meet at the attributes level.

### EC4: Quality Attributes in Use

Applying the same mapping procedure to the quality approaches in use, the level of recurrence of the characteristics and sub-characteristics of the ISO/IEC 25010 standard - quality in use was determined (see Table 5). The characteristics *effectiveness*, *efficiency* and *satisfaction* are the most used by the quality assessment approaches for the AAL system with 83.33%; followed by the characteristic *freedom from risk* with 66.67%; and finally, the characteristic *context coverage* with 15.67%.

**Table 5.** Comparative analysis of quality proposals in use.

| Characteristics and sub-characteristics ISO/IEC 25010[*] | QP1 | QP2 | QP4 | QP5 | QP8 | QP11 | Recurrence Percentage |
|---|---|---|---|---|---|---|---|
| **Effectiveness** | x | x | x | x | | x | **83.33%** |
| **Efficiency** | x | x | x | x | | x | **83.33%** |
| **Satisfaction** | x | x | x | x | | x | **83.33%** |
|   Usefulness | × | | | | | | 15.67% |
|   Trust | × | | | | | | 15.67% |
|   Comfort | | | | | | × | 15.67% |
| **Freedom from risk** | x | x | | x | x | | **66.67%** |
|   Health and safety risk mitigation | × | | | | | | 15.67% |
| **Context coverage** | x | | | | | | **15.67%** |
|   Flexibility | × | | | | | | 15.67% |

[*] Only sub-characteristics of the ISO/IEC 25010 standard used by proposals are included.

Mostly quality proposals in use evaluate the ability of AAL systems to efficiently achieve the specific objectives of users and satisfy their needs. However, a worrying result is related to the characteristic *freedom from risk*, since despite the critical nature of AAL systems, a smaller percentage of proposals assess the ability of the systems to mitigate the potential risk in health and safety of the users. In addition, only one proposal has considered the characteristic *context coverage*, whose purpose is to evaluate the ability of AAL systems to operate in contexts beyond those initially identified, being a fundamental characteristic in AAL, due to their highly dynamic and changing environment. As shown, the characteristic *context coverage* included in the ISO/IEC 25010 standard is closely related to the field of context quality research. Hence, a research opportunity is to specialize this standard based on the contributions obtained in the context quality research work. Finally, Bitelli et al. [18] in their approach QP11 propose two relevant quality attributes to assess the fulfillment of the mission of AAL systems: (i) impact of the AAL system on the quality of life of users; and, (ii) impact of the AAL system on saving the social costs of the health system.

At the level of sub-characteristics and attributes, quality proposals in use are very limited. Hence, it is necessary to deepen the research at these levels, as well as to build instruments for their measurement (e.g., questionnaires, metrics).

### EC5: Data Quality Attributes

Table 6 shows the results of the mapping between the attributes of the data quality proposals and the characteristics defined in the ISO/IEC 25012 standard. The characteristics *accuracy* and *completeness* are the most used by the proposals with 80%; followed by the characteristics *currentness* and *confidentiality* with 60%; and finally, the characteristics *consistency* and *understandability* with 40%; as well as the characteristics *efficiency*, *accessibility* and *traceability* with 20%.

**Table 6.** Comparative analysis of data quality proposals.

| Characteristics ISO/IEC 25012[*] | QP10 | QP12 | QP13 | QP14 | QP15 | Recurrence Percentage |
|---|---|---|---|---|---|---|
| Accuracy | × | × | | × | × | 80% |
| Completeness | × | × | | × | × | 80% |
| Consistency | | × | | | × | 40% |
| Currentness | | × | | × | × | 60% |
| Accessibility | | | | | × | 20% |
| Confidentiality | × | × | | | × | 60% |
| Efficiency | × | | | | | 20% |
| Traceability | | | | | × | 20% |
| Understandability | | | | × | × | 40% |

[*] Only characteristics of the ISO/IEC 25012 standard used by proposals are included.

The results of this extraction criterion show that most of the data quality proposals for AAL systems have as priority to evaluate the characteristics *accuracy*, *completeness* and *currentness* of the data, which are even highly dependent on each other. *Accuracy* refers to the degree to which data collected from sensors or other sources are in accordance with values or events of the real-world. While the *completeness* represents the degree to which the data obtained from the sensors or other sources are sufficient and suitable for processing and analysis, in order to achieve the user's requirements or represent reality. Finally, *currentness* measures the degree to which the data obtained from sensors or other sources are current and available on time. The importance given to these characteristics is justified, since the correct functioning of AAL systems, which operate in real time, depends largely on the knowledge inferred of the data collected from the sensors; however, there may be faults in the sensors and communication causing errors, delays or data loss.

In turn, the characteristic *confidentiality* has been considered by more than half of the data quality assessment approaches. This characteristic must assess the level at which data accomplish with confidentiality policies (e.g., access control, encryption protocols in transportation and storage of data) included in the health regulations, in order to avoid misuse or accidental disclosure of data.

In contrast, the characteristics *efficiency, understandability* and *accessibility* have been addressed by few data quality approaches, despite being relevant and pertinent with the intrinsic nature of the AAL systems. In relation to *efficiency*, AAL systems are highly distributed and carry large volumes of data between sensors/actuators and servers. Therefore, quality approaches must assess the capacity of the AAL systems to balance and optimize the use of resources (e.g., energy, CPU, bandwidth) in the collection and processing of data. With regard to *accessibility* and *understandability*, AAL systems are preferentially oriented to vulnerable groups with different needs in the use of information technologies, it being essential that quality approaches evaluate both the degree to which the data of an AAL system is expressed using formats, languages, symbols and appropriate units to be read and interpreted correctly by users, as well as the degree to which data can be accessed by people with some disability.

The characteristic *compliance* included in the ISO/IEC 25012 standard has not been considered in any of the approaches studied. However, AAL systems are composed of a wide variety of devices (e.g., sensors, actuators) with heterogeneous communication interfaces, which transfer large volumes of unstructured data. Consequently, it is desirable that quality approaches assess the degree to which data adhere to current standards, conventions or regulations.

### EC6: Context Quality Attributes

The context quality proposals QP12, QP16 and QP17 are not based on existing quality standards, so only a comparative analysis was made between the proposals, in order to determine the level of recurrence of context quality attributes (see Table 7). An interesting aspect is that data and context quality proposals use similar attributes. For example, they share the attributes: *accuracy, completeness and currentness*. However, the difference is that the data quality approaches guide their evaluation at a low level, that is, they evaluate the data captured from the sensors or other sources in their primary state, while context quality approaches evaluate the contextual knowledge resulting from the aggregation and reasoning operations applied to the data collected. In this regard, it is important the approach QP12 that proposes a multilayer architecture (data, information, contextual knowledge) for the quality assessment of AAL systems.

The attributes *accuracy* and *currentness* have been used in all the proposals of context quality for AAL system (100%); followed by the attribute *completeness* that has

Table 7. Comparative analysis of context quality proposals.

| Attributes | QP12 | QP16 | QP17 | Recurrence Percentage |
|---|---|---|---|---|
| Accuracy | × | × | × | 100% |
| Coverage | | × | | 33.33% |
| Completeness | | × | × | 66.67% |
| Consistency | × | | | 33.33% |
| Significance | | × | | 33.33% |
| Currentness | × | × | × | 100% |

been considered in two proposals (66.67%), while the rest of the attributes: *coverage*, *consistency* and *significance* have been considered for only one proposal (33.33%).

The attribute *accuracy* assesses the degree to which contextual information describes reality, while the attribute *currentness* indicates how old the context information is by using a timestamp; that is, it describes the difference between the moment an event occurs and the moment when the system is aware of it. Although these attributes are of great relevance to ensure the quality of the context and the correct functioning of the AAL systems, it is recommended that the proposals complement each other, including attributes such as: (i) *completeness*, the extent to which contextual knowledge is available and sufficient to represent reality; and, (ii) *significance*, level of importance of contextual information, its value is particularly important to alert in critical situations where people's lives are put at risk.

## 5   Conclusions and Future Work

In this study, a systematic review based on the methodology of Kitchenham [5] was applied to know how the quality of AAL systems is evaluated from the perspectives of software product, in use, data and context. The review was conducted from 2007 and 21 primary studies were obtained, which are synthesized in 17 quality proposals.

To answer the research question; first, the quality proposals were classified according to the measurable quality concept; then, a comparative analysis between the categorized proposals and the existing quality standards was performed. Among the main findings are: (i) Research efforts have been directed to the quality of software product (10 proposals), focusing mainly on the attributes of reliability, security and usability; in turn, the quality in use and data quality has been addressed at a medium level (6 and 5 proposals respectively); and finally, the context quality is the least studied perspective (3 proposals), consisting of an important research opportunity. (ii) Only 58.82% of the quality proposals are aligned to a quality standard, evidencing the lack of consensus between the proposals, starting with the absence of a common nomenclature to name the characteristics, sub-characteristics and attributes, as well as the diversity of hierarchical relationships between these. (iii) Current quality proposals partially consider the characteristics or quality attributes relevant to AAL systems, neglecting important non-functional requirements, such as: software product (interoperability and scalability), in use (freedom from risk), data (efficiency, understandability, accessibility, compliance) and context (completeness and significance). In conclusion, the main contribution of this work is the identification of a set of characteristics or attributes considered as common among quality proposals and/or relevant for AAL systems from a multidimensional vision (software product, in use, data and context).

As future work, the study of the quality metrics used by the selected quality proposals will be deepened. Likewise, a more complete quality model will be built for AAL systems at the level of software product, in use, data and context, which includes all the recommendations generated in this study.

**Acknowledgements.** This study is part of the research projects: (i) Software product, data and context quality model for AAL systems, LIDI - Universidad del Azuay; (ii) Design of architectures and interaction models for assisted living environments aimed at older adults. Case study: ludic and social environments, XVIII DIUC Call for Research Projects; and, (iii) Fog Computing applied to monitoring devices used in assisted living environments; Case study: platform for the elderly, XVII DIUC Call for Research Projects. Thus, we thank Universidad del Azuay and Universidad de Cuenca for their support.

# References

1. Calvaresi, D., Cesarini, D., Sernani, P., Marinoni, M., Dragoni, A.F., Sturm, A.: Exploring the ambient assisted living domain: a systematic review. Ambient Intell. Hum. Comput. **8**(2), 239–257 (2017)
2. AAL-Europe - Active and Assisted Living Programme. http://www.aal-europe.eu/about/. Accessed 09 Nov 2019
3. Memon, M., Wagner, S., Pedersen, C., Beevi, F., Hansen, F.: Ambient assisted living health-care frameworks, platforms, standards, and quality attributes. Sensors **14**(3), 4312–4341 (2014)
4. McNaull, J., Augusto, J., Mulvenna, M., McCullagh, P.: Data and information quality issues in ambient assisted living systems. Data Inf. Qual. **4**(1), 1–15 (2012)
5. Kitchenham, B.: Guidelines for performing systematic literature reviews in software engineering. Keele University and Durham University (2007)
6. Garcés, L., Ampatzoglou, A., Avgeriou, P., Nakagawa, E.: Quality attributes and quality models for ambient assisted living software systems: a systematic mapping. Inf. Softw. Technol. **82**, 121–138 (2017)
7. El Murabet, A., Abtoy, A., Touhafi, A., Tahiri, A.: Ambient assisted living system's models and architectures: a survey of the state of the art. J. King Saud Univ. Comput. Inf. Sci. **32**, 1–10 (2018)
8. European Commission - Ambient Assisted Living - Preparation of an Art. 169-Initiative. https://cordis.europa.eu/project/rcn/71922/factsheet/en. Accessed 09 Nov 2019
9. Garcés, L., Oquendo, F., Nakagawa, E.: A quality model for AAL software systems. In: 29th International Symposium on Computer-Based Medical Systems, pp. 175–180 (2016)
10. Salvi, D., Montalvá Colomer, J., Arredondo, M., Prazak-Aram, B., Mayer, C.: A framework for evaluating ambient assisted living technologies and the experience of the UniversAAL project. Ambient Intell. Smart Environ. **7**, 329–352 (2015)

11. Antonino, P.O., Schneider, D., Hofmann, C., Nakagawa, E.Y.: Evaluation of AAL platforms according to architecture-based quality attributes. In: Keyson, D.V., et al. (eds.) AmI 2011. LNCS, vol. 7040, pp. 264–274. Springer, Heidelberg (2011). https://doi.org/10.1007/978-3-642-25167-2_36

12. Mavridis, A., Katriou, S.-A., Koumpis, A.: An evaluation framework for EU research and development e-Health Projects' systems. In: Weerasinghe, D. (ed.) eHealth 2008. LNICST, vol. 0001, pp. 9–16. Springer, Heidelberg (2009). https://doi.org/10.1007/978-3-642-00413-1_2

13. Omerovic, A., Kofod-Petersen, A., Solhaug, B., Svagård, I.: Elicitation of Quality characteristics for AAL systems and services. In: van Berlo, A., Hallenborg, K., Rodríguez, J., Tapia, D., Novais, P. (eds.) Ambient Intelligence - Software and Applications. AISC, vol. 219, pp. 95–104. Springer, Heidelberg (2013). https://doi.org/10.1007/978-3-319-00566-9_13

14. Goletsis, Y., Chletsos, M.: Towards a unified methodology for the evaluation of e-Health applications. In: 10th International Conference on Information Technology and Applications in Biomedicine, pp. 1–4 (2010)

15. Vitaletti, A., Puglia, S.: System overview of next-generation remote healthcare. In: Maharatna, K., Bonfiglio, S. (eds.) Systems Design for Remote Healthcare, pp. 31–53. Springer, New York (2014). https://doi.org/10.1007/978-1-4614-8842-2_2

16. Zentek, T., Yumusak, C.O., Reichelt, C., Rashid, A.: Which AAL middleware matches my requirements? An analysis of current middleware systems and a framework for decision-support. In: Wichert, R., Klausing, H. (eds.) Ambient Assisted Living. ATSC, pp. 111–125. Springer, Cham (2015). https://doi.org/10.1007/978-3-319-11866-6_9

17. Kara, M., Lamouchi, O., Ramdane-Cherif, A.: A quality model for the evaluation AAL systems. Procedia Comput. Sci. **113**, 392–399 (2017)

18. Bitelli, C., Desideri, L., Malavasi, M.: A quality model for service delivery in AAL and AT provision. In: Andò, B., Siciliano, P., Marletta, V., Monteriù, A. (eds.) Ambient Assisted Living. BB, vol. 11, pp. 3–10. Springer, Cham (2015). https://doi.org/10.1007/978-3-319-18374-9_1

19. Beevi, F., Wagner, S.: Data quality oriented taxonomy of ambient assisted living systems. In: IET International Conference on Technologies for Active and Assisted Living (2015)

20. Beevi, F., Wagner, S., Pedersen, C., Hallerstede, S.: Data quality oriented efficacy evaluation method for ambient assisted living technologies. In: 10th EAI International Conference on Pervasive Computing Technologies for Healthcare, pp. 235–240 (2016)

21. Huzooree, G., Khedo, K.K., Joonas, N.: Data reliability and quality in body area networks for diabetes monitoring. In: Maheswar, R., Kanagachidambaresan, G.R., Jayaparvathy, R., Thampi, S.M. (eds.) Body Area Network Challenges and Solutions. EICC, pp. 55–86. Springer, Cham (2019). https://doi.org/10.1007/978-3-030-00865-9_4

22. Nazário, D., Tromel, I., Dantas, M., Todesco, J.: Toward assessing quality of context parameters in a ubiquitous assisted environment. In: Symposium on Computers and Communications (2014)

23. Nazário, D., Todesco, J., Dantas, M., Tromel, I., Neto, A.: A quality of context evaluating approach in an ambient assisted living e-Health system. In: 16th International Conference on e-Health Networking, Applications and Services, pp. 158–163 (2014)

24. Nazário, D., de Andrade, A., Borges, L., Ramos, W., Todesco, J., Dantas, M.: An enhanced quality of context evaluating approach in the e-health sensor platform. In: 11th Symposium on QoS and Security for Wireless and Mobile Networks, pp. 1–7 (2015)

25. Nazário, D., Campos, P., Inacio, E., Dantas, M.: Quality of context evaluating approach in AAL environment using IoT technology. In: 30th International Symposium on Computer-Based Medical Systems, pp. 558–563 (2017)

26. Nazário, D., Dantas, M., de Macedo, D.: An e-Health study case environment enhanced by the utilization of a quality of context paradigm. In: Symposium on Computers and Communications, pp. 1221–1226 (2018)
27. Sanchez-Pi, N., Carbó, J., Molina, J.M.: An evaluation method for context-aware systems in U-Health. In: Novais, P., Hallenborg, K., Tapia, D., Rodríguez, J. (eds.) Ambient Intelligence - Software and Applications. AISC, vol. 153, pp. 219–226. Springer, Heidelberg (2012). https://doi.org/10.1007/978-3-642-28783-1_28

# Virtual Desktop Infrastructure (VDI) Deployment Using OpenNebula as a Private Cloud

Paúl E. Calle-Romero[1(✉)], Pablo A. Lema-Sarmiento[1],
Pablo L. Gallegos-Segovia[1], Gabriel A. León-Paredes[1],
Paúl E. Vintimilla-Tapia[2], and Jack F. Bravo-Torres[2]

[1] Grupo de Investigación GIHP4C, Universidad Politécnica Salesiana,
Cuenca, Ecuador
{pcalle,plema,pgallegos,gleon}@ups.edu.ec
[2] Grupo de Investigación GITEL, Universidad Politécnica Salesiana,
Cuenca, Ecuador
{pvintimilla,jbravo}@ups.edu.ec

**Abstract.** With the advancement of technology and unlimited access to information through the Internet, traditional teaching models are evolving to become centralized in the student. The objective is to offer personalized education that overcomes any spatial-temporal barrier, achieving a continuous transfer of knowledge. However, under this scenario arises the need for equipment with high performance hardware and software. On the one hand, educational institutions, in most cases, do not have enough capital to migrate to new infrastructures; while, on the other hand, students encounter problems linked to licensing and lack of own resources. Overall, this translates into an impediment for teachers to design innovative activities. Hence, the concept of virtual desktop infrastructure (VDIs) is born, which relies on cloud computing techniques to provide access to remote machines pre-configured according to different storage, processing, network and software requirements. This paper presents an open source VDI solution based on OpenNebula, since the costs associated with using the services of large cloud providers could represent a considerable investment. Among the tests carried out, a pilot experiment stands out that demonstrates the benefits of deploying local VDIs, as well as a comparison of the savings they represent in relation to commercial solutions.

**Keywords:** Cloud computing · e-learning · OpenNebula · Open source · Virtual desktop (VDI)

## 1 Introduction

Today, thanks to the constant advances of Information and Communication Technologies (ICTs), the popularity of Internet-based teaching techniques is

M. Botto-Tobar et al. (Eds.): ICAT 2019, CCIS 1193, pp. 440–450, 2020.
https://doi.org/10.1007/978-3-030-42517-3_33

growing, giving way to the construction of electronic learning environments [4]. Thus, tools are born that intervene in the acquisition and management of knowledge to allow the deployment of new educational paradigms, eliminating the space-time barriers that limit traditional models [5]. However, the growing number of students generates a large amount of data that attacks the computing infrastructure of educational institutions, because they do not support adequate processing. For this reason, and bearing in mind the difficulties involved in investing in hardware or software, when implementing any e-learning application or service, efforts should be focused on achieving optimal allocation and consumption of resources according to highly dynamic demand [15]. In addition, it is essential to ensure an adequate quality of service, since the student's interest could be lost and, therefore, the academic objectives set could not be met [17].

Faced with this situation, a promising alternative is emerging in cloud computing, thanks to the fact that it represents a technological trend that allows resources to be exchanged via the Internet [13]. Different providers offer as a service the capacity of their equipment in terms of processing, storage, network and applications, to meet the needs of different organizations, avoiding investment in new infrastructure [9]. Thus, the benefits of transferring this scenario to educational institutions can be summarized in 4 points [6]:

1. Reduction and rationalization of expenses: the use of cloud-based services simplifies a series of complicated processes depending on the maintenance of the local infrastructure and the deployment of e-learning applications, reflecting a saving of resources and capital.
2. On-demand service delivery: Cloud computing is a technology model that supports the aggregation of resources to meet customers' exponential demand. Thus, at times of peak activity such as evaluations or registration processes, only the service provider should be asked to momentarily allocate a greater processing capacity or network, preventing possible congestion or system crashes.
3. Greener education: by employing third-party hardware, opportunities are offered to reduce energy consumption, giving way to environmentally friendly institutions. For its part, from the provider side, each cloud hosts multiple tenants, so the processing capacity is shared efficiently, indirectly reducing polluting emissions.
4. Improve academic proficiency: Under the infrastructure-as-a-service model, cloud computing can provide each student with a virtual desktop, commonly known as virtual desktop infrastructure (VDI). Teachers can then design activities that require high-performance software without any limitations.

With respect to the last point, the use of VDIs significantly helps to change the traditional concept of teaching, since it makes it easier to overcome the restrictions involved in the use of proprietary software both licensing and equipment (processor, hard disk and RAM) [12]. In few words, a VDI is a cloud computing service that supports virtualization of desktops, including operating systems and software, on remote servers accessed via the Internet [11]. Therefore, it is possible to provide each student with a virtual and personalized environment that has sufficient features to support the development of the tasks assigned by the teacher, ensuring ubiquitous access from any device [7]. In addition, from a practical point of view, infrastructure managers also benefit by reducing equipment setup times, increasing information transfer rates, and mitigating security and compatibility issues [2].

On base the mentioned, it can be said that there is a close relationship with the concept of centralized computing, where users are connected to the host computer through terminals without intelligence that do not have processing or storage capabilities [1]. For this reason, it is essential to know the architecture on which the VDIs are executed, which consists of six components [8]:

1. Management platform: intervenes in the management and provisioning of each client's virtual desktops.
2. Connection Broker: known as session broker, it is used to balance the traffic load generated.
3. Virtualization Application: Allows users to install and interact with virtual applications inside the desktop through end devices. This type of application leads to accelerated deployment, as it consumes server resources rather than local resources.
4. User profiles and data redirection: Traditional computers support configuration of various features and file storage, which is saved in profiles for future access. Continuing with this behavior, within VDIs users can request continuous and non-continuous desktops. The first ones keep the changes made at each login; while the second ones delete any configuration, leaving the desktops "clear".
5. Remote Desktop Protocol: To connect to a VDI, users use dedicated protocols that are involved in managing display functions (updating the display and inputs/outputs from the mouse and keyboard) as well as for multimedia file exchange and multi-screen operation.
6. VDI Gateway: To guarantee remote access, a gateway that receives requests through the Internet, encrypts them to provide security and places them in a format that the internal components understand.

As can be seen, there is not much complexity when implementing the components mentioned, so it is common to find companies focused on cloud computing and virtualization that offer within their products the deployment of VDIs as a service. However, licensing costs cannot be ignored, as they could not be included in the funds of educational institutions with limited budgets. Therefore, this article proposes the development of a system of studio environments and virtual desktops whose architecture is hosted and virtualized in OpenNebula, a private cloud solution. The main objective is to provide tools that allow students to consolidate their knowledge by resolving practices generated in a given context according to learning interests and needs.

The rest of the article is organized as follows. Section 2 presents works that reflect relevant technological proposals aimed at the use of virtual desks to support education. Section 3 describes the diagram of the proposed general architecture, including different modules and services. In Sect. 4, the results obtained in a pilot experiment carried out with students related to the field of Computer Science are analysed. Finally, the main conclusions and future work can be found in Sect. 5.

## 2  Related Works

First of all, the authors of [14] analyze the opportunities and benefits of virtual platforms, which allow students to install, configure, and manipulate remote desktops, safeguarding the stability and security of the physical infrastructure. Thus, it is possible to develop laboratory practices that could compromise the functioning of physical equipment, as a result of the lack of experience in its handling. Hence, emphasis is placed on several important concepts related to virtualization: enabling technologies, security systems, limitations and challenges of use in educational environments. Principally, a business-oriented virtual security system is deployed, with the objective of bringing students closer to the real environment of a company in which security policies are implemented. This process was carried out through virtual laboratories that were accessed through workstations connected to the same network. Each laboratory was equipped with the necessary tools and resources to implement the required practices without difficulty. The results obtained were favorable because the students gained greater interest and a more professional work vision.

For its part, in [10] tries to explain how to make an infrastructure to provide a remote desktop service (Desktop as a Service - DaaS) that is compatible with any operating system. To do this, unlike traditional solutions, several servers hosted in a private cloud are occupied instead of hypervisors, which run virtual machines. In addition, protocols based on virtual networks are specified for end user access. Meanwhile, for cloud administrators, an environment is implemented that deploys tools to support DaaS management. The achieved results expose access facilities to the different desktops, as well as for the handling and storage of information in each one. However, several shortcomings were reported when responding to simultaneous requests, determining a fundamental aspect to keep in mind for future investigations.

Meanwhile, in [16] the authors detail the design of a virtual laboratory architecture capable of providing students with a practical learning experience supported by an online educational offering. In this sense, the design approaches applied are described, addressing criteria for the selection of an optimal implementation method. Thus, each student accesses a virtual desktop through his/her personal computer, being able to install and execute different software solutions, according to the instructions contemplated in the laboratory practices. The evaluation results indicated that the use of VDIs help to improve the performance of the learning environment, supporting multiple users.

Finally [3] explores the practical aspects of migrating to virtual architectures, describing the costs, benefits and challenges of implementing and managing virtual laboratories to support teaching and research in areas such as engineering, computing and information security. For this reason, the alternatives that have been deployed in the private clouds of different universities are analyzed, starting from the description of their infrastructure, application environment, virtualization software, advantages and limitations, relevant characteristics and considerations to take into account for future moves to hybrid or public clouds. In conclusion, the existence of certain risks that involve the movement of a private cloud to the outside is highlighted, so it is recommended to migrate the content in small parts, maintaining adequate administration and performance.

As can be noted, the papers presented describe the use of VDIs as tools that support the educational process. However, they do not take into consideration the aspects or restrictions represented by the use of licensed software, which could slow down technological acceptance by educational institutions with limited budgets. In view of this situation, the following section presents the architecture for the creation of VDIs in a private open source cloud, OpenNebula. The objective is to provide a low-cost virtual study environment in which laboratory practices can be carried out, optimizing existing hardware and software resources.

## 3   Proposed Architecture

When working on the development and design of VDIs as support tools for teaching, it is essential to guarantee their correct functioning, since any error or difficulty could cause a lack of motivation in the students and, therefore, learning deficiencies that prevent the achievement of the objectives set in each subject. In this way, the Fig. 1 reflects the basic hardware and software components involved in the deployment of VDIs, which can be summarized in 7 elements:

1. User access: access to each VDI is via any device with an Internet connection. To do this, it is essential to have credentials (username and password), which have been previously specified by the VDI administrator. This is due to the fact that the desks are personalized since each student has their own activities such as laboratory practices on specific topics.
2. VDI Manager: is in charge of managing the desktops, so it has sufficient permissions to deploy and configure virtual machines with operating systems and pre-installed software. In addition, you must have the minimum capabilities to perform license management tasks, package update, and repository addition. The objective is to provide each student with a tool with the configuration required for the development of the activities proposed by the teacher.
3. End Devices: are devices through which you can access, view, and interact with VDIs. It should be noted that their processing or storage characteristics are not of major importance, since all the tasks in execution consume the resources of the server that hosts the private cloud.
4. Physical server: is the host for the installation of the private cloud, which is divided into two virtual servers that will do the functions of front and node. On the one hand, the front is involved in the installation of the Sunstone

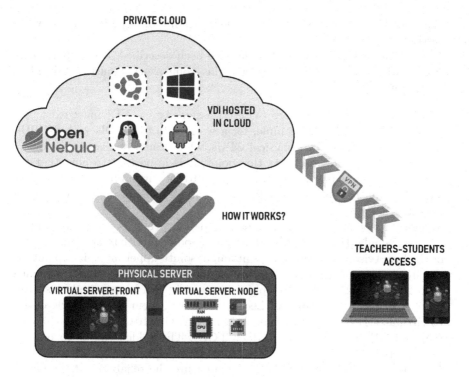

**Fig. 1.** Conceptual operation of VDIs on private cloud.

OpenNebula interface (a GUI that simplifies typical administration operations) to manage the cloud through a Web browser. Meanwhile, the node provides underlying resources such as processing, storage, RAM and network for the deployment of virtual machines, ensuring their proper functioning.

5. VPN: commonly known as virtual private network, allows to add a layer of security of data in transit, thanks to the extension of the local network of the private cloud over the Internet.
6. VDI Application: contemplates the virtual machines that are given to each student for the development of the tasks stipulated by the teachers.
7. Private Cloud: The implementation of VDIs is supported by a private cloud solution known as OpenNebula, as it has an open source software license, provides a virtual infrastructure and serves as a resource orchestrator.

The reasons for choosing OpenNebula in relation to similar alternatives such as Cloudstack, Eucalyptus and Openstack, are justified in the improvements it presents in terms of management and administration of existing resources, as it has an infrastructure that offers a greater degree of openness and scalability. In addition, it presents significant benefits in terms of operational savings, as the execution and grouping of server nodes on low-performance hardware reduces the occupation of physical space, facilitates the development of management tasks and optimizes energy consumption. Finally, it relies on a free software license, protected by Apache v2.0, which grants the possibility of using its features without restrictions.

Once the advantages of OpenNebula have been described, it is important to analyze the dimensioning of the VDIs. For this, some aspects must be taken into consideration:

- CPU: Each virtual CPU core (VCPU) assigned to a VDI must exist as a physical CPU core. For example, for a workload of 10 VDIs with 2 CPUs, OpenNebula will need 20 physical CPUs, which could be distributed over 2 servers with 10 cores each. At this point, it is important to note that the CPU indicates the physical CPUs assigned to the virtual machine; while the VCPU establishes the virtual CPUs that will be made available to the guest operating system.
- Memory: its planning is simple, since, by default, there is no excess memory in OpenNebula. However, it is advised as a good practice to account for 10% of the hypervisor overload (this is not an absolute upper limit, it depends on the hypervisor). Therefore, to maintain a workload of 10 virtual machines with 2 GB of RAM, 20 GB of physical memory will be required. Also, the number of hosts is important, because they will incur a 10% overload due to virtualization. For example, 10 hypervisors with 10 GB of RAM will contribute 9 GB each (10% of 10 GB = 1 GB). The golden rule is to have at least 1 GB per core.
- Network: must be carefully designed to ensure the reliability of the OpenNebula infrastructure. The recommendation is to equip with two front-end cards (public and service) and four for each node (private, public, service and storage). In some cases, fewer cards may be required depending on the storage and network configuration.
- Storage: will depend on the size assigned to VDI. While generally working with 100 GB, OpenNebula allows you to add more capacity if necessary.

In the following section, a pilot experiment will be described to help validate the use of VDIs on OpenNebula as educational tools.

## 4   Pilot Experiment and Preliminary Results

To validate the proposed development of VDIs on OpenNebula, a pilot test was conducted to simulate an educational environment, the objective of this test is to recreate a study environment that requires deploying eight virtual laboratories: one, known as "main", will have three VDIs, and, in the remaining, will install a single VDI each of the machines deployed contain different operating systems or installed packages to perform laboratory practices (see I). At this point, different subnets were organized, users were created with access to the labs, and two test scenarios were defined (Table 1).

In the first one, a local study ecosystem was simulated with several students. In this case, 15 students from the university master's degree in Telematics of the Universidad Politécnica Salesiana were selected to access the laboratories.

**Table 1.** Allocation of resources to laboratories for virtual machines.

| Laboratory | Name | RAM (GB) | Disk (GB) | CPU (%) |
|---|---|---|---|---|
| Main | Windows | 4 | 100 | 0.57 |
| | CentOS | 4 | 80 | 0.57 |
| | Asterisk | 4 | 100 | 0.57 |
| Laboratory 1 | CentOS | 4 | 80 | 0.57 |
| Laboratory 2 | Ubuntu | 4 | 80 | 0.57 |
| Laboratory 3 | CentOS server | 2 | 50 | 0.30 |
| Laboratory 4 | Ubuntu server | 2 | 50 | 0.30 |

In this way, they have specific tools to elaborate practical proposals on mathematical modeling and configuration of e-mail and VoIP servers (Voice /IP). The experiment demonstrated that, considering the dimensioning aspects of cloud services in non-dedicated hardware, the work developed in each practice and the access of the 15 students simultaneously during 20 working hours distributed in 4 working hours during 5 days, an expected behavior of hardware and software is achieved, as can be observed in Fig. 2. Therefore, it can be stated that OpenNebula supports the workload of the VDIs, exposing a window of the remaining 10% for peaks with overload and sustainable performance. This means that 100% of the storage and memory allocated to the laboratories is used, maintaining a 90% occupation of the real or underlying resources Fig. 3.

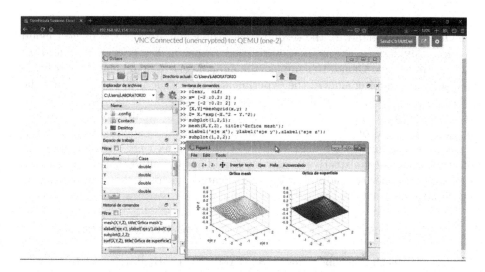

**Fig. 2.** Conceptual operation of VDIs on private cloud, work on a VDI using mathematical software

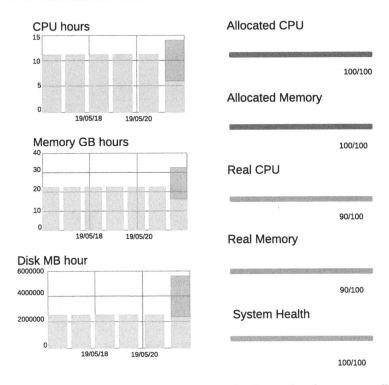

**Fig. 3.** Conceptual operation of VDIs on private cloud, use of real resources, allocated resources and overall system health

On the other hand, in the second stage, the calculators of the biggest cloud service providers in the market were used: Amazon Web Services, Microsoft Azure and Google Cloud, to compare the annual cost of deploying the hardware and software requirements of the experimental infrastructure. Table 2 shows the relative cost increase of the alternatives paid with respect to OpenNebula (local). It is interesting to note that the cost per year in a local architecture is a product of the acquisition of servers and administrative variables such as power, maintenance and trained personnel. While you might think that buying equipment only generates administrative costs, you should keep in mind that a scalable system supports the local addition of non-dedicated machines that lend resources, increasing the annual investment.

**Table 2.** Machine/price comparison with existing commercial solutions.

| Services | Machines number | Host O.S. | RAM memory | Hard disk | Relative cost |
|----------|-----------------|-----------|------------|-----------|---------------|
| Local    | 2               | CentOS    | 32 GB      | 3 TB      | 1 USD         |
| AWS      | 2               | CentOS    | 32 GB      | 2 TB      | 3.59 USD      |
| Azure    | 2               | CentOS    | 32 GB      | 2 TB      | 2.80 USD      |
| Google   | 2               | CentOS    | 32 GB      | 2 TB      | 2.71 USD      |

# 5    Conclusions

The VDI is presented as a greatally of educational institutions to narrow the technology gap and better help ensure the security of all data, necessary for the development of the daily work of all its students. When a student does not have enough technological resources at his disposal, it is a brake on learning capacity. No matter how much internal organization an educational institution has, a student will never perform as well on the move as in front of his own computer, with its programs, its files and its documents.

VDI software removes space barriers in educational institutions and a student who attends a class, a conference or a meeting with a teacher can work from anywhere with the same documents, programs and operating systems he has on his home computer. When an institution enjoys the advantages of VDI, the learning of its students is not altered by travel or any incident, because if you can not work with one computer, you switch to another and ready.

This article describes a proposal that constitutes a support tool for practical activities for students, as it provides teachers with opportunities to improve their teaching methods without incurring high costs. In a simple way, VDIs can be connected from anywhere with uninterrupted availability, increasing productivity and collaboration among those involved in an educational process. Finally, it can be mentioned that the pilot test presents a virtual education process, aiming to provide a low-cost infrastructure capable of providing remote access to computing resources. Thus, the important advantages of the implementation of an open source cloud computing platform such as OpenNebula were observed. Consider the current scenario of the experiment and try to exploit more benefits of being able to configure and consume services in a private cloud environment. Based on the proposed project, it is motivated to expand, develop more tools or use existing ones so that ICTs can be exploited for the benefit of education.

As future work, the incorporation of virtualized graphic processing units (vGPUs) is proposed, in such a way that the execution of high-performance software is guaranteed.

**Acknowledgements.** To the Universidad Politécnica Salesiana del Ecuador, Campus Cuenca, especially to these research groups GIHP4C and GITEL for their support during this research.

# References

1. Agrawal, S., Biswas, R., Nath, A.: Virtual desktop infrastructure in higher education institution: energy efficiency as an application of green computing. In: 2014 Fourth International Conference on Communication Systems and Network Technologies, pp. 601–605. IEEE (2014)
2. Alagappan, A., Venkataraman, S., Sivakumar, S.: Virtual desktop infrastructure for rendering education technology in multifaceted learning platforms—a case study at Botho University. In: 2016 International Conference on Signal Processing, Communication, Power and Embedded System (SCOPES), pp. 1717–1720. IEEE (2016)

3. Burd, S.D., Luo, X., Seazzu, A.F.: Cloud-based virtual computing laboratories. In: 2013 46th Hawaii International Conference on System Sciences, pp. 5079–5088. IEEE (2013)
4. El Mhouti, A., Erradi, M., Nasseh, A.: Using cloud computing services in e-learning process: benefits and challenges. Educ. Inf. Technol. **23**(2), 893–909 (2018)
5. Ewuzie, I., Usoro, A.: Exploration of cloud computing adoption for e-learning in higher education. In: 2012 Second Symposium on Network Cloud Computing and Applications, pp. 151–154. IEEE (2012)
6. Gaur, A., Manuja, M.: Implementation framework for cloud based education-as-a-service. In: 2014 IEEE International Conference on MOOC, Innovation and Technology in Education (MITE), pp. 56–61. IEEE (2014)
7. Hirasawa, S., Koizum, D., Nakazawa, M., Kondo, T.: Learning styles for e-learning systems over virtual desktop infrastructure. In: 2014 IEEE International Conference on Systems, Man, and Cybernetics (SMC), pp. 3241–3246. IEEE (2014)
8. Ibrahim, A.A.Z., Kliazovich, D., Bouvry, P., Oleksiak, A.: Virtual desktop infrastructures: architecture, survey and green aspects proof of concept. In: 2016 Seventh International Green and Sustainable Computing Conference (IGSC), pp. 1–8. IEEE (2016)
9. Jayapandian, N., Pavithra, S., Revathi, B.: Effective usage of online cloud computing in different scenario of education sector. In: 2017 International Conference on Innovations in Information, Embedded and Communication Systems (ICIIECS), pp. 1–4. IEEE (2017)
10. Kibe, S., Koyama, T., Uehara, M.: The evaluations of desktop as a service in an educational cloud. In: 2012 15th International Conference on Network-Based Information Systems, pp. 621–626. IEEE (2012)
11. Kim, S., Choi, J., Kim, S., Kim, H.: Cloud-based virtual desktop service using lightweight network display protocol. In: 2016 International Conference on Information Networking (ICOIN), pp. 244–248. IEEE (2016)
12. Li, J.Y., et al.: The implementation of a GPU-accelerated virtual desktop infrastructure platform. In: 2017 International Conference on Green Informatics (ICGI), pp. 85–92. IEEE (2017)
13. Li, J., Liu, X.: Research on the access control in the education private cloud. In: Proceedings of 2nd International Conference on Information Technology and Electronic Commerce, pp. 192–194. IEEE (2014)
14. Lunsford, D.L.: Virtualization technologies in information systems education. J. Inf. Syst. Educ. **20**(3), 339 (2009)
15. Makoviy, K., Proskurin, D., Khitskova, Y., Metelkin, Y.: Server hardware resources optimization for virtual desktop infrastructure implementation. In: CEUR Workshop Proceedings, vol. 1904, p. 178 (2017)
16. Son, J., Irrechukwu, C., Fitzgibbons, P.: Virtual lab for online cyber security education. Commun. IIMA **12**(4), 5 (2012)
17. Upadhyaya, J., Ahuja, N.J.: Quality of service in cloud computing in higher education: a critical survey and innovative model. In: 2017 International Conference on I-SMAC (IoT in Social, Mobile, Analytics and Cloud) (I-SMAC), pp. 137–140. IEEE (2017)

# Open Source Cloud Platform for Academic Systems Monitoring Software

Rubén Nogales⦿, Paul Tandazo, Franklin Mayorga⦿, David Guevara$^{(\boxtimes)}$⦿, and Javier Vargas⦿

Facultad de Ingeniería en Sistemas Electrónica e Industrial, Universidad Técnica de Ambato, Ambato, Ecuador

{re.nogales,ptandazo6197,fmayorga,dguevara,js.vargas}@uta.edu.ec

**Abstract.** The research consists in the study of the problem arises from the improper use of software, which triggers an excessive investment in tools that do not represent an academic benefit for an institution of higher education. This work proposes the development of an adaptive system which captures the data generated from the execution of any computer application in the laboratories. At the same time, the modules send the data to a server hosted in the cloud where the activities are stored in offline files. On the other hand, the monitoring system tabulates these data and presents them through reports following the XP methodology to facilitate their maintenance. The implementation of the monitoring system made it possible to determine the use of the applications executed in a given time, for the proper control of academic systems.

**Keywords:** Monitoring system · Adaptive system · Cloud

## 1 Introduction

The use of informatics in education has evolved as developing countries have focused on improving the quality of education systems [1]. Although Ecuador is governed by Decree 1425, which recommends the use of open standards and free software [2], several higher education institutions have opted to allocate a portion of their budget to the acquisition of educational software licenses, this economic distribution is limited by the limited information generated on the impact of software use on educational outcomes and productivity. For example, a MatLab annual license is at \$275, i.e. if you consider a laboratory with just 10 machines, the total investment for a single educational program would be \$2750, despite the high cost, the total time the software was used is still uncertain. The situation ends up being more critical if the data obtained previously are multiplied by the different classes in an educational center, the tendency would clearly mark a great increase.

The scarce information on the use of computer applications in laboratories does not clearly show how students are using the investment made by universities, another more obvious example of this situation are the virtual libraries that have a high cost, but little competition for students. The inappropriate use of software within an educational entity

M. Botto-Tobar et al. (Eds.): ICAT 2019, CCIS 1193, pp. 451–465, 2020.
https://doi.org/10.1007/978-3-030-42517-3_34

triggers an excessive investment in tools that are ultimately not used by students or that their use does not represent the investment made by the institution of higher education.

In the Facultad de Ingeniería en Sistemas, Electrónica e Industrial de la Universidad Técnica de Ambato there is no method to know in detail the use of the software products installed in each of the laboratories of the faculty, which in the end are goods financed by the state, and even less is known about the incidence caused by the misuse of tools installed in student performance. In the development of this paper generates a solution to address the problem that arises from the inadequate use of software in the laboratories of the faculty.

## 2  Related Work

The practices to know with exact data the actual use that has the software within a public or private entity has been used in various ways. For example, in the research carried out by Gonzalo Ruiz, a control and monitoring system was proposed to improve the laboratory management processes. At the end of the study, the result was an improvement in the laboratory management processes, since it went from one manual control and monitoring to another [3].

One step further is SIMCUS, a software developed in JAVA by Fernando Galarza that proposes the monitoring of assigned computer programs to be used by an employee at certain times to then present information that reflects the level and degree of use of the programs within the institution and then implement control measures. In the specific case of this research, the data collected are the percentages of CPU use that the programs occupy when they are opened and used [4].

Regarding research on the monitoring of computer equipment, we can take as a precedent work [5], which proposes the monitoring of rules for systems of multiple agents, what is sought with these rules was that the monitoring itself be carried out by the agents involved in the system, so that in this way the monitoring prevents the publication of content that goes against the interests of the main system.

This research presents several results, first there is the case in which perfect monitoring is achieved that prevents the established norms from being violated, but there is also the other case in which the application is not perfect and the probability of violation of the norm is relatively minimal.

A study by Kutare et al. uses a solution that combines both monitoring and data analysis for virtualized systems and cloud infrastructures (Monalytics). This solution through an integration of functionality with Xen seeks to manage large-scale data centers and service clouds efficiently, which necessarily included some consideration of scalability in time and space. According to Kutare et al., to obtain monitoring and analysis of data at multiple levels of abstraction, the ability to dynamically adjust and deploy functionality must be sought. Through experimental evaluations, it was demonstrated that actions can be simple if integrated with monitoring, particularly when it comes to scalability issues [6].

A very interesting related work is the one made by Taylor and He, which proposes a monitoring of network resources based on push, the research is based on the evolution of the switches that today went from admitting only the use of SNMP protocol, by using an extensible operating system that allows to implement a push based approach, to monitor a network, this solution seeks to solve the problems of intensive use of data, involving the transmission and analysis of massive volumes of data from large sensor networks or other acquisition devices, simulations or social networks. Although the monitoring proposed in this study [7] is innovative, the results obtained show that the strategy used is insufficient in terms of scalability and performance.

A study that is somewhat more centralized and directed to a specific type of monitoring is carried out [8], in its research it clearly proposes to deal with scientific applications or those used for experiments, where it seeks to monitor the production side of scientific applications in a way that is efficient and that produces usable information on the calculation, both for scientists and for system administrators, in order to solve the inconvenience in which a request for execution is sent to a computational resource, and this request eventually ends, possibly fails or is stopped and needs to be restarted. While it is running, nothing is known about what that request is doing, other than what might appear in the output files it might be creating. Commercially there are applications such as Kickidler [9], iMonitor EAM [10], ActivTrak [11] that offer constant monitoring of actions executed by software, usage times, reports, recordings, tracking, keylogger, security, remote control and other features.

In the systematic search for literature they present applications that focus on monitoring activities, some proposals present problems due to a totally different approach, while in other cases the parameters captured in the monitoring stage are uncertain. Finally, existing tools that could be applied to the required needs present cost as a major obstacle. It is also important to emphasize that on the free software side there is no program that fully adapts to the identified needs. Therefore, this background leads to the idea of solving the problem with the development of an open source monitoring system.

## 3   Methods

### 3.1   Analysis Phase

As a solution to detect and obtain real data from the use of software in a certain equipment, the development of a monitoring system based on Fig. 1 is presented as a solution proposal. This system acquires specific data, which have been generated from the computer applications that are executed in a team of the laboratories of the Facultad de Ingeniería en Sistemas, Electrónica e Industrial (FISEI).

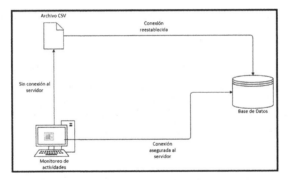

**Fig. 1.** General scheme of the monitoring system.

The developed software is in full conditions to adapt to a data structure that retains the same characteristics for the operation of the software. During the investigation it was determined that the computer activities are generated by the students who use the different programs in the equipment of the laboratories of the FISEI, since it is these people who when executing the desktop applications and navigators generate a great amount of useful data for the present work.

The collection process is carried out by means of applications installed directly in each one of the computers of the laboratories and its purpose is to capture and store in a database server, the information of the applications used during certain periods of time, as shown in Fig. 2.

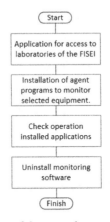

**Fig. 2.** Flowchart of the general process to get the data.

### 3.2 Execution Phase

As described in Fig. 1, the system is developed taking into account aspects such as team execution, connection to a CentOS server, implementation of backups in flat files, everything framed in the use of XP as an agile methodology to produce software to offer technical excellence and team collaboration practices during the software development stage [12]. The user stories described in Table 1 are the basis on which a system is based that is developed with XP or any other agile methodology [13]. For the developed project, user histories were defined detailing the initially planned requirements:

**Table 1.** User history.

| No. | Description | Priority |
|---|---|---|
| 1 | Capture desktop application computing activities in real time | High |
| 2 | Storage of desktop data in the Cloud | Medium |
| 3 | Implementation of backups for offline data | High |
| 4 | Transfer of the backed up data to the server | High |
| 5 | Recognition and identification of web pages visited | High |
| 6 | Web data storage in the Cloud | Medium |
| 7 | Report generation | High |

Since the monitoring system needs to obtain data and also represent them, the solution is developed by modules, the first modules will consist of agent programs that run in the background in Windows operating systems and will be responsible for feeding the server with the computer activities generated in the computers that have the software. Another module only focuses on representing the data collected by the agents in simple reports that use the functionalities of an open source server.

### 3.3 Management Phase

The fulfillment of each one of the User Stories, it must be taken into account that it is necessary to fulfill activities that in the end trigger useful parts of the software. Taking in reference the definitions made in the user histories, in order to store the data of the applications executed in the desktop computers, the tables "Monitoreo_Software_Inicio – Monitoreo_Software_Cierre" were added. In order to measure the use of the software installed in the equipment of the laboratories, it is fundamental to consider an environment: in which the applications executed have a start and a close (Fig. 3).

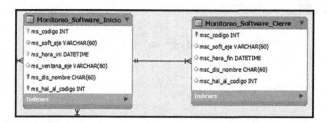

**Fig. 3.** Tables to store desktop data.

In addition, the "Software_Autorizado" entity may store the applications that were installed with the authorization of the teachers who teach classes in a specific laboratory, as indicated in Fig. 4:

**Fig. 4.** Table for Authorized Software.

The "Monitoreo_Sitios" table described in Fig. 5 was created in order to store the addresses accessed from the different computers where the agent programs are installed:

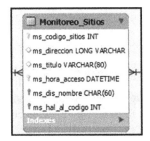

**Fig. 5.** Tables to store web data.

For the development of the project it must be taken into account that the computer activities constitute specific information that is generated when a program is started in a laboratory equipment or any web page is accessed. Based on the requirements described in the user stories, the system must capture and store the data frames described in Figs. 6 and 7:

|  | ID of the executed software | Name of the executed software | Date, time (start and end time) of the program | Window's name | Equipment's name | Laboratory |
|---|---|---|---|---|---|---|
| Maximum length of characters | 10 | 260 | 19 | 260 | 60 | 11 |

**Fig. 6.** Data frame to be captured in desktop monitoring.

| | ID of the web page | URL | Web page title | Date and time of access | Equipment's name | Laboratory |
|---|---|---|---|---|---|---|
| Maximum length of characters | 10 | Unlimited | 80 | 260 | 60 | 11 |

**Fig. 7.** Approximate plot of data to capture in web monitoring.

The information is stored in a database server or in files with a limited space, the maximum length of each parameter in Fig. 6 is given by the documentation of the language to use and the operating system that executed the application, for example the "Code of the executed program" has a maximum length of 11 characters, this random code is the one that allows to differentiate a program from another and to be a value of type Int32 can only cover values of −2,147,483,648 to 2,147,483,647.

According to the Windows documentation the maximum size in characters to name a file is 260 so the parameter "Name of the executed software" which is the executable with which the application starts and the "Name of the window" are governed to this limitation.

For the case of the frame captured in web browsers, the limit of some parameters differs from each browser is why the frame has fairly large limitations that exceed the possible information captured, for example, the tag can reach approximately a length of 55 characters [14]. In the case of the "Web Address" the recommended maximum is 2000 characters especially in popular browsers, some extremely long addresses usually generate errors, but also through tests of [15] it is known that although it is not recommended can exceed the "limit" established.

In the theme of "Date and time of access" for both Figs. 6 and 7 the maximum size in characters is governed by the count of each of the characters that compose the date and time in which the code captures any computer activity, which is based on the format MM/dd/yyyy HH:mm:ss. Other parameters that have been conceived under the same perspective are the "Name of the equipment" and "Laboratory" are lengths established based on the needs of the location in which this research is applied.

### 3.4 Storage Phase

e storage of application data in real time depends on the connection to the network, there is the possibility that this connection is not available at a given time, so you will need to back up the data on the local disk of the computer on which the monitoring application was installed. In order to determine the best alternative, it was decided to compare the performance of the application in similar environments, save 5513 records between a SQLite database (the same used by browsers for histories or mobile devices) and a flat file, as shown in Table 2:

**Table 2.** Comparison between SQLite – CSV.

| Backup. | SQLite | CSV file | Selected |
|---|---|---|---|
| Number of data | | 5513 | |
| Creation of the file | 766 ms | 11 ms | CSV |
| Writing time | 1.234 ms | 757 ms | CSV |
| Process memory | 41,2 MB–5,435 s | 38,7 MB–3,143 s | CSV |
| CPU (% processors) | 4 times in 50% | 3 times in 50% | CSV |
| File size | 1.264 KB | 1.191 KB | CSV |
| Data handling | Database properties | Database without properties | SQLite |

Because the monitoring system must be imperceptible and have as little effect as possible, the impact that the application has on the performance of the equipment must be taken into account. In addition, it is important to highlight the behavior of offline storage from the growth ranges in Process Memory, the SQLite tests showed a maximum of 41.2 MB, while in CSV a maximum of 38.7 MB, as described in Figs. 8 and 9.

**Fig. 8.** Process memory for CSV storage.

**Fig. 9.** Process memory for SQLite storage.

After the tests described in Table 2, Figs. 8 and 9 performed in development time, it was determined that the best alternative for response times is to back up the information in a CSV (comma delimited file).

### 3.5 Data Storage

The storage of data that are of importance and relevance for the development of the present project will depend on the database engine that has been destined by the faculty for the execution of the project and has characteristics defined in Table 3.

**Table 3.** Cloud platform Database Server.

| Type | Description |
|---|---|
| Server | Localhost through of socket UNIX |
| Data Base | MariaDB |
| Version | 5.5.56-MariaDB-MariaDB Server |
| Protocol version | 10 |

## 3.6  Programming Phase

Analyzing features between Visual Studio and NetBeans for the software development stage, the Visual Studio IDE was used, which after the revision generated important advantages for this specific case, such as: native support for Windows operating systems, essential for the execution and adapters for stable connections with MySQL, which is currently being used as the main database in the environment where the tool will work. The most important turning point is the fact that the application is intended for computers with an operating system that has been developed by the same manufacturer as the programming IDE.

The program developed in Visual Studio has the following purposes: to identify the applications that are executed at a certain moment and to store this information in a database. For the identification of started applications, C# inside Visual Studio has integrated libraries that allow to determine the information of the applications started and ended in the computer, through the classes Win32_ProcessStartTrace and Win32_ProcessStopTrace [16, 17]. In order to access and retrieve the definition of the Win32_ProcessStartTrace and Win32_ProcessStopTrace classes that are WMI class events, the ManagementEventWatcher class can be used to receive notifications based on how the events consulted with the EventArrived method occur, as if it were an SQL query as shown in the code in Fig. 10:

```
ManagementEventWatcher startWatch = new ManagementEventWatcher(
                new WqlEventQuery("SELECT * FROM
Win32_ProcessStartTrace"));
        startWatch.EventArrived += new
EventArrivedEventHandler(startWatch_EventArrived);
        startWatch.Start();


ManagementEventWatcher stopWatch = new ManagementEventWatcher(
                new WqlEventQuery("SELECT * FROM Win32_ProcessStopTrace"));
        stopWatch.EventArrived += new
EventArrivedEventHandler(stopWatch_EventArrived);
        stopWatch.Start();
        startWatch.Stop();
        stopWatch.Stop();
```

**Fig. 10.** Main method of the application developed.

For the processing of data generated from a web browser, the application interacts directly with the browsers installed on the computer where the data monitoring is performed, as described in Fig. 11, the code allows access to the history generated on the local disk by reading the SQLite file that is simply based on a traditional database. Once the data is accessed, it is possible to store the information in a native object of the C# language and then by means of calls to the method to store the objects in simple or complex data structures.

```
public  DataTable ExtreerDesdeTabla(int identificador, string fecha)
{
    try
    {
        conexion.Open();
        SQLiteDataAdapter sd = new SQLiteDataAdapter("select visits.id as id,
urls.url as link, urls.title as titulo, " +
                " datetime(visits.visit_time / 1000000 + (strftime('%s',
'1601-01-01')), 'unixepoch', 'localtime') as fecha " +
                " from urls, visits" +
                " where  urls.id = visits.url " +
                " and visits.id != " + identificador +
                " and datetime(visits.visit_time / 1000000 + (strftime('%s',
'1601-01-01')), 'unixepoch', 'localtime') > '" + fecha + "'; ", conexion);

        DataSet datos = new DataSet();
        sd.Fill(datos);
        return datos.Tables[0];
    }
    catch (SQLiteException excepcion)
    {
        throw excepcion;
    }
    finally
    {
        conexion.Close();

    }
}
```

**Fig. 11.** Method of access to web browsers.

In addition to the applications that capture the information, the monitoring system presents a graphical part where reports are generated from the data captured by the monitoring modules for computer applications, data that reside on a database server. Because the system will grow in the future, it is important to establish simple designs that do not require a large number of changes, as shown in Fig. 12:

**Fig. 12.** Prototype of general user interface of the web system [18].

## 4   Results and Discussion

The solution to monitor the computer activities is clearly based on a Windows application, it is important to specify the performance in development time that reached the different methods considered to perform the desired function:

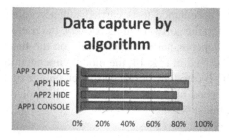

**Fig. 13.** Application performance to capture data (algorithm).

In order to capture data from a specific computer, 4 options were considered, all oriented to a windows operating system but with differences in execution and performance. For example, and describing Fig. 13, the first program based on reading the Process class of the C# language was executed as a Console Application, when generating a window, the application increased the consumption of resources such as memory, CPU percentage and as described in Fig. 13 it captured only 70%.

For the third case was used the same algorithm of the first case but with a different execution environment, i.e. the application captured data for the same time as a Windows Application, i.e. in the background and captured 10% more than with the first version. From these first results it is possible to emphasize that the consumption of resources on the part of the application affects the volume of captured data.

For the second case the application reads directly the native classes of the operating system Win32_ProcessStartTrace and Win32_ProcessStopTrace designed to detect and control the applications that have been started or completed on the computer, so that with a background execution is reached 90% performance in data captured with totality, the same case but with different execution is reflected in the fourth case, the application that runs accompanied by a window captured 80% of the possible data, i.e. about 24 data 30.

Since it is practically impossible to know the hardware conditions of all the equipment of the institution intended for testing, the alternative that retrieves information is the application of the second case, through this option it was determined that as far as possible its operation is unperceivable in the normal performance of the equipment and at the same time can guarantee a higher data storage than in other options.

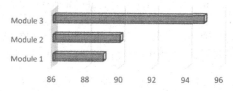

**Fig. 14.** Application performance to capture data (modules).

On the basis of the acceptance tests carried out according to the methodology described above to develop the software in its entirety, the usefulness and performance of each of the modules depends net and exclusively on the functionalities detected in the testing stage. As described in Fig. 14, the module intended to capture desktop data based on the plot in Fig. 6 (module 1) reached a percentage of around 89% in a total of 15 tests. While the second module that captures the frame described in Fig. 7, i.e. browser data, reached almost 90%.

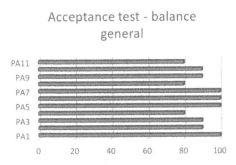

**Fig. 15.** Percentage of acceptance tests.

An important point to note is that during the total of acceptance tests performed as shown in Fig. 15, at least 91% of them were satisfactory, from the beginning of the application in the background to the storage in various facets (online - offline) the application stores at least 9 of every 10 open programs, the remaining 9% information is incomplete, i.e. in cases is saved the beginning of the software but not the end or vice versa, the entire stage to test the software was developed on computers with different characteristics, so the more capacity has the computer more activities are captured.

In XP compliance it is essential as a final step to test all the code developed in order to know if the software does what was planned in the user stories. With the tests it was possible to determine that the .EXE application runs normally.

It is feasible to use the tool developed in an environment that has computer equipment with Windows operating system. Because the application has no direct interaction with the user, i.e. does not have a GUI, the usability is clearly governed by the impact that the program has on the overall performance of the equipment, which through tests run on computers FISEI did not detect problems and inconveniences.

The system at the same time contemplates an adaptive web module that is available in a private server with CentOS and where it is feasible to review the data that have been collected by the monitoring modules previously developed. By means of the reports, it is possible to access information that is clearly oriented to report the use that the programs have had in a certain class time, always taking as a reference whether the programs have authorization from the person in charge of the class, that is, they were requested by the teachers in minutes defined by the institution, as shown in Fig. 16.

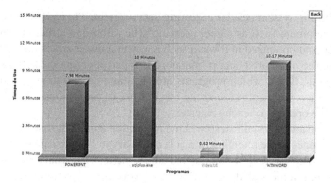

**Fig. 16.** Unauthorized program usage time report.

By means of the tests of functioning of the monitoring system, computer activities were captured between December 4 and 5, 2018, in the laboratory 5 of the FISEI. The data allowed to graphically represent the behavior of the computer programs during certain class hours.

The final results of the tests conducted under the authorization of the faculty, had computer activities where they were captured during 13 h of class on 5 different computers, from the data collected was determined that 4.37 h are used in the execution of unauthorized software, i.e. computer programs outside the acts of conformity of the software installation, as shown in Fig. 17.

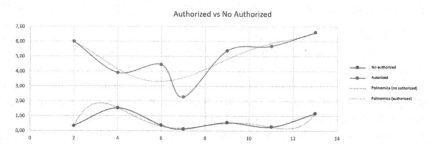

**Fig. 17.** Data analysis.

Applying a trend line on Fig. 17 based on a grade 5 polynomial function on the data obtained, it was determined that the time of use could increase as more class hours are dictated. It is also important to emphasize that the function used does not adjust adequately to the data due to the irregularity and the lack of representativeness of these data around the overall class hours dictated during a semester. On the other hand, the data generated from authorized software represent 34.28 h of execution, that is to say, it was verified that the type of software that was most used in the testing laboratory was the one requested by the teachers, as described with the orange line in Fig. 17.

The monitoring system besides capturing data is oriented to add other fields that are relevant by equipment such as name, user, etc. The information that is generated in a team is filtered and organized in rows in such a way that under any concept the integrity and validity of the monitored data is guaranteed. When applying the solution proposal, it is practicable to define which programs are class at a certain time, and on the basis of that information you can to found the level of use of the applications demanded by educators by the opening of each semester.

In order to be able to establish some kind of relationship, in the use that the software has and its incidence in the retention rate, it is necessary to capture data for a longer time, so that it is possible to find a polynomial that adjusts better to the function given based on the information captured with the monitoring and so a trend can be found according to the data stored in the project server. The deployment of monitoring applications for a much longer time will allow a greater volume of data and thus generate a more comprehensive data analysis following the implementation of tools such as Big Data that allow the requirements to generate other reports at the site of the CloudIoT Platform could vary or increase over time.

## 5   Conclusions

The monitoring system made it possible to capture imperceptibly and cause the least possible effect on the performance of the data generated by the equipment from the beginning and closure of applications that were used by students in Windows operating systems inside the laboratories of the faculty.

With the data collection in a certain period of time, it was verified that the desktop and web modules could establish connection with the Platform server and store the data in a normal way. The collected data allows to graphically represent the use of the software at a given moment of the faculty class. Throughout the development phase, the modules that make up the Open Source monitoring system consider the use of an agile methodology as a proven measure to make a correct interpretation of the requirements requested by the client in the planning phase. The information generated by the monitoring is represented graphically through reports that contribute greatly to determine the use of the software at a given time of class in the laboratories of the faculty, based on the total operation of the Cloud Platform.

In the academic field, obtaining this type of information regarding their systems has generated a mining of relevant data of the potential uses of the academic software installed in each laboratory. These data allow us to make administrative decisions on the installation, execution and termination of these programs. On the other hand, at the application level it is possible to estimate the time of use in memory, CPU, disk, etc., for each process of the software installed.

**Acknowledgments.** The authors gratefully acknowledge the financial support provided by Universidad Técnica de Ambato for the development of the research project "Plataforma CloudIoT de control y monitoreo del uso de equipamiento y programas informáticos en aulas y laboratorios", and the research project PFISEI24 "Integración de Machine Learning y Visión por Computadora para la Manipulación de Objetos Aplicados al Youbot Kuka".

# References

1. Barrera-Osorio, F., Linden, L.L.: The use and misuse of computers in education: evidence from a randomized controlled trial of a language arts program 1 (2009)
2. Correa, R.: Reglamento para la adquision de software por parte de entidades contratantes del sector público. https://www.elcomercio.com/uploads/files/2017/05/24/Decreto-1425-2017_mayo_prelacion.pdf
3. Ruiz, G., Morales, E.: Sistema de control y monitoreo para mejorar los procesos de administración de los laboratorios de las Carreras de Sistemas. Electrónica e Industrial en la FISEI-UTA (2014). http://repositorio.uta.edu.ec/jspui/handle/123456789/8112
4. Galarza Molina, F.X.: Sistema para monitoreo y control de uso de software en la empresa (2007)
5. Alechina, N., Halpern, J.Y., Kash, I.A., Logan, B.: Decentralised norm monitoring in open multi-agent systems (2016)
6. Kutare, M., Schwan, K., Eisenhauer, G., Talwar, V., Wang, C., Wolf, M.: Monalytics: online monitoring and analytics for managing large scale data centers. In: ICAC 2010 Proceedings of the 7th International Conference on Autonomic Computing, pp. 141–150 (2010)
7. Groves, T., Arnold, D., He, Y.: In-network, push-based network resource monitoring. In: Proceedings of the Third International Workshop on Network-Aware Data Management, pp. 8–16 (2013). https://doi.org/10.1145/2534695.2534704
8. Cook, J., Sharifi, H., Farrahi, A.: Towards production monitoring of application progress. In: Proceedings of the 4th International Workshop on Software Engineering for Computational Science and Engineering, pp. 56–57 (2011). https://doi.org/10.1145/1985782.1985792
9. Kickidler: Tarifas de las licencias. https://www.kickidler.com/es/price.html
10. IM Software: Licencia iMonitor EAM. https://es.imonitorsoft.com/employeemonitoring-software.html
11. ActivTrak: Free Employee Monitoring Software. https://activtrak.com/pricing/
12. Letelier, P., Penadés, M.C.: Métodologías ágiles para el desarrollo de software: eXtreme Programming (XP) (2006)
13. Wells, D.: User Stories. http://www.extremeprogramming.org/rules/userstories.html
14. Girón, B.: Tamaño límite title y description. https://www.borjagiron.com/seo/tamano-limite-title-description/
15. Dixon, P., Community: What is the maximum length of a URL in different browsers? https://stackoverflow.com/questions/417142/what-is-themaximum-length-of-a-url-in-different-browsers
16. Microsoft: Win32_ProcessStartTrace class. https://docs.microsoft.com/enus/previous-versions/windows/desktop/krnlprov/win32-processstarttrace
17. Microsoft: Win32_ProcessStopTrace class. https://docs.microsoft.com/enus/previous-versions/windows/desktop/krnlprov/win32-processstoptrace
18. Tisalema, A., Urvina, K.: Sistema Embebido IoT para la Facultad de Ingeniería en Sistemas, Electrónica e Industrial aplicando Programación Limpia y Patrones de Diseño (2017). http://repo.uta.edu.ec/handle/123456789/26222

# Using Subject-Specific Reference Cyclograms on the Gait Evaluation of a Cerebral Palsy Patient

Pedro Sá Cunha[2] , João P. Ferreira[1,2(✉)] , A. Paulo Coimbra[2] ,
Manuel M. Crisóstomo[2] , and César Bouças[2]

[1] Department of Electrical Engineering, Superior Institute of Eng. of Coimbra, 3030-199
Coimbra, Portugal
ferreira@isec.pt
[2] Department of Electrical and Computer Engineering, Institute of Systems and Robotics,
University of Coimbra, 3030-290 Coimbra, Portugal

**Abstract.** Cyclograms are parametric curves composed by the angle trajectory curves of two joints and are an easy way of visualizing and condensate information. The features of Hip-Knee cyclograms can be used to evaluate and asses patient deviation from normality and to track treatment progress. Different joints of the patient can be used for the generation of this parametric curves, as well as the same joint for dominant and non-dominant limb. This former type of cyclograms are called bilateral cyclograms and provide insights of patient symmetry through their geometric properties. The present gait evaluation method is based on the comparison of patient cyclograms with healthy subject cyclograms. In order to obtain a reliable comparison, healthy subject-specific cyclograms should be used instead of generic standard cyclograms because joint angle curves are heavily influenced by subject characteristics (age, height, weight) and gait speed. In the present work, subject-specific knee and hip healthy reference curves are generated for a patient diagnosed with Cerebral Palsy using an Extreme Learning Machine. In this way features of importance to patient gait evaluation can be extracted and compared against several healthy reference cyclograms.

**Keywords:** ELM · Cerebral Palsy · Subject-specific profiles · Cyclograms

## 1 Introduction

Cyclograms, commonly referred as angle-angle graphs, are far from being a novelty in gait analysis and assessment. This type of parametric curve is generated by plotting the angle of different markers, such as hip and knee, or the same marker for both dominant and non-dominant limb, being the former named bilateral cyclogram. By creating such plots, we can get clear insights of the gait symmetry and quality. The generated geometries of such plots enable us to distinguish a normal from an abnormal gait pattern and condenses information such as range of motion that might be important for gait evaluation. Cyclograms fall in one of two categories regarding their construction: synchronized

M. Botto-Tobar et al. (Eds.): ICAT 2019, CCIS 1193, pp. 466–479, 2020.
https://doi.org/10.1007/978-3-030-42517-3_35

and unsynchronized. In order to understand such differentiation, it should be noticed that in a gait cycle the angles of both limbs are nearly complementary, i.e., legs move approximately out-of-phase. In order to synchronize a cyclogram the moment of heel strike for both limbs need to be found before plot one gait cycle against the other. In a synchronized cyclogram the angle of the right knee, when the right heel touches the ground, corresponds to the angle of the left knee when left heel touches the ground. An example of a synchronized knee cyclogram is presented in Fig. 1 at left and unsynchronized knee cyclogram at right.

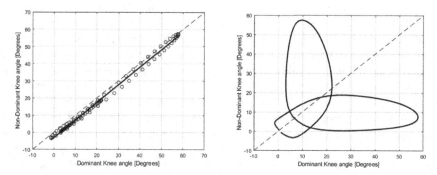

**Fig. 1.** Synchronized and unsynchronized knee cyclograms.

The use of this of this type curves is particularly useful in comparing and measuring deviations. Nevertheless, to do it in a reliable manner it need to be ensured that factors such as subject characteristics and gait speed are taken into consideration in the generation of this curves. Some of the recent literature surpasses this problem by using computational Intelligence methods, modelling in many forms the relation between subject characteristics and angular curves of the knee, hip and ankle joints.

Błażkiewicz et al. [1] trained an Artificial Neural Network (ANN) to simulate the sagittal plane angle of the knee when the hip and ankle sagittal plane angular curve are given as input. The hip and ankle angles were increasingly reduced by 20%. The results for the several combinations of the two joints angles reductions were compared with targets using the correlation coefficient. The lowest correlation obtained was of 0.70. A quasi-Newton optimization method was used for the learning.

In Kutilek et al. [2] a neural network was trained with segments of a cyclogram in order to predict the missing values of the parametric curve. The neural network received as inputs the angles of the cyclogram segment, the angular accelerations of the joint, and subject's weight and age. This procedure was done for knee-hip and knee-ankle cyclograms.

In a subsequent article Kutilek et al. [3] displayed bilateral synchronized cyclograms properties in gait symmetry evaluation. Similar procedures were used by Sobral et al. [4] with Vertical Ground Reaction Forces (VGRF). A synchronized bilateral cyclogram was created for the VGRF and a Symmetry Index (SI) was obtained through percentual relative difference of the slope that fits the cyclogram and the ideal symmetrical gait gradient (45° Degrees).

Some of the most relevant and accepted measurements in clinical gait analysis for gait normality deviation are based on kinematic and spatial temporal measurements. Nevertheless, gait symmetry measurements [3–5] and indexes as GDI-Kinetic [6], based on kinetic data, are also commonly used. The Normalcy Index (NI) or Gillette Gait Index (GGI) stand out as being one of the oldest most accepted indices in gait assessment. It serves as a measure of the severity and normality deviation of the patient pathological gait. Furthermore, GGI allows the analysis of treatments effectiveness by quantifying the changes on the pathological gait. This index makes use of the PCA applied to 16 independent discrete variables [7]. From the 16 variables, 3 are temporal-spatial parameters, (time of toe off, walking speed, cadence) and 13 are kinematic variables (mean pelvic tilt, range of pelvic tilt, mean pelvic rotation, minimum hip flexion, range of hip flexion, peak hip abduction in swing, mean hip rotation in stance, knee flexion of initial contact, time of peak knee flexion, range of knee flexion, peak of ankle dorsiflexion in stance, peak of ankle dorsiflexion in swing, mean foot progression angle). GGI has been extensively used and validated in both clinical and scientific environments, predominantly in children with CP. Despite the common use in children with CP, GGI has also been used for other pathologies such as PD, Multiple sclerosis and strokes. One of the limitations of this index it's the lack of evidence in the choice of the 16 discrete variables as being the most adequate ones. As well as GGI, indexes such Gait Deviation Index (GDI), and Gait Profile Score (GPS) make use of kinematic variables such as the pelvis and hip in the three planes and the knee and ankle in the sagittal plane as well as the foot progression. These indexes require acquisition systems capable of detecting the 3-dimensional position of the markers on the patients. Such acquisition vision systems are naturally more complex and expensive. The methodology used in the present work makes use of the knee and hip angles in the sagittal plane and it is of possible execution with lower cost vision systems with 2 cameras only.

Symmetry is a main feature of gait. Asymmetric gait is correlated with gait pathologies [8, 9] and an evaluation of it can bring great insights of the patient state and situation. Despite the importance, up to date there is no standard for SI, neither for the calculation nor the parameters to use [5]. Some commonly used approaches are based on bilateral cyclogram. In the present work, bilateral cyclograms will be used for symmetry evaluation, as well as some features of hip vs knee cyclograms will be used to show the potential of such approaches.

Both bilateral and regular cyclograms present features of interest for gait analysis and assessment. The most relevant aspects are presented below along with the insights they can provide in a subject's gait evaluation.

(A) **Area:** The enclosed area of the cyclogram is a direct repercussion of the range of movement of both joints in analysis. This feature encodes all possible pair of angles during the gait cycle. When evaluated in sections the diagram permits the identification of phases where conjoint movements happen, and area is naturally more expressive.

(B) **Perimeter:** While the area reflects changes based on conjoint movement, increasing one joint angle solely might keep the area unchanged while drastically modifying the cyclogram. The perimeter of the cyclogram, would nevertheless, reflect this change making the evaluation based on this characteristic more robust. This property permits to identify uncoordinated movements in the gait.

(C)  $P_A = \frac{Perimeter}{\sqrt{Area}}$ : This dimensionless ratio presents a relation with the cyclogram shape, although the value by itself cannot ensure a unique specific shape.

If the diagram shape remains the same $P_A$ will remain the same even if the area changes drastically [10–12].

The previous referred characteristics are of interest mainly for the hip vs knee cyclograms since the conjoint movement of two different markers is of interest. Nevertheless, when using bilateral cyclograms the focus is shifted for a symmetry evaluation and the perimeter and $P_A$ ratio are no longer of such importance. With bilateral cyclograms the deviation from both limbs to the perfect symmetry line (45° degrees line) can be noticed at several moments of the gait cycle.

A different approach for symmetry evaluation can be done with unsynchronized cyclograms. Besides bringing a different visualization, perhaps more intuitive of the patient limb conjoint movement, this approach takes into account the phase shift occurring between joints of both limbs [5].

## 2  Methodology

Data from a cerebral palsy patient with 23 years was obtained and made publicly available by authors [13]. This data contains anthropometric data of the patient, EMG and force plate data, and kinematic data. This kinematic file contains the displacement of 15 markers of the patient lower body in the $x$, $y$ and $z$ coordinates. It was recorded using Vicon motion analysis system (Vicon Motion Systems, Inc., Lake Forest, CA) at 50 Hz for the duration of 1.50 s. All files types given were only compatible with Gaitlab software, which is currently deprecated. OpenSim was the chosen software for this purpose. Using excel and Matlab, the kinematic file (.kin) was read and organized into a matrix. The columns contained the several markers coordinates and the lines correspond to the value of that coordinate for the respective time of sampling. Every marker displacement data was filtered using an 4°th order zero-phase-shift Butterworth filter. The cut-off frequency was 6 Hz and was chosen by residual analysis [14, 15]. Once again, Excel was used to create a trace (.trc) file required to visualize the experiment in OpenSim software. OpenSim GUI rotation method was used to match data orientation with OpenSim coordinate system. Furthermore, OpenSim was used to solve the Inverse Kinematics (IK) problem that yield both knee and hip angles. This open source software contains several human body models that can be scaled using anthropometric information and markers displacement data emulating the recorded patient trial.

Force plate information was used to extract heel strike and toe off moments for both limbs and is displayed in Fig. 2.

The available force plate information contains only one step of each limb, since a complete gait cycle encloses the moment of heel strike up to the subsequent moment of the same limb heel strike. OpenSim was used to visually obtain such events times and confirm force plate information.

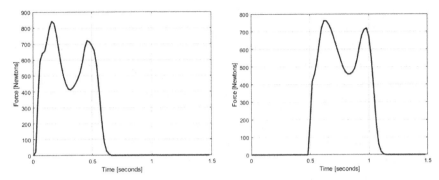

**Fig. 2.** Force plate information.

With these events times, the knee and hip angles were reduced to one gait cycle and interpolated to 100% in order to allow comparisons. Results of the right hip and knee angles for the patient are presented in Fig. 3.

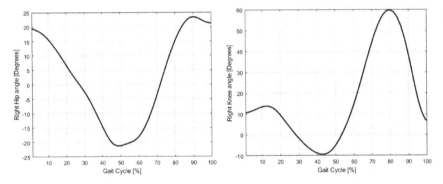

**Fig. 3.** Right hip and knee angle curve for cerebral palsy patient.

The authors from where displacement data was obtained, present an entire chapter dedicated to this patient [13], from the medical history to the kinematic and kinetic evaluation. Even though, only the right limb curves are presented. A very close match was obtained for knee angle curve when comparing the obtained with presented results. Nevertheless, right hip angle curve results needed an offset correction. It is common for authors to consider neutral position as a pelvic tilt of 12° to 13° degrees, nevertheless, OpenSim model Gait2354 considers 0° degrees pelvic tilt with respect to the ground. This will then reflect in an offset in hip flexion that needs to be corrected. A 10° degrees offset was added to the hip flexion. This is a typical tilt value and is recommended in OpenSim user manual when comparing curves [16].

## 2.1 Symmetry Analysis Using Bilateral Cyclograms

SI was, in a first approach, calculated as the ratio of ROM of the non-dominant limb to ROM of the dominant limb.

$$SI = \frac{ROM_{Non-Dominant}}{ROM_{Dominant}} \tag{1}$$

In order to improve the analysis, the same methodology was applied to the ELM generated curves, permitting this way a comparison of the patient results to what would be expected if such subject was healthy (ELM generated curve). The difference of the SI of patient and the SI of ELM is represented and calculated as:

$$\Delta SI = SI_{Patient} - SI_{ELM} \tag{2}$$

The same comparison philosophy was applied to the unsynchronized cyclograms. Similar methodology to the one used in [5] was applied to make a more accurate alternative of the symmetry evaluation with unsynchronized cyclograms.

The unsynchronized cyclograms are built by plotting right versus left limb like shown in Fig. 4.

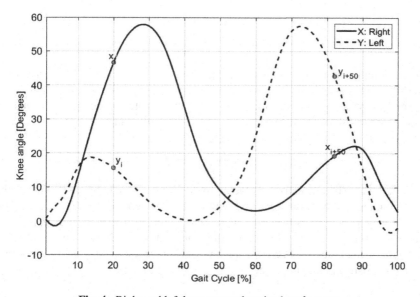

**Fig. 4.** Right and left knee unsynchronized angle curve.

For each pair moment of the gait cycle, i.e., $(x_i, y_i)$ for the right limb and $(x_{i+50}, y_{i+50})$ for the left limb (see Figs. 4 and 5), the Euclidean distance to $45°$ degrees line is calculated ($c_j$ and $d_j$ respectively). Furthermore, the ratio of the distance from $(x_i, y_i)$ and $(x_{i+50}, y_{i+50})$ to the origin ($a_j$ and $b_j$ respectively) is taken into account yielding the symmetry equation for both hip and knee marker.

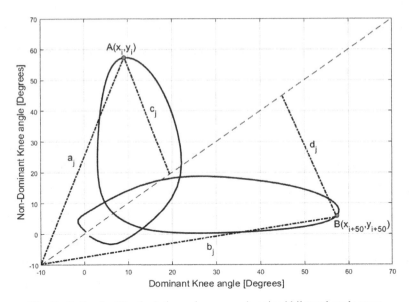

**Fig. 5.** Ratios for SI calculation using unsynchronized bilateral cyclogram.

$$S_{Marker} = \frac{\sum_{j=0}^{50}\left(\frac{\frac{a_j}{b_j}+\frac{c_j}{d_j}}{2}\right)}{N} \tag{3}$$

Where $j$ represent every instance of the gait cycle and $N$ is 101, the total number of instances.

Overall symmetry was visualized in polar coordinate system [5]. The adapted equation used to calculate the overall symmetry is the following.

$$S = \frac{\sqrt{S_{Knee} + S_{Hip}}}{1.41} \tag{4}$$

Where 1.41 is the normalization factor so that $S$ is a value between 0 and 1. When using SI together with unsynchronized cyclograms in such way, it can be considered the phase shift occurring between joints of both limbs. Furthermore, this approach is sensitive to variations of the right and left limb range of motion because of the point-by-point comparison. Later, when analyzing the results, it becomes clear the importance of such characteristics in making an accurate evaluation of the patient symmetry.

## 3   Results and Discussion

### 3.1   Hip-Knee Cyclogram Analysis Using ELM

The patient and ELM hip-knee cyclograms were compared using Dynamic Time Warp (DTW). Furthermore, the standard curves of the hip and knee used in [13] were used to generate the standard cyclogram and to evaluate the results of a comparison using subject-specific curves counterposed to a standard curve.

When comparing DTW results between ELM and the patient curve to standard curve, DTW's for the knee show a difference of 592.48° degrees, being both ELM and literature reference curve very similar in shape. The hip results show a substantial difference of 545.74° degrees. ELM learned correctly the influence of speed on hip range of motion. The increase of speed seems to accentuate hip flexion and decrease/narrow extension. On the other hand, the standard curve used in [13] from Winter et al. [15] was age matched, but did not take into account the several other parameters that influence gait and thus does not constitute a reliable curve for comparison. Results from the DTW comparison are presented in Table 1. Hip-knee cyclograms for the right/dominant limbs are presented in Fig. 6 for ELM, Fig. 7 for the reference cyclogram from literature, and Fig. 8 for CP patient. Area of the dominant limb cyclogram for the patient was bigger than the ELM cyclogram. This might be due to the fact that patient presented a knee extension of approximately 10° degrees together with greater amounts of hip extension. One should notice that knee recurvatum is a sign of pathological gait. These two factors might have led to a bigger conjoint movement since knee curvature happens nearly at the same time that hip achieves minimum angle, translating in this way, in a bigger area and the stretched look of the cyclogram.

**Table 1.** Dynamic time warp right limb cyclograms.

| Joint | ELM-CP patient | Literature reference-CP patient |
|-------|----------------|---------------------------------|
| Knee  | 454.5          | 651.5                           |
| Hip   | 794.6          | 308.0                           |

Patient knee and ELM curve are similar and hip curves, although very distinct, present similar ROM. Due to the fact that perimeter is more sensitive to individual joint changes than area, the differences between patient and ELM generated cyclogram perimeter weren't so accentuated. Nevertheless, patient cyclogram displayed a bigger perimeter than his healthy expected equivalent generated using ELM (Table 2).

The $P_A$ ratio, as mentioned previously, gives an indication of the shape. It can be seen that ELM healthy expected profile has a ratio closer to the literature reference curve than to the patient curve. The shape of the patient is difference from a healthy expected cyclogram, and such reflects slightly in the $P_A$ ratio.

### 3.2 Symmetry Analysis Using Bilateral Cyclograms

ELM generated cyclograms give us support in discerning what is an acceptable deviation from perfect symmetry. SI presented in Table 3. SI based on Range of Movement results Table 3 is based on [3] and is calculated as the ratio between ROM of non-dominant limb and ROM of dominant limb. Furthermore, difference of patient SI to ELM generated cyclogram SI is calculated for comparison (see Eqs. (1) and (2)) replacing the previous comparison measure, the ideal symmetry (SI = 1).

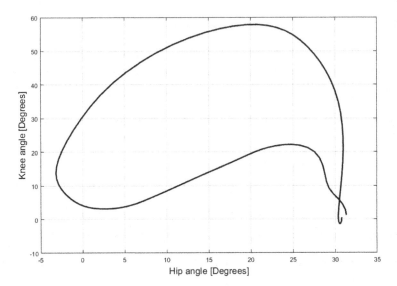

**Fig. 6.** Dominant hip-knee cyclogram generated using ELM.

The $\Delta$SI was of 0.0652 for the knee and 0.1052 for the hip. Naturally, greater the difference, greater will be the asymmetry. It can be noticed that for a comparison with the ideal symmetry (SI = 1) results would be more symmetrical. In the following figures are displayed the unsynchronized cyclograms of both patient and ELM (Figs. 9, 10, 11 and 12).

By visualizing both Cyclograms together with the 45° degrees perfect symmetry line, we can have a better understanding of the differences between the pathological and correspondent healthy. By visualizing the unsynchronized cyclogram we can easily identify the discrepancy between right and left limb. SI based on unsynchronized cyclograms will penalize the abnormal knee negative extension since it contributes to a bigger range of movement of the right limb while left limb remain fairly normal. SI of the hip values were almost the same for ELM and patient, nevertheless, knee symmetry was 1.6 times lower for the patient, emphasizing the presence of some abnormality. The results for overall SI for both ELM generated curve and patient are present in Table 4.

SI results are considerably different using unsynchronized cyclograms than when ROM's are used. When unsynchronized cyclograms were used, $\Delta$SI of the knee was of 0.2410 and 0.0699 for the hip. Overall $\Delta$SI is then of 0.1 which is a much less symmetrical gait than ROM's based SI indication. This results seem to be coherent with patient gait evaluation present in [13], furthermore, Pilkar et al. [5] results were also shown to be lower when using such approach.

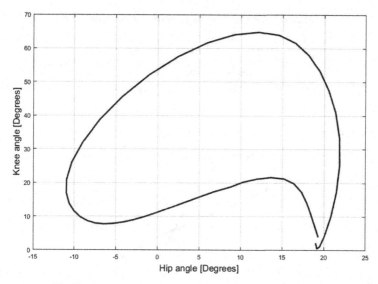

**Fig. 7.** Dominant hip-knee literature reference cyclogram.

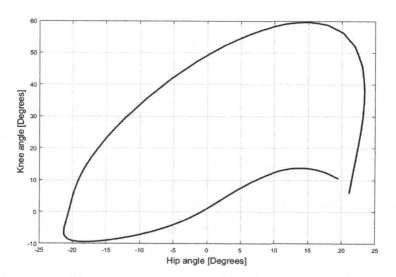

**Fig. 8.** Dominant hip-knee cyclogram of cerebral palsy patient.

**Table 2.** Right limb area, perimeter and $P_A$ of hip-knee cyclograms.

| Feature | ELM | Literature reference curve | Patient |
|---------|-----|----------------------------|---------|
| Area | 1197.2 | 1292.0 | 1828.5 |
| Perimeter | 184.7 | 182.5 | 194.4 |
| $P_A$ | 5.3 | 5.0 | 4.5 |

**Table 3.** SI based on range of movement results

| SI | ELM | Patient |
|---|---|---|
| Knee-Knee | 1.0243 | 0.9591 |
| Hip-Hip | 1.1115 | 1.0063 |

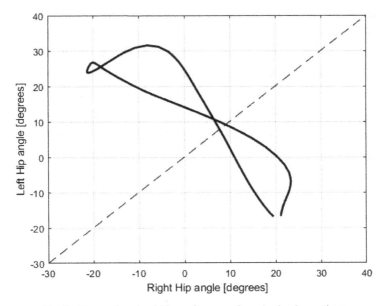

**Fig. 9.** Unsynchronized hip cyclogram of cerebral palsy patient.

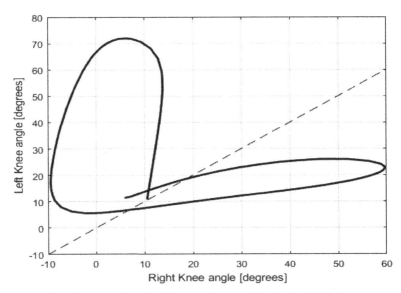

**Fig. 10.** Unsynchronized knee cyclogram of cerebral palsy patient.

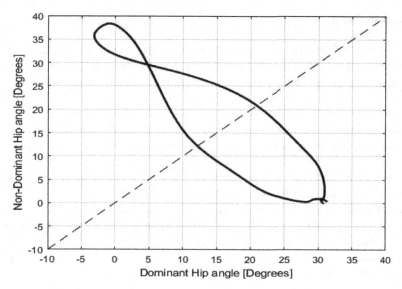

**Fig. 11.** Unsynchronized hip cyclogram generated using ELM.

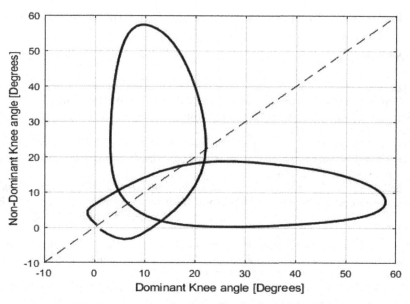

**Fig. 12.** Unsynchronized knee cyclogram generated using ELM.

**Table 4.** Overall SI for ELM and patient.

|    | ELM  | Patient |
|----|------|---------|
| SI | 0.67 | 0.57    |

## 4  Conclusions

The use of the several types of cyclograms implied in the work permitted the visualization and extraction of data of relevancy for the gait analysis and assessment. The use of bilateral cyclograms and the Symmetry Index (SI) extracted allowed the comparison between the patient and subject-specific curves generated by ELM. This analysis brought insights on patient symmetry and its distance to his healthy expected results instead of the ideal unattainable symmetry. Furthermore, the SI obtained by unsynchronized cyclograms shown to be more sensitive to variations of the right and left limb range of movement (ROM) due to the point-by-point comparison. The SI based on unsynchronized cyclograms takes into consideration the phase shift occurring between joints of both limbs that is not considered in the SI based on ROM.

Further validation should be done when using unsynchronized cyclograms based SI and in using ELM healthy expected generated cyclograms as reference for comparison. Also, would be of interest to do a selection of main cyclograms features that would allow a deviation index out of ELM generated cyclograms, originating this way a subject-specific gait deviation measure.

**Compliance with Ethical Standards.**

**Conflict of Interest.**  All authors declare that they have no conflict of interest.

## References

1. Błażkiewicz, M., Wit, A.: Artificial neural network simulation of lower limb joint angles in normal and impaired human gait. Acta Bioeng. Biomech. **20**(3), 43–49 (2018)
2. Kutilek, P., Farkasova, B.: Prediction of lower extremities' movement by angle-angle diagrams and neural networks (2011)
3. Kutilek, P., Viteckova, S., Svoboda, Z., Smrcka, P.: Kinematic quantification of gait asymmetry in patients with peroneal nerve palsy based on bilateral cyclograms. J. Musculoskelet. Neuronal Interact. **13**(2), 244–250 (2013)
4. Sobral, H., et al.: Two new indices to assess gait disturbances applied to anterior cruciate ligament reconstructed knees. In: 8th Annual IEEE International Conference on CYBER Technology in Automation, Control, and Intelligent Systems CYBER 2018, pp. 701–706 (2019)
5. Pilkar, R., Ramanujam, A., Chervin, K., Forrest, G.F., Nolan, K.J.: Cyclogram-based joint symmetry assessment after utilization of a foot drop stimulator during post-stroke hemiplegic gait. J. Biomech. Eng. **140**(12), 121005 (2018)
6. Rozumalski, A., Schwartz, M.H.: The GDI-kinetic: a new index for quantifying kinetic deviations from normal gait. Gait Posture **33**(4), 730–732 (2011)
7. McMulkin, M.L., MacWilliams, B.A.: Application of the gillette gait index, gait deviation index and gait profile score to multiple clinical pediatric populations. Gait Posture **41**(2), 608–612 (2015)
8. Yogev, G., Plotnik, M., Peretz, C., Giladi, N., Hausdorff, J.M.: Gait asymmetry in patients with Parkinson's disease and elderly fallers: when does the bilateral coordination of gait require attention? Exp. Brain Res. **177**(3), 336–346 (2007)
9. Wafai, L., Zayegh, A., Woulfe, J., Mahfuzul, S., Begg, R.: Identification of foot pathologies based on plantar pressure asymmetry. Sensors (Switzerland) **15**(8), 20392–20408 (2015)

10. Hershler, C., Milner, M.: Angle–angle diagrams in the assessment of locomotion. Am. J. Phys. Med. **59**(3), 109–125 (1980)
11. Hershler, C., Milner, M.: Angle-angle diagrams in above-knee amputee and cerebral palsy gait. Am. J. Phys. Med. **59**(4), 165–183 (1980)
12. Oberg, K., Lanshammar, H.: An investigation of kinematic and kinetic variables for the description of prosthetic gait using the ENOCH system. Prosthet. Orthot. Int. **6**(1), 43–47 (2009)
13. Vaughan, C.L., Davis, B.L., OConnor, J.C.: Dynamics of Human Gait, vol. 2. Human Kinetics Publishers, Leeds (1992)
14. Sinclair, J., Taylor, P.J., Hobbs, S.J.: Digital filtering of three-dimensional lower extremity kinematics: an assessment. J. Hum. Kinet. **39**(1), 25–36 (2013)
15. Winter, D.A.: Biomechanics and Motor Control of Human Movement, 4th edn. Wiley, Hoboken (2009)
16. Simtk-confluence.stanford.edu: Gait 2392 and 2354 Models - OpenSim Documentation. https://simtk-confluence.stanford.edu:8443/display/OpenSim/Gait+2392+and+2354+ Models. Accessed 25 Aug 2019

# Bio-mechanical Analysis of Knee Stresses Based on Finite Elements Approach

Gustavo Caiza[1] ![ORCID], David Lanas[2] ![ORCID], Juan Lanas-Perez[3] ![ORCID], Luis E. Mayorga[4] ![ORCID], and Marcelo V. Garcia[5(✉)] ![ORCID]

[1] Universidad Politecnica Salesiana, UPS, 170146 Quito, Ecuador
`gcaiza@ups.edu.ec`
[2] Instituto Superior Tecnológico Superior Cotopaxi, IstCotopaxi, 050108 Cotopaxi, Ecuador
`rlanas@institutos.gob.ec`
[3] Universidad de las Américas, UDLA, 170125 Quito, Ecuador
`juan.lanas@udla.edu.ec`
[4] Universidad Estatal de Quevedo, UTEQ, 120301 Quevedo, Ecuador
`lmayorga@uteq.edu.ec`
[5] Universidad Tecnica de Ambato, UTA, 180103 Ambato, Ecuador
`mv.garcia@uta.edu.ec`

**Abstract.** Software tools based on finite element analysis are widely used for structural mechanical analysis and even in other areas such as medicine. This research analyzes the efforts that occur in the two most important bones that are part of the knee joint from computerized axial tomography (CT) and proposes a methodology based on finite element meshes to obtain these efforts. From the simulation of the geometry of a real knee, stress-strain curves have been developed. The results obtained from the simulation showed that the stress pattern is at a value of 10.97 Mpa in the area between the intercondylar eminence and the intercondylar notch and a unit strain of $1.05 \times 10 - 2$ mm for the femur and $8, 5 \times 10 - 4$ mm in warm.

**Keywords:** Articulation · Finite elements · Stress · Strain · Computed axial tomography (CT)

## 1 Introduction

The Finite Element Analysis (FEA) software is a very useful tool in the field of mechanical engineering, because it allows to perform stress analysis on many prototypes. More specifically, in the field of human biomechanics, the object's geometry needs to be well defined to create the most realistic simulation possible. That is why, a precise definition of the human knee's geometry is necessary by using a simulation from a Computerized Axial Tomography (CAT or CT) scan and determine the possible causes of injuries analyzing the results [5].

Nowadays, medicine is strongly related to engineering and technology. This interconnection among the three sciences gains more and more importance.

M. Botto-Tobar et al. (Eds.): ICAT 2019, CCIS 1193, pp. 480–492, 2020.
https://doi.org/10.1007/978-3-030-42517-3_36

Thanks to the progress in these fields, virtual medical operations can now be carried out, as well as better design and production of orthopedic implants, more similar to the human body's anatomy [15].

This close relationship between computer assisted engineering and medicine, has resulted in the fact that by using the finite element analysis software, the possibility of having a heart attack can be determined thanks to the Computational Fluid Dynamics (CFD). It is also possible to know if artery issues are related to possible congenital causes which could lead to the death of the person [1].

Biomechanics is a very important object of study because the human body is a complex mechanism that, when moving, generates effort, from both the kinematic and the dynamic point of view. For this reason, studying these kinds of stresses from a mechanical perspective, will make possible to determine the maximum permissible stress on many joints like the knee, and consequently determine the causes of injury [21].

This research aims to obtain a 3D knee model in CAD format from a CT (Computed Tomography) scan. Thus, by using the FEA, a stress test of the human knee joint is carried out for determining possible injuries in this joint.

This study is divided in 7 sections including Introduction. In Sect. 2 work is presented, documenting the research status, both worldwide and locally. In Sect. 3, the state of the art is depicted, and a detailed, conceptual study is made on this topic. In Sect. 4, the proposed methodology is presented for developing studies like knee stress and fatigue. In Sect. 5 the obtained results are listed. In Sect. 6, a brief discussion and a critical analysis of the results are presented. Finally, in Sect. 7, the conclusions are described.

## 2   Background Literature

The aim of this section is to discuss the technologies that can be adapted to a knee mesh reconstruction from a CT scan. In this sense, a general view is given with respect to related studies, paradigms and implementation technologies, that is, software architectures aiming to perform human body stress studies using FEA.

In studies like the ones made by Scherer et al. [20], a relation is established between the knee-centered Clinical Coordinate System (CCS) and a Biomechanical Coordinate System (BCS) based on the Mikulicz line. This study is based on the data obtained from a knee CT scan. A group of CT images corresponding to 45 lower extremities is evaluated. Using the VG Studio Max software - a visualization and measurement software - each data set corresponding to a CT scan is aligned accordingly to the CCS and BCS systems. After overlapping both aligned data sets, the deviations of both coordinate systems in the three planes are measured by selecting the center of the knee as the origin of the measurement. This software allows to corroborate that the CCS method is the optimal for determining the medical conditions related to stresses on the knee.

Due to the diversity of the experiments found on previous studies, the individual differences of the subjects and the relatively small changes introduced by the orthosis modelled by CT, no consistent results were achieved [1,11,12,15]. In the present, computer modeling methods, particularly those based on FEA gradually show advantages when exploring the biomechanical responses of the internal structures in the joints. Excessive stress on the cartilage layers and menisci predicted by the finite element model, should be a direct indicator of knee loading. Stress reduction at any level should decrease the accumulated, compressive strain on the knee joint.

There are many studies developing models of human extremities based on the FE method, as shown for the cases of the foot and ankle [5–7,13,23], that have contributed to understand the mechanical interaction between the foot and the foot supports. It has been proven that the finite element modeling could expand the knowledge on foot biomechanics and improve the design of foot supports using parametric information. Concerning the knee joint, the FE modeling of the complete joint or of the knee joint structures in clinical applications has also demonstrated the potential of the finite element method in the field of knee biomechanics with specific research interests [3,8,17,18,21].

As we can see, there is a lot of research on the use of finite element modeling of upper and lower extremities, but there is no critical analysis for the possible disorders of the patient. For this reason, this paper aims to bring new and different approaches on the knee joint biomechanics, focusing on the injury prevention.

## 3   State of the Art

In this section, all concepts related to the development of this research will be explained.

### 3.1   Knee Loading States

The knee is the biggest, most flexible and complex joint of the human body. The knee is a trochlear joint, which means that the end of a bone is inserted on an osseous support like a pulley, allowing two movements: flexion and extension.

The biomechanics of the long bones shows that most of the stresses take place on the joints. The knee joint must meet the following requirements: (i) Resist the impact on the foot when it touches the ground and (ii) provide the forces and moments needed to overcome the inertial forces during the phases of the walking cycle (stance and swing phases).

In many studies related to the analysis of contact forces with the ground, it was proven that during different ambulatory activities, contact forces vary from 1.3xBW (Body Weight) during normal walking, up to 2xBW in race walking. During the phases of the walking cycle, the contact forces change in direction: forces will be directed upwards and backwards in the hill strike position; while during the mid-swing position the forces are pointing forward. In both cases, the knee moment value is in correspondence with the real rotation center or with the contact point of the joint [2,22].

## 3.2    Computer Models of the Knee Joint

The knee joint models can be classified as analytic and computational. Analytic models are used for describing the kinematics of the knee and extracting information about the joint's kinetics. Deformation of the tissues, except the ligaments, are usually ignored in these models, being studied the rigid-body movements only.

This methodology is often called inverse dynamics (inverse rigid-body dynamics) and can be classified as analytical because it only requires a numeric work without excessive computational cost for the solutions. Several analytic models with different degrees of precision have been published in many studies. These models are used for describing the joint movements and the kinematics in 2D/3D and for predicting loads on the muscles, tendons and ligaments [4,14].

In some of these models (mainly in 2D), simple contact algorithms are used like the contact approach by Hertz for describing tissue interactions [16,22]. Some analytical models have considered the geometric non-linearities and have often included the inertia effects on the bones [10,24]. More recently, the studies of rigid-body musculoskeletal models were combined with the finite element method for studying the contact mechanics of the knee and the role of the menisci in the performance of the joints [9].

The validation is a necessary step in the development of the model. The established validation dataset can help the researchers to validate their kinematic and rigid-body models. Although analytical models offered robust approaches for determining the kinematics of the knee, they had limitations for describing stress/deformation patterns of cartilages, menisci and ligaments in 3D configurations. In addition, the non-linear, anisotropic and time-dependent response of the soft tissues could not be captured using these models. The analytical models were not adequate for simulating the knee contact mechanics which is highly non-linear between knee joint surfaces that usually have big deformations. A more complete revision on the analytical models can be found on the study by Räsänen et al. [19].

## 3.3    Generation Methods for the Knee Mesh

The geometry of the knee joint is normally reconstructed from images obtained by means of Magnetic Resonance Images (MRI), Computerized Axial Tomography (CAT or CT) or Micro CAT of the joint. The MRI images are generally preferred for the soft tissue reconstruction, while the CT images are more precise for hard tissues (bones). The essential process in a successful geometry reconstruction is to precisely select the tissue limits from the obtained images. This process is called segmentation and can be done manually or automatically. After extracting the initial geometry of the images, an additional edition is normally needed for improving the model's precision and smoothing the surfaces. This is generally done by eliminating the compression artefacts such as borders/redundant vertices, little spaces and sharp borders, that can lead to impossible or unnecessarily dense meshes [19].

The FE based mesh can be generated using the integrated functions of the image processing software. The choice between using the mesh tools provided by an image processing software or a third-party mesh software is mainly based on the type of mesh required. Normally, triangular or tetrahedral elements are generated in the mesh or a combination of tetrahedral and hexahedral elements. In this sense, the mesh information (node coordinates and number of elements) can be exported to an FEA software for performing an finite element analysis. However, since the exported mesh (generally called orphan mesh) does not include all geometric data of the reconstructed knee, important changes in the mesh or mesh regeneration can only be made on the image processing software.

# 4    Proposed Methodology

This paper aims to determine the maximum permissible force that the knee joint can bear when receiving the action of external forces during two specific activities: light jogging and weightlifting.

Nowadays, the contribution of engineering to medicine is very important being the relationship between both disciplines stronger every day, not only concerning the hospital equipment and devices, but also in the amount of research made on the mechanics of the human body, a science called biomechanics. For this reason, a methodology based on the finite element analysis is used for knee reconstruction in three dimensions (3D).

The modeling process starts from a CT scan of the knee. Then the CT image is converted to a CAD file (format corresponding to Computer Aided Design). The CAD file defines the 3D objects geometry, excluding some information like color, texture or physical properties (STL format). The CAD File is modified as needed during the process, delimiting the knee joint components. After this, the knee mesh is reconstructed by using the finite element method, which allows to perform the corresponding knee stress analysis. The methodology proposed is summed up in Fig. 1.

The progress in biomechanics and in 3D modeling represents an important contribution to the medicine field, because medical procedures and treatments have now minimum risks for the patients which leads to a better medical service.

## 4.1    Finite Element Mesh Validation

The FE method is a numerical method that generates solutions for problems of engineering that would be impossible to solve using the classic mathematical methods. The FEA algorithm allows to analyze any object of any type or geometry, obtaining the tenso-deformational field inside the object, and predicting if this object meets the expected structural requirements.

Once the matrix structural analysis is made to the load vector, it is possible to know the components of the vector associated to the load applied directly to the solid parts. On the contrary, the vector components associated to the reaction forces originated by the existing ligaments are unknown. With respect to

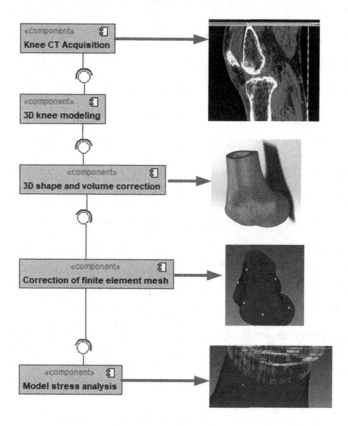

**Fig. 1.** Proposed methodology architecture

the nodal displacement vector, only the components resultant from the existing ligaments are known. The FE method only provides calculations on a limited number of points (finite) and then interpoles the results for the whole domain (surface and volume).

To determine the type of mesh required for this research, using the Hyperworks™ FEA software, we must study the mesh carefully, for obtaining more reliable results. Using a very coarse mesh or a very fine mesh will not lead to adequate results, that is why we decided to study three mesh types: (i) coarse mesh (ii) medium mesh and (iii) fine mesh, all of them generated with hexahedral elements (see Fig. 2). Based on previous studies by [21], an isotropic material was selected for the bones, the soft tissues and the ligaments forming the lower extremity.

As shown in Fig. 2, when comparing the fine mesh with the coarse mesh, the differences in the displacement values are under 20%, which allows to select a fine mesh for this study, because it will lead to more accurate and reliable results.

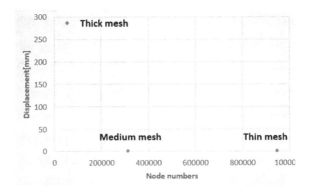

**Fig. 2.** Comparison between the types of mesh used

## 4.2 Mesh Convergence Study

In the finite element method, a more refined mesh leads to more accurate results, however, the computer resources required to run your simulation also increase as the mesh is refined, and the calculation time also will be higher.

The mesh convergence study allows to obtain an accurate solution with a sufficiently dense mesh and without demanding an excessive computational cost. For this paper, the mesh convergence study was made taking the stress values and the degrees of freedom. The obtained results are shown in Fig. 3.

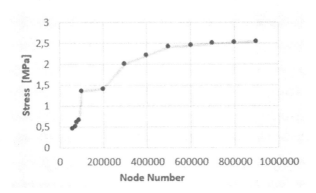

**Fig. 3.** Mesh convergence

As it can be seen in Fig. 3, the mesh is convergent because by reducing the element size and increasing the number of nodes and elements, we obtain a solution that tends to the exact one. Furthermore, the mesh starts to refine when the number of elements is above 40000. This mesh refinement causes that the processing time is extremely high because of the complexity of the elements chosen for the study.

# 5   Results

For this study a CT scan file in DICOM fomat (Digital Imaging and Communication in Medicine) is converted to IGES format using the 3D Slicer™ software, in order to be handled by any mechanical design software. Later, with the Hyperworks™ program, changes are made in the FEA mesh for eliminating the unwanted holes that stop the mechanical analysis to be done by the software. For the stress analysis a distributed load is suggested, according to the following equations (see Eqs. 1 and 2)

$$Load = \frac{Bodyweight}{N^o\,of\,nodes} = \frac{70\,kg}{271\,nodes} = 0.25\frac{kg}{node} \tag{1}$$

$$N^o\,of\,equations = N^o\,of\,nodes \times 6\,degrees\_freedom = 43500 \times 6 = 2610000 \tag{2}$$

In the knee stress analysis three different loads were used: 70 kg, 300 kg and 500 kg. Two graphics are presented (i) The first graphic shows the displacement analysis: in this study loads are applied on a solid object, this solid is deformed and the effect of the pressure is transmitted through the solid. What simulation does is to induce internal forces and reactions from the external loads for rendering the solid on a balanced state. (ii) The second graphic shows the Von Mises stress analysis, which allows to detect fatigue on different elements of the knee joint, while repeatedly applying and removing loads. This process weakens the knee over time, even when the induced tensions are considerably lower than the permissible tension levels. Both stress studies were carried out on the femur (see Fig. 4) and on the tibia (see Fig. 5).

# 6   Discussion of Results

The FEM allows an approximate solution which gets close to the displacement values through polynomic functions that are defined using the values of the sample points placed in the solid. This is very helpful because it is possible to have reliable numerical models which simulate the knee bones behavior, like the femur and the tibia. In this study, the osseous tissue has been considered as an homogeneous material, linear and isotropous, since in previous studies limitations in the model have been found and focus on the anisotropy of the spongy bone in the proximal tibia, without taking into account the possible effects of the anisotropy on the final results. In the 6 models, for the tibia and for the fibula, loading and overloading situations are simulated for a normal subject in daily activities. These simulations compare both deformation and stress, showing in which part of the knee the highest pressure is applied being a possible cause of fracture or injury in the future.

The displacements and stress distribution have been analyzed in monopodal support with the knee in full extension and in $0^o$. It has been proven that the

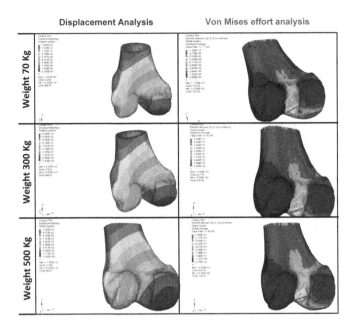

**Fig. 4.** Analysis of displacement and von Mises of the femur

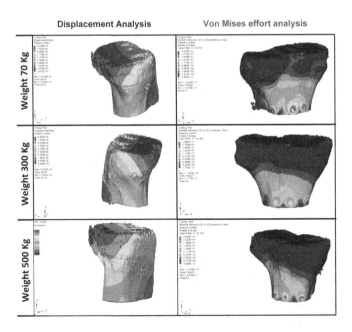

**Fig. 5.** Analysis of displacement and von Mises of the tibia

obtained displacements on the tibia are more relevant than in the femur. In the femur, when the three loads were applied the displacement remained steady. This was not the case for the tibia, where greater changes in the displacements were found (see Fig. 6).

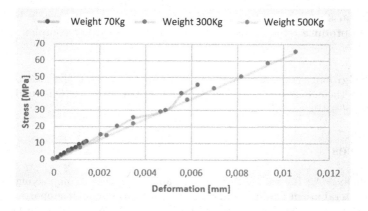

**Fig. 6.** Effort comparative deformation diagram between the three weights

It is important to consider that the displacement will vary according to the knee flexion angle, keeping the same support conditions and load distribution. For instance, it was found that in the full extension, when the three loads were applied the femur tended to move to the previous position, which produces a higher work for the crossed ligaments. If a knee flexion was produced, for example a 10° flexion, the femur would tend to move backwards, generating more work for the quadriceps and the patellar tendon.

Concerning the tensions produced by the osseous tissue, the stress distribution is more uniform, although it was proven that the highest concentration of these stresses occurred on the femoral head. It must be considered that tension distribution is transmitted from the femur to the tibia through the menisci, in a way that the contact area of the femoral condyles is the maximum possible.

## 7   Conclusions and Ongoing Work

The simulation using the FE method allowed to establish the zones where the stress concentration is the highest. In the study, these zones were on the rotular surface and on the intercondylar eminence. The study allowed to establish a methodology for the stress analysis simulation in the knee joint by means of a mesh reconstruction and refinement which brings more accurate results.

In addition, it is important to say that choosing the adequate mesh is vital for a better result. The results of this research show that when comparing the displacement values, they do not have significant changes, despite the variation in the loads affecting the knee. According to the obtained data, it is proven that the knee joint is capable of bear up to three times the bodyweight of a person in monopodal phase. However, this creates damage in the menisci and in the muscles of the lateral zones.

Specific models based on FE analysis can predict the complex, non-uniform stress and strain fields that occur in biological soft tissues and the kinematics of the human knee joint. As future work, this approach could easily be adapted in order to produce realistic biomechanical models of other complex joints and systems.

**Acknowledgment.** This work was financed by Universidad Técnica de Ambato (UTA) and their Research and Development Department (DIDE) under project CONIN-P-256-2019.

# References

1. Abdallah, A.A., Radwan, A.Y.: Biomechanical changes accompanying unilateral and bilateral use of laterally wedged insoles with medial arch supports in patients with medial knee osteoarthritis. Clin. Biomech. **26**(7), 783–789 (2011). https://doi.org/10.1016/j.clinbiomech.2011.03.013, https://linkinghub.elsevier.com/retrieve/pii/S0268003311000957
2. Barreto Andrade, J., Villarroya-Aparicio, A., Calero Morales, S.: Biomecánica de la marcha atlética. Análisis cinemático de su desarrollo y comparación con la marcha normal. Revista Cubana de Investigaciones Biomédicas **36**(2), 53–69 (2017)
3. Beillas, P., Lee, S.W., Tashman, S., Yang, K.H.: Sensitivity of the Tibio-femoral response to finite element modeling parameters. Comput. Methods Biomech. Biomed. Eng. **10**(3), 209–221 (2007). https://doi.org/10.1080/10255840701283988
4. Butler, A.B., Caruntu, D.I., Freeman, R.A.: Knee joint biomechanics for various ambulatory exercises using inverse dynamics in OpenSim. In: Biomedical and Biotechnology Engineering. American Society of Mechanical Engineers, Tampa, Florida, USA, vol. 3, November 2017. https://doi.org/10.1115/IMECE2017-70988
5. Cheung, J.T.M., Zhang, M.: A 3-dimensional finite element model of the human foot and ankle for insole design. Arch. Phys. Med. Rehabil. **86**(2), 353–358 (2005). https://doi.org/10.1016/j.apmr.2004.03.031, https://linkinghub.elsevier.com/retrieve/pii/S0003999304004708
6. Cheung, J.T.M., Zhang, M.: Parametric design of pressure-relieving foot orthosis using statistics-based finite element method. Med. Eng. Phys. **30**(3), 269–277 (2008). https://doi.org/10.1016/j.medengphy.2007.05.002, https://linkinghub.elsevier.com/retrieve/pii/S1350453307000884
7. Cheung, J.T.M., Zhang, M., Leung, A.K.L., Fan, Y.B.: Three-dimensional finite element analysis of the foot during standing–a material sensitivity study. J. Biomech. **38**(5), 1045–1054 (2005). https://doi.org/10.1016/j.jbiomech.2004.05.035, https://linkinghub.elsevier.com/retrieve/pii/S0021929004002842
8. Farrokhi, S., Keyak, J., Powers, C.: Individuals with patellofemoral pain exhibit greater patellofemoral joint stress: a finite element analysis study. Osteoarthr. Cartil. **19**(3), 287–294 (2011). https://doi.org/10.1016/j.joca.2010.12.001, https://linkinghub.elsevier.com/retrieve/pii/S1063458410003985

9. Guess, T., Razu, S., Jahandar, H.: Evaluation of knee ligament mechanics using computational models. J. Knee Surg. **29**(02), 126–137 (2016). https://doi.org/10. 1055/s-0036-1571954
10. Hatano, G., Krzysztof, K., Sauer, P., Morita, Y.: Kinematic simulator of e-Knee robo that reproduces human knee-joint movement. In: 2019 12th International Workshop on Robot Motion and Control (RoMoCo), Poznań, Poland, pp. 74–79. IEEE, July 2019. https://doi.org/10.1109/RoMoCo.2019.8787349, https:// ieeexplore.ieee.org/document/8787349/
11. Kakihana, W., Akai, M., Yamasaki, N., Takashima, T., Nakazawa, K.: Changes of joint moments in the gait of normal subjects wearing laterally wedged insoles. Am. J. Phys. Med. Rehabil. **83**(4), 273–278 (2004)
12. Kerrigan, D., Lelas, J.L., Goggins, J., Merriman, G.J., Kaplan, R.J., Felson, D.T.: Effectiveness of a lateral-wedge insole on knee varus torque in patients with knee osteoarthritis. Arch. Phys. Med. Rehabil. **83**(7), 889–893 (2002). https://doi.org/10.1053/apmr.2002.33225, https://linkinghub.elsevier. com/retrieve/pii/S000399930200000X
13. Liu, X., Zhang, M.: Redistribution of knee stress using laterally wedged insole intervention: finite element analysis of knee-ankle-foot complex. Clin. Biomech. **28**(1), 61–67 (2013). https://doi.org/10.1016/j.clinbiomech.2012.10.004, https:// linkinghub.elsevier.com/retrieve/pii/S0268003312002318
14. Madeti, B.K., Chalamalasetti, S.R., Sundara siva rao Bolla Pragada, S.K.: Biomechanics of knee joint – a review. Front. Mech. Eng. **10**(2), 176–186 (2015). https:// doi.org/10.1007/s11465-014-0306-x
15. Maly, M.R., Culham, E.G., Costigan, P.A.: Static and dynamic biomechanics of foot orthoses in people with medial compartment knee osteoarthritis. Clin. Biomech. (Bristol, Avon) **17**(8), 603–610 (2002)
16. Naghibi Beidokhti, H., Janssen, D., van de Groes, S., Hazrati, J., Van den Boogaard, T., Verdonschot, N.: The influence of ligament modelling strategies on the predictive capability of finite element models of the human knee joint. J. Biomech. **65**, 1–11 (2017). https://doi.org/10.1016/j.jbiomech.2017.08. 030, https://linkinghub.elsevier.com/retrieve/pii/S0021929017304529
17. Peña, E., Calvo, B., Martínez, M., Doblaré, M.: A three-dimensional finite element analysis of the combined behavior of ligaments and menisci in the healthy human knee joint. J. Biomech. **39**(9), 1686–1701 (2006). https://doi. org/10.1016/j.jbiomech.2005.04.030, https://linkinghub.elsevier.com/retrieve/pii/ S0021929005002113
18. Ramaniraka, N., Terrier, A., Theumann, N., Siegrist, O.: Effects of the posterior cruciate ligament reconstruction on the biomechanics of the knee joint: a finite element analysis. Clin. Biomech. **20**(4), 434–442 (2005). https://doi. org/10.1016/j.clinbiomech.2004.11.014, https://linkinghub.elsevier.com/retrieve/ pii/S0268003304002888
19. Räsänen, L.P., Mononen, M.E., Lammentausta, E., Nieminen, M.T., Jurvelin, J.S., Korhonen, R.K.: Three dimensional patient-specific collagen architecture modulates cartilage responses in the knee joint during gait. Comput. Methods Biomech. Biomed. Eng. **19**(11), 1225–1240 (2016). https://doi.org/10.1080/10255842.2015. 1124269
20. Scherer, T.P., Hoechel, S., Müller-Gerbl, M., Nowakowski, A.M.: Comparison of knee joint orientation in clinically versus biomechanically aligned computed tomography coordinate system. J. Orthop. Transl. **16**, 78–84 (2019). https://doi.org/10.1016/j.jot.2018.07.005, https://linkinghub.elsevier. com/retrieve/pii/S2214031X18300779

21. Shirazi, R., Shirazi-Adl, A.: Computational biomechanics of articular cartilage of human knee joint: effect of osteochondral defects. J. Biomech. **42**(15), 2458–2465 (2009). https://doi.org/10.1016/j.jbiomech.2009.07.022, https://linkinghub.elsevier.com/retrieve/pii/S0021929009004266

22. Valencia-Aguirre, F., Mejía-Echeverria, C., Erazo-Arteaga, V.: Desarrollo de una prótesis de rodilla para amputaciones transfemorales usando herramientas computacionales. Revista UIS Ingenierías **16**(2), 23–34 (2017)

23. Yu, J., Cheung, J.T.M., Fan, Y., Zhang, Y., Leung, A.K.L., Zhang, M.: Development of a finite element model of female foot for high-heeled shoe design. Clin. Biomech. **23**, S31–S38 (2008). https://doi.org/10.1016/j.clinbiomech.2007.09.005, https://linkinghub.elsevier.com/retrieve/pii/S0268003307002082

24. Zhang, R., Liu, H., Meng, F., Ming, A., Huang, Q.: Cylindrical inverted pendulum model for three dimensional bipedal walking. In: 2018 IEEE-RAS 18th International Conference on Humanoid Robots (Humanoids), Beijing, China, pp. 1010–1016. IEEE, November 2018. https://doi.org/10.1109/HUMANOIDS.2018.8624984, https://ieeexplore.ieee.org/document/8624984/

# Author Index

Printed in the United States
By Bookmasters